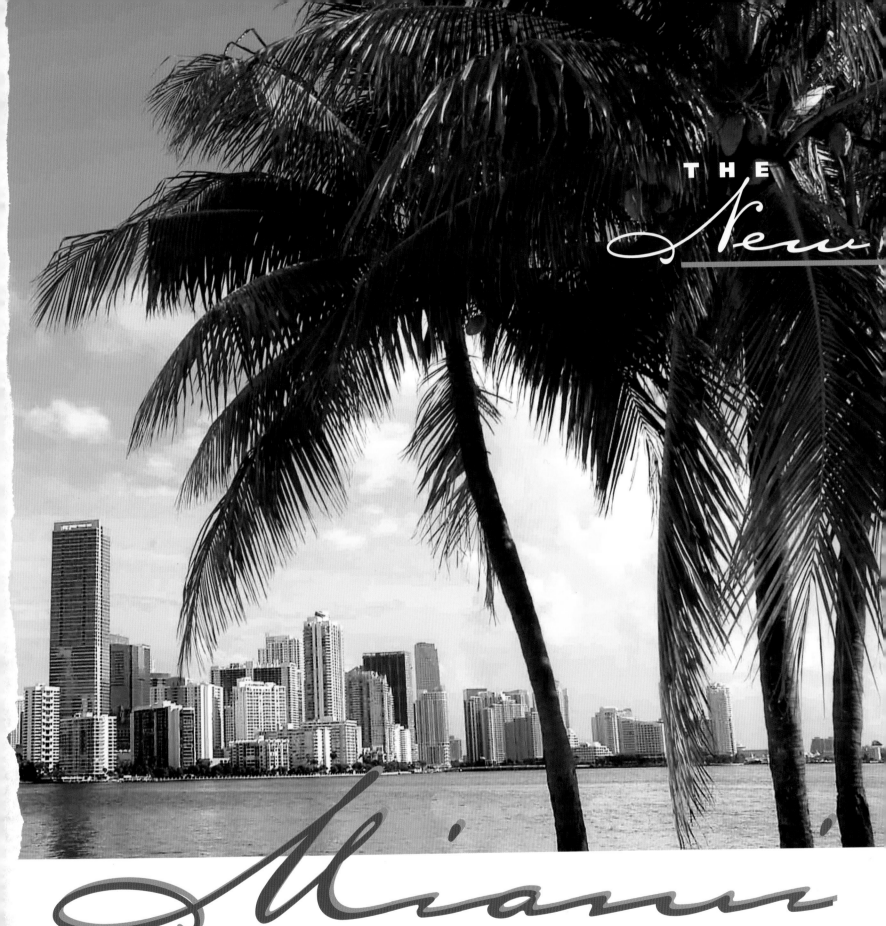

THE New

Miami
THE MAGIC CITY

by Arva Moore Parks

THE NEW
Miami
THE **MAGIC** CITY

by **Arva Moore Parks**

©Copyright 2008
Arva Moore Parks

For my husband Bob McCabe

History Consultants:
Howard Kleinberg
Dorothy Jenkins Fields
Laura Pincus
Larry Wiggins

History Editors:
Patty Shillington
Laura Pincus
Sue Edmiston

History Designer:
Rhondda Edmiston
Mixed Media, Inc.

Illustrative Handcoloring:
Eleanore Keim
Cecy Williams

Production Assistant:
Nuria Santizo

Publisher:
Community Media
1395 Brickell Avenue Suite 800
Miami, Florida 33131

Director of Administration:
Helen Nelson

Project Manager:
Sally Kamman

Profile Writers:
Beverly Bidney
Michelle Solomon
Dale Hutchings

Pofile Designer:
Sean Keenan

Profile Editor:
Britton Marie

Library of Congress Cataloging
in Publication Data
LC: 2008939911
Parks, Arva Moore

Miami, the Magic City
1. History—Florida
ISBN #0-9717649-3-X

Sculpture: Manuel Carbonell
El Centenela del Rio (SP)

Cover photo: Harry Emilio Gottlieb
End sheet photo: Randall Groh

Printed in Korea
By Global Print Services, Inc.
www.globalprintservicesinc.com

HERE WE GO AGAIN

This is the third time I have written an introduction for my book *Miami: The Magic City* which was first published in 1980. In my first introduction, I talked about "My Miami"—the city of my birth and place where I have spent my entire life. In the 1991 edition, I changed the focus to "Our Miami" because we had become a multiracial, multiethnic community, quite unlike "My Miami" of a decade earlier. As I write the third introduction, I once again assess the place I call home. This time, I have redone the entire book and have added "The New" to the book's title. Yes, it is a "new" book—a "new" edition. But most importantly, Miami is once again a "new" place.

Many, like me, have lived through the changes of the last 15 years. But I have learned that one does not gain understanding by just regurgitating facts and chronicling events. This is what I call "one foot in front of the other kind of history." The historian has a harder job. He or she must study the people and the events in context to learn how each relates to the past and impacts the future. In short, an historian must consider the big picture.

As I wrote about Miami's more recent history, I was ever mindful that it was too soon to write the definitive history or even risk an evaluation of the present. As one friend remarked, "the jury is still out" on the new Miami and the people who created it. But one thing is for sure. We have witnessed unprecedented change—even by Miami standards. We have watched a city transform itself right before our eyes. We have made history.

Writing Miami history may not be easy but it is never boring. Just as I was finishing the first edition of *Miami: The Magic City* in May 1980, tragedy struck. Ugly rioting broke out. Innocent people died. Parts of the city were ablaze. More than 125,000 new Cuban refugees hit town—including 25,000 criminals. Never in my memory had Miami, or any other American city for that matter, experienced such trauma. I tried and tried to write an upbeat ending to the history that I had been working on for years. It was impossible. I finally wrote something about "temporary setbacks" and how history proved that Miami could survive any storm—those created by nature and those created by man.

Ten years later, as I began updating the book, I realized that my original conclusion was right on target. As I researched the 1980s, it became very clear that, despite continuing tragedy and pain, Miami not only survived; it thrived.

The new chapter, entitled "Transformation," once again begins with tragedy and ends with uncertainty. But many positive, history-making events occurred between 1992 and 2008. Despite uncertainty, we live in an exciting new Miami—a Twenty-first Century city with potential to surpass the great cities of the Twentieth Century. We have experienced a Renaissance in art and culture. We have experienced a history-making boom that dwarfs all others. We see a breathtaking new skyline that includes almost 50 new high-rise buildings. With 36 buildings over 500 feet, we now come in third after New York and Chicago. But more important than what we build is what we are. We are America's laboratory, a place that author T.D. Allman called "A City of the Future." In short, we are the face of America's future.

But as I have written in each edition, despite our problems, we have proved that we know how to overcome adversity and absorb a continuous flow of people who come from someplace else. Our greatest strength continues to be our ability to adapt to change. "It is not the strongest of the species that survives, nor the most intelligent," Charles Darwin reminded us, "but the one most responsive to change."

My friend and fellow historian Howard Kleinberg once noted that Miami's history should be written in a loose-leaf notebook. No one has said it better. Before the ink is dry on this edition, new people and new places and new history-making events will shape our future. What will the next Miami be like? We may not know that answer but history has taught us one thing. There will be another "new" Miami and the future looks bright. We are in the right place at the right time with the right people. As we say in Miami: "Stay tuned."

Arva Moore Parks
September 18, 2008

BUSINESS PROFILES

The following Miami firms, organizations and institutions have helped make this historic book possible and thereby expressed their commitment to the past, the present and the future of this great city. --

1 FirstBank	406	Goldstein Schechter Koch	448
Associated Photo & Imaging	460	Goodwill Industries of South	336
AvMed Health Plans	380	Florida, Inc.	
BAC Florida Bank	403	Greater Miami Chamber	326
Bacardi	470	of Commerce	
Badia Spices	472	Gulliver Schools	360
Bank of America	402	Hall, Lamb and Hall, P.A.	456
BankUnited	404	Harvey Bilt Photography	463
Baptist Health South Florida	382	Helm Bank	408
Barry University	352	Hill York	430
Beckman Coulter	378	Jackson Health System	390
Belen Jesuit Preparatory	354	Johnson & Wales University	364
School		Kane & Company, P.A.	452
Brickell Motors	480	Leon Medical Centers	391
Business Centers International	459	McKinley Financial Services	462
Carlos Albizu University	356	Medica Healthcare Plans	395
Carrollton School of the	358	Mercedes-Benz of Coral Gables	478
Sacred Heart		Mercedes-Benz of Cutler Bay	
Century Homebuilders of	420	Miami Children's Hospital	392
South Florida		Miami Children's Museum	486
Christopher Columbus	353	Miami Country Day School	366
High School		Miami-Dade Chamber of	329
Dade Community Foundation	324	Commerce	
Dade County Federal	400	Miami Dade College	342
Credit Union		Miami Downtown	332
Del Monte Fresh Produce	474	Development Authority	
North America		Miami International Airport	330
Esslinger-Wooten-Maxwell, Inc.	428	Miami International University	368
Fairchild Tropical Botanic	484	of Art & Design	
Gardens		Miami Jewish Home &	394
Flagler Dog Track	485	Hospital	
Florida East Coast Realty	416	Miami Parking Authority	335
Fortune International	414	Miami River Inn	498
Fuerst, Humphrey, Ittleman	454	Miami Science Museum	488

Monsignor Edward Pace	348	Sunrise Community, Inc.	396
High School		Supermix Concrete	436
Morgan, Lewis & Bockius LLP	450	Terra Group	433
Morrison, Brown, Argiz &	446	The Allen Morris Company	438
Farra, LLP		The Cushman School	374
News Café	496	The Ferraro Law Firm	449
Northern Trust	405	The Graham Companies	422
Olympia Theater at Gusman	487	The Oceanaire Seafood Room	494
Center		The Related Group	424
Orange Bowl Committee	333	The Rusty Pelican	500
Palmer Trinity School	370	The Samuel Scheck Hillel	362
Perry Ellis International	490	Community Day School	
Port of Miami	331	United Way of Miami-Dade	334
R.J. Heisenbottle Architects	434	University of Miami	350
Ransom Everglades School	340	University of Miami Hospital	388
RCI Group	492	University of Miami Health	386
Rilea Group	432	System/Leonard M. Miller	
Rok Enterprises, Inc.	426	School of Medicine	
Rowland Coffee Roasters	476	Victoria & Associates Career	458
Ryder System, Inc.	466	Services	
Shook, Hardy & Bacon L.L.P.	442	Wachovia	410
South Florida Hispanic	328	Wometco Enterprises	499
Chamber of Commerce		Zumpano, Patricios &	451
St. Stephen's Episcopal Day	363	Winker, P.A.	
School			
St. Thomas University	372		

For eons, the bluffs rose fortress-like on the bay until they were replaced with the bulk-heads and lawns of Miami's "Millionaire's Row." Today, thousands of people live in towering condominiums unaware of the beauty that once was. (MC)

*R*alph Munroe's beautiful photograph of the mouth of the Miami River in 1884.
Twelve years later, the north bank, shown here, would become the City of Miami. (MC)

TABLE OF CONTENTS

1. *La Florida* — 1
2. Bloody Red, White & Blue — 21
3. Carpetbaggers & Homesteaders — 43
4. "Never a Town" — 77
5. "The Magic City" — 107
6. Boom, Bust & Blow — 143
7. The Morning After — 160
8. Getting Ready — 197
9. "New World Center" — 219
10. *City of the Future* — 245
11. Transformation — 275
   Business Profiles — 320
   Acknowledgements — 508
   Selected Bibliography — 509
   Photo Credits — 511
   Index — 512

■ *South Dade's Cutler Fossil Site revealed a 10,000-year-old carnivore den where dire wolves dragged a hapless peccary for an afternoon feast. Jaguars, mammoths, horses and llamas also roamed the hospitable land as Paleo-Indian hunters watched the drama and prepared for the hunt. (HMSF)*

Chapter One

La Florida

"And the Lord God planted a garden eastward in Eden."
Genesis 2:8

NO OTHER PLACE IN THE UNITED STATES IS LIKE SOUTH FLORIDA. GEOLOGICALLY, IT IS AN AFTERTHOUGHT, A

late baby. Eventually, it managed to lift itself out of the ocean that still hungrily laps at its shores. The receding sea left its mark—firmly stamped into the bedrock.

Before modern man arrived, little dry ground existed in South Florida except for a narrow coastal ridge. The ridge served as the eastern rim of a huge bowl that contained a vast "River of Grass"—the Florida Everglades. In several places along the rocky rim, years of pressure from the Everglades eroded the rock, creating small rivers and streams that spilled fresh water into the bays surrounding the southern tip of the peninsula.

Long before people lived in South Florida, heat-loving plants, animals and insects flourished in the moist subtropical climate. Although the top soil was thin, organic material accumulated in natural indentations in the bedrock, forming fertile pockets that spawned hammocks—beautiful subtropical forests filled with an incredible profusion of life.

Human beings—destined to be misnamed Indians—discovered South Florida more than 10,000 years ago. Anthropologists believe that Asian natives may have wandered across the Ice Age bridge between Siberia and Alaska and through the years trekked southward, pulled by the warmth of the sun.

Like primitive people everywhere, South Florida's first humans settled on the banks of rivers. Judging from archaeological remains, we now know they had a substantial settlement on both sides of the Miami River near its mouth. They were not just a simple band of hunters and gatherers but also master fishermen who built seaworthy dugout canoes for fishing and hunting expeditions along the coast and into the Everglades. They also traded with other tribes and created their own distinctive art.

The first historical description of Florida's native people comes from the Spanish who encountered them as early as 1513. Later Spanish accounts described the natives as living in a large village on the north bank of the Miami River. Recent archaeological discoveries, however, tell the story of more than 4,000 years of habitation and provide new clues about the lifestyle of Miami's first residents.

■ *Lake Okeechobee and the Everglades were created 5,000 years ago when the Ice Age caps melted. Humans lived on the ridge and on island villages in the Everglades. Here, a fishing party in a dugout canoe returns to the village with the day's catch. (HMSF)*

■ More than 3,500 years before the arrival of the Spanish, Miami's native people occupied both sides of the Miami River. In 1998, archaeologists discovery numerous postholes carved in a 38-foot circle. Called the Miami Circle, this discovery added to present-day knowledge of more than 4,000 years of human habitation on the Miami River. (HMSF)

■ A conch shell lashed to a stick made a useful weapon. (HMSF)

The 1998 discovery of what has been called the "Miami Circle" revealed that humans lived on the south bank of the Miami River in a series of circular huts as early as 750 B.C. The site included a structure, 38 feet in diameter, supported by between 75 and 100 wooden posts thrust deep into the bedrock. This structure was most likely a public or sacred building perhaps near the home of the cacique or chief. For some unknown reason, by 1200 A.D., the Indians had abandoned this settlement but remained on the north bank of the river.

Recovered artifacts from both the north and south banks of the Miami River reveal that Miami's first people traded with other prehistoric people as distant as northern Georgia and the Appalachian Mountains. These objects also indicate a robust trade with North Florida tribes as well as their South Florida neighbors.

The Spanish wrote that Miami's native people were tall, handsome and well-developed. The men wore simple breech cloths, and the women fashioned skirts from Spanish moss. Their Garden of Eden, filled with pine and hardwood forests, was home to an abundance of bear, deer and wild fowl. Inexhaustible fresh water bubbled up in the rocky land and even in the salty coastal waters. The sea and the rivers teemed with fish, manatee, turtles, oysters, clams and conch. They also made bread from starch extracted from the native comptie (zamia integrifolia).

Although no metal and little usable stone were present in South Florida, the native people created a variety of weapons and tools from the abundant shells. Lashed to a stick, a heavy conch shell became a club, its sharp lip an ax, its spiral center a pick. They also obtained harder stone from other tribes in North Florida and in the southeastern United States.

THE COMING OF SPAIN

In the early Sixteenth Century, Juan Ponce de León discovered Florida's first people. Ponce was a remarkable man, imbued with the same kind of curiosity and dreams of glory that propelled Christopher Columbus to discover the New World in 1492. He joined Columbus on his second voyage in 1493 and helped him establish the first permanent settlement in the New World on the Caribbean island of Hispaniola.

Ponce de León was not content to remain a follower. In 1508, he, too, became a discoverer when he found and named the island of Puerto Rico. After he lost the governorship of Puerto Rico to Columbus' son Don Diego, Ponce decided to move on. He heard the Indians whisper about an island to the north that they called Bimini. Spurred by their belief that the island had a magical spring that gave eternal youth, Ponce de León set out for a new frontier and what he hoped would be a new life.

On March 3, 1513, Ponce de León left Puerto Rico to search for the legendary island of Bimini. He missed Bimini but, after sailing 25 days, sighted a large body of land to the west. A week later, he stepped ashore (somewhere between present-day Saint Augustine and Jacksonville) on what he believed was another new island. He did not realize that he had actually discovered the southern shore of a huge new continent.

He named the new land *Pascua Florida* after the Feast of the Flowers at Easter time.

Three months after Ponce de León discovered Florida, he sailed into today's Biscayne Bay and wrote in his journal, "reached Chequescha." It was Miami's first recorded name. At the same time he also named a large offshore island Santa Marta. Today it is known as Key Biscayne. Ponce did not record whether or not he came ashore and met the people living there but it seems likely that he did. He remained in the area for almost two weeks and, from that time forward, the Spanish called the Indians of the southeast Florida coast Tequestas. In 1521, Ponce de León tried to colonize the southwest Florida coast but the native Indians mortally

wounded him and drove the Spanish away.

During the next 40 years, several other brave Spaniards tried to conquer Florida. They, like Ponce de León, were no match for Florida's native people. When the Spanish discovered gold and silver in Mexico and Peru, their interests shifted to those more lucrative ventures.

By mid-century, 50 years had passed since Spain claimed Florida—which at one time included most of the eastern United States. For most of that time, Spain was so powerful that no other European power dared question that control—even though *La Florida* had never been completely explored, much less occupied, by the Spanish.

At first, other European powers—through their pirates and privateers—were content to prey on the homeward-bound Spanish treasure fleet. Before long, however, European royalty coveted unsettled Spanish territory as well. In 1562, the French established an outpost near present-day Jacksonville that they named Fort Caroline. To meet the challenge to Spanish territory, King Phillip II named Pedro Menéndez de Avilés *adelantado* (governor) of Florida and commanded him to drive out the French and secure Florida for Spain.

In 1565, Pedro Menéndez de Avilés attacked and vanquished the French from Fort Caroline and founded Saint Augustine, the first permanent settlement in what is now the United States. Once he expelled the French, Menéndez built a few outposts to bolster Spanish control and left soldiers behind to hold the positions. In 1566, with these steps taken, Menéndez looked to South Florida.

■ *Juan Ponce de León (upper left) made history when he discovered Florida in April 1513. Three months later he wrote that he "reached Chequesta," Miami's first recorded name. (HMSF)*

■ *In 1564, French artist Jacques LeMoyne came with explorer Jean Ribalt to Fort Caroline near Jacksonville, Florida. He was the first European to draw Florida's native people (left). In 1591, Theodore DeBry made engravings and published a book of the drawing. (APC)*

■ *Cartographer Alain Manesson Mallet published this map of Florida (facing page) in 1683 in his Description de L'Univers. (JF)*

FIGURE CXXVIII.

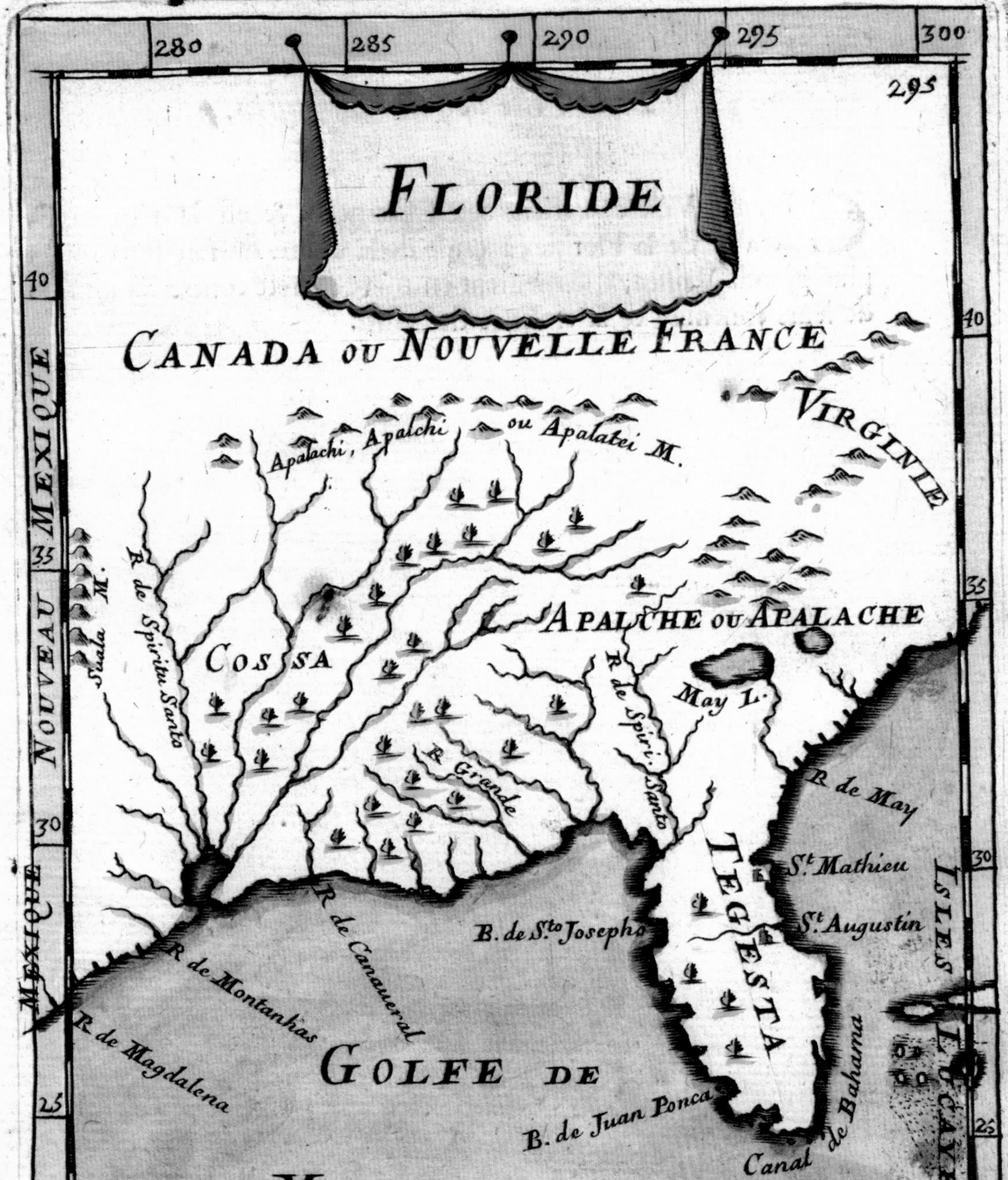

FLORIDE

CANADA ou NOUVELLE FRANCE

VIRGINIE

Apalachi, Apalchi ou Apalatei M.

APALCHE ou APALACHE

Cossa

R. de Spiritu Santo

Suala M.

May L.

R. de Spiri. Santo

R. de May

R. Grande

St. Mathieu

TEGESTA

St. Augustin

NOUVEAU MEXIQUE

MEXIQUE

ISLES LUCAYES

B. de Sto Josepho

R. de Canaueral

R. de Montanhas

GOLFE DE

R. de Magdalena

B. de Juan Ponce

Canal de Bahama

MEXIQUE

ISLE CUBA

280 285 290 295 300

40

35

30

25

South Florida had intrigued the Spanish from the time of Ponce's discovery. They believed it was the best site to control the Florida Straits and guard the treasure fleet. But it had a mysterious and foreboding aura because hundreds of shipwrecked Spaniards had disappeared on its shores.

Pedro Menéndez de Avilés' own son was one of the missing. Spurred by the lingering hope that his son might be alive, Menéndez sailed to Florida's southwest coast near the place Ponce de León landed 45 years earlier.

In February 1566, as Menéndez prepared to go ashore, a startled lookout spied a dugout canoe rapidly coming toward them. Standing in the canoe was what he described as a "naked and painted" Indian wildly waving a crucifix. The Indian, as it turned out, was not an Indian at all but a shipwrecked Spaniard, Hernando d'Escalante Fontaneda, who had been stranded in Florida for 17 years. He was one of the few survivors of more than 250 Spaniards who washed ashore from wrecked ships. (Menéndez never found his missing son.) d'Escalante Fontaneda traveled all over the area, visiting and recording the names of many different Indian villages. He also learned their languages. When he became Menéndez's interpreter and guide, Menéndez had an advantage over other would-be-conquerors. (Eventually d'Escalante Fontaneda returned to Spain and wrote his memoirs.)

D'Escalante Fontaneda was not Menéndez's only stroke of good luck. Soon after he landed, he met Chief Carlos, principal chief of all the South Florida Indians. Chief Carlos was so impressed with the dashing Spaniard that he wanted to give him his sister for a wife. Menéndez was no fool. Even though he had a wife in Spain, he agreed to marry Carlos' sister if she would convert to Catholicism. His newly christened bride, Doña Antonia, became his first Indian convert and, at least temporarily, the key to his unprecedented success.

Menéndez had big plans for South Florida. Before he left the west coast, his soldiers built two small outposts—one at Carlos and another at Tocobaga near Tampa Bay. After returning to his supply base at Havana, he planned to sail to the east coast to a place d'Escalante Fontaneda said was ruled by a chief named Tequesta. Menéndez, however, was not the first Spaniard to arrive triumphantly in Tequesta and write the first chapter of Miami's recorded history. That honor fell to other men.

MISSION AT TEQUESTA

Miami's first Europeans were not ordinary pioneers. They were mutineers on the run from the Spanish fort at San Mateo (near present-day Jacksonville). When their drinking water ran out, they anchored in Biscayne Bay in order to send a party ashore to look for a fresh supply. While some of the men were ashore, the soldiers on the ship took advantage of favorable winds and sailed away, leaving their comrades stranded.

But the winds blew the fleeing mutineers right into the hands of the Spanish, who were searching for them in the Florida Straits. When the Spanish captured the mutineers and took them to Havana, they told Menéndez about the men left behind at Tequesta. Menéndez sent his nephew, Pedro Menéndez Marqués, to investigate even though he did not expect to find anyone alive.

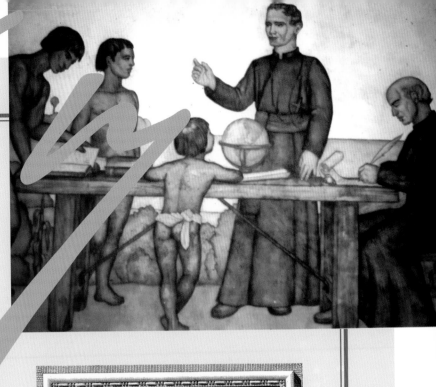

An Historic Beginning

■ *In February 1567, Jesuit Brother Francisco Villareal (top right) opened a mission at Tequesta. At first, the native people were friendly and eager to learn. (HMSF)*

■ *Pedro Menéndez de Avilés (bottom right) founded Saint Augustine in 1565 and two years later sent his men to the Miami River to open a mission at the place he named Tequesta after the native chief. (HMSF)*

■ *Chief Tequesta welcomed Pedro Menéndez de Avilés and his men when they arrived at the Tequesta village on the north bank of the Miami River in early 1568. During his four-day stay, the native children entertained him with a religious drama. (HMSF)*

PEDRO MENENDEZ DE AVILES.
Natural de Avilés en Asturias, Comendador de la orden de Santiago, Conquistador de la Florida, nombrado Gral de la Armada contra Inglaterra. Murió en Santander N.º 1574, á los 55 de edad.

uban-born artist Manuel Carbonell created the inspiring 53-foot-tall bronze statue of a Tequesta family as part of the new Brickell Avenue Bridge designed by the architectural firm of Portuondo, Perotti and Associates. The column includes additional bas-relief images of Florida's native people. Ironically, just a few years after it was dedicated, archaeologists discovered an unknown Tequesta site nearby that they called the "Miami Circle." (APC)

Pedro Menéndez Marqués arrived in Tequesta in October 1566. He found the mutineers not only alive but enjoying their new life with the Indians. The mutineers told the incredible story of their landing and subsequent meeting with the Tequesta Indians. Fortunately, Chief Tequesta knew about Menéndez's marriage to the Indian princess who was his relative. Because of this marriage bond, Tequesta treated the mutineers like family and honored guests. When Chief Carlos sent his men to Tequesta to bring the Spanish to his village on the southwest coast, the Tequesta Indians fought to keep them.

Many of the mutineers did not want to leave. If they went with Menéndez Marqués, they would surely be charged with treason. Besides, Chief Tequesta treated them very well. He seemed to like them. He even announced that he wanted more Spanish to come and live in his village. To prove his good intentions, he sent his brother to Havana with Menéndez Marqués to personally invite Adelantado Pedro Menéndez de Avilés to come to Tequesta.

In February 1567, Pedro Menéndez de Avilés sent a party of 30 men to Tequesta to join several of the mutineers who, in return for amnesty, agreed to stay. The head of the expedition was not a soldier but a Jesuit, Brother Francisco Villareal. Menéndez wanted Brother Villareal to establish a mission in order to pacify the Indians and convert them to Christianity.

At first, things went well at the new mission. The Indians helped Brother Villareal raise a large pine cross in the village. They also helped the soldiers build 28 simple houses within

After his first visit, Pedro Menéndez de Avilés took several native people with him to Seville, Spain to be baptized in the cathedral famous for its Giralda Tower. (APC)

FISHING TEQUESTA STYLE

"*In winter all the Indians go out to sea in their canoes to hunt for seacows [manatee]. One of their number carries three stakes fastened to his girdle and a rope on his arm. When he discovers a seacow he throws his rope around its neck and as the animal sinks under the water, the Indian drives a stake through one of its nostrils and no matter how much it may dive, the Indian never loses it because he goes on its back.*"

Don Hernando d'Escalante Fontaneda, c1569

a large stockade. Soon after they completed the work, Pedro Menéndez de Avilés arrived to check the mission's progress. He called the Indians "affable" and was impressed with their hospitality. The soldiers and the Indians, under Brother Villareal's direction, entertained him with a religious drama. After a four-day visit, he took Tequesta's brother and several other Indians with him to be baptized in the great cathedral in Seville, famous for its Giralda Tower.

For awhile, the mission at Tequesta looked as if it would be the most successful in Florida. But the soldiers disliked South Florida. The climate was unbearably hot and the mosquitoes almost drove the men crazy. When fishing and hunting expeditions did not go well, the Spanish often went

hungry. Bored, discontented and miserable, the soldiers harassed the Indian women, bothered the men, insulted the elders and made fun of Indian customs. Inevitably, the Indians demanded that the Spanish leave.

Perplexed, Brother Villareal tried to make the soldiers behave but one pious brother had little effect on the restless men. Besides, he had his own problems. His religious instruction faltered. His high hopes for conversion had not materialized. He could not teach the Catholic doctrine to recalcitrant subjects who were constantly on the move. If he gave the Indians gifts, they would listen, but his only converts were among the very young or the dying.

The situation at Tequesta grew tense. After a disgruntled soldier killed a tribal elder over an alleged insult, the Indians struck back, killing four of the soldiers. Undoubtedly, all the Spaniards would have been killed if a Spanish supply ship had not arrived in time to save them and take them to Havana.

But all was not lost. A few months after their frantic departure from Tequesta, the Spanish gained an unexpected ally. Tequesta's brother—fresh from his baptism in Spain—returned to Florida as Don Diego, Christian. He told the Indians glowing stories about his royal reception in Seville. He talked them into giving the Spanish another chance. As a sign of reconciliation, Don Diego had the Indians erect another cross in their village and wear red crosses at their throats. Encouraged, the Spanish returned to Tequesta and reopened the mission in 1568. Little is known of the second mission at Tequesta except that it was short-lived. In 1570, the Jesuits decided to concentrate their efforts on more willing subjects outside Florida.

Even though the mission at Tequesta (and a similar one on the southwest coast) lasted only a few years, the missions profoundly affected the course of history. During the brief settlement, the Spanish and the Indians became friendly. The Spanish worked hard to cement the alliance. They invited the South Florida Indians to Saint Augustine for feast days. On these occasions, the Spanish governor of Florida entertained the Indians like visiting heads of state. This special treatment paid off. When Spanish ships wrecked on the Florida reef, the Indians often came to their assistance. When ships of other countries foundered, the Indians killed any survivors. Sailors learned that if they washed ashore, they must pretend to be Spanish if they wanted to live. This charade was not always easy because many of the Indians learned to speak Spanish.

The Indians became expert salvagers of Spanish shipwrecks and often traded their bounty back to the Spanish. The Indians also had contact with Cuban fishermen and even traveled to Cuba in their dugout canoes. As the years passed, other European powers challenged Spain for New World supremacy. By the early Eighteenth Century, Spain's arch rival, England, had firmly established 13 colonies that would later become the nucleus of the United States. In Georgia and the Carolinas, British colonists settled on Creek Indian land, driving many Creeks across the border into Spanish Florida. Once in Florida, the Creeks threatened both the Spanish and the Florida natives.

Even without this new challenge, the South Florida natives were in serious trouble. European-introduced diseases, such as smallpox, ravaged thousands of families. Internecine wars and human sacrifice reduced the population even more. Large quantities of rum, taken from shipwrecks and traded by Cuban fishermen, dimmed the spirit of the once-proud warriors. What remained was only a small remnant—an easy target for Creek war parties who were slowly pushing down the Florida peninsula.

When the Creeks arrived in South Florida, they plundered and burned the native villages. They captured women and children and forced them into slavery. Trying to escape this wily new enemy, the native Indians retreated to the extreme southern coast and onto the Keys. Before long, the Creeks even threatened these island strongholds.

With their backs to the sea, the native South Florida Indians made a desperate choice. If they wanted to live in freedom, they would have to leave their native land and seek refuge elsewhere. In 1711, several chiefs went to Havana to ask if they could immigrate to Cuba. The Cuban leaders agreed that something had to be done to help their Florida friends. They sent several Cuban ships to investigate the situation. When the ships appeared off the Florida coast, the captains discovered 2,000 Indians waiting on shore. Unprepared for such a deluge of refugees, the ships could only hold 270 Indians. The rest were left behind.

When the first wave of Florida refugees arrived in Havana, the Cubans took them into their homes and promised them a place of their own in Cuba. Before they could be resettled, however, another disaster struck. The Indians had no natural immunity against alien diseases. One by one, the newcomers contracted a violent illness that killed all but 70. Frightened and homesick, many survivors returned to their Florida home.

But the conditions that sent the Indians to Havana only grew worse. A few years later, the remaining South Florida Indians decided once again to go to Havana. The Cubans sent two more ships to Florida but this time, for some reason, the Indians abandoned ship before they sailed. The first boatlift had ended badly; the second was a total failure.

The outraged Cubans believed that the Indians had taken advantage of their goodwill. As a result, sentiment in Havana changed. It might be better, the Cubans reasoned, to help the Indians on their native soil. Then the Cubans would not have to deal with a large number of destitute refugees with alien customs. It better served the Spanish national interest to keep friendly Indian allies in Florida as a buffer against the invading Creeks who sided with the hated English.

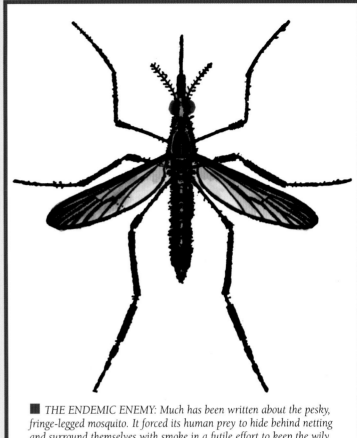

■ *THE ENDEMIC ENEMY: Much has been written about the pesky, fringe-legged mosquito. It forced its human prey to hide behind netting and surround themselves with smoke in a futile effort to keep the wily enemy at bay. (HMSF)*

TRIAL BY MOSQUITO

Like the serpent in the Garden of Eden, the mosquito was the spoiler in South Florida's tropical paradise. "I and the others have constantly remained healthy, glory be to God, which helps us endure with little difficulty some of the burdens of the land that otherwise would seem insufferable," wrote Brother Villareal in the first known correspondence from what later became Miami. "I am referring to the three or more months of mosquitoes we have endured, in which I passed some nights and days without being able to sleep for an hour…Our sleep during all that time was around the fire and immersed in clouds of smoke, as one could not survive in any other way."

Brother Francisco Villareal
Tequesta, January 23, 1568

UNCOMMON SUFFERINGS

In 1748, Briton Hammon, a black man from Massachusetts, and eight other men shipwrecked on the reef near what later became Miami. As some of the crew rowed to shore in a small boat, 60 Indians in 20 canoes intercepted them and killed everyone except Hammon. They took Hammon back to their village and, according to Hammon, "they intended to roast me alive…But they were better to me than I feared and soon unbound me, but set a guard over me every night. They kept me with them about five weeks during which time they used me pretty well and gave me boiled corn which is what they eat themselves."

When the captain of a Spanish ship rescued Hammon and took him to Havana, the Indians went to Havana and demanded that the governor return Hammon to them. The governor resolved the conflict by paying a ransom of $10 for Hammon. Eventually, Hammon made it back to Massachusetts and published a pamphlet about his "uncommon sufferings."

Narrative of the *Uncommon Sufferings and Surprising Deliverance of Briton Hammon*
Boston, 1760

CHANGES OF HEART

With such considerations in mind, the Spanish returned to South Florida. In the summer of 1743, Father Joseph Maria Mónaco, Father Joseph Xavier de Alaña and a group of Spanish soldiers arrived at the old Tequesta settlement with plans to build another mission. This time, the Spanish built a substantial, triangular stockade with mortared corners and three wall guns. They christened it *Pueblo de Santa Maria de Loreto*. It was the second place name given to Miami.

Only about 180 Indians—remnants of the Tequestas and other scattered bands—remained in the villages on the Miami River. (In the Eighteenth Century, the Spanish called them Costa Indians.) Although their population diminished, the remaining Indian families continued to live as they had for generations. Their attitude toward the Spanish, however, changed. What the Spanish called the "kind, affable" Indians were now angry and bitter. They no longer welcomed the Spanish. The braves spewed epithets at the priests and demanded rum and fine clothing. The Indian priests argued with their Spanish counterparts and flaunted the religious practices, which the Spanish found especially repugnant. They demanded that the Spanish pay a tribute if they wanted to remain in South Florida.

Despite such hostility, the priests believed that the *Pueblo de Santa Maria de Loreto* had a promising future. In a lengthy report, the priests predicted that if the Crown would send more soldiers to pacify the Indians and farmers to till the soil, the pueblo could become the largest settlement in Florida. The Crown, however, was not impressed with future possibilities; the present situation was untenable. The king ordered the fort destroyed and the mission abandoned. Once again, the chance for a permanent settlement at the future site of Miami was lost.

Twenty years after the Spanish gave up on Miami, they also gave up on Florida. At the 1763 Treaty of Paris that ended the Seven Years' War (Americans called it the French and Indian War), Spain used Florida to ransom back Havana from the English who had captured it a year earlier. After more than two centuries of Spanish rule, Florida became an English colony. This switch was the last straw for South Florida's natives. The remaining families—numbering only about 80—

Father Joseph Xavier de Alaña prepared this map, Pueblo de Santa Maria de Loreto, *at the time of the 1743 mission. It highlighted the forks of the Miami River as it entered the Everglades (near the upper quarter) and what is now Miami Beach (the narrow peninsula on the right). (UF)*

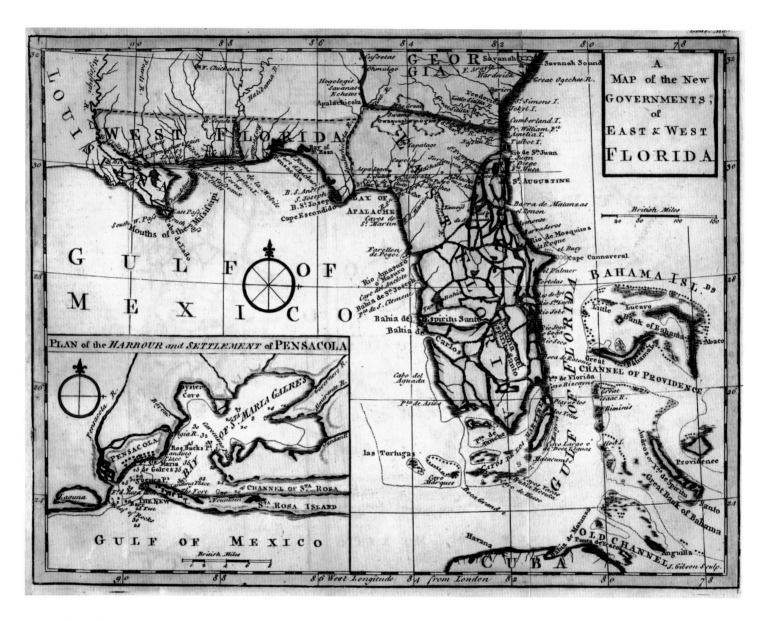

gathered at what is now Key West and prepared to leave their ancestral home. When the Spanish pulled out of Florida, the last of the South Florida Indians followed them to Cuba.

The British were the real victors at the Treaty of Paris. In addition to Florida, they received Canada from the French, rounding out their American empire from the Atlantic Ocean to the Mississippi River. Although Spain lost Florida, they regained Cuba, which they clearly considered the better part of the bargain.

Under the Treaty of Paris, Spanish subjects had the option of either departing or remaining in Florida. Most of the Spanish residents distrusted British rule and considered the Anglican religion heretical. They believed their future would be more

secure in Cuba. Thus, the British took over a new territory almost devoid of people. The largest group left in Florida were bands of runaway Creeks who, from the time of the British occupation, would be called Seminoles (meaning renegade).

The first order of business for the British was to survey their new territory and locate suitable land for European settlement. For administrative purposes, they divided the area into two sections—East Florida (from the Atlantic Ocean to the Apalachicola River) and West Florida (from the Apalachicola River to the Mississippi River). In 1764, East Florida Governor James Grant appointed William Gerard De Brahm surveyor general. Between 1765 and 1771, De Brahm carefully surveyed and mapped Florida's entire east coast and changed many of the Spanish place names to English. Biscayne Bay became Sandwich Gulf after the Earl of Sandwich. The Rio Ratones (Miami River) became the Garbrand River.

Another British surveyor, Bernard Romans, also came to South Florida. He noted the remains of the pueblo on the north bank of the Miami River and called the river Ratton.

While De Brahm and Romans commented on the absence of any kind of permanent settlement on the South Florida mainland, both noted that people from the Bahamas, whom they called "New Providence men," frequented the area. The English first settled the Bahama Islands in 1647 when a group of men known as the Elutherian Adventurers came from Bermuda to establish a colony. For many years, Nassau was the base of pirates and privateers who plagued the Florida Straits and the Bahama Channel. After Bahamian Governor Woodes Rogers drove out most of the pirates and established a semblance of order in the Bahamas, the hearty souls who stayed still made their living from the sea. The nearby and uninhabited Florida coast became a natural rendezvous for Bahamian wreckers and fishermen.

The English were eager to populate Florida in order to round out their stronghold on the eastern coast of North America. Because they succeeded in other colonies, they had every reason to believe settlers would flock to what one enthusiast called "the most precious jewel of his Majesty's American dominion." To ensure immigration, the government placed glowing advertisements in London newspapers offering free land to proprietors who promised to bring settlers to Florida. The Crown gave several proprietors huge grants that included much of what is now Greater Miami.

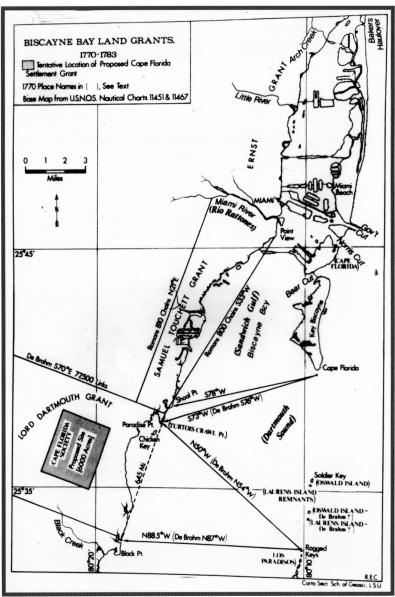

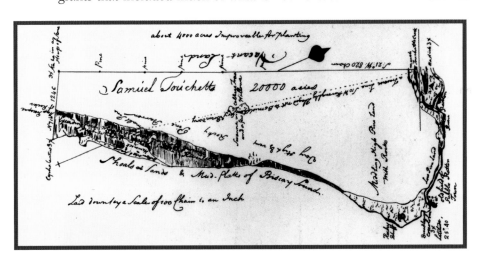

■ *During Florida's British Period (1763-1783), cartographer John Gibson created this map of East and West Florida (facing page). It was published in Gentleman's Magazine in November 1763 shortly after England traded Cuba to Spain for Florida following the Seven Years' War (French and Indian War). (JF)*

■ *A 1771 survey prepared by Bernard Romans (left) included 20,000 acres south of the Ratton River (Miami River) and the "old field of Pueblo Ratton Town" at the bottom of the river's north bank. (LC)*

■ *Although no settlers came, the Crown awarded several large land grants (top right) during the British Period to encourage settlement in their 13th American colony. The area between today's Arch Creek and Black Point was divided among three men: John Ernst, Samuel Touchett and the Earl of Dartmouth. (RC)*

"AMERICAN ROYALTY"
Time & Time Again

1564

Jacques LeMoyne drawing of Florida's native people. (APC)

2007

American Royalty, new works of art modeled after LeMoyne drawings and created by artists Brad Cooley and his son Brad Cooley Jr. to honor Florida's native people, stand on the grounds of the R.A. Gray Building in Tallahassee, Florida. Governor Charlie Christ, with members of the Seminole Tribal Council, unveiled the statues on March 15, 2007. (SPA)

In 1766, Samuel Touchett received 20,000 acres south of what is now the Miami River. He hired Bernard Romans to survey the grant on which he planned to raise indigo, sugar, rice and "anything else that would grow."

The king also granted 20,000 acres between the Miami River and Arch Creek to John Augustus Ewan, a German Protestant who lived in England. He agreed to bring large numbers of Swiss and German Protestants to settle it.

William Legge, the Second Earl of Dartmouth made the most ambitious proposal. It involved 40,000 acres of South Dade land in the present Kendall area. Lord Dartmouth set aside 6,000 acres in the middle of the grant for a planned settlement he called the Cape Florida Society.

The principals in the Cape Florida Society were Lord Dartmouth, the surveyor Gerard De Brahm and two Swiss Protestants. In order to promote the venture, De Brahm wrote an extensive eyewitness account of South Florida, pointing out some of the problems would-be settlers might face.

> *As to wild beasts, they are never known to have hurt a person, unless when they being attaqued, was obliged to defend themselves, they all will flye, at the Sight of a human species, except Basilisks [rattlesnakes] they cannot flye, but when a person comes near them, they will give warning with rattling their tales, which is equal to the noise of the mounting of a watch, at which noise one may Stand of. Crocodilles in deed will attaque a person but not otherwise than in the water.*

He also warned immigrants not to listen to rumors and cautioned them that the Bahamian fishermen would try to scare them away so they could keep the area for themselves.

The proprietors organized the society into what they called a "small community of twenty households, made up of honest, industrious and resourceful" Protestants from Switzerland, England, Scotland and Italy. The planned community would operate on a democratic framework similar to the Mayflower Compact.

If all these proprietors—or even one of them—had settled their claims as planned, Miami probably would have developed a century before it did. For one reason or another, none of the grantees confirmed their grants and there are no records of British settlers in South Florida during the British Period.

Lasting from 1763 to 1783, the British period was simply too short. Revolution brewed in America, and outright war was on its way. But the two Floridas—part of his Majesty's 14 colonies and the 15 American colonies—played an unusual role in the American Revolution. They became a haven for Tories, or Loyalists who refused to rebel against the Crown. When the Loyalists became as unpopular with the American rebels as the British army, many had to flee. At first, the refugees trickled into British Florida. But as the war progressed, the trickle turned into a flood. Saint Augustine became a boom town after nearly 12,000 Loyalists arrived from other American colonies. Even more Loyalists poured into Florida at the end of the war. Then, with no advance warning, the Crown announced that the British would exchange Florida for the Bahamas, which Spain had captured during the war. Like the Spanish before them, the British in Florida faced a dilemma. They could either take their chances in Spanish Florida or move to another British colony where the Crown offered free land in return for their loyalty. Thousands of Loyalists chose the Bahamas, swelling the island population to more than 11,000 by 1789.

During the Second Spanish Period (1784-1821), Spain adopted a more liberal land policy than previously. They permitted foreigners and non-Catholics to receive land grants if they pledged their loyalty to the Spanish Crown. Two individuals received Spanish grants in the Miami area. The first grant was to Pedro Fornells for 175 acres on *"Cayo Biscaino"* (Key Biscayne). The second was to John Egan for 100 acres on the north bank of the *"Rio nombrado de aquadulze"* (Miami River).

HOTBED OF DISCONTENT

Miami was anything but deserted during the Second Spanish Period. Even though Spain had legal title to South Florida, it was clearly in Bahamian hands. The Bahamians were a thorn in the side of the Spanish. Nassau was a hotbed of discontented Loyalists determined to retake Florida. Adventurers, such as William Augustus Bowles, led raids into Florida to harass the Spanish, slipping in undetected on deserted South Florida beaches.

THE GOOD SAMARITAN OF CAPE FLORIDA SETTLEMENT

In 1819, a Cape Florida resident put the following notice in the Bahamas Royal Gazette *to assist mariners who wrecked on the reef.*

"Having observed in the course of long experience that several masters of vessels, who had the misfortune to be cast away on the Martyrs and the Coasts of Florida, ignorant of the existance [sic] of any settlement at Cape Florida, have attempted to proceed to the Northward in their boats, deprived of every sustenance, we feel it incumbent upon me to inform such as may hereafter experience a like misfortune, that if they pass to the North of Key Biscayne, they will find the entrance to Boca Ratones [Norris Cut], through which they can safely go with their boats and they will see the Houses in front on the mainland.

"In case of Shipwreck, to the northward of Boca Ratones, at the distance of two miles there from, they will perceive mangroves thickly scattered from where the houses may be seen; and in this situation on making a signal with fire or otherwise, they will obtain assistance.

"If it should happen to the Southward of New River they may proceed southward along the Beach where they will meet every four miles, and posts fixed in the ground, on which there is an inscription in English, French and Spanish indicating where Wells of fresh water have been properly dug."

When the Spanish captured Bowles, several of his men remained in South Florida, squatting undisturbed on Spanish land.

Charles Lewis was one of Bowles' men. Once he arrived in Florida, he decided to stay. He moved his family from Nassau to the banks of the New River (now Fort Lauderdale). The Lewis settlement included a house, a barn for his horses, a blacksmith shop and a chicken coop. In the early 1800s, the family moved to the Miami River settlement, taking up residence on the south side near today's Vizcaya. They were joined by several other Bahamian families who settled on both sides of the river and on Key Biscayne. Of these, only John Egan bothered to file a claim with the Spanish government. Before the Second Spanish Period ended, the *Nassau Royal Gazette* referred to the Miami area as The Cape Florida Settle-

ment. The Bahamians, in fact, considered South Florida almost part of the Bahamas. Bahamian merchant ships did a thriving business there. People from the Cape Florida Settlement went to Nassau to sell their venison hams and alligator skins. Often, they helped Bahamians wrecked on the Florida reefs, prompting one ship captain to publicly express his gratitude in the *Royal Gazette.*

Bahamians also came to South Florida to salvage the ever-increasing number of shipwrecks on the reef. Every visitor commented on the numerous wrecking vessels always on the scene. One reported seeing 27 wrecking boats anchored in what is today called Hurricane Harbor at Key Biscayne.

When a ship hit the reef, the "wreckers" were quickly dispatched to aid the distressed, salvage the remains of the ship and its cargo and return to Nassau with the prize. Between wrecks, the seamen busied themselves by fishing, turtling and cutting the Keys hardwood. The Spanish could not stop the Bahamian interlopers. The Bahamians were a minor problem, however, compared to American encroachment from the north that ultimately doomed Spanish Florida. American adventurers harassed the Spanish and agitated for annexation. One point of contention between the two was the large number of runaway slaves that the Spanish allowed to escape into Florida and join the Indians. One visitor reported that he met 61 runaways living on Key Biscayne with as many Indians. Another reported that more than 300 blacks, or what some called black Indians, left Cape Florida for the Bahamas. They later established a village on Andros Island called Red Bay where their ancestors still live today.

American animosity against Spanish Florida even reached the Cape Florida Settlement. Once, Levi James, an American privateer from Savannah, attacked the settlement under the excuse that he was teaching "the Spanish rascals to keep their place." The fact that the people whose houses he burned were not Spanish was of little consequence. They lived on Spanish land and that was enough. When the residents resisted, James flayed William Lewis with a cat-o-nine tails and "almost deprived him of his life."

By 1819, the Spanish were ready to get out of Florida. As far as they were concerned, the Americans could have it if they wanted it. In 1821, with formalities concluded, Florida joined the United States.

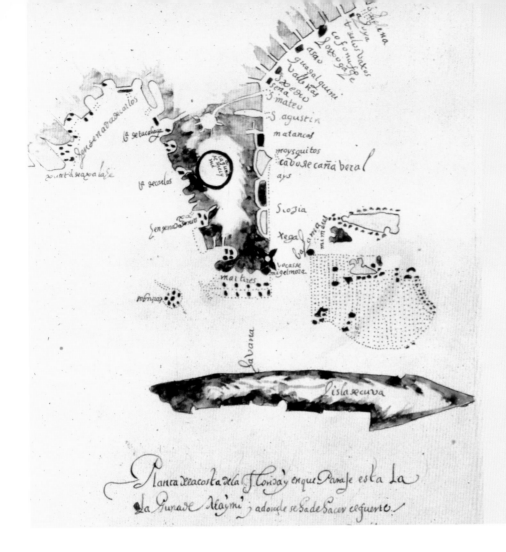

WHERE DID THE NAME MIAMI COME FROM?

People often wonder about the origin of the name Miami. It is an Indian name (translated as either big water or sweet water) given to the huge body of water we call Lake Okeechobee. An early Spanish map, Mapa De La Florida y Laguna de Maimi, 1565-1600 (left) is one of the first to document its use. With passing years, the name made its way down to what we call the Miami River because early explorers thought the Miami River was a tributary of the lake. It was not used as a place name until the 1840s and then only briefly. But from that time until the founding of the City of Miami in 1896, it kept reappearing—often with different spellings. (JF)

THE CHANGE of FLAGS ~ JULY 10TH 1821

"Florida, sir, is not worth buying. It is a land of swamps, of quagmires, of frogs and alligators and mosquitoes! A man, sir, would not immigrate into Florida— no, not from Hell itself."
Representative John Randolph of Virginia

■ *Despite generally negative feelings about Florida, the U.S. government acquired it from Spain in 1821 (left). (SPA)*

■ *Late in the afternoon of July 23, 1836, Indians attacked the Cape Florida Lighthouse. Assistant Lighthouse Keeper John Thompson miraculously survived and the crew of a Navy schooner rescued him from the top of the tower. His assistant, Aaron Carter, died in the skirmish. The lighthouse remained out of service for the balance of the Second Seminole War. (HMSF)*

Chapter Two

Bloody Red, White & Blue

"After all, Florida is certainly the poorest Country that ever two people quarreled for."

Dr. Jacob Rhett Motte, U.S. Army Surgeon, Second Seminole War, 1838

N 1821, WHEN THE SPANISH LOWERED THEIR FLAG AND THE UNITED STATES OF AMERICA RAISED THE

Stars and Stripes, one observer predicted that settlers would "pour in from all parts of the Union to enjoy the advantages so liberally bestowed by nature upon Florida." The United States could not open Florida to newcomers, however, until they settled private land claims. Under the treaty of Spanish cession, the U.S. government had to confirm all Spanish land grants issued before January 24, 1818. In order to honor the treaty, the U.S. government formed a special commission to judge individual claims.

The land commission met for two years before word of its existence reached the Cape Florida Settlement. Few North Floridians knew that settlers lived on the Miami River. Most Americans, in fact, believed South Florida matched the land office description of "a place of half-deluged plains, deep morasses, and almost inaccessible forests...a home or shelter only for beasts, or for men little elevated above beasts." When the U.S. government suggested building a road from Saint Augustine to Cape Florida, the surveyor, James Gadsden, questioned the

need for such a road beyond the Saint Lucie River because the southern tip of Florida was beyond "the ultimate limit of population...(excepting such establishments as may be made for the object of wrecking and fishing near the Cape)."

Despite its isolation, the Egans, Lewises, Pents and a few other Bahamian families called this southern tip of Florida home. When they learned about the commission, they sent a petition to Congress requesting title to the land on which they had been living for more than 15 years. James Egan received 640 acres, including his father John's Spanish land grant, on the north bank of the Miami River. (John Egan had drowned a few years earlier in the Nassau harbor.) His widowed mother, Rebecca, acquired another 640 acres on the south bank. When the Egans received their papers, they discovered the land commission recorded their name as Hagan instead of Egan. They were not concerned about the mistake since, as Bahamians, they pronounced it Hagan anyway.

■ In this 1846 U.S. Surveyor General map (left), the "donations" refer to federal land grants dating back to the 1820s. Two members of both the Egan and Lewis families received the grant after they proved they were living on the land when acquired by the United States. (APC)

■ Naturalist Francis Comte de Castelnau, visited Florida in 1837 and included this view of Key West (far left) in his notes published in 1843. Key West was Florida's largest city. (HMSF)

■ Commodore David Porter (facing page) of the U.S. Navy Anti-Pirate Squadron. (USN)

■ CAPE FLORIDA: In 1851, the Coast Survey Team prepared this drawing of the Cape Florida Lighthouse and keeper's cottage. The masts of a ship are visible in today's Hurricane Harbor. (APC)

Immediately south of Rebecca Egan's grant, the commission validated Mary "Polly" Lewis' claim for 640 acres, along with her brother-in-law Jonathan Lewis' claim for another 640 acres immediately south of her tract. Even though they had large tracts of land, they probably lived near each other in what later became known as the "Punch Bowl"—a natural spring on the bluffs just south of today's Rickenbacker Causeway. Jonathan Lewis' widowed mother, Frankee, received title to the original Lewis homestead on the New River (Fort Lauderdale). The commission denied Bahamian Temple Pent's claim, probably because it conflicted with Jonathan and Polly Lewis' grants. Despite this setback, Pent and his family remained in the area. The only other confirmed grant was on Key Biscayne. Mary Ann Davis received title to 175 acres through purchase of the original Spanish grant from Pedro Fornells for $100. Except for these six grants—a little more than 3,000 acres—the rest of South Florida was in the public domain.

The Egan and Lewis family grants were milestones in the history of Miami. From that time forward, the river on which they lived would be called the Miami River and the chain of title began to the land that someday would be the City of Miami.

A KEY FOR CIVILIZATION

Miami was not destined to be South Florida's first real community. That honor fell to the island of Key West. Soon after Florida became a territory, American John Simonton received title to the former Spanish island of Cayo Hueso. In 1823,

the United States, eager to bring some law and order to this watery frontier, opened a naval depot in Key West. The depot became the temporary headquarters for the U.S. Anti-Pirate Squadron that came to rid the Florida Keys of the predators who had ruled the Florida Straits for generations.

That same year, the territorial government instituted a semblance of civil order when it created Monroe County, with Key West as the county seat. This huge new county included most of South Florida from Charlotte Harbor on the west coast to the Hillsborough inlet on the east. Next, the U.S. government sought to control the formerly wide-open wrecking industry. They built a lighthouse and customs house at Key West and, in 1828, established a U.S. District Court there. The court required all wreckers to obtain a U.S. license and to bring their salvage to Key West for adjudication.

One of Key West's first settlers was young Richard Fitzpatrick from Columbia, South Carolina. He quickly became a leading citizen. Fitzpatrick was elected to the town council and appointed clerk of the court, a member of the grand jury and deputy auctioneer. For awhile, he tried to develop a salt-making industry in Key West, turning acres of low lands into salt ponds. As his influence spread, Monroe County voters elected him representative to the Florida Territorial Council and one of Key West's first streets bore his name. (In addition to his long list of Key West activities, Fitzpatrick later became the dominant figure in the Cape Florida Settlement.)

Soon, the Cape Florida Settlement also attracted attention. In 1825, the U.S. government acquired three acres of land on Key Biscayne from Mary Ann Davis for $225, although the deed was not confirmed until 1827.

AUDUBON IN FLORIDA

In April 1832, John James Audubon, the famous painter and naturalist, came to the Florida Keys in search of new species for his Birds of America series. His first stop was at Indian Key where he hired James Egan (formerly of the Cape Florida Settlement) as his guide. During the next month, Egan became Audubon's indispensable companion. In Audubon's Ornithological Biography, he credited Egan for the success of his Florida venture. He described him as a "person of great judgment, sagacity and integrity," and added that "besides knowing him to be a good man and a perfect sailor, I was now convinced that he possessed a great knowledge of the habits of birds and could without loss of time lead me to their haunts." Egan introduced Audubon to the magnificent Great White Heron and was with him when he saw his first American Flamingo. "Ah, Reader," wrote Audubon, "could you but know the emotions that then agitated my breast! I thought I had now reached the height of all expectations."

WRECKERS ON THE REEFS

Charleston, North Carolina physician Benjamin Strobel came to Key West in 1829. Besides being the town's chief physician, Dr. Strobel also became editor of the Key West Gazette. His fascination with Key West's wrecking industry prompted him to write several articles for Charleston newspapers.

"From all I had heard, I expected to see a parcel of dirty, pirate-looking vessels, officered and manned by a set of black-whiskered fellows, who carried murder in their very looks. I was agreeably surprised on discovering the vessels were fine large sloops and schooners, regular clippers, kept in first-rate order. The captains generally were jovial, good-natured sons of Neptune, who manifested a disposition to be polite and hospitable, and to afford every facility to persons passing up and down the Reef. The crew were hearty, well-drest and honest-looking men.

Dr. Benjamin Strobel
Charleston Mercury
June 22, 1833

Boston builder Samuel Lincoln arrived to construct a 65-foot-tall brick lighthouse and a separate keeper's cottage. The lighthouse, which began operating in December 1825, did little to deter wrecks. Sailors complained that it was a bad light, and a "sailor would go ashore looking for it." John Dubose, the first keeper, did little to help the light's reputation. He was constantly criticized for neglecting his duty and engaging in the wrecking trade—hardly an acceptable sideline for a lighthouse keeper. Dubose kept up a lively correspondence with the lighthouse authorities, declaring his innocence of any wrongdoing. He blamed the mosquitoes for his absence and claimed that low government pay forced him to seek other work to feed his 12 children. Although he continued as the official keeper, he spent less and less time at the lighthouse.

Dubose was not the only South Florida wheeler-dealer. No one could compare to Jacob Housman. Housman arrived from Staten Island on a boat he stole from his father. He ensconced himself on the 12-acre island of Indian Key where he carved out his own little empire. Before long, he challenged Key West for the wrecking trade and succeeded in getting Indian Key made a port of entry. Next, he laid out a town that had stores, a hotel, a billiard parlor and substantial houses, including his personal mansion. This touch of civilization—halfway between the Cape Florida Settlement and Key West—was a powerful lure to people living on the Miami River. James Egan was the first to decide that he was ready to move. He bought a house at Indian Key and placed an advertisement in the Key West paper offering to sell his "valuable plantation" on the Miami River.

Richard Fitzpatrick took Egan up on his offer and purchased his 640-acre tract for $400. Even though Fitzpatrick was a Key West leader, he remained a planter at heart. He grew up on one of the largest plantations in South Carolina and owned many slaves. He dreamed of recreating his South Carolina plantation on the banks of the Miami River. Soon after he purchased Egan's grant, he acquired all the other privately owned properties on the South Florida mainland as well. For a mere $1,840, he purchased four square miles of the most desirable land in the Miami area and added a square mile in Fort Lauderdale (the Frankee Lewis donation) for another $500. He then hired James Wright as overseer and young Stephen Mallory (later a U.S. senator and secretary of the Navy for the Confederacy) as assistant. Wright and Mallory moved to the Miami River along with 60 of Fitzpatrick's slaves. They turned the formerly lethargic Cape Florida Settlement into a beehive of activity.

JOHN DUBOSE

■ John Dubose (top left) was the first lighthouse keeper at Cape Florida. (JGB)

■ In 1829, James Egan put an advertisement (left) in the Key West Register offering his "valuable tract of land" for sale. Richard Fitzpatrick purchased the 640 acres for $400. (APC)

■ An early lithograph (far left) depicted a romantic view of the Cape Florida Lighthouse with an ever-vigilant "wrecker" on the shore. (APC)

THE CAPE FLORIDA LIGHTHOUSE
Time & Time Again

1838

Built in 1825 and reconstructed after the Seminole Wars, the Cape Florida Lighthouse is Miami's oldest historic structure. In 1838, Army Captain J.R. Vinton sketched the earliest known view of the tower. (APC)

2008

The Cape Florida Lighthouse is part of Bill Baggs Cape Florida State Park that opened on Key Biscayne in 1967. During a 1996 restoration, the tower's red brick walls were repainted white to match the original color. (RG)

The slaves cleared several hundred acres of hammock land south of the river and planted sugarcane, corn, sweet potatoes and pumpkins in the virgin soil. Fitzpatrick added to Egan's lime and coconut groves and harvested more than 500 barrels of limes and thousands of coconuts. The Fitzpatrick plantation included more than 20 buildings. A large wooden plantation house dominated the north bank of the river and the south side had 12 slave houses and numerous outbuildings. One visitor described the enterprise as one of the "finest plantations in Florida."

Building a plantation was not Fitzpatrick's only dream. He also became Miami's first real promoter. He led a one-man campaign to convince the government to survey the area so it could be opened to other planters. "It is really a matter of astonishment to me," he wrote, "that such an immensely valuable tract of Country should have been so

long neglected…There is a very large proportion of the best lands in the United States within this section…A few weeks ago gentlemen from the neighborhood of Tallahassee came to Cape Florida to examine the land and so well satisfied were they, that they immediately picked out such places for their plantations, and will remove their Negroes the ensuing fall."

When the next fall came, Richard Fitzpatrick was in Tallahassee looking for prospects from the planter class who had moved into North Florida from Georgia and the Carolinas. He also was slated to chair the Legislative Council that, next to the governor, was the most important territorial office. The residents of Cape Florida and Indian Key petitioned the council to create the new county called Pinckney out of part of Monroe County. Fitzpatrick's chairmanship assured its passage. But by the time the Legislative Council met in January 1836, there were far more serious problems to consider.

INDIAN TROUBLES

In December 1835, Seminole Indians ambushed and killed Major Francis Langhorne Dade and 109 of his men while they were on a routine march between Tampa and Ocala. It was not surprising considering the fact that soon after Florida became a territory of the United States, the government signed a series of treaties with the Indians, guaranteeing them separate lands of their own. But land-hungry Florida frontiersmen refused to give the Indians even what they considered wasteland. They amended and broke treaties or stacked them in favor of the white man. President Andrew Jackson believed that the Indians were a menace, an evil, an obstacle in the way of America's Manifest Destiny. He supported the plan to remove the Indians from Florida and to send them to a reservation in the West.

At first, many Indians agreed to move west. But when a group of Seminoles refused to go and retreated southward, the long, painful and ultimately unresolved Seminole Wars began. As the Indians' desperation increased so did the conflicts. Sooner or later, the Indians would be pushed into direct confrontation with the South Florida settlers.

Even though the Legislative Council raged against what they called the "Dade Massacre," business went on as usual. Early in the session, they tentatively approved a bill for the new county but with one change—it would be called Dade County in honor of Major Dade and his men. Before the new county could be officially created, however, it was vacated.

On January 6, 1836, the Seminoles attacked the William Cooley family who lived on Richard Fitzpatrick's New River plantation. They killed everyone in the Cooley family except William Cooley, who was in Key West. The only survivor was a young slave named Peter who managed to escape by hiding in a palmetto thicket. Peter could have run away a free man but instead, he set out to warn the Cape Florida Settlement that the Indians were on the warpath. He made his way down the coast, swimming across swift, alligator-infested rivers, wading through swamps, cutting his bare feet on the rocky pinelands, traveling by night to avoid the ever-present eyes of Indian scouts. Finally, he reached the Miami River and spilled out his frightening story. The people fled to the

FITZPATRICK AND THE SEMINOLES

After the outbreak of the Second Seminole War ran Richard Fitzpatrick off his plantation, he served as General Duncan L. Clinch's aide-de-camp during the war's first major campaign. After General Clinch retired, Fitzpatrick became aide-de-camp to General Richard Keith Call of the Florida militia. Fitzpatrick's association with Call continued after Call became Florida's territorial governor in 1838. Unhappy with the war's progress, Call decided to take matters into his own hands. He came up with the idea of using bloodhounds to track down the elusive Indians. Call raised more than $5,000 to finance the project and sent Richard Fitzpatrick to Cuba to buy the dogs. After Northern newspapers reported that Fitzpatrick had returned to Florida with 33 bloodhounds and five Cuban trainers, a storm of controversy broke out all over the United States. People argued that it was inhumane to use vicious dogs against Indian women and children. Although Fitzpatrick and Call claimed that the dogs would be muzzled and used only for tracking, the controversy continued. As it turned out, the dogs proved ineffective and Call abandoned the plan.

Hunting Indians in Florida with Blood Hounds (LC)

lighthouse for protection, where they remained until Stephen Mallory brought a ship from Key West to transport them to safety. James Wright sent word to Richard Fitzpatrick that everything had been left behind except the slaves. The men took them to Key West to keep them from joining the Indians.

Once again, the Indians controlled the South Florida mainland. Only the acting lighthouse keeper, John Thompson, and his black assistant, Aaron Carter, remained at Cape Florida. (The regular keeper, John Dubose, had taken his family to Key West and refused to return unless the United States sent soldiers to protect them.)

Late in the afternoon of July 23, 1836, as Thompson went from the kitchen to his dwelling house, he spied a large group of Indians about 20 yards away. He yelled for Carter to join him in the tower. With the Indians in pursuit, the two men barely made it inside. While Carter held the door, Thompson climbed the stairs and fired from the windows, keeping the Indians at bay until dark. Under the cover of night, the Indians lit a fire at the base of the tower. Fed by spilled lantern oil oozing from the bullet-ridden storage tanks, the fire spread quickly to the wooden doors and then ignited the wooden stairway. With flames roaring around them, Thompson and Carter climbed to the top of the tower and out onto the two-foot-wide platform. The lantern itself was now full of flames, with the lamps and glasses exploding under the intense heat. Thompson, his flesh roasting, threw a keg of gunpowder down the tower, hoping to end their suffering. The ensuing explosion caused the burning woodwork to drop to the base of the tower and miraculously the fire went out. The Indians, believing that the men were dead, left the still-smoldering lighthouse and returned to the mainland.

Aaron Carter lay dead. Although wounded, John Thompson was still alive but stranded at the top of the tower. Fortunately, the flames attracted the attention of the sailors on the schooner *U.S.S. Motto*. They arrived the following day and managed to reach Thompson with a line suspended from a kite. Slowly they lowered him to safety.

Soon after the destruction of the lighthouse, the Navy sent Lieutenant L.M. Powell to South Florida to reconnoiter the area. He set up his base of operations on Key Biscayne and sent a search party to the mainland to seek out the Indians. The search party reported that Fitzpatrick's plantation had been burned to the ground but they found no Indians.

In July 1837, the government sent Bostonian Winslow Lewis to rebuild the lighthouse. When Lewis arrived and realized that the Indians were firmly in control of the area, he refused to stay, leaving the lighthouse dark and abandoned.

DALLAS ON THE MIAMI

In the fall of 1837, Powell returned to the Miami area. Powell and Army Captain L.B. Webster of Company C, First Artillery (which had been sent to Key Biscayne), picked a site for a fort on the north bank of the Miami River and started building three log houses. They named the installation Fort Dallas after Navy Commander Alexander James Dallas. Soon after they completed the fort, Dr. Henry Perrine, a noted New York horticulturist, made a visit. Perrine had just received an entire township from the U.S. government on which he planned to introduce tropical plants from around the world. When he arrived in 1836, he discovered that the Indians controlled the tract. While he waited for the war to end, he moved his family to Indian Key. He was particularly interested in Fort Dallas because it was on the site of Fitzpatrick's plantation. Although the Indians destroyed the plantation buildings, many trees—banana, coconut and lime—still flourished. Perrine also wanted to encourage the troops because they were the key to his South Florida future.

So many problems developed at Fort Dallas that the men had little time to pursue Indians. Supply boats, sent to stock the fort, ran aground on the huge sandbar that almost blocked the river's mouth. The Army had to hire wreckers to get the boats off the bar. Finally, in desperation, the Army abandoned the half-finished fort and moved the troops to Key Biscayne, where a supply depot already existed. Under the shadow of the gutted lighthouse, the soldiers pitched their tents and lined their campfires with bricks from the keeper's burned house. They named this new installation, little more than a bivouac, Fort Bankhead.

A year later, they decided to reoccupy Fort Dallas because of its proximity to the Everglades. Company B, Third Artillery, under the command of Captain J.R. Vinton, arrived to complete the fort. Soon after the troops settled in, Captain Vinton sent Captain S.L. Russell up the Miami River to establish another fort, Fort Miami, on the south fork of the river in order to secure the entrance to the Everglades. After a few days at Fort Miami, Captain Russell and his men prepared to return to Fort Dallas. As they paddled down the river, the Indians attacked. The soldiers raced for cover but in the melee an arrow hit its mark and Captain Russell was killed—

the first casualty at Fort Dallas. His comrades buried him on the Tequesta Indian mound near the mouth of the river.

During the next year, the soldiers again abandoned Fort Dallas and returned to Key Biscayne. They renamed Fort Bankhead Fort Russell in honor of their fallen comrade. In October 1938, when Indian fighting increased on the mainland, they returned and reopened Fort Dallas. By this time, most of the Seminole Indians had been captured and transported to the West. Some, however, escaped into the deepest, uncharted depths of the Everglades.

In August 1840, the Indians attacked Indian Key, completely destroying Jacob Housman's island empire. Some believed that Housman's proposal to the U.S. government to kill the remaining Seminole Indians for $200 a head prompted the attack. Dr. Henry Perrine was one of seven people who died. Before personally confronting the Indians, he managed to save his family by hiding them in a turtle kraal under the wharf. After his young son slipped through some loose boards and sought help from a passing ship, the navy rescued the distraught family. On their way home to New York, the Perrine family stopped at Fort Dallas. Their plight touched the soldiers who not only gave them clothing but also collected money to help them. Guilt probably motivated this outpouring of sympathy. Securely locked in the guardhouse was "Negro John," who had been living with the Seminoles. He had warned the soldiers of the impending attack on Indian Key but they ignored him.

The soldiers at Fort Dallas were now under the command of Lieutenant Colonel William S. Harney. He vowed revenge against the Indian leader Chekaika who led the raid on Indian Key. Chekaika embarrassed Harney and his men in an earlier sneak attack at the Caloosahatchee River. During this raid, Harney barely escaped death and had been forced to flee in his underwear. Only Chekaika's death could assuage his rage.

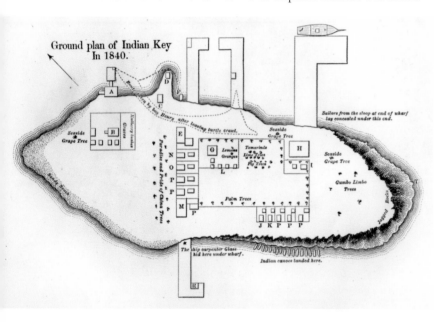

■ Jacob Housman's 1840 plan for Indian Key (top left) included Housman's mansion (building "H" on North West Street) and the Tropical Hotel (the large building on Fourth Street). (HMSF)

■ During their stay on Indian Key, the Perrine family lived in a house owned by Charles Howe (bottom left). While Dr. Perrine tried to reason with the Indians, his wife and children escaped into the turtle kraal under the dock. (APC)

I REMEMBER INDIAN KEY
By Henry E. Perrine

*Y*oung Henry E. Perrine moved to Indian Key with his family on Christmas Day 1838. His father, Henry, had received an entire mainland township from the U.S. Congress on which he planned to introduce tropical plants. Because of the Indian War, the family moved temporarily to Indian Key. In August 1840, young Henry was one of the few survivors of an Indian attack. He later wrote of his experience in a book entitled *A True Story of Some Eventful Years in Grandpa's Life* (1885).

We saw on the distant horizon the top of palm which appeared at first as though floating in the air, there seeming to be a space between the sea and the feathery fronds of the palms…Soon the tops of houses could be seen, and then the whole island of Indian Key in all its beauty greeted our eager eyes…A large warehouse three stories in height, and crowned with a lofty cupola, was the most prominent object. A short distance beyond, stood the two-story mansion of Captain, Houseman, the proprietor of nearly all the island and the various cottages, about forty buildings in all, none of them of pretentious architecture, but nearly all having either the graceful palm trees, or others of a tropical or semi-tropical nature near their doors. Three large wharves stretched out from the northeastern side of the island; beyond these was a small neck of land, upon which stood a carpenter's shop and a blacksmith shop. About a hundred feet beyond, stood a two-and-a-half story house with a cupola upon it…Right opposite this house, which was to be our home, stood the low one-story house and negro dwellings…On the southwestern side of the island, another wharf stretched out of deep water. The side of the island towards the gulf consisted of jagged coral rock, while on the opposite side was a sandy beach.

In 1871, J.B. Holder wrote a series of articles entitled "Along the Florida Reef" for *Harper's New Monthly Magazine*. He included the drawing (above) entitled "The Wrecker's Rendezvous." (APC)

1888

Artist James Hutchinson's emotional painting recalls Lieutenant Colonel William S. Harney's controversial foray into the Everglades to track down and kill Chief Chekaika. Dressed as Indians, the soldiers, aided by "Negro John," surprised and killed Chekaika and his men. (HMSF)

Early on December 4, 1840, Lt. Col. Harney and 90 of his men left Fort Dallas with their former prisoner, "Negro John," who agreed to lead them to Chekaika's camp deep in the Everglades. Up the dark waters of the Miami River they paddled, into the south fork where the saw grass grew tall. For several days, the soldiers pushed, shoved and dragged their canoes through the ooze and shallow water. Finally, John sighted Chekaika's island. Ignoring the conventions of civilized warfare, Harney ordered his men to don Indian attire and paint their faces. Whooping and hollering, the U.S. Army "Indians" attacked and shot and killed Chekaika along with many of his braves. At sunset, they hung two braves and the lifeless body of Chekaika from a tall oak and left them for the buzzards. They took the squaws and children to Key Biscayne where boats waited to take them to Tampa and on to the new lands in the West.

LT. COLONEL HARNEY

Besides his hatred of Chekaika, Major Harney had another reason for wanting to rid South Florida of Indians. Even under the worst of circumstances, Harney was one of the first to recognize the area's potential. A few years earlier, he purchased several lots in the "Town of Key Biscayen" from the Davis family who had come from Texas to survey and plat their island possession. He also showed interest in acquiring land at Cape Sable.

Activity at Fort Dallas continued to increase as the Army, Navy and Marines tried to capture the last of the Indians hiding in the Everglades. The Indians and the Everglades, however, could not be conquered. Finally in 1842, the exhausted and frustrated U.S. government gave up and left. For the time being, the war was over and lawmakers looked to the new Armed Occupation Act to restrain the Indians. Under this act, the government offered 160 acres free to any head of a family that agreed to move into Indian country, clear the land, plant crops and stay for five years. This new law spurred South Florida development. Several "armed occupants" took up tracts of land there on both sides of the Miami River. Others settled in Little River.

Even the arrival of new settlers was not enough to encourage Richard Fitzpatrick. He had enough of South Florida and wanted out. He also demanded that the U.S. government compensate him for his losses and began what was to become a long struggle to make the government pay him for their unauthorized occupation of his plantation. While the bill made its way through congressional committees, he sold his huge holdings to his nephew, William F. English, for $16,000.

LAND OF PROMISE

William F. English moved to the former Fitzpatrick plantation in 1842 with big plans for the future. He dreamed of a great city, and in 1843, he platted the Village of Miami on the south bank of the river and sold several lots on Porpoise Street for $1—on the condition that the buyer build a good frame building on the site. English was the first to call the area Miami. The new village did not go unnoticed. In 1843, the *Saint Augustine News* reported it was a:

> site suitable for a town, combining the exquisite advantages of proximity to the ocean, and communicating with the interior of the country…extraordinary fertility of soil…very inducement to active industry—these capabilities we are gratified to learn are being properly appreciated, and an activity already prevails at the river…a town is laid off on its southern banks, opening in front upon Key Biscayne Bay and some coontie [sic] mills are in progress of rapid completion. The settlers, already numerous, are every day increasing and there is no doubt at no very distant day the inhabitants of the new city in Dade County will be more numerous than this.

There were other reasons for optimism in the new village. In March 1844, the legislature moved the Dade County seat to the "Miami River where it empties into Biscaino Bay." Voters at the "Town of Miami" helped elect their favorite son, William English, state senator. Navy Master Edward Anderson, who sailed into the area, described English and the new town:

> A senator of Florida, Mr. William F. English is the chief cook & bottle washer of the establishment. He is lame of leg & intends flooding the United States and Key West with Coonti [sic] & sugar or whatever else his productive plantation that is to be will produce. Mr. E. is a Colonel, of course, as are all the natives of this region. The settlers are 'armed occupants'…They are very sanguine of establishing eventually a flourishing settlement & have laid out a town…yet to be built. I have no idea however that Miami will ever be more than it is for there are but few facilities and no capital either at present or in prospect…I have never in all my travels met with such immence number of horseflies & other insects as are to be found here.

MOSQUITOES, MOSQUITOES, MOSQUITOES

Dr. Benjamin Strobel, who visited the Miami area in the late 1820s, described his own personal war with the mosquitoes. "But of all the places in the world for mosquitoes, Key Biscayne is entitled to the preference saying nothing of the sand flies. Their everlasting hum never ceases…We were surrounded with smoke pans, and enveloped in smoke, but still found it necessary to keep our hands and feet in active motion to avoid the assaults of the enemy. After supper I went on board of our sloop—our beds were brought on deck, and our mosquito nets spread, and we ensconced beneath them. But, alas, it was fruitless labor. The enemy stormed and assailed us in every direction. One of the sailors swore that they had divided into two gangs, and one hoisted the net, whilst the other got under and fed, and I verily do believe there were enough of them to have done it."

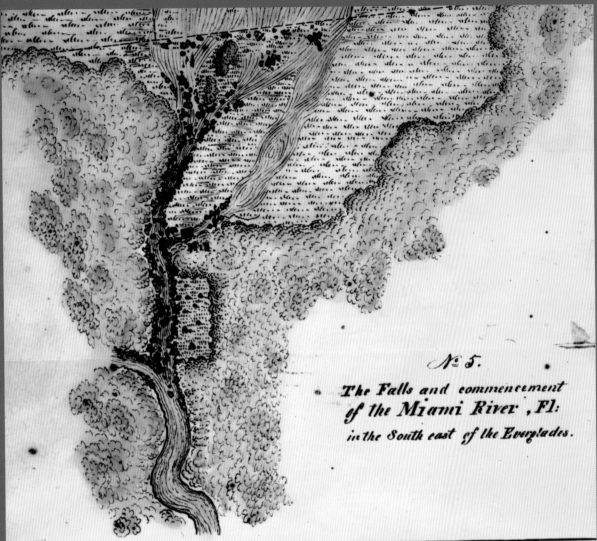

N.º 5.

The Falls and commencement of the *Miami River*, Fl: in the South east of the Everglades.

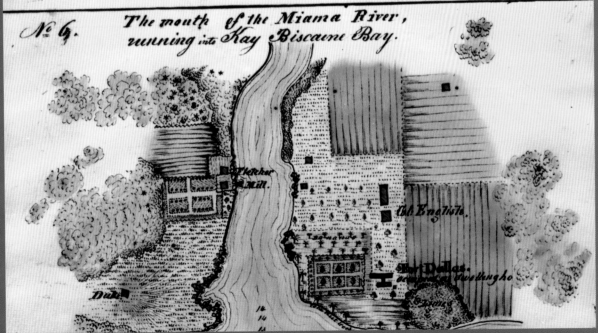

N.º 6. The mouth of the *Miama River*, running into *Kay Biscaine Bay*.

Fletcher Mill.

Col. English.

Fort Dallas.

Duke

In 1849 F.H. Gerdes, of the U.S. Coast Survey, drew the first known map of what William English called the Village of Miami. It included Fort Dallas and William English's home and slave quarters on the north bank, as well as Dr. R.R. Fletcher and Reason Duke's homes on the south. The upper portion of the map highlighted the Miami River falls and George Ferguson's comptie mill. (APC)

Even though there was no sign of new capital pouring in, the situation continued to look up. In 1846, the government heightened and rebuilt the Cape Florida Lighthouse and keeper's quarters. A year earlier, after Florida became a state, Robert Butler came to Miami to complete the long-awaited survey. As a result, several men purchased land from the government for $1.25 an acre.

Dr. R.R. Fletcher, formerly of Indian Key, opened a store and trading post on the south bank of the river and his home became the courthouse. George and Thomas Ferguson, also from Key West, built another store and trading post at the rapids of the river (near what is now 27th Avenue). They constructed a huge, water-powered comptie mill and hired 25 men. The Fergusons produced 300,000 pounds of comptie starch in one year, selling it in northern markets and netting more than $24,000.

In early 1849, a team of men from the U.S. Coast Survey visited English's plantation and drew the first map of the new town. They reported that English was building himself a large rock mansion on the north bank of the river with rock slave quarters nearby.

Just as the settlement at Miami began to grow and prosper, word came that the Indians had killed the U.S. inspector at Indian River. This new crisis rocked the community. Once again, everyone fled to the lighthouse for protection. When the survey team returned a short time later, they found the town deserted.

In response to the threat, the government sent troops back to South Florida. In September, Company F, Second Artillery, arrived at English's plantation to reopen Fort Dallas. They completed his two rock buildings, repaired the log houses still standing from the original Fort Dallas and built two more officers' houses on the mound near the river's mouth. (This occupation of Fort Dallas has been generally overlooked in history because the soldiers had almost no contact with the Indians.) After a year of boredom, dysentery and drunkenness, the troops left.

While the Army occupied his land and the Indians ran off all the settlers, William English followed the Gold Rush to California, hoping to find the capital he needed to build his city. He caught gold fever after his former neighbor, Thomas Ferguson, returned from the gold fields a wealthy man.

FERGUSON'S FLORIDA ARROW ROOT.

REFINED AND PREPARED

Expressly for the Table.

THIS ARTICLE can at all times be had at my Dwelling in Key West, or at my Mill at Miami, in any quantities, neatly put up into paper parcels with full directions for preparing; and is

Warranted fully Equal to the

BEST ARROW ROOT IN USE.

either as to whiteness, purity, or substance; and as the various preparations from Arrow Root are recognized as the very highest delicacies and only kept from universal use by the high price at which it has heretofore been sold, we hope to introduce this staple production of Florida into every family in the country, as its price is sufficiently low to recommend the inferior qualities for use as common starch.

The Refined Arrow Root peculiarly commends itself to strangers visiting Key West as a memento of Florida to their absent friends.

G. W. FERGUSON.

March 12, 1859.   6m

PAPER

COMMISSION WAREHOUSE,

AND

PRINTERS' DEPOT.

■ *Lt. Robinson's 1854 map of what is today Greater Miami (far left) listed almost every structure and every resident in the area, including Ferguson's Mill. (NA)*

■ *George Ferguson ran a profitable water-powered comptie mill at the falls of the Miami River. In 1850, he reported earning $24,000 from his starch enterprise that was located at today's Paradise Park. (APC)*

Although of a later date, Charles Peacock's horse-powered comptie mill produced the same kind of arrowroot starch earlier settlers produced. The Seminole Indians taught the settlers how to extract the starch from the comptie roots. The comptie grew wild in the pinewoods; making starch from its root was South Florida's first industry—an industry that continued into the Twentieth Century.

GEORGE FERGUSON

English arrived in California in April 1851. Filled with dreams of his new city, he established the Kentucky Ridge Mine in Grass Valley, California. Even though California was a free state, he brought as many as 100 slaves with him to work the mines. He never saw Miami again. On August 27, 1852, he died in a suspicious accident. The newspapers reported that he was thrown from his horse and killed when his weapon accidentally discharged. Others believed that he had been attacked by highwaymen who had stolen his gold-filled saddlebags. His slaves settled in Grass Valley as free men. Their ancestors still live there today.

With English gone, George Ferguson assumed leadership of the small community that regrouped on the Miami River once the Indian scare passed. Claiming the patience of Job, he fired off a petition to the government demanding that the United States take responsibility for removing the Indians from South Florida. "If it wasn't for that menace," he wrote, "South Florida would soon become what nature has so evidently designed upon other genial climates, fresh pure streams, rich hammocks, and other numerous spontaneous products."

Ferguson had a plan for developing South Florida. He petitioned the Florida Legislature to grant him thousands of acres of Everglades land. In return, he promised to drain it and open it for settlement. (It was the first local proposal for an enterprise that would dominate South Florida thinking for the next century.) The legislators ignored his request.

The U.S. government was well aware that the Indians still controlled South Florida's destiny. In January 1855, they reactivated Fort Dallas. The troops returned to find the rock buildings stripped of lumber, a prize commodity on the frontier. They rebuilt the rock houses and added five new officers' quarters, a hospital, guardhouse, magazine, stables and other outbuildings to the complex. A visitor wrote that Fort Dallas was now "a beautiful sight; the stars and stripes floating from [a] tall flagstaff erected on the parade ground, all clean and covered with Bermuda grass...All around was

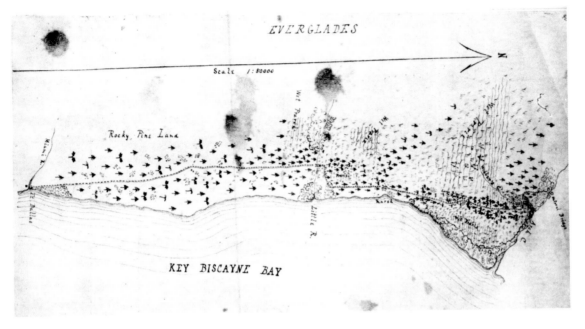

EVERGLADES

Scale 1:80000

Rocky, Pine Land

KEY BISCAYNE BAY

planted in flowers, shrubbery and vegetables of all kinds." For the first time, Fort Dallas was a fort worthy of its name. The residents of Miami felt secure with such a large defense facility in their midst. But this sense of security ended tragically in January 1856 when the Indians ambushed and killed Peter Johnson and Edward Farrell at their home in today's Coconut Grove. The soldiers quickly rounded up the panic-stricken Miamians and took them to Fort Dallas for protection. For many settlers, this was the final blow. Once again, families abandoned their homes, packed up their belongings and left.

Most of the soldiers at Fort Dallas spent their time on search-and-destroy missions into the Everglades. Their most significant accomplishment in the Miami area during what is now called the Third Seminole War (1855-1858) was construction of the first road between Miami and Fort Lauderdale. Led by Army Captain Abner Doubleday (later famous as the father of baseball), the soldiers built a corduroy road through the swampland, constructed bridges across the rivers and streams and chopped through the difficult pine and palmetto country. The few people who stuck it out were ecstatic. Everyone believed that as soon as the Indian war ended, the road would open up Miami for the development William English predicted. But by the time the troops withdrew from Fort Dallas in 1858, a different kind of war gathered force.

By 1860, the name Miami no longer appeared in public records. The 1860 census reported 60 souls "in the district of Fort Dallas," which included the entire area that later would become Greater Miami. A few people remained from the "Village of Miami" era but the constant Indians wars drove the less committed away. A few new residents arrived at the end of the Third Seminole War. Some were former soldiers who decided to stay. But for all practical purposes, Miami was back where it started and the Village of Miami was an idea whose time had passed.

DOUBLEDAY FATHER OF BASEBALL

Captain Abner Doubleday, "The Father of Baseball," came to Fort Dallas in 1855 as commander of the Company B, First Artillery of the United States Army. Sixteen years earlier, he had been credited with "inventing" baseball when, as a Cooperstown, New York schoolboy, he modified "town ball" into the present game of baseball. The National Baseball Hall of Fame and Museum is located in Cooperstown in his honor along with Doubleday Field. During his two-year stay in Miami, he was in charge of constructing and preparing a map of the first road between Fort Lauderdale and Fort Dallas. In June 1858, he removed to Charleston, South Carolina, where he remained until the first shot was fired at Fort Sumter in April 1863—the beginning of the Civil War. Some historians credit him with firing the first shot.

Captain Abner Doubleday (HMSF)

OF THE BLUE AND THE GRAY

During the three years between the end of the Third Seminole War and the beginning of the Civil War, the isolated people on the Miami River were barely aware of the serious problems ripping at the nation. When the Civil War actually broke out in April 1861, however, they felt the effect almost immediately. Rebel guerrillas, including Miamian James Paine, took over the Cape Florida Lighthouse. They ran off the keeper, Simeon Frow, and destroyed the lighthouse. Soon, the federal blockade completely cut off the remaining settlers from the outside world. The government suspended the monthly mailboat that had served as a lifeline to Key West since 1856. Even though Florida joined the Confederacy, Key West never left Union hands. While North Florida united in its secessionist sentiment, South Florida remained more like a border state. Opinion was as varied as the make-up of its citizens. Prominent Key West Senator Stephen Mallory became the Confederate secretary of the Navy. Other Key West citizens took up the Union cause. The guns at Fort Taylor and the growing blockade squadron were powerful inducements to embrace the red, white and blue.

Most Miamians cared little about either side and tried to remain neutral. One wrote that the men "took to the woods" when the blockaders came. They soon learned that the best rule was to lie low, keep quiet and avoid suspicion.

There were a few notable exceptions. Dr. Robert Fletcher, who lived on the south bank of the river, was a strong Southern sympathizer. His sons fought for the Confederacy. George Lewis, son of early settler Jonathan Lewis, was a Confederate blockade runner. Isaiah Hall, who settled just south of what is now Matheson Hammock Park, became a pilot for the Union's blockade squadron. Local Southern sympathizers made life so difficult for his wife and children still living in Miami that a boat from the blockade squadron picked them up and took them to more neutral ground in Fort Lauderdale.

CAPTAIN EARL ENGLISH

The leaders of the blockade squadron believed Miami could be a possible entry point for Bahamian blockade runners. But the bay was so shallow that most used the Indian River instead. Occasionally, Captain Earl English and a group of sailors from the blockader *Sagamore* came ashore looking for the wily blockade runners. On one such foray up the Miami River, they destroyed George Lewis' house and store. This action apparently had the desired effect on other would-be Confederates. When Fletcher saw the flames leaping from Lewis' house, he became a much subdued Southern patriot. Before the war ended, at least two Miamians—George Lewis and John Adams—found themselves in federal prison.

When the war ended, all types of people came to and through Miami. To apprehend Confederate leaders fleeing to foreign soil, the federal government sent a Union gunboat to Key Biscayne to guard Bear Cut. Despite the blockade, Confederate Secretary of the Treasury John C. Breckenridge made his escape through Miami. One of the men in the Breckenridge party wrote that the abandoned Fort Dallas buildings were packed with men "of all colors, from Yankee to the ebony Congo, all armed, a more motley and villainous crew never trod the Captain Kidd's ships…deserters from the Army and Navy of both sides, a mixture of Spaniards and Cubans, outlaws and renegades."

Despite the turmoil, the war was over, and once again, Miami stood on the brink of change.

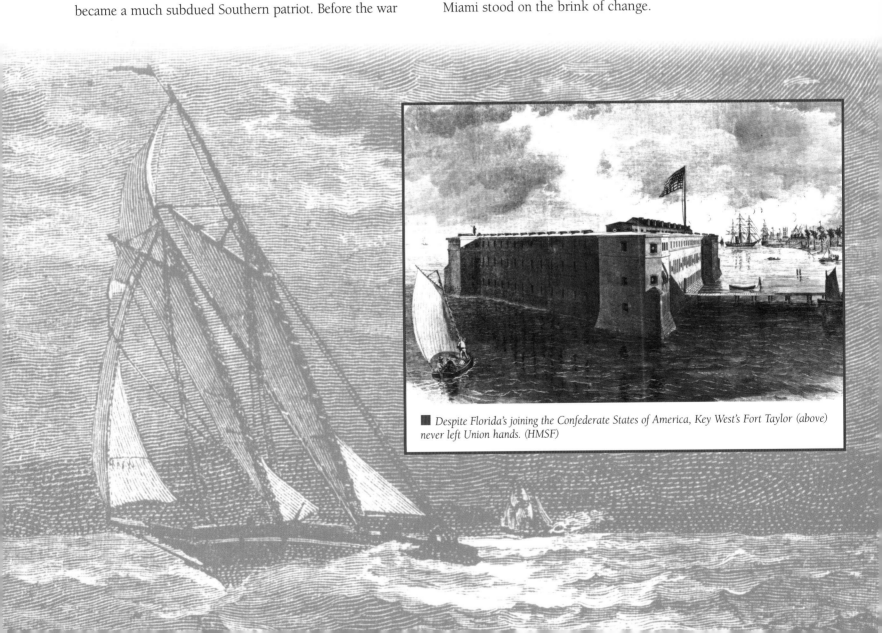

■ *Despite Florida's joining the Confederate States of America, Key West's Fort Taylor (above) never left Union hands. (HMSF)*

■ *Before the railroad came to Miami in 1896, William and Mary Brickell's Indian trading post on the south bank of the Miami River was the first stop for visitors coming to Miami by boat. (LW)*

Chapter Three

Carpetbaggers & Homesteaders

"A fair proportion of well balanced folk, genuine pioneers of civilization were trying to get a foothold against great odds."

Ralph M. Munroe

AFTER THE CIVIL WAR ENDED, THE POPULATION OF THE MIAMI RIVER SETTLEMENT DROPPED TO ONE OF ITS LOWEST

points. The big dreamers departed. Even the military, who at least spurred some activity in the area, left. What remained was a handful of hangers-on who chose to live in the wilderness and enjoy quiet, simple lives. These old-timers, however, fully expected to see the day when someone else would discover Miami and get things moving again. They did not have long to wait.

In 1865, a group of men from the Freedman's Bureau came up with a plan to turn South Florida into another Liberia. (Liberia, Africa had been colonized by former U.S. slaves.) Abraham Lincoln established the Freedman's Bureau in 1865 primarily to help former slaves adjust to their new life as free men. Under the 1862 Homestead Act that offered 160 acres free to any citizen who would live on public land for five years and improve it, the bureau proposed to place 50,000 for-

mer slaves in South Florida where most of the land remained in government hands. In early 1866, the Washington bureau chief sent two men to South Florida to investigate the area. This ambitious project died because one of the bureau's men, William H. Gleason, left Miami with some plans of his own.

In July 1866, a large schooner anchored off Key Biscayne. The handful of people in Miami, always eager for visitors, gathered on the north bank of the river to greet the strangers making their way to the Miami River in a small boat. They recognized William H. Gleason from his earlier visit but were surprised to see him arrive with a sizeable group of strangers. Gleason's entourage included his wife and two sons, his friend William H. Hunt and family and four hired men. The biggest surprise of all came when Gleason announced that they were all moving to Miami.

One Too Many Governors

William H. Gleason

For the next several days, the people watched as Gleason unloaded what resident Rose Wagner Richards called his "Noah's Ark" and moved everyone and everything into the unoccupied Fort Dallas buildings. First came the cows, horses and mules. Then he unloaded hay rakes and farming implements, bags of seed, tins of food, boxes of books and even a printing press.

William H. Gleason was a remarkable young man. In his 36 years, he had already made and lost one fortune and had started on another one. A native of New York, he moved to Wisconsin where he studied law, founded the town of Eau Claire and became president of its first bank. When he acquired a somewhat shady reputation in Eau Claire, he left Wisconsin and started over again in New York. After a series of involvements, he allied himself with a group of radical Republicans who saw the prostrated former Confederate states as fair game. Carpetbags in hand, Gleason and company moved into Florida.

With William H. Hunt in charge of his Miami operations, Gleason quickly became embroiled in Florida Reconstruction politics. In 1866, he was elected Florida's lieutenant governor under the carpetbag regime of Harrison Reed. Two years later, allied with the more radical Republicans, Gleason engineered impeachment proceedings against Reed and declared himself governor. Reed refused to be intimidated by Gleason and his gang. As a result, Florida had two men claiming to be governor. Reed holed up in his Capitol office while Gleason, in possession of the state seal, played governor from a hotel across the street. Before the episode ended, the legislature cleared Reed and impeached Gleason because he had not lived in Florida the requisite three years to hold office.

■ *On the South Florida frontier, the sailboat was the covered wagon. (MC)*

And Then There Were Mosquitoes

In 1865, the Freedman's Bureau sent brevet Lieutenant Colonel George F. Thompson and William H. Gleason to South Florida to study its suitability as a home for former slaves. In his final report, Thompson waxed eloquently about South Florida's potential as the "garden of the United States" but noted that the ever-present insects were a serious problem. "During the entire year mosquitoes and sand flies seem to vie with each other in their efforts to torment humanity," he wrote. "While we were there in the winter they were almost intolerable, and during the summer months are said to be more numerous and aggressive. To sleep at night without mosquito bar would be nearly as fruitless as to attempt to fly without wings."

■ *In 1879, artist Cornelia Adele Fassett painted the remarkable 60 x 75 inch* Florida Case Before the Electoral Commission *to document the history-making event that settled the disputed election of 1876. The painting had 256 people including commission members, senators, representatives, Supreme Court justices, members of the press and friends. The commission declared Rutherford B. Hayes the winner, just two days before his March 4, 1877 inauguration. (USS)*

DR. JEPTHA V. HARRIS

Despite this political setback, Gleason's two years as lieutenant governor had their reward. He began acquiring state land for his Southern Inland Navigation and Improvement Company, which proposed building a canal between Fernandina and Key West. Before he finished, his company acquired 1.35 million acres of Florida "swamp and overflow" land for six cents an acre. He also handpicked all the Dade County public officials who, under the Reconstruction Constitution, were appointed by the governor.

Back in Miami, Gleason proceeded to perfect his control. Under his role as county clerk, the Dade County public records—almost nonexistent before his regime—suddenly came to life. He disbursed public funds for his various duties as county surveyor, tax assessor and school board member. (There were no schools at the time.) As tax assessor, he levied taxes on abandoned property, and when the taxes were not paid, he bought the tax certificates. Before long, he acquired an enormous amount of Dade County real estate.

The county offices not held personally by Gleason were held by his colleagues. William Hunt held several positions, and his black associate, Andrew Price, became both a county commissioner and a member of the school board.

For many years, Gleason's hold on Dade County went almost unchallenged even though he became more and more unpopular with local residents. Occasionally, someone took him on, only to discover that he was not only unscrupulous but extremely clever.

In 1869, Louisianan Dr. Jeptha V. Harris purchased the 640-acre tract on the north bank of the Miami River from the heirs of William English. This purchase put Harris into direct confrontation with Gleason, who had not only lived on Harris' property for three years but claimed he held a special government lease on it. Eventually, Harris and his shotgun forced Gleason off his land. Furious, Gleason moved to Hunt's place (now Miami Shores) and planned a comeback.

When Gleason left the Miami River, he took Miami with him—at least he took the Miami post office, the name of which he changed to Biscayne. For the next few years, Miami was wiped off the map and Biscayne took its place.

■ *Jeptha Vining Harris, M.D. (top left) was the first to challenge Gleason. Harris forced the wily Gleason off the Fort Dallas property by producing a legitimate deed. (FK)*

■ *Among Gleason's many enterprises was the mailboat Governor Gleason (left) that operated between Miami and Key West. Its captain was Andrew Price, right, a black homesteader whom Gleason named county commissioner and a member of the school board. (TP)*

■ *A WPA mural in the West Palm Beach post office (facing page) depicts the so-called "barefoot mailman" who walked the mail down the beach from Lake Worth. Once, Gleason joined him on the trek. (HMSF)*

The mail came to the Biscayne post office in Hunt's house, by foot or by boat. The mailboat, *Governor Gleason,* captained by Andrew Price, arrived from Key West once a month. The "barefoot mailman" walked the mail up the beach to the small settlements at Fort Lauderdale and Lake Worth and then back to Biscayne.

Although the Biscayne settlement grew rapidly, Gleason did not give up on Miami. By 1871, he figured out a way to regain possession of the Harris property. Gleason discovered that someone named James Fletcher Hagan lived in Key West. Using the mistaken spelling of the original grantee (James Egan's name as James Hagan), he wrote the land office in Washington, D.C., claiming to be Hagan's attorney and asking to add the initial "F" to Hagan's name. With the amended title papers in hand, Gleason arranged to "purchase" the property from Hagan's unwary heirs who were still living in Key West.

Next, he confronted Harris with his supposedly legitimate title to the property and demanded that he vacate the premises. Harris, however, did not give up easily. First, he challenged Gleason to a duel. When Gleason refused, Harris whipped him with his cane. Those who witnessed the alter-

cation reported "vicarious satisfaction" for all of Gleason's misdeeds. Finally, Harris convinced the government that he was the legitimate owner of the Fort Dallas tract and received another amended title. Even though Gleason lost that round with Harris, he continued to cloud the property's title.

Gleason's schemes to acquire South Florida real estate proliferated. Occasionally, however, his self-interest helped others. He not only informed the earlier settlers about the U.S. homestead laws, but he helped them file their claims. Sometimes he received part of the claim for his services. Often, after someone filed a legitimate claim, he "took it off their hands" for what, to them, seemed like a lot of money. Regardless of his motives, he spurred development. After 1868, a flurry of homestead claims appeared in South Florida. Ownership gave people a new commitment to the Miami area.

Dan Clarke, who for many years had been squatting on land just north of what is now N.E. 20th Street, was the first of the old settlers to file. Others followed in quick succession. Edmund Beasley, longtime resident of what is now Coconut Grove, claimed his 160 acres and William Wagner of Wagner's Creek (a tributary of the Miami River) filed for only 40 acres because he thought that was enough for anybody. In 1876, Wagner built a small Catholic chapel on his property—the first church on the South Florida mainland.

Gleason also attracted new settlers to Miami. Well-known poet Sidney Lanier in *Florida: Its Scenery, Climate and History* wrote, "Those desiring to know more of this portion of Florida [South Florida] would doubtless be cheerfully informed upon application of letter or otherwise to Rev. W. W. Hicks of Fernandina, Florida or Hon. W. Gleason, Miami Florida, who seem to be the stirring men of Dade County."

EPHRAIM T. STURTEVANT

■ **FAMOUS SETTLERS:** *Union physician Horace P. Porter (background) was the unwitting "founder" of Coconut Grove when he opened the "Cocoanut Grove" post office in 1873.* (MC)

■ *Ephraim T. Sturtevant (inset), the father of the "Mother of Miami," Julia Tuttle, lived in Biscayne and was a carpet-bag legislator from 1872 to 1876.* (TP)

■ *Artist George W. Potter, who later moved to Lake Worth, painted his Biscayne home—typical of many other pioneer dwellings. (TP)*

In 1870, two men from Cleveland, Ohio—William Barnwell Brickell and Ephraim T. Sturtevant—arrived in Miami. Brickell purchased the Rebecca Egan and the Jonathan and Polly Lewis donations on the south side of the Miami River from the heirs of William F. English. (Brickell may have learned about South Florida from William English because he joined the California Gold Rush at the same time as English and left California for Australia just eight days after English's untimely death.) In 1870, Brickell built his home on the south bank. After Sturtevant had a falling-out with Brickell, he acquired a homestead in Biscayne and became a confidant of Hunt and Gleason. (Sturtevant's later claim to fame was through his daughter, Julia Tuttle, who visited him on the bay as early as 1875.)

Many of the newcomers were homesteaders. In 1872, Dr. Horace P. Porter, former Union surgeon from Connecticut, arrived in South Florida. At first, he rented Edmund Beasley's improved homestead (in today's Coconut Grove), which had been abandoned when Beasley died. Porter filed for 80 acres adjacent to Beasley's claim and moved into Beasley's house with his wife and daughter. The elderly widow Anna Beasley, who lived in Key West, sent Porter what she believed were her title papers so he could purchase her property. When Porter received the papers, he realized that the Beasley homestead had never been "proved up," even though Beasley had lived there for more than 30 years. Porter took advantage of Anna Beasley's shaky legal position and wrote Washington to amend his homestead application by adding 80 acres from the Beasley grant to his claim.

When word reached Anna Beasley that Porter was trying to jump her claim, her grandson fired off an angry letter to Washington claiming that Porter "was endeavoring to defraud her and refused to agree even to pay for the improvements and wished to keep house, plants and all without paying one cent." The land office sympathized with Anna Beasley and awarded her the land. Porter decided the unimproved acreage was not worth the effort and left the area in January 1874, never to return. In his brief stay, however, Porter became the unwitting founder of today's Coconut Grove. In January 1873, he opened a post office by the name of "Coconut Grove." When he left the area in 1874, the post office was closed and temporarily forgotten.

In the 1870s, Miami probably had more medical doctors per capita than any other area in the United States. In addition to Drs. Porter and Harris, another medical doctor, Richard B. Potter and his brother George arrived in 1874 and homesteaded in the Biscayne area. Because there were so few patients, Potter, like the rest of the physicians, dug comptie, helped build houses, became a U.S. marshal and did a little wrecking, along with practicing medicine.

Everybody in Miami did a little wrecking if the opportunity presented itself. Even though wrecking without a government license was against the law, it was a law most people ignored. Several famous wrecks occurred during the 1870s and 1880s. For years, pioneers remembered the legendary "wine wreck," and the rip-roaring party that followed. They also recalled the *Three Sisters'* wreck as one of the few times the government caught anyone illegally wrecking. The U.S. marshal made a surprise visit and arrested half the men in Miami and hauled them off to jail in Key West for illegally salvaging the ship's lumber cargo. For years, the "Three Sisters' House" stood in Coconut Grove (some of the lumber had been hidden) in defiance of what the frontiersmen considered government interference.

THE GREAT WINE WRECK

In the late 1880s, a bark sailing out of Bordeaux, France to Havana, Cuba, wrecked on the reef. For weeks after, the South Florida beaches were strewn with pipes, casks, kegs and barrels of wine. "The entire population of the southeast coast declared whole-holiday and moved to the shore en masse, and oh! what a time everybody had!" wrote Ralph Munroe in The Commodore's Story. "For many months there was scarcely any solid food consumed, and no traffic on the Bay save rafts of casks. "Jolly Jack Peacock was an especially successful collector, so much that there seemed no possibility of drinking the entire stock; he finally took the heads out of some of the casks, and bathed in the wine, thinking it would help his rheumatism…Even the Indians flocked out from the Everglades, and in some cases sawed casks in two, losing half the contents, and then balanced the resulting tub between two canoes and boated it up the river."

TINKERERS AND TRADERS

Although the government tried to catch illegal wreckers, it stopped trying to catch Indians. In fact, the government appeared to have forgotten about them. By the 1860s, the few hundred Seminole Indians remaining in Florida were living unmolested and free in the Everglades. They were, however, very much a part of the Miami settlement. Almost every week, they paddled down the Miami River to visit the Indian trading posts that sprung up on both sides of the river. The Indian families would usually camp out on the trading post grounds. Old Alec, Billy Harney, Miami Jimmy, Old Tigertail and Cypress Charlie were especially popular attractions at the trading posts.

MARY BRICKELL

The most prosperous trader was William Brickell. His large building on the south bank of the river became the center of activity. His wife, Mary, who managed family and business affairs, ran the trading post as well. The Brickells traded cloth, hats, beads, watches, silver coins and liquor for the Indians' venison, alligator skins and egret plumes.

Contact with the trading posts began to affect the Indians' lifestyle. Beads and white man's clothing changed their native dress. Liquor—always available at the trading posts—caused more serious problems. Frequently, the Indians and a group of frontier bachelors went on prolonged drunken sprees. George W. Parsons, a New York visitor who witnessed a particularly wild party wrote, "What a subject for a temperance lecture this place is."

■ When newcomers arrived on the south side of the Miami River, their first impression of the tropical wilderness came via the Brickells' canopied walkway (left). (MC)

■ The Brickells operated their first trading post from their home that can be seen in this rare 1883 view of the Miami River (background). (MC)

■ In 1884, the Brickells built a new trading post at the river's mouth (below). (APC)

■ Seminoles (left) paddled their canoes down the Miami River from their Everglades homes to trade egret plumes and alligator skins for items of clothing, alcohol and beads. (MC)

GUAVA JELLY AND FEATHER BEDS

*W*hen J.W. Ewan arrived on the bay in 1874, William H. Gleason took him on a tour. The two spent a night with the Francis Infinger family who lived near what is now Matheson Hammock Park.

J.W. EWAN

"There were ten visitors," Ewan recalled, "so we sat in all thirteen men. We were offered by the ladies, venison steak, liver and home cured bacon—and such bacon fed on hammock mash! Oh, it was sweet. Corn bread, Jonnie or Johnsie cake, sweet potatoes, Indian pumpkin— better than the nicest squash—coomptie [comptie] pudding and guava jelly—all in good style and great abundance and all were made welcome. After supper we sat on the porch of the old log house. Some ate bananas, some chewed sugar cane; others smoked, and we talked and listened for we were nearly all newcomers and strangers to each other from different parts and anxious to know what could be done here. Just before retiring we were asked into the main room, and the Bible was read, a hymn or two sung and a prayer of good length was said by our host. Then we were assigned our places for the night. Governor Gleason and myself were assigned the couch of honor—a large bed with a cheese cloth bar. The Governor retired first. We had to do this in turns. When my time came, I looked for the Governor but could not find him. So I crawled in and found myself gradually disappearing. I was on a feather bed and there was soon a great mountain between the Governor and myself. I hailed him good night and asked him to look me up in the morning and help me out of the feathers."

New people continued to arrive. A group of Georgians who called themselves the Biscayne Bay Company purchased the Fort Dallas tract from Harris. In 1874, the company applied enough pressure on the post office department to reopen the Miami post office. J.W. Ewan, however, insisted that it be listed as "Maama" because it was the correct Indian spelling. Ewan and British newcomers Charles and Isabella Peacock, who came to Miami in 1875, operated an Indian trading post in William English's old slave quarters. Henry E. Perrine, son of Dr. Perrine, came to Miami in 1876 to develop his father's grant on what the locals called "the Hunting Grounds" or "Addison's Landing" (named after the area's well-known squatter, John Addison). Perrine and his sister, Hester Perrine Walker, planned to build a new town called Perrine. They published an 18-page advertising brochure that they distributed in New York. The first 35

people who agreed to settle permanently at Perrine and plant at least one tropical plant would receive a free lot. The venture was a total failure. After eight hard months in the wilderness, featuring one hurricane and an extremely cold winter, Henry Perrine gave up on South Florida and returned to New York.

■ *J.W. Ewan (facing page) was fondly called the "Duke of Dade" because he replaced "King" Gleason in the Florida Legislature. He later wrote a series of articles about pioneer days for Miami's first newspaper. (EPM)*

■ *Ewan managed the Biscayne Bay Company property on the Miami River's north bank. For awhile, the long building (below), once William English's slave quarters, was the Dade County Courthouse and Ewan, right, was the county clerk. Today, the building is preserved in Lummus Park. (MC)*

■ *Because most of South Florida was uninhabited, the U.S. government opened it for homesteading. Citizens could acquire free 160-acre quarter sections if they lived on the land for five years and improved it. The homestead map (right) records the homesteaders in what became parts of Coconut Grove, Coral Gables and South Miami. (EPM)*

■ *John Addison, a former Seminole War soldier, and his wife, Mary, homesteaded in South Dade near today's Charles Deering Estate (bottom right). (MC)*

Other Northerners were also interested in planting tropical plants. Three men from New Jersey—Henry B. Lum, Ezra Osborn and Elnathan T. Field—came to South Florida with plans to establish a giant coconut plantation. They purchased all the vacant beach land between Jupiter and Cape Florida and planted over 300,000 coconuts. The ever-present rats, rabbits and raccoons ate the tender green coconut shoots and ended the lofty dreams of the coconut planters. (A few plants did survive, and long after the coconut planters departed, Miami Beach would have the appearance of a tropic isle.)

The coconut planters would probably have agreed with writer F. Trench Townsend's 1875 description of Miami. "Throughout Florida," he wrote, "the settlement of Miami on Biscayne Bay is represented as a sort of terrestrial paradise, cultivated like the Garden of Eden…In reality it is a very small settlement on a ridge of limestone [and] the multitude of insects makes life hardly endurable."

South Florida remained an inaccessible wilderness. It was so isolated and underdeveloped that in 1875 the U.S. government felt it necessary to build a house of refuge on the beach to provide shelter for people who were shipwrecked. (Four other houses were built between Miami and Jacksonville.) The keeper patrolled the beach after every blow to look for survivors. Besides providing shelter for the shipwrecked, the Biscayne House of Refuge, built on Miami Beach near today's 71st Street, was a popular day's outing for those who lived in Miami.

The U.S. government had other major projects in the area. In 1875, government engineers came to build a lighthouse on Fowey Rock. When completed three years later, the lighthouse board darkened the old Cape Florida Lighthouse and returned the land to the original grantees. At this time, William Harney, now an Army general, surfaced to claim the lots he purchased on Key Biscayne during the Second Seminole War. In the process of investigating his claim, the government agents wrote, "No possible value can be attached to [the lands on Key Biscayne] except for building purposes and the project, once entertained of a town to give value to the lots has long sense [sic] fallen hopelessly through, so the grounds have remained and undoubtedly always will remain in their wild, barren condition."

■ *A group of men from New Jersey purchased all the vacant oceanfront land between Jupiter and Key Biscayne in the early 1880s and began planting coconuts. Their camp (below) added a picturesque touch of life to the desolate beach. (MC)*

ACROSS THE BAY: To help those shipwrecked on the isolated South Florida coast, the U.S. government built five Houses of Refuge between Indian River and Biscayne Bay. House Number Five (above), completed in 1876, was located on today's Miami Beach near 71st Street. (BL)

A few years after Ralph Munroe took this 1883 picture, the discouraged coconut planters gave up and moved away. The rats and rabbits ate most of the young coconut sprouts and only a few of the thousands of trees they planted remained to mark their efforts. (MC)

"WHERE IN THE HELL IS DADE?"

William Gleason added supervisor of U.S. Life Saving Service District No. 7 to his long list of local, state and federal offices. But the main thing that Gleason supervised was the Dade County elections. If the voters did not select the candidates he handpicked, he figured out a way to put them in office anyway. Ultimately, this election tampering became his undoing. By 1876, the people of South Florida finally organized against him.

The upcoming national presidential election was a hotly contested fight between Democrat Samuel J. Tilden and Republican Rutherford B. Hayes. Locally, the people were only interested in their own contest for the state legislature. Four years earlier, Gleason claimed voting irregularities and stole the election from two popular local candidates, Israel Stewart and John Brown. He and Ephraim T. Sturtevant took office instead. This time, the local citizens were determined to put Brown and Stewart in office.

In November 1876, Dade County recorded 73 registered voters, including all of what is now Broward and Palm Beach and part of Martin County. One precinct was at Jupiter, the second at Lake Worth and the third, which served the Miami area, was at the home of Michael Sears (located in what is now Bay Point).

When the votes were counted after the election, Stewart and Brown won once again. But before the official canvass of the polls, Gleason challenged the results, thus delaying the tally of Dade's votes. Unknown to most of the electors in Dade County, the presidential election was as heated and controversial as their own. Samuel Tilden went to sleep on election night believing he had been elected president. Even the *New York Tribune* announced his victory in banner headlines. Then an incredible thing happened. John C. Reid of *The New York Times* did some arithmetic. Tilden was one electoral vote short of election, with three states left to report—Florida, South Carolina and Louisiana—the three states still under radical Republican control.

By the time the official tally began in Tallahassee, national attention focused on Florida—a situation that would be repeated more than a century later. Within a week, when all the Florida votes had been counted except Dade's, Dade County landed on the front page of *The New York Times*. The missing Dade votes held up the final count of the Florida electors, and the missing Florida electors held up the outcome of the presidential election.

The people in Dade County were unaware of their sudden national notoriety. They only cared about the local election. Tempers flared when the Dade County Canvassing Board met and threw out the Sears precinct (just as Gleason wanted) and reversed the outcome of the election. Gleason was re-elected to the Florida Legislature along with his associate, John Varnum.

Meanwhile, the people in Tallahassee were still waiting for Gleason to bring them the Dade County returns. With the Sears precinct thrown out, Dade had only 14 votes, hardly enough to affect the outcome of the national election. Still the election could not be certified without Dade's return.

As the nation waited for the Florida count, the national press had a field day with Dade County's missing votes. Suddenly, every major U.S. newspaper carried a story about the mysterious Southern county. One story called the area the "Kingdom of Dade," another speculated on the Indian vote, while a third—not understanding the sudden interest—wrote, "Where in the hell is Dade?"

After the state board officially tallied Dade County's votes and Florida went for Hayes, *The New York Times* headlined, "The last straw for the Democratic camel, Dade comes in with a Republican majority."

The national election controversy was not over—only Dade County's part in it. The final outcome was not settled until the evening before the inauguration when Tilden, eager to unite the nation, conceded to Hayes if he would agree to end Reconstruction in Florida, South Carolina and Louisiana.

When Reconstruction ended in Florida, the old guard threw the Republicans out of office. The new Democratic-controlled legislature refused to seat most of the Republican legislators. As a result, the legislature and the courts removed Gleason from state office for the second time. This time, however, his influence also ran out in Dade County.

In 1877, the people in Dade County held a special election to select a new county commission. (The governor no longer appointed county officials.) The voters removed all of Gleason's men, brought the courthouse back from Biscayne

to the Miami River and changed "Maama" back to Miami. A young visitor named Ralph Munroe witnessed the emotionally charged transfer of power and wrote that the people were "armed to the teeth" and ready to stop Gleason and his men if they tried to regain control.

Gleason, however, decided to leave. Never one to put all his eggs in one basket, he had another kingdom waiting for him in Brevard County where he founded the city of Eau Gallie and eventually settled down to a sort of baronial respectability.

TWO COCONUTS MAKE A GROVE

ISABELLA PEACOCK

Ralph Munroe came to Miami after hearing about Biscayne Bay from longtime resident Ned Pent, who was visiting the offices of the wrecking firm Merritt and Chapman in New York. Munroe, a sailing enthusiast, viewed his 1877 trip only as an exciting adventure and had no interest in coming to Miami to live. He returned to his Staten Island home in New York, married and started a successful oyster planting business. But in 1880, Ralph Munroe's young wife, Eva, who had recently borne a little girl, contracted tuberculosis. Remembering the warmth of the South Florida winter, he took her to Miami in a last desperate attempt to restore her health.

Ralph and Eva Munroe, her sister Amelia Hewitt and a companion arrived in late 1880. At first they lived in a home in today's Coconut Grove but it was so isolated they moved and set up camp on the north bank of the Miami River in front of the rock buildings owned by the Biscayne Bay Company. Isabella Peacock, who lived with her husband Charles and her three sons in one of the buildings, befriended the young Munroes and tried to nurse Eva, whose health worsened rapidly. Unfortunately, the warm winter did not help. She died in April 1882 and was buried nearby. (Her body was later reinterred in Coconut Grove where it remains today next to the Coconut Grove Library— Miami's oldest marked grave.)

Artist Ken Hughes captured the spirit of early "Cocoanut Grove" with his oil painting of a Seminole Indian canoe arriving at Charles and Isabella Peacock's Bay View House wharf. The Bay View House, which later became the Peacock Inn, was located in today's Peacock Park. (APC)

"Cocoanut Grove"

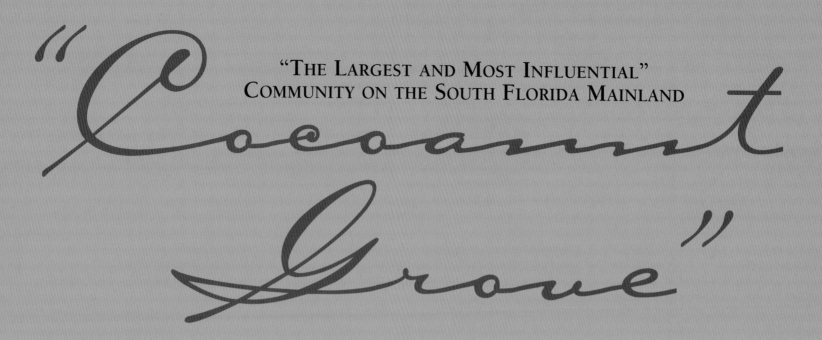

"THE LARGEST AND MOST INFLUENTIAL"
COMMUNITY ON THE SOUTH FLORIDA MAINLAND

The Peacock Inn (facing page) attracted a variety of sophisticated winter visitors. (APC)

The Jimmy family (above) posed on the Coconut Grove bayfront near the two famous coconut trees. (MC)

Paul Ransom opened Pine Knot Camp in Coconut Grove in 1896. From its beginning in this pioneer dwelling (above right), it became the Adirondack-Florida School in 1903 and eventually metamorphosed into today's Ransom Everglades, still located on the original site. (MC)

Isabella Peacock organized community picnics (right) to support her Sunday school. Most of Coconut Grove's pioneer families including Peacocks, Frows, Pents, Alburys and Thompsons, came to the gathering. Mariah Brown, the first black resident, stands in the background. (MC)

HOPING FOR A CURE

On February 8, 1882, Addie Hewitt wrote a friend about her life on the banks of the Miami River. A few months earlier, she and her sister Eva Munroe, who both suffered from tuberculosis, had come to South Florida hoping for a cure. Their brother Tom Hewitt, Eva's husband Ralph Munroe and a companion joined them. Sadly, two months after she penned her letter, Eva died of the disease and a short time later Addie too succumbed. Ralph buried Eva on the north bank of the Miami River. Several years later, he moved her body to Coconut Grove and re-buried her next to the today's Coconut Grove Library.

"I am now sitting under a coconut tree in a hammock," Addie wrote. "I left my sister lying on my cot. She is very delicate, so weak, has a chill almost every day and she is so thin I fear she will never be well again. We are on the banks of the Miami River and just across the river is the post office a half a mile from our encampment. We must row over for our mail. Our mail is brought each week by schooner from Key West. It seems strange to receive the mail only once a week. How much we do enjoy it. The mail here has increased they tell us since we came. When I read of the cold weather north I feel thankful I am here.

Last week we all went over to Mrs. Gilbert's place to spend the day, had the use of the house. Eva had a chill and she found it very nice to go into a parlor and lie down. Eva and I drink coconut milk every day. It is said to be very good for invalids…the jelly is also very nice.

Ralph and Tommy have just come in from fishing, had good luck, caught a number of different kinds of fish, red snapper, grouper, running jacks and schoolmaster, expected to have caught some of our favorite king fish, but it was too rough outside. I have seen some of the Seminole Indians of which I will tell when I write again.

I am to have a cart ride on Saturday to the pine woods. They are a mile from us. I amuse myself with walking out some. I have made a flower bed. I am now gathering daisy seed to take north. I will enclose a diagram of our place, perhaps you can get some idea from it how we live. Do not laugh at us.

Addie

■ *Eva Amelia Hewitt Munroe rests peacefully beside the Coconut Grove Library in Miami's oldest marked grave.* (HG)

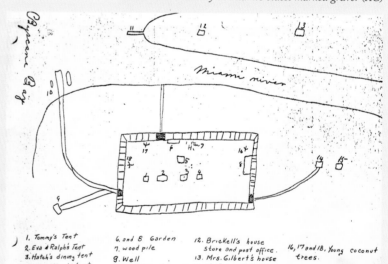

1. Tommy's Tent
2. Eva & Ralph's Tent
3. Hatch's dining tent
4. Mrs. O'Dea's tent
5. Palmetto Kitchen
6. and 8. Garden
7. wood pile
9. Well
10. Dock & boats
11. Brickell's dock
12. Brickell's house store and post office.
13. Mrs. Gilbert's house
14. Mr. Peacock G. Evan
15. Store
16, 17 and 18, Young coconut trees.

Ralph Munroe sadly prepared to return home. On the way back, his sister-in-law became desperately ill with the same disease and died just as the ship pulled into New York Harbor. More tragedy awaited Munroe in Staten Island. In his absence, his infant daughter Edith, who stayed behind with her grandmother, also died, leaving Munroe devastated and alone.

The following year, Munroe decided to return to South Florida where he had buried his wife. During this trip, he urged Charles and Isabella Peacock to find some bayfront property and build a hotel because there was no public lodging in the area. He offered to help by bringing Northern tourists to Miami.

At first, the Peacocks considered buying property in "Billy Mettair's Bight," an area that later developed into Lemon City. Munroe, however, encouraged them to move to "Jack's Bight" instead. Jack's Bight was near the former Beasley property and Jack, who lived nearby, was Charles Peacock's brother. Jack Peacock had encouraged his brother and family to move to Miami from England in the first place, having wandered into the area after being stranded in Key West.

Charles Peacock bought 31 acres from John Frow, who purchased the entire Beasley homestead from Anna Beasley for $100. Peacock's purchase included all the land from the south border of what is now Peacock Park, north to Grand Avenue and Mary Street. On this large tract, they built theBay View House—the first public lodging place in the Miami area.

The Bay View House was not really a hotel but simply a large home. On the South Florida frontier, however, it looked grand. When the Peacocks built it, they launched the first real community in the Miami area. The long, wooden dock that jutted out into the bay became the settlement's front door.

Charles Peacock hired black Bahamians, who had moved to Key West, to work at the hotel. The first to come, Mariah Brown, from Upper Bogue, Eleuthera, lived on the hotel property. When more black Bahamians arrived, they built a small settlement a short distance away on land bought from homesteader Joseph Frow, John Frow's brother. Known as Kebo, it became the first black settlement on the South Florida mainland.

About the same time, Ralph Munroe accidentally discovered the existence of Horace Porter's Cocoanut Grove post office which Porter had abandoned a decade earlier. Because reopening this previously existing post office was easier than applying for a new one, the community expeditiously rechristened itself "Cocoanut Grove"—even though only two coconut trees grew in the entire area. The new post office opened in a room in the Bay View House and Charles Peacock became the postmaster.

Charles and Isabella Peacock, who came to Coconut Grove from England, sit with their three sons, left to right, Alfred, Harry and Charles John. (MC)

"CAPTAIN DICK" CARNEY. THE JOKER OF "COCOANUT GROVE"

"Captain Dick" Carney was Coconut Grove's resident practical joker. He played his best joke one night during a dance at the Housekeepers Club. It was customary at all the community dances for families to bring their young children with them and put them to sleep in the adjoining room. One night, while the parents were enjoying themselves at the dance, Carney slipped into the room of sleeping babies and exchanged their blankets and clothing and shifted them about. When the dance was over, the unsuspecting mothers picked up the wrong babies and took them home. Author Kirk Munroe told the story to Owen Wister who incorporated it into his novel, The Virginian.

Dick Carney (MC)

Like a good tourist, Mrs. Thomas Hine posed for the photographer on the mysterious steps next to the famous Punch Bowl. (TG)

BRICKELL HAMMOCK
Time & Time Again

1896

2008

The whole Brickell area was once a dense tropical hardwood forest known as a hammock. It was filled with lush vegetation and wild animals like panthers and fox. In the 1890s, William and Mary Brickell hacked a wagon trail through the jungle (now Brickell Avenue) from their property on the Miami River to Coconut Grove. Today, it is still possible to experience this natural masterpiece at Simpson Park Preserve on South Miami Avenue. (APC)

THE FIRST BLACK SETTLEMENT ON THE SOUTH FLORIDA MAINLAND

In 1900, Reverend John Davis opened the first school in Kebo (left) in the Methodist Church on Charles Avenue, then called Evangelist Street. (KSD)

The residents of Kebo (facing page), most of whom came from the Bahamas, stood proudly in front of Ralph Munroe's boathouse for this historic photo. Many of their ancestors still live in Coconut Grove. (MC)

The Reverend Samuel A. Sampson (left) organized and built the St. Agnes Baptist Church on Thomas Avenue in 1895. Count Jean D. Hedouville, who lived on the bayfront, donated the land. As the congregation grew, the church built a new sanctuary on Charles Avenue (right), which became the Macedonia Baptist Church. (KSD)

Samuel Sampson's brother, Nat, shown with pioneer resident Alice Burrows, worked at the Peacock Store. Alice Burrows' house still stands on Charles Avenue. (MC)

Just as he promised, Ralph Munroe encouraged many of his Northern friends to visit "the Grove." Soon the Bay View House filled with visitors.

Titled noblemen, world-famous scientists, writers and preachers (including Charles Stowe, the son of Harriet Beecher Stowe) made the Grove their winter haven.

The special atmosphere of the Bay View House and the warmth and good humor of Charles and Isabella Peacock kept people coming. As a result, the Bay View House expanded into the Peacock Inn after they added several new imposing structures.

The Peacocks also encouraged permanent settlement. They gave Ralph Munroe part of their land to convince him to stay in Coconut Grove year-round. Before long, many of their most famous visitors also became Coconut Grove's first families, including Kirk Munroe (no relation to Ralph), a noted author of boys' books, his wife Mary Barr and Flora McFarlane.

OF SAILBOATS AND SUNDAY SCHOOLS

Many of the Northern tourists came to Coconut Grove on their yachts or sailboats. This prompted the founding of the area's first organization—the Biscayne Bay Yacht Club. In 1887, Ralph Munroe and Kirk Munroe established the club after the community held a Washington's Birthday sailboat race and dinner at the Bay View House. (Charles Peacock and his son Alfred were charter members of the club.)

Yacht clubs were fine for visitors, but Isabella Peacock despaired because there was no house of worship. In 1887, she collected enough donations from her guests to build a Sunday school building. Two years later, it became the first public school building in what is now Dade County. (The school itself had opened in a private home a year earlier.)

FLORA McFARLAND

In 1891, Ralph Munroe donated some of the land the Peacocks gave him for a new church that became known as the Union Chapel. Charles Stowe preached there. At first, blacks and whites worshipped together in the picturesque building. Reverend Samuel Sampson later organized Saint Agnes Baptist Church—the first church in the black community (now Macedonia Baptist).

That same year, Flora McFarlane—South Florida's first woman homesteader and the Grove's schoolteacher—organized the Housekeepers Club for the women in the community. Sturdy pioneer women who grew up on Biscayne Bay with little formal education met with former Northerners who grew up in fancy Eastern drawing rooms. The club raised most of the money for "village improvement and uplift," held cultural events, sponsored most social events and provided outstanding leadership.

In 1895, Housekeepers Club member Mary Barr Munroe organized the "Pine Needles Club" for young girls. Through Kirk and Mary Barr Munroe's leadership, the Pine Needles established the area's first library in a donated room on the second floor of Charles Peacock and Son's store. By 1894, the Lake Worth newspaper, *The Tropical Sun*, wrote that Cocoanut Grove was the "largest and most influential" community on the South Florida mainland.

■ *In 1887, Ralph and Kirk Munroe organized the Biscayne Bay Yacht Club, South Florida's oldest institution. Kirk's wife, Mary, made the club's "25-N" flag that was hoisted for the first time at Munroe's boathouse. (MC)*

THE FIRST SEASON

■ Biscayne Bay's first winter visitors—a harbinger of what was to come—launched South Florida's enduring tourism industry (left). Front row, left to right: Kirk Munroe, Count Jean D'Hedouville and Alfred Munroe; middle row: Dr. Tiger, Ralph Munroe, Mrs. E.P. Brown, Miss Brown, Charles F. Stowe, Thomas A. Hine, Count James L. Nugent and E.P. Brown; back row: Ellen Munroe, Flora McFarland, Mary Barr Munroe, Edward A. Hine and Mrs. Thomas Hine. (MC)

■ The same season, the Peacock's held a party at the Bay View House for the tourists and everyone else who lived on the bay. It was South Florida's first community gathering (above). (MC)

1884

THE BARNACLE
Time & Time Again

1891

Ralph Munroe built his house, the Barnacle, high off the ground with wide porches. It was not a typical pioneer dwelling but a home built to take advantage of South Florida's unique environment. (MC)

1908

When his growing family needed more room, he jacked up the original house and built a new first floor underneath. (MC)

2008

Today, the Barnacle is an historic state park. Residents gathered for the annual Fourth of July celebration that Munroe inaugurated more than 100 years ago. (APC)

BILLY METTAIR'S BIGHT

Five miles north of the river in "Billy Mettair's Bight," another settlement grew just as rapidly. "Buffalo Bill" Mettair, who moved to the area in 1874 with his trusty rifle and his horse Prince, was a living legend. For 16 years, he was either sheriff or deputy sheriff of Dade County and dealt with many frontier characters. He also was the town blacksmith.

Edward "Ned" Pent, another early resident of Mettair's Bight, was the son of Temple Pent who had moved to the Miami area in the early 1800s and served as the Cape Florida Lighthouse keeper. Ned Pent was one of the "barefoot mailmen," walking the mail down the beach from Lake Worth. He was also a licensed wrecker and the settlement's coffin maker. He tried to claim a homestead in Mettair's Bight, but it conflicted with William H. Gleason's claim for excess land. When Pent lost the contest, he moved to Cocoanut Grove to live near his brother, John. His nephew William Pent homesteaded just west of the main part of the settlement. (Today, Pent family heirs are the oldest pioneer family in the Miami area.)

Bahamian John Saunders also lived at Mettair's Bight. He arrived in 1876 and in 1889 homesteaded the land on which he had been squatting. Even before final proof, he started selling lots. Eugene C. Harrington, an enterprising newcomer, bought a half-mile strip of Saunders' land and subdivided it into Lemon City.

A year later, Mettair platted another Lemon City on the banks of the Little River. This new area died and the Harrington's subdivision became the nucleus of the Lemon City community.

By 1895, Lemon City had three short business streets. The main street was Lemon Avenue with Saw Dust Street to the north and Biscayne Avenue to the south. Fifteen buildings included several substantial houses, two small hotels, two or three saloons, one restaurant, a blacksmith shop, a real estate office and one saw mill.

Lemon City also had at least three small, but thriving, black communities. They included Nazarine, Knightsville and Boles Town. Each occupied part of the land north of Lemon Avenue (62nd Street) between the railroad track and today's N.E. Second Avenue.

CENTERBOARDS FOR CEMETERIES

For many years, Ned Pent was the only person on the bay qualified to build coffins. He was regularly called upon to perform this duty, but as time went on, he became less and less enthusiastic about the job. In order to keep him working, he would be locked in a room at nightfall with a jug of whiskey and a pile of lumber. In the morning, the whiskey would be gone and the coffin completed. His career came to an end after one coffin-building binge when he got too drunk. The next morning, the bereaved family found Pent passed out next to a nicely made coffin, complete with a retractable keel often used on sailboats known as a centerboard.

Ned Pent, left, with his brother John. (MC)

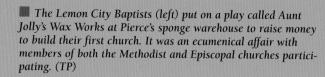
The Lemon City Baptists (left) put on a play called Aunt Jolly's Wax Works at Pierce's sponge warehouse to raise money to build their first church. It was an ecumenical affair with members of both the Methodist and Episcopal churches participating. (TP)

Carrie Barnes Johnson (below) grew up in Nazarine, Lemon City's black community. She was one of the first black women to register to vote. (TP)

Solomon James Peters had a large home in Lemon City-Little River at N.E. Second Avenue and 75th Street (below). The family became major tomato farmers and later moved their packinghouse to South Dade where the settlement of Peters still bears their name. (TP)

Lemon City residents built a new school in 1907 to replace the one-room schoolhouse that was located near N.E. Fifth Avenue and 59th Street. The Miami Metropolis opined that it was "a credit to Lemon City and the pride of her citizens." By 1907, the new school had more than 70 students (right). (TP)

The heart of Lemon City (facing page), although never incorporated, was at N.E. 62nd Street between N.E. Second Avenue and Biscayne Bay. Lemon City was the first of Miami's pre-railroad communities to claim connection to the north by both road and rail. It also had the area's deepest water, making it a natural stopping point for incoming boats. (TP)

THE LURE OF THE UPPER BAY

Lemon City

REMEMBERING LEMON CITY
Time & Time Again

Young John Gordon DuPuis came to Lemon City in 1898 right out of medical school. He opened an office and Lemon City's first drug store in a small board and batten house near the bay at 62nd Street. He later owned the White Belt Dairy and in 1917 founded Lemon City Agricultural High School (now Miami Edison).

Dr. DuPuis' original office. (above). (TP)

The Lemon City Drug Store (right). (CWP)

Color picture (below). (APC)

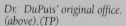

1939

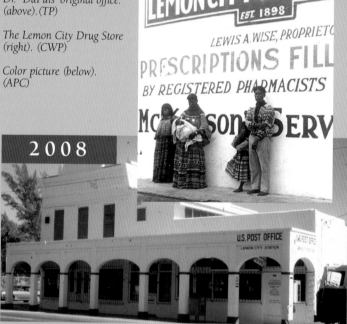

2008

In 1902, Dr. DuPuis built a new office and drug store at N.E. Second Avenue and 61st Street. It also served as the Lemon City post office. In the early 1930s, he leased the drug store to Lewis W. Wise, who operated it until the 1970s. Although its future is uncertain, it remains today as a rare example of early commercial architecture and one of the last remnants of the once-thriving pioneer community.

■ *The William Freeman family lived on the Little River. Family members included, left to right, George, Mr. Freeman, Ethel, Rebecca, Edison, Mrs. Freeman and Cora. (TP)*

Lemon City's advantage was its accessibility. It had a relatively deep harbor and was the first part of Miami to be connected to another part of the state by road. In 1892, Dade County built a road between Lemon City and Lantana on the south end of Lake Worth. A stagecoach line that ran three times a week connected the two settlements.

Prior to the arrival of the railroad, Lemon City had a school whose students were taught by the Brickells' daughter, Alice. In 1890, Ada Merritt moved to Lemon City from Kentucky and became the schoolteacher. Ada Merritt, who had a strong influence on the community, also organized Lemon City's first Sunday school.

By 1895, both Lemon City and Coconut Grove were thriving communities as another settlement in South Dade known as Cutler began to prosper. The future site of the City of Miami, however, was still little more than a wilderness. The two rock buildings on the north bank, the Brickells' home and trading post on the south bank, and a few other scattered pioneer houses were the only structures.

In 1891, Cleveland widow Julia Tuttle purchased the 640-acre Fort Dallas tract from the Biscayne Bay Company and moved there with her two grown children. She brought a dream with her—a dream that had been germinating since she first visited her father, Ephraim T. Sturtevant, on the bay in 1875. With great determination, she planned to build a city on the Miami River. By this time, it was a dream whose time had come, and she would be the one to turn it into reality.

Shortly before she left her Cleveland, Ohio home and moved to Miami, Julia Tuttle, left, had a formal picture taken with her mother Frances Sturtevant and daughter Fanny. (HMSF)

■ *MIAMI'S BEGINNING: In order to clear the land for the Royal Palm Hotel, Flagler's workers, led by John Sewell, in shirt sleeves, cart away the bones from the Tequesta Indian burial mound that people said stood "like a mountain" at the mouth of the Miami River. The men included (but in no order) A.W. Brown, Philip Bowman, John Hawkins, Warren Merridy, Richard Mangrom, Romeo Fashaw, Scipio Coleman, Sam Anderson, Davie Heartly, J.B. Grown, William Collier and Joe Thompson. Back row left to right: J.E. Lummus, C.T. McCrimmon, L. Townley and E.G. Sewell. (APC)*

Chapter Four

"Never a Town"

"Marvelous Miami...the coming Metropolis of South Florida."
Miami Metropolis, Vol. 1, No. 1, May 15, 1896

THE INFANT CITY OF MIAMI WAS THE REMARKABLE PROGENY OF REMARKABLE PARENTS. IT DID NOT DEVELOP

slowly like other cities; it arrived in a railroad car, howling and kicking.

Miami's mother, Julia Tuttle, discovered Biscayne Bay in 1875 when she was only 26 years old. She and her two young children, along with her friend Mrs. Davis and her child, came to visit Julia Tuttle's father, Ephraim Sturtevant, at his homestead in today's Miami Shores.

The arrival of the two ladies from Cleveland, Ohio created quite a sensation in the small Miami settlement. Very few women lived in Miami—especially cultured and refined ladies. Many people thought that it was rather shocking for married women to travel so far without their husbands.

Local tongues wagged when bachelor J.W. Ewan, manager of the Biscayne Bay Company property, took it upon himself to show the women around in his boat, *The Zenobia*.

"Mrs. T. very young and both [Mrs. Davis] quite good looking and lively…pleasant ladies," George Parson, another local bachelor, wrote in his diary. "It is a very great pleasure to meet with such ladies way down here in this desolate country and I appreciate their society. Mrs. Tuttle is younger, full of life but not very discreet and seems to favor E's [J.W. Ewan] attention. Rather unbecoming conduct in a married lady. She is unaffected though and possesses a stout heart I think."

■ Through a stroke of luck and a lot of persistence, Julia Tuttle convinced Henry Flagler to continue his railroad from Palm Beach to Miami. Her land and his money launched the fledgling City of Miami. (HFM)

■ Soon after she moved to Miami, Tuttle (facing page), fourth from the left back row, invited a group of tourists and community leaders to a tea party at her home on the Miami River. Coconut Grove icons Isabella Peacock, sitting at the far left, and Flora McFarlane, sitting at the far right, had much in common with Julia Tuttle's determination. (MC)

Julia Tuttle and her children returned to Cleveland where her husband Frederick's family was prosperous and well-established. Frederick was a partner in the family's pioneer ironworks which grew as America industrialized. Had he not become ill, Julia Tuttle would probably have remained a proper Cleveland society matron.

At that time, Cleveland was a bustling industrial city. Besides iron, two other minerals—coal and oil—came together in the Cuyahoga Valley. The city's nascent oil industry included a company formed by three young men—John D. Rockefeller, Samuel Andrews and Henry M. Flagler. The company became the foundation of the Standard Oil Trust and the men were soon among America's wealthiest.

A series of personal tragedies brought Julia Tuttle and Henry Flagler together. When Henry Flagler's wife Mary became ill, her doctor suggested he take her to a warmer climate. So in 1878, the Flaglers spent the winter in Jacksonville, Florida, the railroad's southern terminus.

In 1881, shortly after his wife died, Flagler married her nurse, Alice Shourds, and took her to Saint Augustine on their honeymoon. During this happy interlude, he fell in love with Florida. In 1885, Flagler built the luxurious Ponce de Leon Hotel in Saint Augustine, launching the career of architects John Carrere and Thomas Hastings who at the time worked for the legendary McKim, Mead and White. Flagler's Spanish-style hotel set a style that Florida would claim as its own in the years to come.

Next, Flagler purchased a small-gauge railroad and expanded it so that he could bring his private railroad car to Saint Augustine. Saint Augustine quickly became the darling of the private-car set. Millionaires poured into Flagler's new winter resort. Flagler realized that this unique combination of railroad and luxury hotel was a winner. Because the rest of the Florida East Coast south of Saint Augustine was mostly undeveloped, and the State of Florida offered thousands of acres of land to potential railroad builders, he saw an opportunity to build more hotels, create settlements around them and connect the new towns with his ever-expanding railroad.

A LONG WAY FROM TAMPA

Meanwhile, back in Cleveland, Frederick Tuttle died, leaving his wife in financial straits. To survive, she turned her Fairmont Avenue mansion into a rooming house and ladies luncheon facility. As her financial condition continued to deteriorate, she called upon her friend John D. Rockefeller to intercede on her behalf by writing Henry Flagler to offer her services as the head of his housekeeping staff at the Ponce de Leon Hotel. He turned her down. When her mother died, she inherited some money, as well as a half of the Sturtevant Florida property. In 1891, "stout-hearted" Julia Tuttle decided to forge a new life for herself in Miami. Instead of settling on her family's homestead in today's Miami Shores, she set out to buy the most impressive piece of real estate she had seen in Miami. It was on the north bank of the Miami River near its mouth that, by this time, the Biscayne Bay Company was happy to unload.

Julia Tuttle did not go blindly into the new venture. She consulted with James E. Ingraham, president of Henry B. Plant's Florida railroad whom she had met at a dinner party in Cleveland. At the time, Plant was Florida's premier railroad builder. His Jacksonville, Tampa and Key West Line reached Tampa in 1883 and was the closest line to Miami. "Some day," she told Ingraham, "someone will build a rail-

road to Miami and when they do I will be willing to divide my properties there and give one-half to the company for a town site. Perhaps, you will be the man."

Ingraham replied that Miami was a long way off, but added, "stranger things have happened, and possibly I some day may hold you to that promise."

On November 13, 1891, Julia Tuttle, her 23-year-old daughter Fannie and her 21-year-old son Harry came floating into Miami on a barge loaded down with all their possessions. J.W. Ewan was there to greet her and transfer the Biscayne Bay Company property into her hands. She moved her family into the two-story rock building that William English had built almost 50 years earlier, and, like him, she began to plan a city. "It may seem strange to you," she wrote a friend in Cleveland, "but it is a dream of my life to see this wilderness turned into a prosperous country."

After only four months, Julia Tuttle received the good news that James E. Ingraham and a group of Plant railroad men had started across the Everglades from Fort Myers to Miami. She hoped this was the beginning of Plant's railroad expansion. The venture went badly. Finally, after almost a month of wandering through saw grass and swamp, the exhausted party reached Miami. Julia Tuttle welcomed the men by raising the American flag and setting off firecrackers.

Although Miami did not have much to offer, Tuttle impressed the men. "She has shown a great deal of energy and enterprise in this frontier country," one wrote, "where it is almost a matter of creation to accomplish so much in so short a time."

When the party returned to Tampa with their report, however, Henry B. Plant decided that he was not interested in taking on the Everglades just to reach a tiny east coast settlement. Undaunted, Julia Tuttle turned to Florida's other railroad builder, Henry M. Flagler, who had just begun to extend his railroad south of Saint Augustine.

For the next few years, Julia Tuttle besieged Flagler. She went to Saint Augustine to talk to him but he ignored her offer. She wrote him regularly, pointing out the advantages

In 1887, Henry Flagler opened his luxurious Hotel Ponce de Leon in St. Augustine (facing page). It was designed by two young architects—John Carrere and Thomas Hastings—from the prominent New York firm of McKim, Mead and White. The hotel's popularity launched a new style of architecture that remains popular in South Florida. Its success also prompted Flagler to extend his railroad south of Saint Augustine and build additional hotels along the way. (APC)

want to bring his railroad to Miami but it was years away and he did not want to tie up her property. His railroad, however, kept getting closer. By 1893, it was on its way to Palm Beach where he was building the Royal Poinciana Hotel. Now that the tracks were only 66 miles away, Julia Tuttle bombarded Flagler with letters. His opinion of her lessened with every note. In the end, her persistence and a stroke of luck turned his head.

During the winter of 1894-95, a terrible freeze hit Florida and destroyed the north and central Florida citrus groves. Julia Tuttle saw the freeze not as a disaster but as an opportunity. She wrote Flagler, reminding him that Miami was untouched by the cold weather. For the first time, Flagler listened. He sent J.E. Ingraham, whom he had hired away from Plant to manage his land department, to investigate. When Ingraham reached Miami, Julia Tuttle presented him with orange blossoms from Kirk Munroe's grove to take to Flagler as proof

that Miami was unaffected by the freeze. When Flagler saw the orange blossoms and photographs of the region taken by pioneer photographer Ralph M. Munroe, he decided to check out Miami himself. When he arrived in June 1895, Julia Tuttle took him to lunch at Coconut Grove's Peacock Inn and took her hard sell to a new level. Before the day was over, Flagler agreed that the time was ripe to bring his railroad to Miami.

In the final contract, Tuttle gave Flagler half her land—300 acres—if he agreed to build a luxury hotel and lay out the town around it. It included 100 acres on the bay and river fronts, with the exception of her 13-acre home lot and a 200-acre plot she believed would be the business district of the new town. The 100-acre tract included land from the bay on the east (at the time the bay came to the western side of today's Biscayne Boulevard) to S.W. Third Avenue on the west and S.W. First Street to the north. The boundaries of her home lot were the Miami River on the south, South Miami Avenue on the west, S.E. Second Avenue on the east and S.E. Second Street on the north. To insure development of this business district tract, she cleverly gave Flagler alternate lots. It included land between the Miami River on the south and southwest and N.E. and N.W. 11th Street on the north.

Flagler signed a separate contract with William and Mary Brickell who added part of their holdings on the south bank of the river, as well as part of their Fort Lauderdale property. Flagler agreed to build a bridge over the Miami River and also subdivide the Brickell land with alternate lots. The boundaries of the Miami property were the Miami River on the north and South Miami Avenue on the east, S.W. and N.W. Eighth Avenue on the west and S.W. 15th Road and S.W. 11th Street on the south. Like Tuttle, the Brickells reserved their home lot as well as all the land between the bay and South Miami Avenue.

When word spread that the railroad was coming, the news had the same effect on Miami as the Gold Rush had on Sutter's Creek, California. Men, especially refugees from the freeze, poured into Miami. When this army of "95ers" descended on the little settlement, they pitched their tents and waited for the railroad.

■ *North Florida men (above) survey the damage to their citrus crop caused by the "Killer-Freeze of 1894-1895." (SPA)*

■ *Many of Miami's founding fathers spent their first days on* The Rockledge—*Captain Vail's floating hotel (above). It was docked at the foot of Avenue D, now Miami Avenue. (HMSF)*

THE LAST DAYS OF THE FRONTIER

In 1895, William B. Brickell had the only store in Miami. His shelves were soon empty. The newcomers also cleaned out Charles Peacock and Son's store in Coconut Grove and D.K. Knight's Lemon City establishment. The Tuttles frantically started constructing a huge barn-like building to house the workmen. Before it was finished, they decided to turn it into a makeshift hotel they called the Hotel Miami. Early-bird arrivals eagerly awaited the coming of Flagler's men. Trouble with the land titles, thanks to William Gleason's machinations a decade earlier, held them up. In the interim, Julia Tuttle hired some of the men to begin clearing the hammock. They swatted the mosquitoes and horseflies, cursed the palmetto stumps that refused to budge and wondered what they were doing there. Many left in disgust.

Even though Flagler's men had not yet arrived, the railroad was on its way. The would-be city builders waiting in

WILLIAM B. BRICKELL

Miami were kept apprised of its progress. By September, it was south of West Palm Beach, carving its path of steel southward into the wilderness.

Finally, on March 3, 1896, Flagler's men, led by John Sewell, arrived. The party included only 17 men—five white men and 12 blacks—whom Sewell had handpicked for the job. Sewell's first impression of the site was that it was all woods. Julia Tuttle had laid out one street, Avenue "D" (Miami Avenue), on which several stores neared completion. The Miami Hotel was still not finished. Fortunately, Sewell was able to stay on Captain Vail's floating hotel, *The Rockledge*, which had docked two days earlier at the foot of today's Miami Avenue.

Sewell's first task was to clear the site for the new Flagler Hotel that he named the Royal Palm. Realizing the historic importance of the event, Sewell hired pioneer photographer J.N. Chamberlain to record the ground-breaking ceremony. The crowd cheered as A.W. Brown, leader of the black labor force, threw the first shovel of dirt. Miami was on its way.

The first spadeful of dirt was only the beginning of a series of firsts. During the next month, entrepreneurs vied to become the first merchant, banker, printer, livery stable owner, druggist, hardware store owner and professional man. "Buildings are springing up in every direction as if by magic," wrote Isidor Cohen, one of the first three Jewish residents.

WHILE AWAITING THE RAILROAD, JULIA TUTTLE BUILT MIAMI'S FIRST BUSINESS STREET— AVENUE D (MIAMI AVENUE) ON LAND SHE RESERVED FOR HERSELF.

▪ E.L. Brady, one of Miami's first grocers had a store on Avenue D (right). It was located next door to the Bank of Bay Biscayne. The tragic Christmas morning fire of 1896 started here. (HMSF)

▪ Tuttle also built the Hotel Miami (below) on Avenue D. It opened before the Royal Palm and gave workers a slightly better alternative to Vail's floating hotel. (LW)

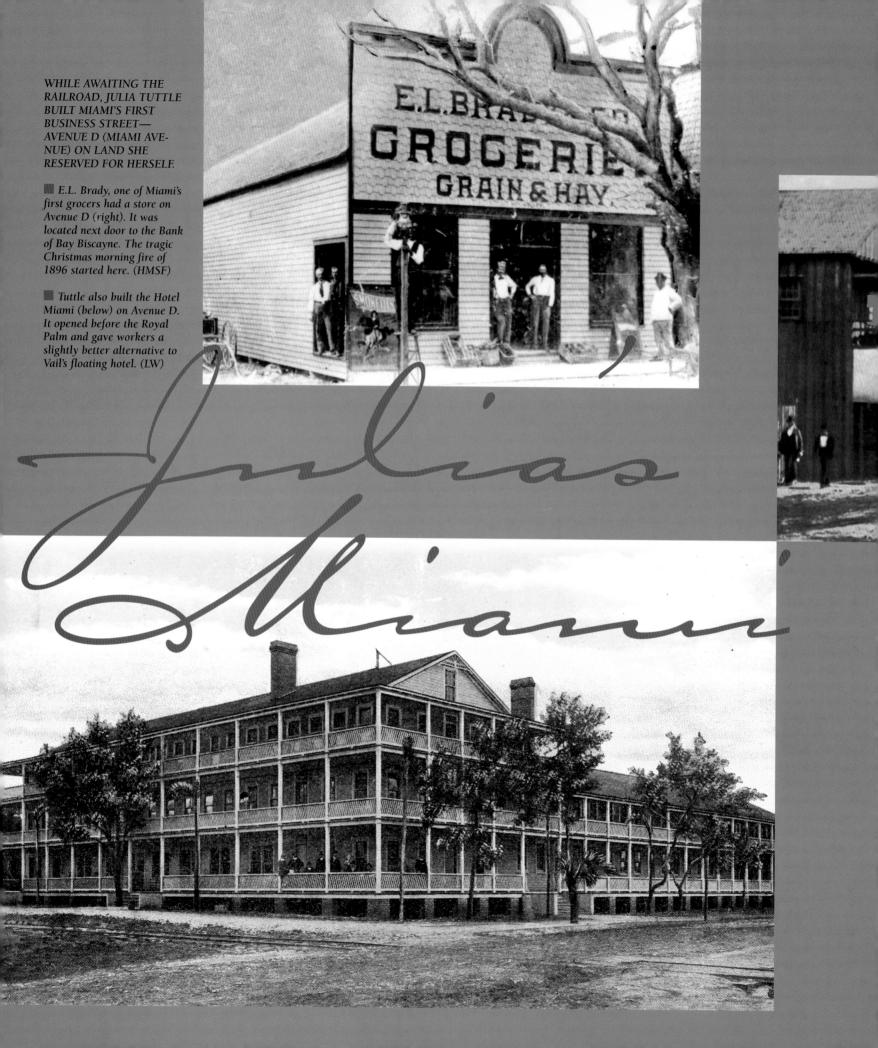

Julia's Miami

Sewell's "black artillery" posed for Miami's pioneer photographer J.N. Chamberlain on not-yet-paved Avenue D. It looked more like a western frontier town than what promoters called "The Magic City." Chamberlain later made this postcard from his photograph. (LW)

William M. Brown, right, and Charles H. Garthside stand in the doorway of the Bank of Bay Biscayne, Miami's first bank. It opened on May 2, 1896 at what is now S.E. Second Street just east of Miami Avenue. (HMSF)

Lula Lummus (LL)

MIAMI—MAY 1896

Lula Lummus, wife of J.N. Lummus, who worked for Henry Flagler and later helped develop Miami Beach, came to Miami shortly before the railroad arrived.

We now live at Miami, Florida, the terminus of the East Coast Railroad. I feel like I am in another world, but the novelty is fascinating and interesting. Miami is situated on the Miami River and beautiful Biscayne Bay. It is decidedly a "boom" town. This place is only a few months old and has a population of several hundred people.

Everything is crude and we have few comforts of civilization, but I'm enjoying living near to nature's heart. Twenty business houses are going up, and in a few years everyone predicts this place will be equal to Tampa. Boats run three times per week from Key West, and crowds arrive on every train to see the much talked of place.

I had the thrill of my life when I stood and watched the first train come in! All rejoiced to see that important mark of civilization…

Mr. Flagler is having the ground prepared for his new hotel. It will be built on a point facing the bay.

Mrs. Julia Tuttle's home, with its well kept lawns and lovely tropical flowers and luscious fruits, shows what can be done down here in Dixie land! The old Fort Dallas within her grounds is of much interest to sightseers. It is a picturesque sight crumbling away and covered with beautiful ivy.

Mrs. J.N. Lummus
Written for the Sanford Chronicle at Hotel Miami, May 1896

GOING FULL TILT

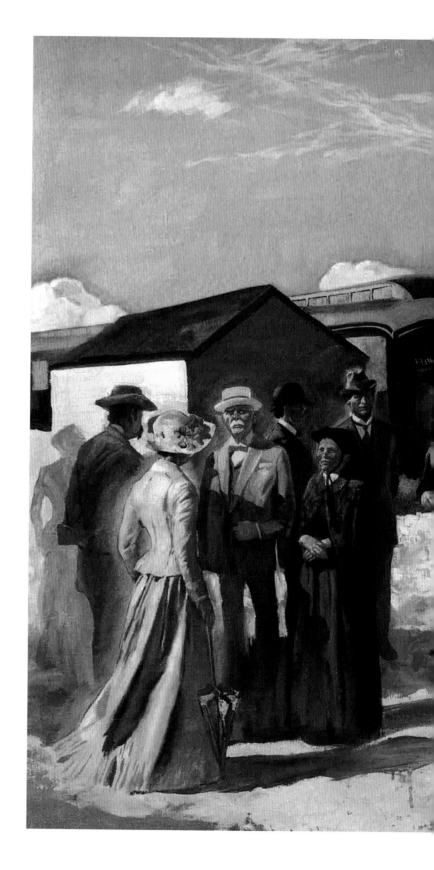

The most important first occurred April 13, 1896, when the first train arrived with Henry M. Flagler and other railroad and hotel dignitaries aboard. The entire town—about 300 people—came out to greet the new age that arrived on iron-shod feet. The train "puffed its way into the village over wobbly tracks," wrote one witness, J.N. Lummus. "With its big bell top, [it] was spouting smoke and the whistle and the bell were going full tilt." Some old-timers who had never seen a steam engine took off for the woods.

HENRY M. FLAGLER

Within a month, Miami's first newspaper, *The Miami Metropolis* (named by Henry Flagler) published its first issue. The Bank of Bay Biscayne organized just in time to make the front page. (Before it opened, John Sewell kept everyone's money in a small safe in the shoe store he and his brother E.G. opened.) Dr. James M. Jackson, whom the Flagler interests brought to Miami from Bronson, Florida, set up a temporary office in the shoe store and in the new Townley Brothers drugstore until he could build a permanent office and relocate his bride. "This Miami spirit is a great thing," he wrote his wife. "It is infectious."

During the summer of 1896, the Royal Palm Hotel began to rise skyward. Workmen leveled the large Indian mound, which stood like a small mountain near the mouth of the river, to make way for the hotel's veranda. John Sewell and his work force discovered several graves near the top of the mound and 50 or 60 skeletons in the center. He temporarily stored the bones in a tool house and later buried them at an undisclosed site. At the time, no one realized that the men had carted away Miami's past.

On July 28, 344 voters met at the Lobby Pool Room—the largest room available—to incorporate the City of Miami and elect Flagler man John B. Reilly mayor. The first on the list of electors was Silas Austin, a black laborer. (One hundred and eighty-one of the signers were black men.)

■ *Artist Ken Hughes' painting captures April 13, 1896, when the first train, bearing Henry Flagler and other dignitaries, chugged into Miami. Henry Flagler and Julia Tuttle are shown on the left with William Brickell and one of Sewell's "black artillery" on the right. From that day forward, Miami grew, as Isidor Cohen said, "as if by magic." A penchant for and history of continuous, sudden and sometimes unexpected change continue to define Miami. (HMSF)*

From the time of incorporation, two clear factions emerged in Miami—the "Flagler Gang" and the others who dubbed themselves the "Antis." Isidor Cohen was an "Anti." "The railroad crowd is certainly taking control of politics in this neck of the woods," he wrote. It was a very accurate assessment because John Sewell enlisted the support of his black laborers who recently moved to Miami to help build the new city. Through what Sewell called his "black artillery," Flagler controlled the election and put his men into office.

When Flagler received word of the event, he sent the new city leaders a congratulatory telegram.

I congratulate the citizens of Miami upon the harmony which marked the election yesterday and trust that the auspicious beginning will result in future prosperity which will equal the most sanguine expectation of the people of the new city.

Boosters promoted the fact that Miami was never a town but was incorporated as a full-fledged city. (The definition of a city was 300 or more voters.) "Miami: the city that was never a town" became its first motto.

■ *Miami's first merchants lined up on Avenue D. The City of Miami was incorporated in the tall center building, then the home of the Lobby Pool Hall. Most of these buildings burned down during the Christmas morning fire of 1896. (HMSF)*

■ *Miami was not yet incorporated and had only 300 residents when its first newspaper, The Miami Metropolis, published its first issue on May 15, 1896. The newspaper's office was located at what is now Miami Avenue and S.W. Third Street. The weekly eight-page paper recorded Miami's history from its earliest days. (MN)*

1896

RECORDING HISTORY

ATLANTIC OCEAN

DADE COUNTY

COCOANUTS

The Miami Metropolis

MIAMI, DADE COUNTY. FLORIDA. (25 Deg. 20 Min. North Latitude.) FRIDAY, MAY 15, 1896.   PRICE 5 CENTS

KEEP THIS PAPER AS A
SOUVENIR.

It is the first paper ever
published on

Beautiful Bay Biscayne.

The most southern newspaper on the
mainland of the United States, published at the most southern railroad
point in Uncle Sam's domain, and
at the most southern telegraph terminal and express office on the mainland, at

MARVELOUS MIAMI

The town with over a thousand souls
and the survey of the place not yet
completed. The coming

Metropolis of South Florida.

This is a paper that stands with a
list of subscribers larger than any
paper south of Jacksonville on the
East Coast; with all the advertisements
we could put in type or have space for
in our first issue. The reading matter
speaks for itself.

We want 10,000 subscribers!
We want them now!
We want you!

Watch Miami. Watch THE METROPOLIS.

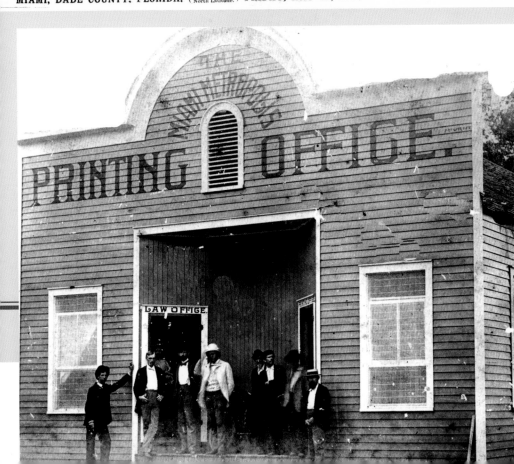

PRINTING OFFICE

LAW OFFICE.

■ Many people who arrived before the railroad lived in shacks and palmetto-thatched enclosures (above). (HMSF)

■ The Sturgiss Boarding House (left) was home to many of Miami's bachelor frontiersmen. (HMSF)

The new city covered two square miles—one square mile on each bank of the river. The city fathers made their first mistake when they laid out the streets. Instead of putting First Street on the riverfront, the city planners made it the northern border of the city (today's N.W. 12th Street). They created avenues in alphabetical order, starting west of the bayfront road (Biscayne Drive) until it curved around the Royal Palm Hotel and became Boulevard. Once the city began to push northward and westward, this street system created problems.

Flagler was a benevolent dictator. He did more than just fulfill his end of the bargain, which included laying out the streets and building the water and power companies. Whatever the young city wanted, he provided. He deepened the channel into the Miami River and gave the city land for a

city hall, market, jail and school. When he discovered that some of his managers could not find a place to live, he built two streets of houses for middle-class residents. He also built a hospital for his employees.

Of Bibles and Book Learning

Young men dominated the town during Miami's early years. Yet, despite a rather wide-open frontier atmosphere, it was a moral town. Julia Tuttle required an anti-liquor clause in all her deeds and she convinced Flagler to do the same. When someone opened a saloon in defiance of her liquor clause, she sent the sheriff to close it down. Once would-be saloon owners realized that the lady meant business, they moved their establishments just north of the city limits. "North Miami," as it was called, was soon filled with saloons, brothels and other frontier-style establishments.

But many of the new arrivals were devout, church-going people determined to set up proper religious establishments. The Congregational Church raised a gospel tent in Miami even before the railroad arrived. A short time later, the Presbyterians opened another tent-church and allowed other denominations to use it on alternate Sundays. Most of the churches began in the Presbyterian tent.

Because Flagler was a Presbyterian, the denomination soon had one of the finest church buildings in Miami. Flagler, however, had an ecumenical outlook. About the only church that did not receive his aid was the Episcopal Church. Episcopalians organized in Julia Tuttle's home and built their church on land she provided.

The few Jewish families observed their High Holy Days in private homes. But despite small numbers, the Jewish community had a strong influence in the young city. Of the 16 merchants in 1896, all but four were Jewish.

When the sheriff arrested several Jewish merchants for operating their businesses on Sunday, *The Miami Metropolis* showed their outrage by reminding the town of the importance of the First Amendment.

READIN,' WRITIN,' AND RITHMETIC'

The first year of school for Miami children ended on May 4, 1897. To celebrate, the two teachers planned an all-day outing and picnic at Arch Creek. Teachers, pupils and friends drummed up interest by parading down the streets of Miami led by a brass band.

(HMSF)

■ *Almost every church in Miami got its start in the Presbyterian tent. It was located in the woods south of today's S.E. First Street just east of Avenue D (Miami Avenue). In 1897, the Presbyterians, aided by the Baptists, took down their tent and built a pavilion (left). (HMSF)*

(HMSF)

ISIDOR COHEN
THE CONTINUING SAGA
OF THE MOSQUITO

The more Miami changed, the more the mosquitoes remained the same. "Business better than ever," pioneer merchant Isidor Cohen wrote. "We have a big demand for mosquito bars. The pests are with us day and night. During the day we defend ourselves by burning rags and insect powder. We are also tormented by a vicious breed of giant horseflies. Excursion trains brought in a large number of people from all parts of the state who, on arrival, were attacked by the mosquitoes that found no available spots on the bodies of our home folk. These poor victims begged the railway officials to take them back to civilization."

■ *Isidor Cohen established a clothing store on the south bank of the Miami River in early 1896. (HMSF)*

Miami's first school opened in the fall of 1896 even though the county superintendent voiced disappointment at the lack of community interest and remarked that he certainly did not want to force a school on anyone. The new school opened in a rented building near what is now N.E. First Street near Miami Avenue. Despite its location in the piney woods, 38 children showed up the first day. By the third day, there were 49 pupils, and within a month, 79 enrolled. Most were newcomers who had never laid eyes on each other until the first day of school. A school for black children opened west of the railroad tracks in a part of town Henry Flagler and Julia Tuttle had reserved for "colored people only."

By December 1, 1896, the young city was well on its way. Workmen hurried to complete the Royal Palm Hotel and everyone looked forward to its January opening. "Miami looks like a real town," Isidor Cohen wrote. "Both sides of Avenue D [Miami Avenue] are lined with store buildings…and the merchants are doing a good business." *The Miami Metropolis* extolled its pre-Christmas message: "May no sickness or distress or adversity darken your doors this Christmas. May you be happy and gay."

But no one in Miami was happy and gay on Christmas night, 1896. At 4 a.m., a fire broke out in Brady's grocery store on 14th Street and Avenue D (Miami Avenue and S.W. Second Street). It quickly spread to the Bank of Bay Biscayne next door and then on to Chase's Pool Hall. Before it burned itself out, 28 buildings—almost the entire business district—burned to the ground. Everyone, including Julia Tuttle, turned out to fight the fire. There was no fire department but the Tuttles had their own equipment for the Hotel Miami. Their rudimentary pump and a frantic bucket brigade had little effect on the flames as they roared unchecked through the flimsy, hastily constructed wooden buildings. Miami was wiped out before it had a chance to begin.

For the first time, tragedy tested the city's mettle. Imbued with the "spirit of Miami" that impressed young Dr. Jackson six months earlier, the people bounced back. *The Metropolis* wrote, "Miami Arises from its Ashes" and called the fire a blessing in disguise. Most of the crude, barn-like frontier storefronts burned down. The city could now rebuild with finer, more attractive buildings.

■ *THE SEMINOLES: Newcomers and the city's early photographers were fascinated with the Seminole Indians, who were as interested in witnessing the birth of the new city as any other resident. People liked to pose with the Seminoles and early photographers created postcards that were sent all over America. (APC)*

A REMNANT OF ANOTHER ERA

Time & Time Again

1886

(MC)

2008

(APC)

Resting undisturbed in Miami's Lummus Park is William English's c1849 slave quarters that the military later occupied during the Seminole Wars as part of Fort Dallas. When the Seminole wars ended, it housed transients and briefly served as the Dade County Courthouse. When Julia Tuttle purchased the property in 1891, she used it first for storage and later rented it to a family for their home. In the 1920s, the Daughters of the American Revolution moved it from its original location on the Miami River west of the Second Avenue Bridge to Lummus Park.

INTERVIEW WITH JULIA TUTTLE 1896, E.V. BLACKMAN

In late 1896, E.V. Blackman, a Methodist minister and editor of Henry Flagler's newsletter, *The Florida East Coast Homeseeker*, interviewed Julia Tuttle. It provides a rare glimpse of an extraordinary woman and her vision.

Many thought Mrs. Tuttle a dreamer—a chaser of shadows—but the passing years have proven beyond question that she was a woman of great foresight, a woman who had vision of the future that others were not permitted to see. I remember one evening, in the latter part of 1896, Mrs. Tuttle sent me a note inviting me to come to her home. It was a pleasure for me to grant her request. On my arrival at her home, she said: "I have a new inspiration regarding the future of Miami and I want to tell it to you, for I know that you will remember it and some time use it." We were seated in her living room, she occupying a large settee on the south side of the room. "Now," she said, "I want to talk to you, and don't laugh at my predictions, for I feel sure they will all come true. All these years I have had but one thought and that is to see Miami grow to one of the largest, if not the largest, city in all the southland. I have had many discouragements— discouragements that perhaps to one of a different temperament might have proven fatal—but the one thought and belief that at some future time these dreams of Miami's greatness would prove true has urged me on during all these years."…

Mrs. Tuttle had equally bright visions regarding the port of Miami. Along this line she said, "It will not be many years hence when Miami will be the most important port on the Atlantic Coast in the South…South American vessels will finally ply between their home ports and Miami, and Miami will become the great center of the South American trade. Vessels from all ports of the world will call at Miami, making Miami the greatest commercial center in all the southland. This may seem far-fetched to you, but as surely as the sun rises and sets all of this will come true." Again, we ask, was this a day dream or was it vision or inspiration?

Julia Tuttle: "Mother of Miami." (TC)

"Miami's Only Reason for Being"

MARJORY STONEMAN DOUGLAS

THE ROYAL PALM HOTEL

AMERICA'S SUN PORCH

Three weeks after the fire, the magnificent Royal Palm Hotel opened. Flagler's new hotel was very grand indeed. Like most other hotels in the Flagler chain, it was painted "Flagler yellow" in "modern colonial style." The huge clapboard building was five stories tall, almost 700 feet long and had a red mansard roof. A lookout tower and platform topped the six-story center section. From there, guests could view the Cape Florida Lighthouse to the east, the mysterious Everglades on the west and the burned-out town.

The hotel's most distinctive exterior feature was a 578-foot veranda that wrapped around the eastern end of the hotel. The porch was the favorite spot of the ever-present rocking chair brigade that assembled to catch the breeze.

The hotel grounds were especially impressive. Hundreds of coconut palms, brought full grown from Elliot Key, gave the hotel instant tropical ambiance. Other exotic plants intrigued Northern visitors. Hotel guests enjoyed a clock-golf course and a separate bathing casino with an enormous, bay-water swimming pool that measured 40 by 150 feet.

The impressive interior, described by one witness as the "acme of elegance," was painted a gleaming white. The hotel had electric lights, two electric elevators, 350 guest rooms with another 100 rooms for maids and hotel staff. Added to this were 200 bathrooms, a main dining room that seated 500 and three other dining rooms—one for maids and children, one for black and one for white hotel workers. A writing room (with special stationery for ladies), a billiard room and a reading room completed the interior chambers.

Forty townspeople turned out for the Royal Palm's inaugural dinner on January 17, 1897. The elegant setting included fresh flowers, fine linen and sparkling crystal. The gourmet menu listed everything from green turtle soup to tutti-frutti ice cream.

Townspeople who did not attend the dinner stood outside and watched the arrival of the elegant guests and marveled at the twinkling electric lights that illuminated the veranda and the grounds. The hotel appeared a veritable fairyland—the magic touch that brought the city to life.

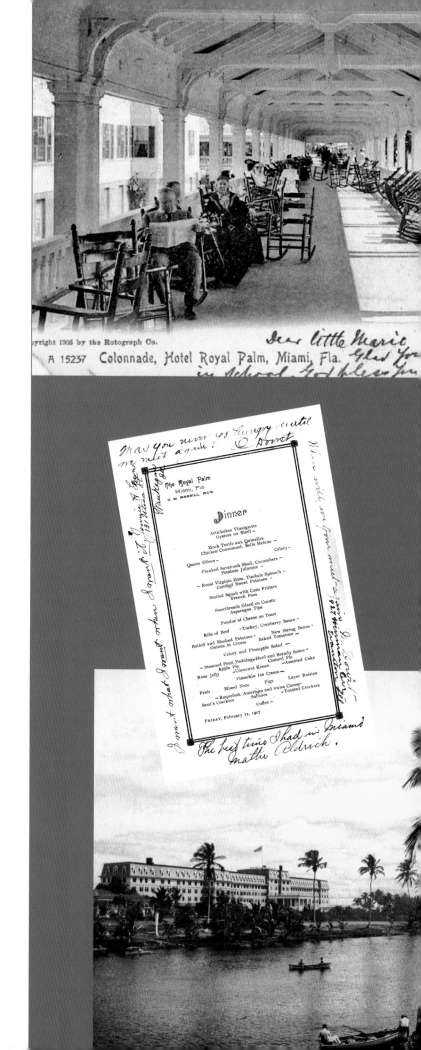

The Royal Palm's 578-foot veranda (left) wrapped around the eastern end of the hotel. It was a popular gathering place for tourists eager to catch the breeze. (APC)

The hotel also had a clock-golf course (right) on the hotel grounds. (HMSF)

The hotel opened on January 17, 1897 with a gala dinner (facing page). (APC)

Henry Flagler promoted the hotel in a variety of publications he created to draw tourists to Florida. Romantic hand-colored photographs (below) and postcards were a way to show the Royal Palm in all its tropical glory. (APC)

Miami's first swimming pool and bathing casino (left) took up the northwestern edge of the hotel property. It was 40 feet wide by 150 feet long, surrounded by a gallery where spectators gathered to watch the fun. Locals were allowed to swim during the off-season. Adults paid 25 cents and children 15. (APC)

The Royal Palm

Even though the Royal Palm's first season lasted little more than a month, Miamians benefited immensely from the attention it brought their town. Not only was the Royal Palm the center of everything, it was, as Marjory Stoneman Douglas remarked, "the city's whole reason for being." Everyone looked to the future. "Just wait until next year," they said, "things will be even better."

During 1897, the city continued to grow. Another freeze brought more people to "America's Sun Porch," the city's latest name for itself. To encourage immigration, the Florida East Coast Railroad refunded the cost of the train ticket to anyone who bought land in Miami. Besides inexpensive town lots, many newcomers took advantage of cheap land in what was called the "back country"—anything west of the railroad tracks. There was still an abundance of free government land available for homesteading, especially in South Dade. The Perrine family received title to the old Perrine grant and the Florida East Coast's Model Land Company opened it for development.

Before long, agriculture also became a vital part of the economy. When the International Tobacco Growers held a convention (Miami's first) at the Royal Palm in 1897, E.V. Blackman organized a Dade County Fair to show off local agricultural products and tout the city as the only place in the world to hold an agriculture fair in the winter. Henry Flagler paid all fair expenses and offered a $75 prize for the best display of home-grown vegetables. But even though agriculture flourished, tourists remained the most important commodity. Time was calculated by the tourist seasons—January to March. Between seasons, the city fathers rushed to improve the city and get ready for its lifeblood—the tourists—to pour back into town.

The urge to please the tourists brought many changes. The city built the first bridge across the river at Avenue G (S.W. Second Avenue). Workmen paved new streets with crushed Miami oolite which emitted a blinding glare and choking dust. When the merchants rebuilt their burned-out stores, the center of town shifted to 12th Street (Flagler). Soon, 12th Street eclipsed Avenue D as the "in" address.

When the Royal Palm opened its second season in January 1898, Miami had surpassed its pre-fire status. Eager to show off the city, Flagler wired his rival, Henry Plant, and invited

OLMSTEAD 1, GATOR 0

After a hard day's labor, pioneers often cooled themselves off with a swim in the Miami River. On one occasion, a 14-foot alligator attacked James Olmstead near the present Miami Avenue Bridge. The alligator grabbed Olmstead around the chest and submerged with the frantic man held firmly in his jaws. When Olmstead stuck his fingers in the gator's eyes, the alligator turned him loose and the bleeding man made it to the river bank. But the alligator followed him ashore. Olmstead made it to safety as the gator disappeared back into the river. The workman vowed to kill the creature. Every night, the stitched-up Olmstead sat up by the riverbank waiting. About a week later, the creature reappeared and Olmstead shot and killed the alligator who had almost had him for dinner. The whole town turned out to see Olmstead's prize.

him to Miami. Plant wired back, tongue in cheek, "Where on earth is Miami, and how do I get there?" Flagler responded, "Go to the terminal in Jacksonville and follow the crowd." No one realized that within a few months, an unprecedented and unimagined crowd would be on its way to Miami.

ARMED CAMPS AND YELLOW JACK

On February 7, 1898, the *U.S.S. Maine* was blown up in the Havana Harbor, sending the nation head-on into war with Spain. Because of Miami's location, its residents panicked. Mayor John Reilly wrote Washington demanding that the government build a fort to defend the city. While Reilly waited for Washington to reply, a 150-man home guard ("The Miami Minutemen") organized to defend the city. The volunteer soldiers held daily drills on the Royal Palm grounds. When the first Spanish prisoners of war passed through on their way to federal prison, the whole town turned out to view the enemy. One entrepreneur bought the buttons off the soldiers' uniforms and sold them to the crowd as souvenirs.

After Henry Flagler lobbied his friends in Washington, the U.S. government agreed to build a fortification in Miami on William Brickell's bluff south of today's 15th Road. Henry Flagler offered the use of his dredge to pump large quantities of bay sand up on the bluff to build the fort and create earthworks.

Flagler viewed the war as a way to attract more people to Miami and to "put it on the map." He wrote Washington, promoting the town as the perfect site for a large troop encampment. He called Miami "the most pleasant place south of Bar Harbor to spend the summer." Everyone knew better considering the heat and mosquitoes, and most Miamians wanted to get out of town in the summer. Even after visiting government men wrote a negative report, Flagler remained undaunted and began preparing for the troops' arrival. He hired 100 men to clear the palmetto and extend the northern and western limits of the settlement. They built roads and laid water pipes to the proposed campsite. Sure enough, by the time the campsite was ready, Washington announced that troops would be sent. The crowd that Flagler wanted was on its way.

On June 24, the first of 7,000 troops arrived. Even though Miamians gave the men a hero's welcome, the soldiers were quickly disillusioned. On the way down on Flagler's railroad, the soldiers received promotional brochures about the Royal Palm depicting Miami as a tropical paradise. One look at the small town, however, shattered all illusions. The Royal Palm was closed for the summer. All that was left were 1,200 to 1,500 permanent settlers and a raw frontier settlement.

"There was a most magnificent and gorgeously appointed hotel right in the midst of a perfect paradise of tropical trees and bushes," one soldier wrote. "But one had to walk scarce a quarter of a mile until one came to such a waste wilderness as can be conceived of only in rare nightmares."

Even though the Royal Palm reopened as the headquarters for the officers and press, Miami was clearly not the place to send 7,000 restless soldiers in the middle of the summer. The terrible heat and the ubiquitous mosquitoes made camp life unbearable. The water in the exposed water pipes was too hot to drink and tasted and smelled like sulphur. Because the hard rock kept soldiers from building a decent latrine, sanitary facilities consisted of buckets and barrels. Usually, the soldiers simply took to the woods. One soldier summed up the troops' feeling when he wrote, "If I owned both Miami and Hell, I'd rent out Miami and live in Hell."

Even though the merchants enjoyed the added business, the soldiers caused serious problems. The churches tried to entertain the men but most of the soldiers found North Miami—with all its attendant evil ways—more inviting. Rowdyism proliferated. Townspeople started carrying guns and a murder occurred almost every night. No decent family would let their womenfolk out of the house alone. The members of the black community fared the worse. Whenever the soldiers became bored, they harassed the blacks who lived near the camp. Once the entire black community fled to Coconut Grove for safety. One black man barely escaped lynching.

REMEMBER THE MAINE.

■ *Nervous Miamians lobbied the U.S. government for a fortification (inset below). Finally, the government responded and built what locals called "Fort Brickell." It was located on the bluff near the present site of the Santa Maria condominium on Brickell Avenue. In reality, Fort Brickell was little more than a half-finished magazine and bunker. At war's end, it became a popular attraction for children's play. (TP)*

■ *Troops who came to Miami during the war with Spain stayed in tented camps on the outskirts of the new town. Local residents often visited the campgrounds to watch drills and talk to the visiting soldiers (bottom). (TP)*

During the Spanish-Cuban-American War, soldiers drilled in Royal Palm Park (left). (TP)

Spanish prisoners of war, captured in Cuba, stopped in Miami on their way to federal prison in Atlanta, Georgia (background). (HMSF)

An American soldier in Miami (below). (WS)

War with Spain

"THE BATTLE OF MIAMI"

(WS)

MAIN STREET MIAMI – STYLE
Time & Time Again

1896

(APC)

2008

In early 1900, 12th Street, now known as Flagler, became the city's main business street. In those days, Biscayne Bay lapped at what is now the western edge of Biscayne Boulevard. J.N. Chamberlain, the city's first photographer, set up shop in his home on the corner of today's Flagler and Biscayne Boulevard. Today, impressive new skyscrapers like 50 Biscayne dominate the western edge of the Boulevard as the City of Miami transforms itself once again.

(HG)

Fortunately for everyone, the Spanish-Cuban-American War was brief. Two months after the troops arrived, they were gone. The war was over by the end of August. Miami's home guard never fired a shot and the little fortification that was dubbed "Fort Brickell" was not even finished until after the war ended. Miamians, however, felt as if they had been through a war just the same. One wag wrote that he was glad the "Battle of Miami" was over.

A month after the troops left Miami, Julia Tuttle died unexpectedly. Miamians felt shock and sadness. Stores closed, and hundreds of people followed the funeral cortege to the Miami City Cemetery that she had gifted to the people of Miami. Julia Tuttle, "the mother of Miami," was the 12th person buried there.

Things always looked up with the coming of each new year. In 1899, Miami received a psychological boost when it mustered enough voters to outvote Palm Beach for the county seat of Dade County. (It had been removed to Juno a decade earlier.) After the election, a fish house on the Miami River became the temporary Dade County Courthouse.

■ *When Dade County electors voted to return the county seat to Miami in 1899, a fish house on the Miami River and Avenue D (Miami Avenue) housed the courthouse and all the Dade County offices, including the jail. (MN)*

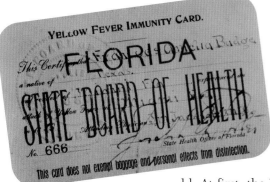

Then tragedy struck once again. In the fall, yellow fever broke out. For three months, Miami was quarantined, shut off from the rest of the world. At first, the Hotel Miami, where one of the first cases was diagnosed, became a makeshift hospital for the "yellow jack" victims. Before the scare ended, a public-spirited citizen, W.W. Prout, erected a frame "pest house," 18 by 88 feet, on his property. It was Miami's first public hospital.

The rush of people who wished to leave town had to stay in a "refugee detention camp" for two weeks before they could proceed. Flagler established the first camp on his steamer *Santa Lucia* anchored in Biscayne Bay. When it became overcrowded, another camp opened at Fulford (N.E. 166th Street) and accepted "people of all races." Armed guards patrolled both camps.

When a person became ill, the family had to fly a yellow flag. If someone died, city personnel burned all their personal belongings. Before long, suspicious fires broke out all over town. In November, someone set fire to the Hotel Miami and it burned to ashes. In early January 1900, another mysterious fire broke out on 12th Street and destroyed a large part of the business district for the second time in four years.

To keep people busy and Miami afloat until the epidemic subsided, Henry Flagler poured money into the construction of new streets, sidewalks and other municipal improvements. By January 15, the crisis passed and the city lifted the quarantine. In just three months, more than 200 Miamians contracted the disease. Miraculously, only 14 died.

Miami entered the Twentieth Century with little fanfare. The Royal Palm opened for its third season and, despite the numerous setbacks, few residents felt anything but optimistic about the city's future.

■ DISASTERS: Only the yellow fever immunity card (top) allowed people to travel in and out of Miami during the three-month quarantine in 1899. (WS).

■ Miami was proud of its new 12th Street (Flagler) business district (below) that replaced Avenue D after the 1896 fire. Budge's popular hardware store was one of the "first of the bricks." (LW)

■ Just as Miamians celebrated the beginning of the new century, the city experienced its second devastating fire in four years. Budge's store, which sat on the northeast corner of today's Flagler Street and Miami Avenue (left), burned to the ground along with several others. (HMSF)

■ *Elegant patrons of the Royal Palm Hotel came to experience Miami's magic. (LW)*

Chapter Five

"The Magic City"

"Miami—springing up as if by magic, and appropriately called from the beginning, 'The 'Magic City.'"

Official Directory of the City of Miami, 1904

N THE EARLY YEARS OF THE TWENTIETH CENTURY, MIAMI LOST ITS FRONTIER BOOMTOWN ATMOSPHERE

and began to take on the appearance of a respectable small town. Dade County's new rock courthouse, completed in early 1904, added to the sense of Southern respectability. A Confederate monument sat on the front lawn, and solidly Democratic politics reigned inside. "Mi-am-ma" spoke and thought "Southern" and few people believed that "damn Yankee" was two words. The homes and businesses of Miami's pioneer families clustered around what is now the core of downtown Miami. Twelfth Street (Flagler) was not only the center of business; it was also one of Miami's finest residential addresses. Harry Tuttle subdivided

his mother's home place and platted Fort Dallas Park, Miami's first exclusive walled subdivision.

Most of the town was sandwiched between the river and the railroad station (now N.E. Sixth Street). At first, people were slow to move across the Miami River to what was called Southside. After the city built a new bridge at Avenue D (Miami Avenue) and Mary Brickell opened up Brickell Avenue, Southside became a popular residential area. Before long, Brickell Avenue was one of the most fashionable areas and Miami's first "Millionaire's Row."

■ Miamians were proud of their new "coral rock" court-house with its impressive red dome. (LW)

IRON AWNINGS AND WOOD BLOCK STREETS

Around 1905, the Tatum brothers—J.H., B.B., J.R. and Smiley—built a toll bridge across the river at Flagler Street and developed Riverside. Anyone buying a lot in Riverside could cross the toll bridge for free.

In July 1906, the Tatums launched Miami's first trolley. The line had one car that ran on second-hand rails. It commenced near the railroad station at Sixth Street and Avenue B (N.E. Second Avenue) then ran south to 12th Street (Flagler) and west to the Miami River. After a year of continuous problems, including several collisions with horse-drawn wagons, the Tatums shut down the system.

The hub of Miami's growing business district was at the corner of 12th Street and Avenue D (Miami Avenue). Brady's Grocery Store, the Fort Dallas National Bank, Budge's Hardware Store and the Biscayne Hotel and Pharmacy were the four corner businesses. Almost every store had a corru-gated iron awning that covered the sidewalk to protect shoppers from the heat and rain. Because most commercial buildings were less than three stories, church steeples and the cupola of the new public school, which graduated its first high school class of three in 1904, dominated the skyline. (Miami High did not have its first native graduate until 1917.)

To eliminate the blindingly white, crushed-rock streets, city fathers paved many streets with wooden blocks. This created an entirely new set of problems. Every time it rained hard, the blocks expanded, turning the street into a washboard. Swollen wooden blocks sometimes popped up and floated away.

■ *The 1906 Miami City Council was a Who's Who of early Miami. Left to right front row: R.B. Gautier, C.L. Huddleston; middle row: M.R. Kellum, J.I. Wilson, John Sewell (mayor), F.W. Wharton (fourth mayor), J.C. Crossland, Ben Hinton: back row: J.F. Jaudon, J.E. Lummus (second mayor), J.C. Tucker, T.E. Cheatham, W.W. Chaille, J.B. Reilly (first mayor). (HMSF)*

■ *A rare 1904 view of Miami (bottom), probably taken from the dome of the new courthouse, shows Miami as it emerges from its raw frontier beginnings. Twelfth Street, now Flagler, right, had been rebuilt after the 1900 fire and by 1904 had many new brick and rock buildings. (APC)*

The castle-like Halcyon Hotel (originally called the White Palace) (left) opened in 1906 and was the first, and only, hotel to rival the Royal Palm. It was torn down in 1938 to make way for the DuPont Building. (TP)

Every time a tourist sent a postcard of the fairy-tale hotel back home (below), it lured others to come on down and stay awhile. (APC)

Prohibitionist Carrie Nation, with her infamous ax (facing page), prompted souvenir makers to create a metal sign with the slogan: "All nations welcome except Carrie." (APC)

The Royal Palm was no longer the only large hotel in town. By 1906, the impressive, white stone Halcyon Hall offered visitors a grand alternative. Other smaller hotels sprang up as well. Less affluent tourists flocked to the San Carlos, Green Tree Inn, Biscayne and Gralynn. Numerous boardinghouses catering to newcomers and family visitors dotted the downtown area.

On Saturdays, everyone came to town to shop, see and be seen. Besides E.L. Brady, several other grocers—Girtman, Leffler, Lummus and Gautier—enjoyed a thriving trade. John Seybold ran a popular bakery and ice cream parlor. Phillip Ullendorf had most of the meat business. Numerous dry goods and specialty stores—including two rival Burdines (W.M. Burdine and Burdine and Quarterman)—vied for the shoppers' dollars. Other popular stores included E.B. Douglas, John Sewell and Brother, Chailles' "Racket Store" and Isidor Cohen's Men's Ware. The Red Cross and Biscayne pharmacies and Seybold's Ice Cream Parlor became popular meeting places for the afternoon soda crowd.

In 1904, Miami set the first speed limit for automobiles at 8 mph, even though few people had cars. Despite the new horseless carriages, Miami was still a more-than-one-horse town. Five livery stables and four blacksmith shops did a big business downtown. Bicycles were the newest rage and several downtown bicycle shops rented wheels for a dollar a day.

TRAPPINGS OF CIVILIZATION

Miami also grew in other ways. In 1901, the First National Bank built an impressive columned one-story building on 12th Street to rival the Roman temple built by the Bank of Fort Dallas and the more mundane old-guard Bank of Bay Biscayne. Several newspapers gave the town lively and divergent points of view. The most prominent paper was *The Miami Metropolis*. Its strongest rival was *The Miami Evening Record* (later *The Miami Herald*) edited by Frank M. Stoneman, father of future author and environmentalist Marjory Stoneman Douglas.

Saloons arrived soon after Julia Tuttle's death when her son Harry sold a few lots without the liquor clause. Once the clause was broken, Miami had its share of brass rails. Exotically named establishments—the Ben Hur, Majestic and The Ideal Saloon—opened downtown. But they did not go unopposed. Between 1907 and 1913, the well-organized Anti-Saloon League and Women's Christian Temperance Union (WCTU) forced three wet-dry elections and brought Carrie Nation into town to preach on the evils of alcohol. Even though the drys lost the first two elections, the WCTU succeeded in getting an ordinance passed that limited saloons to men only and prohibited any obstruction that would block the interior of the bar from view, thus making tippling open to public scrutiny. Finally, in 1913, the drys won and Miami became dry—at least on paper.

"Wee Tappie Tavern".

NO MORE TAPPING

Until 1913, when ardent prohibitionists succeeded in voting Miami dry, Miamians came to William Ogden's Ye Wee Tappie Tavern to imbibe. Although rumors persisted that Ogden continued to sell liquor, he gave up in 1916 and sold the property. In the deed, he required a bronze plaque that he created to remain on the property in perpetuity. It read:

> *Here lies 'les restes' of Ye Wee Tappie Tavern—*
> *Once a hotel, gaudy, gilded cavern—*
> *Born in champagne in Nineteen and Eleven.*
> *Died in limeade before she was seven.*

After Howard Kleinberg wrote about the deed requirement in his series of articles for the Miami News, *the owner of the Flagler Street property put the plaque back. Sadly, a short time later, vandals stole it and today, it is nowhere to be found.*

The temperance ladies also went after North Miami where saloons, gambling establishments and bawdy houses proliferated. In 1908, Dan Hardie was elected sheriff on a reform ticket that promised to close down North Miami. Hardie's aggressive raids temporarily cleaned up North Miami but before long, the wily entrepreneurs moved a little farther north in an area that became known as "Hardieville."

By 1906, Miami had several moving picture theaters. Two of the earliest were Kelly's and the Alcazar. The owner of the Alcazar came up with the novel idea of air-conditioning by putting a ton of ice under a perforated floor and then installing large fans to blow the cooled air into the audience. When this did not prove practical, some theater owners built open-air theaters with canvas roofs that could be rolled back to let in the breeze.

Miamians and the increasing number of tourists loved the bayfront. Flagler's Dade County Fair Building, located on the bay just south of today's Flagler Street, dominated the shoreline. It was the site of many civic events besides the fair itself, held every February. For awhile, the Fair Building also housed Miami's first public library, organized by the Miami Women's Club. In 1912, Flagler gave the group land on 12th Street for a clubhouse with the understanding they would provide space for a free public library.

Piers also lined the bayfront. Some included buildings, like the Biscayne Bay Yacht Clubhouse, perched on pilings in the bay. Four times a day, the ferries to Ocean Beach plied between a dock at the foot of 12th Street and Smith's Casino, which opened on the south end of what is now Miami Beach. Smith's Casino not only had a beautiful ocean beach; it also sported a saltwater swimming pool.

Other naphtha launches took tourists up the Miami River to view the river rapids and the beginning of the Everglades. In 1907, John Roop built an observation tower on Musa Isle to give people a better view. (At the time, the Everglades began at what is now N.W. 27th Avenue.) Other tourist boats took passengers to the Arch Creek Natural Bridge, the Cape Florida Lighthouse and the Biscayne House of Refuge.

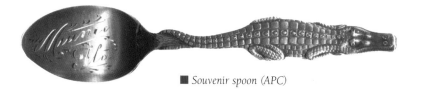

■ *Souvenir spoon (APC)*

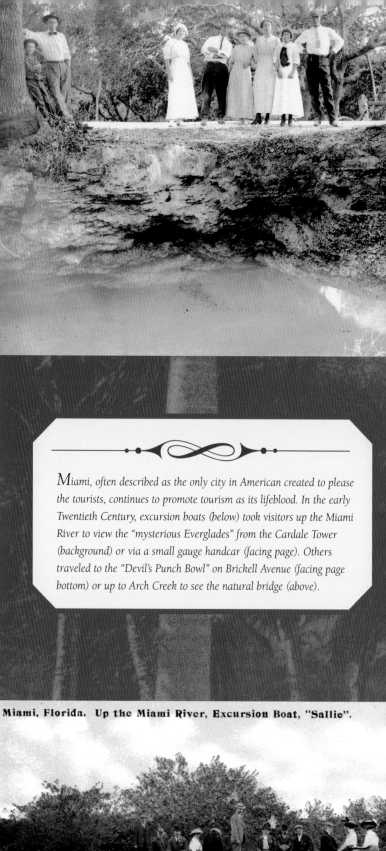

Miami, often described as the only city in American created to please the tourists, continues to promote tourism as its lifeblood. In the early Twentieth Century, excursion boats (below) took visitors up the Miami River to view the "mysterious Everglades" from the Cardale Tower (background) or via a small gauge handcar (facing page). Others traveled to the "Devil's Punch Bowl" on Brickell Avenue (facing page bottom) or up to Arch Creek to see the natural bridge (above).

Miami, Florida. Up the Miami River, Excursion Boat, "Sallie".

Y'all
Come!

A 15259 A Short R. R. in the Everglades, near Miami, Fla.

Baseball was Miami's favorite sport. The entire town turned out for baseball games in Royal Palm Park. It made no difference whether the games were between two sandlot teams or the popular Miami Magicians. As soon as someone yelled "Play ball!" a crowd gathered.

Royal Palm Park, which spread out in front of the Royal Palm Hotel, was the scene of many civic gatherings. The city built a pavilion in the park where, after 1915, Arthur Pryor's Band played regular concerts and three-time presidential candidate William Jennings Bryan taught his famous weekly Sunday school.

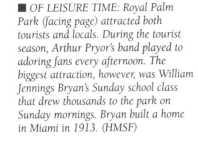

■ OF LEISURE TIME: Royal Palm Park (facing page) attracted both tourists and locals. During the tourist season, Arthur Pryor's band played to adoring fans every afternoon. The biggest attraction, however, was William Jennings Bryan's Sunday school class that drew thousands to the park on Sunday mornings. Bryan built a home in Miami in 1913. (HMSF)

■ Miami was a baseball town. People flocked to Royal Palm Park to watch the Miami Magicians (left) and other local teams play. (HMSF)

■ Once automobiles arrived on the scene, motorcades, parades and Sunday afternoon drives became a popular pastime. The first group of Miamians to own automobiles lined up for an historic photograph (below). (CSP)

THE PESKY CRITTER STINGS ON

In 1904, S. Bobo Dean came to Miami as editor of The Miami Metropolis, forerunner of the Miami News. His daughter Dorothy Dean Davidson was five years old at the time.

"It was a wonderful life," she recalled years later. "The only flaw in it…was the mosquitoes. It was my household chore to keep the punk piles burning—little saucers of mosquito powder which sent up smoke and odor repulsive to the mosquitoes. We placed these saucers underneath the dining table, the bed, and just outside the front and back doors. We used mosquito nettings over our beds and sometimes put newspapers under our clothes."

Dorothy Dean (DDD)

■ THE LURE OF DOWNTOWN: The image (left) from a rare hand-colored glass "magic lantern slide" (an early way to project photographs) of Royal Palm Park captured one of Miami's first traffic jams. (APC)

■ Miamians also loved the newest fad: "Moving pictures" flickered in a variety of downtown theaters. To combat the heat, some theater owners installed a canvas roof that rolled back to let in the breeze. Others put ice under the seats. The Airdome (top right) took over the former Hippodrome—barely covering up the first theater's name. In 1925, the new Olympia Theater (now Gusman Theater for the Performing Arts) occupied the site. (HMSF)

■ John Sewell claimed that he was Miami's first merchant. He opened his initial store on Julia Tuttle's Avenue D. When the business district moved to today's Flagler Street, Sewell, left, and his brother E.V. "Ev" opened a men's store there (above). Few, if any, pioneer merchant contributed more to Miami's development than the Sewell brothers. Both John and Ev were Miami mayors and worked to make their adopted hometown better. (HMSF)

■ The Tatum Brothers launched Miami's first streetcar on Wednesday, July 25, 1906 as part of the city's 10th birthday celebration. Although it operated little more than a year, it gave Miamians one more reason to think of Miami as a real city. (APC)

■ Avery Smith came to Miami from Norwich, Connecticut in 1908. He purchased land on mostly uninhabited Miami Beach, then called Ocean Beach, with plans to open a bathing casino on the ocean near today's Fifth Street. Because there was no bridge, he operated naphtha launches (bottom) from Henry Flagler's Fair Building to take bathers to his new facility. (MCSP)

■ He also built his family a "coral rock" home on today's Washington Avenue at 10th Street. Despite a doubtful future, it survives as Miami Beach's oldest home. (MCSP)

AVERY SMITH

CAPTAIN CHARLIE AND THE "MONSTER OF THE DEEP!"

Charlie Thompson, son of an early lighthouse keeper, was Miami's most popular fishing guide. He guided many famous people including four presidents of the United States—Grover Cleveland, Teddy Roosevelt, Woodrow Wilson and Warren Harding. He was also popular with industrialists such as John Jacob Astor and Cornelius Vanderbilt. On June 23, 1912, "Captain Charlie" made headlines of his own after he caught the "Monster of the Deep" off Knight's Key. Captain Charlie was guiding a group of tourists when "the monster" caught his line and began dragging the boat out to sea. For 39 hours, Charlie fought the incredible fish. Five harpoon thrusts and 151 bullets later, the creature was finally subdued, but it took five days to die. When Thompson brought the fish in, over 5,000 people turned out at the Avenue D [Miami Avenue] docks to view the 45-foot, 30,000-pound creature. The Smithsonian Institution sent an expert to mount the specimen which they identified as Rhino don Typicus—a whale shark. At first, Thompson exhibited his monster at Elser Pier and "next to Burdine's big store." William Jennings Bryan came to see it and announced that its name should be changed to "the Smell." Later Thompson took it on a national tour that continued under different owners until 1932.

A FEW FACTS CONCERNING
Capt. Chas. H. Thompson's

MONSTER Of the Deep!

The Largest Fish in the World.
The Only One Ever Captured.

This Sea Monster is the largest ever captured. It differs entirely from any other that has ever been caught. A specimen well worth seeing. Indorsed by all Institutes of Natural History.

Now On Exhibition at
406 WABASH AVE.
Next to Meyers Bros. Clothing Store
4th and Wabash Avenue
TERRE HAUTE, INDIANA

(LW)

EMPIRE OF THE EVERGLADES

Prior to 1909, most Miamians lived on the coastal ridge which was South Florida's highest land. Mangrove swamps on the east and saw grass swamps on the west surrounded this four-mile-wide rocky rim. The original pioneer settlements of Cocoanut Grove and Lemon City grew up on the ridge, along with several other early outlying communities such as Cutler, Buena Vista, Little River, Fulford (North Miami Beach) and Larkins (South Miami). In 1905, several important events occurred that not only changed the settlement pattern but actually changed the face of the land.

Everyone expected a man with a name like Napoleon Bonaparte Broward to take charge. In 1904, he was elected governor of Florida on a drainage platform that promised to turn Florida's wetlands into the new "Empire of the Everglades." After Broward's election, this grandiose plan (kicked around for years by private developers) became a state responsibility.

Draining the Everglades sounded so simple. All the state had to do was cut a few canals through the swampland to Lake Okeechobee and then open the flood gates and watch the Everglades disappear into the sea. When the first shovelful of muck flew in November 1905 on the New River in Fort Lauderdale, residents eagerly awaited the arrival of the dredge.

Miamians perpetually lobbied for a deeper harbor. The same year that dredging began on the New River, they convinced the U.S. government to dig "Government Cut" across a 700-foot strip of land near the lower end of the long thin peninsula that was to become Miami Beach. In the summer of 1905, Mayor John Sewell declared a holiday so that everyone could witness what he described as "the mingling of the muddy waters of Biscayne Bay with the turquoise blue of the Atlantic Ocean." Miamians assembled on both sides of the ditch to watch the final thrusts of the great dredge. When the big dipper dug its iron nose into the sand and stalled out, the crowd roared with disappointment. Mayor Sewell grabbed a spade and began digging in front of the dredge.

■ *In 1905, Mayor Sewell declared a holiday so Miamians could watch the dredge dig through the last few feet of land to create Government Cut. Smith's Casino is in the background. (HMSF)*

■ *By 1913, the Miami Canal, right, had been cut through the Everglades on its way to Lake Okeechobee. The drainage canal made it possible for the early cities of Hialeah, Miami Springs and Opa-locka to be built on dry land—at least for part of the year. As the water tabled lowered, most of then-unincorporated Dade County west of Red Road and north of the Miami River also opened for development. The natural north fork of the Miami River at 27th Avenue is on the left. (APC)*

Soon the crowd joined in, and sand began to fly. In less than 30 minutes, a little stream of bay water inched toward the ocean. The startled cut-diggers were almost washed to sea as the bay roared into the ocean, gobbling up sand and shoreline in its path. Within a few hours, the pressure from the bay had opened up a 500-foot-wide cut. "Government Cut" improved access to the port of Miami, then on the bayfront at the site of the future Museum Park, and created Fisher Island.

Once Miamians discovered that the dredge could do more than deepen channels in the bay and river, pressure mounted to get the Florida Everglades reclamation crew into Miami. To help finance the endeavor, the state sold large quantities of wetland to private developers. In Miami, the

enterprising Tatum brothers purchased 80,000 acres of Everglades at $1.25 an acre and started selling watery lots even before the drainage canals opened. To increase sales, the Tatums brought their own dredge to their sales office (located on what is now N.W. 22nd Avenue and the river). When they fired up the dredge, the black smoke was visible all over town. Advertisements invited the public to watch the Tatum brothers drain the Everglades. Many local residents recognized the slightly shady scheme. "They just operate the dredge on the days that they put ads in the papers," early resident Hoyt Frazier recalled. "One week they put the soil on the right bank and the next week they take it off the right bank and put it on the left bank." The gimmick worked, however, and the Tatums did a big business in underwater lots.

MARY BARR MUNROE

The real dredging began in 1909, after the state engineers started digging the Miami Canal. When the canal opened and they removed the restraining dam, the Everglades water flowed like a torrent out of the canal, down the Miami River and into Biscayne Bay. The water table dropped dramatically and most of the beautiful springs dried up. With the barrier removed, the Everglades muck slid into the once-clear waters of the Miami River and Biscayne Bay. Just as the salesmen predicted, the Everglades drainage created new land and new plans. Miamians were so enthusiastic about drainage that *The Miami Herald,* founded in 1910, campaigned to change the name of the Everglades to something more exotic—"Florida Nile" or "the Prairie Garden."

Soon after drainage began, Mary Barr Munroe of the Coconut Grove Housekeeper's Club, began to lobby the Florida Federation of Women's Clubs to lead the effort to save Paradise Key—a natural hammock in the Everglades. In 1916, led by former Florida First Lady May Mann Jennings, the federation acquired 4,000 acres which they called the Royal Palm State Park on Paradise Key. This early preserve later became the nucleus of Everglades National Park.

ROYAL PALM LODGE, ROYAL PALM STATE PARK, HOMESTEAD, FLORIDA.

■ *CELEBRATING VICTORY: Coconut Grovite Mary Barr Munroe, number 5, and former Florida First Lady May Mann Jennings, number 10, organized the movement by the Florida Federation of Women's Clubs to preserve Paradise Key and create Royal Palm Park. Women's Club leaders gathered at its 1916 opening. Royal Palm Park became the nucleus of the future Everglades National Park. (HMSF)*

■ *The women also raised the funds to construct Royal Palm Lodge (above) as a park building for visitors and a home for the superintendent. (APC)*

FLAGLER'S LAST STAND

In 1905, Henry Flagler began construction of what he called the Key West Extension to connect Key West to the mainland via a series of bridges. He pursued what some called an impossible dream to capitalize on increasing Cuban trade and tourism. By this time, his Florida East Coast Railroad (FEC) had already reached Detroit (Florida City), opening South Dade to farmers and creating a string of railroad station communities right down the line. Farmer Thomas J. Peters took advantage of the new means of transportation and launched a large-scale operation in the rich farmland that was so successful that he earned the title "Tomato King."

Between 1905 and 1912, the construction of the overseas section of the railroad, known as "Flagler's Folly," pushed south and west despite mosquito-infested summers and three terrible hurricanes. Swarms of work crews, dredges, seagoing cranes, floating cement mixers and pile drivers left Miami to join in the history-making project. Miami expanded to meet the demands of the thousands of workers who piled into town every weekend.

■ *In 1905, Henry Flagler began construction of the overseas portion of his Key West Extension. It involved 128 miles of rock islands and open seas. Pigeon Key (background) was the base camp for the workers who built the Seven Mile Bridge that some called the eighth wonder of the world. Today the Pigeon Key Foundation operates a museum and marine center there. (SPA)*

■ *On January 22, 1912, 10,000 people gathered in Key West to welcome Henry Flagler and the first train. (IP)*

Concrete bridges and earthen causeways crept from key to key. By 1908, the railroad reached the halfway point at Knight's Key. Work then began on "the great one"—the Seven Mile Bridge just below Knight's Key. Before it was finished, chief engineer J.C. Meredith died suddenly and was replaced by second-in-command William J. Krome. Krome, who had been in charge of the first feasibility survey in 1902, was devoted to Flagler and his railroad. He desperately wanted to complete the railroad to Key West before Flagler died. Krome set January 1912 as his goal—an 82nd birthday present for his boss. Krome pushed the workers at both ends of the line. Electric lights blazed all night as the crews caught Krome's single-minded drive to reach Key West at all costs.

Krome and his incredible workforce succeeded. Early on the morning of January 22, 1912, the "Extension Special" left Miami for Key West. Five passenger cars filled with notables trailed the engine and its tender. The last car was Flagler's own, "The Rambler," bearing the 82-year-old man whose dreams had come true. The railroad had "gone to sea."

In Key West, 10,000 people came to watch the train chug into the "Island City." Bands played, whistles blew, and children threw roses in Flagler's path. *The Miami Herald* called Flagler's feat "The Eighth Wonder of the World." The enthusiastic crowd deeply touched the old man. "We did it," he said with tears in his eyes. "Now I can die in peace." A year later, Henry Flagler slipped and fell down the marble steps of his Palm Beach mansion. He never recovered from the fall and died May 20, 1913, from "old age and exhaustion." Miami, and all the Florida East Coast, lost its father figure and greatest mentor.

A MEETING OF LAND AND MONEY

Fortunately for Miami, other remarkable people waited in the wings to take over where Flagler left off. One was Carl Graham Fisher. Fisher came to Miami in 1910, fresh from making his fortune with Prest-O-Lite, the first bright automobile headlight. He purchased a house on Brickell Avenue and named it the "Shadows." Fisher watched with wonder as his neighbor, L.T. Highleyman, dredged up bay sand and threw it on the shore to create Point View from a former

CARL G. FISHER

mangrove swamp. Seizing upon opportunity, Fisher invested in Highleyman's Point View. It quickly became one of Miami's most upscale neighborhoods. Meanwhile, another remarkable man was building what everyone in town called "Collins' Folly." In the 1880s, John Collins, a New Jersey Quaker, invested in Lum and Osborn's ill-fated coconut planting venture on what would become Miami Beach. In 1909, Collins bought out the other investors and became the sole owner of a spit of land he called Ocean Beach. Like the coconut planters, Collins was primarily interested in growing things. He decided to abandon the coconut scheme and focus on avocados. He planted an Australian pine windbreak (today's Pine Tree Drive) back from the beach and started planting avocado trees.

Before he was finished, his son, Arthur, and his son-in-law, Thomas J. Pancoast, wrote that they came down from New Jersey to see "what the old man was digging into and what was digging into the family savings so rapidly." When the men saw Collins' beautiful ocean and bayfront wilderness, they decided to move to South Florida and get in on the action. As the farming continued, Pancoast created a plan for marketing Miami Beach real estate under the name Miami Beach Improvement Company. By 1912, Collins, who was almost as old as Flagler, decided that he too would build a bridge that connected an island paradise to the mainland. He sought financing from Miami's Southern Bank and Trust Company and the Bank of Bay Biscayne. The Lummus brothers (J.N. and J.E.), as presidents of the respective banks, loaned Collins the money and bought for themselves 580 acres on the southern tip in the vicinity of Smith's Casino. The Lummuses platted Ocean Beach, then formed a real estate company that sold land even before Collins completed the bridge. Unfortunately, when John Collins' bridge was half-finished, he ran out of money.

John Collins came to South Florida as a farmer from New Jersey and stayed to transform his farmlands into Miami Beach. (HMSF)

Miss Helen Lummus hoisting first flag at Ocean Beach March 17, 191-
Compliments of John H Welsh
Resident Agent.

Opening of Collins Bridge,
over 3 miles long, Miami, Fla.

■ On March 17, 1913, Helen Lummus (top right) hoisted the flag to officially open the Lummus brothers' Ocean Beach Real Estate Company—the first to sell lots on what later became Miami Beach. (HMSF)

■ On May 22, 1913, enthusiastic Miamians gathered to watch the first autos set out from Miami across the Collins Bridge to Miami Beach (left). Thomas Pancoast and his family had the honor of being the first to cross. Ironically, the causeway did not quite reach Miami Beach but instead stopped at Bull (now Belle) Island. When the automobiles reached the island, they had to turn around (top left) and return to the mainland. (HMSF)

The coming together of Carl Fisher and John Collins was a perfect combination of a man with plenty of cash and no land meeting a man with plenty of land and no cash. They were an unlikely but unbeatable combination. Fisher loaned Collins $50,000 to finish his bridge. In turn, Collins gave Fisher an 1,800-foot-wide strip of land across the island. Fisher added to his holdings by buying additional land from the Lummuses. He also helped them fill in the mangroves, improving both their holdings.

Fisher's cash transfusion gave a boost to Collins and the Lummus brothers. In February 1913, the brothers hired land auctioneer Edward E. "Doc" Dammers to auction off newly created beach real estate. Miami developers discovered Dammers in Palm Beach and brought him to town in 1911 to run a land auction for Highland Park, a subdivision near the present Jackson Memorial Hospital complex.

Dammers was a master showman. He attracted people to the auction by staging balloon ascensions and parachute drops and giving away silver, opera glasses, dinner sets and other valuable merchandise. He became so popular that when an advertisement appeared in the paper announcing a Dammers land auction, half the town showed up to join in the fun. The Ocean Beach sale was no exception. Even though the bridge to the beach was still not complete, Dammers sold $66,000 worth of lots in three days. (Dammers later remarked South Florida kept him from being a liar. No matter how high-blown his predictions, they eventually came true.)

On June 12, 1913, Collins arranged a ceremony to open his new bridge that Miami's mayor claimed rivaled Flagler's Overseas Railroad. A parade of motorcars chugged clickity-click over the low, wooden bridge, climbed across the draw span and onto Bull Island (now Belle Isle) where the bridge temporarily stopped. Unceremoniously, everyone jumped out of their cars and turned them around to return to Miami.

Meanwhile, Carl Fisher was busy remaking the Miami Beach landscape. No one held a ceremony to mark the beginning of the dredging even though some thought it was the single most important event in Miami Beach history. During

the summer of 1913, teams of black workers descended on the mangroves, hacking their way through the swamps, fighting off mosquitoes, snakes and horseflies. As soon as they leveled the mangroves, Fisher's dredge began pumping around the clock. The dredges threw millions of cubic feet of sand on the rapidly increasing land from Fisher's own private sand pile on the bottom of Biscayne Bay. The decaying small sea creatures that came up with the sand created a dreadful odor. It took days of sun and rain to complete what the workmen called the "sweetening process." This man-made frontier no longer had a tropical, jungle feeling. It looked more like a hard-packed layer of snow—one that created a blinding glare in the hot sun.

Once Fisher got things going on Miami Beach, he returned to his hometown of Indianapolis to promote his other "baby"—the Lincoln Highway, America's first east-west, cross-country roadway. Fisher was not the kind to be satisfied with only one iron in the fire. "Carl was all speed," his wife Jane wrote. "He was the essence of the new age of wheels…Living with Carl was like trying to watch the events of the racetrack on Speedway Day." As soon as the Lincoln Highway reached San Francisco, Fisher launched a plan to build a north-south highway connecting Chicago with Miami. If Henry Flagler could build a railroad to his resorts, Fisher could certainly build a road to Miami Beach.

Fisher, as usual, had his way and began building what he called the Dixie Highway. On October 25, 1915, he led the motorcade of Dixie Highway Pathfinders from Chicago into Miami. More than 1,000 Miamians in decorated cars joined the Pathfinders as they entered Dade County and followed them into town for a grand celebration at the Halcyon Hotel. The press predicted that "a stream of people would soon be pouring into Florida with new blood and new money."

■ *The Dixie Highway Pathfinders, led by Carl Fisher (facing page), drove a 15-car cavalcade from Chicago through Indianapolis, French Lick, Louisville, Nashville and Chattanooga to Miami, arriving on October 25, 1915. (HMSF)*

A LADY AND HER CAMERA

Alice Wood became Miami's first professional woman photographer when she purchased the Hand Studio in 1915. One of her first assignments was to record the triumphant arrival of the Dixie Highway Pathfinders. She also completed a series of remarkable photographs on the building of Vizcaya.

ALICE WOOD

■ *William Jennings Bryan and his wife, Mary (right).*

■ *The Pathfinders (below) entered Miami though the Buena Vista arch.*

■ *Captain James F. Jaudon, "Father of the Tamiami Trail," second from left, joined the surveyors who were charting a course through the Everglades.* (SPA)

About the same time, Captain James F. Jaudon began promoting a highway across the Everglades to connect Miami and Tampa. Someone in Tampa suggested calling the proposed roadway the Tamiami Trail in honor of the two cities. A writer in the *American Eagle* claimed the name sounded like "a bunch of tin cans tied to a dog's tail and clattering across cobblestones."

He added that anyone who liked the name Tamiami Trail would like to change the Jacksonville-to-Miami length of the Dixie Highway to the "Jackiami Joypath!" Despite its detractors, work on the Tamiami Trail began in 1915.

PLAYGROUNDS FOR THE PEOPLE

Citizens incorporated the City of Miami Beach in 1915, combining Collins and Pancoast's Miami Beach Improvement Corporation, the Lummus Brothers' Ocean Beach and Fisher's Alton Beach. The town's 33 voters elected J.N. Lummus mayor. From the beginning, Ocean Beach took on a different character than the other developments. It became the "people's playground." Smith's Casino still operated near the southern tip of the Lummuses' property. In 1914, Sheriff Dan Hardie opened Hardie's Casino nearby. A few rows of small homes already lined the beach. Many of the homeowners were Miamians who built second homes there. The Lummuses were not interested in building a fancy resort. They sold lots to anyone who was "white and law-abiding." They also sold the city 20 acres of oceanfront land for a park. Years later, Lummus Park would be an oasis in a desert of concrete.

Another Miami Beach institution was born during this era. Joe and Jennie Weiss, Hungarian immigrants from New York, came to South Florida and operated a restaurant in Smith's Casino. Within a few years, the enterprising mom-and-pop team opened their own restaurant at 213 Biscayne Avenue (now called South Pointe Drive). Today, it is the world-renowned Joe's Stone Crab.

Farther up the beach, Fisher and Collins envisioned a playground that catered to a different type of clientele—the new American industrial rich like Fisher himself. To add snob appeal, they restricted sales to "Gentiles" only. Fisher became Miami's first P.T. Barnum of real estate. He took over Collins' rustic casino (located on what is now 23rd Street and Collins Avenue) and turned it into the fancy "Roman Pools." Pancoast and Fisher built substantial homes for themselves, hoping to attract others. Fisher also carved out

Lincoln Road, which he planned to turn into the Fifth Avenue of the South. As a gimmick, he brought Carl and Rosie the elephant into town to help with construction. Soon Rosie and Miami Beach appeared in newspapers all across the country. He put Miami Beach on the sports map with golf courses, tennis courts, a speedboat regatta and a polo field. He also promoted sports fishing by opening the Cocolobo Club at Caesar's Creek, making weekend fishing excursions available for his rich friends.

■ *In April 1913, a second bathing casino (right) opened between Biscayne and First Street on what would become South Beach. Hardie's Casino, named after Miami's popular sheriff, Dan Hardie, had a pool, 104 changing rooms, 400 bathing suits for rent, a dance hall and dining room. (LW)*

■ *Feeling the competition, Smith's Casino (below), "The Pride and Joy of Miami Beach," also expanded. Joe and Jennie Weiss operated a restaurant there before opening Joe's Stone Crab nearby. (APC)*

■ *Jennie and Joe Weiss (facing page) stand in front of their famous eatery that has been a Miami Beach institution for almost 90 years. (JB)*

Meanwhile, across the bay, Miami was growing even faster than Miami Beach. By 1915, the city found its first super-promoter in pioneer merchant E.G. "Ev" Sewell. Although Miami had always had its share of boosters, Sewell was considered the drum major at the head of the parade.

In 1911, Sewell demonstrated his promotional genius by staging Miami's first airplane flight to celebrate the city's 15th birthday. A few days before the July 20 event, the Wright brothers sent a biplane to Miami by train. A group of men hauled the plane out to the Royal Palm golf links (where the Richard E. Gerstein Justice Building and Jackson Memorial Hospital complex now stand). About 5,000 residents jammed the grounds to get their first glimpse of the "flying machine" and "birdman" Howard Gill. As the bands played, the fragile plane lumbered down the fairway, slowly left the ground and climbed into the sky. The crowd went wild. The following day, everyone returned to watch Sewell bravely perch himself on the wing of the airplane and become Gill's first and only passenger. Infected with what he called "aeroplaneitis," Sewell then sought to convince the Wright brothers to open a flying school in Miami. When they turned him down, he went after America's other flying ace, Glenn Curtiss, and talked him into the idea. Before long, Curtiss' planes buzzed merrily over Miami and Miami Beach and the whole town contracted Sewell's "aeroplaneitis."

Sewell was the first person to devise a plan for advertising Miami across the United States. Merchants contributed to the city's first real advertising campaign. It worked like a charm. New tourists poured into South Florida. To add to the tropical image, Sewell encouraged everyone to follow his lead and dress year-round in light-colored summer clothes.

Ev Sewell (facing page bottom) was a promoter extraordinaire. He made the news when he brought in a Wright brothers' airplane—the first to fly over Miami— as part of Miami's 15th birthday celebration. On July 20, 1911, "Birdman" Howard Gill (left) took off from the Royal Palm Golf Links (now Jackson Memorial Hospital Complex) as thousands looked on. Sewell also organized a decorated automobile parade (facing page top). (HMSF)

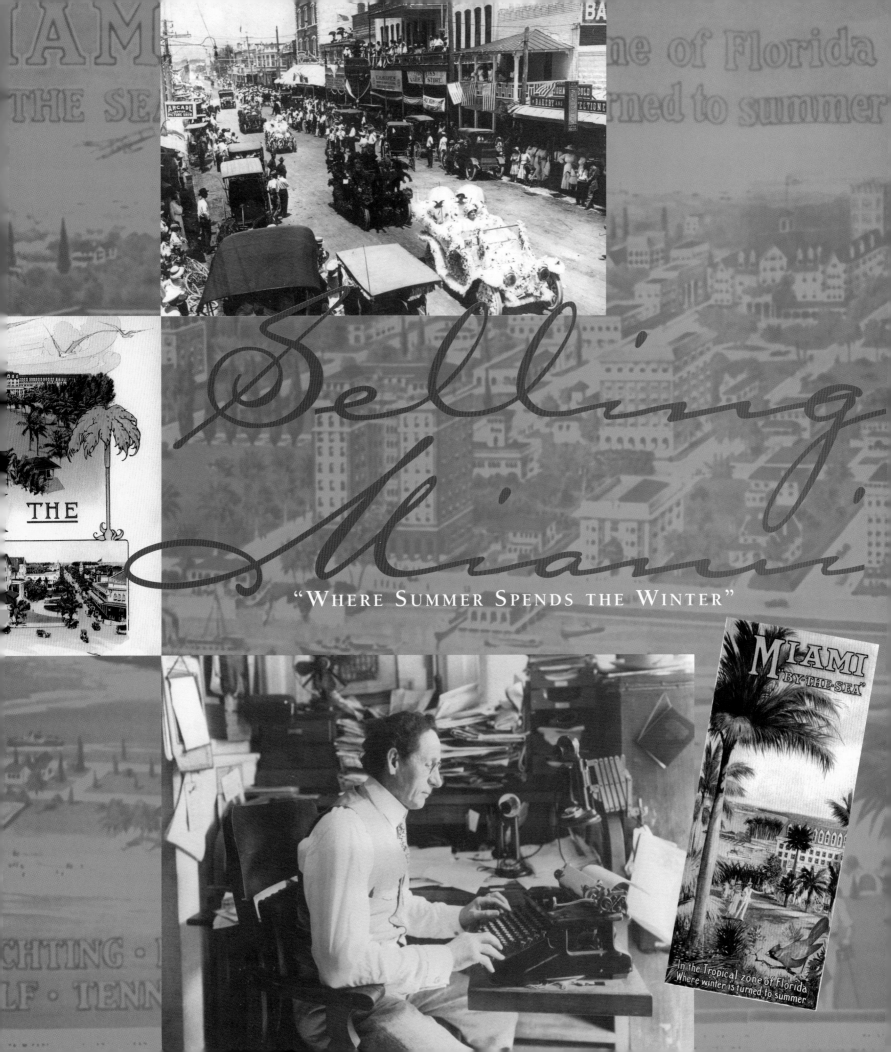

Selling Miami

"Where Summer Spends the Winter"

The crowds of tourists created real problems. They filled every hotel to capacity making it difficult for visitors to find a place to stay. To ease the situation, the city created a temporary tent city near the depot and preachers asked church members to take tourists into their homes.

Sewell was not Miami's only promoter. In fact, Miamian and promoter were practically synonyms. In 1913, a group of men organized themselves into the "Magic Knights of Dade" to promote the Magic City. In 1915, they held a Mid-Winter Festival to entertain tourists. One of the events was an historic parade depicting the city's founding. Riding on one of the floats were six of John Sewell's original 12 black laborers who had cleared the land for the Royal Palm Hotel. This was the first major wintertime festival that under a variety of names would endure for years to come.

Miami also attracted national luminaries. The newspapers loved to list all the famous people visiting the city. They included literary giants like James Whitcomb Riley and Zane Grey, renowned politician and orator William Jennings Bryan and a variety of industrial magnates with names like Rockefeller, Vanderbilt and Matheson. Many built palatial estates on Brickell Avenue and Coconut Grove bayfronts.

None of the homes could compare to the one that farm machinery millionaire James Deering built on 180 acres of prime Brickell hammock land. Designed by architect F. Burrall Hoffman Jr., the grand Italian showplace, named the "Villa Vizcaya," was a godsend for the young city. It improved Miami's image and gave thousands of people employment. Deering's palatial estate included beautiful formal gardens designed by Diego Suarez, as well as a farm and farm village to make the estate self-supporting. Miles of paths snaked

JAMES DEERING

■ *BUILDING A LANDMARK: International Harvester magnate James Deering hired thousands of Miamians to build his Villa Vizcaya, designed by architect Burrall Hoffman. His original estate included today's Museum of Science, Mercy Hospital and Bay Heights. (APC)*

■ *Alice Woods documented construction and immortalized some of the workers (top) who hauled, un-molded and installed the garden's statuary. (AW)*

■ *Architect Burrall Hoffman Jr. (facing page). (AW)*

through the hammock land (painstakingly preserved) and into the gardens. The plan also redirected Brickell Avenue around the main house and created South Miami Avenue.

When James Deering arrived on Christmas Day, 1916, to spend the season in his new home, Miamians felt just as proud of the masterpiece on Biscayne Bay as he did. The beautiful Villa Vizcaya gave the town an entirely new identity. It would also become the area's favorite style of architecture—a love affair that continues today.

The 1916-1917 season was the city's most successful. Mrs. E.C. McAllister started building the McAllister Hotel at the foot of today's Flagler Street and 87 new stores opened downtown. Miami had one automobile for every 13 people, and traffic officers stood on downtown corners under colorful umbrellas to direct automobile traffic. A new trolley system operated with a fleet of cars. The county started construction on a County Causeway to Miami Beach. New subdivisions like Riverside Heights, Miramar, Biltmore and Grove Park expanded the city's

■ *Miamians flocked to Matthew Elser's new pier that jutted out into the bay at the foot of Flagler Street. It had a dance hall, a shooting gallery, an exhibition hall and a photography studio famous for its alligator props. It was torn down in the 1920s when the bayfront was filled to create Biscayne Boulevard and Bayfront Park. (APC)*

boundaries and horizons. Several movie companies came to Miami and people predicted that Miami would soon become the motion-picture capital of the world. Elser Pier, billed as "the largest recreation pier on the south Atlantic coast," rose at the foot of 12th Street. Clearly, the town was on its way to becoming the "Great American City" of everyone's dreams.

THE INDEPENDENT ENTERPRISE OF "COLORED TOWN"

Another downtown flourished just north and west of Miami's main business section. The original "Colored Town," laid out by Henry Flagler and Julia Tuttle in 1896, encompassed the area west of the railroad tracks between today's N.W. Sixth and 12th streets. By 1915, most of Miami's 5,000 blacks lived in this general area because strict laws designated where "colored people" could live. Other "colored districts" included a small south-side neighborhood on what is now S.W. Eighth Street, sizeable communities in Coconut Grove and Lemon City and several other pocket neighborhoods in South Dade farming communities. All these communities considered Colored Town's business district their downtown. (The area eventually became known as Overtown.)

Colored Town's main street was Avenue G (N.W. Second Avenue). Pioneer merchants owned more than a half million dollars in real estate. A thriving Colored Board of Trade encouraged the development of the 100-plus black-owned businesses. In one year, merchants added 30 new stores and a modern hotel on the corner of Sixth Street and Avenue G. They included groceries, meat and fish stores, drugstores, restaurants and "refreshment parlours," tailor and dressmaker shops, bicycle shops, two undertakers, a furniture store, several barbers and "hair parlours," an ice dealer, a savings and loan association, a real estate investment company, two insurance agencies and a theater.

The businesses operated in many fine stone buildings, but the most impressive was the four-story Odd Fellows Hall that had four storefronts on the first floor. Geder Walker, who owned the landmark Lyric Theater, advertised it as the "most beautiful and costly playhouse owned by colored people in all the Southland."

Colored Town also had its share of professional men, including six doctors, several registered pharmacists and an attorney. Nine ministers watched over their flocks from the various churches, which included Saint Agnes Episcopal (with a private day school), Mount Zion and St. John's Baptist, Bethel A.M.E., Ebenezer M.E., the English Wesleyans, the Holy Jumpers and the Seventh-Day Adventists.

Community uplift was in the hands of the many civic clubs. One of four women's clubs ran a day nursery for working mothers. Everyone worked to improve the public school—Washington Graded and High School—that only went to the eighth grade. In 1915, Tuskegee graduate R.W.

Gordon was principal of the 370-student school.

Besides Geder Walker, one of Colored Town's most prosperous citizens was D.A. Dorsey. Dorsey came to Miami to farm in 1895. He soon became one of the wealthiest people in Miami. His real estate portfolio included an island (now called Fisher Island). In 1918, he announced plans to develop a high-class "colored resort." The resort was never built, but Fisher Island became a black bathing beach until Dorsey sold the island in the 1920s. Another black man, E.W.F. Stirrup of Coconut Grove also grew wealthy through astute real estate purchases.

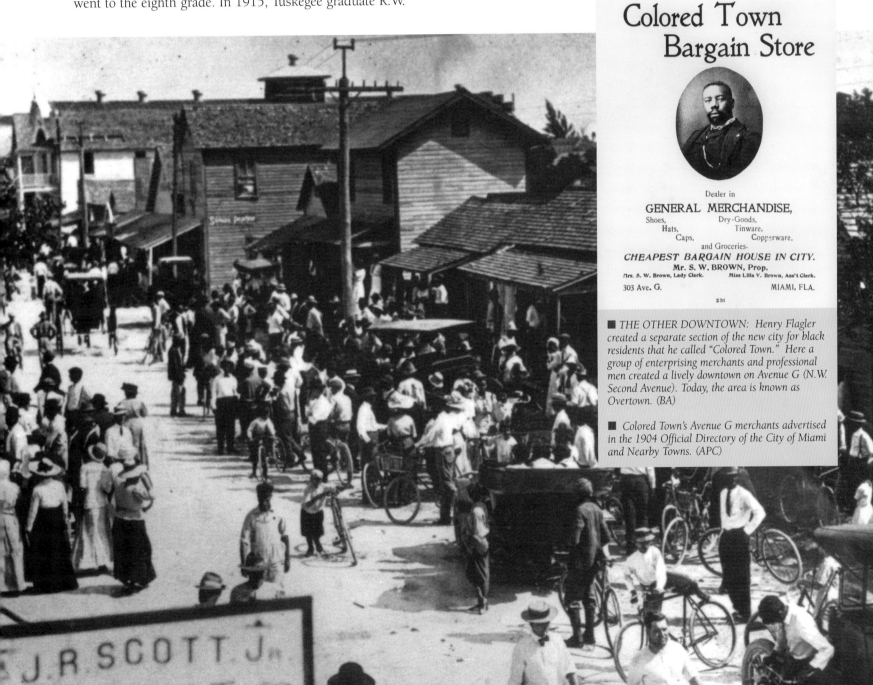

Colored Town Bargain Store

Dealer in

GENERAL MERCHANDISE,

Shoes,   Dry-Goods,
Hats,   Tinware,
  Caps,   Copperware.
and Groceries.

CHEAPEST BARGAIN HOUSE IN CITY.

Mr. S. W. BROWN, Prop.

Mrs. S. W. Brown, Lady Clerk.   Miss Lilla V. Brown, Ass't Clerk.

303 Ave. G.   MIAMI, FLA.

236

■ THE OTHER DOWNTOWN: *Henry Flagler created a separate section of the new city for black residents that he called "Colored Town." Here a group of enterprising merchants and professional men created a lively downtown on Avenue G (N.W. Second Avenue). Today, the area is known as Overtown. (BA)*

■ *Colored Town's Avenue G merchants advertised in the 1904 Official Directory of the City of Miami and Nearby Towns. (APC)*

1916

(SPA)

2008

(SP)

In 1916, Margaret Burlingame purchased a five-acre spoil bank she named Burlingame Island. For decades, little changed on this scraggly spit of land except it got bigger with each deepening of the Miami River entrance. By the time Edward N. Claughton purchased it in 1943 and renamed it Claughton Island, it had grown to 20 acres. His son, Edward Jr., began development of the island but sold it to the Hong Kong-based Swire Properties in 1970. Swire renamed the island Brickell Key and transformed it into a luxury enclave of apartments, restaurants, and the five-star Mandarin Oriental Hotel.

THE CITY GOES TO WAR

In April 1917, Miami's dreams shattered when President Wilson asked Congress to declare war on Germany. Even though the war appeared as an unwelcome interruption in Miami's new golden age of progress, loyalty to the country came first. Construction slowed and developers shelved plans as the town embraced the war effort. In May, 3,800 men registered for the draft and a large number of young men enlisted. Marjory Stoneman Douglas, a young reporter for *The Miami Herald*, went to cover a story on the Navy enlistment, got caught up in the excitement and ended up joining the Navy herself.

Sometimes war fever went too far and anti-German feeling flared. John Seybold, a popular baker of German ancestry who had lived in Miami more than 20 years, felt the heat. When someone accused him of putting glass in his loaves of bread, he took out full-page newspaper advertisements to defend himself against the charge. Editorial writers attested

to Seybold's loyalty. Emotions remained high. Some zealots even criticized the White Temple Methodist Church for performing the *Messiah* because composer Handel was German.

Despite the war, Ev Sewell continued to promote Miami. Like Flagler before him, he saw the war as a special chance to bring in new people. Because of the success of Curtiss' Flying School, he convinced the Navy that they should open a flying school in Coconut Grove. In October 1917, the United States government purchased 31 acres of Coconut Grove lowland at Dinner Key and began filling in the marsh to create a school for the Navy's "Flying Boats." An Army school opened in Cutler, and Glenn Curtiss trained Marine aviators at his airport (near today's N.W. 17th Avenue and the Miami River).

■ *Patriotic Miamians and members of the Miami chapter of the American Red Cross lined up in front of a WWI billboard on the Halcyon Hotel grounds to support the war bond drive.(HMSF)*

PATRIOTS IN "COLORED TOWN"

*D*uring World War I, many young men from Colored Town volunteered or were drafted into the Army. Before each group left for boot camp at Tuskeegee Institute in Alabama, the community held a parade down Avenue G (N.W. Second Avenue) to honor the young doughboys. The Magic City Coronet Band led the parade, followed by Junior Red Cross boys and girls. As the parade passed, enthusiastic onlookers threw money, cigarettes, chewing gum and pencils to the children who collected the items and presented them to the departing men.

Colored Town also formed a Home Defense Service composed of 40 men. Led by attorney R.E.S. Toomey, a black lieutenant in the Spanish-Cuban-American-War, the Home Defense members trained their ranks to protect Colored Town in case war came to Miami. The Home Defense Service, as well as the churches and the Colored Town Board of Trade, also led the drive for Liberty Bonds.

James Grant was one of many black soldiers who fought in WWI and returned to Miami at war's end. (BA)

1919

DINNER KEY
NAVAL AIR STATION
COCONUT GROVE

■ *W.T. Price operated a bus line (left) between Miami and Coconut Grove. Sailors from the Dinner Key Naval Air Station were his best customers. (HMSF)*

■ *Navy photographer Joe Pero (seated far right) took aerial photographs from a camera mounted on the nose of the plane. He married Mayor Reilly's daughter, Eleanor, and moved to Miami at war's end. (JP)*

■ *Miami's young women cheered the arrival of the "dashing young men in their flying machines." Miamians, like Dr. James M. Jackson and his wife, far left, entertained the young officers. Several of Miami's most popular belles, including Bess Burdine and Ethel Jackson, married officers they met at local parties (below). (TP)*

■ *The facility, which encompassed all the bayfront from today's Aviation Avenue to Peacock Park, included hangars, barracks and support buildings. Navy seaplanes (left) took off from the Dinner Key beach. (JP)*

Dinner Key Naval Air Station had barracks with a capacity of 750 men, but, by 1919, 1,367 men lived there. The hum of the 128 Navy seaplanes based at the station filled the air—much to the displeasure of the people in Coconut Grove who bore their discomfort in stoic silence (at least during the war). The intrusion into their ordinarily calm lifestyle, however, caused residents to incorporate as a city so that they would have more clout against the expanding City of Miami. (The newly incorporated Town of Coconut Grove, dropped the "a" from the original Cocoanut Grove spelling.)

Occasionally, serious mishaps occurred at the Naval Air Station. In late 1918, 77-year-old John Frow, former keeper at Cape Florida Lighthouse and owner of the original Beasley homestead in Coconut Grove, was killed when an airplane accidentally landed on his fishing boat in Biscayne Bay. Sometimes a pilot forced to ditch his craft in the bay would swim to shore and hitchhike back to the station with one of the many Miamians whose car bore the windshield sticker, "Ride with me."

The influx of Naval officers added a certain aura of glamour to the town. Women's clubs held socials for the dashing young aviators. Romances flourished and some of Miami's most popular belles married the young men. Bess Burdine, daughter of department store mogul William Burdine, married Albert Cushing Read who later became a world-famous aviator. Ethel Jackson, daughter of Dr. James M. Jackson, married Thomas W. Hutson who became a well-known Miami physician, and Eleanor Riley, daughter of Miami's first mayor John Reilly, married Joe Pero.

■ *In 1918, the U.S. Marines opened a second pilot training facility in Miami at the Curtiss Flying School in today's Curtiss Park on the Miami River. Lieutenant W.A. Spratt (right) stands next to a legendary Curtiss "Jenny." (HMSF)*

The war years also had their tragedies. Many families lost their sons and fathers. In October 1918, the terrible Spanish flu that spread around the world hit Miami. Schools shut their doors, churches called off Sunday services and all public gathering places closed. The city's new hospital opened in the present Jackson Memorial Hospital complex just in time to be overcrowded with victims of the Spanish flu epidemic. (Edith Brickell, the daughter of pioneers William and Mary Brickell, succumbed to the disease.) By the first of November, the worst was over. Schools reopened and life returned to normal.

Early on November 11, the town awakened to blaring whistles. The war was over and the town went wild. Colored Town's Magic City Coronet Band held an impromptu parade down 12th Street. (*The Herald* reported it was Miami's first racially mixed procession.) *The Miami Metropolis* and *The Herald* printed extra editions almost every hour to keep the people informed. At 2 p.m., the town assembled to witness the "official" victory parade. Four prisoners broke out of jail,

but nobody seemed to mind. Everyone with a "flivver" joined the parade. One writer compared the resulting traffic jam to that of New York City. Ev Sewell put on an Uncle Sam costume and waved at the cheering crowd as the Naval Air Station Band played martial tunes. A Kaiser in effigy was stomped, dragged and turned into a volleyball at the hands of the happy crowd. Anyone could make a speech at the pavilion in Royal Palm Park and many did. It was a day no one would ever forget. Miami's suppressed momentum had broken loose and was gearing up to roar unchecked into the 1920s.

Mayor's Proclamation

TO EVERYBODY:

The Beasts, Kaiser William and his "Me Too" son, Prince Frederick William. have not only abdicated and renounced all rights to the throne of Germany, but fearing for their lives, at the hands of their own people, have shaken the soil of Germany from their "big boots", and are now "On The Run". Let us hope that they keep going until they reach the shores of this God fearing, liberty loving country, where their troubles will end, and the Kaiser's Creed. "Me und Gott" will be a reality.

That we may show, in our humble way, however, our appreciation of the splendid and magnificent work done "over there" by our boys and our allies. I hereby declare **Monday, November 11th, 1918, to be a Holiday.** I ask all work, all business and schools to suspend for the day.

―――――

At Two o'clock the Big
Victory Parade

will form at the court house and "do some marching". Everybody and every car must be in this parade.

At 4 o'clock "Short Talks" at the Royal Palm Park.

The festivities to close tonight with a dance, mask or otherwise, on 12th Street between Avenue B and the Boulevard.

Dance commences at 7:30.

Come on out. everybody, as there is "Glory Enough for All"

J. W. WATSON,
MAYOR.

■ *Jubilant Miamians took to the streets for the noisy Armistice Day celebration, November 11, 1918. (MN)*

3502 12th Street Looking East,
Miami, Florida.

(APC)

(TP)

WATCH THE ALLIGATOR…AND SMILE!

Early Miamians were fascinated with the alligator. Postcards with the alligator motif were popular with the tourists. Tourists also flocked to see Alligator Joe's Great Crocodile and Alligator Farm that was located at the intersection of Wagner Creek and the Miami River. Alligator Joe (a.k.a. Warren Frazee) was famous for subduing and roping an alligator with his bare hands. He also sold baby alligators, sprouting coconuts and alligator hides. The alligator was such a popular icon that photographers included a stuffed alligator in their props. Tourists and residents alike loved to have their pictures taken with the fierce-looking creature.

"Alligator Joe" at Alligator Joe's Farm. (LW)

■ *The serenity of Miami's post-Boom skyline belies the frenetic building spree that created it and transformed a small Southern town into a real city. (LW)*

Chapter Six

Boom, Bust & Blow

"Behind the boom, behind frenzied speculation, behind even those ludicrous charabancs crowed with shirt-sleeved 'realtors' selling lots on time-payment to the music of the saxophone, there is something happening in Florida that is very significant and very real."

Theodore Weigall, *London Daily Observer*

DURING THE 1920S, THE AMERICAN PEOPLE WITNESSED PROFOUND CHANGES IN THEIR LIVES, MORALS AND MANNERS.

But nothing could begin to compare to the mania that struck Miami. Miami became the epitome of "flaming youth." She stood up, threw off past conventions, bobbed her hair, shortened her skirts, rolled down her stockings and yelled "Whoopee!" She would never be the same.

As soon as the government loosened the war-imposed fetters, Miamians raced to pick up where they had left off in 1917. As the tempo increased, Miami's boundaries exploded. New streets with names that read like a "Who's Who" of developers cut through farms, groves and strawberry patches. Streets north of today's N.E. 12th Street, west of S.W. 12th Avenue and south of 20th Street had names, not numbers, and some streets sported different names in different subdivisions, creating a postman's nightmare.

The Miami City Council, which wrestled with the antiquated street system for years, seemed paralyzed. Finally, in 1921, the post office threatened to discontinue mail service if they did not remedy the situation. In response, the council adopted the "Chaille Plan," created by Councilman Josiah Chaille. The plan divided the city into four sections—northeast, northwest, southeast and southwest. Twelfth Street (renamed Flagler Street) became the north-south dividing line, and Avenue D (renamed Miami Avenue) separated the city east and west.

That same year, voters, pumped up by Chamber of Commerce prophets who touted Miami as a "coming metropolis," abolished the small council. They adopted the progressive commission-manager form of government and then elected five bank presidents to lead them into the promised land.

A DEVELOPER'S DREAM

By 1923, even the most high-blown predictions for Miami's future seemed to be coming true. Population doubled in only three years. The McAllister Hotel, completed after the war, was no longer the city's only skyscraper. As soon as one record-breaking building was completed, developers broke ground on another. The Bar Association and the Chamber of Commerce lobbied for a new skyscraper-courthouse to replace the existing squat, red-domed building that was too small and totally out of character with the city's new image.

Many people in the Chamber of Commerce believed that almost every 10-year-old building was out of character. The newspapers joined the chorus of boosters who wanted a face-lift. By the time they were finished, the face-lift gave Miami an entirely new face.

First, the city acquired all the bayfront land from the Royal Palm Hotel to N.E. Sixth Street. Next, they demolished the quaint bayfront docks, brought in the dredges and began pumping the bay bottom to create land for a bayfront park and wide boulevard designed by legendary landscape architect Warren Manning.

Flagler Street took on a new appearance after the demand for downtown property sent prices sky-high. Few people were immune to the lure of quick profit. The Miami Women's Club and several local churches considered and eventually gave in to offers to buy their downtown sites for unheard-of profits that easily financed even finer edifices farther out of town. As developers demolished pioneer buildings, new "modern" structures rose in their place. Established merchants who did not sell enlarged and updated their stores or transformed them into arcades—the newest shopping rage.

Not everyone saw the new Miami as a developer's dream: Some had a different vision. Dr. John G. DuPuis headed a committee of influential citizens who wanted to open a Pan American University. Another group opened the Miami Conservatory of Music and a third planned a civic theater.

With change came inevitable growing pains. New construction and the love affair with the automobile turned narrow downtown streets into a living nightmare. Drivers thought nothing of parking cars in all directions and angles, totally disregarding the new no-parking signs. Desperate to create order, the police came up with a novel idea. They simply removed the front seats from all illegally parked cars. Errant drivers had to go to the police station and pay a fine to retrieve the seats. The situation downtown became even worse after the city acquired the trolley system and started laying new tracks making the roads almost impassable. The city also installed the first traffic lights, traffic towers and one-way streets. But the downtown traffic snafu showed no signs of letting up.

By all normal standards, Miami was booming. But in two years, this mild case of boom fever seemed almost subnormal compared to the spiking, red-hot temperature that took over the town. By 1925, Miami's boom fever turned into an epidemic. And before it subsided, the entire nation had contracted the disease.

The Great Boom did not just happen; it was created by Miami's incomparable climate, an abundance of available land and an extremely clever group of promoters. Some of these ebullient gentlemen were the get-rich-quick, buyer-beware variety whose slick, fly-by-night real estate deals sent prices soaring. Others were true visionaries. They may have razzled and dazzled the world with promises of an earthly paradise but some actually delivered on the promise.

■ *If drivers ignored the new no-parking signs in downtown Miami, the police removed their car's front seat. The hapless offender had to pay a fine and retrieve the car seat from the police station. (HMSF)*

THE BEST OF THE LOT

George Edgar Merrick was the best of the lot. He was a rarity among men—half-dreamer, half-planner and all-doer. There was nothing slipshod, hasty or mercenary in his plans for what he called "Coral Gables, Miami's Master Suburb." His plan included strict adherence to what he called "Mediterranean" architecture, described by a writer as "part Spanish, part Italian…a combination of what seemed best in each, with an added touch of gaiety to suit the Florida mood." He believed wide boulevards, decorative entrances, plazas and an abundance of tropical verdure were more important than personal profit.

GEORGE E. MERRICK

Merrick arrived in South Florida as a 13-year-old in 1899 when his father, Solomon, a Congregational minister from Massachusetts, and his artist mother Althea purchased a homestead in what was called the Coconut Grove backcountry. Solomon Merrick dreamed of turning the pineland into a

profitable grapefruit grove. During the early years, George peddled guavas and sold vegetables via mule-cart to the Royal Palm Hotel. He did not attend school but worked side-by-side with a Bahamian workforce that lived on the Merrick property and in Coconut Grove. By 1907, the groves had begun to bear just as Solomon Merrick predicted and George was able to go to college. After two successful years at Rollins College in Winter Park, Florida, Solomon Merrick encouraged George to go to law school in New York City. George did not want to be a lawyer, but instead, wanted to become a writer. During his first year of law school, he lived with his artist uncle Denman Fink.

While he was away, the Merrick family completed a beautiful new home designed by Althea. Built of what the natives called "coral rock," which was quarried nearby, the family named their new home Coral Gables.

During the summer of 1910, when Solomon Merrick's health deteriorated, George came home to manage the family groves. After his father died in the following year, George took over management of the newly named Coral Gables Plantation. The plantation continued to prosper under George's leadership as the largest vegetable and citrus enterprise in South Florida.

By this time, the idea of creating a planned development was percolating in George's fertile brain, in concert with his uncle, Denman Fink, who had moved south when George began planning. In order to gain experience in real estate,

George created a real estate firm and later joined Realty Securities Corporation, Miami's largest developer. On his own and with the Realty Securities, he completed more than 20 Miami subdivisions. At the same time, he purchased additional acreage around Coral Gables, expanding the original 160-acre homestead to 1,200 acres.

In 1916, in the midst of this hurricane of activity, George married beautiful Eunice Peacock, granddaughter of Coconut Grove pioneers Charles and Isabella Peacock. They moved a short distance from his family home into a new rock bungalow that his bride named Poinciana Place.

Poinciana Place became the gathering place for the talented group of people Merrick attracted to plan Coral Gables. Merrick's concept began to take shape with the help of his uncle, Denman Fink; his first cousin, architect H. George Fink; and well-known landscape architect Frank Button.

In July 1921, workmen started clearing the grapefruit groves to prepare the right-of-way for the Gables' first streets—Coral Way and Granada Boulevard. At their intersection, Fink and Button designed Ponce de León Plaza, the first in a series of beautiful Mediterranean plazas replete with fountains, pergolas and tropical plantings.

In November 1921, Merrick took out a full-page newspaper advertisement to announce the opening of his new Coral Gables subdivision. He sent two buses into downtown Miami to bring interested parties to the sale. It commenced

SONGS OF THE WIND

ripple the fronds of the coconut palms,
As I join with the voice of the sea,
The somnolent swell of the mystical psalms,
That breathe from the quivering tree.
I hush to the cries of the wandering crane,
Out over the shimmering lee;
The murmuring moan of the faraway main,
And the hum of the hovering bee;
Then I leap to the crest of the towering pine
And I sing of the life that I see.

George Merrick
Songs of the Wind on a South Shore
and other Poems of Florida, 1920

George Edgar Merrick: Poet, dreamer, city builder. (MM)

■ *Before George Merrick developed Coral Gables, his Coral Gables Plantation encompassed 1,200 acres and had become South Florida's largest grapefruit and vegetable-growing enterprise (top). (APC)*

■ *In 1913, George Merrick (facing page bottom) became vice president of the Realty Security Company, Miami's largest real estate firm. Before he started Coral Gables, he developed more than 20 Miami subdivisions. (MM)*

THE GOLDEN GALLEON

THE GREAT CORAL GABLES ABSOLUTE

AUCTION SALES

Monday, Tuesday, Wednesday, Thursday, Friday and Saturday of this week—at 2:30 p. m. each day

DAMMERS & GILLETTE and **HARRY A. BU**

Selling Agents for George E. Merrick Properties

MERRICK BLDG.   158 E. FLA

To Buy Right, Buy at Auction

FREE!

This Ticket Entitles the Holder when signed by our Representative to one

SIGHT-SEEING TRIP
To
CORAL GABLES
(Without Obligation)

Express Buses and Autos leave the Office of Coral Gables, Merrick Bldg., 158 E. Flagler St., daily (except Sunday) at

9:30 A. M. AND 2 P. M.

Dammers & Gillette and Harry A. Burnes extend to you all of the delights of this Big Sight-
seeing Trip in the interest of the magnificent
development in homes and groves which is cen-
tered in Western and Southern Miami District.
As our guest on this trip you will see at best
advantage:

The Oldest and Largest Grapefruit Groves in
Dade County
The Greatest Building Activity in Miami
Largest Guatemalan Avocado Groves and Over
Fifty Varieties of Tropical Fruits
The Finest Residential Sections of Greater Miami
A Million Dollar's Worth of Artistic Spanish
The Wonderful New Plazas at Coral Gables
The 210-Foot Old World Entrance
The Historic Old Indian Mound Trail
Two Fine Modern Golf Courses
The 4½ Mile Alhambra Plaza
The New Spanish Tea Room
The Six Mile White Way
Coconut Grove—The Millionaire's City
Silver Bluff and its Ocean Drive

Dammers & Gillette and Harry A. Burnes

M. J. GRIMES
Representative

Name
Miami Address
Permanent Address

FREE!

at 2:30 p.m. sharp on November 28 under the
direction of super-salesman Doc Dammers.

Many who came to the sale had never been
to Coral Gables. In 1921, it was still considered
part of Miami's backcountry farmland, reached
only by a narrow country road.

Merrick's promise of a Mediterranean paradise was greeted with
skepticism; not even Dammers'
razzmatazz could sell real estate
that far out of town.

The stark Spanish plaza in the
wilderness only added to the make-
believe atmosphere. Merrick's master
suburb looked more like a Hollywood
set for a low-budget Don Quixote
(complete with actors wandering
through the crowd in pantalones) than
a place where he promised "Your Castles
in Spain Are Made Real." But Merrick
had as much faith in himself as he did in
Coral Gables. And he set about to make
his dreams come true.

Northwest of Miami, another farmer-turned-developer was selling lots in Hi-a-le-ah, the Seminole Indian name for "pretty prairie." James Bright came to Miami from St. Louis in 1909 and purchased 14,000 acres of Everglades land from the Tatum brothers. By 1915, Bright had transformed the wetlands into a huge cattle ranch. In 1917, Bright became partners with aviator Glenn Curtiss after Curtiss moved his flying field onto Bright's property. Together, the two men platted the subdivision of Hialeah and in 1921 began selling lots on the banks of the Miami Canal.

JAMES BRIGHT

By 1924, subdivisions spread so rapidly farmers who did not want to sell their land to developers put up not-for-sale signs. Most groves and farms close to town succumbed to the pressure of development. In Buena Vista, T.V. Moore, the "pineapple king," watched as his Buena Vista pineapple fields became Biltmore. In North Dade, the land near Captain Fulford's homestead turned into Fulford-by-the-Sea even though there was no sea in sight. (Critics called it Fulford by the F.E.C.) The 79th Street avocado groves of T.A. Winfield became Shorecrest. Near Allapattah, Joachim Fritz turned his Melrose dairy into Melrose Gardens and Melrose Heights. The western portion of former Flagler farmland blossomed into Flagler Lawn, Flagler Terrace, Flagler Manor and Flagami. Not even Doc Dammers could keep a straight face when he sold lots in what he termed "Central Miami" west of Red Road. (The coral rock entrances to Central Miami still stand at Red Road and the Coral Gables Canal.)

These smaller subdivisions were small potatoes compared to giants like Coral Gables and Miami Beach. By 1925, Miami Beach's population soared to over 15,000 permanent residents. New luxury hotels and lavish mansions transformed the man-made frontier into a spectacular winter playground. Fisher—a born promoter—hired publicist Steve Hannagan and super-salesman C.W. "Pete" Chase to sell Miami Beach to the world. Once Hannagan discovered that bathing beauties garnered more newspaper space than Fisher's elephants, he replaced "pachyderms with pulchritude," giving Miami Beach a new image.

■ Curtiss and Bright chose the Seminole word Hi-a-le-ah, which meant pretty prairie, for their first subdivision. Following the Seminole theme, they used a huge photographic image of Jack Tigertail, headman at Coppinger's Indian Village, to point the way. Sadly, Tigertail was murdered in March 1922 but his image lives on in the City of Hialeah seal. (APC)

(APC)

Although Miami Beach was incorporated in 1915, the Roaring Twenties brought it to life. Carl Fisher enticed millionaires, yachtsmen and polo players to what he promoted as "America's Winter Playground."

■ A natural-born publicity magnet, Fisher acquired two baby elephants, including the legendary Rosie (below) that he used in thousands of publicity photographs and films. (APC)

Miami Beach

AMERICAS WINTER PLAYGROUND

Fisher also built the posh Roman Pools that attracted the more affluent tourist. Its famous windmill was located on the ocean just south of today's 23rd Street. (APC)

The Land of Palms and Sunshine (APC)

MIAMI
By the Sea

Winter Touri
November

MIAMI
BEACH
Florida

Is Calling You

AND STILL MORE MOSQUITOES

*W*ill Rogers, the famous humorist, was a frequent visitor to South Florida during the Boom. In one of his monologues, he told how Carl Fisher solved the mosquito problem. "Had there been no Carl Fisher, Florida would be known today as the Turpentine State. . . But Carl drained off the water-moccasins, and the Turpentine and replaced them with a Hotel and New York prices. He put in a Jazz Orchestra and one-way Excursions; advertised free heat the year round; fixed up the chug-holes so the Fords could get in; rehearsed the mosquitoes til they wouldn't bite you until after you bought; shipped in California oranges and tied me to the trees; whispered under his breath that you were only ninety miles away from Palm Beach with its millionaires and its scandal."

(HMSF)

LAND BY THE GALLON

In December 1924, a third giant development—Miami Shores: "America's Mediterranean"—cashed in on the Coral Gables phenomenon and became its chief competitor. Hugh Anderson, Roy Wright, Ellen Spears Harris and James B. Jeffries, fresh from their successful creation called Venetian Isles, formed the Shoreland Company and opened up 2,800 acres of Miami Shores for development. The first lots in the Bay View section went on sale December 4, 1924 at Shoreland's lavish Mediterranean offices in downtown Miami. A fleet of 10 new Cadillacs stood ready to transport prospective buyers to the newest promised land. Many buyers wasted no time and bought their lots sight-unseen. Before the first day of sales ended, $2.5 million of Miami Shores real estate had

sold, setting a new Miami record.

By this time, every big developer in Miami and Miami Beach vied to see who had the most luxurious real estate offices in downtown Miami. Hundreds of salesmen poured into the streets to lure innocent passersby with lofty promises backed up with brand-new blueprints and grandiose drawings. Some salesmen even sold real estate on proposed island paradises "by the gallon." Buyers were encouraged to get in on the "wet floor" by purchasing lots even before dredging began.

Miami's island building mania began in 1918 after Carl Fisher discovered that a spoil bank from channel digging could hold a real estate sign. After Fisher developed Star Island, developers rushed to turn Biscayne Bay into a modern-day Venice. The process was simple enough. Would-be developers bought a hunk of bay bottom from the State Internal Improvement Fund, applied for a dredge permit from the Corps of Engineers, staked out their claim with wooden pilings, built a steel bulkhead around the open water and started the pump. Palm Island, Hibiscus Island, Fair Isle, La Gorce and Sunset islands and Venetian Isles rose from the water onto the burgeoning real estate pages of the local newspapers.

In Miami Shores, the Shoreland Company's grandiose plans included the creation of a chain of islands in Biscayne Bay. The company produced an incredible master drawing that clearly showed a causeway from the foot of Grand Concourse (at 125th Street) to the proposed islands of Miami

MIAMI SHORES
America's Mediterranean

Miami Shores
"AMERICA'S MEDITERRANEAN"

■ In December 1924, the Shoreland Company opened an impressive headquarters at 125 East Flagler Street—across the street from Coral Gables' downtown office—and began promoting Miami Shores: "America's Mediterranean." By the end of 1925, Miami Shores had recorded sales of $25 million, second only to Coral Gables.

■ Miami Shores highlighted Shoreland Boulevard, now N.E. 96th Street, and filled it with impressive Mediterranean-style homes (top) designed by the firm of Kiehnel & Elliot. (MSV)

■ Like other developments, Miami Shores had a fleet of buses to transport prospects. They also took community groups like the American Legion Drum and Bugle Corps (left) to public events. (MSV)

A MEDITERRANEAN DREAM

Time & Time Again

1926

2006

(MSV)

(APC)

The Shoreland Company announced: Miami Shores "America's Mediter-ranean" in December 1924. Their plans for luxury hotels and apartments, causeways and wide boulevards brought Coral Gables its only local com-petition. Although the company boasted more than $75 million in sales, the only luxury apartment building completed before the end of the Boom was the Grand Concourse Apartments designed by well-known architect Robert Law Weed. Listed on the National Register of Historic Places in 1985, the Grand Concourse Apartments at 421 Grand Concourse give cur-rent residents a glimpse of what might have been.

Shores—later Indian Creek and Bay Harbor Islands. (The causeway was not built until the 1950s.) At the height of the Boom, Miami Shores opened the Arch Creek section, although it was not contiguous to the other Miami Shores development. It sold out in one day.

Meanwhile in Coral Gables, George Merrick's master sub-urb was starting to look like the promised American Riviera. A business district—all in the Mediterranean manner—was rising on Alhambra and Ponce de León Boulevard. By this time, Spanish street names and Spanish and Mediterranean-style architecture caused one pundit to quip that Coral Gables looked as if Ponce de León had conquered Florida after all.

The creative geniuses of Merrick, Button, Denman and H. George Fink, and newcomer Phineas Paist were busy wiping all traces of ugliness from Coral Gables. Even the water towers were beautiful. Lowland became golf courses, and an unsightly rock quarry right in the middle of the suburb became Venetian Pool and Casino. The Douglas, Granada, Country Club Prado and Alhambra entrances to Coral Gables set a new standard of beauty and lavishness. Other notable architects like Walter DeGarmo, Martin Hampton and Richard Kiehnel entered the scene. Even with fierce competition from Miami Shores, Coral Gables remained without peer except in the work of Addison Mizner in Palm Beach and Boca Raton.

Feeling the competition from Miami Beach and Miami Shores, Merrick pushed to acquire some waterfront property in his landlocked subdivision of Coral Gables. First, he dredged a series of canals creating waterfront lots in rocky pineland. Next, he purchased from James and Charles Deering a huge tract of land south of Bird Road extending from today's Cocoplum to Chapman Field. Called the Biscayne Bay section, it gave Merrick seven miles of genuine waterfront lots. When he acquired Key Biscayne and added it to Coral Gables, he immediately advertised that Coral Gables had "forty miles of Waterfront"—more than any other devel-opment. (Key Biscayne was de-annexed in the 1940s.)

Merrick poured most of his phenomenal profits back into developing Coral Gables. By 1925, he had spent over $100 million on improvements, $5 million in advertising alone. Merrick took out full-page ads in national magazines and *The New York Times*. He rented billboards in Times Square and opened an office nearby. He also had grandiose branch offices in other major cities and on the boardwalk at Atlantic City. This unprecedented promotional splurge not only put Coral Gables on the national map but also helped vault the Florida boom into a national phenomenon.

So many people wanted to come to Coral Gables that the railroad put on special Coral Gables cars to take would-be buyers to Miami. Merrick's fleet of 86 buses brought in hundreds of people a day from all over the South.

Merrick, like Carl Fisher, capitalized on big-name personalities to sell his dream suburb. For $100,000, Merrick hired William Jennings Bryan to give special promotional lectures at Venetian Pool on the future of Coral Gables. Such well-known orchestra leaders as Jan Garber and Paul Whiteman played "When the Moon Shines on Coral Gables" at the Coral Gables Country Club and Venetian Pool—often with a national radio hookup.

■ *Ponce de León Boulevard was Coral Gables' main street. By 1926, it had a variety of distinctive Mediterranean-style buildings, including the now-demolished Coral Gables Theater (below). (CG)*

■ *In 1923, Merrick hired the firm of Kiehnel & Elliot to design the new Grammar School (top right). When the school board refused to pay for his design, Merrick built it with his own funds. It remains today as an active elementary school listed on the National Register of Historic Places. (APC)*

■ *The first commercial building in Coral Gables stood on the southeast corner of LeJeune Road and Alhambra Circle (middle right). Designed by Walter DeGarmo, it housed the Ground Sales Office and a variety of shops. (APC)*

Denman Fink, George Merrick's artist uncle, designed all of Coral Gables' entrances and plazas, including the DeSoto Fountain and Plaza (above). The Biltmore Hotel is visible in the background. (APC)

Coral Gables

"MIAMI'S MASTER SUBURB"

Notables gathered on March 13, 1925 to break ground for the Biltmore Hotel (facing page). Charles Flynn, vice president of Bowman-Biltmore Hotel Company, turned the first shovel of dirt. He was joined by Eunice Merrick, center, and William Jennings Bryan, fifth from right, who was the featured speaker. George Merrick was not there. He was in New York raising money. (SPA)

In early 1923, members of the Merrick family, including Eunice Merrick, fourth from left, posed for a history-making advertisement announcing the opening of the Coral Gables Golf and Country Club. (APC)

Denman Fink (right) considered Venetian Pool (below) his finest work. Because he was an artist and not an architect, all his masterpieces began as paintings. (APC)

GLENN CURTISS

Meanwhile, Glenn Curtiss and James Bright were busy turning Hialeah into South Florida's most exciting sports and amusement center. They built the area's first dog track then created the Hialeah Jockey Club, followed by Miami's first jai alai fronton. Nearby, they opened the Miami Studios, a motion picture production company that promised to turn Hialeah into another Hollywood. While Hialeah metamorphosed into the center of all sorts of fun and games, Curtiss and Bright opened quiet residential sections in Country Club Estates (now Miami Springs) across the Miami Canal.

Just north of Hialeah, another type of development was taking place. In 1919, the Tatum brothers convinced the Pennsylvania Sugar Company to take over 300,000 acres of Everglades muck land for growing sugarcane. In 1921, they sent mining engineer Ernest R. Graham to Miami to oversee the growing, though problem-plagued, operation. By 1924, the company had added a large sugar mill to its operation and started refining sugar. In an era when Miami farmland was shrinking faster than women's skirts, the Pennsylvania Sugar Company's enterprise was a unique new venture.

By 1925, Miami's own four-year boom had spread across Florida. That year "Boom" became a proper noun, and whatever innocence the 29-year-old city had left vanished forever. By that time, the nation had discovered Florida. "Everybody is telling stories of Florida and the wonderful real estate developments there," *The New York Times* opined. "Hardly anybody talks of anything but real estate, and one is led to believe that nobody in Florida thinks of anything else in these days when the peninsula is jammed with visitors from end to end and side to side—unless it is a matter of finding a place to sleep. Ten minutes to half an hour in any spot in the state would convince the most skeptical eyes and ears that something is taking place in Florida to which the history of developments, booms, inrushes, speculation, [and] investment yields no parallel."

■ *Pennsylvania Sugar Company's huge sugarcane-growing operation was in the reclaimed, though still rather wet, Everglades (below). When the venture closed, manager Ernest R. Graham purchased the land and opened a dairy. The Graham family later turned their land holdings into the New Town of Miami Lakes. (APC)*

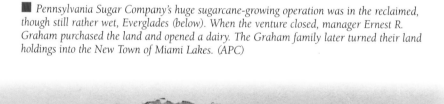

■ *Hoping to create a more exclusive area than Hialeah, Curtiss and Bright also developed Country-Club Estates that later became Miami Springs. It had strict architectural controls that mandated pueblo-style architecture. The Pueblo Hotel was Curtiss' most extravagant project in the Hialeah-Miami Springs area. In 1929, John Kellogg purchased it and turned it into the Battle Creek Sanitarium. Today, it is a retirement home. (APC)*

1925

"THE BEDLAM THAT WAS MIAMI"

"My first impression, as I wandered out into the blazing sunlight of that tropical afternoon into that bedlam that was Miami, was of utter confusion. Everywhere there was building going forward at express speed; and mingled with the perpetual screeching of the motor horns a thousand drills and hammers and winches added to the insane chorus. Everywhere there was dust. Hatless, coatless men rushed about the blazing streets, their arms full of papers, perspiration pouring from their foreheads. Every shop seemed to be combined with a real estate office; at every doorway crowds of young men were shouting and speech making, thrusting forward papers and proclaiming to heaven the unsurpassed chances, which they were offering, to make a fortune. "

T.H. Weigall,
Boom in Paradise

(APC)

■ *Verne O. Williams was one of Miami's best boom-time photographers. He arrived in early 1925, just in time to capture the peak of the Boom for posterity (above). His photographs are easily identifiable by both their quality and the fact that he often signed and dated each image. (APC)*

BINDER BOYS AND BAD REPUTATIONS

Although all of Florida experienced the Boom, Miami was at the epicenter. Flagler Street became one frenzied real estate exchange. As the crowds increased, it was not unusual for the city to issue more than 50 real estate licenses a day. Then a new type of real estate salesman arrived on the scene. The so-called "binder boys" were slick real estate operators who sold "binders" (or 10 percent deposits) on parcels of real estate to hold them until the necessary formalities could close the deal, usually 30 days later. Kenneth Ballinger in his wonderful book, *Miami Millions*, described this new breed of salesman as "an individual slightly under normal height, never very clean or neat, bending every effort to make a lot of money in a hurry without the slightest pretense of remaining in Florida once that was done."

When the binder boys discovered that binders were just as good as property, they started selling the same binders over and over again, each time at a marked-up profit. Sometimes, a binder would change hands eight or 10 times in one day—often increasing a four-digit profit to five and even six digits before the final sale occurred.

Excitement was infectious. Huge crowds milled around in downtown Miami and made the sidewalks almost impassable. Hundreds of subdivision buses charged into town and clogged the narrow streets. All around the city, skeletons of giant skyscrapers dominated the skyline.

But the skyscrapers were not confined to the traditional downtown area. The Rand Company broke ground for the Roosevelt Hotel on the corner of N.E. Second Avenue and 14th Street (later the home of Dade County Schools). Joachim Fritz started the Fritz Hotel at his former dairy on N.W. 27th Avenue, south of 36th Street. George Merrick announced the groundbreaking for Coral Gables' first skyscraper—the Miami-Biltmore Hotel.

■ *Often Verne Williams turned his photographs into postcards, like the view of today's Flagler Street just west of Miami Avenue. (LW)*

(Several other mega-buildings were on the drawing board.) The Biltmore's focal point would be a replica of Seville's famous Giralda Tower.

Ironically, at the time Merrick announced the Biltmore, former Ohio governor and presidential candidate James M. Cox was already building another Giralda Tower on Biscayne Boulevard to house his newspaper, *Miami Daily News and Metropolis* (formerly *The Miami Metropolis*). A third Giralda Tower was going up on Miami Beach as part of N.B.T Roney's lavish Roney Plaza Hotel.

■ *The* Miami Daily News *entrance lobby (below) was a beautiful example of boom-time spare-no-expense Mediterranean architecture. (MN)*

MIAMI DAILY NEWS
1896   1925
NEW HOME EDITION   MIAMI BEACH SECTION

■ *OF SPANISH TOWERS: In the mid-1920s, the South Florida skyline was filling up with Giralda Towers. In one year, the architectural firm of Schultz and Weaver designed three impressive replicas—the Miami Daily News Tower (left) the Miami-Biltmore Hotel and the now-razed Roney Plaza on Miami Beach. (MN)*

■ *When the News Tower formally opened on July 26, 1925, the paper published what it claimed to be the largest edition ever printed. Each section cover was full color. (MN)*

All institutions felt the effects of the Boom. Bank deposits increased 48 percent between June and September 1925. The post office struggled to keep up with the increased volume of mail. Voters passed million-dollar bond issues to meet the demand for public services. Richard Kiehnel completed the drawings for a grandiose Mediterranean-style high school, and citizens chartered the long-awaited new university—the University of Miami—to which Merrick donated 160 acres of land and pledged $5 million. *The Miami Herald* led the nation's papers in advertising. The *Miami Daily News* opened its news tower and celebrated the city's 29th birthday with the largest single issue of a newspaper in history—504 pages in 22 sections.

For a time in the summer and fall of 1925, everything seemed possible. After a September 5 referendum, the city annexed Buena Vista, Allapattah, Lemon City, Little River, Silver Bluff and Coconut Grove, creating Greater Miami. Only Coconut Grove voted against the expansionary move, but it was swallowed anyway. About the same time, Hialeah and Coral Gables upgraded from subdivisions to cities. Greater Miami was riding high on the crest of a wave.

But signs of impending doom were clearly visible. The cost of living skyrocketed. Finding a place to live was next to impossible. To help ease the housing crunch, several Miami businesses opened company apartments for their employees. The demand for housing became so great that entrepreneurs created a "hot bed" system and rented a cot to two people, each with a 12-hour shift.

SUBDIVIDING HELL

One man told the story that he dreamed he had died and gone to Hell. The devil received him graciously and personally escorted him around Hell, pointing out all the interesting and important spots. At last they came to a big iron cage in which about 50 men were incarcerated. He asked the devil, "Who are these men and why are they imprisoned in such a way?" The devil replied, "Oh, they are real estate men from Miami. I do not dare let them out because they would subdivide Hell and sell it all within two hours."

Cora S. Maxwell
Miami of Yesterday, 1956

Cora Maxwell and son Richard

■ *After the Florida East Coast Railroad announced a freight embargo in August 1925 to repair overburdened tracks, the masts of tall ships (left) soon dominated the skyline as developers hired everything afloat to bring in building supplies. (LW)*

■ *City Manager and former Mayor Frank H. Wharton gave the key to the city to "Ponce de León" during the 1926 Fiesta of the American Tropics (facing page top). (RC)*

■ *In January 1926, the German brigantine* Prinz Valdemar *capsized in the middle of Government Cut—completely blocking it for 25 days (facing page bottom). People later called it "the ship that stopped the Boom." (RC)*

Then came the Internal Revenue Service. Agents carefully noted profit takers and slapped Miami's new paper millionaires with huge tax bills. The biggest blow came in August 1925 when the Florida East Coast Railroad (FEC) announced a temporary freight embargo in order to repair and enlarge their overburdened tracks. The edict cut off the arrival of building materials, forcing contractors to idle their crews. Anything that would float—from antique steamships to wooden windjammers—was pressed into service. Bootlegging lumber became as popular as bootlegging booze. Before long, the skeleton masts of the tall wooden ships stood out in stark juxtaposition to the iron bones of the fleshless skyscrapers.

Making matters worse, a strong, anti-Florida campaign swept the nation. The state of Ohio passed "blue-sky" laws and warned its citizens of the dangers of speculating in Florida real estate. Every major magazine in America did an exposé on Florida. To counteract the damaging articles, Florida Governor John W. Martin and a group of prominent developers, including Carl Fisher and George Merrick, held a lavish banquet and news conference at the Waldorf-Astoria in New York City to defend Florida against the charges. Miami rushed to pass laws to drive the binder boys out of town and salvage the city's bad reputation.

Overly optimistic rhetoric increased in direct proportion to depressing events. Overt boosterism reached its all-time climax in the joint proclamation issued by the mayors of Miami, Miami Beach, Hialeah and Coral Gables declaring the last day of 1925 and the first two days of 1926 as "The Fiesta of the American Tropics—our Season of Fiesta when Love, Good Fellowship, Merry Making and Wholesome Sport shall prevail throughout Our Domains… The most Richly Blessed Community of the most Bountifully Endowed State of the most Highly Enterprising People of the Universe."

The three-day extravaganza, which had its roots in the 1915 "Magic Knights of Dade" and "The Palm Fete" held in the early 1920s, included a grand parade down a newly opened section of Biscayne Boulevard. Held in Merrick's new Coral Gables Stadium, the Fiesta Football Game—between the "Four Horsemen and Seven Mules" of Notre Dame and the ex-Princeton All-Stars—drew a huge New Year's Day crowd. Ten days later, the "Richly Blessed Community" had a serious setback when the brigantine *Prinz Valdemar* capsized in the middle of the ship channel. For 25 days, nothing bigger than a rowboat could get in or out of the Miami Harbor. This accident, combined with the railroad embargo, sent builders into a tailspin. By the time the old hulk was towed to shore, the damage was done and the red-hot boom had turned ice-cold.

THE LAST OF THE RED-HOT BOOM

If Merrick suspected such a turn of events, he certainly did not show it. On January 16, the beautiful Miami-Biltmore Hotel opened and set off a whole new wave of Merrick-based optimism. Elegant first-nighters, whose finery matched the opulence of the grand ballroom, marveled at the hand-carved ceilings and wide balconies that overlooked the hotel's two Olympic-sized swimming pools. The pools flowed together at right angles, creating the illusion of a quiet tropical lagoon. Several gondolas—brought from Venice for the event, each with its own gondolier—floated in the pools. Gondolas also ferried guests down the Coral Gables "Grand Canal" decorated with striped Venetian lampposts. The canal connected the Biltmore Hotel with Tahiti Beach under construction in the Biscayne Bay section.

Not to be outdone by Coral Gables, Arthur Voetglin's glittering Pueblo Feliz (Joyful City) opened the following day in the Arch Creek section of Miami Shores. The Pueblo Feliz was a walled replica of a Spanish village, complete with small shops and cafes. Its focal point was the grand Teatro de Alegria that reportedly could seat more people than Carnegie Hall. Each night a cast of 150 performed *Fountania*—a grand recital of Florida history with enough feathered dancing girls to rival the Ziegfield Follies. During the breathtaking finale, 48 beautiful girls, each representing a different state, paraded onstage. With the beauties poised, the chorus danced a lively Charleston as the Magic City rose majestically from cardboard waves.

Another attraction just north of Arch Creek in Fulford-by-the-Sea was even more extraordinary. In late 1925, Merle C. Tebbets, developer of Fulford, started a huge, million-dollar raceway for automobiles. The compound included a 1.25-mile wooden track, a grandstand, bleachers and garages. On February 22, 1926, the track saw its first and only race. Pete de Paola, winner of the 1925 Indianapolis 500, led the pack in his Dusenberg Straight 8 and set a new world's record at 129.19 mph.

By the summer of 1926, sales even slumped in Coral Gables. To generate activity, Merrick announced that the American Building Corporation, headed by former Ohio Governor Myers Y. Cooper, was undertaking a $175 million building program in the Riviera section. For the first time, Merrick allowed homes in Coral Gables without Mediterranean-style architecture. Architectural experts arrived to plan Chinese, American Colonial, French, Italian, Dutch South African and Persian villages that would be tucked into secluded pockets. The tempo quickened in the university section of Coral Gables after ground was broken for the new University of Miami campus in February 1926 and work commenced on the lavish main building.

Not to be outdone by George Merrick, super-developers Anderson and Wright purchased the Charles Deering estate in Buena Vista and announced plans for Bay Plaza (today's Bay Point), a luxurious development they planned to locate between Biscayne Bay and the wide boulevard they were building north of N.E. 15th Street. Harrison Construction Company began the massive project by carving a swath through quiet neighborhoods. Before they were finished, they moved 12 buildings, trimmed the front yards and porches from countless others and leveled 100 additional structures, including two hotels, a $100,000 mansion and a synagogue.

In the waning days of summer, Glenn Curtiss announced one of the last grandiose projects of the Boom—the new town

of Opa-locka, built around a theme from the Arabian Nights.

Domed palaces fit for the grandest potentate rose from the flat Everglades muck land surrounded by rows of small homes, each with a distinctive Arabian motif. Nowhere else in the world could a person live on Sesame Street in a modest bungalow with two bedrooms, one bath and a minaret.

Even though new projects continued to be announced, it was hard to deny that the Boom was almost over. Ever optimistic, Miamians described the slump as a temporary lull to allow the frenzy of over speculation to settle. "Florida they say may suffer from a slight case of colic due to swallowing more than she can really digest," claimed a *New York Times* writer. "But the attack won't be serious. Reverses may come, they say, but Florida as a great vacation state is here to stay."

■ *FULFORD'S FOLLY: Merle Tebbets also built the Fulford-Miami Speedway, a 1.25-mile wooden raceway for automobiles. Racers, pitmen and friends lined up for a history-making picture before the first race. No one knew it would be its only race. (HMSF)*

■ *Pete de Paola (above), winner of the Indianapolis 500 the preceding year, won the Carl Fisher Cup and $12,000 prize money. (TP)*

1926

(APC)

2008

(APC)

Opa-Locka, founded by legendary aviator Glenn Curtiss in 1926, may have more "Moorish Revival" architecture than any other American city. More than 20 Opa-Locka buildings are listed in the National Register of Historic Places. Curtiss hired renowned architect Bernhardt Muller to design the buildings and Clinton McKenzie to do the town plan. The City Hall, completed in 1926 and restored in 1987, is the centerpiece of Opa-Locka Moorish architecture.

THE WINDS RAGE

In July, a 100-mph hurricane grazed Miami—the first in 14 years. Damage was slight. Down in Coconut Grove, pioneer Ralph M. Munroe, who had spent years pleading with developers to consider the inevitability of hurricanes when planning their dream cities, saw the small storm as a blessing. It was "made to order for me," he wrote, "blowing just enough energy to put the fear of the Lord into the scoffers and very possibly make them see the light." Unfortunately, the mild July storm had the opposite effect. When another storm was sighted two months later, only a few old-timers like Munroe took the warning seriously.

On the evening of September 17, 1926, although The *Miami Daily News* and *Miami Tribune* carried a banner headline warning residents to prepare for a tropical storm, life

went on as usual. By the time people went to bed, the wind was blowing briskly, noisily flapping the thousands of canvas awnings that covered almost every window. By midnight, the city plunged into darkness. Thousands awoke, lit candles and asked, "What the hell is going on?" For eight sleepless hours, the storm raged. In the morning's gray light, the wind suddenly stopped. The clouds parted and people came out to check the damage and thank God it was all over. What they saw was sickening. Rubble and broken glass filled the streets and many buildings were simply shells. Trees were flattened and those that remained standing were stripped naked by the fierce wind, giving the scene an eerie deathlike quality.

This devastation was simply a dress rehearsal of what was to come. Most people did not realize that they were in the eye of the storm. Suddenly, without warning, the raging wind returned with even greater strength from the opposite direc-

tion. Thousands became stranded on causeways and without shelter. Before the last wind gauge blew away, the windspeed reached 128 mph. Next came the angry waters. Docks flew by like canoes shooting rapids. Boats seemed to leap out of the bay and onto the bayfront. The ocean roared across Miami Beach, smacked into the bay and raced to overtake Miami.

Late in the afternoon of September 18, the morning tempest started to die down. People emerged from their tattered homes through darkness and debris to view what seemed like almost total destruction. Many homes that the first half of the storm spared were toppled by the second. Everywhere, buildings gaped open, exposing household chaos and half-clothed men and women picking up the pieces of their lives. Miami had been brought to its knees.

■ *The legendary 1926 hurricane caught everyone by surprise and left death and destruction in its wake. Miami Beach's Ocean Drive was especially hard hit. (APC)*

■ *Artist Denman Fink created* Law Guides Florida Progress, *a mural 11 by 26 feet for the main courtroom of the 1933 Miami Post Office, Courthouse and Federal Building. When it was installed in 1941, his nephew George Merrick was Miami postmaster. (APC)*

Chapter Seven

The Morning After

"Out of the night that covers me, Black as the pit from pole to pole
I thank whatever gods may be, For my unconquerable soul."

Invictus. William Earnest Henley
Reprinted in *Miami Tribune*
September 19, 1926

O

N SUNDAY, SEPTEMBER 19, 1926, NATIONAL HEADLINES SCREAMED, "MIAMI IS WIPED OUT!" MANY WRITERS PREDICTED

that the ruined city would soon become a ghost town. Others believed that the hurricane was divine retribution for the city's evil boomtime ways.

Miamians, stunned and sobered, awoke to face the morning after. The city lay in ruins. Every downtown building suffered damage—especially the half-finished Meyer-Kiser Building that emerged from the storm twisted and broken.

Shattered glass littered the streets. Biscayne Boulevard looked like a yacht basin, with boats washed up against palm trees. All through the night, a steady stream of injured arrived at the makeshift emergency hospital in the McAllister Hotel. Volunteers stacked more than 100 recovered bodies in filled-to-capacity morgues and funeral homes. Many of the victims remained unidentified.

ROYAL PALM PARK MIAMI
AFTER THE STORM.

OUT OF THE RUBBLE

People, newly homeless, wandered aimlessly through the streets looking for loved ones and searching for food, water and a place to sleep. Schools, hotels, even department stores, took in thousands of victims.

Conditions were even worse in Miami Beach. The sea swept through oceanfront buildings, leaving sand and fish in its wake. On South Beach, the storm surge lifted many of the old wooden casinos and flimsy, Coney Island-style amusement parlors off their foundations and simply washed them away. "The sight of torn and bleeding Miami Beach that greeted us was enough to break the spirit and heart of a battle-scarred soldier," wrote one resident.

Other areas were also devastated. Hialeah was underwater as if the Everglades had risen up to reclaim it. In Coconut Grove, the angry bay carried away buildings and turned streets into ships' graveyards. The storm destroyed Miami Shores' famous tourist attraction Pueblo Feliz and Fulford's wooden automobile racetrack resembled a pile of matchsticks. Although Coral Gables' strict building code proved equal to the wind's force, "The City Beautiful" looked anything but beautiful. The wind played jacks with roof tiles, shredded the bright canvas awnings and turned tree-lined boulevards into wastelands.

Out of the confusion and near-hysteria, Miami Commissioner James H. Gilman stepped forward to take charge.

■ *After the hurricane (top), Miami's bayfront looked more like a yacht basin than a park. (APC)*

■ *The Miami News Tower (facing page) stood tall amid the destruction around it. (HMSF)*

■ *An "open-air" bathroom after the storm (facing page inset). (APC)*

■ *Miamians made a valiant effort to carry on (bottom) despite the destruction. (APC)*

"THE CARDBOARD COLLEGE"

■ HIGHER EDUCATION: *The new University of Miami opened on schedule in October 1926 (above) although it was forced to move the campus to the bankrupt Anastasia Hotel and Apartments.* (APC)

■ *The first students saw themselves as pioneers and knew they were making history in what they lovingly called "The Cardboard College."* (MN)

(Mayor Ed Romfh and many other public officials were away on vacation.) Gilman's leadership had a positive effect on the battered populace as they began the massive cleanup.

On Monday, the newspapers printed encouraging articles in an attempt to raise sagging spirits. "Shed a tear for the dead you loved," wrote the *Miami Tribune*, "pause a moment over the industrial, commercial or artistic monument you have erected, and then look bravely toward the future." "Pessimism is routed from the city," the *Miami Daily News* added. "Optimism, born of the will to do, reigns."

Despite what seemed to be overwhelming problems, a new spirit arose amidst the devastation. A grocer put a sign in his shattered window, "NO ADVANCE IN PRICE OF GROCERIES, if you're destitute it's FREE." Railroad man John Burke scrawled, "Wiped out but still smiling" on the fallen walls of his home. "A great many of us realize," a Miami Beach resident wrote, "probably for the first time in our lives, what a real brotherhood of man means." The hurricane, like nothing else in the city's history, brought people together. No one would ever forget the camaraderie.

One week after the storm, Mayor Romfh (who had raced home on the first train) declared, "This city has come back with a speed that is absolutely amazing." He predicted that Miami would be restored in time for the next tourist season—only three months away. Some criticized Romfh for minimizing the damage, claiming that his statement cut off some much-needed outside relief. But in the final analysis, Mayor Romfh's optimism—which many called simply whistling in the dark—set the tone for recovery. The 1926 season opened with the slogan, "Miami By the Sea is Ready."

The University of Miami was not ready, but opened anyway on October 15. The university abandoned the half-finished main campus, and instead, began classes on schedule in a bankrupt apartment hotel hastily converted into classrooms with thin cardboard partitions. In spite of this inauspicious beginning, what students lovingly called "The Cardboard College" gave South Florida a new kind of leadership and became a rallying cry for those determined to carry on.

In 1928, Miamians welcomed the National Shrine Convention and parade that transformed the just-opened Biscayne Boulevard and Bayfront Park into an Arabian delight. (APC)

Giant Sphinx decorated the parade route and provided a photo opportunity of costume-clad women. (APC)

For a time, the rush to complete the tattered leavings of boom-time projects and hurricane-damaged buildings masked the city's increasing economic woes. The new Everglades and Robert Clay hotels opened for the 1926-27 season and people thrilled to the twinkling lights and vaporous clouds on the ceiling of the Olympia Theatre, the Boom's last gasp of grandeur. The temporary building boom, however, had as much substance as the Olympia's starry night. For every building repaired or completed, two or three others were abandoned, leaving eerie skeletons of half-finished dreams bleaching in the sun. Miamians felt one last burst of optimism when the northern leg of Biscayne Boulevard opened in 1927. Steel magnate Henry Phipps with his family's Bessemer Properties took over the bankrupt Biscayne Boulevard Corporation and finished the roadway.

The feeling lingered after the Chamber of Commerce convinced the Shriners to hold their 1928 national convention in Miami. The Shriners built an amphitheater in Bayfront Park—complete with minarets—and constructed monolithic Egyptian statues all along the Boulevard. Businesses and schools closed so everyone could witness their spectacular parade down Biscayne Boulevard.

That same year, workers finally completed the Tamiami Trail across the Everglades, linking Miami to Florida's west coast. But the road and the new Seaboard railroad were hardly needed. By late 1928, it was clear that the Boom was over. For the first time in the city's short history, more people left than arrived.

"LEAKIEST SPOT IN AMERICA"

Even though the construction and population booms crashed, Miami's "bootleg boom" continued stronger than ever. After the passage of the 18th Amendment in 1920, the nation became officially dry. Few realized how impossible it would be to enforce such a law—especially in Miami. Rumrunners bought liquor in Bimini and easily smuggled it into the city via fast boats. Miami quickly gained the reputation as "the leakiest spot in America."

In the early years of Prohibition, bootleggers and rumrunners took on the mantle of modern-day Robin Hoods, jousting with blue-nosed government for the good of the thirsty masses. When a Coast Guard boat chased a liquor smuggler up the Miami River with a barrage of gunfire, onlookers cheered the rumrunners and castigated the Coast Guardsmen for what the press called "reckless, needless and uncivilized" behavior. The mayor of Miami called the Coast Guard a "serious menace."

Feelings against the Coast Guard continued to fester after a cutter chased Miami Beach's favorite bootlegger, Duncan W. "Red" Shannon, onto the lawn of Carl Fisher's Flamingo Hotel and shot him down in front of hundreds of horrified tourists.

The Dade County grand jury indicted the Coast Guardsmen for murder but they were later acquitted by the trial jury.

Local law enforcement officers ignored a host of prohibition-bred industries. Speakeasies appeared all over town and in every luxury hotel. Outlying pinelands sported hundreds of "alky cookers" and moonshiners. Although the police made some arrests, operators simply paid a fine and went back to business the next day. In fact, the city depended on the fines to keep it going. Almost $170,000 in bootlegging and gambling fines eased the city's economic woes.

Louis Nuta turned his Miami shipyard into a rumrunner's dream when he created an incredibly fast "booze boat" from surplus World War I airplane engines. With two Liberty Engines, a 34-foot boat could reach Bimini in an hour and return to Miami fully loaded two hours later. Nothing in the Coast Guard flotilla could compete with Nuta's boats until the Coast Guard confiscated a Nuta boat for its own use.

Coconut Grove and Coral Gables' canals became some of the rumrunner's most popular entry points. Occasionally, as the Coast Guard patrol neared, a rumrunner would throw the hams (six bottles of liquor wrapped in burlap) overboard in shallow water, planning to come back later to retrieve them. Many upright citizens took advantage of the situation and waded out into the bay, picked up the hams and carted them away. Beachcombing had not been as much fun since the "great wine wreck" of the late 1800s.

AL CAPONE

In the late 1920s, the good-natured game of hide-and-seek turned into a deadly war. After bootlegger Horace Alderman, known as "The Gulf Stream Pirate," killed several Coast Guardsmen in a bloody battle in the Gulf Stream, citizens began to re-evaluate their liberal attitude. Alderman was hanged for his misdeeds.

Miami's wide-open reputation brought a new group of shady characters into town. In 1928, Al "Scarface" Capone, "King of the Underworld," moved into a mansion on Palm Island. At first, Miamians tried to ignore Capone, but after he was linked to Chicago's St. Valentine's Day Massacre, uneasy citizens tried to run him out of town. Even the Civic Theatre (a local little theater group) joined the movement by producing *Storm Warnings*, an anti-gangster play written by Marjory Stoneman Douglas

and William Muir. (On opening night, the nervous actors recognized several of Capone's men sitting in the front row but the play went on without incident.)

Capone's bevy of lawyers went to court to stop what they called harassment. They described him as a law-abiding citizen who only wanted to be left alone. The standoff continued until 1932 when the federal government convicted Capone of income tax evasion and hauled him off to federal prison. By that time, however, the damage had been done. Organized crime firmly controlled Miami's myriad of illegal fun-and-games establishments.

Even though many criminals moved into South Florida, city leaders refused to admit that the situation was out of hand. Most believed South Florida needed gambling to survive. When Governor Doyle Carlton threatened to close down Miami's illegal gambling establishments—including the Hialeah Jockey Club—newspapers protested the move and lobbied for a change in the law. (Until the law changed, racetracks skirted it by selling stock on the animals and paying dividends to the winners.)

■ *Florida Governor Doyle E. Carlton shook hands with a Seminole Indian during the formal opening ceremonies of the Tamiami Trail in April 1928 (facing page top). (MN)*

■ *Law enforcement officials opened "hams" (facing page bottom) and destroyed bottles of bootlegged booze on the lawn of Miami City Hall. (RC)*

■ *Miamians were not pleased when Al Capone, "King of the Underworld," moved to Palm Island. His son, Sonny, attended Miami Beach's St. Patrick's School and invited his classmates (right) to join him for a birthday party at his home. (HMSF)*

With the backing of *The Miami Herald*, Dade County legislator Dan Chappell introduced a bill into the Florida Legislature to legalize pari-mutuel gambling. After Governor Carlton vetoed the bill, Chappell obtained enough votes to override the veto by promising to divide the profits among all Florida counties. For the first time, Miami's horse and dog tracks and jai alai frontons were legal. The depression-poor state even legalized slot machines. As soon as the law passed, almost every store on Flagler Street put in a one-armed bandit. During the following legislative session, however, public outcry forced the lawmakers to change the law.

Horseracing took on a new image in 1932 after Joseph Widener purchased the Hialeah Jockey Club and transformed it into Hialeah Park. Widener's million-dollar transfusion into Miami's faltering economy turned him into a local hero.

■ In 1932, Joseph Widener purchased the Miami Jockey Club and transformed it into Hialeah Park (above). (APC)

■ Gleason Waite Roomer, one of Miami's premier photographers, captured Hialeah Park's elegant ambiance (left). (RC)

■ Hialeah Park prompted Miami's souvenir entrepreneurs to create a compact (upper left) highlighting the park's famous flamingos. (APC)

■ In 1928, Biscayne Boulevard was completed (facing page), opening up what developers called Miami's "Fifth Avenue." The new buildings were all designed in what is now called Art Deco. (APC)

CLOSED DOORS AND OPEN SKIES

Other developments brought more good news. In 1931, Colonel Henry L. Doherty, founder of Cities Service Gas Corporation, purchased the Miami-Biltmore, the Roney Plaza and the Key Largo Angler's Club and formed the Florida Year Round Club. He hired publicist Carl Byoir to promote his properties and to entice anyone who had any money left to return to South Florida. Byoir's genius put Miami and Miami Beach back into the news as the "nation's playground."

Bessemer Properties, in sharp contrast to other developers who had either gone under or left town, continued to pour millions of dollars into Biscayne Boulevard, "the Fifth Avenue of the South." During the worst of the Depression, Bessemer built a group of buildings between N.E. 13th and 16th streets that introduced a style of architecture described "as streamlined as tomorrow."

HOW LONG CAN THEY LAST?

During the Great Depression, Miami's Cinderella Ballroom became a popular gathering place for dance marathons. The rules were simple. Participating couples had to touch, stay upright and in motion for 40 minutes. After a 15-minute rest, they began the same ritual again, sometimes going nonstop for several months. Spectators paid 25 cents to watch the grueling, almost sadistic, endurance contest that continued until one pair remained standing. The winning couple received a cash prize. Recently, some colleges have revived the craze. (TP)

■ *Ralph O'Neill of the New York Rio and Buenos Aries Airline (NYRBA) convinced the City of Miami to turn Dinner Key into a commercial air base and anchored his houseboat terminal just offshore. O'Neill piloted "Cuba" (above) on February 25, 1929 that brought the first airmail to Miami from South America. (RC)*

■ *After a year of bitter rivalry, Juan Tripp's Pan American Airways purchased the NYRBA in 1930 and took over its Dinner Key operation. Pan Am built a new terminal (right) that opened to the public in 1934 and became an instant tourist attraction. (APC)*

The Phipps' Bessemer Properties also encouraged Miami's cultural climate by building a permanent home for the Civic Theatre. On opening night in January 1930, the cream of the business and social community flocked to see *Miami Herald* classified ad man and future movie star "Jo" (later Joseph) Cotton star in *The Green Goddess*. But the Depression took its toll on the Civic Theatre. When the trustees were unable to pay the mortgage, the Phipps interests reclaimed the property and renovated it into the Mayfair movie theater (torn down in 1973 to make way for the Omni Complex).

When the 1930s began, Ed Romfh was the only one of the famous 1920s banker-commissioners who still had a bank to manage. His First National Bank survived a series of bank runs caused by panicked depositors withdrawing their funds.

Some of the city's most prominent businessmen lost everything. The Sewell brothers (both mayors of Miami) closed the doors to their pioneer retail store. George Merrick, who poured millions of his own money into Coral Gables trying to keep it going, was penniless. He and his wife moved to the Keys where they ran an upscale fishing camp.

Yet in the midst of all the personal tragedy and corporate death, Miami's aviation industry emerged. A Depression child, aviation became a lonely bright star in what seemed like dark, endless night. In 1925, the federal government passed the Kelly Air Mail Act establishing airmail contracts

for specific routes. It gave airline companies a much-needed source of income spurring several Florida corporations into action. In 1926, the Florida Airways Corporation founded by World War I air ace Eddie Rickenbacker received the airmail contract between Miami, Tampa and Jacksonville. The lack of passengers, however, coupled with the dearth of mail, killed Florida Airways within a few months.

In Key West, Juan Terry Trippe's Pan American Airways received the first foreign mail contract between Key West and Havana. On October 28, 1927, Pan Am's Fokker trimotor F-7, the "General Machado," opened regular service between the two cities. Soon after its inaugural flight, Pan Am moved its headquarters to Miami. Trippe purchased 116 acres of reclaimed Everglades land (at N.W. 36th Street and LeJeune Road) and built Pan American Field. Between 1928 and 1930, the airline added many Latin cities to its Caribbean network, making Miami the "Gateway to the Americas."

In 1928, Harold Pitcairn picked up the remains of Florida Airways, renamed it Pitcairn Airways and hired Eddie Rickenbacker to help run it. In 1930, the airline—renamed Eastern—began the first passenger service from Miami to points north. Miami's aviation history took another giant leap forward after the Greater Miami Air Association, a group of local air enthusiasts, convinced Glenn Curtiss to give his 160-acre field at N.W. 112th Street and 42nd Avenue to the city for a municipal airport. The Air Association promoted the All American Air Maneuvers that opened in January 1929. Aviation luminaries such as Amelia Earhart and Charles Lindberg brought 5,000 people to the municipal airport to witness the "Olympics of Aviation." (In July 1937, Amelia Earhart took off from the Miami airport on her ill-fated, around-the-world flight. After her disappearance, the airport was renamed Amelia Earhart Field in her honor.)

Even surprisingly good tourist seasons could not cure all of Miami's problems. Dade County schools faced huge deficits and teachers received only partial salaries. Miami and Coral Gables defaulted on their bonds. Many people lost their homes at tax sales on the steps of the impressive new courthouse that opened in 1928. Property values fell so drastically that a person could buy a house as cheaply as a Ford V-8, but few had money for either.

Volunteers from the Dade County Welfare Board launched a campaign to collect "a penny a day to keep hunger away from somebody out of a job." The city opened a camp in Opa-locka that provided room and board for unemployed men willing to work 30 hours for 90 cents. When the camp filled, the sheriff sent unemployed transients away on the "hobo express"—a plan for each county sheriff to pass vagrants from one county to the next until they reached the state line.

■ *Amelia Earhart, third from right, nicknamed "Lady Lindy" because of her achievements comparable to those of Charles Lindbergh, left Miami in her twin-engine red-winged Electra on June 1, 1937 for her ill-fated around-the-world trip. Her disappearance over the Pacific Ocean remains a mystery today. (HMSF)*

THE GATEWAY TO AMERICA
Time & Time Again

1931

(APC)

2008

© Dan Forer

In 1931, Pan American Airways moved from their 36th Street facility to Dinner Key and completed what some described as the largest and most modern seaplane terminal in the world. Designed by Delano and Aldrich, the Streamline Moderne building has been Miami City Hall since 1954. Although many of the original features are gone, the commission chambers underwent an extensive restoration under the supervision of preservation architect Richard Heisenbottle.

The airline also constructed three large hangars nearby that served as maintenance and storage facilities for their "Flying Clippers." Today, they house marine facilities and a Fresh Market.

"My Friends and Enemies…"

When the presidential election of November 1932 rolled around, people flocked to the polls and voted for change. Democrat Franklin Delano Roosevelt and his "New Deal" won in a landslide. A few weeks prior to his March 1933 inauguration, President Roosevelt vacationed in South Florida on the yacht of his friend Vincent Astor. At the end of the 12-day cruise, the yacht docked at Miami's Pier 1 to allow Roosevelt to disembark and catch a train for New York.

On the evening of February 15, 1933, 18,000 Miamians assembled to greet the president-elect who stopped at the Bayfront Park band shell on the way to the train station. At 9:15, Roosevelt and Miami Mayor R.B. Gautier entered a Buick convertible and headed down Biscayne Boulevard toward Bayfront Park. To give the crowd a better view, the Secret Service lifted the president-elect to the top of the back seat. Arriving at the park, the president, tanned, relaxed and smiling his famous grin, waved to the crowd and began his speech from the open convertible.

"Thank you, Mr. Mayor, my friends and enemies," he began. Unnoticed in the fourth row was Guiseppe Zangara, an unemployed Italian bricklayer with a hatred for wealth and authority. Because Zangara was barely over five feet tall, he climbed up on the bench to see over the crowd. As he stepped forward, the bench wobbled, startling Lillian Cross,

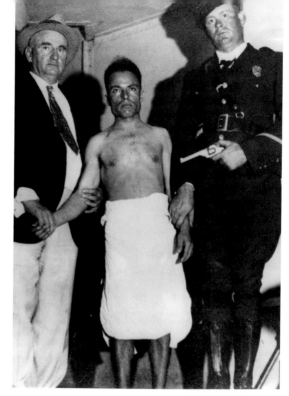

A CLOSE CALL: President-elect Franklin Delano Roosevelt (bottom left) came to Miami for a vacation just a few weeks before his March 1933 inauguration. On February 15, while addressing a rally of 18,000 Miamians in Bayfront Park, Guiseppe Zangara attempted to assassinate him. Vigilant spectators foiled the presidential assassination but Zangara mortally wounded Chicago Mayor Anton Cermak and hit four others. (APC)

The unrepentant Zangara posed with his captors at the Dade County jail (left). (MN)

a tiny, bespectacled 48-year-old woman who was already standing on it. "Don't do that," she cried, "you're knocking me off." Ignoring her remark, Zangara reached into his pocket, pulled out and raised an $8 pistol he purchased from a Miami Avenue pawnshop. "Here, young man," she screamed, "what are you doing with that gun? Put it down!" Just as she spoke, Zangara pulled the trigger and a shot rang out. Instinctively, Lillian Cross grabbed for Zangara's wrist and tried to push up his hand as he fired four more times.

The first bullet hit Mabel Gill, wife of the president of Florida Power and Light, who was sitting on the band shell platform. She screamed, grabbed her chest and fell to the ground. Seconds later, Miami chauffeur Russell Caldwell, who was sitting in the row behind Zangara and 30 feet to his left, clutched his forehead and fell backward, blood pouring down his face. (The almost-spent bullet lodged in his skull.) Nearby, Margaret Kruis, a visiting showgirl, lay semiconscious on the ground; the third bullet pierced her hat and grazed the back of her head. Bill Sinnott, a vacationing New York police detective pressed into service at the last minute to help guard Roosevelt, was the fourth to fall with a bullet wound in his forehead. The fifth shot hit Chicago Mayor Anton Cermak who was standing only a foot from Roosevelt. The bullet entered just under Cermak's right armpit and lodged in his lung.

Miami policeman Fitzhugh Lee, who was Roosevelt's chauffeur for the night, started the car's engine and had the car moving before the last shot. The Secret Service gathered around Roosevelt as one agent shouted to Lee, "Get the hell out of here!" When the car lurched forward, Roosevelt screamed, "Stop!" and demanded that the Secret Service put Cermak in the car next to him. As the president-elect tried to reassure his fallen friend, the car raced Cermak to Jackson Memorial Hospital.

Meanwhile, Zangara had been subdued, his clothes almost ripped off, and his gun taken away. Someone yelled, "Kill him! Kill him!" as the police opened a path through the angry crowd. They dragged Zangara to a nearby car that contained several men, including Vincent Astor and the wounded Russell Caldwell. Because the car interior was full, the police threw Zangara on the luggage rack and sat on top of him.

With Zangara prostrate on the back of the car, the police drove Caldwell to the hospital before they took Zangara to jail.

Justice was swift. Within a week, a jury indicted, tried and convicted Zangara of attempted murder and gave him the maximum sentence—80 years in prison. On March 6, Cermak, expected to recover, died from pneumonia and gangrene. The other victims survived. Another jury immediately indicted Zangara for murder. Two days later, he was tried and convicted. There were no appeals and no psychiatric examination. Before Judge Uly O. Thompson pronounced the death sentence, he spoke out for gun control legislation. Thirty-three days after Zangara almost changed the course of history, the unrepentant assassin died in the electric chair at Raiford State Prison.

HISTORY REVEALED
Time & Time Again

1933

Criminal Court of Record Judge Ernest Clyde Collins (center) presided over the first Zangara trial for attempted murder for which he received a sentence of 84 years. A short time later, when Mayor Cermak died, Zangara was charged with murder, found guilty and executed on March 20, 1933. *(HMSF)*

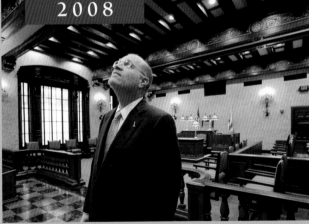

2008

Courtroom 6-1, the site of the Zangara trial, is Miami's most historic courtroom. But its elegant ambiance suffered from years of unsympathetic remodeling. Miami-Dade Circuit Judge Scott Silverman, above, led the effort to return the once-beautiful courtroom to its original grandeur. Silverman also helped found and heads the new 11th Judicial Circuit Historical Society. *(SS)*

An Alphabet Soup of Agencies

On March 4, 1933, Franklin Delano Roosevelt became president of the United States. As soon as the inauguration ceremonies ended, he proclaimed a bank holiday and set his aggressive New Deal into motion. Miami benefited almost immediately from what people called the New Deal's "alphabet soup agencies," instituted to get the economy moving. After the government released FERA (Federal Emergency Relief Agency) funds to aid the unemployed, 16,000 Miamians received assistance.

Community leaders encouraged the government to establish a CCC (Civilian Conservation Corps) camp in Miami. (The CCC enrolled young, unemployed single men to work in the nation's parks.) In Miami, the CCC boys, under the direction of landscape architect William Lyman Phillips, went to work at Matheson Hammock that William J. Matheson had recently given to Dade County. (The county purchased additional acres.) They built rock walls and outbuildings and cleared spots in the hammock for picnickers. They also helped to construct walls and buildings next door at Fairchild Tropical Garden. In North Dade, the CCC transformed A.O. Greynold's former rock pit property (also a gift to Dade County) into Greynolds Park. There, the CCC built rock buildings and wooden bridges across small streams that meandered from Snake Creek (now Oleta River) and bisected the property. To camouflage Greynolds' abandoned, rusted, rock-crushing machinery, the workers covered it with earth and created Miami's only mountain topped with its own rock fortress. These two parks, pushed by County Commissioner Charles Crandon and park director A.D. Barnes, became the nucleus of Dade County's future park system.

Within two years, the PWA (Public Works Administration) also operated in Miami. As a result, Miami acquired many new public buildings including the Miami Beach Post Office, the Miami Shores Golf Club, the Coral Gables Municipal Building, the Coral Gables Woman's Club and Library, an additional Jackson Memorial Hospital building,

■ *President Franklin Delano Roosevelt smiles in a cartoon showing his New Deal "alphabet soup" agencies that he created to help the nation out of the Great Depression. (APC)*

THE FAIRCHILD TROPICAL GARDEN

COCONUT GROVE, FLA.

PLAN

SHOWING THE PROPOSED DISPOSITION OF MASSES
ROADS, WALKS, BUILDINGS, LAKES AND VISTAS.

WILLIAM LYMAN PHILLIPS
LANDSCAPE ARCHITECT
NOEL CHAMBERLIN
LANDSCAPE ARCHITECT, CONSULTING

■ South Florida benefited from the Civilian Conservation Corps (CCC) that hired young, unemployed men to work in state, local and federal parks. Under the leadership of A.D. Barnes and William Lyman Phillips, the CCC built Greynolds and Matheson Hammock Parks and the lodge at Royal Palm State Park. They also built the limestone wall, pergola, gatekeepers' lodge, overlook and amphitheater at Fairchild Tropical Garden. (MM)

■ George E. Merrick and his wife, Eunice, center, celebrate the 1938 public opening of Fairchild Tropical Garden. (MM)

■ Roosevelt's Public Works Administration (PWA) was also active in South Florida. It constructed many notable public buildings, including (right) Coral Way Elementary (NA) and Miami Shores Elementary (left). (LM)

Shenandoah Junior High School, and North Beach and Coral Way Elementary Schools. Besides creating impressive new buildings, this unprecedented program gave jobs to thousands of unemployed construction workers.

The PWA also built Liberty Square, Florida's first public housing project. Father John Culmer and the Negro Civic League spurred the project by convincing *Miami Herald* editor Frank Stoneman to do a series on the plight of local black families. When Liberty Square opened in 1937 with James E. Scott as administrator, it was touted as one of the finest black communities in America. The PWA did a similar project for white residents called Edison Courts.

Another important agency, the WPA (Works Progress Administration), hired unemployed artists and writers. Artists created beautiful murals and sculptures for public buildings and taught art to needy children. Writers prepared a *Guide to Miami and Environs* and unemployed actors and musicians joined the federal theater and federal music projects.

■ The PWA also built Liberty Square (above). It was Florida's first public housing project. Father John Culmer led the effort to provide affordable housing for Miami's African-American community. Liberty Square underwent extensive renovation in the 1990s. (BA)

■ Liberty Square prompted the development of Liberty City, which Alonzo "Pop" Kelly (left) had acquired years earlier. When Liberty Square opened, many families who had previously lived in Overtown moved to the new subdivision. (BA)

The Farm Security Administration (FSA), headed by Roy Stryker, hired photographers to document the desperation of Americans and the help of the New Deal agencies during the Depression. Photographer Marion Post Walcott came to South Florida and captured not only the poor, but also the so-called "idle rich" who passed through the era somewhat unscathed. Her pictures spoke for themselves.

The government sent unemployed World War I veterans to the Keys to work on the new Overseas Highway. On Labor Day 1935, the strongest hurricane ever to hit Florida struck the Keys and caught the veterans, who were living in tents, unaware. An incredible tidal wave washed more than 400 workers to a watery death and swept the rescue train from Miami off its tracks. Despite this tragic setback, the new highway to Key West opened for traffic in 1938.

The hurricane also obliterated George and Eunice Merrick's Caribee Lodge on Upper Matecumbe Key. Once again, George Merrick faced unexpected disaster.

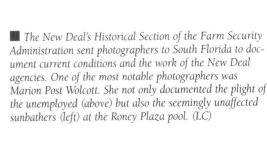

■ *The New Deal's Historical Section of the Farm Security Administration sent photographers to South Florida to document current conditions and the work of the New Deal agencies. One of the most notable photographers was Marion Post Wolcott. She not only documented the plight of the unemployed (above) but also the seemingly unaffected sunbathers (left) at the Roney Plaza pool. (LC)*

CELEBRATING CIVIC ARTS
Time & Time Again

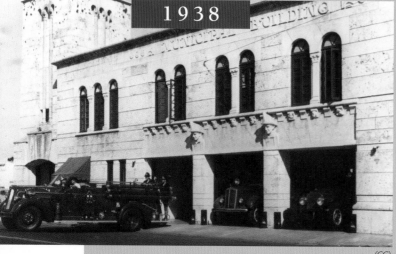

1938

In 1938, the Public Works Administration built a new municipal building for the City of Coral Gables. It served as courthouse, jail, police and fire station until 1973. Designed by Phineas Paist and Harold Steward and built of oolithic limestone, the building also included relief and sculpture by Works Progress Administration artist Jon Keller. In 1977, when the city manager proposed removing the sculpture and filling in the fire engine bay, the City of Coral Gables Preservation Board led the successful effort to preserve the building's unique features and historic integrity. Today, the former municipal building is home to the new Coral Gables Museum and is undergoing restoration under the supervision of architect Jorge L. Hernandez.

(CG)

2007

2008

City officials and administration join Coral Gables Museum board members, architects and contractors to celebrate the beginning of the restoration of the Old Police and Fire Station. (JS)

(APC)

ORANGES TAKE THE DAY

Although Florida entered the Great Depression before the rest of the nation, by the mid-1930s, as the rest of the nation continued to suffer, Miami showed signs of recovery. "If one were to judge Florida by the appearance of Miami," reported a writer for *The Nation*, "one would have to say the Depression is over."

The harbinger of the city's resurrection was an increase in tourists. Pan American Airways, which took over the New York Rio and Buenos Aires operation at Dinner Key, moved its operation there from its 36th Street Airport making Miami the jumping-off place for international flights. Pan Am's "Flying Clippers" brought in thousands of Latin tourists. A writer for the *Miami Daily News* noted, "The little signs in store windows *Aqui se Habla Espanol* are proof that Miami has come to the front as a cosmopolitan city and gateway to Latin America."

Eastern Airlines, which took over Pan Am's 36th Street field, accommodated large numbers of Northern tourists. Two newer airlines—National and Delta—also grew along with Miami. But the airlines could not compete with the new streamlined diesel trains—still the most popular mode of travel in and out of the city.

Miami's Orange Bowl Festival became another important tourist attraction. For years, the city tried to create a special winter event, from the 1915 Magic Knights of Dade Festival to the 1920s Palm Fete (later Palm Festival) and Festival of the American Tropics. In 1933, Palm Fete boosters convinced Colonel Henry L. Doherty to put up $3,000 to finance "The First Annual New Year's Day Football Classic" at Moore Park between the University of Miami and Manhattan College. The following year, the University of Miami met Bucknell University in a New Year's Day game held at the site of the future Orange Bowl Stadium. (The Tatum brothers built Miami's baseball stadium nearby in 1916.)

The Orange Bowl in Miami, Florida   31

■ *The first Orange Bowl Parade (top) passed by the Dade County Courthouse on New Year's Eve day, 1936. (MN)*

■ *In 1935, the first Orange Bowl game was held at the site of the Orange Bowl Stadium, demolished in 2008. Fans sat on secondhand bleachers left over from the American Legion convention parade. In 1937, the PWA built a new 25,000-seat stadium that sports writers considered one of the best in the country (above). (APC)*

The **HURRICANE GRIDIRON**

The First Annual
ORANGE BOWL TOURNAMENT

Dedication of
MIAMI STADIUM
New Years Day

UNIVERSITY of MIAMI vs. BUCKNELL UNIVERSITY

2:30 *p. m.* ★ ★ ★ ★ ★ ★ ★ ★ ★ **10** *cents*

Lyrics by LEO ROBIN • Music by RALPH RAINGER

MIAMI

Don
AMECHE
Betty
GRABLE
in

MOON OVER MIAMI

A 20th Century-Fox Picture with
ROBERT CUMMINGS
CHARLOTTE GREENWOOD
JACK HALEY • Carole LANDIS
Directed by Walter Lang
Associate Producer Harry Joe Brown
Photographed in TECHNICOLOR

(APC)

"MOON OVER MIAMI"

*I*n 1936, the whole nation was singing about Miami—"Moon Over Miami" was number one on the Hit Parade. Burdines Department Store designed a special "Moon Over Miami" fabric, and before long, half the town was not only singing "Moon Over Miami" but also wearing it. In 1942, Miamians swooned when movie pin-up girl Betty Grable starred in a movie with the same title.

(MN)

The 1934 football stadium consisted of a roughed-out playing field and secondhand bleachers, purchased from the 1933 American Legion convention held in Miami.) The Palm Festival became the Orange Festival in 1934 with the Orange Bowl Football Classic as its main event.

The Orange Festival added the first downtown Orange Bowl Parade on New Year's Eve day 1936. Three years later, the PWA built the 25,000-seat Roddy Burdine Stadium giving the Orange Bowl a permanent home. Thus, in the middle of the Great Depression, Miami created its most enduring winter event.

SHIFTING GEARS

In Miami Beach, the construction of more than 100 hotels and apartment buildings accelerated the road to recovery. In contrast to boomtime buildings, however, most of the new structures had stark "moderne" lines. Unfortunately, beneath the façade, a strong wave of anti-Semitism emerged. Miami Beach had a long history of anti-Jewish sentiment. From the beginning, Carl Fisher and John Collins restricted their part of the beach. Through the years, however, deed covenants became difficult to enforce and Depression-weary sellers cared little about a person's religion. As a result, Jews moved in north of 14th Street, the old line of demarcation.

In the late 1930s, the arrival of a large number of Jews to South Beach created a fierce anti-Semitic backlash. "Restricted" and "Gentiles Only" signs appeared in hotel and apartment lobbies. Promotional brochures blatantly proclaimed "No Jews Allowed." Ironically, South Florida's new wave of anti-Semitism reached its height at the same time Adolf Hitler rose to power in Germany.

After Hitler invaded Poland in September 1939, war broke out in Europe. As the 1940s began, however, few consciously admitted that the United States would be drawn into the conflict. But before 1940 ended, the reality of war touched Miami. The Bahamas—only 45 miles off Miami's shores—was an English colony already at war with Germany.

The new Bahamian governor was the Duke of Windsor who had charmed the world when he gave up the British crown for the woman he loved. He and his wife made frequent trips to Miami to promote England's war efforts. In late 1940, a group of Royal Air Force pilots came to the city for training at the University of Miami and with Pan American Airways. Spurred by the need to train aviators for the war, Paul Riddle took over the old unfinished Fritz Hotel that stood as the last reminder of the bust and transformed it into Embry-Riddle Aviation School.

On Sunday, December 7, 1941, *The Miami Herald* wrote optimistically about the coming season. "We've crossed our fingers," the lead column read, "and donned rose-colored glasses today as the curtain goes up for the best tourist season in history." The rose-colored glasses shattered at 2 p.m. when an announcer broke into the scheduled radio program to report that the Japanese had attacked Pearl Harbor. As the news spread throughout South Florida, crowds gathered at Flagler Street and Miami Avenue under the pine boughs and brightly colored

Christmas balls and lights (made in Japan). Before the day ended, the Dade County Defense Council organized and soldiers with fixed bayonets patrolled the waterfront.

The following day, throngs of enlistees swamped the military recruiting offices. John Pennekamp, editor of *The Miami Herald*, noted the change in attitude and wrote, "Grimly, earnestly and willingly, Miami assumed the mantle of a community at war."

After the initial fear of invasion passed, life seemed to return to normal. The Orange Bowl Festival took place as planned although parade floats quickly changed to pro-war themes like "Remember Pearl Harbor." As the tourist season progressed, however, war visibly affected Miami's sun-and-fun economy. To make matters worse, in February, German submarines torpedoed a tanker in full view of Florida shores, sending remaining tourists scurrying for safer ground.

Fear, patriotism and empty hotels spurred Miamians into action. If the government would make Miami and Miami Beach major training centers, they reasoned, South Florida could be saved from another depression. The government did not need much convincing. Miami Beach's famed hotel row was a perfect place to house military personnel because the area's year-round temperate climate was conducive to rapid training.

■ *In 1942, burning tankers were a common sight in the Florida Straits as Hitler's undersea raiders grew bolder and bolder. (NA)*

In April 1941, the U.S. Army invaded Miami Beach and soldiers replaced swank in 70,000 Miami Beach hotel rooms. More than 150 hotels metamorphosed into barracks for the Army Air Forces officer's candidate school, an officers training school and a basic training center. Before the war ended, one-fourth of the Army Air Force officers and one-fifth of the enlisted men trained at Miami Beach.

The tourist-oriented city made a remarkably smooth transition from a fun destination to a war camp. The men flooded the streets and traffic halted while endless parades of singing soldiers marched by. Golf courses turned into drill fields. Fancy restaurants and clubs became mess halls. Military classes opened in churches and synagogues.

The officers trained in three months of 16.5-hour days. Many of the so-called 90-day wonders were celebrities, including movie stars Robert Preston and Gilbert Roland. None, however, could compare to Clark Gable, the country's hottest matinee idol. Word quickly spread every time someone sighted Clark Gable and women lined the streets just to get a glimpse of him.

SUBMARINES OFF THE COAST

Early in 1942, the headquarters for the Navy's Gulf Sea Frontier moved from Key West to Miami. The Navy command took over two entire floors of the city's only post-boom skyscraper, the Alfred I. Dupont Building, which they dubbed the U.S.S. Neversink.

With most American ships tied up in the Pacific, German submarines practically took over the Florida Straits, Gulf Coast and Caribbean. In 1942 alone, the Germans torpedoed more than 25 tankers between Cape Canaveral and Key West—four in full view of Miami residents. Even though the Navy tried to conceal the submarine activity off Florida, they could not hide burning tankers. Sometimes pleasure boaters rescued sailors from burning ships and brought them to safety. Everyone feared the Germans would fire on Miami Beach. When oil and flotsam floated onto the beaches, a cold shiver went up the community spine. (No one complained of environmental pollution.) Rumors of German sailors walking freely through Miami added to the scare.

136—Officers of the Army Air Forces Technical Training Command, showing their Hotel Quarters in Background, Miami Beach, Fla.

■ WORLD WAR II: During the war, thousands of Army Air Force men transformed a former sunbather's domain into a training camp. (LW)

■ The Navy built the world's largest wooden hangar (facing page) to house blimps at Richmond Field, now the site of Miami Metrozoo. (MN)

THE KING OF HOLLYWOOD

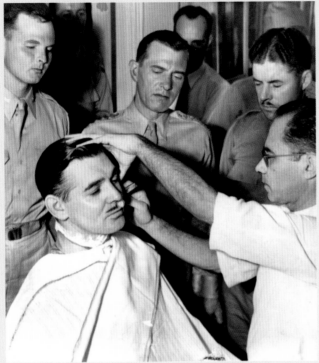

Clark Gable (MN)

In August 1942, movie idol Clark Gable, known as the "King of Hollywood," arrived in Miami Beach for Army Air Forces officer's candidate school. Grieving from the loss of his wife, movie star Carole Lombard, who died in a tragic airplane crash while on war bond tour, Private Gable moved into the Collins Park Hotel with other recruits. Although he determined to be a regular soldier, fans watched his every move including the fateful day when he had to shave off his legendary mustache. Gable received his commission on October 28, 1942 and gave the commencement speech. After attending gunnery school, he went to England and saw action with the Eighth Air Force 351st Bombardier Group. He also made a documentary Air Force film, Combat America, to help recruit others to the cause.

A huge map of what the Navy called the Gulf Sea Frontier hung between the Dupont Building's eighth and ninth floors. (The ceiling had been removed to make one huge space.) The map told the story of sightings, sinkings and patrols. By 1943, the chart revealed that the Navy had driven most of the German submarines away from Florida coasts.

One reason for the Navy's effectiveness was the opening of the sub-chaser school (dubbed the "Donald Duck Navy") at the Port of Miami. More than 50,000 Navy recruits trained in classrooms along the waterfront and then climbed into PT boats to chase real German submarines offshore. Navy personnel bunked in Miami hotels. Barricaded Biscayne Boulevard parking islands became the drill fields for thousands of sailors.

Besides the sub-chaser school, the Navy had another weapon against the German submarines. At Richmond Field in South Dade (the site of Metrozoo), the Navy built the world's largest wooden hangar to house blimps. During one blimp patrol off Miami, a German submarine surfaced and shot the blimp down as a number of local anglers watched in horror.

The Army Air Force Transport Command took over the 36th Street Airport and a new air base at Homestead. The base at 36th Street became the terminus of the Caribbean division and beginning of the "Fireball Run" to India and China. Miami was also a supply center for other domestic military bases. Local aviation industry personnel became an adjunct of the military by training personnel and flying for the Air Transport Command.

D. C. 135—"Off to Study," Army Air Force
Technical Training Command,
Miami Beach, Fla.

▓ Army Air Force officer candidates, with book in
hands, march by Miami Beach's famous hotel row
(left). (APC)

▓ Distraught wives bid their Navy husbands goodbye
at the Port of Miami (below), which was turned into a
Navy training center. (NA)

▓ Future Army Air Force pilots learned the basics at
Miami Beach's officer training school (facing page top).
(NA)

World War II

10 CENT

DEFENSE STAMP ALBUM

For the purchase of

UNITED STATES DEFENSE SAVINGS BONDS

10¢ STAMPS $25 BONDS

■ To help do their part, Miamians held War Bond drives and schoolchildren filled Defense Stamp Albums (bottom left). (APC)

■ At war's end, General Dwight David Eisenhower visited the wounded at the Army Air Force Regional Hospital No. 1, formerly the Biltmore Hotel (below). (SDL)

WE'RE BUYING AT LEAST 10 4TH WAR LOAN DRIVE Miami Airwood

WORLD WAR II ON MIAMI BEACH

At age 18, having volunteered for Army Air Corps Aviation Cadet training, I reported for active duty in summer 1943, to Air Corps Basic Training Center, Miami Beach, Florida. With great excitement, I arrived Miami by train, where we were greeted by Air Corps drill sergeants and loaded aboard Army trucks. As we passed over MacArthur Causeway, I was enthralled by the blue-green water of the bay and the islands with colorful houses.

Arriving South Beach, we put on uniforms and were billeted in a hotel on Ocean Drive and 3rd Street. We drilled on the closed-off streets, we sang while marching, did physical training on converted golf courses, and trained as Air Cadets. We were young, patriotic, excited at the prospect of flying, and we were surrounded by beautiful Miami, which was to us a tropical paradise.

Hugh MacRae II

■ *Miami's women organized clubs to help the service members. First Lady Eleanor Roosevelt, in the white hat, visited the servicemen's club in Overtown.* (BA)

The Army took over several South Florida luxury hotels and turned them into hospitals. At the end of the war, all the hotels, except the Miami-Biltmore, returned to civilian use. The Biltmore remained Pratt General Veterans Hospital until the VA built a new facility in 1968.

The U.S. government sent hundreds of German prisoners of war to Miami for incarceration. German prisoners from POW camps in Kendall, a former CCC camp, and in Homestead repaired streets and did other menial community jobs. When the war ended, Miamians learned that more than 25 prisoners had escaped undetected.

The overwhelming military presence and the German submarine menace galvanized Miamians behind the war effort. A group of Miami Beach women organized the Servicemen's Pier on South Beach to give servicemen a place to relax. Before the war ended, more than four million personnel visited the Servicemen's Pier. Other civic groups opened similar facilities. The City of Miami built a structure at the north end of Bayfront Park for servicemen's activities. Because black soldiers could not go to the white clubs, the black community opened a club of their own in Overtown.

Filled with patriotism, residents raised millions of dollars in War Bonds and on 161 Saturdays, the city held "Victory Parades" down Flagler Street. With the slogan, "Slap the Japs with Your Scrap," workers collected all types of scrap metal from flattened tin cans to a bronze pirate cannon. With great fanfare, the city donated its first steam fire engine, "The Dan Hardie," to the cause, along with the old bronze fire bell. Miami Beach threw in the World War I cannon that formerly sat on the front lawn of its City Hall.

Citizens met "blackouts" and "dim-outs" with enthusiasm. Defense leaders promoted the slogan, "Kill the Lume," to lessen the probability of submarine attack. Everyone painted automobile headlights and streetlights half-black and turned off illuminated signs. Within a year of Pearl Harbor, one out of every 14 Miamians went to war. Women took over many previously all-male jobs to keep the city functioning. By war's end, more than 18,000 Miami women held full-time war-related jobs.

Rationing was in full effect as early as 1942. Schools closed at 1 p.m. and teachers handed out ration books for sugar, butter, meat and certain canned goods. Automobiles bore "A," "B" and "C" stickers, each designating a certain weekly gas allotment. The average homeowner had an "A" sticker for only 1.5 gallons of gas per week. The government also banned all nonessential driving. As a result, cities canceled public activities and social life revolved around neighborhoods.

The military even cleaned up Miami's rackets. Strict curfews regulated nightspots. The Military Police closed houses of prostitution and shut down illegal gambling clubs. The posh bayfront Royal Palm Club became Coast Guard headquarters.

As the war effort geared up, it became clear that the nation's war economy brought the country out of the Depression. Citizens with full pockets looked for ways to spend their money and tourists started returning. The new influx caused some hotel owners to lobby for return of their properties to civilian use. This so-called profiteering caused South Florida a great deal of bad press.

The national press also criticized Miami for its treatment of black soldiers. In May 1945, Otis Munday led a group of blacks to Baker's Haulover Beach to challenge the strict segregation rule, which prohibited black swimmers. (At that time, no place in Miami or Miami Beach allowed blacks to swim.) Three months later, the county opened a "Colored Only" beach at Virginia Key—although the only way to get there was by boat. (Construction of the causeway to Key Biscayne, started before the war, but stopped when war broke out.) A ferry transported black bathers to Virginia Key from a dock on the Miami River at N.W. Fifth Street. Despite its inaccessibility, Virginia Key Beach was popular with the black community.

In May 1945, Miamians celebrated V-E Day (Victory in Europe) amid ongoing and increasingly intense conflict with Japan. On the morning of August 6, 1945,

an American B-29 commanded by Miamian Paul Tibbits took off from the Marshall Islands. The plane, named the Enola Gay (after the pilot's mother who was living in Miami), headed for Hiroshima, Japan and a rendezvous with history. At 8:15 a.m., the Enola Gay released an atomic bomb. Within seconds, it destroyed a city, sealed Japan's fate and ushered in a frightening new age. Three days later, another American bomber dropped an atomic bomb on Nagasaki, Japan. Finally, on August 14, within an hour of President Truman's announcement that Japan had surrendered, 30,000 Miamians descended on Flagler Street to celebrate the peace. The war was over and Miami's warriors would soon be coming home— except for the 515 who gave their life for their country.

■ *In 1945, black leaders succeeded in securing a "Colored Only" beach on Virginia Key (above). For the first time, black Miamians had a place to swim. (BA)*

■ *A group of sailors (below) cheers the end of the war at a jubilant celebration on Flagler Street attended by more than 30,000 people. (MN)*

■ *During the 1940s and 1950s, Miami's promotional department used bathing beauties to sell the city to Northern tourists seeking "Fun in the Sun." (APC)*

Chapter Eight

Getting Ready

"Get ready Miami, the world is coming your way"

The Miami Herald
December 20, 1942

World War II changed Miami as much as any other event in its history. Even before it ended, people sensed the beginning of a new era. In 1942, a *Miami Herald* writer predicted, "political, economic and geographical factors slowly are swinging Miami into a position that will make the Indian wars, coming of the railroad, the land boom and even the present military cauldron look like a quiet Sunday afternoon on a Swiss Alp."

When the war began, Miami had just begun shaking off the small-town atmosphere that had returned at the end of the Boom. Of the 268,000 people living in Dade County, 63 percent resided within the Miami city limits. The boondocks began west of Red Road and north of 125th Street. Downtown Miami remained the center of everything. Almost every religious denomination had a large downtown facility. The after-church crowd caught up on the latest gossip while waiting in line at the M&M and Polly Davis cafeterias. Every Saturday, teenagers from the three major high schools, all within the city limits, congregated under the clock at Burdines Department Store.

Burdines Tea Room was a popular gathering place for shoppers and "ladies who lunched." Parents rewarded good little children with the tea room's most popular item, the Snow Princess—a delicious concoction of ice cream covered with whipped cream and silver balls and topped with a Madame Pompadour china doll. Children also flocked to Bayfront Park to feed the pigeons and watch the charter fishing boats coming in to Pier 5. Riding the ponies at N.E. 15th Street and Biscayne Boulevard, a visit to Policeman's Park or a trip on the Island Queen to the Musa Isle Indian Village were favorite childhood excursions. Nothing was as exciting as the Olympia Theater, which had a vaudeville show in addition to regular movies. Lucky spectators would often be asked on stage to join the performers—hold a stick for a jumping dog, be a foil for the magician or try to out-sing, out-whistle or out-dance the paid performers. (One performer was a young, unknown, stand-up comic named Jackie Gleason.)

■ *Pier 5 on Miami's bayfront was a popular gathering place. (LW)*

DREAMS COME TRUE: In 1946, the University of Miami was finally able to return to its original campus in an area of Coral Gables that was still mostly undeveloped (above). (UM) Three years later, architects Robert Law Weed and Marion I. Manley transformed the "skeleton" of Merrick's original Mediterranean confection into the sleek modern Merrick Building (right). (APC)

A LAW AND HOME FOR ALL

The Miami that Johnny came marching home to in late 1945 and early 1946 was different from the Miami he left to go to war. No longer did he call everyone on Flagler Street by their first names. Ten strangers followed every familiar face. Even though the city might have looked almost the same, its people and its image of itself had changed dramatically. The hopeful 1896 prediction that Miami was the "coming metropolis" was actually coming true. It was coming true because Johnny and Jane did not come marching home alone. Thousands of young men and women who trained in South Florida during the war discovered what locals called "sand in their shoes" and decided to stake their future with the Magic City. South Florida's population soared. Between 1940 and 1950, it nearly doubled, and then it almost doubled again the next decade.

The GI Bill of Rights caused one of the greatest social changes in the nation's history. The bill—passed to help veterans settle down after the war—actually helped them to settle upward. Every returning veteran now had a rich "Uncle Sam" willing to finance a college education, a new business or a new home.

While the postwar woman donned the "new look" with lower hemlines, wasp waists and full skirts, Miami took on a new look all its own. Neat little rows of identical GI houses

appeared in former farmland and pine forests like rows of citrus trees. For no money down, veterans could acquire a piece of South Florida real estate and a boxlike pink, yellow or blue concrete block home. The GIs' newfound educational opportunities transformed the University of Miami into a major educational institution.

After hanging on for 20 years through depression and war, the university had more students apply than they could accommodate. In 1947, the university moved to its vacant main campus, built the Memorial Classroom Building and added other temporary wooden classrooms that were leftover Army barracks acquired from the government. Two years later, UM completed the last boomtime skeleton—the original Merrick Building— that for 20 years had been home to only creeping vines and small creatures.

Petsy Gautier models a dress made from Burdines' custom-made Orange Bowl fabric. (CM)

Several black subdivisions—including Bunche Park in North Dade and Richmond Heights in South Dade—gave thousands of black veterans an alternative to crowded ghetto housing. Blacks also made other important gains within Miami's strictly segregated society. John Milledge became Miami's first black police officer in the "colored district" and the government hired black mail carriers. Dr. Elmer Ward had the honor of being the first black man on a Dade County grand jury. In 1950, the city created an all-black municipal court and appointed a black attorney, L.E. Thomas, judge. For the first time, the city admitted blacks into the Orange Bowl Stadium although they were restricted to the end zone. Once the causeway to Key Biscayne opened in 1947, blacks finally found Virginia Key Beach accessible.

Like the rest of Miami, Overtown's downtown also benefited from the postwar boom. Famous black entertainers like Cab Calloway, Nat King Cole, Billie Holiday and Ella Fitzgerald stayed in Overtown when they came to Miami to perform in white nightclubs. While they were in town, they also performed in black night spots like the Mary Elizabeth Cabaret and the Harlem Square Club.

Overtown was also the scene of several new special events. Because they were all but excluded from Orange Bowl activities, the black community organized its own Coconut Festival. As the Orange Bowl queen led the parade down Biscayne Boulevard, the Coconut Queen led the parade down N.W. Second Avenue. The Coconut Festival also held an all-black football game at Dorsey Park. In 1949, the Coconut Festival became the Orange Blossom Classic. The parade continued down Second Avenue, but the football

game between the Florida A&M University Rattlers and a visiting team was played in the Orange Bowl Stadium. For that one event, blacks were allowed to sit out of the end zone.

In Coconut Grove, Elizabeth Virrick, wife of a prominent architect, joined Christ Church's Father Theodore Gibson to form the Coconut Grove Citizens' Committee for Slum Clearance. This biracial effort—one of the first in Miami's history—forced a referendum that helped clean up the Coconut Grove slums.

THE ENVIRONMENT WINS...
AND LOSES

Amid the whirlwind of activity suddenly overtaking Miami, an incredible number of natural whirlwinds blew into town. Between 1945 and 1950, six hurricanes—the largest number in history—struck or grazed Miami. The first occurred just a month after V-J (Victory in Japan) Day. Although the full force of the hurricane bypassed the city, 150-mph winds hit Richmond Field causing three wooden blimp hangars to burn to the ground in one of the most cataclysmic fires Miami had ever seen.

In the fall of 1947, Miami experienced two more hurricanes only a month apart. Although with minimal winds, both storms were extremely wet. The second one hit October 11 and turned 80 percent of Dade and Broward counties into a lake. Even longtime residents had never seen a harder rain. The Everglades, already brimming over from the September storm, rose up, plunged over its man-made boundaries and spilled like a flood tide into Hialeah, Miami Springs, Opa-locka and the western parts of Miami. Airport runways disappeared underwater. The identical GI homes in subdivisions west of Red Road resembled rows of houseboats in a lake. Water stood two feet deep in the Orange Bowl Stadium. Red Cross workers in motorboats chugged down flooded streets to rescue flood victims. Water moccasins and rattlesnakes, washed out of the Everglades, plagued relief workers.

■ *In 1948, Elizabeth Virrick, wife of a leading Miami architect, organized the Coconut Grove Citizens' Committee for Slum Clearance with Father Theodore Gibson (top right). (EV)*

■ *Between 1945 and 1950, six hurricanes struck South Florida. The 1947 hurricane was particuclarly wet. (right). (HMSF)*

The 1947 hurricane profoundly affected South Florida. County leaders sought federal help for flood control and in 1948, Congress authorized the Army Corps of Engineers to begin a study. The next year, the Corps began a $208 million flood control plan. The plan proposed dredging additional canals with locks and levees. When completed, it would dry up much of the eastern Everglades, creating hundreds of thousands of acres of new habitable land. In the years to come, more than a million people would live on the reclaimed land. The price of the project, however, would be tragically high. Serious problems developed that would threaten South Florida's water supply, the remaining Everglades and the area's unique, subtropical environment.

Two months after the 1947 hurricane set the stage for the new drainage program that would severely alter the Everglades, President Harry S. Truman dedicated the Everglades National Park. It was a victory for a dedicated group of citizens who had tried for 30 years to preserve the natural environment. In 1928, Ernest Coe, a retired landscape architect, became the leader of a long struggle to create a national park. The following year, the Florida Legislature made Coe chairman of a state National Park Commission. Although Coe worked tirelessly, interest lagged through the Depression and the commission eventually died.

One of the Everglades' greatest allies was Florida Governor Spessard Holland. Before he left office in 1945, he convinced Governor-elect Millard Caldwell to continue to push for a national park. The Florida Federation of Women's Clubs gave the state Royal Palm Park and the state offered the federal government all the state-owned wetlands. The state also reduced the size of the original proposal. (Coe had pushed for a two-million-acre park.) But even with reduced acreage, the government still needed to acquire another 400,000 acres of privately owned land to complete the park. *Miami Herald* editor John Pennekamp became a driving force in getting the legislature to put up the $2 million for the land. Once the State of Florida put in its contribution, the federal government moved ahead and the Everglades National Park was born.

■ *EVERGLADES NATIONAL PARK: Miami Herald editor John Pennekamp (above) helped create Everglades National Park and preserve the last of the living Great Florida Reef. (MN)*

■ *When President Harry S. Truman (facing page) dedicated the Everglades National Park on December 6, 1947 he spoke the following…"Here is land, tranquil in its quiet beauty, serving not as the source of water, but as the receiver of it. To its natural abundance we owe the spectacular plant and animal life that distinguishes this place from all others in our country." (MN)*

1944

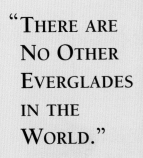

> "THERE ARE
> NO OTHER
> EVERGLADES
> IN THE
> WORLD."
>
> *Marjory Stoneman Douglas*

(RG)

The Everglades:
RIVER OF GRASS

BY

Marjory Stoneman Douglas

ILLUSTRATED BY

Robert Fink

RINEHART & COMPANY, INC.
NEW YORK · TORONTO

In 1945, Miami Mayor Leonard K. Thomson began a push to join the City of Miami and Dade County into a single governmental entity. Although voters rejected the idea, consolidation began in many ways. The county commission, led by Charles Crandon, took over the former municipal sewer board and Jackson Memorial Hospital. The county also created the Dade County Port Authority, which purchased Pan American Field, merged it with the Army Air Transport field and created the present site of Miami International Airport. Dade County schools, which operated in 10 districts, merged into a consolidated county school system. Although consolidated government was a decade away, the handwriting was on the wall. By 1950, only 31 percent of the people in Dade County lived in the City of Miami.

CLOSING THE DOORS

In the late 1940s, Miami began to recover its magic. But part of its magic was more like an evil spell. Miami's longtime, wide-open attitude toward gambling had created a monster. Hoodlums—including the Mafia and Capone gang members — moved into town and quietly took over several locally owned gambling casinos. They gained control of most slot machines in more than 40 private clubs including one on city-owned property. The newly arrived big-time gangsters were masters at paying off public officials and law enforcement officers who either looked the other way or, as one policeman said,

"went fishing." Occasionally, police raided known gambling establishments (usually ones that the mobsters did not control), thus forcing them to join the gang for protection. When police hauled known gamblers into court, punishment was never more than a fine. Still, in 1950 alone, the city figured a half-million dollars in gambling fines into their budget.

Bookmaking created other serious problems, including loss of tax revenue from legitimate parimutuel betting. An inordinate amount of money fell into the hands of illegal operators. The "bookie" kingpin was the S&G Syndicate, with principals Jules Levitt, Samuel P. Cohen, Harold Salvey, Charles Friedman and Eddie Rosenbaum. The S&G Syndicate operated like a legitimate business from a plush

office on Miami Beach. It controlled more than 200 bookies in Miami and Miami Beach who worked openly in almost every Miami Beach hotel. One well-known bookie did business from a newsstand across the street from the Dade County Courthouse.

In 1948, a group of influential citizens who called themselves the "Secret Six" decided to stop Miami's illegal gambling. The group included *Miami Herald* publisher James L. Knight; *Miami Daily News* publisher Dan Mahoney; McGregor Smith, president of Florida Power and Light Company; George Whitten, president of Burdines; John Clark, principal owner of Hialeah Race Track; and Frank Katzentine, owner of radio station WKAT. They hired Daniel P. Sullivan, a former FBI agent, to investigate the burgeoning crime scene. A short time later, the Secret Six merged with a Dade County Bar Association committee and formed the Crime Commission of Greater Miami, headed by Sullivan.

Once the group organized, they put several carefully orchestrated plans into action. *The Herald*, which eventually won a Pulitzer Prize for its campaign, and The *Miami News* began a relentless campaign to expose the people responsible for Miami's illegal gambling activities. Articles named names, including those of corrupt public officials, published gambler's home addresses, divulged the gory details of their previous careers and generally exposed the underside of Miami life. Radio stations WKAT, WQAM, WIOD and WGBS broadcast a program called "The Sinister Plot" that exposed a different gangster each week.

As the heat increased, the Capone gang closed down their casinos and shipped the gambling paraphernalia to Cuba. By this time, many of the gang leaders owned plush hotels, homes and real estate on Miami Beach. The investigation came to a climax in July 1950 after the Crime Commission brought Senate crime fighter Estes Kefauver to Miami to investigate. Many public officials had already been exposed by the newspaper and radio campaign. The exposé revealed that every level of government had been touched by graft and corruption. Even Florida Governor Fuller Warren had accepted an illegal contribution from a known gambler. Before the Senate committee finished its hearings, Dade County Sheriff "Smiling Jimmy" Sullivan and several other public officials were implicated and removed from office.

The Kefauver investigations marked the end of an era. No longer would free-wheeling hoodlums have carte blanche in the city. Although the commission did not totally eradicate organized crime, citizens proved what they could accomplish by working together. For the first time since Miami's founding, residents closed the door on the formerly wide-open city.

One reason Kefauver was so successful was that Miamians watched the hearings on television. Television arrived in March 1949 when Florida's first television station, WTVJ, began broadcasting. Although few Miamians had television sets, half the town turned up at appliance stores to glimpse the new age. To handle the overflow crowds, store owners put sets in their windows so everyone on the sidewalk could see. Even though the first night had several broadcast interruptions and programming lasted only a short time, Miamians—like everyone else in America—fell instantly in love with the exciting new medium. Before long, more antennas than chimneys dotted the skyline.

■ *Ralph Renick, Miami's popular veteran WTVJ news anchorman, began his broadcasting career in 1950 (below). (HMSF)*

ARTHUR GODFREY: AMERICA'S FAVORITE REDHEAD

In the early 1950s, the Arthur Godfrey show was one of the most popular programs on radio and television. At the height of his popularity, with an estimated audience of more than 40 million, Godfrey boasted that he "goes into more homes in America every morning than the milkman." In 1953, publicist Hank Meyer convinced Godfrey to move his television and radio show to Miami Beach. During the first radio and television simulcast transmission from the Kennilworth Hotel in Bal Harbour, Godfrey had the largest audience ever reached over the airways. When asked why he brought his show to Miami Beach, Godfrey quipped, "When I like something I like my friends to enjoy it, too." To honor Godfrey for millions of dollars of free publicity, a grateful Miami Beach City Council renamed 41st Street Arthur Godfrey Road.

During the late 1940s and early 1950s, a new type of national paranoia spread into every part of the country. Old certainties disappeared and peace remained elusive. Deep inside the national psyche was a nagging fear that the Cold War would suddenly turn hot. When the Russians acquired the atomic bomb in 1949, America's feeling of military superiority faded. The growing Communist expansion in Europe and Asia and the wide-eyed ranting of Senator Joseph McCarthy, who announced that the government was crawling with Communists and "fellow travelers," unleashed unprecedented fear and suspicion across America.

Floridians were not immune. In 1950, Miamian George Smathers challenged incumbent U.S. Senator Claude Pepper who had been a staunch supporter of the New Deal. The campaign drew national attention because Smathers' campaign called Senator Pepper "Red Pepper" and pictured him as soft on Communism. In the fervor of the campaign, Smathers questioned Pepper's Americanism and went as far as saying, "the Communist party has found in my opponent a man to suit their evil designs." Only two Florida newspapers backed Pepper. Even *The Miami Herald*, in an editorial supporting Smathers' candidacy, felt the storm of fear. "At a

■ *George Smathers, second from left, celebrated his 1950 Democratic nomination to the U.S. Senate over Claude Pepper. (HMSF)*

time when Communism is the greatest of all threats to our freedom and democracy," the editorialist opined, "it does not make sense to place in a position of power a voice that has defended Stalin, spoken out for fellow travelers and echoed the beliefs of the Communist front organizations." George Smathers swept into office and served until his retirement in 1968. (In 1962, Claude Pepper, who moved to Miami from Tallahassee, won a seat in the U.S. House of Representatives where he served until his death in May 1989.)

The outbreak of the Korean police action in June 1950 only added to the climate of fear and intolerance. Miamians joined hundreds of other young soldiers in the fields of Korea. Before the conflict ended in 1953, 114 died and 30 more remained missing in action.

Before the "Red Scare" passed, those who wanted to maintain the status quo called most dissidents "Communists" or "fellow travelers." Blacks, beginning to press for change, felt the sting worse than most other groups. The NAACP (National Association for the Advancement of Colored People) became especially suspect. Father Theodore Gibson chose jail over giving NAACP membership rolls to the FBI. The court released him and upheld his stand.

In 1951, intolerance turned to violence. Angry segregationists bombed Carver Village, a black housing project in a formerly all-white neighborhood. They also targeted several synagogues whose congregants were sympathetic to the problems of local blacks. The Ku Klux Klan burned a cross on the lawn of Miami Shores Community Church because of the congregation's alleged pro-black stand. But the terrorist actions backfired. "Miami is ashamed, afraid and disgraced," wrote *The Miami Herald*. Citizens organized the first Dade County Council for Human Relations and tried to wrestle with the problems created by 50 years of segregation.

Although the Carver bombings exposed the worst side of Miami, other gains for blacks showed that many people were seriously trying to bring about change. Florida Governor LeRoy Collins, in sharp contrast to most other Southern governors, spoke out saying "segregation is morally wrong."

■ *Dr. John O. Brown, a leading ophthalmologist, was one of the giants of Miami's civil right movement. In the late 1950s, as head of the Miami chapter of the Congress of Racial Equality (CORE), he led the successful effort to integrate downtown lunch counters.* (BA)

■ *The bombing of Carver village in 1951 caused Miamians to form the city's first Human Relations Board.* (MN)

Amid the turmoil brought on by long-overdue change, Dade County made the first-ever commitment to developing Miami's cultural institutions. In 1951, the county opened both the Dade County and Miami Beach Auditoriums—the performing arts centers of the era. For the first time, opera, ballet and classical music had a venue other than high school auditoriums. In 1952, world-renowned contralto Marian Anderson integrated Dade County Auditorium by refusing to sing to a segregated audience.

In 1954, the U.S. Supreme Court's Brown decision outlawed segregation in public schools. Although the white establishment adopted the theory of "gradualism," in 1959 Orchard Villa Elementary and the Homestead Air Force Base Elementary School integrated.

In 1956, Maggie Gorman, with the help of the NAACP, sued to end restricted seating for blacks in buses. A few years later, Dr. John O. Brown, president of CORE (Congress of Racial Equality), led a series of sit-ins which eventually opened all downtown lunch counters and restaurants to people of all races. Besides Gibson and Brown, the Reverend Edward T. Graham, Dr. George Simpson, G.E. Graves, Dr. Ira P. Davis and other black professionals led the integration effort.

S. HUROK

PRESENTS

MARIAN ANDERSON

January 25, 1952   Miami, Florida

■ In 1951, Dade County built not one but two performing arts centers—the Dade County and Miami Beach Auditoriums. Previously, institutions like the symphony, ballet and opera had to perform at Miami High School. In 1952, Marian Anderson integrated Dade County Auditorium when she refused to sing to a segregated audience. (CM)

(CM)

Downtown Miami, 1950 (APC)

(LW)

Seminole Family Group. Tropical Hobbyland. Miami, Fla.

TOURISM 1950s STYLE

The arrival of air-conditioning made South Florida a year-round tourist destination. This spawned a completely new group of tourist attractions geared to the family trade. Although the Parrot and Monkey Jungles had been entertaining locals and visitors for a generation, the addition of the Seaquarium, the Serpentarium, the Rare Bird Farm and the Wax Museum gave Miami new ways to entertain the crowds.

CM

A Full-Fledged Metropolis

By the mid-1950s, Miami's "unincorporated area" had grown dramatically. Most of the new suburbanites were newcomers who poured into South Florida in record-breaking numbers. One farmer commented that his crops had suffered from an "iron problem"—the iron of bulldozers turning former farmlands into subdivisions. In response to the sprawling population, developers built new shopping centers and, for the first time, challenged downtown for the shoppers' dollar.

The phenomenal suburban growth and the rising cost of government once again spurred the effort to create a Dade County metropolitan government. In 1953, after citizens narrowly defeated a city-county consolidation move, the city created the "3M Board" (Metropolitan Miami Municipal), which hired the University of Miami to study the growing cost of government. This study was the basis of the home-rule bill passed by the Florida Legislature, making it possible for Dade County to create a metropolitan form of government if voters approved it.

The battle lines between "centralists" and "pro-city" factions were clearly defined. Both of Miami's major newspapers backed metropolitan government. *Miami Herald* editor John Pennekamp and lawyer Dan Paul became two of the most outspoken proponents for change. The pro-metro forces, led by *The Miami Herald*, had stiff opposition from the municipalities. "Never was an experiment in government, outside of communism or fascism, more bitterly condemned or more stubbornly fought by its enemies," wrote Nixon Smiley in his book *Knights of the Fourth Estate*. In the spring of 1957, the Metro Charter squeaked by with a 1,782-vote margin.

■ In 1956, the Florida Legislature created the new Metropolitan Charter Board (top) with members appointed by the governor. This board and their attorney, Dan Paul, prepared the charter that went to the Dade County voters in May 1957. Following a close election, Metro government began two months later. (CM)

■ Downtown, with Flagler Street as its center (above), remained the hub of business and commerce. (APC)

Miami goes Modern

Eden Roc (LW)

Fontainebleau

Americana (LW)

Fontainebleau (LW)

bal harbour / miami beach
THE HOTEL OF ★ THE AMERICAS
americana
OCEANFRONT AT 98th STREET.

americana

MORRIS LAPIDUS: "TOO MUCH IS NEVER ENOUGH"

With the opening of Miami Beach's Fontaine-bleau Hotel in December 1954, Morris Lapidus (below), the controversial former New York store designer, hit the big time. Although barely mentioned during the construction, the Fontainebleau eventually made him a headliner. Critics lined up to lambaste what he called his signature "woggles and cheese holes" lobby design. Despite mixed reviews, within three years, Lapidus redefined the Miami Beach luxury hotel market with the addition of the Eden Roc and the Americana. He also redesigned Miami Beach's Lincoln Road into a pedestrian mall. Lapidus outlived most of his critics and before his death in 2001 at age 98, his contribution was not only appreciated but honored. In 2007, the Fontainebleau closed and underwent a multimillion-dollar restoration for a 2008 re-opening. Ironically, the Americana, later renamed the Sheraton Bal Harbour, was torn down in early 2008 at the same time mid-century Miami Modern architecture (MiMo) received historic status and renewed appreciation.

(HMSF)

l -- Main Lobby

The early years of metropolitan government were stormy. Those who wanted to weaken Metro's new powers forced several referendums. Despite the onslaught, the metropolitan concept, although diluted, survived. Consolidation did occur in many areas, such as the building code, creation of a new seaport, road and expressway construction and hospital expansion. But the municipalities never "faded away" as the proponents predicted. Despite the problems, the newly organized Metro Commission became the most influential local political body.

As the 1950s ended, no one would have disputed that Miami was no longer a "sleepy Southern town," but a genuine full-fledged metropolis. Dade County's population was nearing a million and counting. Air-conditioning had transformed a winter tourist Mecca into a year-round playground. New luxury hotels like the Fontainebleau, Eden Roc and Americana gave Miami Beach grandeur unknown since the 1920s. Superstars like Frank Sinatra and Dean Martin performed in the new Miami Beach hotels and gave Miami a national dateline. Even the historic Olympia Theatre, under the direction of band director Les Rhode, brought in luminaries like pop star Rosemary Clooney and the "King" himself, Elvis Presley.

■ *Elvis 'the King' Presley filled the house with screaming teenagers when he appeared in August 1956. (HMSF)*

BRING IN THE STARS

■ From 1951 to 1957, I Love Lucy was television's most popular show. Miamians swooned when stars Lucille Ball, center; her Cuban-born husband Desi Arnez, who grew up in Miami, right, and co-starts Fred Frawley, left, and Vivian Vance, right, came to Miami. Miami Mayor Randall Christmas gave the dignitaries a key to the city. (CM)

■ Pop singer Rosemary Clooney (below), left, aunt of George Clooney, greets her fans with Olympia Theatre impresario and band leader Les Rohde (right). (PR)

■ Soon after the Americana Hotel opened, NBC chose it as the place to celebrate its 30th anniversary (below). Many of the country's most popular singers and movie and television stars came to Miami Beach to join in the fun. Left to right: William Bendix, Ann Jeffries, Laraine Day, Jinx Falkenberg, Vaughn Monroe, Bob Sarnoff, president of RCA, Perry Como, Debbie Reynolds, Eddie Fisher, Gina Lollobrigida, Johnnie Ray, Dave Garroway, Helen O'Connell, Jan Murray, Helen Forest and Mrs. Graucho Marx. (CH)

The 1950s had been good to most people even though many familiar things like miles of open sand dune and sea oat beaches had been replaced with a string of thematic motels. Highway engineers sacrificed mature banyan trees on Dixie Highway to accommodate increased traffic. Burdines' familiar neon Santa Claus and Miami High's local football supremacy vanished.

On the positive side, changing laws and attitudes removed the most visible reminders of past inequities. "Gentiles Only" signs disappeared from Miami Beach and "Whites Only" signs no longer hung on countless drinking fountains, restrooms and commercial establishments. But Miami had always been accustomed to change. The city's entire history had been written in short paragraphs. No one, however, was prepared for the changes the 1960s would bring.

On November 24, 1950, thousands of Miamians turned out for the lighting of Burdines' giant neon Santa Claus. For the next 10 Christmas seasons, Santa waved and blinked at holiday shoppers. (DB)

(MN)

THE NIGHT NEXT YEAR CAME

For many years, attending the Thanksgiving night football game between the Miami High Stingarees and the Miami Edison Red Raiders was as mush a part of Miami's Thanksgiving ritual as turkey and cranberries. For 28 straight Thanksgivings, the Stingarees reigned supreme and for 28 straight years Edison fans shouted "Wait til next year!" On Thanksgiving night 1952, 40,000 local football fans watched as Edison finally defeated Miami High, 21-7. Some Miami High fans were so distraught they required medical assistance. Jubilant Edison fans raced onto the field and hauled down the goal posts. Thousands of shouting Red Raiders paraded behind their prize as fans carried the goal posts in a triumphant procession from the Orange Bowl to Bayfront Park for a victory rally. Today, the goal posts still stand in the patio of beautifully restored Miami Edison Middle School (below), formerly Miami Edison Senior High.

© Dan Forer

This 1959 aerial view of Biscayne Boulevard and Bayfront Park shows the new City of Miami Library and refurbished amphitheater. The Boulevard's famous hotel row included, left to right, the McAllister, Columbus, Miami Colonial, Everglades, Biscayne Terrace, Alcazar and Parkleigh. The Mayflower coffee and donut shop, far left, was a popular gathering spot famous for is "Optimist Creed", which ever-changing Miami understood more than most.

As you ramble through Life. Brother,
Whatever be your goal.
Keep your eye upon the doughnut
And not upon the hole."

For Miami, it was good advice. (LW)

■ *The calm before the storm: Miami skyline in 1959. (SS)*

Chapter Nine

"New World Center"

"Someday…Miami will become the great center of South American trade."

Julia Tuttle, 1896

ON DECEMBER 31, 1958, MIAMIANS HARDLY NOTICED WHAT SEEMED LIKE THE USUAL NEW YEAR'S EVE CACOPHONY OF

horns and raucous cheering. But on the first day of 1959, the merriment showed no signs of letting up. Throughout the day and into the night, hundreds of cars roared through town with horns blaring. This prolonged and unprecedented exuberance had nothing to do with the new year and everything to do with the fall of Cuban dictator Fugencio Batista and the rise to power of a 32-year-old revolutionary named Fidel Castro.

Most longtime Miamians paid little attention to the shouts of "Viva…Viva…Fidel…Fidel!" They were accustomed to the vicissitudes of Cuba's seesaw politics. The city had become a popular, albeit temporary, haven for a variety of Cuban exiles. It was not unusual for deposed Cuban presidents to live in Miami between revolutions. In fact, at the time of the Castro revolution, former President Carlos Prio, overthrown by Batista in 1952, lived on Miami Beach. What people did not realize, however, was that this revolution was different. It would not only change the course of Cuban history, but Miami's history as well.

Many of the Cuban exiles who had been living in Miami rushed to return to their homeland. Every flight to Havana was completely booked. Hundreds of pro-Castro supporters waited in the airport for available flights. Local police had to protect arriving Batista exiles from the exuberant Castro supporters.

For a short time in early 1959, many in both the United States and in Cuba hailed Castro as the conquering hero. *The New York Times* supported the new regime. A U.S. congressman called Castro our *"Nuevo Amigo"* (new friend). But television station WTVJ newsman Ralph Renick, one of the first to interview the new leader in Havana, reported a nagging uneasiness about Castro. Films of the kangaroo-court trials and the sickening deaths by firing squad told a different story than Castro's pronouncements of freedom and democracy.

As terrorism continued in Havana, an ever-growing stream of exiles flowed into Miami. Many were Cubans who had quickly become disenchanted with their new leader. Once Castro began showing his true colors (decidedly red), the stream of refugees increased and Miami opened its heart and its doors.

By the summer of 1960, six packed planes a day arrived from Havana. Most of the passengers were destitute, having been forced to leave everything behind. Many arrived with no more than $5 and the clothes on their backs. The U.S. government gave them modest assistance. Each head of a household received food stamps and $100 a month.

■ *Heartbroken Cuban refugees arrived in Miami after Fidel Castro took over the Cuban government and announced his Communist regime. (MN)*

WELCOME

ERNATIO

■ *Miami's Cuban refugees wait at Miami International Airport to greet friends and family fleeing Cuba. By the late 1960s, a new Cuban refugee arrived in Miami every seven minutes.* (MN)

The Coast Guard rescued many refugees in makeshift boats adrift in the Florida Straits (left). (MN)

In the summer of 1962, the U.S. government took over the old Miami News Tower (facing page), renamed it the Freedom Tower and transformed into the Cuban refugee services center. It became Miami's own Ellis Island and Statue of Liberty to hundreds of thousands of Cuban refugees. (MN)

Refugees line up at the Freedom Tower to be processed (facing page bottom inset). (CM)

The Cuban refugees were hardworking, dedicated people, eager to become self-supporting. They moved into declining neighborhoods, like the old Riverside neighborhood between Flagler Street and the Tamiami Trail, where rent was cheap. They would take any kind of job available. It was not uncommon to find a former Cuban Supreme Court justice running an elevator or a professional man working as a waiter or janitor. Cuban women, many of whom had managed a staff of servants in Havana, became domestic servants themselves. Others who had learned lady-like handwork as children went to work in Miami's growing garment industry.

In the early years, most Miamians were extraordinarily tolerant of the new arrivals. They respected the Cuban family values and empathized with their plight. But as the stream of refugees turned into a flood, attitudes changed. Cuban workers displaced many black workers, causing friction between the two groups. The school system struggled to absorb and educate thousands of Spanish-speaking Cuban children. As the refugee influx continued and the sound of Spanish filled the air, many old-timers began to complain. "I feel like a stranger in a foreign land," one resident wrote. "But it's not a foreign land, it's my own hometown."

DOOMED TO FAILURE

Until 1961, most Cubans believed they soon would be able to return home. The feeling intensified after the CIA organized a brigade of exiles into an invasion force to free Cuba. Members of the Democratic Front trained in the Everglades with CIA and U.S. military supervision. Early in 1961, the brigade departed from Miami's Opa-locka airport to Guatemala for further training. (After Carlos "Carlay" Rodriguez Santana, number 2506 in the brigade, died in a training accident, the group of freedom fighters called themselves "Brigade 2506.")

The rag-tag brigade included professional soldiers, mercenaries, former politicians and idealistic young men, many still teenagers. One common bond—the hatred of Fidel Castro—welded the group together. Although the brigade numbered less than 1,300, the full power of the United States was behind them—or so they believed.

On April 17, 1961, Brigade 2506, with the help of the American Navy, landed on the south coast of Cuba near the Bay of Pigs. Unfortunately, the invasion was doomed from the start. The U.S. government called off the promised U.S. air support, which was the key to success. Eighty members of Brigade 2506 died in the fight, another 37 drowned when their ship sank and 1,180 others were taken prisoner.

Gloom fell over Miami's refugee community. Sons, husbands, brothers and fathers had been sacrificed for nothing. Miami's Cubans believed that the United States—which had recruited, trained and funded the freedom fighters—had betrayed them.

The problems with Cuba soon accelerated. In the fall of 1962, secret U.S. reconnaissance planes discovered Russians building missile pads in Cuba. Before the missile crisis became public, Miamians watched as their town turned into an armed camp. Rumors flew as Army trucks rumbled through the streets. Long trains chock-a-block with military equipment tied up traffic at railroad crossings. Tent cities sprang up in the outskirts of town, and missiles sprouted in South Dade tomato fields.

Finally, on October 22, 1962, President John F. Kennedy appeared on national television to explain the military buildup. When he ordered the Navy to blockade Cuba to stop further landing of Russian war materiel, the United States went on wartime alert. Not since the German sinking of freighters during World War II had Miamians been so frightened. The possibility of World War III loomed menacingly. Some left town. Others started building bomb shelters. Many signed up for Red Cross disaster courses. Almost everyone, fearing the worst, stocked up on canned food and bottled water.

On October 28, after unprecedented negotiation between President Kennedy and Russian leader Nikita Khrushchev, the Russians agreed to remove the Russian missiles from Cuba if the United States promised not to invade—or allow anyone else to invade—Cuba. The agreement had a profound effect on Miami's Cuban community. For the first time, Miami's 100,000 Cuban refugees realized that a long time would pass before they could return home—if ever. Later information would reveal how close the world had come to nuclear war. If it had occurred, Miami would have been the first city to be obliterated. Not all the news was bad. The Bay of Pigs prisoners, still languishing in Cuban jails, came home in late 1962 in exchange for $62 million in food and medical supplies.

■ *Cuban refugees in Miami gathered around a radio for news of the April 1961 Bay of Pigs invasion. (MN)*

1962

THE WORLD ON THE BRINK

"It shall be the policy of this nation to regard any nuclear missile launched from Cuba against any nation in the Western Hemisphere as an attack on the United States, requiring a full retaliatory response upon the Soviet Union."

President John F. Kennedy
October 22, 1962

■ *Jubilant families welcome Bay of Pigs prisoners returning home on Christmas Eve, 1962 (above). (MN)*

■ *President Kennedy and his wife Jacqueline (below) greeted thousands of Cuban refugees and returning POWs at an emotional December 29 ceremony at the Orange Bowl. (APC)*

■ *Soldiers erected tent cities in South Dade during the Cuban Missile Crisis, 1962 (left). (MN)*

protest and uncontrolled passion. The unpopular Vietnam War added to the turmoil. Frightened young people called themselves flower children and made the peace symbol their national emblem. Coconut Grove began to look like San Francisco's Haight-Ashbury, then hippie capital of the United States. Long-haired "love children" filled Peacock Park and spilled over into the streets. Many Coconut Grove residents felt as if their town had been invaded by aliens from another world. Many of the young people joined a growing drug cult—

■ *"Peace," a symbol of the 1960s, is painted on a shirt at a gathering in Coconut Grove's Peacock Park that quickly became Miami's "Hippie Capital" (left). (MN)*

President Kennedy arrived in Miami to honor the men personally in an emotional ceremony attended by 30,000 in the Orange Bowl. Kennedy returned to Miami in November 1963, just four days before he was cut down by an assassin's bullet in Dallas.

After the new Lyndon Johnson administration negotiated with Castro, what the Americans called the "Freedom Flights" began in December 1965. They consisted of two flights per day, sponsored by the U.S. government. Before they ended in April 1973, the 3,048 flights brought more than 150,000 Cubans from a list put together by the exiles and the U.S. State Department. This new program increased Miami's Cuban population to almost 300,000. Sixty-four percent of the new refugees were wives and children joining husbands and fathers who had come to Miami earlier.

In the late 1960s, a Cuban refugee arrived in Miami every seven minutes. The often-traumatized newcomers lined up at the old Miami News Tower, renamed the Freedom Tower, to be processed. By the end the decade, 400,000 Cuban refugees lived in Dade County.

AWAKENING FROM CAMELOT

After President Kennedy's death, Camelot—as his term in office had been called—soured. The nation experienced an unprecedented period of disillusionment and division,

MIAMI'S MODERN ICON

The City of Miami's Ralph M. Munroe Marine Stadium arrived on the scene in 1963. The $2 million structure, designed by Hilario Candela of the architectural firm Pancoast, Ferendino, Skeels and Burnham, became a popular gathering place for boat races, Pops on the Bay, sunrise services and a Miami-like stage for superstars like Jimmy Buffet. (APC)

the 1960s worst legacy. As the demand for illegal, mind-altering drugs increased all over the United States, South Florida faced the same impossible task it had faced in the 1920s. The air age made drug-runners even harder to apprehend than rumrunners. South Florida's miles of coastline could not be patrolled effectively. Drugs and an incredible amount of money poured into Miami. It was the bootleg boom all over again, but this time with deadlier stakes.

About the same time, black Americans' patience began to run out. The promised "New Frontier" and "Great Society" were slow in coming. With the assassinations of Martin Luther King and Robert Kennedy, the last thread of hope and reason seemed to vanish. The nation erupted in violence.

Miamians held their breath while Los Angeles' Watts burned, Cleveland went up in flames and Chicago boiled over. But despite the turmoil, some tenuous gains emerged. The 1964 Civil Rights Act broke down the last vestiges of lawful segregation. Athalie Range became the first black and second woman on the Miami City Commission and Joe Lang Kershaw was elected to the Florida Legislature.

Urban renewal—President Lyndon B. Johnson's "Great Society's" panacea for the future—created a new set of problems. In Overtown, many blacks lost their homes and had to move to other crowded ghettos while promised new housing lagged. Expressways cut Overtown in half and caused many homes to be plowed under. Liberty City, once considered a model black community, received most of the overflow. Serious overcrowding, substandard housing and lack of hope turned Liberty City into a time bomb. Through the long, hot summer of 1968 the time bomb ticked away in the heat of frustration.

■ In the name of progress, Miami entered the express-way era as swaths of concrete and steel mowed down pine forests and farms, divided neighbor-hoods and left miles and miles of pylons supporting a stream of bumper-to-bumper automobiles. (CM)

In August, the Republican Party held its presidential nominating convention at Miami Beach. Miamians had a special interest in the convention because one of their most famous winter visitors, Richard Nixon, was the front-runner for the nomination. Many considered Nixon, who had spent his vacations on Key Biscayne, almost a native son. Just as he was giving his acceptance speech at the Miami Beach Convention Hall, Liberty City's time bomb exploded and Miami experienced its first racial riot. Local police with the help of the National Guard quelled the disturbance, confined mostly to the Liberty City area.

The young and the blacks were not alone in their disillusionment. Other groups shared their frustration. The Seminole Indians sued the federal government for stolen land and broken promises. The Miccosukees who lived on the Tamiami Trail demanded to be treated as a separate tribe. Dade County school teachers went on strike for higher pay and better working conditions. Even the elderly on Miami Beach organized to seek change.

WARMING THE PASSING YEARS

From the time of Henry Flagler, South Florida's warm semi-tropical climate lured thousands of retirees to Miami and Miami Beach. As a result, people over 65 made up a large part of the area's population. In North Miami Beach, Miami Beach, Key Biscayne and along Brickell Avenue, affluent retirees filled luxury condominiums. Others were not so fortunate. More than 50,000 senior citizens clustered in South Beach below Lincoln Road. Of these, 85 percent were Jewish, 20,000 of them Russian Jews. The area became a warm-weather replica of New York's Lower East Side, complete with fish markets, kosher meat markets, delicatessens and newsstands selling Yiddish papers.

The political clout of these senior citizens was legendary. It was not unusual for 90 percent of these South Beach registered voters to turn out in an election. Most of the more affluent condominium dwellers voted in equal force, and several larger condominiums constituted an entire voting precinct.

■ *The Republicans held their convention on Miami Beach in August 1968 (top). (MN)*

■ *Richard Nixon and his wife Pat were frequent Miami visitors when he was vice president (above). (CM)*

THE BEATLES...
"YEAH, YEAH, YEAH"

In May 1964, a new English rock group, The Beatles, travelled to Miami Beach to perform on the Ed Sullivan Show. *The show, broadcast live, was their second American television appearance. When they arrived at the Miami International Airport, thousands of teenagers skipped school to greet the new rock stars who were destined to transform the music and hairstyles of an entire generation.*

Left to right: George Harrison, John Lennon, Ringo Starr and Paul McCartney pondered their Florida souvenirs during a Miami Beach visit for their second U.S. television appearance on the Ed Sullivan Show. *(MN)*

Ed Sullivan, left, and The Beatles at the Deauville (below). (MN)

MOSTLY A GOLDEN TIME

Despite the turmoil, the 1960s were not all bad. Dade Junior College opened, making a college education available to almost everyone. Both the colleges and the public schools integrated without serious incident. When Jackie Gleason began broadcasting his weekly television show from Miami Beach, South Florida basked in his reflected glory. Miami's new professional football team, the Miami Dolphins, arrived. The new seaport at Dodge Island opened, making Miami a first-class port. Cruise ships soon filled every berth. The Jackson Memorial Hospital/University of Miami Medical School complex was rapidly becoming one of the finest medical centers in the nation.

On February 20, 1962, the population of Dade County reached a million. (Ironically, Nick Nicolades, chosen as "Mr. Millionth Resident," grew up in Miami and had recently returned. He left again four months later.) Throughout its history, Miami loved growth and development. Whatever developed the city was good; whatever hindered development was bad.

■ Publicist and icon Hank Meyer, left, convinced Jackie Gleason to bring his television show to Miami Beach. "How sweet it is," Gleason remarked. (MN)

Suddenly, in the 1960s, developers became suspect for the first time. Newly organized environmentalists, who were concerned not only with natural beauty but with the relationship of all living organisms to their environment, challenged government's laissez faire attitude. Ecology became a watchword. Crusading groups such as the Audubon Society, the Sierra Club, the Isaac Walton League and the newly created Friends of the Everglades stopped the proposed jetport in the Everglades, killed a proposed oil refinery in South Dade and slowed down the dredge—long the symbol of South Florida growth. For the first time, mangroves and estuaries had equal billing with man-made canals, fill and waterfront lots.

Local citizen groups also worked to clean up, protect and revitalize South Florida waters. The U.S. government created the Biscayne National Monument to prevent the Upper Keys from becoming another Miami Beach. The State of Florida opened John Pennekamp State Park to protect the last of the living Florida reef. The state also saved the Cape Florida Lighthouse and opened Bill Baggs-Cape Florida State Park on the tip of Key Biscayne.

As the 1960s drew to a close, Floridians felt a part of one of the nation's most historic events—the July 16, 1969 launching of Apollo 11 from Florida's Cape Canaveral. Five days later, astronaut Neil Armstrong took "one giant leap for mankind" when he bounded onto the surface of the moon. For one brief moment, differences disappeared and the nation came together to celebrate.

■ SAVING THE ENVIRONMENT: For the first time in Miami's history, a group of newly organized environmentalists took on development and stopped the Everglades Jetport and an oil refinery (left) in South Dade. (MN)

■ Congressman Dante Fascell (top right) greeted supporters during his successful crusade to create Biscayne National Monument in the Florida Keys (bottom right). It became Biscayne National Park in 1980. (MH)

NEAR THIS SITE GROUND WAS BROKEN SEPT. 18, 1968 FOR THE WORLD'S FIRST ALL-NEW JETPORT for the SUPERSONIC AGE CONSTRUCTED THROUGH COOPERATIVE EFFORTS: DADE COUNTY PORT AUTHORITY, THE FEDERAL AVIATION ADMINISTRATION, THE AIR TRANSPORT INDUSTRY, COLLIER COUNTY AND THE STATE OF FLORIDA

DADE COUNTY PORT AUTHORITY

A GOLDEN TIME

During the early 1970s, Miami experienced what some called a "Golden Age." First, the city was booming again and the decline of downtown seemed to be over. The Miami Dolphins were in the middle of an incredible winning streak and a perfect season. Between 1972 and 1973, the Dolphins won 18 straight games and two Super Bowl titles. Nothing in recent history had been able to draw the city's diverse population together like the unbeatable Dolphins. Miamians were proud that President Nixon chose a home on Key Biscayne as his "vacation White House." When President Nixon was in town, Miami became a national dateline.

The last "Freedom Flight" ended in April 1973 and most Miamians believed that it marked the end of the uncertainty created by the constant arrival of new Cuban refugees. Most early arrivers forged bright new lives. After years of retraining, Cuban professionals could practice again in Miami. Cuban entrepreneurs opened thousands of profitable businesses. Miami's "Trail" (S.W. Eighth Street) became Calle Ocho, a lively, vibrant, thoroughly Latinized "Little Havana."

(MS) (MD)

HOMETOWN BOY MAKES GOOD

Miami native Joe Auer gave the Miami Dolphins a spectacular send-off during the first play of the first game of the Dolphins' first season on September 2, 1966. "Auer grabbed the opening kickoff and raced back 95 yards to score," wrote Miami Herald *sports editor Jimmy Burns. "The game was only 15 seconds old and the fans had fallen in love with their Dolphins." Frolicking in his tank in the end zone was the team mascot, Flipper—a live dolphin. Every time the Dolphins scored, Flipper danced on his tail. Danny Thomas, part owner of the team, began the slogan, "Win this one for the Flipper." Despite the auspicious beginning, the Dolphins lost the game to the Oakland Raiders, 23-14.*

■ *THE ONE AND ONLY PERFECT SEASON: Don Shula led the Miami Dolphins to its perfect 17-game victory streak in 1972, providing Miamians with a strong dose of optimism and togetherness. Miamians joined in the celebration (left). (DS)*

TORCH O,F FRIEND

MARCH FOR M.L. KING

THE TORCH OF FRIENDSHIP

DEDICATED BY THE CITY OF MIAMI TO THE EVERLASTING FRIENDSHIP OF OUR NEIGHBORING COUNTRIES

1960

COMMISSIONERS

ROBERT KING HIGH MAYOR
HENRY L. BALABAN
GEORGE W. DUBREUIL
JOSEPH X. DUMOND
B. E. HEARN

MELVIN L. REESE   CITY MANAGER

Following Martin Luther King's assassination, people gathered at the Torch of Friendship for a memorial service. (CM)

(APC)

WE SHALL OVERCOME

THE TORCH OF FRIENDSHIP

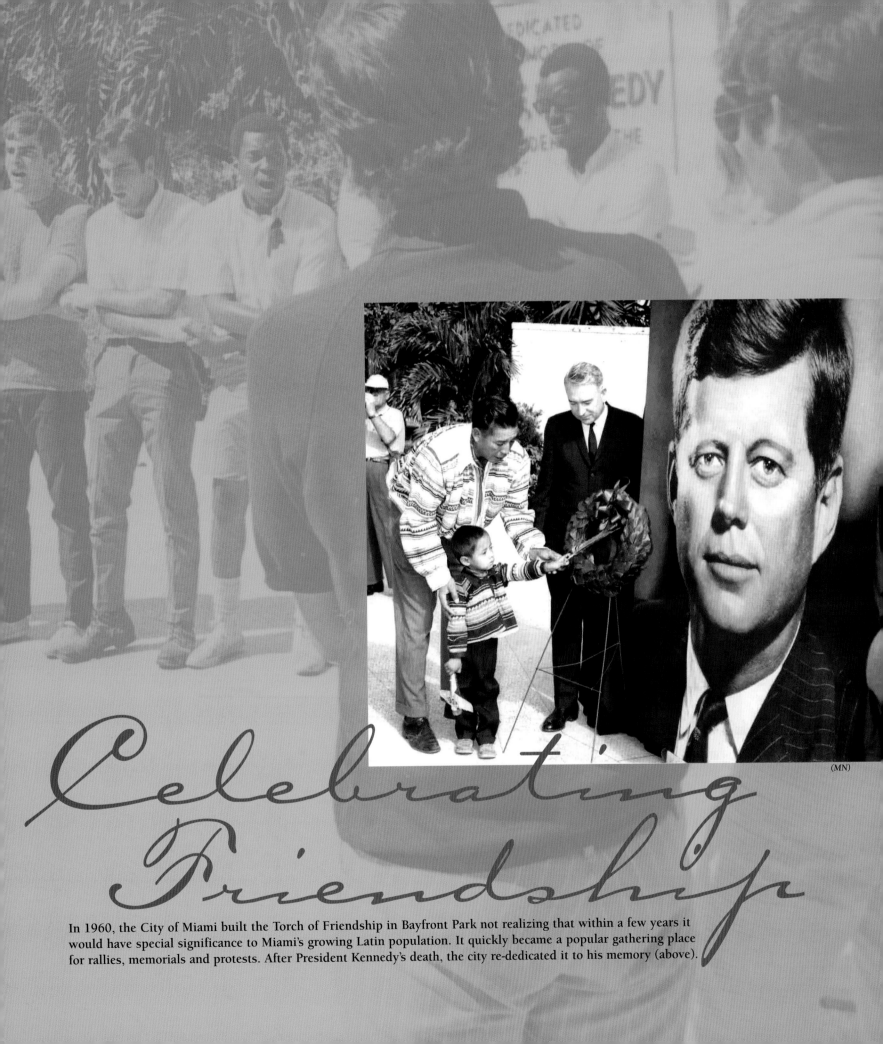

(MN)

Celebrating Friendship

In 1960, the City of Miami built the Torch of Friendship in Bayfront Park not realizing that within a few years it would have special significance to Miami's growing Latin population. It quickly became a popular gathering place for rallies, memorials and protests. After President Kennedy's death, the city re-dedicated it to his memory (above).

"THE GREATEST" ON MIAMI BEACH

In the early 1960s, a young black boxer named Cassius Clay trained on South Beach with Angelo Dundee. He was a colorful character, called himself "The Greatest" and recited original poetry before each fight. In 1964, Clay proved that his description of himself was correct. On February 25, he knocked out heavyweight champion Sonny Liston in the seventh round of a bout at Miami Beach to become the new world heavyweight champion. A short time later, he embraced the black Muslim religion and changed his name to Muhammad Ali.

■ *In June 1965, the new Port of Miami on Dodge Island (above right) opened with Dade County Vice Mayor Arthur H. Patten Jr. cutting the ribbon and, left to right, Port Director Arthur Darlow, Commissioners Newton Greene, Joe Boyd and Lew Whitworth. (MN)*

■ *The new port quickly became a popular cruise ship terminal (top left). (HMSF)*

Cuban restaurants had a large Anglo clientele as Miamians developed a taste for lechon asado, café Cubano and frijoles negros. Citizens felt proud of the way Dade County schools educated refugee children. In a spirit of optimism and brotherhood, the Dade County Commission declared Dade County a bilingual, bicultural community. No one protested.

Black Miamians also felt a new sense of hope when in 1970 U.S. District Judge C. Clyde Atkins ruled that the staff, faculty and administration in Dade County schools must be integrated. The following year, he paired a group of formerly all-white schools with a group of formerly all-black schools, greatly decreasing the number of schools made up of one race. Although some "white flight" occurred, the overall feeling was one of success as thousands of black and white children learned together.

In 1972, Florida International University opened its doors, giving Dade County its long-awaited state university. Meanwhile, Dade Junior College grew by leaps and bounds. A second campus opened in South Dade, followed by the announcement that a third campus would be built in downtown Miami.

ROXCY BOLTON

Women, too, made gains in the early 1970s. Coral Gables resident Roxcy Bolton organized the Miami chapter of the National Organization for Women (NOW) and became a spokesperson for women's rights. She pushed NOW principles at commission meetings, in board rooms and into community consciousness. During the 1970s, female faces appeared in political offices, in police forces, in board rooms and formerly all-male dining rooms.

■ "I am woman hear me roar:" In 1971, Roxcy Bolton, Miami's pioneer feminist, led a demonstration against the insensitive treatment of rape victims (above). As a result of these protests, Jackson Memorial Hospital opened a Rape Treatment Center that became a model for America. (HMSF)

■ From humble beginnings in 1963 (below), the Coconut Grove Arts Festival has become one of the nation's premier outdoor fine arts festivals. (CM)

EXPANDING HORIZONS

Caught up in the wave of optimism, voters passed an ambitious "Decade of Progress" bond issue. It promised a rapid transit system, an improved sewerage system, new street lighting, new libraries, museums and even a cageless zoo. Bright green oases appeared in the city's often maligned cultural desert. Miami's first art museum, the Lowe, was joined by the Bass Museum in Miami Beach and the Miami Art Center. Every February, the streets of Coconut Grove turned into a sidewalk art show that gained national attention. Important private galleries opened all over town. The beautiful Villa Vizcaya, purchased by Dade County in 1952, became a showplace of decorative arts. The Historical Museum of Southern Florida found a new home next to the Museum of Science, which the Junior League of Miami had started in 1952 as the Junior Museum. The University of Miami turned over its Symphony Orchestra, founded in 1926, to the community. The Miami Opera Association, founded in 1941, became one of the nation's finest opera companies. The Miami Ballet Society brought world-famous dancers into town, and support increased for the new Ballet Concerto. Legitimate theater lovers flocked to local venues, such as the Coconut Grove Playhouse, the Miami Beach Theater for the Performing Arts and the University of Miami Ring Theatre. Meanwhile, civic leaders were working toward the creation of a downtown cultural center.

Then came recession, the most serious since the 1930s, and the bottom fell out of the financial bucket. Construction projects ground to a halt and skeletons of half-finished buildings once again dotted the skyline. Miami's newest and tallest skyscraper—One Biscayne Tower—went bankrupt. By 1975, the unemployment rate had risen to almost 14 percent.

In Washington, D.C., police arrested four Miamians in a bizarre break-in at Democratic Party headquarters in a building named Watergate. Before the investigation ended, President Nixon was implicated and forced to resign from office. A short time later, he sold his vacation White House on Key Biscayne and the new owners demolished it.

Not even the trauma of Watergate could dampen the nation's enthusiasm for its bicentennial. Miami was selected as one of the nation's three official bicentennial cities. "Third Century U.S.A.," Miami's local bicentennial organization, coordinated a myriad of exciting activities as the city painted itself a glorious red, white and blue. On July 4, the city dedicated the Bicentennial Park on the bayfront with hoopla and fireworks. The most meaningful celebration, however, occurred when 7,300 people, mostly Cuban refugees, became U.S. citizens in one emotional ceremony.

During the worst of the recession, Alvah Chapman, president of *The Miami Herald*, summoned 27 educational, business and government leaders to an early-morning meeting in the barren, unfinished and vacant 38th floor of One Biscayne Tower—Miami's "Black Elephant" (black for its dark glass siding). Leaders studied maps, charts and proposals for downtown revitalization. They listed every possible source of funding—public and private—that could be used to start things rolling again. By 4:30 that afternoon, they had a plan and a new committee, the Downtown Action Committee of the Greater Miami Chamber of Commerce, to implement it.

■ *One of the highlights of Miami's 1976 Bicentennial Celebration occurred when President Gerald Ford presided at the naturalization ceremony (top left) for 1,121 new citizens.(APC)*

■ *In 1975, Miami became one of the official Bicentennial cites and adopted the theme "Third Century" for its part of the celebration (left). Miami Mayor Maurice Ferre, left, and Dade County Mayor Steve Clark, right, launch the effort at a press conference. (CM)*

Working with the Downtown Development Authority, the committee had goals loftier than just revitalizing downtown. Like Julia Tuttle and other former boosters, they dreamed of the day Miami would take its rightful place at the center of Latin American trade, tourism and commerce. Even though Miami had always been in the right place, the dream remained elusive. By the 1970s, however, a quirk of history had given the city an irresistible pull—its own Latin beat. Ironically, this magic ingredient had been suggested in 1943 when Mariano Font, an international trade expert with Dunn and Bradstreet, came to Miami to help an earlier generation make the city the center of the Western Hemisphere. "If you want to trade with these countries [in Latin America]," he advised, "learn to speak their language…that gives you an entree you can't acquire any other way."

DISCOVERING A NEW WORLD

*D*uring the worst of the 1970s recession, Alvah Chapman, then president of The Miami Herald, *called community leaders together to address the problem. They created a new action committee and called upon publicist Hank Meyer to come up with a logo for their coordinated efforts. From this beginning, the "New World Center" concept was born.*

(AC)

■ *On July 4, 1976, Miamians gathered on the bayfront to dedicate Bicentennial Park, built on the site of the former Port of Miami. The U.S. Coast Guard tall ship came to help in the celebration. (CM)*

the new world center

(APC)

INTERAMA: WHAT MIGHT HAVE BEEN

As World War II ended, Dr. William H. Walker, president of Miami's First Federal Savings and Loan Association, had a dream. He proposed that Miami build a great Inter-American Center that would bring the countries of the Western Hemisphere together for trade and understanding.

In 1950, a cadre of well-known local architects, including Russell Pancoast, Robert Law Weed, Alfred Browing Parker and Robert Fitch Smith, designed the massive project for the so-called "Graves Tract" in North Miami just east of Biscayne Boulevard and 151st Street. A sign went up, landfill began but no Interama appeared.

But Interama was an idea that refused to die. In the early 1960s, another group of influential people with the same mission organized under the leadership of then-Governor Farris Bryant. The new Inter-American Center Authority for the State of Florida prepared an impressive document that highlighted four areas—international, industrial, cultural and festival. The proposed center would rise on the Graves Tract. The festival proposal included a major theme park along the idea of what Walt Disney would later build in Orlando. But once again, the project stalled.

The final push came in the 1970s when yet another group of luminaries proposed a less-ambitious plan to finally get the project underway in time for the nation's 1976 bicentennial. But the bicentennial came and went and still no Interama. Florida International University, however, opened its Interama Campus in 1977 (renamed Biscayne Bay in 1999) on the Graves Tract amid the barely begun trade center.

Today, Florida International, the Oleta River State Park and the proposed Biscayne Landings housing development occupy the site once slated to become the nation's first permanent Inter-American exposition.

BOB GRAHAM:
WORKING FOR GOVERNOR

*I*n 1979, Bob Graham became the first Miamian to be elected governor of Florida. During the campaign, Graham worked at a hundred different jobs all over the state. His "workdays" captured the imagination of the voters, and he came from behind to win the election.

Graham's interest in politics and government came from his father, Ernest R. Graham. "Cap" Graham (for his World War I service) had been Dade County's only state senator between 1937 and 1943. In 1944, Ernest Graham ran for the Democratic nomination for governor but was defeated by Millard Caldwell.

Ernest Graham came to Florida in 1921 to manage the Pennsylvania Sugar Company's operation in the Everglades. When the Pennsylvania Sugar Company pulled out of South Florida, Graham bought their land and turned it first into a vegetable farm and later into a dairy.

Bob Graham grew up in a coral rock house that still stands on the family farm in Pennsuco, named after the Pennsylvania Sugar Company. He attended Hialeah Elementary School and Junior High and later became president of the Student Council at Miami Senior High School. He married native Miamian Adele Khoury, his college sweetheart at the University of Florida, and returned to Miami after attending Harvard Law School. In the 1960s, Bob and his brother Bill began developing their cow pastures into the "New Town of Miami Lakes"—the first planned community in South Florida since Coral Gables. Once Miami Lakes was launched, Bob Graham was elected to the Florida House of Representatives in 1966 and in 1970 became a state senator like his father. In 1987, he was elected U.S. senator and served in Washington until 2005.

■ *A Bob Graham "workday."*

In late 1975, sensing Miami was on the brink of becoming a truly international city, the Downtown Action Committee asked people to suggest a new logo that would reflect the city's growing international status. The committee selected publicist Hank Meyer's "New World Center" concept, depicting Miami's future as the center of Columbus' New World—the Western Hemisphere.

In true Miami fashion, by 1977, the recession began turning into another boom. The Omni International Complex—one of the city's most ambitious projects to date—opened on Biscayne Boulevard. It contained a luxury hotel, a multistoried shopping mall, theaters and restaurants. It was in the same area that the Phipps family had developed in the late 1920s. Fifty years later, their prophecy that Biscayne Boulevard would become the Fifth Avenue of the South, at least for the moment, seemed to be coming true.

■ *Pundits said it would be a "cold day in Hell" when a South Floridian was elected governor of Florida. Bob Graham (left) reminded the audience on the very cold inauguration day January 2, 1979, but to his supporters, it seemed more like Heaven. (Bob Graham)*

TOWERING OVER HISTORY
Time & Time Again

1966

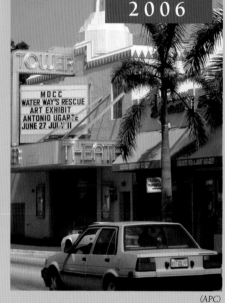

2006

The Tower Theater, located at S.W. Eighth Street and 15th Avenue, opened in 1926 and received its current Art Deco remodeling in 1931. Generations of Miami children spent their Saturdays watching movies, serials and cartoons in this popular neighborhood venue. In the 1960s, as thousands of Cuban refugees moved into the area, it became a gathering place and the first movie theater in Miami to have Spanish subtitles and later Spanish-language movies. Early refugees acknowledge the Tower's role in introducing them to American culture and language.

The Tower closed in 1984 and, after a series of owners, the City of Miami purchased it in 1991. The architectural firm of Bermello, Ajamil & Partners restored the theater in 1997, honoring its historic Art Deco design while adapting it into a center for art, film and culture. In 2002, Miami-Dade Community College (now Miami Dade College) entered into a management agreement with the city to operate the theater and promote its mission as a multicultural, multi-ethnic arts center.

(CM)   (APC)

BIG CITY UPS AND DOWNS

As Miami entered the 1980s, the New World Center was taking shape. Construction began on the new rapid transit system and, for the first time since the 1920s, the steel skeletons of buildings dominated the skyline. Banking laws aimed at foreign dollars turned Miami into an international Wall Street, with banks opening on almost every corner. Hundreds of blue-chip U.S. companies made Coral Gables their Latin American headquarters. The City of Miami-University of Miami's new James L. Knight International Conference and Convention Center on the north bank of the Miami River neared completion. Ground was broken west of the Dade County Courthouse for an impressive cultural center, designed by world-renowned architect Philip Johnson, which would include a Center for the Fine Arts, the Historical Museum of Southern Florida and a new central library. North of the cultural center, the planned government complex rose skyward. Clearly, Miami the New World was on the horizon. But many people felt uncomfortable in the New World. Anglos—the Miami vernacular for white non-Hispanic Americans—often longed for the good old days when they were firmly in control. (In the past Miami's only refugees were from the frozen North, and bilingualism meant being able to speak "Mi-am-ee" for the Northern tourists and "Mi-am-uh" for the mostly Southern home folks.)

Ironically, some of the most vocal critics of the New World were relative newcomers. Old-timers often seemed more adaptable. If they could survive booms, busts, hurricanes and hordes of new-comers, they could survive any other kind of change as well.

Although black Miamians made gains in the New World, they also lost something. Overtown—once the psychological and geographical heart of black Miami—was dying and part of the soul of the black community seemed to be dying with it. Booker T. Washington High School, the first 12-year school for blacks in South Florida and at one time the pride of the community, became an integrated junior high. Most of Overtown's older merchants went out of business or moved elsewhere. Urban renewal and expressways tore up their town and integration sent black shoppers into downtown. Worst of all, blacks had the sinking feeling that they had become third-class citizens in a tricultural society.

Most of the Cuban community felt comfortable in the New World that they, more than anyone else, helped create. Still, they faced the sting of prejudice, hate and misunder-standing. The bilingual ordinance that passed in 1973 was rescinded in 1980 because of an anti-Cuban backlash. Although a Latin majority was elected to the Miami City Commission, Cubans often remained outsiders in other politi-cal and community bodies. The older generation of Cubans felt uneasy and fought to hang on to their Cuban heritage as they watched their children become Americanized.

Despite the pain, Miamians had a sense of pride at how well they handled the events of the past 20 years. Few cities had been faced with such sudden change. South Florida

MIAMI'S ART DECO COMES OF AGE

On May 14, 1979, Miami Beach's Art Deco District became the first Twentieth Century district on the National Register of Historic Places. Art Deco, sometimes called "the last complete style," was defined by the 1925 Paris International Exhibition of Modern Decorative and Industrial Arts. During the Great Depression, it took on a smooth style reminiscent of the streamlined trains and sleek silver airplanes. Miami Beach's Art Deco buildings helped bring South Florida out of the Depression several years before the rest of the nation. In the mid-1930s, Miami Beach experienced a tremendous building boom. Between 1935 and 1940 alone, almost 200 hotels and apartments were built on the beach in the new "moderne" architectural style. The Art Deco District remains the nation's premiere storehouse of this unique Twentieth-Century phenomenon.

Even though favorite Art Deco motifs—the curve of a wave, the flamingo and the circle of the full moon—seemed to have been created especially for South Florida, the district had a greater national follow-ing than a local one. Deco devotees often clashed with developers over the future of Art Deco on Miami Beach, despite untiring efforts of the Miami Design Preservation League, chief supporters of the district.

A stroll through the Art Deco District is a return-trip to the 1930s and 1940s, when couples could swing and sway to the sound of the big bands, to a time when young officer candidates filled every hotel room and marched, singing, down the middle of the street.

In the late 1970s, residents of the nation's youngest historic district were the nation's oldest people, averaging 70 years. Sixty percent of the elderly lived alone on small fixed incomes. Yet they supported the preservation of their neighborhood as strongly as the young Deco fanciers who were not yet born when it was created.

■ *Jerry Sanchez, owner of the Break-water Hotel, commis-sioned this mural to immortalize the leaders of Miami Beach's Art Deco movement. The warriors for the cause surround Barbara Captiman, sitting center right. (MDPL)*

Building
"the New World"
Center

accommodated more than 500,000 Cuban refugees who helped transform a medium-sized Southern city into a vibrant international metropolis. Blacks, escaping the bonds of segregation, slowly gained status. Dade County had a black superintendent of schools, Johnny Jones, and it was no longer unusual for blacks to hold public office. Janet Reno became the first woman state attorney and many women held local or state political offices. Jeanne Bellamy Bills was the first woman elected president of the Greater Miami Chamber of Commerce.

As the 1970s came to an end, the media, as usual, recounted the decade's major events and brought out the soothsayers to predict what Miamians could expect in the new decade. Sylvan Meyer, writing in *Miami Magazine*, believed, like many other wishful thinkers, that the Cuban migration was about over and by the end of the 1980s, Cuban children would be so acculturated that their ethnic identity would fade. Many supported the proposition that, while Miami might not be a melting pot, it was a salad bowl.

The Miami News entitled its special section "Dade's Seismic Seventies," but the title seemed chosen more because seismic alliterated with seventies than because the decade was so earthshaking. The earth may have moved a bit in the 1970s, but seismic events that would almost split the city asunder still lay in the future. Miami seemed right on track, speeding toward the eighties. Pessimists were hard to find, and the few who surfaced worried more about the energy crisis than anything else. Everyone sensed that something extraordinary was happening to the Magic City. No one, however, dreamed that the 1980s would absolutely, positively, unequivocally and completely make Miami over and change it for all times.

■ *Architects Aldolfo Albaisa, left, and Lester Pancoast look over the new City of Miami Police Station that their firm designed (top left). (DDA)*

■ *Left to right: Henry King Stanford, president of the University of Miami; James L. Knight, publisher of* The Miami Herald; *Miami Mayor Maurice Ferre and developer Earl Worsham look over the plans for the new City of Miami University of Miami James L. Knight International Center, completed in 1982 (center left). (DDA)*

■ *The City of Miami University of Miami James L. Knight International Center on the Miami River (center right). (DDA)*

■ *By the end of the 1980s, plans were unveiled for the Philip Johnson-designed Miami-Dade Cultural Center (bottom right). The county also planned a new administration building just north of the center. (DDA)*

■ *Two buildings—the AmeriFirst Building (facing page bottom left) and One Biscayne Tower—changed Miami's skyline and gave the downtown area the first new "Class "A" offices in 30 years. © Steven Brooke*

■ *Architect Hugh Stebbins added his signature to Dade County's Administration Building (facing page top left). (DDA)*

■ *In 1984, artist Rockne Krebs transformed the Metrorail Bridge over the*
Miami River into a work of public art entitled The Miami Line. © *Steven Brooke*

Chapter Ten

"City of the Future"

"The travails of recent years have given Miami a lot of pain. But they've also given it something else—a strength of character, a gritty resourcefulness and an ability to rebound from the worse kinds of crises, which is one of the city's most attractive qualities."

T.D. Allman
Miami: City of the Future

THE NEW DECADE BEGAN AUSPICIOUSLY ENOUGH, EVEN THOUGH THE WEATHER WAS AN UNUSUALLY COOL 58

and Oklahoma whipped Florida State in the 47th Orange Bowl Classic. As tourists poured into town and workers poured concrete into foundations for new downtown skyscrapers, it looked as if Miami were on another roll. No one knew that unimaginable obstacles lay ahead that would stop the heady momentum.

In February, the Dade County Grand Jury indicted Johnny Jones, the popular superintendent of schools, for attempted theft of school property in what became known as the "gold plumbing case." It was a great loss. Jones was the highest-ranking black public official and, arguably, the most respected black leader in Miami. Jones' indictment followed a series of similar events in which other black leaders had been removed from office.

The next trauma came by sea. On April 4, Fidel Castro, in retaliation against the Peruvians for giving asylum to Cuban nationals, removed the guards from Peru's embassy in Havana. Within days, more than 10,000 Cubans crowded into the embassy grounds seeking political asylum. Then, in a complete reversal of policy, Castro announced that anyone who wanted to leave Cuba could do so through the port at Mariel. When President Jimmy Carter offered what he called an "open heart and open arms" policy to all Cubans seeking freedom, the stage was set for the most incredible sea rescue since World War II's Dunkirk.

Miami's Cuban community responded immediately. Within hours, what the press called a "freedom flotilla," made up of thousands of small boats—almost anything that would float—struck out across the Florida Straits, heading for Mariel. It did not take long, however, for the noblest rescuers to figure out what Castro was doing. In addition to allowing Miami Cubans to pick up their relatives, Castro forced them to take what he called the *scoria* (scum). As a result, of the 125,000 Marielitos who came to South Florida, at least 25,000 were social misfits, picked up from the streets and out of Cuban jails and mental hospitals.

■ THE FREEDOM FLOTILLA: When Fidel Castro opened his borders in May 1980, Miamians responded with everything that would float to rescue Cubans who wanted to come to America (facing page). (MN)

■ Cuban refugees crammed into the boats that would bring them to Florida (left). (MN)

MIAMI COMES TO THE RESCUE

■ The City of Miami opened a refugee assistance center at the Orange Bowl. Thousands of new refugees lined up for processing (top left). (MN)

■ Miami City Manager Cesar Odio (above), with bullhorn, led the humanitarian effort to help the new arrivals. (CM)

■ The faces of the new refugees reflected the trauma of an uncertain future in a new land. (CM)

While all this was going on, an all-white jury convicted Johnny Jones and sentenced him to three years in prison. Three weeks later, at the same time the Mariel refugees were arriving on Miami shores, an all-white Tampa jury acquitted four white policemen of the December 1979 beating death of black Miami insurance agent Arthur McDuffie. The McDuffie and Jones verdicts, along with several other confrontations between police and blacks, provided the spark. Within hours, the powder keg, its seams already splitting, exploded like never before. For three very long days, Miami experienced the worst riot in its history. Eighteen people died, more than 1,000 were injured and property damage exceeded $50 million.

The anger that swirled among the rioters was even more frightening than the smoke of burning buildings that rose skyward. The smoke and flames could be extinguished, but the heavy gray cloud of fear and despair that hung over the city would not go away. For a time, the combination of events seemed to overwhelm Miami. As strong as a hurricane, winds of rage and hate screamed in the maelstrom.

Fires burned at Ramblas Station in Liberty City as Miami experienced the worst riot in its history. (HMSF)

NOT THE BEST OF TIMES

Miamians, who had always prided themselves on their grit and ability to overcome adversity, were in shock. Even the most optimistic had nagging, if unspoken, thoughts that this time Miami might not recover. In a matter of days, the city's carefully crafted sun-and-fun image vanished and a new picture of turmoil, refugees and racial unrest took its place.

The federal government offered little assistance in dealing with the refugee influx and, once again, the city had to fend for itself. As the Mariel criminals settled in, Miami's crime rate soared. Before the year ended, the city had the nation's highest murder rate. *The Miami Herald* and the *Miami News* ran constant editorials trying to prod Miamians out of their malaise and depression. Nothing seemed to help.

Incredibly, the economy continued to boom. "There is enough frenetic building going on in Metropolitan Miami," *The Herald* reported in a full page editorial, "that the place,

like the hair on a corpse, will keep growing even if we allow the fire [riots] and the water [Mariel] to consume its soul."

Spirits hit bottom in the fall of 1981, when a dilapidated Haitian boat sank in rough seas and, while tourists watched, 33 bodies washed ashore. It did not matter that the incident occurred in Palm Beach County. The tragedy, the horror and the headlines hit home. At the time, Miami had 1,000 Haitians retained in the federal government's Krome Avenue North Detention Center. The Haitians, whose only crime was not to have been granted political asylum like the Cubans, went to the detention center awaiting deportation while most of the Cubans went free. The differences in the nation's immigration policy vis-a-vis Haitians and Cubans went unnoticed almost everywhere except in Miami.

Then *Time* magazine hit the news-stands with its infamous cover story on Miami entitled: "Paradise Lost?" Miamians protested loudly and passionately, believing *Time* kicked them when they were down.

■ *More than 10,000 Haitians arrived in Miami (left) between May and September 1980. (MN)*

■ *Haitian leaders in Miami (top) protested U.S. immigration policy that refused them political refugee status. (HMSF)*

Fighting mad, Miami started its comeback. Bill Cullom, who took over the presidency of the Greater Miami Chamber of Commerce just weeks before the *Time* piece, must have wondered if he had made a terrible mistake. The chamber, in the absence of strong political leadership, had been trying desperately to do something about the situation. It brought in a Minnesota group, called Capital Ventures, to tackle the monumental task of rebuilding Liberty City. The black community did not like this out-of-town approach and the plan faltered. The chamber also organized the Greater Miami Citizens Against Crime. By the summer of 1982, the chamber, with the leadership of Cullom and builder Charles Babcock, raised $6.9 million from local businesses to help Liberty City. This effort set a national record for the largest amount of money ever raised from private sources for an inner-city project. The chamber hired Newell Daughtrey, the city manager of Opa-locka, to head the new Business Assistance Center. The center's mission was to help black businesses and encourage new entrepreneurs. By this time, many of the worst of the hard-core Marielito criminals were back in jail and the crime rate had stopped its upward climb.

■ Citizens launched "Miami's for Me" to remind people that Miami was still a good place to live (top). (APC)

(BS)

SEE THE NATIVE NO MORE

In February 1981, workers shredded 27,000, controversial "See it Like a Native" posters that had been locked up for two years. The county banned the tourism poster after women objected to what they called the "sexist totally misleading and blatantly distasteful" picture of the backside of a topless scuba diver. (MN)

IN THE PINK

For better or worse, Miami was certainly attracting national attention. Suddenly, it seemed that every magazine in America carried an article about Miami. Three books on Miami for national consumption were in progress by well-known authors. Most of the publicity, however, was a public relation nightmare. "Here we go again," people would say as the next negative article hit the newsstands. In the spring of 1983, most Miami politicians braced themselves for what they thought would precipitate another national drubbing. Some "kook" wanted to wrap some islands in Biscayne Bay with pink plastic. Only in Miami.

As early as 1981, a Bulgarian artist named Christo Javacheff had tried to get a permit to wrap the islands with 6.5 million square feet of pink polypropylene. Environmentalists lined up against him, art critics rolled their eyes and politicians ran for cover. But Christo would not give up. Ten permits, seven public hearings, four court appearances and three separate manatee tests later, he prevailed and was ready to begin creating what he called "Surrounded Islands."

It took several days to surround the islands. Hundreds of volunteers—old and young, black, Hispanic and Anglo, old-timer and newcomer—braved thunderstorms and winds, critics and naysayers and just kept wrapping the islands. When they finished and a skeptical city viewed "Surrounded Islands" for the first time, an incredible thing happened. Miami smiled for the first time in three years.

■ *COLOR ME PINK: Christo Javacheff, at one of his many public hearings, sought support from a dubious public for his "Surrounded Islands." (MH)*

■ *The "Surrounded Islands" in Biscayne Bay reminded people of French artist Claude Monet's water lilies. © Steven Brooke*

Out in California, two television producers, Peter Yerkovich (of TV's *St. Elsewhere* fame) and Michael Mann, came up with the idea of making Miami the locale for a new television series. Yerkovich saw Miami as a sort of tropical Casablanca—full of intrigue and drama. Mann, on the other hand, saw Miami as bright and beautiful: a pink paradise starring pink flamingos, pink sunsets, pink flowers and pink buildings.

At the time, Miami was still decidedly a beige-and-brown town. Beth Dunlop, architectural critic for *The Miami Herald*, had been leading her own crusade against this drab, boring 1970s color palette. She wrote that beige and brown were completely wrong for South Florida, which was known for its bright light, lush vegetation and vibrant skies. She lobbied for the same tropical colors that George Merrick selected for Coral Gables in the 1920s. Without knowing it, Michael Mann and Beth Dunlop agreed. The first thing Mann told his production crew when it arrived in Miami to film the new television show was, "No earth tones." The rest, as they say, is history.

On September 16, 1984, Mann and Yerkovich's image of Miami, which they called *Miami Vice*, hit the airwaves. They compacted almost every bright, beautiful, fun thing Miami could offer into the opening credits. In only two hours, Michael Mann had reinvented Miami! For the next five seasons (107 shows, not counting reruns), this new, young, beautiful image of Miami flashed into the nation's living rooms every Friday night at promptly 9 p.m. Miami, as usual, immediately began reinventing itself to match its newfound image. The city painted itself pink and blue, aqua and purple. It installed neon, glass brick and palm trees. It donned crushed white linen and threw away its ties. It brought out the tropical shirts, which had been in storage since Arthur Godfrey went off the air. Sure enough, before long, Miami looked like *Miami Vice*. There were hardly any earth tones left in sight.

Miami loved Mann's Miami, but was less enthusiastic about Yerkovich's Vice. Having lived through so much of the real thing, the shoot-'em-up episodes, too close to truth for comfort, made many Miamians uneasy. But then, most rationalized, Miami did look beautiful and exciting. Tourism picked up and the magazine editors took a new look at the city.

In 1985, just a short time after *Miami Vice* made the cover of *Time* magazine, Governor Bob Graham presented Vice star Don Johnson the Florida Entertainment Writers' Carbonnell Award "in recognition of the phenomenal positive effect" the show had on South Florida's image. Everyone agreed that *Miami Vice* made Miami look better, but most had nagging doubts about what the Vice did to the world's perception of Miami.

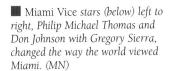

■ Miami Vice *stars (below) left to right, Philip Michael Thomas and Don Johnson with Gregory Sierra, changed the way the world viewed Miami. (MN)*

LOOKING GOOD

The Miami depicted in the early episodes of *Miami Vice* was more fantasy than reality. By 1988, however, Miami had a genuine, new, dramatic architectural presence. The whole world began to notice that Miami had become a totally different city. Several local architects made what was described as "an astounding leap from obscurity to renown." In 1976, four bright young architects, Bernardo Fort-Brescia, Laurinda Spear, Andres Duany and Elizabeth Plater-Zyberk, joined Hervin Romney and formed Arquitectonica International. Before they split up in 1980, their earliest Brickell Avenue buildings were already on the drawing board. Fort-Brescia, Spear and Romney stayed with Arquitectonica and gained attention for their imaginative, modernist, "sky's the limit" design style. (Romney left the firm in 1984.) Duany and Plater-Zyberk, who favored more traditional architecture, formed their own firm and received national attention as well—especially for their town planning philosophy called New Urbanism. Through the University of Miami School of Architecture, Duany and Plater-Zyberk, who became dean of the school, had a tremendous influence on a new generation of architects, and gained attention for themselves and for the college.

When it came to apartments, Arquitectonica clearly dominated the Brickell Avenue skyline. The Atlantis, Imperial, Palace and Babylon made a dramatic statement—as if Arquitectonica had the skyline all to itself. Realizing this, neighboring developer Nicholas Morley, whose building paled between two Arquitectonica structures, hired the Israeli artist Agam to create a Jacob's-coat-of-many-colors scheme for his Villa Regina. Brickell Avenue, once one of the most staid and traditional streets in town, had suddenly become playful and avant-garde.

The commercial section of Brickell Avenue became Miami's Wall Street, a grand boulevard of impressive buildings with a bank or two in every block. Although the Brickell and downtown skylines merged in the 1980s, the earth-connection began when ground was broken for the Brickell and Omni links of the Metromover extension, completed in 1994.

■ Arquitectonica's famous Atlantis became a Miami icon after Miami Vice featured it in its opening credits. (A)

■ Two of Arquitectonica's dazzling Brickell Avenue condominiums—the Imperial and the Palace—frame the Villa Regina, painted as a work of art by Israeli artist Yaacov Agam (facing page top). (HG)

Bernardo Fort-Brescia and Laurinda Spear
created innovative new designs that put Miami on
the architectural map. (A)

Meanwhile, what *Progressive Architecture* called "designer architects" were busily recreating the Miami skyline. Legendary modernist and AIA gold medalist Philip Johnson, with John Burgee, shocked and disappointed many Miamians when he selected his personal reinvention of Mediterranean style for the new Cultural Complex. Next door, Hugh Stubbins (of Citicorp fame) created the huge Metro-Dade Administration Building. Skidmore, Owings and Merrill (SOM) left its mark on not one, but three Miami skyscrapers. The legendary firm designed the Interterra and One Brickell Square on Brickell Avenue and the Southeast Financial Center—then South Florida's tallest building. Pietro Bellusschi designed the Ball Building (Miami Center) and its matching hotel (now the Intercontinental). Some thought that his style was to cover everything that stood still in beige travertine marble. All the buildings had their followers, but as soon as they turned on the lights, I.M. Pei's World Trade Center became the undisputed local favorite.

Andres Duany and Elizabeth Plater-Zyberk brought traditional values and human scale back to architecture and city planning. (DPZ)

CenTrust CEO David Paul hired New York lighting expert Douglas Leigh, who had illuminated the Empire State Building, to do the same for CenTrust. One hundred seventy-eight 1,000-watt halide lamps later, Miami's skyline took on a whole new kind of magic. Adding to the serendipity, the building changed its colors on command. It turned orange and green when the University of Miami won the national championship, blue and white for Hanukkah, and red, white and blue on the Fourth of July (and when the Resolution Trust Corporation took over after David Paul fell from grace).

The 1980s also witnessed a new birth for Overtown/ Park West, located just north of downtown. Miami attorney Martin Fine conceived the idea of doubling the documentary stamp tax to fund new low-cost housing, and then lobbied for its passage in Tallahassee. This new source of funding made it possible to build new housing in Overtown/Park West.

When Metrorail, "Miami's billion-dollar baby," began operation in 1984, Miami took another step toward the future. Two years later, Metromover started looping around downtown, making Miami look like a futurama exhibit that had suddenly come to life. Miamians pinched themselves to make sure it wasn't a dream. The change had come so quickly.

Speaking of dreams, Kitty Roedell, who worked for the Downtown Development Authority, took it upon herself to convince the city that Bayfront Park needed a major face-lift and that Isamu Noguchi was just the man to do it. Noguchi, a world-famous sculptor who had trained with the legendary Brancusi, came up with a $30 million plan that included two amphitheaters, a playground, a laser tower, an undulating fountain, an expansive baywalk and lots of concrete. Cost overruns and aesthetic disagreement slowed progress on Noguchi's controversial design. Sadly, he died before seeing his last major work completed.

In 1985, the Rouse Company, which won a competition to develop the north end of the park into a specialty market-place, broke ground for Bayside. When Bayside opened in 1987, downtown Miami had a major bayfront gathering place for the first time since the 1920s, when Elser's Pier was torn down to make way for Biscayne Boulevard.

A FUTURE FOR THE PAST

From the time of its founding, Miami paid scant attention to its past. During the 1980s, however, this tear-'em-down philosophy began to change. For the first time, South Floridians realized that most of their historic buildings had been altered or demolished. The City of Coral Gables, which passed a Preservation Ordinance in 1973, was the only place in town where anyone paid any attention to their architectural heritage. This was soon to change. In 1979, Barbara Capitman and the Miami Design Preservation League managed to get a group of Miami Beach's Art Deco buildings listed on the National Register of Historic Places. But even with the impressive credential of being the nation's first Twentieth Century district, Miami Beach officials showed little respect for or interest in the area. (The city did not create a local preservation district until 1986.) The Art Deco District's greatest support came, ironically, from outside Miami and the preservation league struggled to keep the district intact.

In 1981, Dade County Commissioner Ruth Shack decided that it was time for Dade County to adopt a county-wide preservation ordinance. What she thought would be a motherhood-and-apple-pie issue quickly turned into a hot potato. After months of hearings and haranguing, the ordinance squeaked through. For the first time, South Florida had a strong, comprehensive preservation ordinance.

The most important part of the new ordinance was the requirement that each of Dade's 27 municipalities had to pass a similar ordinance or the county law would apply. This spurred the municipalities into action and, eventually, every municipality either created its own ordinance or adopted the county's. Some cities, including Miami and Miami Beach, were slow in securing and enforcing their ordinances. This prompted the county to institute lawsuits to force the errant municipalities to comply. The Dade County ordinance did not work miracles but, for the first time, all of Dade County had to accept historic preservation as policy.

Ironically, *Miami Vice* did more than anything to advance preservation of Miami's unique Twentieth Century architecture. By the time Michael Mann saw the Art Deco District,

"Designer Architects"

A Group of Inernationally Know Architects Left Their Mark on Miami's Skyline During the 1980s.

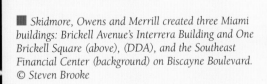

■ Skidmore, Owens and Merrill created three Miami buildings: Brickell Avenue's Interrera Building and One Brickell Square (above), (DDA), and the Southeast Financial Center (background) on Biscayne Boulevard. © Steven Brooke

■ Isamu Noguchi, designer of the new Bayfront Park, stands by the plaque he designed in memory of the Challenger 7 crew. Dade County school children, who raised over $65,000 for the memorial, joined the celebration (top right). (DDA)

■ CenTrust Tower (left), I.M. Pei © Steven Brooke

■ Cultural Arts Center (right), Philip Johnson (DDA)

THE LURE OF THE BAY
Time & Time Again

1920

In 1917, Matthew Elser built Elser's Pier that became downtown Miami's most popular venue for shopping and entertainment. It was torn down in 1925 in preparation for the construction of Biscayne Boulevard and Bayfront Park. (HMSF)

1987

When the Rouse Company opened Bayside Marketplace in 1987, people once again flocked to the bayfront to shop, dine and enjoy the tropical ambiance. (DDA)

Leonard Horowitz had already secured a grant to highlight the Art Deco features on a block of Washington Avenue buildings. This new rainbow of pastel colors created such a stir that Friedman's Bakery, which looked as if it were covered in pastel icing, appeared on the cover of *Progressive Architecture*.

At this time, the Art Deco District was still primarily an enclave of elderly Jews, mostly former New Yorkers, who were living in small rundown hotels and apartments. A few brave pioneers began renovation and were barely hanging on with the hope people would discover and appreciate the district. Once Michael Mann's cameras zoomed in on some of South Beach's Art Deco details—porthole windows, etched-glass sea horses and pastel towers—Miami, and an array of national and international tourists, not only discovered Art Deco, they fell in love with it. Suddenly, it seemed that half the world was coming to South Beach (SoBe) looking for Art Deco. The 1990 census documented what everyone suspected. The Beach not only looked younger, the people who lived there were younger. South Beach was no longer what had been derisively called "God's waiting room." The success of the Art Deco District convinced even the severest critic that preservation had real merit after all.

By the 1980s, preservation in Coral Gables, for the most part, had already become a way of life. The city created historic districts and restored Venetian Pool, City Hall, the Alhambra water tower and its entrances and plazas. The city finally saved the deteriorating, abandoned Biltmore Hotel by leasing it to a private developer. When the beautifully restored Biltmore Hotel reopened in 1986, it helped solidify Coral Gables' Mediterranean character.

The Gables became so enraptured with its historic Mediterranean style that it passed an ordinance destined to "re-Mediterraneanize" the city. The new ordinance gave zoning bonuses and variances to downtown developers who built in the Coral Gables Mediterranean style. The ordinance was the brainchild of the late Mayor Bill Chapman, whose father had sold lots for George Merrick in the 1920s. Chapman mourned the loss of the historic Coral Gables ambience and not only promoted historic preservation but spurred the effort to bring the character back in new construction as well. Before long, even the residential neighborhoods, which were not included in the ordinance, began to re-Mediterraneanize.

Coconut Grove, Miami's most historic neighborhood, changed dramatically in the 1980s. Villagers bemoaned the loss of the old charm as Coconut Grove turned trendy and became the hottest spot in town. Most of the change from unpretentious to upscale occurred after the Coconut Grove Master Plan went into effect. Mayfair, the first major project under the new plan, brought luxury retailing into the Grove along with a high-end hotel. When the five-star Grand Bay Hotel opened, the Grove had yet another upper-crust enclave.

This new luxury market lured the middle-range market back to the Grove. As the crowds increased, the Grove filled with boutiques, art galleries and sidewalk cafes. It became an entertainment destination for both locals and tourists looking for South Florida's tropical, outdoor ambience. CocoWalk, which opened in 1990, connected the older part of downtown Coconut Grove with the new and reintroduced a 1920s town plan that included a Mediterranean-style town plaza. Although the Grove changed for all time, it retained its unique character and its independent spirit. As the new decade got underway, Grove activists were still complaining about the City of Miami's 1925 takeover of the Town of Coconut Grove and threatening to secede from Miami and become an independent municipality. They were encouraged by the success of the citizens of Key Biscayne, who created the new Town of Key Biscayne in 1991 from unincorporated Dade County.

MOTHER OF ART DECO

Barbara Capitman (below left) and Matti Bower, who later became Miami Beach mayor, mourn the loss of the Senator Hotel, which was demolished to become a parking lot. Capitman started a one-woman crusade to make the world appreciate Miami Beach's unique Art Deco architecture. Before her death in 1990, she saw her dreams come true as Miami Beach came back to life and her Art Deco Society became a national movement. (MN)

■ *In 1981, Deco supporter Teresa Gordon exchanges words with anti-Deco picketers in front of the doomed New Yorker Hotel. (MH)*

MAURICE FERRE

The Miami City Commission, for the most part, was not very sympathetic to the past. Despite this problem, many historic buildings in Miami were saved during the 1980s. Zaminco International spent millions restoring Miami's beloved Freedom Tower, formerly the Miami News Tower, but failed to make it viable. In Overtown, the Black Archives led the effort to restore the historic Lyric Theater as the centerpiece of its Folk Life Village. Preservationists persuaded the federal government to incorporate the historic Chaille Block into a new federal prison. In northeast Miami, Morningside became the city's first historic district and Buena Vista East, the second.

Plans moved forward to create a Latin Quarter in Little Havana—the historic Riverside neighborhood. Nearby, Sallye Jude opened The Miami River Inn, which included a grouping of early Twentieth Century buildings.

In South Dade, off Old Cutler Road, archaeologists discovered a deep sink hole (solution hole) that contained 10,000-year-old Ice Age fossils. This site turned out to be one of the oldest human habitation sites ever found in the southeastern United States and moved Dade County's known human history back 6,000 years. Nearby, the Charles Deering Estate at Cutler came into public ownership. The new park included natural, archaeological and historic treasures and soon became one of Dade County's favorite parks.

MORE THAN SKIN DEEP

Everyone could see that Miami completely changed the way it looked in the 1980s but the change was more than new-skyscraper-and-pastel-colors-deep. For better or worse, the 1980s changed the whole style and character of the Magic City. By the middle of the decade, three well-known national authors, Joan Didion, David Reiff and T.D. Allman, all wrote books about the Miami phenomenon. Each, not surprisingly, explained Miami. differently. Miami was so mercurial that

trying to describe it was like the fabled blind men trying to describe an elephant. One's perspective on Miami depended on where and how and when one looked at it and to whom one spoke. T.D. Allman, author of *Miami: City of the Future*, said it best: "...practically everything everyone says about it [Miami], both good and bad, is true!"

It was easy enough to note the demographic changes. In one decade, Greater Miami's Hispanic population became the predominant group. Greater Miami was on the verge of becoming the first metropolitan area in America to have a Hispanic majority. By Miami standards, overall growth was minimal (16 percent), and the historic majority group, non-Latin whites, actually decreased by 192,000. New Miamians included 120,000 additional blacks and 370,000 Hispanics. The majority of the Hispanics did not come from Cuba, but from other Latin American countries. Not counting the Mariel boatlift, which added more than 100,000 Cubans in one month, only 65,000 new Cubans came to South Florida—many from places like Chicago and New York. One hundred seventy-eight thousand new Hispanics (half the total population of the City of Miami) arrived from other Spanish-speaking countries— principally Nicaragua and Colombia.

Other Hispanic gains were also easy to track. Although 10 Hispanics held elected office in Dade County in 1980, this number was misleading. The Miami City Commission already had a Latin majority, but Mayor Maurice Ferre was a longtime Miamian of Puerto Rican birth who became mayor long before anyone counted Hispanic surnames. His political support came mostly from blacks and Anglos. Ferre was a man of vision who had predicted Miami's international future earlier than most and pushed the city in that direction. For many years, he was a bridge between Miami's diverse people.

Cuban-American leaders came into their own during the 1980s. By the end of the decade, most of the "first Cuban" history had been made and many Cuban-Americans were established community leaders. The power shift was especially dramatic in the Florida Legislature. In 1980, the Dade delegation had no Hispanic members. By 1990, 10 Cuban-Americans served. Gains in appointed positions were equally impressive. Amazingly, this Cuban-American advancement into Miami's highest positions of power and influence occurred in one decade.

PEOPLE MAKE A DIFFERENCE

■ *Dade County Commissioner Ruth Shack (left) spearheaded Dade County's preservation ordinance that forced the county and the municipalities to consider their historic resources. (RS)*

■ *Jubilant Ileana Ros-Lehtinen (right) learns that she is victorious in her race for Congress. (MH)*

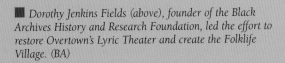

■ *Dorothy Jenkins Fields (above), founder of the Black Archives History and Research Foundation, led the effort to restore Overtown's Lyric Theater and create the Folklife Village. (BA)*

■ *Bob Carr (right), Dade County archaeologist, surveys a bayfront burial site. (BC)*

ONLY IN MIAMI

Many saw this dramatic change as a Cuban takeover or the "Cubanization of Miami." T.D. Allman saw just the opposite. He believed that instead of Cubanizing Miami, Miami had Americanized the Cubans faster than any group of immigrants had been Americanized in the history of the United States. Only in Miami had a large group of immigrants advanced from penniless refugees to affluent leaders in the first generation. It was the classic American success story fast-forwarded in a tropic land.

The Cubans arrived with intelligence, grit, determination and unparalleled entrepreneurial ability. But it was the American economic system, the American political system, the American educational system and American stability that made it possible for the Cubans to create in Miami what they never had in Cuba. It was Miami, with its traditional openness to new people and new ideas, which brought the pieces together. Miami gave life to what the Cubans called "The Miami Miracle."

No person, no place can experience sudden change without fear and pain. To Cubans, no matter how wonderful life was in Miami, the loss of homeland remained a dull heartache. Anti-Communism and anti-Castro emotion ran deep in the Cuban-American psyche and often surfaced in ways that long-time Americans could not understand. Many non-Latins bemoaned the fact that Miami appeared to be the only city in America that had a foreign policy.

In the late 1980s, some American blacks started calling themselves African-Americans. This identification was difficult to use in Miami because many of Miami's blacks were not yet Americans and an even larger percentage did not come to America directly from Africa, but had a stop along the way. In fact, Miami's earliest black residents had come from the Bahamas, even before the City of Miami was born. (They celebrate their Bahamian roots each June at the Goombay Festival in Coconut Grove.) In recent years, the largest group of new black residents came from the Caribbean—principally Haiti and Cuba. Thus, identifying Miami's diverse black community as "African-American" was as much a misnomer as identifying Miami's diverse non-Latin white community as "Anglos."

During the 1980s, the negative feelings of blacks, or African-Americans, toward Cuban-Americans, intensified. The historical timing of the Cubans' arrival in the early 1960s, at the very moment Miami was dismantling its historically segregated society, did not help. The rising expectations of African-Americans, and their desire to escape the bondage of stereotypical menial labor, created a vacuum that the Cubans eagerly filled. As the need for bilingualism increased in the workplace, many African-Americans (as well as Anglos) believed the need to speak Spanish put another barrier in the way of their quest for jobs. As the Cubans' stars rose and their socioeconomic

FROM REFUGEE TO COMMUNITY LEADER
THE 1980S: A DECADE OF CUBAN-BORN FIRSTS

Paul Cejas: Member, Dade County School Board, 1981

Roberto Casas: Member, Florida House of Representatives, 1981

Armando Codina: President, Greater Miami Chamber of Commerce, 1989

Margarita Esquiroz: Female judge, Dade County Circuit Court, 1984

Rosario Kennedy: Female member, Miami City Commission, 1985

Modesto A. "Mitch" Maidique, President, Florida International University, 1986 (first Cuban-born president of a four-year university in the United States)

Raul Martinez: Mayor of a city (Hialeah) with a population of more than 100,000, 1981

Marta Montes: Member, Hialeah Gardens Council, 1982; (first Cuban-born woman to hold municipal office in U.S.)

Alex Muxo: Homestead city manager, 1980

Gilda Oliveros: Mayor of Hialeah Gardens, 1989; (first Cuban-born female mayor in U.S.)

Eduardo Padron, PhD: Vice President (title later changed to President) of Wolfson Campus, Miami Dade Community College, 1980

Jose Garcia-Pedrosa: Miami city attorney, 1982

Sergio Pereira: Miami city manager, March 1985; Dade County manager, November 1985

Ileana Ros-Lehtinen: Florida House of Representatives, female member, 1982; U.S. House of Representatives, 1989

Xavier Suarez: Mayor of Miami, 1985

Jorge Valdes: Dade County commissioner, appointed 1981; elected 1982

Celebrating Diversity

■ Crowds gather at the Holocaust Memorial on Miami Beach (background), designed by artist/architect Ken Treister (right). (KT)

■ The City of Miami built the colorful Charles Harrison Pawley-designed Caribbean Marketplace in Little Haiti (top right). (CP)

■ Calle Ocho Open House draws thousands of Miamians to Little Havana for the annual celebration (above). (HG)

■ A spirited Junkanoo band celebrates South Florida's Bahamian heritage (left). (HG)

FOUNDING THE MIAMI TIMES

In early 1919, Henry Ethelbert Sigismund Reeves moved to Miami from Nassau, Bahamas. Because he had been a printer at the Nassau City Press, he wanted to get into a similar business in Miami. In partnership with the Reverend S.A. Sampson, Dr. Alonzo P. Holly and M.J. Brodie, Reeves formed a printing company and published a newspaper for the black community called the Miami Sun. When World War I made it difficult to get newsprint, the newspaper went out of existence after only eight months.

Reeves launched another weekly newspaper, the Miami Times, that has been published every week since it began in 1923. He also formed the Magic City Printery which made enough profit to keep the newspaper going through the Depression. Today Reeves' son, Garth C. Reeves Sr. and his grand-daughter, Rachel Reeves, left, continue to own and operate the weekly paper. (MH)

HENRY E.S. REEVES

level improved, many African-Americans felt left out of the American dream once again.

Anger, frustration, expectations—first raised and then dashed—joblessness and real and perceived problems within the criminal justice system all created a volatile atmosphere that sparked three more racial disturbances between 1982 and 1989. In 1990, a group of Haitians protested the alleged mistreatment of a Haitian by a Latin storekeeper at a North Dade shopping center. After several days of restraint, the police forcefully dispersed the crowd. Miamians were troubled by the confrontation and, once again, held their breaths. In December 1990, violence also broke out in Wynwood, a predominantly Puerto Rican neighborhood, after police were exonerated in the death of a Puerto Rican. On the positive side, for the first time in history, Miami had an African-American police chief, Perry Anderson. When Anderson resigned, another African-American, Calvin Ross,

took his place.

The 1980s did little to improve the nagging economic disparity between Miami's black, Latin and Anglo communities. The decade was not without its victories, however, as many blacks made impressive gains. George Knox became the City of Miami attorney and by the end of the decade, Dade County's legislative delegation had five African-American members. Other African-American leaders included: William Turner, chairman of the Dade County School Board; and Roy Phillips, president of Dade Community College's new Homestead campus. Miami lawyer Frank Scruggs became Florida's secretary of labor and Garth Reeves, publisher of the *Miami Times*, completed a record-setting 18 years on the Dade Community College Board. African-Americans, as well as women and Hispanics, also became members of many longtime Miami institutions such as the Orange Bowl Committee.

Throughout the 1980s, Miami's political cauldron bubbled and, sometimes, the volatile mixture boiled over. All of Miami seemed divided into three parts and, more often than not, people voted along racial and ethnic lines. In the 1985 election for Miami mayor, however, African-Americans abandoned their anti-Cuban voting record and voted for Xavier Suarez over Maurice Ferre, whom they had helped keep in office for an unprecedented six terms.

FLOWERS IN THE DESERT

For most of its history, Miami was considered a cultural desert, even though it always had an oasis or two, like the Greater Miami Opera Association. Dependent on tourism for survival, Miamians traditionally put more energy into pleasing the tourists than into raising the cultural level of the local population. In the 1980s, however, the desert began to flower. In 1981, Ted and Lynn Arison, who at the time lived in Miami, founded the National Foundation for the Arts. The foundation honored talented young people from all over America and gave Miami an impressive cultural connection. The following year, when Miami's self-esteem was at one of its lowest points, Frank Cooper created the New World Festival of the Arts. Although this overly ambitious festival may have been premature (and ill-timed, since it was held in the heat of summer), the event gave the city a taste of future possibilities.

Another arts event was more successful. The Miami Film Festival, which began in 1985, continued to attract attention with a variety of film offerings. Miami also became an increasingly popular locale for major feature films.

Art took on many new dimensions. Although Dade County adopted its Art in Public Places law in 1971, the construction boom of the 1980s created many opportunities for more public art. Each new Metrorail station featured a different artist and style. The late Carlos Alfonzo, who created the tile mural at the Santa Clara station, was one of the many talented artists who came to Miami in the Mariel boatlift. Rockne Krebs' oft-photographed Miami Line, a rainbow of neon that crossed the Miami River on the Metrorail bridge, was another favorite. By decade's end, the Art in Public Places ordinance had created more than 400 new pieces of art all around the county.

Trompe l'oeil artist Richard Haas left his mark on Miami with his Havana Landmarks in the Harry Cain Towers and private commissions at the Fontainebleau Hotel on Miami Beach and the Bakery Center in South Miami, now demolished. One of his best paintings, executed on the construction fence at the Museum Tower, depicted Miami's architectural and developmental history.

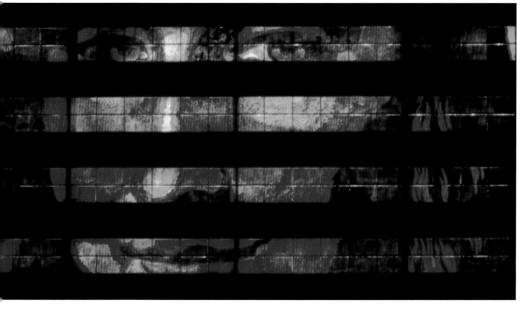

■ ART FOR EVERYONE: World-class artists Claes Oldenberg and Coosie van Bruggen's "Dropped Bowl of Oranges in Slices and Peels" (top right), next to the Dade County Administration Building, was a favorite addition to the art scene. (DDA)

■ Mona Lisa smiles at Miami from the Museum Towers opening (left). (MT)

When the building was completed, the fence was dismantled and moved to the University of Miami School of Architecture. In 1987, the developers of the Museum Tower gave Miamians the decade's most unique public art. For one month, an illuminated reproduction of Leonardo da Vinci's Mona Lisa flashed her enigmatic smile from the side of the new building.

Even the sidewalks were to become works of art. In 1988, the city commissioned Brazilian artist Roberto Burle Marx to create a dramatic design for Biscayne Boulevard from the Miami River to the Omni complex. As the decade ended, some portions of the sidewalk were in place and plans for the completed design moved forward.

Ken Triester's emotional Holocaust Memorial on Miami Beach attracted national and international attention and thousands of visitors. South Florida, with one of the largest Holocaust survivor populations in the world, raised the money to create the monumental outdoor masterpiece as homage to the six million Jews who perished under the Nazis. In February 1990, Eli Wiesel, Nobel laureate and South Florida resident, spoke at the memorial's dedication.

New galleries and co-op efforts such as the Bakehouse Complex and Lincoln Road's South Florida Art Center also elevated Miami's art scene. Many of the new galleries specialized in Cuban-American artists who were receiving national acclaim.

South Florida music and dance lovers also found reason to shout "Bravo!" even though Miami lost its resident philharmonic orchestra. In 1985, the Miami City Ballet began its first season under the dynamic directorship of Edward Villela. Three years later, the unique New World Symphony, an advanced, three-year training orchestra for 21- to 30-year-olds, launched its first series of concerts under the direction of Michael Tilson Thomas. The Miami City Ballet and the New World Symphony were two of the decade's greatest success stories and helped change the way the world looked at Miami's cultural scene.

South Florida culture received another boost when the new, tax-financed Cultural Center opened in 1984. It included the Center for the Fine Arts, the Historical Museum of Southern Florida and a new main library. The new library also housed the Louis Wolfson II Media History Center, which had a growing collection of television and film footage—including the CBS Channel 4 film archives.

The following year, the library, along with Dade Community College, inaugurated "Books by the Bay" at the college's Wolfson Campus. By the end of the decade, the Book Fair, under the leadership of Dr. Eduardo Padron and Mitchell Kaplan, became one of the most successful literary events in America.

■ *Dade County Mayor Steve Clark joins Governor Bob Graham and Miami City Commissioner J.L. Plummer (above) for the ribbon-cutting ceremony at the new Historical Museum of Southern Florida. Actors portraying Julia Tuttle and Henry Flagler join in the fun. (DDA)*

■ *Internationally recognized Brazilian artist and landscape designer Roberto Burle Marx (left) created a new look for Biscayne Boulevard's sidewalks and gardens. (DDA)*

■ *Artist Richard Haas (below) in front of his history-making construction fence at the Museum Towers. (MT)*

■ AN INTELLECTUAL OASIS: Miami-Dade Community College President Dr. Robert H. McCabe (left) and a group of students celebrate Miami-Dade being named the number one community college in America. (MDC)

■ Mitchell Wolfson Jr., founder of the Wolfsonian Museum, launched the first public exhibition of his Decorative and Propaganda Arts at the Wolfson Campus of Miami-Dade Community College. (MDC)

■ Toby Lerner Ansin, "mother" of the Miami City Ballet, shares a quiet moment with founding Artistic Director Edward Villella in front of their Lincoln Road storefront studio. © Ray Fisher

That same year, Mitchell Wolfson Jr. opened a gallery at Dade's Wolfson Campus to highlight his Decorative and Propaganda Arts collection. The exhibits were so well received that in 1986 he formed the Wolfsonian Foundation and purchased the old Washington Avenue Storage Building on Miami Beach to house a new museum. Wolfson also created the Columbus Discovery Commemorative Fund and agreed to match money raised for the endowment funds of the Historical Association, Museum of Science and Greater Miami Opera Association.

In 1987, Dade Community College, in concert with the Dade County Public Schools and Florida International University, opened the New World School of the Arts at its Wolfson campus. This unique school trained talented young people from 10th grade through college in the visual and performing arts. From its inception, the school, the deans, the faculty, staff and students received national recognition.

Miami's varied higher educational institutions also added to the cultural and intellectual scene. The University of Miami grew into a major national research university. Barry College transformed itself from a small women's college into a premier parochial university. Florida International experienced the greatest growth of any university in Florida and expanded to a more comprehensive mission. St. Thomas University had a new law school and Florida Memorial gained stature as one of the United Negro Colleges. Dade Community College also garnered the honor of being named the top community college in America.

Clearly, Miami's cultural and intellectual life came of age in the 1980s. It was a phenomenal decade, full of dreams come true and visions of future possibilities. At decade's end, one major issue remained unresolved. The debate continued on where and when and how the county would build its long-awaited performing arts center.

To Toby — What a lovely beginning & what a lovely memory With deep appreciation — Edward Villella

FUN AND GAMES

The 1980s will also be remembered as a golden era for sports. The area's weather, its geography and its reputation for vitality and variety cast Miami as a national sport phenomenon. The Miami Dolphins celebrated their silver anniversary in 1990 and, despite a lackluster record for the previous five years, retained their history-making position as the only team ever to have had a perfect season (17-0). Although not as successful as in the 1970s, the Dolphins won two AFC championships, taking them to the Superbowl in 1983 and 1985. Coach Don Shula celebrated his 20th year with the Dolphins and was consistently rated one of the two greatest coaches in professional football history—second only to Vince Lombardi. Quarterback Dan Marino made history of his own as NFL records fell to his superior talent.

After failing to reach an agreement with the City of Miami on the Dolphins' continued use of the Orange Bowl, owner Joe Robbie moved his team to a brand-new stadium in North Dade. Joe Robbie Stadium, the first facility of its kind to be privately financed, opened with the 1988 season in time to host Superbowl XXIII in 1989. Despite racial unrest in Miami, the Superbowl proceeded without incident and was lauded as a great tribute to the resiliency and spirit of Miami, as well as the Dolphins organization. When Joe Robbie died in 1990, Miami lost a sports legend.

The University of Miami Hurricanes also made sports history in the 1980s. They achieved the honor of being one of the best (and, as far as Miamians were concerned, THE best) college teams of the decade. In 1983, 1987 and 1989, Miami was the number one college football team in America. The Hurricanes' legacy of outstanding quarterbacks—Jim Kelly, Bernie Kosar and Heisman-winner Vinny Testaverde—stands unmatched. The Hurricanes baseball team won the College World Series in 1982 and 1985. Coach Ron Fraser's teams helped establish him as a national, and even international, baseball figure. As a result, he was named head coach for the U.S. baseball entry in the 1992 Olympics.

The Orange Bowl Game continued to dominate the post-season bowls. Four times in the 1980s, the outcome of the Orange Bowl decided the national college champs. (In the 1984 Orange Bowl, the Hurricanes earned that honor by defeating Nebraska's Cornhuskers.) In 1990, after much discussion, the Orange Bowl Committee turned down an opportunity to switch its event to Joe Robbie Stadium. That year, the Blockbuster Bowl debuted at Joe Robbie Stadium, giving South Florida two bowl games.

Miami also added to its sport offerings. In 1983, Ralph Sanchez, who came to the United States from Cuba in 1961 as an unaccompanied minor, talked the City of Miami into allowing him to run an International Motor Sports Association-sanctioned automobile race right through the middle of town. The first Miami Grand Prix got off to a shaky start when one of the worst cloudbursts in recent memory caused the race to be called before it was completed. Not even an act of God, however, could discourage Sanchez. "If you wait long enough, try hard enough, hope desperately enough," Sanchez told T.D. Allman, "eventually the sun will smile down on you here in Miami." And shine it did. By the end of the decade, the Miami Grand Prix became a major national event that brought thousands of race enthusiasts into downtown Miami each year.

World-class tennis also garnered a Miami dateline after the Lipton Tennis Tournament moved to Key Biscayne. A success from the start, it appeared that the Lipton was here to stay. Miami also made tennis headlines with its hometown superstars: Gabriela Sabatini and Mary Joe Fernandez.

One of the most popular additions to Miami's sports scene was the new NBA basketball team, the Miami Heat. Miamians had been trying to get a professional basketball team for decades. The situation improved in 1983 when the Florida Legislature approved a 3 percent economic development tax for convention and sports facilities. As soon as the tax passed, Miami established

■ *MAKING SPORTS HISTORY: In 1983, drivers and mechanics make ready for the first Grand Prix in downtown Miami (facing page top right). (JK)*

■ *Jubilant University of Miami Hurricane football fans celebrate their first national championship with a January 1984 ticker-tape parade down Flagler Street (facing page center). (UM)*

■ *Joe Robbie Stadium (background), home of the Dolphins, the Blockbuster Bowl and the new Florida Marlins. (MN)*

■ *The new Miami Heat (facing page bottom left) shows its spirit. (MH)*

■ *Dolphins quarterback Dan Marino (facing page bottom right) set records and made NFL history. Miamians considered him one of their own. (APC)*

■ *New fans Jennifer Ricardo and her son Matthew show off a Florida Marlins T-shirt at Joe Robbie Stadium (facing page middle right). (MH)*

A Golden Era

as the Doral Open Golf Tournament and the Breeders Cup carried a Miami dateline. Many local teams at all levels had phenomenal success.

A NICE PLACE TO VISIT

From the beginning, the Magic City was in the business of attracting people. As a result, Miamians were always a little celebrity crazy. In the 1920s *The Miami Herald* even ran a front-page profile almost every day that highlighted Miami's visiting and resident rich and famous. South Florida people-watchers had a field day during the 1980s and early 1990s when some of the most important people in the world visited Miami. Other notables either moved to Miami or were hometown heroes who became famous.

The Pope and three presidents of the United States all came to Miami during the 1980s. (President Reagan had a street named after him—12th Avenue in Little Havana.) Miami's diverse population cheered Pope John Paul II, who paraded through town in his "Popemobile." He showed a special understanding of Miami by speaking in English, Spanish and Creole. Not even a terrible thunderstorm, which halted the open-air mass for 150,000 at Tamiami Park, could dampen his enthusiasm for Miami or Miami's for him.

a Sports and Exhibition Authority, chaired by George Knox. Three years later, ground was broken for the Miami Arena. In 1987, Miami finally received the long-awaited NBA franchise for the 1988 season and the Miami Heat was on its way.

The new Miami Arena opened in Overtown/Park West in July 1988 with a rousing concert by superstar Julio Iglesias, a Miami resident. Four months later, a sell-out crowd of 15,677 welcomed the new Miami Heat.

Along with professional basketball, South Floridians had long dreamed of having a major league baseball team. In 1991, more than 90 years after Royal Palm Hotel workmen played Miami's first baseball game in Royal Palm Park, the real thing came to South Florida. Wayne Huizenga, who had bought part of Joe Robbie Stadium and the Dolphins in 1990, mounted a convincing campaign before the National League Expansion Committee, surpassing the efforts of two other local groups hoping to bring major league baseball to Miami. In the summer of 1991, Huizenga led a proud city in celebration of its new Florida Marlins, who would begin play at Joe Robbie Stadium with the 1993 season.

The variety of sporting events in Miami was as diverse as the community itself. Prestigious offerings such

■ *The new Miami Arena opened with a Julio Iglesias concert in 1988. (APC)*

■ *Her Majesty Queen Elizabeth II, flanked by Dade County Mayor Steve Clark and Booker T. Washington Middle School Principal John Williams, attends a performance at the school during her historic May 1991 visit to Miami. (MH)*

The May 1991 stopover by Her Majesty Queen Elizabeth II of England—Miami's first-ever opportunity to play host to the British monarch—had the same positive effect on the city as the Pope's visit. Miami put its best foot forward during her one-day whirlwind tour. She attended a play at Booker T. Washington Middle School in Overtown, enjoyed a reception at Vizcaya and held a party for VIPs aboard her yacht, *Britannia.* Everyone was sure she went home with nothing but good things to say about her former colony. (After all, Florida was loyal to the Crown during the American Revolution—a fact few even realized.)

Often, people in Miami's multicultural community could not agree on who should receive the traditional key to the city. This frequent difference of opinion turned into a serious problem during Nelson Mandela's July 1990 visit. After Mandela, appearing on ABC's *Nightline*, acknowledged Fidel Castro for his anti-apartheid support, the City of Miami withdrew its official greeting and no high-ranking public officials were on hand to welcome him. As a result, members of the African-American community, led by Miami lawyer H.T. Smith, instituted a black boycott of Miami tourist and convention facilities until Mandela received an official apology.

Miami also acquired many famous new residents. During the filming of *Miami Vice*, most of the cast, including Don Johnson and Philip Michael Thomas, lived in Miami. Miami claimed Vice's Gina, Sandra Santiago, as a hometown

INTO THE LIMELIGHT

Miami's favorite pop star, Gloria Estefan, has come a long way since her days of being a shy Cuban refugee. In 1975, as a University of Miami coed, Estefan joined the Miami Latin Boys band on a lark. Three years later, she married the percussionist, Emilio Estefan, and the renamed group—the Miami Sound Machine—was launched. Estefan and the Miami Sound Machine put Miami on the world's musical map. The group won the American Music Award in 1989 as the favorite pop-rock group. After she, her husband and son were involved in a serious bus accident in March 1990, just two days after being guests at the White House, Miami took their injuries to heart and cheered their recovery. In 1989, Estefan and the Miami Sound Machine received the first star in the Calle Ocho Walk of Fame. (MN)

"I'M NOT MAKING THIS UP"

In 1982, when Miami really needed a sense of humor, *The Miami Herald* flew Dave Barry in from Philadelphia to make us laugh at ourselves. It worked. Four years later, Barry actually moved to Coral Gables ("where most human activity is illegal"). In 1988, Barry won the Pulitzer Prize for commentary.

(MH)

WHY I LOVE SOUTH FLORIDA
by Dave Barry

I like the Miami skyline at night, even though I imagine that as a taxpayer I'm now helping to pay for illuminating the CenTrust Tower. I like hardly ever having to wear a tie to restaurants or even necessarily funerals. I like watching the cruise ships go out, loaded with happy Indianapolis people, and I like it when the ships come back and the passengers have to be unloaded via cranes because they've been eating 17 meals per day and their arms and legs have turned into small useless appendages. I like Bayside and the Grove and Tobacco Road at 1:30 a.m., which is what time it always is inside Tobacco Road, even on Monday afternoon. I like the Book Fair and the Columbus Day Totally Nude Regatta and of course the King Mango Strut, a wondrously demented event that each year proves the important and reassuring scientific law that there is no direct correlation between age and maturity. I even like the Orange Bowl Parade after a certain amount of rum. I like conch fritters. I like being represented by the baddest-ass college football team in the nation. I like being at a Heat game when the crowd is going nuts because we're down by only 15 points going into the fourth quarter and if the team plays really hard there's an outside chance that we can cut it to just 10 by the end of the game. I like South Beach on a Saturday night when the bars are busy and the bands are playing and the Beautiful People are strolling past beautiful yet somehow comical architecture and the world-famous Atlantic Ocean is right there.

I like all these things, and many more. But they're not what makes me sometimes love South Florida. What makes me sometimes love South Florida is this: It's weird.

girl. Popular movie stars Andy Garcia and Mickey Rourke also lived in Miami and baseball superstars Jose Canseco and Dennis Martinez called Miami home.

Latin superstars also gravitated to Miami. Julio Iglesias built a mansion on Indian Creek Island and Jose Luis Rodriguez "El Puma" built a home here as well. Miami's favorite pop star, Gloria Estefan, of the Miami Sound Machine, not only grew up in Miami but lived in a mansion on Star Island. Until his death in 1987, Jackie Gleason continued as one of the area's greatest resident promoters.

THRIVING ON CHANGE

"History doesn't look like history when you are living through it," wrote John W. Gardner in his book, *No Easy Victories*. "It always looks confusing and messy and it feels uncomfortable." During the 1980s, when Miami made history faster than ever before, life was confusing, messy and uncomfortable—to say the least. Part of the time, it was downright depressing and even scary. But when the 1990s began, and people caught their breaths and looked back, they were proud of their city. In one decade, Miami absorbed the shock of refugees and riots. It witnessed an orderly changing of the guard, a revolution of sorts, without missing a beat. It changed the way it looked, thought, felt and dreamed. It took advantage of the good and endured the bad. It refused to be paralyzed by disaster or the happenstance of history. It fought back and made the best of whatever came its way. And when everything seemed to go wrong, it hung on by its fingernails. Miami was a survival town. It had grit.

Sometimes, there was reason to cry. Giants, who changed things for the better, passed away—Claude Pepper, Mitchell Wolfson Sr., Father Theodore Gibson and Governor Leroy Collins, to name a few. When death took former television anchorman Ralph Renick and *Miami Herald* columnist Charles Whited, Miami lost part of its soul. Barbara Capitman died, but what she had created lived on in Miami Beach's Art Deco District. When the *Miami News* folded on December 31, 1988, 92 years after its founding, Miami lost an important voice and a link with its beginning. Other cornerstones like Eastern Airlines, which had long been a part of the history of Miami as well as the history of aviation, closed and left another void. Bankruptcy and an uncertain future for other pioneer companies, like Burdines and Pan American Airways, caused more pain.

As the 1990s began, Miamians continued to grapple with nagging problems that had no easy or quick solution. Language remained a volatile, emotional issue. Although both the crime rate and drug use were down, the level of each remained intolerable. In response, a diverse group of people organized the Miami Coalition for a Drug-Free Community and took bold new steps toward tackling the drug problem, which was also linked to crime.

When the 1980s real-estate boom collapsed, many people and institutions were deeply hurt by Miami's perpetual real estate roller-coaster. Miami, however, had a history of dealing with boom and bust and learned years ago to hang on and wait out the downturn.

In many ways, the 1980s had been like no other decade in Miami's history. Never before, not even during the Boom of the 1920s, had Miami changed its whole being politically, economically and socially—along with its skyline. In other ways, however, the 1980s were just one more typical chapter in the Miami's history of change, change, change. "If you want sustained stability, don't come to Miami," Governor Bob Graham once remarked. "But," he added, "if dealing with change is a challenge, Miami is for you."

Some cried for the loss of the comfortable, familiar Miami of their youth. The 1980s changed the old Miami almost beyond recognition. But the new Miami was alive and beautiful and full of promise. Off it went, unafraid, gambling on a different kind of future that surpassed the wildest dreams of even its most visionary pioneers. No longer at the end of something, Miami was at the center of everything—the connector of the Americas, the center of the New World. But another new Miami was on the horizon and even more dramatic change was on the way.

■ *In 1987, Charlie Munroe, grandson of founder Commodore Ralph M. Munroe, serves chowder at the Biscayne Bay Yacht Club's 100th Washington's Birthday Celebration at the Charles Deering Estate in South Dade. (APC)*

The Miami News
Saturday, December 31, 1988   A Cox Newspaper   25¢

FAREWELL, MIAMI
City's oldest newspaper folds as lawsuit, sale efforts fail

■ *THE END OF AN ERA: After 92 years, Miamians mourned the demise of the* Miami News. *(MN)*

■ *Editor, Howard Kleinberg. (MN)*

TRANSFORMATION: *change in form, appearance, nature or character.*

TRANSFORMACION: *cambio en forma, apariencia, naturaleza o carácter.*

TRANSFOMASYON: *chanjman nan aparans, charakte, oubyen pesonalite ou...*
Yon chanjman natirel ou spirityel.

Chapter Eleven

(RG)

Transformation

"Miami is one of the country's newest big cities, and it's still in formation. It is dynamic and contrasting—a center of popular Latin music and the only city in the U.S. to recently open classical, world-class opera and concert halls. With the wave of Latin American and Caribbean immigration, the last 20 years have finished the transformation of the bilingual, bicultural city into a multicultural metropolis."

Alberto Ibargüen, President and CEO
John S. and James L. Knight Foundation

AS THE 1990S BEGAN, MIAMIANS TOOK A DEEP BREATH AND REMINDED THEMSELVES HOW WELL THEY HAD SURVIVED THE

crippling and often cataclysmic events of the previous decade. It did not take long, however, for new problems to surface. Before the decade celebrated its third birthday, some of South Florida's most valued businesses vanished. First came CenTrust, the bank with its bold Joseph-coat-of-many-colors tower. Ironically, when its president was indicted and its assets seized by regulators and sold to Great Western, the tower blazed a patriotic red, white and blue. This subtle flag-waving did not lessen the nagging fear that more bad news was on the way. Next, like a row of falling dominoes, came the demise of Eastern and Pan American Airlines, followed by Southeast Banking Corporation, Florida's largest and most influential bank. This blow was even worse than the loss of CenTrust because Eastern, Pan Am and Southeast had deep South Florida roots. Their demise was more than a business failure. It felt like the death of a member of the family.

CAUGHT UNAWARE

As South Florida reeled from each new disheartening event, another disaster lurked nearby. Its name was Andrew and it was destined to become even more destructive than the corporate meltdown. It had been 27 years since a hurricane hit Miami. Many newer residents had never even witnessed a severe tropical storm. During those intervening years, people had become complacent and the county's vaulted hurricane-proof building code had been ignored or compromised. Many new homes were poorly constructed and did not have hurricane shutters. Of even greater consequence was the fact that many homeowners were unaware that their new roofs lacked vital hurricane straps.

Andrew was not your average hurricane. In fact, it wasn't even a hurricane until the day before it made land-fall. Once it gained hurricane status and picked up speed, television news morphed into emergency mode. Andrew was heading for South Florida like an arrow to a bulls-eye. On August 23, *The Miami Herald* arrived with a bold "Bigger, Stronger, Closer" banner headline. Many heeded the warnings and followed the prescribed drill. They bought hurricane lanterns, filled their bathtubs with water and cleaned out all the batteries, water and canned food in local stores. But the prevailing opinion was that Andrew was little more than an inconvenience—something to endure but not to fear. Few boarded up their windows or secured their sliding glass doors. That was a big mistake. With each passing hour, Andrew, fueled by warm South Florida waters, intensified—110—120—130-plus miles per hour. It became increasingly clear that the long anticipated "Big One" was out there poised to strike.

In the early hours of August 24, Andrew slammed into Florida City with all its now Category 4 (some say Category 5) might. It even took the hurricane forecasters by surprise. They predicted that Andrew would strike downtown Miami, Aventura and Miami Beach and feared a potential 10-foot storm surge. Miraculously, some said, it bypassed most of the densely populated coastal areas and, instead, focused its fury on less populated South Dade.

■ *On August 24, 1992, Hurricane Andrew slammed South Florida with its vicious winds. (NOAA)*

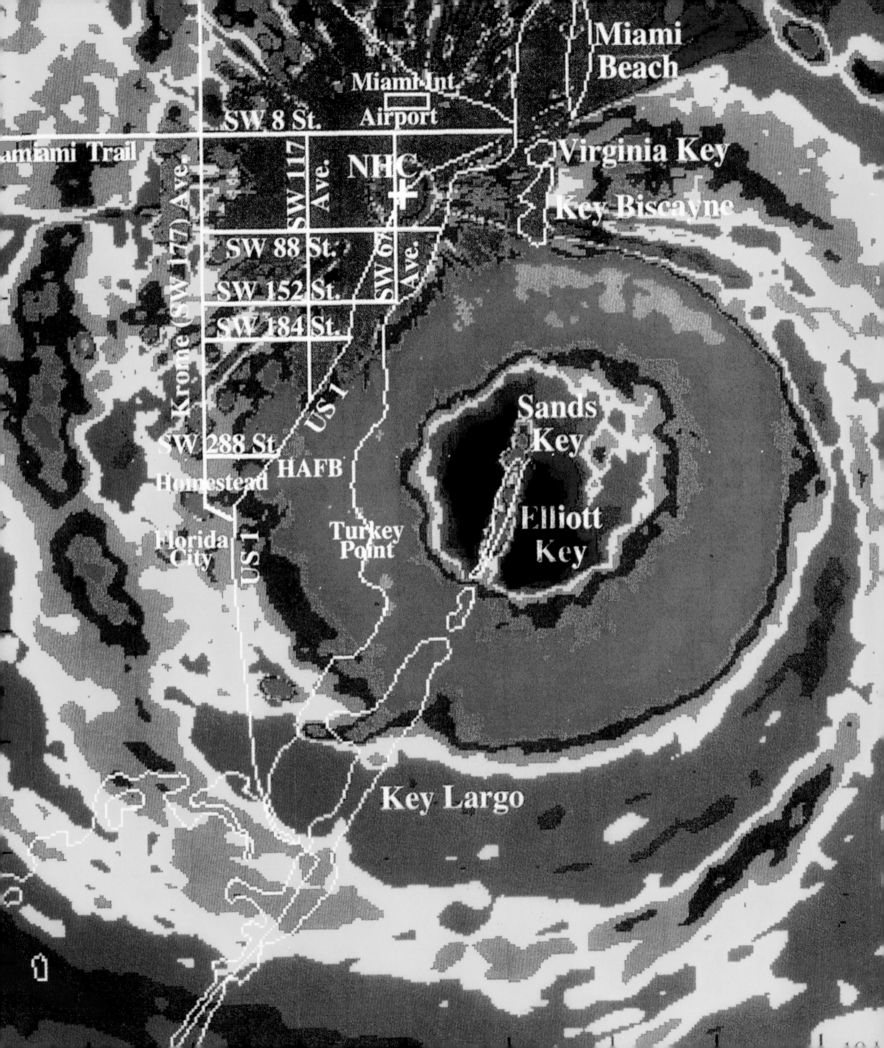

ANDREW

BLOWN APART, BLOWN TOGETHER

■ *Brian Norcross, WTVJ television weather forecaster, became the voice of calm amid the storm (facing page top right). (MH)*

■ *Sharon Hench looks up in horror at what once was the roof of her Country Walk home (facing page top left). (MH)*

■ *Destruction at the Homestead Trailer Park (background). (LW)*

■ *Dade County Emergency Director Kate Hale (below) delivers her dramatic plea for federal help. (MH)*

FINAL EDITION

The Miami Her

SUNDAY, AUGUST 23, 1992

Bigger, stronger

TRACKING HURRICANE ANDREW

In the midst of the increasing whirlwind, a new hero emerged. Bryan Norcross, the WTVJ television weather forecaster, became the voice of calm and reassurance. Even before the hurricane struck, he encouraged people to prepare a "safe room"—a room without outside windows or doors. Fortunately, many took his advice. Although most lost their electrical power, the station simulcast on radio. After the storm passed, many credited Norcross with saving their lives.

When dawn broke, people emerged from their homes to see the kind of destruction Miamians had not witnessed since the horrific 1926 Hurricane. As expected, trees and power lines were down, cutting electricity to more than 1.5 million people. But that was a minor problem compared to what many described as "total devastation." Journalist and historian Howard Kleinberg, who rode out the storm holding a mattress against a buckling door at his son's South Dade home, recalled Andrew's wrath in his book *The Florida Hurricane and Disaster 1992.* His son's home, he wrote, was "dissected bit by bit, pane by pane, shingle by shingle."

Many experienced even more trauma than Kleinberg. It was as if someone had drawn a line at North Kendall Drive and decreed that nothing south of that line should be spared the attack of what Kleinberg's son Eliot called "a vicious beast." Newer neighborhoods suffered the most. Thousands of homes lost roofs and many condominiums lost at least one wall. Mobile home parks resembled a bombed out war zone. The flimsiness of modern building material—plastic, drywall, particle board and pink insulation—was exposed, in more ways than one. Country Walk, an idyllic new community with front porches and gazebos, lay in ruin. Homestead and Florida City appeared almost blown away. Andrew's victims stood stunned in a state of shock.

Without power, communication was difficult. At first, those who lived north of the zone of destruction did not realize the extent of the damage. Most went about normal post-hurricane chores—cleaning, mopping, sawing, hauling trees and looking for ice. Once they learned the horror of South Dade's plight, those less affected rushed to help. Volunteers also poured in from out of town and out of state—a portable soup kitchen from a Georgia church, linemen from South

Carolina and Red Cross workers from every-where. The federal government was less responsive even after President George H.W. Bush flew in within hours of the hurricane's passing and promised immediate federal assistance. But when four days passed and federal help remained elusive, Kate Hale, Dade County Emergency director, took to the airways with a dramatic "Where the hell is the Calvary?" Her emotional plea got federal attention. Two days later, *The Herald* reported: "On the fourth day, they begged for the Calvary. On the fifth day, it rode to the rescue by land, by sea, by air."

A month after the storm, *The Herald* summed up the hurricane's destruction. Miraculously, only 50 people had lost their lives but property damage exceeded $20 billion. This made Hurricane Andrew the most destructive storm in U.S. history, a title that stood until Katrina struck New Orleans more than a decade later. But dollars did not tell the entire story. Andrew's strike was personal. It made more than 150,000 people homeless. Thousands sought refuge elsewhere. Many never returned.

As soon as South Florida began its long journey toward recovery, a remarkable spirit of caring and cooperation emerged. Ethnic and racial disagreements and suspicions evaporated as people rallied to help anyone who needed assistance. With other means of communication difficult, *The Miami Herald* delivered 40,000 free copies of the paper. It contained both news and information about hurricane relief. *The Herald,* in conjunction with WTVJ, launched a campaign called "Neighbors Helping Neighbors" to connect volunteer with victim. President Bush asked Alvah Chapman, retired chairman and CEO of Knight Ridder, to lead the local private recovery effort. Again, Chapman pulled together business and community leaders to tackle a myriad of post-Andrew problems. With two dozen committees, 60 board members and more than 800 volunteers, the group raised almost $30 million and leveraged much more. Superstars like Gloria Estefan and her husband, Emilio, also joined in the recovery efforts. They organized a hurricane relief concert that brought in other luminaries like Whoopi Goldberg, Paul Simon, Celia Cruz, the Bee Gees and Crosby, Stills and Nash. Although the event raised more than $2 million, its real value was to give storm-weary Miamians a chance to laugh, sing and believe Gloria Estefan when she introduced her song, "Coming out of the Dark."

THE WINDS OF CHANGE

Unfortunately, the Andrew spirit did not last long because a different kind of storm with even more lasting consequences hovered nearby. The same day that Andrew turned into a hurricane, the Metro Commission voted not to appeal U.S. District Judge Donald L. Graham's August 14 ruling that declared Metro's at-large elections diluted the rights of blacks and Hispanics. At the time, the nine-member Dade County Commission had one Hispanic, one black and seven non-Hispanic white members. After the county presented several plans, Graham approved single-members districts and enlarged the commission to 13. Following six months of continuing turmoil and uncertainty, including a failed appeal by a group of citizens, the new history-making commission took office in April 1993. It had six Hispanic, three black and three non-Hispanic white members. This transformation not only marked the end of an era but also the end

■ Miami-Dade County's history-making new commission took office in April 1993. Left to right: Pedro Reboredo, Javier D. Soto, Dennis C. Moss, Bruce Kaplan, James Burke, Natasha Milan (Seijas), Sherman Winn, Chairman Art Teele, Maurice Ferre, Miguel Diaz de la Portia, Alex Penelas, Betty Ferguson and Larry Hawkins. (M-DC)

"La Petite Haiti"

"LITTLE HAITI"

During the 1980s, thousands of Haitian immigrants transformed Miami's historic Lemon City neighborhood into "Little Haiti." The award-winning Caribbean Marketplace, designed by Charles Pawley, stamps N.E. Second Avenue with the style and vibrant colors of Haiti's world-famous primitive art. Adding to the Haitian ambiance, the City of Miami opened a new Little Haiti Soccer Park (left) and Cultural Complex designed by Zyscovich Architects. © Morris Moreno (ZA)

City of Miami Commissioner Michelle Spence-Jones, third from left, joined by Port-au-Prince, Haiti Mayor Jean Yves Jason, far right, Commissioners Angel Gonzales and Tomas Regalado, City Manager Pete Hernandez, other elected officials and members of the Little Haiti community celebrate the opening of the little Haiti Soccer Park and pre-opening of the Cultural Complex (above). © Jorge R. Perez (CM)

Mural at Little Haiti Cultural Complex (below). (APC)

of veteran Mayor Steve Clark's 20-year run as Metro mayor. African-American Art Teele took over leadership as commission chairman—a position he would hold until the new executive mayor was elected in 1996. One of the commission's first actions was to unanimously repeal the 13-year-old ordinance that required only English in public documents. It confirmed what everyone knew—the old order had indeed passed. Other public bodies like the Dade County School Board and the City of Miami soon followed suit and switched to single-member districts producing similar ethnic and racial changes. Miami would never be the same.

When Steve Clark stepped down as mayor of Metropolitan Dade County, most wrote his political obituary. But Clark was not inclined to go quietly into a political graveyard. In the fall of 1993, he was elected mayor of Miami, besting a black and a Hispanic opponent.

Nineteen ninety-three also marked the end of the three-year-old black tourism boycott. Organizer H.T. Smith, with Knight Ridder CEO Jim Batten who had spearheaded the negotiations, announced a May settlement that included the formation of Partners in Progress, a citizens' group dedicated to 20 goals that addressed critical issues in the black community. One of the most ambitious was to foster a black-owned convention hotel on Miami Beach.

"A MAGIC MOMENT"

Although the first years of the new decade had been stormy, the December 1994 Summit of the Americas gave Miamians an opportunity to put divisive issues aside. With historic predictability, the community worked together to welcome the Western Hemisphere's 34 democratically elected leaders. The event proved to be what many called "a magic moment" for Miami. The world rediscovered Miami, experienced its diversity and acknowledged it as a laboratory and harbinger of the future. "There is truly a spirit of Miami," President Bill Clinton reminded everyone at the closing ceremony, "and in future years, when the difficulties mount up, when it is difficult to sustain the hope…May future leaders remember the spirit of Miami."

Two years later, following an aggressive campaign by local leaders, the United States Southern Command moved its headquarters to Miami from Panama. Hailed as another example of Miami's future as the center of the Western Hemisphere, SouthCom also highlighted the city's increasing international reputation and geographic advantage.

Spirits continued to soar when Miami celebrated its 100th birthday in 1996. Launched with the December 31, 1995 Orange Bowl Parade and followed by a fundraising Centennial Ball a month later, the yearlong series of events reminded everyone that there was "Something to Celebrate," just as organizers promised. For at least a year, the notion that Miami had no history vanished. Newspapers produced special sections and historic churches and synagogues held commemorative services as the centennial drew Miami people together to reflect on their separate and collective past. When the official AT&T Birthday Extravaganza commenced in Bayfront Park on July 28, thousands came to join in a once- in-a-lifetime birthday party. Three stages of non-stop entertainment filled the park with the sounds of Miami's diverse cultures and food booths gave participants a true taste of Miami's people.

Ironically, just as Miami basked in the glow of its 100 candles, there was a growing movement afoot to abolish it and place the city under the jurisdiction of the Dade County Commission. The effort gained momentum in late 1996 after a city commissioner and the city manager were indicted following a FBI investigation dubbed "Operation Greenpalm." Reeling from the negative publicity, the remaining elected officials convinced former county manager Merrett Stierheim to step in as interim city manager. Stierheim, who was a popular county manager for nine years, took a leave of absence from his leadership at the Greater Miami Visitors and Convention Bureau to answer the call. He quickly discovered that the city had even more serious problems than anyone realized. For a start, it had a $68 million shortfall in its smoke-and-mirrors budget. The situation was so dire that the State of Florida appointed a blue-ribbon oversight board to monitor the city's efforts and, if it failed to resolve the problem, take over. Stierheim enlisted 40 community leaders—executives from major corporations and accounting firms—to help prepare a recovery plan that the state oversight board would approve. Despite the unprecedented crisis at city hall, Miami residents voted overwhelmingly against abolishing the city. A short time later, in a separate election and with only-in-Miami irony, voters approved the changing of Dade County's name to Miami-Dade County.

Just when everyone thought the worst was over, more political turmoil erupted. When Steve Clark died in June 1996, the city commission could not agree on a successor and called a special election. Commissioner Joe Carollo, whom *Herald* staff writer John Dorschner described as "Miami's most electrifying, controversial and unpredictable politician," won. This event was quickly followed by the indictment of yet another city commissioner and a string of here today-gone tomorrow city managers. After former mayor Xavier Suarez beat Carollo in the 1997 mayoral election, the election was thrown out because of voter fraud and Carollo again became mayor.

■ *Jim Morin, The Miami Herald's* Pulitzer *prize-winning political cartoonist, poked fun at the ill-fated effort to abolish Miami. Jim Morin © Miami Herald Media Company, 1997*

■ *The Univeristy of Miami awarded former Secretary of the Treasury Robert E. Rubin, a graduate of Miami Beach High School, an honorary Doctorate of Laws at a May 2008 ceremony (inset). (UM)*

■ *During the 1994 "Summit of the Americas," Miami played host to the leaders of the Western Hemisphere. After three days of discussion, they posed for a history-making photograph in Vizcaya's gardens (facing page). (DDA)*

■ *Three Miamians, Attorney General Janet Reno, front row, right, Environmental Protection Agency Director Carol Browner, second row, right, and Secretary of the Treasury Robert Rubin (inset) served in President William J. Clinton's Cabinet. In 2001, Secretary of Health and Human Services Donna Shalala, second row, fourth from right, became a Miami resident when she was named the University of Miami's fifth president. (DES)*

"Something to Celebrate"

■ Bobbi Mumford and her husband Bobby looked elegant in 1890s formal attire (facing page top left). (BD)

■ Nancy Bahn, as Julia Tuttle, and an actor portraying Henry Flagler greet the crowd as an historic train rolled into town to commemorate the April 1896 arrival of Henry Flagler's railroad (below). (APC)

■ Dominating the celebration in Bayfront Park was Miami's Official Birthday Cake that highlighted different eras of Miami's history (bottom). (APC)

■ School children join pop-artist Romero Britto and three of the Miami Centennial Co-Chairs, Commissioner J.L. Plummer, left, Arva Moore Parks and Thomas G. Abraham, to introduce the official Centennial mascot, "Sunny," created by Britto (facing page bottom). (TA)

■ Following the dedication ceremonies in May 1996, Commissioner Katy Sorenson (right) stands in front of the county's Art in Public Places sculpture—the "M"—created by Roberto M. Behar and Rosario Marquardt. (M-DC)

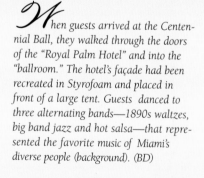

the miami centennial ball
1896~1996

Saturday, February 24, 1996, 8:00 p.m.

Grand Ballroom, Royal Palm Hotel
200 Southeast Second Street
Miami, Florida

Ticket must be presented for parking
and admittance

When guests arrived at the Centennial Ball, they walked through the doors of the "Royal Palm Hotel" and into the "ballroom." The hotel's façade had been recreated in Styrofoam and placed in front of a large tent. Guests danced to three alternating bands—1890s waltzes, big band jazz and hot salsa—that represented the favorite music of Miami's diverse people (background). (BD)

1925

1998

First National Bank, c1925 (LW)   *Flagler First Condominiums, 2008 (RK)*

When the new First National Bank building opened in 1922 on the site of its 1904 offices, it was billed as "Miami's Most Modern Building." Its brick walls and Corinthian columns spoke to the bank's preeminence. In the late 1950s, First National built a new building on Biscayne Boulevard and First Street and then, 30 years later, built a fourth home, now the Wachovia Bank building, across the street.

After CenTrust Savings and Loan acquired the building in the 1980s, workers painted the brick gray, covered the Corinthian columns with marble and put aluminum screening on the façade. Today, Rok Enterprises has restored the exterior to its 1920s' grandeur and transformed it into the Flagler First Condominiums.

A New Beginning

A year later, archaeologists made a startling discovery on the south bank of the Miami River that reminded everyone how insignificant their brief and often tumultuous history looked compared to the scope of thousands of years of human life in Miami. After the Dade County Preservation Ordinance passed in 1981, and the City of Miami added protection in 1996, the disturbance of known archaeological sites required an archaeological survey before construction could proceed. When county archaeologist Robert Carr noticed the demolition of the 1950-era Brickell Apartments in preparation for construction of a new high-rise building, he notified the owner. No one anticipated what lay beneath the surface. "Whether serendipity or fate," Carr wrote, county archaeologists had found what would turn out to be the most important archaeological discovery in South Florida history.

Dubbed the "Miami Circle," archaeologists and community volunteers uncovered a circular feature that measured 38 feet in diameter. Carefully spaced postholes indicated it was the remains of a large circular structure—perhaps a public or sacred building. Radiocarbon dated the Miami Circle c.200 A.D. and overall human habitation on the site as early as 750 B.C. Archaeologists and historians had long been aware of the Tequesta Indian site on the north bank of the river that the Spanish described in 1567. The newly discovered site on the south bank changed Miami's prehistory and added new knowledge, as well as new questions, to the saga.

In stark contrast to Miami's 1896 leaders who leveled the huge Indian mound on the north bank and hauled away the bones and artifacts, Dade County leaders, spurred by Mayor Alex Penelas, Dade Heritage Trust, native people and community activists, sought an injunction to stop construction. Ultimately, the county, the State of Florida and the Trust for Public Land acquired the property through eminent domain for $27 million.

Several years before archaeologists uncovered the Circle, artist Manuel Carbonell had created a 53-foot column and statue of a Tequesta warrior on the new Brickell Avenue Bridge. As the Circle awaited future evaluation, the silent Tequesta sentinel seemed to watch over the site. Carr reminded people that the Miami Circle represented "the deep taproot of prehistory that is the spiritual undercurrent of Miami's cultural landscape."

■ *Archaeologists at work at the Miami Circle (below). (AHC)*

■ *State of Florida archaeologist Jim Miller and Christopher R. Eck, director of the historic preservation division of Miami-Dade County, bow their heads as Catherine Hummingbird-Ramirez of the Carib Nation says a prayer at the Miami Circle (facing page inset). Carl Juste © Miami Herald Media Company, 2001*

MAKING HISTORY

For John Ellis "Jeb" Bush, politics is certainly a family affair. The second son of former President George H.W. Bush and the younger brother of President George W. Bush, Jeb has built an impressive political resume of his own.

His Florida career began in 1980 after he moved to Miami to stake his claim in the real estate market. Four years later, he became chairman of the Dade Republican Party and then Florida Secretary of Commerce. Bush made his first run for Florida's governorship in 1994 but lost a close race to incumbent Lawton Chiles.

The defeat was simply an intermission. In 1998, he handily defeated Lt. Governor Buddy MacKay to win the governorship. He was reelected in 2002. Jeb Bush was the second South Floridian to reach the state's highest office, following in the footsteps of Bob Graham. *(EF)*

■ *Miami has always attracted stars—Oprah Winfrey, Rosie O'Donnell, Cher, Ricky Martin and Matt Damon, to name a few. In the early 1990s, Madonna and Sylvester Stallone caused a stir when they moved almost next door to each other on Brickell Avenue. As the sightseers increased, adjoining residents sought to close the street to keep the tour buses away. Stallone often participated in local events and gave to community causes. In 1996, he presented Gusman Theater board member Rosario Kennedy with a check for $75,000 to help restore the historic Olympia Theater. (RK)*

Never a Sure Thing

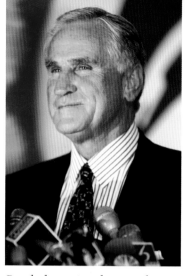

As the 1990s drew to a close, Miamians, despite having been stuck on what seemed like a perpetual roller coaster ride, looked to the future with shaky optimism. "It was a kaleidoscope decade," *Herald* sports writer Edwin Pope wrote, "like a Disney World ride, up and down, up and down, up and down. So wild, so unimaginable, so theatrical, nobody could have possibly thought this up in their dreams." Although Pope was writing about sports, it was an apt description of the decade itself. That is not to say that Miami's ever-changing sports scene did not experience its own wild ride. In one decade, the city witnessed the debut of the Florida Marlins and watched in disbelief as the four-year-old team won the World Series and triumphed again five years later. The Panthers, a National Hockey League team, roared into town and left for Sunrise, west of Fort Lauderdale, five years later. Although Ralph Sanchez ended his downtown Grand Prix, he built the $58-million, 65,000-seat Homestead Speedway with a public-private partnership. The Speedway not only became a major national racing venue, it gave Homestead a much-needed boost toward recovery from Hurricane Andrew. Meanwhile, the University of Miami continued to dominate the college football world with a 1991 championship and a winning streak of 58 home games. UM baseball added to the excitement by again becoming national champions and spawning off players to the major leagues. After a legendary career with the Miami Dolphins, Don Shula retired with a history-making 325 wins, two Super Bowl championships and an unmatched reputation.

At the time, change came so suddenly it was difficult to keep track. Joe Robbie's heirs sold the Miami Dolphins to Wayne Huizenga and Wayne Huizenga sold the Florida Marlins to John Henry. The Orange Bowl Game moved out of the Orange Bowl Stadium and in celebration of the new millennium, the impressive new AmericanAirlines Arena—Miami's second arena in little more than a decade—opened on New Years' Day 2000. Six years later, the arena's home basketball team, the Miami Heat, won the National Basketball Association championship.

Miami's favorite hometown superstar, Gloria Estefan, helped celebrate the arrival of the new century and millennium with a sold-out pre-opening concert in the new Arquitectonica-designed arena. New Year predictions included the usual hopeful expectation that the city had finally matured and would no longer be the subject of unflattering national headlines.

■ A beaming Don Shula announces his retirement at a January 1996 press conference (top). © Miami Dolphins, Dave Cross

■ The beautiful new $213-million AmericanAirlines Arena, designed by Arquitectonica, debuted on New Year's Eve 1999 with Gloria Estefan's "Millennium Concert." Two days later, the Heat played their first game in the new facility (left). © Richard Bryant-Arcaid (A)

■ Ralph Sanchez, with his wife Lourdes, daughter Patricia Sanchez-Abril and son Rafael "Rafa," celebrated at the 1995 opening of the Homestead Speedway (facing page top left). (RSAN)

■ A jubilant Miami Marlins and their fans cheer the team's 1997 World Series victory. © Florida Marlins, Dennis Bancroft

■ In 2006, Miami Heat players and fans celebrate the Heat's first NBA Championship (facing page bottom). (NBA)

MERRETT STIERHEIM:
"A MAN FOR ALL SEASONS"

Tim Chapman © Miami Herald Media Company, 2002

*F*ew, if any, have had as long or as positive an impact on South Florida as Merrett Stierheim. His Miami career began in 1959 when he came to the City of Miami as a Wharton graduate intern. Eight years later, as an assistant city manager, he accepted a manager position in Clearwater and later, Pinellas County.

In 1976, with "sand in his shoes" Stierheim returned as Dade County Manager. During his almost-10-year-scandal-free tenure, he oversaw the Decade of Progress voter-approved bond issue that included megaprojects like Metrorail, Metromover and Metrozoo. He also helped Dade County work through the tumultuous 1980s, including racial unrest and the assimilation of 165,000 Cuban and Haitian refugees.

The Women's Tennis Association temporarily lured him away from public service in 1986. But the public sector pulled him back four years later as president and CEO of the troubled Greater Miami Convention and Visitors' Bureau (GMCVB).

When the City of Miami manager was indicted in 1996, the mayor looked to Stierheim for help. With a leave of absence from the GMCVB, he became the pro bono city manager and led the effort to help the city through serious financial and ethical problems. (He also provided pro bono help to the City of Homestead when it struggled with financial issues.)

By this time, Stierheim had garnered the enviable reputation as "Mr. Fix-it." Whenever any public body faced serious problems, it was Stierheim to the rescue. In 1998, when Dade County faced a series of embarrassing scandals, the mayor brought Stierheim back. His temporary assignment quickly became permanent.

After leaving Miami-Dade County in 2001, the new Town of Miami Lakes grabbed him to help them launch the new municipality. While at Miami Lakes, the Dade County School Board recruited him to be Superintendent of Schools after they fired the previous superintendent. Three years later, when he stepped down as school superintendent after 45 years of public service, he continued as an example and a voice for honesty and integrity in public service.

DEALING WITH THE UNEXPECTED

But early in the new century, Miami's penchant for attracting sudden controversies accelerated. What began as a Thanksgiving Day miracle turned into a tragedy. The miracle came on November 26, 1999, when two fishermen rescued a five-year-old boy floating in an inner tube three miles at sea off

Fort Lauderdale. His name was Elián Gonzalez and he was one of three survivors of a Cuban refugee boating catastrophe that killed 10 others, including his mother. At first, the tragic story read like many others. In recent years, a staggering number of Cuban and Haitian children, as well as adults, had drowned or been rescued at sea after risking their lives to reach America. This time, however, it would be different. Elián Gonzalez became a symbol—an emotional linchpin that connected 40 years of pain, longing and unrelenting hatred of Fidel Castro to the fate of a child.

While awaiting final disposition, immigration authorities gave his great uncle Lazaro Gonzalez temporary custody of the boy, and he moved into the family's Little Havana home. At first, Elián's Miami relatives wanted his father, Juan Miguel, to join them in Miami. When Juan Miguel announced that Elián's mother had left without his knowledge and he had no desire to move to Miami but, instead, wanted Elián back, feelings toward him changed. For many, returning Elián to Cuba was out of the question, even if it meant separating him from his father and violating American law.

As the case worked its way through immigration procedures, Elián became more comfortable in the Gonzalez home. Every time he walked outside, an ever-increasing number of photographers captured his every move and his now-smiling face. Christmas and Three Kings Day brought an abundance of American toys, more attention and more smiles. This picturesque idyll came to an abrupt end a month later after immigration authorities ruled in favor of his father.

Nothing since the civil disturbances of the 1980s had fractured Miami's fragile ethnic and racial rapprochement like the Elián controversy. Appeals and counter appeals continued as well-meaning Miamians tried to work out a compromise among the Immigration and Naturalization Service, the Justice Department, Elián's Miami relatives and his father in Cuba. Although many predicted his return was inevitable and just a matter of time before federal and state law demanded he be reunited with his father, the protestors remained of one mind. Elián must stay in America. "The court decision to repatriate Elián approaches like a speeding vehicle careering toward a collision," *Herald* columnist Fred Grimm wrote.

After 20 of Miami's elected leaders, including Miami Mayor Joe Carollo and Miami-Dade County Mayor Alex Penelas, stood together to announce that no local law enforcement officials would help federal authorities remove Elián from the Gonzalez home, Miami's already fractured populace lined up into two unyielding, angry camps. For many non-Cubans, the politicians' stance reminded them of Orville Faubus standing at the Little Rock, Arkansas schoolhouse door in 1957 defying the U.S. government's court-ordered integration. On the other side, many Cuban Americans thought non-Cubans did not understand what Elián would face if he returned to Fidel Castro's Cuba. They felt strong-armed by the U.S. government—especially President Clinton and Attorney General Janet Reno, a Miami native. Many compared sending Elián back to Cuba to sending Jews back to Nazi Germany.

By this time, thousands of people gathered around the Gonzalez home causing one reporter to dub the site "Camp Elián." Under the glare of live television camera lights, well-know celebrities held hands with the protestors. Although some described the scene as having a carnival atmosphere, for the round-the-clock Elián supporters, it was a vigil.

■ A crowd of supporters gathered near the house, upper right with flags, where Elián Gonzalez was staying (left). Tim Chapman © Miami Herald Media Company, 2000

■ Musician Emilio Estefan, actor Andy Garcia, singer Gloria Estefan, Silvia Iriondo of Mothers Against Repression and Maritza Guiterrez joined hands in prayer and solidarity outside the Gonzalez's house (above). Marice Cohn Band © Miami Herald Media Company, 2000

■ Elián Gonzalez watched the crowd outside his Uncle Lazaro Gonzalez's Little Havana home (facing page). © Miami Herald Media Company, 2000

As a nation watched and waited to see how the increasingly dramatic story would end, Attorney General Reno, hoping to find a peaceful solution, welcomed help from a variety of local leaders—lawyers, business executives and two university presidents. Talks continued even after Lazaro Gonzalez defied a court order and said he would never give Elián up. But at 5:15 a.m. on April 22, after Reno set a 5 a.m. deadline for a final agreement and no agreement came, 20 agents from the U.S. Immigration and Naturalization service stormed the Gonzalez home. Within three minutes they removed the frightened boy from the house and sped him away in a white van. Within hours, Elián was reunited with his father, who was waiting for him in the Cuban embassy in Washington. As *Herald* columnist Robert Steinback wrote, "It was all over but the anguish."

The horrifying images of armed marshals and a terrified child further enraged the Cuban-American community and even caused concern among those who supported reuniting Elián with his father. All across American continuous television coverage depicted Miami in a negative light. "Some called it brutal and premature. Some called it proper and overdue," *The Herald* reported the day after Elián's removal. "Virtually everyone," the article continued, "regretted that—somehow, after all this time and all that talk—it had come

to this." Defiant elected officials, while expressing outrage over the action, urged calm.

As superheated emotions played out on the streets of Miami, some incidences of tire burning and bottle throwing prompted more than 250 arrests. As the crowd grew larger, the leaders of 21 exile organizations came together to find a non-violent way to channel the protestors' anger. After a two-hour meeting, their spokesperson, under the glare of television lights, called for a general strike. "We declare Miami a 'dead city' on Tuesday," he said. This action, especially the term "dead city," infuriated non-Cubans including those who had joined Cuban Americans in questioning how Elián had been removed.

Tuesday, April 25 arrived and, as promised, businesses shut down as countless numbers of protestors took to the streets in what *The Miami Herald* called a "river of outrage." More than 4,000 teachers and 100,000 students stayed home. Many Cuban Americans believed that the strike was a way to demonstrate their political and economic power. Those on the other side saw it as an in-your-face affront to the United States and the residents of the city that had welcomed them. They believed that the protestors were showing their gratitude by defying the federal government, breaking the law and calling a strike against the people who had helped them. Although the day passed without serious incident, anger intensified. Neither side offered an apology. Adding to the turmoil, Miami Mayor Joe Carollo fired the city manager because he would not fire the police chief, who Carollo said disobeyed orders by aiding the federal authorities. The police chief quit in protest.

The aftershock continued until the United States Supreme Court settled the matter two months later by turning down an appeal by Elián's Miami relatives to keep the boy in the United States. On June 28, the Gonzalez family, who had been living in seclusion in Maryland, boarded a jet in Washington bound for Havana. A small crowd stood quietly outside Elián's Little Havana home as they watched Elián's departure on television. As the plane climbed and turned south they fell to their knees, wept and cried "No! No! No!" It was over, but the difficult job of healing the raw wounds that separated a community had barely begun.

PICKING A PRESIDENT

In November 2000, during the presidential election between Republican George W. Bush and Democrat Al Gore, Florida again grabbed the headlines. It began on election night when a television anchor declared Al Gore the winner in Florida and then, a short time later, changed his mind and said the election was too close to call. Thus began 36 days of national turmoil as the nation waited for Florida to figure out its final tally and determine who would be the next president. Not since the disputed election of 1876 had Florida played such a pivotal role. As election officials and the courts tried to sort out the mess, super-lawyers, political activists and an army of media personnel poured into the state. Conspiracy theories abounded.

After the Florida Supreme Court ordered a manual recount in four counties—Broward, Palm Beach, Volusia and Miami-Dade—South Florida again attracted national media attention like a moth to a flame. As the clock ticked toward a November 25 deadline, election officials struggled with absentee ballots, butterfly ballots, over votes, under votes and the infamous dimpled and hanging chads.

Chanting crowds gathered in the halls of the Miami-Dade Administration Building, causing some of the vote counters to say that they felt intimidated. Whether because of fatigue, intimidation or simply facing an impossible task in the time allotted, the Miami-Dade Canvassing Board abruptly stopped the count on November 22.

Four days later, the Florida vote became official—at least

for the moment. Out of 5.825 million votes cast for the two main candidates, George W. Bush was declared the winner by 537 votes. But this was not the end of the controversy. A week later in a split decision, the Florida Supreme Court ordered all counties to scrutinize the under votes. Just as the recount began in Florida's 67 counties, the U.S. Supreme Court stopped it and, after legal arguments were heard two days later, sealed Gore's fate. On December 13, Gore decided it was time to concede rather than continue the national uncertainty. "Now the Supreme Court has spoken," he said. "Let there be no doubt, while I strongly disagree with the court's decision, I accept it."

■ *Supporters cry in disbelief after the U.S. Supreme Court refused to block Elián Gonzalez's return to Cuba (facing page). Tim Chapman © Miami Herald Media Company, 2000*

■ *Kendall Coffey, attorney for the Democrats, speaks about the Florida Supreme Court order to manually recount Florida's ballots (top right). Al Diaz © Miami Herald Media Company, 2000*

■ *The Honorable Lawrence D. King, chairman of the Miami-Dade Canvassing Board, center, reviews a questionable ballot as Democrat Jarrett Barrios, left, and Republican Miguel A. De Grandy, right, look on (bottom far right). Jeffey Boan © Miami Herald Media Company, 2000*

■ *Bryan Wilkes of Northern Virginia, dressed as Santa, shows his support for Bush outside the Miami-Dade County Administration Building (bottom near right). C.W. Griffin © Miami Herald Media Company, 2000*

MAKING A COMEBACK

During the time Miamians became embroiled in local, international and national political issues, the cranes returned to Miami without fanfare. They were not the winged variety suddenly flying out of the Everglades. These cranes were construction cranes built of wire and steel. With an almost eerie sense of déjà vu, South Florida was booming again. When humorist Will Rogers viewed a similar phenomenon during the 1920s boom, he quipped that Florida should make the crane the state bird.

The latest chapter of South Florida's boom and bust history began on Miami Beach. In 1998, responding to the increasing number of tourists lured to Miami Beach by the Art Deco District, Loews Hotels, in partnership with the City of Miami Beach, opened the first major hotel built in Miami Beach in more than 30 years. Just four blocks from the Miami Beach Convention Center, the 17-story, 800-room hotel incorporated the adjacent 100-room historic St. Moritz into their plan. Besides attracting new visitors to Miami Beach, the Loews also sparked additional restoration of historic hotels, as well as the construction of new properties.

After a series of delays, in May 2002, black developer Donald Peebles opened the $80-million Royal Palm Crowne Plaza. The new hotel incorporated a replication of the historic Royal Palm and the restoration of the neighboring Shorecrest. Called the "crown jewel" of the settlement to end the black tourist boycott, its first official guest was boycott leader H.T. Smith.

■ *Don Peebles
C.W. Griffin
© Miami Herald
Media Company,
1999*

■ *The rebuilt Royal Palm Hotel and the restored Shorecrest, each with new towers, became the first black-owned luxury hotel in the nation (above). It was considered the "crown jewel" of the settlement of the black boycott. (RTG)*

■ *H.T. Smith, leader of the black boycott, was the first guest to sign in at the opening of the Royal Palm Crowne Resort (left). Charles Trainor Jr. © Miami Herald Media Company, 2000*

■ *The 17-story Lowes Miami Beach Hotel incorporated the historic 1939 Art Deco St. Moritz Hotel into the 780-room convention hotel's design (below). (Lowes Hotel)*

BRICKELL AVENUE
THE BEGINNING OF THE BOOM

■ When the Four Seasons Hotel and Residences was completed on Brickell Avenue in 2003, it became Miami's tallest building at 64 stories and the tallest residential tower on the east coast south of Manhattan (left). (APC)

■ The Espirito Santo Plaza, completed in 2004, had offices, residences and a Conrad Hotel. It quickly became one of Miami's favorite new buildings (right). (APC)

FROM KITSCH TO CONDO
Time & Time Again

1950

(LW)

2008

(SIB)

In the 1950s and 1960s, a beautiful stretch of oceanfront called Sunny Isles filled with elaborately themed Miami Modern motels. With names like Waikiki, Tangiers, Mandalay and Castaways, the middle-class resorts attracted a different type of tourist. They came in their automobile—even in the summer—and often brought their children. The Carlos Schoeppl-designed Sahara Motel, now the Sahara Beach Club Motel, is one of the few that has survived—concrete camels and all.

Today, motel row has become condo row filled with more and more luxury, oceanfront condominiums in the newly incorporated City of Sunny Isles Beach (above), the "City of Sun and Sea."

The flurry of hotel development also spread across the bay. By 2004, Miami's Brickell area had four new luxury hotels—the Mandarin on Brickell Key, and the J.W. Marriott, Conrad and Four Seasons on Brickell Avenue. Some of the new hotels incorporated apartments and offices into their plan.

But this was just the beginning. Seemingly almost overnight, the Miami skyline—from Brickell to Uptown—filled with construction cranes as the skeletons of new condominiums and office building rose skyward. No one in Miami, not even those with memories of Miami's other periods of rampant growth, had witnessed anything like it.

The City of Miami's transformation began with the election of Manny Diaz as mayor. He came into office in November 2001 with a pledge to save the city from the brink of financial disaster and promised renewal and rebirth. Although his first election victory followed a runoff fueled by post-Elián anger, when he ran for re-election four years later, his sky-high approval ratings resulted in a landslide. By this time,

low interest rates and easy credit had joined with Diaz's pro-development point of view to create a full-blown boom. Unlike recent periods of rapid growth that mainly affected the urban core, this boom spread out in all directions.

After officials and community leaders broke ground for the long-awaited Cesar Pelli-designed Carnival Center for the Performing Arts in 2001, it had the same effect on development in Miami that the Loews Hotel had on Miami Beach. As soon as the construction cranes arrived at the Carnival Center, they appeared all over the area. Developers broke ground for a plethora of high-rise buildings—mostly condominiums—on Biscayne Boulevard, into Edgewater, Midtown, Uptown and points north.

As the impressive new skyscrapers rose on Biscayne Boulevard, plans were underway for revitalization of long-neglected Bicentennial Park. Following a series of public meetings and a charette, the city adopted a new master plan for the park that included three new museums—the Miami Art Museum and the Miami Science Museum with a wing for the Historical Museum of Southern Florida. Although not without controversy, the plan moved forward. The City of Miami and Miami Dade County voters passed a multimillion dollar bond issue that included funds for what was now being called Museum Park.

■ Miami Mayor Manuel A. "Manny" Diaz (top left) laid out his plans for a second term following his 2005 re-election. © Jorge R. Perez (CM)

■ Architect Kentaro Ishida of the Swiss architectural firm of Herzog & de Meuron shows Miami Art Museum Trustee Rose Ellen Meyerhoff Greene the model for the new Miami Art Museum in Museum Park (left). (MAM)

■ Model of the Herzog & de Meuron-designed Miami Art Museum in Museum Park (below). Herzog & de Meuron designed Beijing's "Bird Cage" stadium for the 2008 Olympic Games. (MAM)

■ Cooper, Robertson & Partners with Rodriguez and Quiroga completed the master plan for Museum Park (background).

■ MAM Director Terence Riley joins Trustee Aida Levitan, Board Chairman Aaron Podhurst, Trustee Diane Grob, Werner Grog, Dorothy Podhurst, Beverly Parker, Trustee Mitchell Bierman and Trustee William Parker at the unveiling of a model of the new museum in Museum Park (right). (MAM)

■ Historical Museum of Southern Florida Trustee Judge Scott Silverman, right, joined by Laura Morilla, executive director of the Miami-Dade County Commission for Women, looks over the Historical Museum's plans for its new 25,000-square-foot hall as part of the Science Museum in Museum Park (below). (HMSF)

■ Grimshaw Architects won the commission to design the Miami Museum of Science's new $275-million Museum Park facility (left). Left to right: William Horgan, Andrew Whalley and Vincent Chang, of Grimshaw's New York office will be in charge of the plans that will include a three-story aquarium and a plane-tarium. (GA)

■ Grimshaw, which has offices in London, New York and Melbourne, Australia, is known for its concern for the environment and its high-tech modern designs. Their Eden Project in Great Britain (left) is the largest plant enclosure in the world. (GA)

MiMo and BiBo

In 1999, Randall Robinson, a planner with the Miami Beach Community Development Corporation, and Teri D'Amico, an interior designer, coined a new term and launched a new movement they dubbed MiMo. Just as Barbara Capitman had

done in the 1970s with Art Deco, Robinson and D'Amico looked around and liked what they saw. It was Miami Modern—Miami's own version of mid-century Modernism—the angled and cheese-holed architecture of the late 1940s, 1950s and 1960s. Unappreciated and disappearing fast, the movement grew quickly as more and more people saw MiMo in a new light. After years of being ignored and sometimes derided, legendary architects like Morris Lapidus, Norman Giller, Igor Polevitsky, Robert Little, Marion Manley, Robert Law Weed, Rufus Nims, Robert Bradford Browne, Alfred Browning Parker and others received new attention.

■ *Randall Robinson and Norman Giller (above). (RR)*

In Miami, Eric Silverman, with the help of Miami Commissioner Johnny Winton, worked to designate a stretch of rundown Biscayne Boulevard as an historic district. Miami Beach preservation activists Nancy Liebman, Terry D'Amico and Don Worth offered their expertise and helped organize the MiMo Biscayne Association. President Fran Rollason and others began the challenging job of revitalizing the area into both a tourist destination and a nice place to live and work. Combining MiMo with BiBo, for Biscayne Boulevard, the new area dubbed MiMo on BiBo was born.

(FR)

The arrival or expansion of other new museums also indicated that Miami was finally developing a long-sought cultural soul. In 1995, Mitchell Wolfson Jr. opened the Wolfsonian Museum of Decorative and Propaganda Arts in the restored Miami Beach Storage building on Washington Avenue. The following year, he donated the building and his entire collection to Florida International University—the largest private donation in Florida history. The opening of the Jewish Museum on South Beach added another dimension to South Florida's creative and intellectual offerings. Nearby, the Bass Museum added a new wing designed by internationally recognized architect Arata Isosaki.

On Watson Island, a group of community leaders launched the instantly successful Miami Children's Museum. It sat across from the iconic Parrot Jungle Island that moved to the new site from its former Pinecrest home. The city approved plans for a new mega-yacht marina and hotel, much to the displeasure of open-space supporters and nearby residents.

Across the bay, other museums continued to grow in both size and reputation. The University of Miami's Lowe Museum of Art—Miami's first—continued to expand and grow in stature. It complemented Coral Gables' artistic ambiance that included many private galleries. In North Miami, the Museum of Contemporary Art (MOCA) built a Charles Gwathmey-designed gallery, in concert with local architect Jose Gelabert-Navia. Phillip and Patricia Frost's $3 million gift ensured that Florida International University would also have a new art museum designed by the internationally known architect, Yann Weymouth of Hellmuth, Obata + Kassabaum. But the greatest boost to Miami's art scene arrived with Art Basel Miami Beach.

The Wolfsonian-Florida International Museum (background and bottom right). (W-FIU)

The Miami Children's Museum on Watson Island (center). © Dan Forer (A)

The Joan Lehman Building at the Museum of Contemporary Art (MOCA) (facing page bottom right). © Steven Brooke (JGN)

The new Frost Art Museum at Florida International University (right). (FIU)

The Jewish Museum of Florida is housed in the former Beth Jacob Synagogue—Miami Beach's first (left). (HG)

Our Cultural Soul

Art Basel Miami Beach, which *The New York Times* called "an experimental stepchild of a venerable Swiss parent," began in 2002. (Its original 2001 launching had to be postponed because of the tragic events of September 11.) Almost from the moment it opened, people predicted it would become the preeminent North American art fair, especially for contemporary art. One of the reasons for its success was the involvement of South Florida's growing number of private collectors who opened their homes and their collections to collectors from all over the world.

Art Basel also focused attention on Wynwood, Miami's emerging art district that was busy transforming itself from its rather seedy light-industrial past to a major art venue. The first to arrive in the area was the nonprofit Bakehouse Art Complex, founded by a group of artists and art supporters in 1986. Located in an old, abandoned bakery, its nonprofit mission was to provide affordable studio space and exhibition galleries for emerging artists.

Don and Mera Rubell, who moved to Miami from New York in 1993, helped launch Wynwood's renaissance when they converted a former Drug Enforcement Agency building into a gallery for their art collection. After they expanded and incorporated a nearby warehouse into their space, the Rubell Family Collection opened to the public.

Art Basel

THE PREEMINENT NORTH AMERICAN ART FAIR

■ *Art Basel participants admire Michael Vazquez's work at the Snitzer Gallery (facing page top left), one of the many galleries that offered invitation-only opening nights. Pedro Portal © The Miami Herald, 2006*

■ *Admirers take in the art at the Miami Beach Convention Center, 2004 (facing page bottom left). Jeffrey Boan © Miami Herald Media Company, 2004*

■ *Artist Spencer Tunick photographed nude women volunteers on the grounds of the Sagamore Hotel for an installation at the 2008 Art Basel (facing page bottom right). John VanBeekum © Miami Herald Media Company, 2004*

■ *Five-year-old Theodore Watkins is intrigued by Tony Oursler's "YMBI" at the Miami Beach Convention Center in December 2004 (above). Jeffrey Boan © Miami Herald Media Company, 2004*

■ *A visitor enters an Installation at Roberto Clemente Park by SITI Studio at the Scope Miami as part of Art Basel 2007 (right). Hector Gabino © Miami Herald Media Company, 2007*

■ *Art by Niki de Saint Ralle attracted attention during the 2005 Preview day at the Miami Beach Convention Center (right). Jeffrey Boan © Miami Herald Media Company, 2005*

■ *Glass sculpture by Dale Chihuly at Fairchild Tropical Garden (left). (RG)*

■ The Rubell Family Collection was Wynwood's first major private gallery to open to the public (above). (RFC)

■ Don and Mera Rubell (top right). © Simon Hare and Whitewall Magazine.

■ Art Basel comes to Wynwood (right). Al Diaz © Miami Herald Media Company, 2007

■ Tony Goldman, left, artist Hans Van de Bovenkamp and Joey Goldman, right, pose next to Bovenkamp's work at the new Wynwood Sculpture Park. The park is one of 20 Tony and Joey Goldman properties in Wynwood (below). (GP)

■ Craig Robins, president of Dacra Development, stands at the entrance to the re-energized Miami Design District that he spearheaded. Besides showrooms of internationally known designers, the new Miami Design District has also attracted more than 40 architectural and design firms and a group of trendy restaurants. One of his first projects in the Design District was the Moore Furniture Building (facing page top right). Chuck Fadley © Miami Herald Media, 1990

Nearby, real estate mogul Marty Margulies converted another former Wynwood warehouse into a private gallery he called The Warehouse. Once he opened his private collection to the public, Wynwood's future as an art Mecca was assured. "Miami has gone quite bonkers over art," *The New York Times* reported.

Others soon followed including Tony Goldman, who made his reputation as one the New York's SoHo district pioneers. He transferred his skill and passion to Miami Beach's Art Deco District where he restored the Colony and Tiffany Hotels (now The Hotel) and made them trendy gathering spots. After a foray in Philadelphia, he and his son, Joey, purchased more than 20 former warehouses in Wynwood.

A short distance away in the historic Buena Vista neighborhood, Miami Beach native Craig Robins, president of Dacra Development, purchased properties in the down-in-the-mouth former design district. He wanted to create a new Miami Design District that would attract well-known designers the way Wynwood attracted artists and collectors. Robins got his start on Miami Beach where in the 1990s he preserved and restored a series of hotels and commercial buildings on Ocean Drive, Washington Avenue, Espanola Way and Lincoln Road. When he crossed the bay and focused on the Design District, one of his first projects was the restoration of the historic Moore Furniture Building. It became the harbinger of future possibilities.

Just south of the Miami Design District, another major project was underway on the 56-acre former Florida East Coast Railroad storage yard—the largest parcel of vacant land in Miami's urban core. Dubbed Midtown Miami, the massive $1.2-billion new development followed what designer Bernard Zyscovich called "real urbanism." When it opened in 2006, Miami's new "city within a city" became its first planned, mixed-use pedestrian-friendly neighborhood.

■ The Margulies Collection at the Warehouse will launch Huma 1994-1995 (above) an epic figurative environment by renowned Polish sculptor Magdalena Abakanowicz. (MCW)

■ Martin Z. "Marty" Marguiles in his Wynwood gallery. (MCW)

Wynwood
& MIAMI DESIGN DISTRICT

Midtown Miami

"A City within a City"

Model of the Zyscovich Architects Midtown Miami Master Plan (background). (ZA)

A shady walkway at Midtown Miami's retail center (bottom). (APC)

Midtown Miami from the air (left). © Smith Aerial (ZA)

The new 2 Midtown designed by Zyscovich Architects (top left). © New York Focus

The dramatic Cesar Pelli-designed Carnival Center for the Performing Art (above). © Robin Hill (PAC)

Dignitaries join New World Symphony Director Michael Tilson Thomas in raising the baton to officially open the Carnival Center for the Performing Arts, later renamed the Adrienne Arsht Center (facing page top right). © Robin Hill (PAC)

Cesar Pelli addresses the crowd at the dedication of the Carnival Center (facing page middle). © Robin Hill (PAC)

Bravo!

By the time Art Basel Miami Beach opened its fourth season, another history-making event had taken place. The long-awaited grand opening celebration of the new Cesar Pelli-designed Carnival Center for the Performing Arts began on October 5, 2006. Although overdue and over budget, the opening night crowd and those that followed gave it a chandelier-rattling "Bravo!" Besides sleek architecture, Miami-Dade's Art in Public Places ordinance had mandated a percentage of construction costs to go toward art. Art was everywhere in the cavernous halls—on walls, curtains, railings and floors.

Grammy award winner and Miami resident Emilio Estefan produced the opening "Concert for Miami" that honored Miami's diverse populations with performances by many of Miami's favorite residents including Estefan's wife, Gloria.

The celebration continued for three more nights with the debut of the center's resident companies—the pioneer Florida Grand Opera, The Concert Association of Florida, founded by Judy Drucker, and two exciting young institutions, the Miami City Ballet and the New World Symphony. "The resident companies spoke more about Miami than people ever realized," said Sherwood "Woody" Weiser, chairman of the Carnival Center Foundation. "We came together to build this place," added Carnival Center Trust Chairman Parker Thomson. "We are coming together still. This is a new, beautiful day for Miami."

FUTURE POSSIBILITIES

The opening of the Carnival Center served as inspiration for the aspiring students of nearby New World School of the Arts. Launched by Miami-Dade Community College in 1987, the college joined with Miami-Dade County Public Schools and the University of Florida to provide a seamless art-based curriculum for talented students. Graduates quickly made a name for themselves and for the school in both performing and visual arts.

When Miami Dade College President Robert H. McCabe retired in 1995, Eduardo J. Padron, Ph.D., became the college's fourth president and its first Cuban-American leader. After the college began granting a limited number of baccalaureate degrees, Miami Dade College dropped the word "community" from its name but continued its long history of community involvement. With eight campuses and 160,000 students, it continued as the largest and most diverse college in America. Padron inspired a media campaign that highlighted Miami Dade graduates who helped shape Miami. They included Miami Mayor Manny Diaz and Miami-Dade County Mayor Carlos Alvarez, to name a few. It reminded people of Miami Dade College's pivotal role in building Miami's future.

Miami Dade College also did its part to energize Miami's expanding cultural scene. The Miami Book Fair International, which Padron helped found, grew into a major national event. The Book Fair's success spawned Miami Dade College's Florida Center for the Literary Arts. The college also took over and expanded the Miami International Film Festival that attracted world attention. In 2008, Miami Dade acquired the Freedom Tower, one of Miami's most treasured landmarks.

Eduardo Padron, Ph.D.

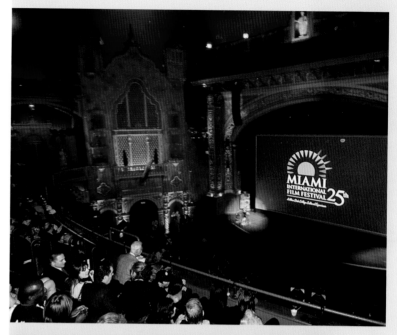

■ *The 25th Annual Miami International Film Festival held its opening night at the Gusman Center for the Performing Arts (top). (MDC)*

■ *Miami Dade College graduates have risen to the highest leadership positions in Miami-Dade County. Left to right, front row, Congresswoman Ileana Ros-Lehtinen, Miami-Dade Mayor Carlos Alvarez, Circuit Court Judge Sarah I. Zabel; row two, Miami Gardens Mayor Shirley Gibson, Marlene Bastien, executive director of Fanm Ayisyen Nan Miami; third row, State Senator Gwen Margolis, Miami Beach Police Chief Carlos Noriega, State Attorney Katherine Fernandez Rundle and Miami Mayor Manny Diaz. (MDC)*

Florida International University was another educational success story. In less than 40 years, Miami's first public university had grown from a 5,000-student upper division commuter-university to a major American research institution. Beginning with only a few graduate programs, by 2008 it had 35,000 students, expanded Ph.D. programs, a college of architecture, a law school, a newly approved school of medicine and a modern residential campus. Much of the change was attributed to the vision and dedication of President Modesto "Mitch" Maidique, who completed his 20th year of leadership in 2006.

■ Florida International University President Modesto "Mitch" Maidique in front of the Green Library (above). (FIU)

■ President Maidique talks with a group of students in front of Argosy by Alexander Lieberman. With more than 30 major sculptures, the campus has become a virtual sculpture garden (left). (FIU)

■ The Wertheim Performing Arts Center (below). (FIU)

■ *Retiring President Edward T. "Tad" Foote with the university's fifth president Donna M. Shalala, Ph.D. (right). (UM)*

The University of Miami celebrated its 75th anniversary in 2001, the same year that President Edward T. "Tad" Foote retired after 20 years at the helm. Foote helped transform what was derisively called "Sun-Tan U" into a nationally recognized research university with a tropical campus and increasingly talented student body. That same year, the university won another national football championship and welcomed its fifth president, Donna M. Shalala, Ph.D., who had just completed eight years as President Clinton's Secretary of Health and Human Services. One of her first goals was to move the university into the top tier of American universities. Within two years of her arrival, she launched an unprecedented $1-billion fundraising campaign to give UM the resources it needed to move from "good to great." Shalala's leadership was particularly apparent at the medical school, which received a $100-million gift from the family of the late Leonard Miller, founder of Lennar Homes and former chairman of the UM Board of Trustees. The renamed Miller School of Medicine attracted a group of internationally known scholars and acquired Cedars Hospital for a new university hospital. To inspire UM students to become involved in public affairs, she brought in an impressive group of national speakers and events, including two national presidential debates. In 2008, President George W. Bush presented her with the Presidential Medal of Freedom—the nation's highest civilian honor.

Other South Florida institutions of higher learning such as Florida Memorial, Barry University and St. Thomas University also continued to thrive with increasingly talented and diverse student bodies and expanded programs. When it came to higher education, South Florida offered something for everyone.

■ *Members of the Miller family join UM President Donna Shalala and "Sebastian," the UM mascot, to celebrate the dedication of the Miller School of Medicine in honor of the late UM Board of Trustees Chairman, businessman and philanthropist Leonard M. Miller (middle). (UM)*

■ *León Krier, an internationally known architect and urban planner, designed the University of Miami's new Jorge M. Perez Architecture Center (above). (UM)*

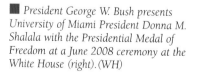

■ *President George W. Bush presents University of Miami President Donna M. Shalala with the Presidential Medal of Freedom at a June 2008 ceremony at the White House (right). (WH)*

DIFFERENT POINTS OF VIEW

When Hurricane Wilma arrived in Miami in 2005, with unexpectedly strong bursts of wind, it again exposed serious structural problems in Miami's new buildings. This time it was the glitzy glass towers on Brickell Avenue that took the hit. After the storm passed, onlookers were shocked to see hundreds of blown out windows with interior curtains fluttering through the gaping holes like flags of surrender. Streets and sidewalks were covered with millions of tiny, jewel-like pieces of safety glass sparkling in the sun.

Hurricane Wilma was not the only storm swirling around town. Citizens organized to oppose what they perceived as over-development—especially in their neighborhoods. The high-rise mania of the current boom was not confined to the downtown area but also worked its way into the suburbs. This spawned the creation of neighborhood associations, the Urban Environmental League and Miami Neighborhoods United—the two largest of the opposing forces. Other citizens joined preservation organizations like Dade Heritage Trust and fought to protect historic neighborhoods and landmarks that were being razed or overshadowed by high-rise buildings. Protecting the Miami River and its marine industry became the cry of other activists. Miami Mayor Manny Diaz and the pro-development members of the commission came under fire. For the first time in memory, citizens filed lawsuits to stop what they considered misplaced or over-development. They took on Miami's update of the State of Florida-mandated comprehensive plan and achieved initial success that forced the city to restudy it. After initial support, many became suspicious of the Diaz-led overhaul of Miami's antiquated zoning ordinance. Dubbed "Miami 21," skeptical residents demanded more study and more meetings in order to understand new concepts promoted by its authors, DPZ, who had received national acclaim for other New Urbanism projects across America.

Next came the sinking realization that the bubble had burst. Thousands of buyers—many who had only purchased units for speculation—backed out when it came time to close. This, in turn, impacted the mortgage and banking industry. As foreclosures mounted, some institutions folded or declared bankruptcy. Seemingly oblivious to previous downturns, the latest generation of speculators, called "Flippers," joined the 1920s infamous "Binder Boys" in Miami's continuing boom and bust soap opera.

DANCINC DOGS & WURLITZERS

The Olympia Theater began its long career with a gala opening night on February 18, 1926. In 1971, Miami philanthropist Maurice Gusman purchased the dilapidated building which was in danger of being torn down. Today, the Olympia Theater at the Gusman Center for the Performing Arts is owned and operated by the City of Miami and is used for a variety of performing arts. After a recent restoration by renowned preservation architect Richard Heisenbottle, it has become, once again, one of Miami's greatest treasures. © Dan Forer

■ *Charettes, a type of collaborative workshop that joins designers with interested parties, became popular mechanisms to bring citizens and a variety of designers into the planning process. Liz Plater-Zyberk, upper right, dean of the University of Miami School of Architecture and principal of DPZ, participates in the Downtown Kendall charette that helped create the new Downtown Kendall master plan (right). (DPZ)*

Everything Old is New Again

Many of Miami's historic buildings have been infused with Twenty-first Century uses and amenities. Overtown's beloved Lyric Theater has a new $5 million Richard Heisenbottle-designed welcome center and exhibit gallery. On Miami Beach, Nichols Brosch Wurst Wolf and Associates have transformed three historic hotels—the Fontainebleau, Eden Roc and DiLido. Fronting on the Atlantic Ocean, the new $1 billion Fontainebleau Resort has 1,540 rooms including the restored original, a 40,000-square-foot spa and two new towers. Next door, the Eden Roc is undergoing a major restoration and addition that will add a new chapter to the historic rivalry of the two hotels, both originally designed by Morris Lapidus and updated by NBWW. On Lincoln Road and the ocean, the restored 1950s DiLido Hotel has found a new life as the glitzy Ritz-Carlton South Beach.

■ *Nichols Brosh Wurst Wolfe and Associates restored the historic DiLido Hotel and transformed it into the Ritz-Carlton South Beach (above). (Ritz-Carlton South Beach)*

■ *The historic Lyric Theater added a new welcome center and gallery designed by Richard Heisenbottle (below). (HG)*

Dealing with Loss

Dramatic change always comes with a sense of loss. The community mourned the passing of familiar people, places and institutions. But not even the seemingly ageless Marjory Stoneman Douglas could live forever. She died at 108, soon after receiving the Presidential Medal of Freedom for her lifetime effort to save the Everglades. With Thelma Peters and Helen Muir's death, Miami lost two talented writers and historians. Three of South Florida's strongest and most effective national advocates—former Senator George Smathers and former Congressmen Dante Fascell and William Lehman—passed away. The Cuban exile community lost a strong national leader with the death of Jorge Mas Canosa. When community builders Athalie Range and Jim Batten, CEO of Knight Ridder, died in 1995, they left a leadership void that remains unfilled. And no one has forgotten the deaths of four Cuban exiles when the Cuban Air Force shot down the humanitarian Brothers to the Rescue plane. Art Teele's shocking suicide in the lobby of *The Miami Herald* gave Miamians yet another reason to mourn.

Just as it was hard to imagine Miami without Steve Clark, it was hard to imagine Miami without Burdines. When Federated Department Stores, which had owned the chain since 1956, changed Burdines' historic name to Macy's, Miami lost a piece of history. Next came the sale of *The Miami Herald* to the McClatchy Company after 69 years of the Knight brothers' and then Knight Ridder's leadership. Although Knight Ridder was gone, the John S. and James L. Knight Foundation remained in South Florida. In 2008, it energized the

■ *Marjory Stoneman Douglas (below) © Michael Carlebach*

community with its $40 million Knight Arts Partnership for endowment and community challenge grants.

Many historic places also disappeared or were threatened. The Coconut Grove Playhouse closed its doors and its future remained in doubt. On a positive note, however, the success of the Actor's Playhouse in Coral Gables' historic Miracle Theatre softened the blow.

Despite Herculean efforts, the Miami Stadium was torn down to make way for affordable housing. People rallied to save the Marine Stadium on Virginia Key, prompting the City of Miami to take a second look. Another proud institution—Hialeah Park—ran its final race in 2001. Hialeah resident Alex Fuentes mounted a countywide effort to save it from demolition.

But the greatest outcry and grief came with the demolition of the Orange Bowl Stadium. Its fate was sealed after the Dolphins and then the Orange Bowl Game moved to Dolphin Stadium and the city deferred maintenance. When the University of Miami played its final game in the historic facility, fans stood at game's end as if to absorb one final view to add to their memory books.

The Orange Bowl Stadium's final games were played in January 2008. First, the Northwestern High School Bulls won the Offense-Defense All American Bowl championship there. On January 26, alumni of the Dolphins and the Hurricanes played a nostalgic final game as a sort of taps to a grand old dame.

Crowds gathered as demolition crews began to hack away at the venerable stadium and its more than 70 years of memories. Some found the piece-by-piece removal too painful to watch. Then after three months of painstaking dismemberment, it was gone.

■ Knight Ridder CEO Jim Batten was a consensus builder who was able to bring the community together. When he died in 1995, Miami, and the newspaper world, lost an important leader. (JB)

GOING, GOING, GONE

In 1935, Miami Parks and Recreation Director Ernie Seiler bargained for leftover bleachers from an American Legion parade and moved them to the site of the baseball field at N.W. Third Street and 15th Avenue. These hand-me-down wooden bleachers launched the memorable history of the Orange Bowl Stadium. The first Orange Bowl Game was played there. The following year, fledging Orange Bowl Committee members went to Washington to seek Depression-era Public Works Administration funds to build a permanent stadium. Miami residents went to the polls and voted in favor of building the new Miami Stadium with WPA funds and Miami bonds. The positive vote gave the city means to build the $250,000 concrete-and-steel 39,000-seat facility. The new stadium opened in time for the 1938 Orange Bowl Game. For the next 70 years, the Orange Bowl, briefly called Burdine Stadium for merchant Roddy Burdine, was expanded until it accommodated more than 75,000 fans. Demolition of the grande dame began in April 2008. By summer, she was gone. (HG)

(HG)

LOOKING BACK, LOOKING AHEAD

But despite loss and the obvious challenges that lay ahead, it was hard not to feel a sense of pride or wonder in what had occurred in the Magic City in such a short period of time. The old Royal Palm Hotel site that remained vacant for almost 80 years was bustling with activity as the first building in Met Miami opened. The Related Company completed Miami One on filled land that had once been the Royal Palm Hotel's marina. Nearby, the 1950s DuPont Plaza Hotel was being replaced with another mixed-use project called Epic.

Across the river, Brickell Key developers announced the island was almost built out as other massive nearby projects like Icon neared completion. On Biscayne Boulevard, a new generation of skyscrapers had replaced the old. As cranes disappeared one-by-one and new buildings welcomed their first tenants, people kept their fingers crossed hoping residents would move in. New downtowners would also reinvigorate the historic shopping streets and transform the area into a major international and urban center. When gas prices soared, the prospect of South Florida abandoning its historic push for suburban sprawl and adopting a new urban point of view improved.

Lead by Mayor Manny Diaz, South Florida also acquired a new "green" point of view. The City of Miami opened Virginia Key Beach Park and honored members of the black community who worked tirelessly to reopen and interpret Miami's only segregation-era "Colored Beach." The city also hired master planners to study the rest of Virginia Key. The city opened a new park, the first in Little Haiti, and created a water park in

■ *Jorge Perez, founder, chairman and CEO of the Related Group (right). (RLG)*

■ *After almost 80 years, MDM Development Group is creating "Metropolitan Miami" on the site of the historic Royal Palm Hotel that was demolished in 1930. Designed by Nichols Brosch Wurst Wolfe & Associates, Met One is completed and Met Two and Met Three are under construction with Met Square to follow. The project gained added attention after NBA superstar Shaquille O'Neal's O'Neal Group joined the development team (top). (MDM Development)*

■ *The Related Group, South Florida's most prolific developer and the largest Hispanic-owned business in the United States, developed One Miami. Designed by Arquitectonica, it sits on filled land that was once the Royal Palm Hotel marina (facing page bottom). © C.W. Craig (A)*

■ *The Epic Condo and Residence, designed by Revuelta Vega Leon and developed by the CMC Group, rises on the site of the Royal Palm Gardens, later the 1950s DuPont Plaza Hotel (middle). © Esteban Koffsman (RL)*

THE NEXT MIAMI EMERGES FROM THE SITE OF HENRY FLAGLER'S ROYAL PALM HOTEL, THE PLACE WHERE THE CITY OF MIAMI WAS BORN LITTLE MORE THAN 100 YEARS AGO.

FULFILLING A DREAM
THE VIRGINIA KEY BEACH PARK

HISTORIC

VIRGINIA KEY BEACH PARK
MIAMI, FLORIDA

Established 1945

After being closed for more than 25 years, Virginia Key Beach Park reopened in February 2008 with a joyous celebration. During the segregation era, Miami's "Colored Beach" was the only beach where blacks could swim. It quickly became the center of local black events—church socials, baptisms and family gatherings. Like Crandon Park, the "white beach," Virginia Key Beach had a mini-train and merry-go-round. The beach closed in 1982 and remained neglected until Enid Pinckney of Dade Heritage Trust, University of Miami Professor Gregory Bush and artist Gene S. Tinnie alerted the black community to the fact it was about to be leased to a private developer. The late Athalie Range and the late Commissioner Arthur Teele organized a group of citizens who convinced the City of Miami to reopen it as a public beach. In 2001, under Range's leadership, the Virginia Key Beach Trust was born. Plans for the park, now listed on the National Register of Historic Places, include an indoor/outdoor museum and cultural center. It will highlight and interpret both the 82.5-acre park's natural features and what Trust Chair Gene Tinnie calls the "rich and remarkable history surrounding Miami-Dade County's onetime only "Colored Beach."

■ *City of Miami Commission Chairman Joe Sanchez, second from left, joined by City Manager Pete Hernandez, left, present Virginia Key Trust Chairman Gene Tinnie, third from left, a proclamation in celebration of the opening of Virginia Key Beach Park. Others on the stage include, left to right, Denise Wallace, Yvonne MacDonald, Vicki Augustus-Fidelia and Trust Executive Director David Shorter. (HG)*

Miami's Own

South Florida's skyline is always changing. In the 1980s and 1990s, the works of what writers called "Designer Architects"—nationally known names like I.M. Pei—dominated Miami's skyline. Today, local architects—many with international reputations—have transformed Greater Miami's Twenty-first Century skyline.

the Grapeland Heights neighborhood. Environmentalists celebrated after the new Village of Pinecrest acquired the lush, former Parrot Jungle and created a community center.

In 2008, the City of Miami and Miami-Dade County announced the so-called $3 billion Mega Plan that would utilize community development funds to build a new port tunnel, a trolley and a baseball stadium and provide money for the Performing Arts Center, Museum Park and economically deprived neighborhoods. Arguing that voters should have a chance to weigh in on the plan, automobile dealer Norman Braman went to court to stop it. The courts deliberated and decided the city and county governments had followed a legal process. But few believed the issue was settled.

As Manny Diaz's approval rates dropped in Miami after a backlash against rampant development, the Mega Plan and city hall problems, they rose nationally. In June 2008, Miami hosted the U.S. Conference of Mayors, where Diaz was installed as president. As a national advocate for cities, Mayor Diaz vowed to promote his green initiative all across America and lobby Congress for more funds for America's cities. When asked about his legacy, Diaz responded to a *Miami Herald* reporter saying, "Opportunity comes every so often, and you have to take advantage of the opportunity."

■ *500 Brickell (facing page top left), Arquitectonica. © Brett Hufziger (RCRS)*

■ *The Murano Grande (facing page background and bottom right), Fullerton-Diaz. © Morris Moreno*

■ *Fontainebleau (facing page, bottom left), Nichols Brosch Wurst Wolfe & Associates.*

■ *Jade (facing page middle left), Revuelta Vega Leon. © Esteban Koffsman (RL)*

■ *Lincoln Cinema, interior (left), Zyscovich Architects. © Steven Brooke*

MAKING A DIFFERENCE

Children's Trust Chairman David Lawrence Jr. with some of the beneficiaries of the Children's Trust. (CT)

iamians proved that people can solve community problems if they get involved. In the late 1980s, the Miami Coalition for a Safe and Drug-Free Community took on rising drug problems that had given Miami the title of "Drug Capital of America." Led by University of Miami President Tad Foote, Knight Ridder CEO Alvah Chapman and Miami-Dade Community College President Robert McCabe, the Coalition orchestrated a community-wide assault on drug abuse. More than 1,000 volunteers, churches, schools, businesses and federal, state and local governments joined the battle. The result speaks for itself. Hundreds of drug houses were flattened, innovative services such as the Drug Court and the Juvenile Assessment Center were established and Miami became a very unfriendly place for drug traffickers. Juvenile drug use plummeted to the lowest of any county in Florida and the lowest of any major U.S. city. Miami's effort became the model for America.

At about the same time the Drug-Free Coalition formed, another group of community leaders tried to organize voter support for additional tax dollars to help children. Although this first effort failed, retired Herald publisher David Lawrence Jr. spearheaded a new program called the Children's Trust that aided all Miami-Dade children. In 2002, voters approved the Trust with a "sunset provision" that gave them the opportunity to vote it up or down six years later. In August 2008, voters gave the Trust a huge "thumbs up" when 85 percent of voters supported the permanent funding of the Children's Trust.

"ONLY IN MIAMI"
Time & Time Again

Everyone loves "then and now" photographs—historic images of long-ago days compared to present views. In Miami, change occurs so rapidly that you have to update your "now" photos almost daily. Case in point: below are four images that document the transformation of downtown Miami. The earliest was taken in 1997. "Only in Miami."

THEN: *Looking north from Freedom Tower, 1997 (DDA)*

NOW: *Looking north from Freedom Tower, 2008 (MSMc)*

THEN: *Looking south from Freedom Tower, 2007 (APC)*

NOW: *Looking south from Freedom Tower, 2008 (MSMc)*

Coming Together

Gepsie Metellus, executive director of the Haitian Neighborhood Center Sant La, stands with proud new citizen Marie Monique Louis (above). Sant La helped her with her citizenship application and test. (SL)

Kendrick Meek, right, was elected to the U.S. House of Representatives in 2002. He succeeded his mother, Congresswoman Carrie Meek, left, who retired after 10 years of service (left). (KM)

In January 2008, Performing Arts Foundation Chairman Emeritus Sherwood "Woody" Weiser, left, and Trust Chairman Ricky Arriola, right, announce businesswoman and philanthropist Adrienne Arsht's $30 million gift to Miami Dade's Performing Arts Center. In recognition of the gift, the center was renamed the Adrienne Arsht Center for the Performing Arts (bottom right). (PAC)

In November 2007, as husband Peter Bower looks on, Judge Peter Lopez, right, swears in a jubilant Matti Herrera Bower as Miami Beach's first Hispanic woman mayor (bottom left). (MB)

Seizing on opportunity has defined Miami from the beginning. Today, Miamians face the challenge of creating a "world-class" city in a changing world. As it inches toward that goal, only ethnic and cultural divisions seem likely to stop its ascent. Harvard Business Professor Rosabeth Moss Kanter used Miami as a case study in her book, *World Class*. "Miami is already starting to build social and civic bridges to improve quality of life," she wrote. "Ultimately, that is the key."

As the new millennium dawned, Miamians watched the city's dynamic urban core rise up, like Isidor Cohen's description of the city's founding, "as if by magic." The next Miami has been launched, sprouting like an adolescent who needs time to fill out, mature and—with hard work, wisdom and a little luck—realize her full potential.

MIAMI
STORM & SUNSHINE

Under the spell of the warm sun a city grows.

From verdant jungle to shining glass reflecting growth—

spontaneous, constant, heightened by the flush.

Only the sky is changeless.

People are drawn to its warmth of opportunity—

Feeling the enchantment of future possibilities in a tropic land.

Transplanted from another place,

They come looking for summer.

No cold winds here—but winds just the same.

Frightening thunderheads form in the heat of a perfect

afternoon, exploding their fury in incredible bursts.

They pass just as suddenly.

The sun reappears as if nothing had happened,

and life goes on renewed.

Arva Moore Parks

Market place

Community Service

Building & Development

Banking & Finance

Health Care

Professional Services

Business & Enterprise

COMMUNITY SERVICES   322

EDUCATION   338

HEALTH CARE   376

BANKING & FINANCE   398

BUILDING & DEVELOPMENT   412

PROFESSIONAL SERVICES   440

MARKETPLACE   464

Education

Economic Development in Miami

*T*here is no place in the world like Miami. Miami is alive. It's an energetic global business center with one of the world's busiest airports, the largest cruise port on the planet and a population excited about the future.

Miami is home to more than 2,000 multinational companies and the only community outside of Switzerland to annually host the world's premiere art fair, Art Basel. Audiences in Miami also experience a wide array of talent at one of the world's finest venues, the new Adrienne Arsht Center for the Performing Arts, as well as the nation's orchestral academy, The New World Symphony and one of the top ballet companies in America, Miami City Ballet.

Miami boasts of two Carnegie University designated Research I universities - Florida International University and the University of Miami. Both have law and medical schools, with cutting edge biomedical advances made daily at the University of Miami's medical campus. Miami has the fourth largest school system in America. And, through a partnership between the Greater Miami Chamber and educational leaders from across the community, a comprehensive strategic plan is being developed to strengthen academic achievement of students from kindergarten through college to ensure competitiveness in today's global environment.

Miami is a sub-tropical paradise with an azure sea, golden beaches and an effervescent mix of cultures, languages and heritage. It is synonymous with recreation and leisure, sex, sizzle and shopping. Whether it's playing on countless golf courses or tennis courts or watching professionals in the World Golf Championship at Doral or the Sony Ericsson Open at Crandon Park; it's all here. And, Miami is one of a handful of American cities to offer a full array of sports franchises: the Miami Dolphins, Florida Marlins, Miami Heat, Florida Panthers and our new professional soccer team, Miami FC.

Miami is also a favored destination of the Super Bowl and

BARRY E. JOHNSON

Barry E. Johnson is president and chief executive officer of the Greater Miami Chamber of Commerce, South Florida's first and largest business organization with more than 100 years of service to Greater Miami. Before joining the Chamber, Barry was vice president of corporate affairs for AT&T, directing the company's public policy initiatives in Florida.

Community Services

DADE COMMUNITY FOUNDATION 324

GREATER MIAMI CHAMBER OF COMMERCE 326

SOUTH FLORIDA HISPANIC CHAMBER OF COMMERCE 328

MIAMI-DADE CHAMBER OF COMMERCE 329

MIAMI INTERNATIONAL AIRPORT 330

PORT OF MIAMI 331

MIAMI DOWNTOWN DEVELOPMENT AUTHORITY 332

ORANGE BOWL COMMITTEE 333

UNITED WAY OF MIAMI-DADE 334

MIAMI PARKING AUTHORITY 335

GOODWILL INDUSTRIES OF SOUTH FLORIDA, INC. 336

the NCAA National College Football Championship at the FEDEX Orange Bowl game. And, each fall, national motor sports championships are determined for NASCAR and Indy Car racing at Homestead-Miami Motor Speedway.

From the Everglades to the Atlantic Ocean, Miami has it all. I invite you to experience the magic of Miami and enjoy our beaches, world class sport fishing and boating. Party with celebrities in South Beach, watch the filming of CSI Miami, or just experience some of the best restaurants and shopping in the hemisphere.

DADE COMMUNITY FOUNDATION

40 years of service to Greater Miami promoting philanthropy and building community.

Community Foundation. Investment performance ranking in the top quartile of all community foundations in the United States. More than 600 charitable funds established by individuals, families, businesses and organizations.

Letter from the President

Greater Miami is a community of constant change. Our economy and culture are influenced by global forces. Every decade Miami-Dade's demographic profile changes, and with those shifts come changes in our neighborhoods, employment, languages and points of view.

Miami's diversity, for many, is what makes our community such a great place to work and live. This place's international flair, lively cultural scene and usually strong economy put Greater Miami in the forefront of world cities. But our diversity and always changing physical and cultural landscape can also create impediments to the cohesiveness a community

needs to thrive. In this environment, Dade Community Foundation is a constant. We are a permanent endowment and institution dedicated to meeting the community's evolving needs. We define those needs not only in the traditional philanthropic terms of food and shelter, education, health and human services, but also in terms of human relationships, understanding, and the way people work together toward common goals.

— Ruth Shack

The mission of Dade Community Foundation is to encourage philanthropy and charitable giving by developing a permanent endowment to meet Greater Miami's emerging charitable needs. More than $110 million in grants distributed to nonprofit organizations during our 40-year history. Educational scholarships totaling more than $4.4 million awarded to more than 3,500 students during the past 15 years. Total assets of $167,464,226 at year-end 2007, an increase of 222 percent during the past decade. More than $35 million from national private funders and government agencies distributed to the Miami-Dade community – dollars that would not have been available if not for Dade

Dade Community Foundation initiatives include:

Partnership & Innovation

In a series of remarkable public and private partnerships, the Foundation has enabled Greater Miami to benefit significantly from the resources of major institutions – among them the Ford Foundation, W. K. Kellogg Foundation, John S. and James L. Knight Foundation, Rockefeller Foundation, Charles Stewart Mott Foundation, Lila Wallace-Reader's Digest Fund and other private funders, as well as government agencies of Miami-Dade County and the State of Florida. In each case, Dade Community Foundation recognized a local need, identified and solicited a source of funding, established a competitive grantmaking program, and reported the results.

DadeFund

The largest single gift in the Foundation's history came from the sale of Hospice, Inc., an organization founded by activist minister Hugh Westbrook and visionary nurse Esther Colliflower. In 1976 the pair started the hospice movement in Miami, committed to providing end-of-life care for the terminally ill. When they sold Hospice, Inc. 16 years later, they allocated $7 million in proceeds to establish DadeFund, part of Dade

Community Foundation's permanent endowment, to address the critical need for early childhood development.

Miami Fellows Initiative

A flagship program of the Foundation, the Miami Fellows Initiative (MFI) was launched in 1999 to address the community's need for effective, ethical, collective leadership. Funded by the W. K. Kellogg Foundation, MFI has also gained significant support from the John S. and James L. Knight Foundation, allowing the program to flourish. MFI cultivates new generations of civic leaders, fostering a culture of collaboration and high ethical standards. Through its first four classes, the initiative has supported new leadership networks across generations, cultures, neighborhoods, professions.

Dade Community Foundation's

MIAMI FELLOWS INITIATIVE

INAUGURAL CLASS 1999

A model of the Kellogg National Leadership Program

Disaster Recovery

When Hurricane Andrew devastated Dade County in 1992, Dade Community Foundation responded to the disaster through its Rebuild Initiative, helping stabilize the nonprofit community and supporting community development corporations in efforts to restore housing and jobs. The Foundation also served as a vehicle for donors in Florida and internationally to support recovery and restoration. Within a matter of weeks, more than $1 million in contributions from

more than 2,900 donors began providing shelter, medical care, clothing and other emergency relief. The Foundation played a major role in community restoration for more than a decade after the storm.

GREATER MIAMI CHAMBER OF COMMERCE

Since 1907, the Greater Miami Chamber of Commerce has built a legacy of leadership for the region it serves.

The first business organization in Miami, the Chamber is still the largest in Greater Miami with a membership of 5,500 individuals from more than 2,500 companies. In fact, it is one of the largest metropolitan chambers of commerce in the Southeastern United States and serves the seventh largest market in the nation. As such, the Greater Miami Chamber of Commerce is the central gathering point for business issues and is the voice of business in South Florida.

Some highlights of the Chamber's activities are events featuring some of America's most influential business and government leaders. Speakers who have addressed the Chamber are diverse and include leaders of commerce, government, industry and education such as the chairmen of General Motors, AMR (the parent company of American Airlines), Secretary of the Army, CEO's of the country's top companies such as Burger King, McDonald's, DHL and the presidents of the universities, like the University of Miami and Florida International University. These monthly events offer members information as well as South Florida's best networking opportunity.

As a volunteer led organization, members create the programming. Over the years, Greater Miami Chamber programs have been launched as independent organizations. The Greater Miami Convention & Visitors Bureau and The Miami-Dade Beacon Council are two examples of success breeding success. Today, the Chamber concentrates its efforts on domestic and international business development, along with programs in governmental affairs and leadership. It can rightly be called an activist chamber for its proactive work plan.

Throughout its history, the Chamber has attracted the top tier of Greater Miami's business leaders. They join and get engaged because they know that serving in leadership -- from a one-year term as chairman of the Chamber or chairman of one of its 35 committees -- provides tremendous business connectivity and the opportunity to make a difference on critical issues facing South Florida.

■ *First Vice Chairman, Maria Alonso, Senior Vice President, Market Development Manager for Miami-Dade/ Monroe, Bank of America*

The largest program area within the Chamber is the Domestic Business Development Group. It includes committees and task forces that address a plethora of business issues including education, healthcare, bioscience, military affairs and the New World Center, which deals specifically with downtown Miami issues. Other focuses of the committees are nonprofit business, small business, sports, technology, transportation and infrastructure.

The International Business Development Group committees concentrate on developing relationships for Greater Miami Chamber members with other chambers and businesses in Latin America, the Caribbean and Europe. The Chamber also partners with Miami-Dade County and Enterprise Florida to provide international business opportunities for members.

■ *Chairman-Elect, Bruce Jay Colan, Partner, Holland & Knight, LLP*

President and CEO, Barry E. Johnson, Greater Miami Chamber of Commerce

Solid international business relationships are formed by creating a dialogue with other nations by travel to their countries and inviting their businesses to come to Miami to conduct business. American Airlines is the Chamber's business partner that makes travel to Latin America and the Caribbean affordable for members. The Greater Miami Chamber the portal for many international companies who wish to explore business opportunities in the United States.

The Advocacy Group committees are focused on local governments in Miami-Dade County, the state legislative process in Tallahassee and the federal programs in Washington, D.C. Members often visit the halls of power and meet with elected officials to better understand and influence the governmental process as it relates to issues in the Greater Miami business community. Other issues the committees address include workforce housing, windstorm insurance, the impact of property taxes and natural resources.

The Greater Miami Chamber's Leadership Programs are renowned for producing the community's top-tier leaders. For 29 years, the Leadership Miami Program has educated more than 9,000 people, many who have gone on to top positions in their fields. Miami Mayor Manny Diaz is but one example of the caliber of leaders educated in Chamber programs. The program allows these future leaders to learn about the issues facing the region, ensuring generations to come will have a complete understanding of the business community's role in Greater Miami. Similar programs for senior executives who are relocated to South Florida help integrate them into the community while offering them a concise education of the local business environment. Both programs offer information about local government, history, culture and the physical environment. A benefit of the program is a strong base for networking; the programs often create lasting friendships and business relationships.

For more than 100 years, South Florida's leading business organization.

There are three levels of membership at the Chamber; General, Trustee and the Chairman's Circle. Regardless of the type of membership, members all understand they will get out of their membership what they put into it. Becoming involved in committees ensures an understanding of the community that isn't possible outside of the chamber. As a tool for businesses, the chamber also offers networking functions and opportunities for members to showcase their products and services throughout the year.

But perhaps the most important thing the Greater Miami Chamber offers its members is access. With a guarantee that a small business owner will have the same access as the Fortune 500 company, membership in the Greater Miami Chamber of Commerce is the right thing to do. The bottom line is its good for business... of all sizes.

Miami skyline, courtesy of the City of Miami Downtown Development Authority.

SOUTH FLORIDA HISPANIC CHAMBER OF COMMERCE

The South Florida Hispanic Chamber of Commerce (SFLHCC) is committed to promoting the South Florida businesses, its tourism industry, and to enhancing the quality of education in the public school system.

The SFLHCC, composed of young, committed, dynamic professionals, since its foundation, has been identified with successful entrepreneurs and as an organization that meets the demands of the rapid-growing and constant-changing businesses. The SFLHCC has a Minority Business & Education Enhancement Program. This program provides business information, training, and technical assistance for small businesses. It also provides annual scholarships and paid internships to both high school and college students. The SFLHCC sponsors business workshops, seminars, lunch and learns, luncheons with high profile speakers, networking receptions, and an annual golf tournament benefiting its scholarship program. These chamber activities have the reputation of being the best networking events of South Florida. The leadership of the SFLHCC strongly believes that by promoting our businesses and our tourism industry we are keeping our economy strong and vibrant.

The South Florida Hispanic Chamber of Commerce (SFLHCC) was founded

by Liliam M. Lopez, Eloy Cepero, Luis Casas, Orlando Romero, Ralph Jacobo and Luis Boue on July 21, 1994 with the mission of promoting the continued growth and development of the business community and the tourism industry of Miami-Dade County. The SFLHCC helps its members expand their business opportunities, encourage mutual beneficial ties with the public and private sectors and serves as an active, strong and visible advocate of the Hispanic business community.

MIAMI-DADE CHAMBER OF COMMERCE

With a strong sense of community and a commitment to helping businesses in the urban core, the Miami-Dade Chamber of Commerce has established itself as the voice of minority business in Miami-Dade.

ounded in 1974 to act on behalf of the emerging black business community, the Miami-Dade Chamber continues to grow along with the changing landscape of the city. Now the chamber supports as its members minority owned businesses run by women, Hispanics, those of Caribbean and Haitian descent, and other under-represented demographics in business.

Miami is a small business town, according to President and CEO Bill Diggs, and it is small business that drives South Florida's economy, he says. As a strategic partner for minority-owned businesses, the Miami-Dade Chamber of Commerce has evolved over the years as a matchmaker of sorts for large businesses who are seeking the services of minority vendors. Businesses know to call on the Miami-Dade Chamber to help them develop partnerships that previously may have seemed unattainable, while member businesses find the advocacy of the Chamber to be a valuable asset for their companies. "We're not just about building businesses, we're about building a community," says Diggs, who took over leadership of the Chamber in 2005.

Its mission is to lead the way towards long-term business prosperity, by providing advocacy, networking, resources, and training to men and women in business in Miami-Dade. The Chamber provides the following services to its members: Technical assistance in business development operations; promotion of trade missions internationally; networking opportunities at business-related forums; exchange events, and business stimulated projects and activities.

Not surprisingly, the Chamber is experiencing strong growth as more and more minority business owners are finding that membership can be a source of empowerment both personally and professionally.

While maintaining its stance to be a solid voice for the minority business community, the Chamber continuously expands its efforts to meet the ever-changing needs of its members and the community. Moving the chamber forward as a 21st century leader, the Chamber has instituted a number of new initiatives including The Women's Business Council, Urban Partnership for Prosperity, Young Professionals Network and the Business Empowerment Series.

As Florida's oldest historically black Chamber of Commerce, The Miami-Dade Chamber of Commerce continues to build on its legacy and provide a world of business opportunities.

The South Terminal's international arrivals lobby welcomes visitors from throughout the globe.

MIAMI INTERNATIONAL AIRPORT

With more flights to Latin America and the Caribbean than all other airports combined and as one of the top three international airports in the United States, Miami International Airport is truly a global aviation leader.

Miami International Airport welcomes visitors from every end of the earth servicing more than 33 million passengers through its doors and shipping more than 2 million tons of cargo. With its $6.2 billion Capital Improvement Program, passengers will find every comfort and convenience they would expect from the place where North America meets the world.

Its latest addition, the new South Terminal, is a wonder of modern style and efficiency. The 1.7 million square foot, five-level expansion includes a new concourse. To offer some perspective, the South Terminal is as big as most mid-sized airports in the country. However, the new terminal is poised to do more than just help transport passengers from one destination to another. Fine dining and shopping await including 61 new food, retail and duty-free concession locations.

An "avenue" of name brand stores in South Terminal makes the airport a full-service mall and a visit to Miami , no matter how quick, wouldn't be complete without a taste of authentic cuisine. At midpoint between the concourses is a glass-walled food pavilion with plenty of choices, including Emilio and Gloria Estefan's Bongos Bar and Grill.

Those are the creature comforts, but there's also an emphasis on efficiency. A high-tech baggage screening system can screen and transport 4,000 bags per hour between ticket counters, aircraft and baggage claim areas. Some 168 ticket counters and 1,040 feet of curbside drop off/pick-up space make it convenient to catch a flight on time. Fifteen gates in Concourse J and 13 in Concourse H serve 19 airlines, with most capable of handling international flights. Additionally, upgrades to the North Terminal should be completed by 2011.

While transporting freight and people is of the utmost importance, there's also the airport's contribution to the economy of Miami-Dade County. The airport creates an estimated 200,000 jobs and is an economic engine jetting more than a billion dollars into the local economy each month.

With capital improvements, routes and airlines being added frequently, an emphasis on the latest technology for safety and security, noise abatement, and environmental concerns, Miami International Airport is truly the airport of the future today.

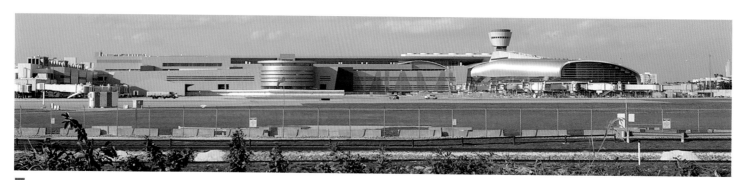
The new South Terminal at Miami International Airport is a wonder of modern style and efficiency.

PORT OF MIAMI

Whether it is a ship full of tourists heading out to sea for the cruise of a lifetime or a load of cargo leaving for lands beyond the horizon, the Port of Miami is the favored port of embarkation.

In fact, it is among America's busiest ports and is often referred to as the Cruise Capital of the World and the Cargo Gateway of the Americas.

Located on the 528-acre Dodge Island between downtown Miami and Miami Beach, the Dante B. Fascell Port of Miami-Dade serves more than 20 shipping and cruise lines, which call on 250 ports in more than 100 countries around the world. In 2007, 3.75 million passengers and more than 7.84 million tons of cargo transited through the seaport. This active port contributes more than $16 billion annually to the South Florida economy and provides approximately 110,000 jobs.

With a striking new sculpture greeting visitors at the entrance, the Port of Miami is dedicated to offering the finest customer service to all those who pass through. Every one of the port's 400 employees is intensively trained in customer service. Cruise passengers embark from convenient, modern facilities; in the cargo sector, vital goods move through secure, state-of-the-art container terminals.

The future looks bright for the port, which has recently partnered with Miami-Dade County, the City of Miami and the State of Florida to design plans to build a port access tunnel. The project, which will allow trucks to avert the streets of downtown Miami and have bridge-free access to the port, is one of the most ambitious public works projects to be undertaken in the Southeast U.S. Improving port access will maintain the Port of Miami's competitive edge in the global marketplace.

Other capital improvements include the Miami Harbor Phase III dredging project, which will deepen the port's south channel from 42 feet to a depth of 50 feet and allow the port to handle some of the world's largest vessels. The momentous project will give the port the ability to increase its cargo operation.

Miami's location at the crossroads of the hemisphere gives the port the geography to succeed. The commitment to improving the infrastructure will ensure the Port of Miami will be a vibrant business center for years to come.

The Port of Miami looking eastward to Miami Beach.

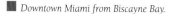
Downtown Miami from Biscayne Bay.

MIAMI DOWNTOWN DEVELOPMENT AUTHORITY

Take one look at the gleaming skyscrapers of Downtown Miami - it is hard to imagine the district that has become the centerpiece of the City of Miami sprang from an isolated trading post at the mouth of the Miami River more than a century ago.

Downtown Miami began as a modest hub for commerce and has evolved into a sophisticated region with an international reputation as a business and tourism capitol.

Business isn't the only thing that has boomed in Downtown Miami; the district has undergone a residential explosion with people moving in every day. All this growth has been promoted and shepherded through by the Miami Downtown Development Authority, a non-profit business organization dedicated to making Downtown Miami the most livable urban center in the nation while strengthening its position as an international destination for commerce, culture and tourism.

Founded in 1965 to create a downtown friendly to merchants, visitors and residents, the Miami DDA has surpassed its early expectations and was instrumental in fashioning the area as it is today. The Miami DDA worked diligently to attract major projects, including Bayside Marketplace, as well as guiding the regulatory infrastructure necessary for the development of new high-rise condominiums and office towers.

What makes the Miami DDA so successful is the partnership between the public and private sectors. Its 15-member Board of Directors is comprised of three public appointees and 12 downtown property owners, business owners, residents and workers. Charged with the mission of ensuring Downtown is compelling and competitive for business; continually improving the quality of life for residents; and expanding the district's economic base, the Miami DDA

has developed a host of programs to support those goals.

The area served by the Miami DDA is vast and encompasses Northwest 24th Street to the north to 15th Road to the south. The district is comprised of four distinct neighborhoods: Brickell, the Central Business District, Park West and Media and Entertainment. The Miami DDA work program includes economic development and research, capital improvements and enhanced services, land use and transportation planning and marketing and public relations.

Businesses, whether in the banking, professional services, real estate or retail sectors, all want to be part of Downtown, and have fueled the area's growth. The grand scale of development in Downtown Miami has created a stunning skyline and a fashionable lifestyle. Its tropical location, directly on the gorgeous turquoise waters of Biscayne Bay, makes it the envy of urban areas around the world.

From its humble beginnings as a lonely outpost to the cosmopolitan city center it is today, Downtown Miami is a story still being told. Because of the work of the Miami DDA, Downtown Miami is an exciting place, which continually evolves to meet the needs of its residents, visitors and stakeholders.

Biscayne Boulevard with the American Airlines Arena

ORANGE BOWL COMMITTEE

Founded in 1935 to promote tourism through an annual college football game, the Orange Bowl Festival has grown into one of the premier events in the nation.

The FedEx Orange Bowl is the culmination of the Festival, which is organized by one of Miami's oldest civic groups, the Orange Bowl Committee.

Although the first game between the University of Miami and Bucknell was watched by only 5,135 fans, it began a proud tradition. Today the FedEx Orange Bowl sells out the 75,000-seat Dolphin Stadium. The FedEx Orange Bowl has hosted 18 National Championship Games and 15 Heisman Trophy winners have played in the game, more than any other college bowl. The 2005 National Championship Game was the only bowl game in which three Heisman Trophy winners competed.

Coaches who have led teams in the FedEx Orange Bowl read like a who's who and include Tom Osborne, Bear Bryant, Bob Devaney, Bobby Bowden, Barry Switzer, Bud Wilkinson, Woody Hayes, Joe Paterno and Darrell Royal. In January 2009, the 75th Anniversary of the venerable game, the Orange Bowl Committee will double host the FedEx Orange Bowl and FedEx BCS National Championship Game a week later.

The Orange Bowl Festival fills the weeks leading up to the big game with activities and events for all to enjoy. Highlights include the Orange Bowl International Tennis Championship, where young athletes from 80 countries will compete for one of the world's top junior tennis titles. Other notable events through the years have included the Orange Bowl Regatta,

a 10K race, a fashion show and luncheon, the Orange Bowl Swimming Classic and the Orange Bowl Basketball Classic, which showcases top college basketball action.

The Orange Bowl Coaches Luncheon includes humorous analysis of the match-up to come as well as inductions into the Orange Bowl Hall of Honor. Fan favorite events include the Orange Bowl Fan Fest the day before the game and the Tailgate Party on game day.

The Orange Bowl Committee is also committed to the youth of South Florida through the work of the Orange Bowl Foundation. The mission of the Foundation, founded in 1998, is to support youth sports through athletic and academic opportunities. Youth programs include the Orange Bowl Youth Football Alliance, in which more than 15,000 five to 15 year old children participate in its football and cheerleading teams.

■ *The Orange Bowl game moved to Pro Player Stadium in 1996. In 2005, the stadium was renamed Dolphin Stadium, which hosted the 2005 National Championship game where USC battled to beat OU.*

UNITED WAY OF MIAMI-DADE

The Community Chest of Dade County, the forerunner to United Way of Miami-Dade, came to life in the mid-1920s, thanks to an estate gift from the William Matheson family.

The early Community Chest was an association of business leaders and a repository for corporate donations. Today's United Way is a leader in building community and improving lives.

As Miami has gone from a small, pioneer city to a diverse and dynamic metropolis, the United Way of Miami-Dade has played a leadership role in responding to the changing needs of the community and its residents both directly and through a network of strategic partners.

When Miami opened its arms to waves of immigrants in the early 1960s, the 1980s and again in the mid-1990s, United Way in partnership with a network of social service agencies, opened its arms, too – establishing special programs and non-profit agencies designed specifically to help immigrants get the best possible start in their new, adopted homeland.

When Hurricane Andrew devastated South Dade County in 1992, United Way and its family of agencies were on the front lines, helping people to rebuild their lives and the community to recover. United Way's role in the aftermath of Hurricane Andrew was a defining moment for the organization, leading to a new mission focused around community building. At the same time, it garnered national attention and changed the way United Ways prepare for and respond to disasters in their own communities.

Today, United Way of Miami-Dade is engaged in a new challenge – changing the way early childhood education is delivered so that all children, ages 0-5, have the best possible educational experience that prepares their minds for lifelong learning. On January 8, 2007, the United Way Center for Excellence in Early Education opened. A national learning, teaching, research, and training facility dedicated to elevating the quality of early care and education, the Center models proven best practices and shares those practices with adult learners including parents, educators, and child care providers. The Center also partners with universities, business leaders, field experts and policymakers to create the public and political will that demands quality early childhood education, and supports sustainable and lasting change.

Throughout its history, United Way of Miami-Dade has been a significant part of the community it serves, earning national recognition as an innovator and model of excellence. It's ability to generate revenues, provide stewardship, apply technical know-how, leverage assets and rally volunteers is a major community resource.

MIAMI PARKING AUTHORITY

Everybody knows Miami is Florida's most cosmopolitan, fashionable and hip city. Convenient parking helps everyone join the fun.

Perched like a jewel on the edge of Biscayne Bay, the city undulates with a rhythm of its own. Miami, a business center with a vibrant downtown, merges a fast-paced urban lifestyle with the more laid back subtropical vibe. In recent years, downtown Miami's popularity has soared. In addition to a real estate boom, the city boasts an abundance of culture, sports, dining and shopping.

The Miami Parking Authority exists to serve the vehicular needs of people who come into the city. Established by a Special Act of the Florida State Legislature in 1955 and incorporated into the city's Charter in 1968, MPA manages and develops on- and off-street parking in the City of Miami. A self-sustaining agency managed by parking industry professionals and financed by parking revenues, MPA is responsible for more than 30,000 parking spaces in 11 garages and 78 surface lots and provides parking for approximately six million vehicles annually. In addition, MPA manages the Olympia Theater at the Gusman Center for the Performing Arts and the adjacent Olympia office building.

Since parking is an integral component of a downtown shopping or cultural outing, MPA's facilities add to the economic base of the city by attracting consumer and commercial traffic into the business districts. However, MPA's responsibilities don't stop at parking; the agency is also involved in enhancing community redevelopment efforts, complementing public transportation initiatives and is committed to the revitalization of downtown Miami.

MPA is engaged in many worthy programs including implementation of Pay and Display and Pay by Phone technology, which keep sidewalks clear of unsightly individual meters; discounted parking for Gusman Center patrons; and support for special events such as the Miami Book Fair International, the Downtown Miami Classic Car Show, the Miami International Film Festival and many Bayfront Park activities. Downtown Miami residents are offered discounted parking and City of Miami residents may register to secure their cars in an MPA garage during hurricane emergencies. For busy holiday-season shoppers, MPA offers a

MPA strategically locates its parking facilities in areas of current and projected high demand.

time extension of one hour of free parking at every on-street parking location during the holidays.

Good corporate citizenship is the cornerstone of MPA's mission. Convenient parking is an important component of every successful downtown, including Miami. Ultimately, the success of MPA will lead to the enhancement of the city's exciting downtown for years to come.

GOODWILL INDUSTRIES OF SOUTH FLORIDA, INC.

Goodwill Industries of South Florida is a lot more than a place to donate used household goods and clothing; it is a place where people with disabilities are rehabilitated and trained to be productive members of society.

In fact, with more than 2,000 employees, Goodwill is one of Miami-Dade county's largest employers.

Founded in 1959 by civic leaders Roy E. Perry, Leonard L. Abess and James A. Ryder, who were inspired by the work being done by Goodwill in other cities, Goodwill Industries of South Florida is the very model of a successful social service organization and tops virtually every list of premiere charitable organizations across the nation. The mission of the agency is simple; it provides rehabilitation, on-the-job training, work experience and placement services to help people with disabilities and special needs overcome barriers to employment and become employed in the community.

Until 1980, Goodwill was located in the old Miami Herald building in downtown Miami. People would drop off their donated items and Goodwill employees would repair and sell them from the site. The focus of the organization changed dramatically when Dennis Pastrana was hired as president and CEO. His vision for Goodwill was to become completely self-sufficient while attaining the organization's worthy goals.

To that end, Goodwill moved to their current 243,000 approximately square foot location, developed a new business plan and strategy to accomplish the plan. The vision was to utilize the free-market and free-enterprise system to develop diversified industrial and commercial activities to fulfill

Goodwill's overall mission, with minimal government support.

Today, the business model is comprised of five divisions, four of which are entrepreneurial. The commercial categories are the donated goods division, including 23 stores; a service contract business for janitorial, ground-keeping and food preparation; apparel manufacturing and a flag manufacturing business. These revenue generating divisions fund the fifth, and perhaps most important, division – rehabilitation and job training.

The apparel division, which started with only one sewing machine, now employs 675 people and produces uniforms for the U.S. Military. The service contract business is responsible for cleaning all federal buildings and busses in the county, Homestead Air Force Station, Key West Naval Station, two Coast Guard Stations and police headquarters and sub stations. In total, more than 150 buildings are cleaned by Goodwill employees.

In only two decades, Goodwill of South Florida has become completely self-sufficient. In fact, 94% of the operating budget comes from the entrepreneurial businesses, making it one of the most cost efficient organizations in the country. To put the numbers into perspective, any agency that puts 65% back into a program is reputable: Goodwill puts back 94%. Goodwill of South Florida is routinely used as a model for other social service agencies to emulate. It's abundantly clear that social service entrepreneurialism works for Goodwill and the people it helps.

The people served by Goodwill have varying degrees of disabilities and often come to the organization without a diagnosis. The agency provides a complete physical and psychological evaluation, from which a rehabilitation program is developed. They are then placed in a work adjustment program, taught the basics of working and ultimately go out into the world. Job coaches and a placement service that represents all industries in the community place more than 1,800 people in new jobs annually. Some people can make it through the program swiftly; others need much more time and are often placed in one of Goodwill's divisions for employment and training.

Goodwill Industries manufactures over 2000 U.S. military uniforms each day.

The rehabilitation program offers six vocational training opportunities; machine operation, bank encoding, food preparation, apparel manufacturing, office clerical, and cashiering. Additionally, every person in the program has a social worker, case manager and job coach. Programs are designed so people are challenged to progress while learning a practical skill. Those who are able are cross-trained in multiple skills so they can advance within a career.

Goodwill of South Florida recently merged with Goodwill of Broward County and plans to expand their successful programs there. The goal is to expand through more businesses, service contracts and commercial opportunities.

With 27 million people in the U.S. with disabilities, there is a huge need for the important work done by Goodwill. When he founded Goodwill in 1902, Edgar J. Helms vowed to be satisfied only when every disabled person in the community has an opportunity to develop to his or her fullest usefulness and enjoy a maximum of abundant living. Those who carry on the important mission of Goodwill embrace that vision in the work they do every day.

Goodwill's Service Contract Division cleans over 110 federal buildings and washes over 10,000 buses each month.

LOOKING TO THE FUTURE

*M*IAMI MOVES TO ITS OWN RHYTHM, AND THE FIELD OF EDUCATION PROVIDES ONE OF ITS MOST DRAMATIC, VIBRANT BEATS. THIS DRUM BEAT HAS ACCELERATED OVER THE YEARS AS MORE AND MORE STUDENTS HAVE FLOODED OUR SCHOOLS AND COLLEGES. THE SOUND OF SCHOOL CONSTRUCTION STRUGGLES TO KEEP PACE WITH THE GROWING CHORUS OF YOUTH.

A century ago, barely a one-room schoolhouse existed in Miami to educate the few entitled to such privilege. But today impressive institutions provide the infrastructure for students of any background. The growth of the past few decades has resulted in the largest college in the nation, Miami Dade College, and one of the largest school districts, Miami-Dade County Public Schools. Together, these institutions serve more than a half a million students annually. Another 38,000 students attend Miami's first public university, Florida International University.

Whereas the growth of these public institutions has been explosive, private institutions were initiators. The college preparatory Ransom Everglades School traces its pioneer origins to 1903. The University of Miami arrived in 1926. Belen Jesuit Preparatory School moved from Cuba to Miami in 1961 during the rise of communism. Many others serve our community tirelessly.

Recent chapters of Miami's education story reflect the massive influx of immigrants during the past 50 years, particularly from Latin America. Bilingualism has become an expectation instead of an approach. For many if not most immigrants, the education system is their primary means of acculturation. This absorption of so many so quickly is

DR. EDUARDO J. PADRÓN
President
Miami Dade College

Dr. Eduardo J. Padrón leads the largest institution of higher education in the U.S., Miami Dade College. Of Cuban heritage, he is recognized internationally as one of the most influential educational leaders of our time.

Education

RANSOM EVERGLADES SCHOOL 340

MIAMI DADE COLLEGE 342

MONSIGNOR EDWARD PACE HIGH SCHOOL 348

UNIVERSITY OF MIAMI 350

BARRY UNIVERSITY 352

CHRISTOPHER COLUMBUS HIGH SCHOOL 353

BELEN JESUIT PREPARATORY SCHOOL 354

CARLOS ALBIZU UNIVERSITY 356

CARROLLTON SCHOOL OF THE SACRED HEART 358

GULLIVER SCHOOLS 360

THE SAMUEL SCHECK HILLEL COMMUNITY DAY SCHOOL 362

ST. STEPHENS EPISCOPAL DAY SCHOOL 363

JOHNSON & WALES UNIVERSITY 364

MIAMI COUNTRY DAY SCHOOL 366

MIAMI INTERNATIONAL UNIVERSITY OF ART & DESIGN 368

PALMER TRINITY SCHOOL 370

ST. THOMAS UNIVERSITY 372

THE CUSHMAN SCHOOL 374

Miami's story and arguably its saving grace. It is difficult to imagine the stability of such a highly diverse population without education to unite them.

The future drum beat of education in Miami should become steadier and stronger. I believe that as awareness of its value to the community grows, education will receive more of the support it needs to thrive. The young people of Miami will transform this Magic City based on what they learn and how they learn. Even with the challenges Miami faces, many conscientious educators are making sure that the doors of priceless opportunity remain wide open.

RANSOM EVERGLADES SCHOOL

In a town as young and forgetful of its history as Miami, Ransom Everglades School is a visual and educational oasis.

he school's origins date back further than the incorporation of the City of Miami. The names of its generations of students are plastered all over the landscape of Miami-Dade County.

In 1893, a young lawyer from Buffalo named Paul Ransom came to Coconut Grove seeking respite for his delicate health. He immediately fell in love with the pine wilderness on Biscayne Bay, and a few years later built a boy's winter sailing camp on seven waterfront acres, called Pine Knot Camp.

In 1903, the boy's camp became the revolutionary Adirondack-Florida School, with campuses in New York and Coconut Grove, for summer and winter migrations. By the 1920s, the school had become the preferred educator for many of the area's most prominent scions. It survived the hurricane that leveled Miami in 1926, and the closing of the school during World War II.

By 1950, the school had been consolidated into one campus, and renamed the Paul C. Ransom School. The 1960s brought an expansion and modernization of the campus as well as a growing reputation as an elite college preparatory school. In the 1970s, Ransom ceased to be a boy's boarding and day school, and welcomed girls as well as its first Cuban refugees. Architect Lester Pancoast designed a grand new swimming pool and the Math-Science complex.

In 1974, Ransom merged with the nearby Everglades School for Girls, founded in 1955 by Marie Swenson. It was a natural partnership, since both were independent schools with a focus on creating strong-minded, well-rounded community leaders.

The new Ransom-Everglades School had 610 students that year, and the faculty spent the next few years combining the best elements of both educational styles to serve students in its Middle and Upper Schools. In the 1980s, Ransom Everglades (with the hyphen removed to indicate a full integration) engaged in an ambitious capital campaign to update the campus once again.

That effort came to fruition in the '90s, with the opening of the Anderson Student Activities Center, the Bowden Library, the Middle School Science Center, Fine Arts Center, and Performing Arts Center.

■ The Lewis Family Auditorium, with over 900 seats, is a fully equipped professional theatre, with state-of-the-art lighting, a full backstage, a 15 x 20 projection screen, sound systems, a digital projection system and two large dressing rooms.

■ *Cheerleaders perform in front of the entire school for an outdoor pep rally. Ransom Everglades School offers a wide range of athletic opportunities with over 70 teams among 18 interscholastic sports.*

Ransom Everglades stepped into its future with the appointment of Ellen Moceri as Head of School in 2001. Moceri was the ideal choice at a critical time in the school's history. She has four decades of experience in independent schools, including heading the prestigious American School Foundation in Mexico City.

This experience gave Moceri an international perspective that melds perfectly with the increasingly diverse student body, which now hails as much from South America as it does from South Florida.

The school's mission is to train a leadership class that will give more to the community than they take from it. That mission is expressed in the school's focus on five principles -- Tradition, Thinking, Teamwork, Talent and Technology. The rigorous curriculum is discussion based, encouraging students to develop not only the right answer, but the right path to the answer.

Although the school is expensive, nearly 15 percent of the students are receiving nearly a full scholarship to attend the school. The board of trustees is a diverse group of community leaders, who work strategically toward a broad vision that protects the legacy of Paul Ransom and all those who came after him, while pushing the school into the future.

Ransom Everglades is much larger than it was, with nearly 600 students in the high school level and more than 400 in the middle school.

But Moceri and her faculty maintain an intimacy by emphasizing team sports, community service and a strong advisory system. The Summerbridge Miami program, which partners Ransom Everglades students and faculty with middle school students in low-income neighborhoods, is the largest of its kind. Ransom Everglades students have also worked for reforestation programs in Haiti, schools in Africa, and numerous local community programs.

The dedication to the waterfront and the great outdoors that lured Ransom to a nascent Miami continues with programs in sailing, marine biology, and green building technology.

More than a hundred years after its founding, Ransom Everglades School lives the axiom that to those to whom much is given, much is expected. Thus far, they have never disappointed.

■ *Students from the Robotics Club present an electrifying exhibition during an All-School Assembly.*

MIAMI DADE COLLEGE

The Great Equalizer:
Democracy's College

An ever-growing student body, unparalleled diversity and renowned degree programs in hundreds of disciplines contribute to Miami Dade College's status as democracy's college.

With more than 165,000 students on its eight campuses, MDC is the country's largest higher education institution, recently welcoming its 1.5 millionth student. The College's commitment to excellence and equal access serves as a model for educational institutions around the world: MDC enrolls and graduates more Hispanic and African-American students than any other college in the nation, and its students represent approximately 180 countries and speak nearly 80 languages.

The College's degree paths are as diverse as its students, with possibilities ranging from associate degrees in aviation and Web design to a selection of high-caliber baccalaureate degrees. Numerous nationally lauded programs enhance these core curricula, including an honors college praised by Time magazine and the Wall Street Journal, the distinguished New World School of the Arts, and a wealth of internship possibilities with established and emerging industries.

Miami Dade College has received many accolades for its combination of academic excellence with a commitment to creating opportunities for all. These include the first Theodore M. Hesburgh Award for excellence in teaching from TIAA-CREF, recognition by the Beacon Council as the best higher education institution in support of workforce development, selection by a University of Texas research study as the best and most innovative college in the nation, inclusion in the New England Board of Higher Education's "Saviors of Our Cities" list for service to the community and acknowledgement by *Yahoo! Internet Life* for being one of the most wired colleges in the nation.

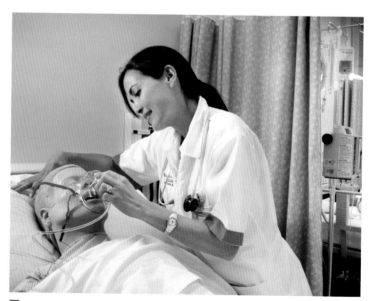

■ *Nursing student practices on a high-tech human patient simulator at Medical Center Campus. Miami Dade College offers a large array of health programs and graduates more nurses than any other institution in the country.*

Background and History

There is much continuity between Miami Dade College's current status and its founding nearly five decades ago. Throughout its history, the College has held fast to a belief in the importance of delivering a high-quality, affordable education that develops students as both independent thinkers and devoted stewards of the community.

The history of the College, founded as Dade County Junior College, reflects a continuous dedication to providing educational opportunities to traditionally underrepresented groups. MDC was the first integrated junior college in Florida, opening its doors to African-Americans at a time when other institutions refused admission. The College gained further recognition for its dedication to equal treatment and open access by providing a means of advancement to newly arrived immigrants. Many of these individuals – including MDC's own distinguished president,

Dr. Eduardo J. Padrón – began their ascent to the top of their respective fields as students of the College.

As Miami's population grew, so too did MDC, becoming Florida's largest institution of higher education by 1967. From its origin in 1960 as a cluster of lackluster buildings in northwest Miami-Dade County, the College has expanded to eight state-of-the-art campuses located throughout the county.

Programs and Services

This commitment to diversity extends to the College's academic offerings, which include more than 300 programs running the gamut from architecture to radio and television broadcast production. The College changed its name from Miami-Dade Community College to Miami Dade College after the addition of baccalaureate degree programs to its academic offerings. Furthermore, students can choose from Associate in Arts degrees in 80 areas of concentration and a comparable

The historic Freedom Tower in downtown Miami is located at MDC's Wolfson Campus.

range of Associate in Science degrees. A wide variety of advanced technical certificates and career credit certifications make MDC a key contributor to the local and regional workforce, providing career and professional development opportunities in dozens of fields.

The College's belief in combining academic excellence with affordability opens the door to upward mobility for many, and a flexible range of course options and venues (from fully online courses through the Virtual College to weekend and evening courses) allows students to accommodate family and work-related obligations. Close to 3,000 faculty members – all recognized leaders in their respective fields – bring their subjects to life using inventive and inspirational teaching strategies.

The College also addresses the training needs of the business community in South Florida and beyond through its Center for Corporate Training, which offers innovative, state-of-the-art professional training tailored to the needs of the corporate client.

◼ *Nobel Laureate and former Soviet President Mikhail Gorbachev addresses students, faculty members and community leaders as part of Miami Dade College's illustrious Miami Leadership Roundtable series, which has brought numerous prominent world leaders and top thinkers to the community.*

Community Outreach

A service-oriented impulse underlies these diverse academic and extracurricular endeavors, a quality that won the College inclusion on the U.S. President's Higher Education Community Service Honor Roll.

Among the flagship programs epitomizing this core value are annual community health fairs that provide free tests and screenings to the public; tutoring and beautification initiatives in financially strapped areas of the city; service-learning grants that enable current and future educators to design and implement community-building curricula; a comprehensive refugee assistance and education program that acts as a lifeline for many of South Florida's newly arrived immigrants; and numerous environmental awareness campaigns and educational outreach projects initiated at the College's Earth Ethics Institute, Kendall Campus' Environmental Center and North Campus' Green Urban Living Center. MDC also consistently positions itself at the forefront of community debate and dialogue on issues of particular local concern, including immigration law reform, the socio-economic repercussions of rising property taxes and the evolving relationship between the United States and Cuba.

This investment in the local community goes hand-in-hand with global outreach initiatives. The College has provided training for health care workers in Saudi Arabia, medical assistance in the Dominican Republic and donations to disadvantaged children in Uganda, to name

◼ *Actor Andy Garcia studied at Miami Dade College's Kendall Campus. He's among the more than 1.5 million people who have attended the College since 1960.*

has grown into the largest and one of the most celebrated in the country. Each year it attracts more than 300 world-class authors, 300 major publishers and half a million fairgoers.

The energy and enthusiasm sparked by this event are rivaled in Miami only by the electrifying film festival, which annually brings together film lovers, directors, producers and actors, and is considered the premier venue in the U.S. market for international and Ibero-American films. In addition to the book and film festivals, MDC delivers a wide range of high-quality cultural programming through its Cultura del Lobo performance series, the Tower Theater in Little Havana, Prometeo Theatre and numerous heritage festivals that celebrate the College and city's trademark diversity.

MDC's Art Gallery System (AGS) – a network of six galleries and three public art spaces that together comprise more than 15,000 square feet – showcases works by emerging artists and established masters. One of the many groundbreaking exhibitions made possible by AGS includes a collection of 218 etchings by Spanish artist Franciso de Goya y Lucientes that had never before been shown in the United States.

■ *Joining dozens of leaders representing a wide range of fields and career paths, celebrated retired Miami Dolphins wide receiver and MDC alumnus Nat Moore was inducted into the Miami Dade College Alumni Hall of Fame in 2006.*

but a few of the most recent projects. MDC is also a well-established destination for international delegates and dignitaries as a result of its frequent hosting of meetings, conferences, workshops and orientations, such as the Fulbright Gateway Program and the National Defense University's International Fellows Program.

The local and global frequently overlap at MDC's varied and much touted cultural offerings, which the New York Times acknowledged as among the best in academia. The College plays an integral part in two particularly renowned annual events: the Miami Book Fair International and the Miami International Film Festival. The long-running book fair

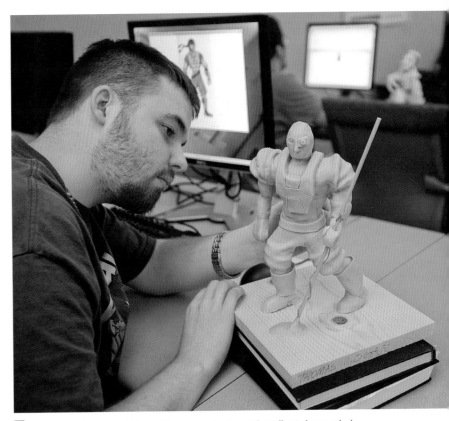

■ *A student works on a model for a video game animation at the College's distinguished Emerging Technologies Center of the Americas.*

■ *The College's acclaimed School of Aviation is one of just 13 institutions in the nation certified by the FAA in air traffic control.*

■ *Pulitzer Prize-winning playwright and MDC alumnus Nilo Cruz got his start on the stage at Miami Dade College and its respected Prometeo Theatre at Wolfson Campus.*

The Future

MDC's pivotal role in hosting these cultural events is in line with its unwavering investment in cutting-edge academic and career-training programs that equip today's students with the expertise to rise to the challenges of tomorrow's job market. South Florida's rapidly growing biotechnology sector is but one case-in-point: with the help of multimillion dollar grants from the U.S. Department of Labor, the College has launched a Biosciences Job Growth Initiative that is providing valuable training to local companies while laying the groundwork for future partnerships. Complementing this initiative is MDC's Biotechnology Program, which offers students a variety of certificate and degree concentrations.

MDC's vital role in supplying technologically savvy employees to South Florida's workforce is universally acknowledged. Its Emerging Technologies Center of the Americas is a leading provider of skilled professionals to the region's Web design, electronics and information technology industries. The College also fills the ranks of South Florida's computer programming, media and entertainment sectors.

The College's dynamic partnerships and regular consultation with local, regional and national companies facilitate a fluid progression from the classroom to rewarding careers. Collaborations with Microsoft, Oracle, Cisco, Unigraphics, Dell, IBM, FPL and many others yield invaluable internship opportunities for MDC students in the

ever-evolving field of technology, while a range of training and educational centers based at the College provide local businesses with a steady stream of skilled employees. Regarding the latter, Wolfson Campus' Center for Financial

■ *Theater students perform during a campus production.*

Training is the largest industry-sponsored education program in the world for the financial services sector, while the Employ Florida Business Assistance Now for New Economy Results Center plays a decisive role in maintaining the health of the South Florida economy.

The College's enduring desire and heartfelt duty to function as the lifeblood of the community motivate these diverse educational endeavors. Miamians daily encounter the fruits of Miami Dade College in the multitude of dedicated employees sustaining and shaping the region's many businesses, banks, health care facilities, schools, law enforcement agencies, tourism and hospitality venues and public service industries. The College is equally omnipresent in the city's cultural offerings, from concerts, art exhibitions and films, to plays, festivals and lectures on topics of local interest. Whatever the context, MDC savors its status as a bedrock educational institution that instills purpose, actualizes potential and creates endless opportunities for enrichment.

■ *Students who earn degrees through The Honors College at MDC transfer to the nation's top institutions, including Yale and Stanford.*

■ *Sunset at North Campus, Miami Dade College's first campus, which opened in 1960.*

MONSIGNOR EDWARD PACE HIGH SCHOOL

Monsignor Edward Pace High School is much more than an educational institution; it is an extended family.

Typically 99% of the graduating class, comprised of approximately 300 seniors, is accepted into the college or university of their choice. Of those graduates, more than one third usually qualify for Florida's Bright Futures Scholarship and many receive a plenitude of additional accolades and scholarships. By and large, a graduating class will amass about $11.5 million in scholarships to colleges around the country.

The guidance department steers the students in the right direction and assists them in making the right decisions for their academic careers. By keeping the same advisor throughout the four years of high school, students form a strong bond with their guidance counselor. In fact, the bonds between students and teachers are also strong, leading to a secure sense of belonging at Pace. Students feel at home at the school, which instills a generous amount of self confidence in them. Pace's formula for success can be put in a simple equation: academics plus faith equals success in life.

About half of the teachers are former students, as is the school principal, which proves the bonds formed in high school can last a lifetime. Owned by the Archdiocese of Miami, Pace High School was established in 1961 and named for the first native-born Floridian to become a diocesan priest. Monsignor Pace, a brilliant student and educator, founded the schools of Canon and Civil Law at Catholic University in Washington D.C.

A National Blue Ribbon School of Excellence, Pace has been on the Catholic Honor Roll twice, placing it among the top 50 Catholic High Schools in the nation. Originated by Marist Brothers, Pace is a Marist school by tradition. Among its first students were children who escaped communist Cuba through Operation Pedro Pan in 1961.

Located on an idyllic 44 acre campus, Pace's student body is comprised of 1,150 children in grades nine through 12. Most students come to Pace from 22 feeder Catholic schools in Miami-Dade and Broward counties. Academic programs at the school, which strives to meet the needs of a diversity of students, include the national Advanced Placement program, dual enrollment opportunities with Florida International and St. Thomas Universities, general education classes and a program for students who may require more individualized instruction.

■ *Monsignor Edward Pace High School, established in 1961, promotes a tradition of excellence in Catholic education.*

The Hennessey Center serves as the Performing Arts Center and Cafeteria.

Student life includes a wide-ranging athletics program. The strong tradition of sports excellence includes 17 state championships in football, baseball, basketball – boys and girls, girl's volleyball, cross-country and wrestling. For those students not interested in participating on a team, a rich variety of clubs and arts programs is available.

Academic success is only one aspect of the Pace environment. The philosophy of giving back to the community is integrated into student life. The students support two sister schools in Haiti, including teacher salaries and school supplies; volunteer for Habitat for Humanity; hold food and toy drives and donate the goods to local churches; and support an after school program at a parish in Miami's Little Havana neighborhood. These good deeds are accomplished through a creative array of fundraisers throughout the year including car washes, bake sales and book sales.

Baseball picture: Pace Varsity Baseball Team, 2006 FHSAA State Champions. Our long standing, prominent baseball program has won 6 FHSAA State Championships.

The combination of academics, religious studies and charitable activities has had a long-lasting impact on Miami. Many leaders are born at Pace, serve the community while succeeding in their respective careers, and often return to the school as guest speakers or teachers. Notable Pace alumni can be found in every niche of society and include business leaders in the fields of health care, international trade, attorneys, doctors, authors, politicians, musicians, actors and star professional athletes.

Dante Navarro Religious Education Center, "Our Chapel", completed in 2007, is the center of our school.

Perhaps the school's most visible alumni is the principal, Ana Garcia, class of 1980. Garcia, who became principal in 2003, grew up in the Catholic school system. After teaching in the public school system, Garcia came to Pace where she was assistant principal for five years. Her husband, who she met as a student at Pace, is principal at a Catholic grade school; her children attended Catholic schools, including Pace. Garcia believes Pace was the foundation which guided and influenced her life and she is proud the same loving, family atmosphere she experienced as a student remains an integral part of the Pace community today.

The alumni, famous or not, are renowned for their continuing support of Pace. Many donate their time, money and resources to assure the campus is maintained and the technology is kept current. Others enhance the curriculum by sharing their experiences with the students as guest speakers. Undoubtedly, the alumni come back to Pace because of the close familial ties to the school. If they are in the business world, they contribute; if they are educators, they

Our nationally recognized Boys Varsity Basketball Team practices in our state-of-the-art gymnasium. The Basketball Program has captured 5 FHSAA State Championships since 1996.

come back to teach. Pace Alumni reunions are plentiful; again demonstrating Pace is a community that truly does last a lifetime.

UNIVERSITY OF MIAMI

One of the nation's leading research universities, the University of Miami is a vibrant community of exceptionally talented individuals engaged in the pursuit of academic excellence, the discovery of new knowledge, and service to the region and beyond.

ore than 15,300 undergraduate and graduate students from around the world call UM home during the academic semesters. Founded in 1925, the University has grown from its original campus in Coral Gables to include the Leonard M. Miller School of Medicine campus near downtown Miami, the Rosenstiel School of Marine and Atmospheric Science campus on Virginia Key, and the South and Richmond campuses in southwest Miami-Dade County as well as satellite facilities in other locations. The University's 12 schools and colleges, along with the Division of Continuing and International Education, offer 114 bachelor's, 104 master's, 55 doctoral, and two professional degree programs. The Coral Gables campus houses eight schools and two colleges, and the Miller School of Medicine campus is part of the University of Miami/Jackson Memorial Medical Center complex. Additionally, other academic programs, including bilingual continuing education classes, are offered at the Koubek Center in Miami's Little Havana area.

Discovery and the creation of new knowledge is one of the highest priorities for a research university. Each day, in laboratories, clinics, and classrooms across the UM campuses, what is known is rigorously challenged in the pursuit of new knowledge. The University's energetic and comprehensive research enterprise generates innovations

and breakthroughs in numerous disciplines such as marine science, medicine, bioscience, and engineering.

Research and sponsored program expenditures exceeded $325 million in fiscal year 2008. The Rosenstiel School of Marine and Atmospheric Science is a leading oceanographic research and education institution. The largest percentage of the University's research takes place at the Miller School of Medicine, which is the nexus of South Florida's growth as one of the world's great bioscience research and development centers.

The Schoninger Research Quadrangle is located in the heart of the Miller School of Medicine campus.

The University has more than 15,300 students from throughout the United States and 110 foreign countries.

Founded in 1952, the Miller School has earned international acclaim for research, clinical care, and biomedical innovations, establishing the University of Miami/Jackson Memorial Medical Center as one of the best in the nation. It is a vital local health care resource, with its 1,300 faculty-physicians handling one million patient visits annually. The new University of Miami Hospital, launched in December 2007, and University of Miami Health System are dramatically increasing the University's patient care activities.

The University has been engaged in the largest construction program in its history, with approximately $986 million in current and planned projects. Major projects that have opened in recent years on the Coral Gables campus include: University Village, a residential apartment complex for 800 students; the M. Christine Schwartz Center for Nursing and Health Studies; the Jorge M. Perez Architecture Center; the Marta and Austin Weeks Music Library and Technology Center; the Myrna and Sheldon Palley Pavilion for Contemporary Glass and Studio Arts at the Lowe Art Museum; and the BankUnited Center, a 7,000-seat arena that is home to the Hurricanes men's and women's

basketball teams and is used for other events. On the Miller School campus, the 15-story Clinical Research Building is re-engineering the way medical research is conducted, and the Biomedical Research Building, slated to open in 2009, will significantly increase basic science space. The University is moving forward with plans to develop a two million-square-foot Life Science Park on land adjacent to the campus, which will help elevate South Florida into the ranks of the nation's elite medical research communities.

With 12,765 faculty and staff, UM is the largest private employer in Miami-Dade County and has a total economic impact of $4.5 billion. The University's growth has been a powerful catalyst for economic development throughout the county and particularly in Coral Gables. The University further enriches the South Florida landscape through its wealth of programs in the arts, athletics, and other areas.

Led by President Donna E. Shalala, who became the University's fifth president in 2001, UM is accelerating its progress in all key areas, including fundraising. In 2006 *Momentum: The Campaign for the University of Miami* reached its initial $1 billion goal 18 months ahead of schedule, and it surpassed its subsequent $1.25 billion goal, raising a total of $1.4 billion by its conclusion at the end of 2007. As the University advances as one of America's top universities, it will continue to be an energetic, driving force in South Florida.

The Rosenstiel School of Marine and Atmospheric Science conducts advanced studies on the F. G. Walton Smith *research vessel.*

BARRY UNIVERSITY

Founded in 1940 by the Dominican Sisters of Adrian, Michigan, Barry University is a cornerstone of the Miami community.

Since its inception as a small Catholic women's college with an initial enrollment of 45 students, Barry has grown into a thriving Catholic University, with 26 satellite sites across the state of Florida and an enrollment of more than 8,000 students from around the world.

Growth in recent years has included the acquisition of a law school in Orlando in 1999. The Dwayne O. Andreas School of Law received full accreditation by the American Bar Association in December of 2006 and has become one of the most respected law schools in the Southeast. In January of 2007, the university broke ground on the Center for Community Health and Minority Medicine. With its three-phase development plan, the Center will serve more than 400 health professional students and will focus on the prevention, treatment and management of diseases that adversely affect minority and underserved communities.

Yet, throughout its history and the many changes that have occurred on campus over the years, the university remains focused on its mission: To provide a quality education with religious dimension, and to serve the community, and provide a caring environment.

This striking sense of community and belief in the transformative power of Catholic higher education is felt everywhere on campus, but is perhaps best illustrated by Barry students themselves and their continued service to the city of Miami and its people. Every Thanksgiving, students at Barry's School of Social Work provide food baskets to Miami's elderly; the Habitat for Humanity student chapter regularly helps build homes in neighborhoods where they are desperately needed; and every year on Martin Luther King Day, students, faculty and staff join together to complete a much needed social service project in the local community.

In short, when Barry students graduate, they leave not only with the skills to realize their dreams, but also with the will to help others achieve theirs.

CHRISTOPHER COLUMBUS HIGH SCHOOL

Christopher Columbus High School is perhaps unlike any other secondary school in South Florida and in most of our nation.

Sure, being an all-boys Catholic school makes it somewhat unique, but what really sets it apart are its extraordinary character, high standards and achievements over the past half-century. A level of excellence that has earned it prestigious distinctions: *CCHS is consistently ranked as one of the top 50 Catholic High Schools in the United States by the Catholic High School Honor Roll.*

School Principal Brother Patrick McNamara notes, "For 50 years, we have practiced an untiring commitment to shaping the moral, spiritual and religious lives of our students in a structured and caring environment. Two-thirds of our faculty have been here for more than 15 years and many are Columbus graduates, and all our teachers share a remarkable ability to bring out in our students their full potential. The result…students come here as boys and leave as men."

Founded in 1958, CCHS is owned and operated by the Marist Brothers, whose calling is to make Jesus Christ known and loved among young people. School President Brother Kevin Handibode says CCHS's faculty and staff take pride in fulfilling this mission, while simultaneously providing a well-rounded education for high school boys at all levels of learning. Programs are available for: the highly motivated; the academically gifted; those with special talents and even students needing educational reinforcement. Columbus' history of success in taking this multi-level approach to learning speaks for itself: *100% of all seniors graduate and go on to college.*

"What further shapes our boys is dedication to community service to our educational family, to Miami, and to the Marist nation," Admission Director Brother Michael Brady notes.

In addition, students are involved in numerous extra-curricular activities and compete in sports on the highest level, 6A – making it the only private Catholic school in Florida to do so.

Christopher Columbus High School: committed to Marist educational excellence in Dade County for 50 years and for many more decades to come.

A typical day in Christopher Columbus High School's Science Lab.

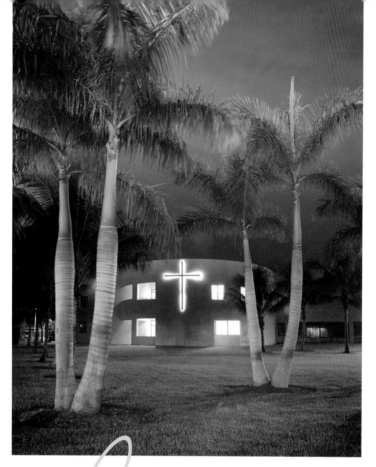

BELEN JESUIT PREPARATORY SCHOOL

From the island of Cuba to the United States, Belen Jesuit Preparatory School has provided young men with the intellectual and moral foundation necessary for a college education.

Jesuit Preparatory School acquired its own building on the corner of Southwest Eighth Street and Seventh Avenue in Miami. Twenty years later, a new school was built on a 30-acre site in west Dade County and in 1981, the school year began with an enrollment of 598 students.

t is an institution steeped in tradition, where students become "men for others," and individuals who care for their fellow human beings. At Belen Jesuit, students achieve excellence in academics, athletics, and extracurricular activities.

Its history is rich. In 1854 a royal charter founded the "Colegio de Belen" (Belen School) in Havana, Cuba, in the building formerly occupied the hospital of Our Lady of Belen. In 1961, Belen Jesuit Preparatory School was established in the United States, under the auspices of Bishop Coleman Carroll. The fourth floor of the Gesu Elementary School, located in what is now the parking lot of Gesu Church in downtown Miami, became the first site of Belen Jesuit Preparatory School. The actual building no longer exists. A year later, Belen

■ *Belen Jesuit follows the Ignatian tradition of excellence.*

■ *Since 1854, Belen Jesuit has provided young men with an intellectual and moral foundation.*

Since then, the school has grown with the inclusion of a language laboratory, two computer laboratories, the Roberto C. Goizueta Athletic Center, the Vincam wing, which hosts a large cafeteria, classrooms, and a guest dining room. Villa Javier, the Jesuit residence, and the Raul and Nidia Rodriguez Science Pavilion were completed in 2002. In the same year, new outdoor basketball and tennis courts were added. In 2004, the Ignatian Center for the Arts opened its doors with seven new classrooms, a music rehearsal hall, the Ophelia and Juan Js. Roca Theater, and the Olga and Carlos Saladrigas Art Gallery.

Belen Jesuit is committed to the service of the Catholic faith and the promotion of justice.

The sprawling campus provides a physical setting that fosters an environment for learning and development for boys in grades six through twelve. Faculty at Belen Jesuit brings strong educational backgrounds and a wealth of experience. Students not only benefit from their teachers' academic credentials, but also from their devotion to the mission of Belen Jesuit. The pedagogy of St. Ignatius of Loyola and his Spiritual Exercises are the basis for the planning and execution of all pedagogical material, as well as faculty training. The needs of students are the primary focus in all decisions that impact the school.

Faith and justice are promoted throughout the curriculum. Character formation takes place through the development of consistent self-discipline and taking full responsibility for personal actions.

Diversity also plays an important role at Belen Jesuit. With bilingual and bicultural settings and curricula, students are better prepared to live and work in a multicultural society. The school adheres to the Catholic faith and Ignatian tradition that every human is uniquely created in the image and likeness of God, and should be treated with respect and dignity.

Today, the school has more than 1,500 students. Its graduates include professors at universities such as Duke, Harvard, Georgetown and the Massachusetts Institute of

Continuing a tradition of over 140 years, the Belen Observatory for Astronomy and Meteorology is at the service of its students and the Miami community.

Technology, bankers and business leaders, entertainers, athletes and journalists, scientists and priests, lawyers, judges and political leaders, including the current mayor of Miami, Manny Diaz.

In 2009, Rev. Pedro Suarez, S.J., a graduate of Belen Jesuit and former teacher at the school will become Rector of Belen. For 25 years, Belen Jesuit was led by Rev. Marcelino Garcia, S.J. who announced he was stepping down in 2008.

Students become well-rounded individuals through their participation in curricular and extra-curricular activities.

Belen Jesuit is accredited by the Southern Association of Colleges and Schools, a prestigious and recognized association. The school has been listed on The Catholic School Honor Roll as one of the top 50 Catholic high schools in the United States.

In addition to its various clubs and athletic offerings, students learn life lessons outside of the classroom as part of Belen Youth Missions. In 1981, Rev. Eddy Alvarez, S.J. took a group of Belen students to the mountains of the Dominican Republic to work alongside the campesinos. For the past few years under the direction of Father Willie Garcia-Tuñón, S.J., Belen Youth Missions has built bridges, aqueducts, schoolhouses, and chapels that have served to improve the communities it has served.

Following the Ignatian tradition of excellence, Belen Jesuit Preparatory School works to guide and support its students in the process of becoming men

Small class sizes ensure higher achievement for Belen Jesuit students.

who are open to growth, and who are intellectually competent, religious, loving, and committed to doing justice, so that they can work as Catholic leaders in a multicultural society.

CARLOS ALBIZU UNIVERSITY

"Love reaches beyond knowledge"
Carlos Albizu- Miranda, Ph.D.
Founder of Carlos Albizu University (CAU)

At the core of Dr. Albizu- Miranda's educational philosophy lies the notion that love reaches beyond knowledge. He believed that knowledge without love is sterile and that it had to be shared in a spirit of cooperation, for it to be meaningful and relevant. Today that mission is kept alive by the faculty and administrators who instill it in their students.

The University upholds the standards of Dr. Albizu-Miranda by educating and training its graduates to work in a multicultural world with the goal of improving the quality of life of the communities where they work. CAU distinguishes itself through an educational philosophy based on a commitment to social responsibility. As a private, non-profit university that bears its founder's name, the University offers programs in psychology, education, speech pathology, and business administration to more than 2,000 students at its campuses in San Juan, Puerto Rico, and Miami, Florida.

Founded in Puerto Rico in 1966 with the specific objective of offering a Master of Science in Clinical Psychology, the institution became a dream realized by

■ *Carlos Albizu-Miranda, Ph.D.*
First President and Founder

Dr. Albizu- Miranda. The founding of the institution by Dr. Albizu-Miranda, a professor of psychology who had obtained his doctorate at Purdue University, was the result of his concern for the lack of culturally competent psychologists in Puerto Rico. There were no graduate programs in clinical psychology in Puerto Rico and he realized that few students from the island were able to pursue graduate studies in the field of psychology in the United States. Those who did study in the U.S. were trained in models and techniques that were not always sensitive to the needs and socio-cultural characteristics of Puerto Rican and other Hispanic populations.

■ *The Carlos Albizu Library.*

The establishment of the CAU Miami Campus in 1980 was in response to a critical need in the United States for graduate psychology programs that could competently train psychologists in the provision of services to a multiethnic population. Twenty years later, in 2000, CAU Miami Campus diversified and expanded its program offerings to include education and business. With more than 40 countries represented in its student body, CAU Miami Campus thrives in a modern facility with 18 acres of university grounds located in the city of Doral.

■ The Miami Campus is a facility of 70,000 square feet within 18.353 acres of land, allowing expansion of the physical facility up to 250,000 square feet.

To reach out to as many students as possible, CAU now offers an extensive array of online courses. These online offerings help to connect students to the campuses in Miami and San Juan, and allows for an opportunity to educate others worldwide.

CAU Miami Campus is committed to Miami-Dade County. Many of its students are involved in the provision of professional services through various internship and practicum sites available in the community. According to Dr. Ileana Rodriguez-Garcia, President of CAU, in many instances, CAU students are offered employment positions prior to graduation.

Another example of CAU's involvement in the community is seen in the work done by students enrolled in its Doctor of Psychology (Psy.D.) Program, through the Goodman Psychological Services Center. The Center, which is a private, non-profit community mental health agency affiliated with the Psy.D. Program at CAU, was established in the early 1980s. It has provided mental health services to over 10,000 residents of our multicultural community

at an annual cost of approximately $500,000. Students at the Center provide clinical services to members of the local community under the supervision of licensed psychologists. The services are specifically designed to be affordable as fees are based on a sliding fee scale.

CAU's programs are recognized both nationally and internationally. A recent article published by The *Industrial- Organizational Psychologist Journal* ranked CAU's master's program in industrial and organizational psychology as one of the best in the country and as the best in the southeastern United States. The ranking is especially significant to the faculty and administration of the University because it is based on student rankings of quality. Additionally, CAU Miami Campus was recently recognized by the prestigious magazine *The Hispanic Outlook in Higher Education* as one of the 100 best universities on the United States for students of Hispanic heritage.

CAU continues its founder's vision by contributing to the growth of human knowledge and the promotion of social justice and a culture of peace through its various academic programs. These offerings provide a unique opportunity for students to obtain a quality education in their desired area of study, while acquiring the multicultural competencies needed to work in a global community.

■ The school is located in a thriving and modern 18-acre campus in the heart of the Doral area in Miami.

CARROLLTON SCHOOL OF THE SACRED HEART

When St. Madeleine Sophie Barat founded the Society of the Sacred Heart in France more than 200 years ago, she envisioned communities of learning where girls would engage in a rigorous academic education, and develop into significant contributors to society.

arrollton School of the Sacred Heart carries forward its founder's mission into the 21st century, preparing students for dynamic learning in the university, professions, and life.

Carrollton is a member of the Network of Sacred Heart Schools -22 in the United States and another 220 in 44 countries. As participants in an international community, Carrollton students are exposed to ways and modes of thinking that are universal. They are prepared to face challenges both academically and spiritually, ultimately to become global citizens.

Unique in the State of Florida as the only pre-K through 12th grade girls' school, Carrollton ensures that students grow in an environment that is culturally rich and diverse in its inclusion of those from all religious and socio-economic backgrounds. The school thrives in the active promotion of the five goals of a Sacred Heart education, which include a personal and active faith in God, a deep respect for intellectual values, a social awareness that impels to action, the building of community as a Christian value, and personal growth in an atmosphere of wise freedom. Carrollton is known for providing a total education that is inclusive of spiritual, intellectual, emotional and physical challenges.

Sited in Coconut Grove on two historic estates totaling almost 17 acres, Carrollton nurtures educational and spiritual enlightenment. Organized into five schools, students move

from each campus to the next, enhancing Carrollton's vitality as an individualized, and also unified learning community. The Barat Campus, home to the Intermediate and High Schools, fronts Biscayne Bay and features El Jardin, one of the first Mediterranean style villas built in Coconut Grove, completed in 1918 and listed on the United States National Register of Historic Places, along with new buildings that retain the spirit of the original historic architecture.

As stewards of the historic structure, the school is an integral part of the Miami community because of its commitment to share El Jardin with Miami's citizens. In addition to its illustrious place in history, Carrollton plans strategically for its future. Significant additions to the campuses include Rose Hall and the Melissa Rodriguez Assembly Hall at Duchesne and the Founders Library and Science-Technology Hall at Barat which opened in January 2007 and is part of a larger master plan entitled "Imagine Carrollton's Tomorrow."

Carrollton is a digital community. The "Anytime, Anywhere Learning" program ensures that beginning in grade 5, each student has her own laptop, a learning toolbox designed to enhance lessons and stimulate accomplishment. Faculty directs these endeavors through Smartboard technology and advanced coursework. The program helps young girls grow into women confident in science and technology. "What we're after is to allow the girls to project themselves into whatever sphere of influence and field

they choose," said Sister Suzanne Cooke, headmistress of Carrollton School, who serves on the National Board of the Anytime, Anywhere Learning Foundation.

Carrollton boasts one of the nation's few all-girls robotics team and the only all-female, championship policy debate team. Foreign languages include Mandarin, as well as French and Spanish. Every student graduates with bilingual capability in text and speech. Championship tennis, golf and sailing augment larger team sports in volleyball, softball, soccer and water polo. Skill and leadership, on and off the field, develop through competition and club sports and activities.

Advancing excellence in every arena, in addition to its long-time Honors and Advanced Placement courses, in 2004, Carrollton joined the society of schools offering the International Baccalaureate diploma program, generally regarded among the most rigorous high school curricula in the world. The IB program emphasizes research, writing and critical thinking across the curriculum. The international diploma is recognized globally to enable students to enroll in the world's leading universities.

The present and future vision of Carrollton school embodies St. Madeleine Sophie Barat's philosophy of education. Carrollton educates girls to change the world with their voice, with their vision and with their faith.

GULLIVER SCHOOLS

Gulliver Schools is recognized as perhaps the best private school in Miami, and for good reason.

hanks to strong leadership and an exceptional faculty, it has earned remarkable achievements in preparing young men and women for college. In 2006, Gulliver had the highest number of Merit Scholar Semifinalist for public or private schools in Miami-Dade County; the International Baccalaureate Program has an outstanding 98 percent diploma pass rate since 1998; 14 National Hispanic Scholars in 2007, and Florida's only 2007 Presidential Scholar.

It's no wonder every student at Gulliver Preparatory and Gulliver Pinecrest Preparatory School is accepted to a four-year college or university, with many continuing on to graduate level studies.

There are a number of reasons for these achievements, as well as other distinguished accomplishments, that vividly depict just how effective Gulliver Schools has been in providing quality education. In part, Gulliver's success stems from its long-standing beliefs of how children should be taught. These include (1) creating an environment that fosters excellence in learning, curricular change and innovation, leadership in interschool relationships, and participation in civic affairs on local, state, national and global levels; (2) nurturing the character and development of young people through a regular emphasis on the Honor Code and LifeSkills® programs, both designed to flourish personal and academic integrity; and (3) maintaining a policy that children learn best within a structured, orderly

framework that encourages the collaboration of faculty and parents; and further, that flexibility within this framework helps accommodate the diverse characteristics of students.

Gulliver Schools: A Growing Presence in Primary and Secondary Education in Miami for Decades

Certainly, the root of Gulliver Schools, dating back to 1926, also plays a major role in the academic success the school has enjoyed for so many years. In 1926, Arthur Gulliver, a resident of Miami's Coconut Grove residential section, established Gulliver Academy. The Academy initially enrolled students

from New England whose families were wintering in South Florida. Many parents viewed Gulliver as a twin school to the prestigious eastern academies in terms of curriculum and focus. Therefore, Gulliver became the ideal choice for where to send their sons or daughters to school, in terms of the best in academic and character-building education. That distinguished recognition remains to this day.

Perhaps the most formative episode in Gulliver's history that has truly allowed the Gulliver Schools' name to become synonymous with high quality education in South Florida was the purchase of the Academy by Marian Krutulis in late 1953. Devoted to the learning styles and educational challenges of Miami's youth, Mrs. Krutulis saw a whole new potential for the school. She envisioned it as one day being a haven for exceptional education, where students and teachers alike would feel part of a caring, challenging family of learners, and she set out to fulfill that vision. The result: in time, Mrs. Krutulis came to personify independent education in Florida, building an environment where care, strength, and candor equaled educational excellence and high-esteem for children.

Her first step in that direction was in 1967, when she moved the Academy to South Dade. This was an area that soon after experienced a population explosion, and hence, a greater need than ever for quality, private schooling to accommodate the children growing up in that community. Today, there are more than 2,000 students learning on five different campuses, all within a three-mile radius in prestigious residential areas of Miami-Dade County. Each campus targets specific grade levels and/or is designed to accommodate students with specific educational needs or athletic interests.

Always Looking Forward To Meet The Needs Of Miami Area Youth

In an effort to ensure its perpetuity well into the future, Gulliver Schools became a 501(c) (3) not-for-profit educational institution in 2000. This transition laid the foundation for a philanthropic culture at the school, with students being the ultimate benefactors of generous community support. A prime example is the ground breaking of a new state-of-the-art Aquatic Center on the Preparatory Campus. Beyond the benefits this provides Gulliver Schools' students, the center will make it possible for Gulliver to continue to serve youth in the surrounding communities, as it has for many years, with swim instruction, safety, and better health. This is a crucial need when you consider that Miami-Dade and Broward County lead the nation in deaths due to drowning for children under age 11.

Gulliver Schools: *synonymous with the highest in quality education for more than 80 years.*

THE SAMUEL SCHECK HILLEL COMMUNITY DAY SCHOOL

THE BEN LIPSON HILLEL COMMUNITY HIGH SCHOOL

THE JUDA AND MARIA DIENER ELEMENTARY SCHOOL
THE HENRIETTA SCHECK MIDDLE SCHOOL

From early childhood through Grade 12, Hillel cultivates and inspires students' interests and talents to prepare them for college admission.

Built in 1970 upon an inspirational vision and a profound commitment to community, today Hillel is the second-largest Jewish community day school in the nation.

While preparing students for higher education, Hillel focuses on the development of individual character. The balanced program is designed to foster children's moral, intellectual, spiritual, aesthetic and physical qualities through a rigorous curriculum, religious and cultural experiences, competitive athletics, comprehensive service learning and enrichment opportunities to explore special interests and develop leadership skills. Hillel offers students a superior academic education, a solid preparation for college and an enduring Jewish identity.

Hillel is about educational excellence. Highly trained, skilled teachers integrate cutting-edge technology along with innovative learning techniques. Nationally recognized programs, faculty and leadership demonstrate how academics are strengthened by traditional values and a vibrant community that prepare students to become knowledgeable adults with deep commitments to Judaism, the Jewish people and the State of Israel.

Extending hands to local service projects as well as communities afar, Hillel students fulfill their roles as members of the next generation on campus, at home and in the global village. Leadership experiences instill ambition and drive so students may reach their greatest potential and discover their individuality and talents within.

Hillel is further enhanced by a commitment to serve all families who seek a Jewish education for their children.

Diversity is a key component of the school's unique environment. Members of the school community are from across the globe, including the United States, Europe, Latin America, Israel and Africa, and are of many denominations within Judaism. Today, the school offers financial support to nearly 30% of its student body. Hillel's celebration of diversity makes it a place where students learn not only from their teachers, but also from each other, speaking to the very soul of the school's mission.

Hillel truly opens doors to opportunity, where hallways are paths to academic achievement, creative development and spiritual growth. Drawing upon a rich history, these are all outcomes of Hillel's ultimate goal to provide children with

Diversity is a key component of Hillel's unique environment.

the finest Jewish educational experience. At Hillel, a sense of belonging nurtures minds, souls and hearts...encouraging the lifelong learning and leadership that continuity requires.

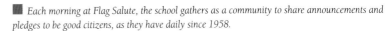

St. Stephen's Episcopal Day School

The essence of St. Stephen's Episcopal Day School is its partnership between the church, the school and the home.

Since its inception in 1958, the school has provided students a strong academic foundation along with a solid moral and ethical background. This is a place where students learn to be leaders with a strong commitment to the community that lasts a lifetime.

Situated on three verdant acres in the heart of Coconut Grove, St. Stephen's prides itself on its individualized attention and small class sizes from preschool to grade six. The academic program is designed to develop strong critical thinking skills along with a life-long love of learning. Steeped in the tradition of the Episcopal Church, the curriculum encompasses academics, values and a spiritual foundation.

An important aspect of the St. Stephen's education is the focus on writing, and critical thinking. Spirituality is at the forefront with chapel services one to three days per week, including a full Eucharist Mass, and sacred studies classes. The latest technology is embraced with smart boards in every classroom. Public speaking is more than encouraged; it is part of every day life at school. Students have ample opportunity to speak in front of their peers, giving them the confidence found in leaders of all ages. Community service is ingrained in the school. Families, students and faculty are involved in a variety of outreach projects throughout the year.

The student body is as diverse as Miami and all cultures are celebrated. Formal Spanish instruction is a priority for all students. St. Stephen's parents are very involved in the school and are always welcome on campus.

The school is committed to preserving the environment and students pledge daily to recycle, conserve energy and reduce water usage. Extra curricular activities include a plethora of enrichment programs such as sports, music, technology, art and even a sailing program on nearby Biscayne Bay.

St. Stephen's is looking toward the future with plans for a new, green building. The façade of the original building, constructed in the early 1900s, will be preserved. By 2010, St. Stephen's will be distinguished by state-of-the-art facilities that support a spiritually-based, multi-cultural educational model which prepares students to embrace the challenges of the 21st century.

For more than half a century, leaders who have made a difference in the lives of South Floridians began their education at St. Stephen's Episcopal Day School. That legacy is one that will continue for years to come.

"St. Stephen's young inquisitive minds at work!"

JOHNSON & WALES UNIVERSITY

As the chief administrator of Johnson & Wales University's North Miami Campus since it opened in 1992, I take pride in what we have done and continue to accomplish in preparing our students for the future."

– Donald G. McGregor, J.D., Campus President

Since 1992, Johnson & Wales University's North Miami campus has helped many thousands of students prepare for careers in some of the fastest-growing industries, including criminal justice, culinary arts, hospitality, marketing and sports/entertainment/event management. To accomplish this, JWU's leadership has hired outstanding faculty, created innovative services and curriculums, and built exceptional facilities, to better teach and prepare students for future employment. It's all part of a simple philosophy instituted by the university early founders that continues to this day which says, "We should teach a thing not for its own sake, but as preparation for what lies beyond."

The university prepares graduates for personal and professional success by integrating rigorous academic and professional skills, community leadership opportunities, and its unique career education model.

Johnson & Wales University's Roots Go Back To Early 1900s

JWU's original campus in Providence, R.I. was founded as a business school in 1914 by Gertrude I. Johnson and Mary T. Wales. Since those early days, this private, nonprofit, coeducational institution has grown in many ways toward fulfilling its ongoing mission: *to integrate general education, professional skills and a career-focused education plan for students.*

Milestones have included in:

• *1954, obtaining accreditation by the Accrediting Council for Independent Colleges and Schools.*

• *1963, granted a charter by the state of Rhode Island to operate as a non-profit, degree-granting institution of higher learning,*

with the ability to award associate degrees in the arts and sciences. (In 1970 this charter was amended allowing the University to award baccalaureate degrees and in 1980 a further charter change occurred, authorizing advanced degrees to be awarded.)

• *1973, the opening of a College of Culinary Arts and the addition of a new associate degree in that field. This proved to be a far-reaching change in the university's educational expansion, leading to two and four year degree programs in hospitality and foodservice.*

• *1992, JWU opens its North Miami Campus to expand its reach to the thriving South Florida business and hospitality communities. The campus opened with one building, 82 full-time students and 20 part-time students.*

• *1993, earning distinguished regional accreditation by the New England Association of Schools and Colleges (NEAS&C).*

- **2006**, *The North Miami Campus and its three sister campuses were named to the President's Higher Education Community Service Honor Roll.*

- **2007**, *Today the North Miami Campus enjoys an enrollment of nearly 2,000 students pursuing bachelor's and associate degrees in business, culinary arts and hospitality.*

Market Driven, Experientially Based, Employment Focused, Student Centered, Globally Oriented

The North Miami Campus operates based on several core values, practiced throughout the university's system, as vividly noted and illustrated in these respective examples. The school is very much:

- **Industry Relevant:** students' needs and the needs of student's future employers are paramount. *Degrees are offered in those areas where many South Florida businesses have identified their greatest future employment demands – business, hospitality, culinary arts, with concentrations in national security, cruise line management, golf management and international hospitality operations management.*

The College of Culinary Arts is one of the three colleges that offers associate and bachelor's degrees at the North Miami Campus of Johnson & Wales University. Students may pursue associate degrees in baking & pastry arts or culinary arts and a bachelor's degree in culinary arts.

Johnson & Wales University is dedicated to preparing students for professional success through rigorous academics and professional skills, community leadership opportunities, and its unique career education model.

- **Experientially Based:** hands-on learning is integrated with a career-focused curriculum, to enable students to gain real-world experience. Numerous students are active in the South Florida workforce through "externship" and cooperative education programs, getting on-the-job experience in their chosen fields as part of their academic work.

- **Employment Focused:** Employment-ready, motivated graduates for world-class employers is an ongoing priority. JWU works directly with corporations such as Marriott International, Inc., Compass Group North America and other industry partners, structuring programs that create experiential learning opportunities.

- **Community Minded:** One of the university's priorities is to develop students who have the skills, training and personal commitment to be strong, ethical leaders in industry and in their communities. Students are encouraged to perform community service in various ways – past initiatives have included "Share Our Strength" benefits to end childhood hunger, the preparation of free income taxes through the Internal Revenue Service's Volunteer Income Tax Assistance program, and Join Work Unite, a pre-Labor Day neighborhood cleanup that more than 500 freshmen participate in annually.

- **Globally Oriented:** Focus is placed to address today's global business environment by fostering multi-culturalism and an international education experience. *The campus' 2,000 students hail from 39 states and 55 countries.*

Campus President Donald G. McGregor, J.D. notes, *"The reason this university has been so successful in South Florida is because we focus our efforts on one key goal -- to provide businesses with highly-skilled, well-prepared graduates to meet their employment needs. That is our goal today, tomorrow…always."*

MIAMI COUNTRY DAY SCHOOL

Miami Country Day School prepares its students for higher learning, and while academics are a priority, the school's mission is to educate the whole child.

The whole child concept recognizes that every individual is endowed with six potentials: intellectual, spiritual, social, aesthetic, physical and emotional. The school helps to develop lifelong learners who are also successful and responsible citizens in a global society.

Started in 1938 as an elementary boarding school for boys by Luther B. "L.B." Sommers and C.W. "Doc" Abele, the school was known as The Miami Country Day and Resident School for Boys. While its first class had only seven boys enrolled, it quickly grew to have a reputation as one of the finest independent institutions in the southeast. Through the 1950s and '60s, day students were added to the school's resident population and in 1972, Country Day became co-educational. The boarding school was eventually phased out and boarding rooms on the 16-acre campus were converted into classrooms to accommodate a rapidly growing population. Originally a K-8 program, the school expanded to include an Upper School and graduated its first senior class in 1981.

Today, the academic program from Jr. Kindergarten through 12th grade includes core curriculum areas and electives that far exceed most college preparatory requirements. However, it's not only in academics where Country Day excels. Extensive enrichment programs give students the opportunity to discover new challenges in a learn-by-doing environment. One of the most popular programs is Miami Country Day's Comprehensive Outdoor Education Program, which features an Experiential Outdoor Adventure based program that reflects the whole child philosophy of Country Day. As an active member of the national and international Association of Experiential Educators, MCDCOEP has established itself as one of the nation's leading outdoor adventure based programs and challenges students in three major areas: academic skills, outdoor and physical tasks, and individual and group leadership development. The Abess Center for Environmental Science (ACES) is an enrichment and resource program

The Comprehensive Outdoor Education Program (COEP) complements and enhances traditional education.

unique to Country Day. Students in grades JK-5 explore biodiversity and environmental issues though exciting hands-on activities. An unusual collection of animals, gardens and a greenhouse provides a living laboratory for budding "avant-gardeners." Through enrichments programs like these at Country Day, students are actively involved in local and international projects.

■ *Sportsmanship, teamwork, tradition, dedication, commitment and self esteem are values fostered by athletics.*

Country Day also offers the opportunity of team building through sports with 37 athletic teams, many of which have gained recognition through district and regional championships. State-of-the-art facilities include an Aquatics Center that was added in 2002 and features a 10-lane, 25-yard competition pool, and the Koch Family Athletic Center, completed in 2005, which utilizes a synthetic turf where baseball, softball, football, lacrosse and soccer are played. For those seeking a different type of outlet, the Fine Arts program at Country Day encourages students to explore the creative process. From Grade 6 and continuing through the Upper School, students choose their arts classes from leveled electives including Advanced Placement classes. Independent study options are also available. Students are empowered to find their instruments or voices and experience the challenges and joys of the creative process through award-winning theater, music and arts programs. The Nathan Hurst Outdoor Amphitheater will open in early 2009.

As technology plays an increasing role in learning, Country Day is committed to providing students with access to the latest technology in order to help them compete in a high-tech world. A state-of-the-art educational facility that is set to open in 2009 will include a library, media arts center, information technology center and student center.

Since the education and lifelong learning of its students is of the highest priority for Miami Country Day, highly skilled and qualified faculty and administration are encouraged to maintain professional standards of excellence. MCDS has recruited each of the 103 faculty from throughout the United States and the world. Each person brings his/her own unique skills, distinct knowledge and well-rounded experiences to the MCDS community and more specifically into the learning environment of the equally diverse student body. Miami Country Day's commitment to retaining and attracting a faculty of excellence is demonstrated in the establishment of the cutting edge MCDS Professional Growth and Compensation plan. Not only does this plan recognize faculty contributions which support the outstanding educational experience of each student, it also requires observation, conversation, and evaluation through a teaching/learning model that defines "best practice". Additionally, the School's commitment to smaller class sizes allows teachers and students to interact more individually. In this "community of learning" environment, teachers motivate students within a fulfilling, dynamic and classic academic program that prepares them for the 21st Century.

Country Day's graduates go on to Ivy League and other top-ranked colleges and universities as a result of a well-guided and thoughtful process in finding the best match for each student's interests and talents.

Miami Country Day School. Preparing students for college and life.

■ *Miami Country Day School's success is based on a philosophy of dedication to academic excellence.*

MIAMI INTERNATIONAL UNIVERSITY OF ART & DESIGN

Since its inception in 1965, Miami International University of Art & Design has been built on a solid tradition of excellence in career-focused education of the applied arts.

This level of excellence is vividly illustrated in the exceptional quality, scope and growth of this institution over the past 40-plus years. From an enrollment in its first year of 47 young women studying Fashion Merchandising, the University has evolved into a multi-faceted higher education institute serving more than 1,700 undergraduate students of all ages and cultures, from over 80 different countries in its degree programs. These programs include Computer Animation, Graphic Design, Advertising, Web Design & Interactive Media, Film & Digital Production, Audio Production, Photography, Visual & Entertainment Arts, Visual Effects & Motion Graphics, Interior Design, Fashion Design, Fashion Merchandising and Accessory Design. Additionally, the University awards Master of Fine Arts degrees in Computer Animation, Film, Graphic Design, Interior Design and Visual Arts.

Guided by an equally diverse faculty, both academically active and work experience in their applied fields, University students are encouraged to develop their creative skills. They also receive a strong foundation in general education and spend the greater part of their studies creating a hands-on portfolio of artistic work. This innovative, teaching formula practiced by the University has produced solid results: *consistently alumni surveys show most graduates find employment in their chosen careers, or pursue an even higher education degree in their fields.*

Early Challenges Stepping Stones To Academic Growth & Success

Founded as International Fine Arts College (IFAC), the first 20-plus years for the College were spent establishing itself.

From 1988 to 1997, IFAC changed its focus, developing

■ *Fashion Design students get to showcase their collections to the media and press at the runway tents of South Beach on Ocean Drive during FUNKSHION: Fashion Week Miami Beach as part of the annual senior show.*

■ *Rebeca Gilling, a recent graduate of the Visual Arts Program, created this ceramic sculpture; this was one of the many pieces included in her Master of Fine Arts thesis exhibition, which was displayed in the University's Main Gallery.*

College Gains Further Credibility With Numerous Accreditations

As IFAC improved, accreditation followed beginning with the Southern Association of Colleges and Schools, Commission on Colleges (SACS), which accredited the school as International Fine Arts College in 1979, making it one of the first two proprietary colleges to earn SACS-COC accreditation. The Executive Director of the Commission on Colleges went on to reaffirm the College's accreditation in 1984 and again in 1995.

After becoming accredited, the College worked to enhance its degree offerings to include baccalaureate degrees, and was granted accreditation to offer such degrees by SACS in 1997. Today, associate's, baccalaureate's and master's degrees programs are available.

With such an array of art and design degree programs being offered, an institutional name change became appropriate. Hence, in 2002, the College became officially the Miami International University of Art & Design. Also that year the University moved its main facility its current site on Biscayne Boulevard; and in recent years two additional campus locations have been added -- The Art Institute of Tampa and The Art Institute of Jacksonville.

Throughout its rich history, the University has overcome challenges time and again, creating a blueprint for success, setting the stage for continued growth and prosperity for many years to come. However, no matter the size or scope it takes shape in the future, the Miami International University of Art & Design will always be based on its tradition of excellence in career-focused education of the applied arts.

clear to the faculty and staff there was a need for a Miami-based, computer animation training facility; hence the school's Computer Animation program was born.

This program was further strengthened in the late 1990s by the College's affiliations with software companies, who began awarding contracts to IFAC to institute training workshops for animation practitioners. In time, this led to the College becoming a beta testing facility, with IFAC having the newest educational software applications available. These capabilities made it possible for ongoing training of faculty in industry-related technology, and subsequently, earned IFAC recognition as a leader in computer art education within the computer industry.

■ *Instructor Luis Crump teaches film students pre-production techniques using industry related equipment in the University product studio's green room.*

Palmer Trinity School, established in 1991, is located on 55 acres of tropical hammock in South Florida.

PALMER TRINITY SCHOOL

Rooted in the traditions and values of the Episcopal Church, Palmer Trinity School in Palmetto Bay, is an institution steeped in quality, sophistication, and vision.

Situated on a campus of extraordinary beauty, students and teachers develop mind, body and spirit with great enthusiasm.

Palmer School (founded in 1972) and Trinity Episcopal School (1983) merged to become Palmer Trinity School in 1991, with a vision that would mutually benefit both schools. After a few years, green and gold Pirates and the purple and white Titans unified as blue and gold Falcons. It became increasingly clear that this new independent Episcopal school was destined to become a premier educational institution.

In 1992, Hurricane Andrew made a direct hit on the Palmer Trinity School campus. The beautiful campus was devastated by the hurricane. Classes started in tents that fall, and the 82nd Airborne (US Army) used Shafer Hall, the current middle school building, as its headquarters.

Post-hurricane landscaping and the school's commitment to environmental preservation are reflected in the serene tropical loveliness of gumbo limbo trees, royal poincianas, palms, ferns, orchids, and other foliage native to the area. The new Yarbrough Humanities building, Music Center, a Gym, Math/Science building, and expanded Library space have been added to the original buildings.

In the years since the merger, the Palmer Trinity student body has steadily grown from 300 to 600 students. The student population is as diverse as the multicultural city of Miami, and includes students hailing from over thirty-five countries. Over fifty percent of the student body is bilingual with thirty percent speaking more than two languages.

An emphasis on spirituality sets Palmer Trinity apart from other schools. Weekly convocations, with frequent emphasis on ethics, encourage spiritual development in each individual, bonding the students in spiritual, as well as academic growth. The school embraces students of all faiths while encouraging them to learn about religions other than their own in an affirming, inclusive atmosphere.

Palmer Trinity's dedication to excellence spans all facets of school life. Academic success can be attributed to the outstanding college preparatory courses, including Honors and AP courses, and the Laptop Program. The demanding

Embracing diversity is a part of Palmer Trinity School's mission

curriculum encourages students to cultivate a greater understanding of themselves and others. Students connect to their lives as well as to their classes through interdisciplinary studies. The school is one of a select few that offers semester-long study abroad opportunities to Australia and Spain. Initiatives in Religion and Ecology reflect Palmer Trinity's commitment to innovative programming alongside strong traditional education. With programs in place like the Advisory system and Peer Counseling, the school focuses on ensuring every student's individual success and happiness.

The celebration of soul and spirit makes Palmer Trinity School unique.

Believing that true learning need not necessarily take place within a classroom, Palmer Trinity's Outdoor Education Program provides an experiential outdoor learning program that embraces our community and natural resources. In a partnership with the University of Miami's Rosensteil School of Marine & Atmospheric Science, students participate in shark tagging trips and intensive studies of the Everglades and Biscayne Bay ecosystems.

The athletic department at Palmer Trinity has always played an important role in school life, and remains competitive by virtue of its many individual and team championships along with significant coaching honors. Much more important however, is the incredible number of students over the years whose lives have been enriched simply through their involvement with one or more of the teams. Participation in athletics allows students to develop leadership traits such as dedication, perseverance, strength, and courage.

The excellent music, drama, and visual arts programs offer students a broad range of options in creative expression. More than 35% of the overall student body is involved in the music program which has been recognized, by the Florida Music Educators Association, for its innovation and diversity of curriculum along with enrollment and retention.

Community service is a significant part of the Palmer Trinity experience. Numerous outreach projects provide hands-on experience. Students grow to be more socially responsible citizens and are expected to spread that spirit in their respective communities. Trips have been organized to build schools, houses and roads in Nicaragua, Honduras and post-tsunami Sri Lanka. Students are expected to connect with a social service agency or begin their own program, as many students have. The school challenges students to make a lasting contribution to the world while developing their potential as scholars.

Palmer Trinity School is a high level educational institution. The school provides the optimal combination of academics, spirituality and social conscience to its college-bound students. Each well-rounded graduate of Palmer Trinity continues to a four-year college or university, attesting to the strong academic programs as well as the school's true commitment to the holistic development of all students.

The teachers at Palmer Trinity lend support to their students both in and out of the classroom.

ST. THOMAS UNIVERSITY

With a diverse, top-tier faculty, it is no wonder that a small, private university in South Florida is "Developing Leaders for Life."

Knowing that leadership can be learned, St. Thomas University challenges and encourages its students to be leaders by emphasizing strategic thinking, undergraduate research, community involvement and service. Students from all creeds and backgrounds learn leadership skills while attending one of the most innovative Catholic universities in the nation.

In addition to being dedicated to developing leaders who contribute to the society in which they live, St. Thomas University is at the cutting edge of higher education. Academic programs are individualized and provide each student a unique level of personal attention while they experience a hands-on learning environment and specialization in a given field. Student to faculty ratio is very low, 13:1, giving students the opportunity to develop their strengths with the guidance of skilled professors.

The curriculum at Biscayne College and the Schools of Law, Business, Leadership Studies, Science, Technology and Engineering Management and Theology and Ministry is as diverse as the students themselves. Graduate level courses in Education include Instructional Technology and Special Education; the Law School has an Intercultural Human Rights curriculum; the School of Leadership Studies offers post-graduate degrees in Hispanic Media, Electronic Media and Art Management. An online religious study program gives students around the world an opportunity to expand their careers and a certificate in Deaf Ministries is unique as well as Homeland Security studies within the criminal justice curriculum.

The university is currently in a growth mode, with new facilities being built at an impressive rate. Opened in August 2008 and funded by private and public sectors, the Carnival Cruise Lines Science and Technology Building features the finest equipment and an innovative academic program, which focuses on undergraduate research. Undergraduates have a rare opportunity to conduct research under the supervision of senior professors. With specialized equipment, much of the research concentrates on spinal cord rejuvenation. In addition, a botany program, with a specialty on the restoration of the Everglades, will have real world applications. Programs like these give students a tremendous advantage for graduate school admissions and to advance in the workforce.

Nursing students sharing information with professor

Another new facility, to be completed in 2009, is the Fernandez Family Center for Leadership and Wellness. This will be an athletic complex combining academic programs in leadership studies with sports administration and recreational activities. The center will include a gymnasium that will seat 1,800 for basketball games and another 1,700 on the floor for events. The facility will be used as a "working laboratory" for the sports administration program that will give students the opportunity to learn how to operate sports facilities and business ventures. Many sports administration graduates are in the business of running professional sports organizations. Internships are available through this program, making it a highly attractive curriculum.

President Monsignor Franklyn M. Casale

St. Thomas University prides itself on the diversity of its student body, which comes from more than 40 countries. The rich, multicultural environment adds to the culture of the school. The student population is indicative of the globalized workforce the students will experience upon graduation.

With a growing student population, new programs and facilities, the future looks bright for St. Thomas University. New professorial degrees, doctoral programs and more majors that meet the needs of the marketplace add to the success of the university.

The school is proud of being an incubator for new leaders. One of the university's goals is to produce leaders and not just graduates who get jobs. Upon graduation, each student will bring the faith-based values they acquired from their Catholic education to their positions of leadership.

Students enjoy campus life and faculty to student ratio.

THE CUSHMAN SCHOOL

Named for Laura Cushman, its founder and principal for nearly fifty-three years, The Cushman School is Miami-Dade County's oldest continuously operating private school.

he school is also recognized as one of the county's most accomplished educational institutions. Like its founder, The Cushman School is known for its idealism, innovation and vision. The school consists of several small buildings, a charming mix of old and new structures, spread across a small but expanding campus in a historic section of northeast Miami. Nearby are the waters of beautiful Biscayne Bay and the 1920s-era neighborhood of Morningside, a gentrified jewel and the city of Miami's first historic district. The Cushman School offers instruction— preschool to grade eight—to nearly 500 students, whose diverse backgrounds reflect the rich ethnic and racial diversity of its host city. The institution's education components consist of the Laura Cushman Academy for students with learning differences, and a primary, elementary and middle school.

The Cushman School opened in 1924, an outgrowth of an earlier school created and administered by Laura Cushman. A native of Iowa, Laura Cushman moved to the nascent city of Miami in the early 1900s. A decorated teacher in the county school system, Laura opened The Cushman School in 1924. Two years later, the school moved into a beautiful Mediterranean-styled building on the present campus. Since then, this seat of learning has introduced innovative approaches to education, including an advanced curriculum and an educational psychology calling for broad student input in the learning process. Laura Cushman was behind every step of the school's development, from its founding until her death

in 1986. She believed that every child was special, that each student was capable of helping to chart his or her educational path. Further, she held that each child possessed the ability, when provided with encouragement and direction, to achieve and succeed in school and in life. Judging by the roster of Cushman alumni, Ms. Cushman's approach succeeded. Former students include those in high-profile professions and businesses, but most have succeeded in life more quietly.

Cushman groomed her successor, Dr. Joan Lutton, who became principal in the early 1980s. An affable intellectual,

■ *All second grade students paint their interpretation of this classic portrait. "Children can paint pictures that feel like the thing they are painting – paint your own way." – Susan Silver, Cushman Art teacher for 30 years.*

Lutton is just as ready with a smile as she is with a solution to a vexing problem. She has continued Cushman's innovative pursuit of excellence, while bringing the school to a much healthier financial position. She presides over an institution that today operates on an annual budget in excess of $8 million, and provides a livelihood for more than 200 employees. Enrollment is capped at 500, which has led to a long list of prospective pupils. The school has recently completed a $7 million capital development program that has transformed the campus radically with three new multiuse buildings, providing for classrooms, art center, and a science laboratory. Additionally, the new additions to the campus include a technology center, individual learning studios, indoor and outdoor occupational and physical therapy playgrounds.

■ *"Laura Cushman speaks with Principal Joan Lutton during a visit at the nursing home where Cushman was recuperating from a stroke, December, 1983"*

■ *Every May 1, all kindergarten students celebrate the start of spring by dancing around the May Pole"*

QUALITY OF LIFE

*W*HEN I MOVED TO MIAMI IN 1969 TO WORK FOR WHAT WAS THEN A SMALL COMMUNITY HOSPITAL IN THE SUBURBS, I FOUND A CITY THAT WAS VIBRANT AND ENERGIZING, SO VERY DIFFERENT THAN THE QUIET OF OHIO WHERE I WAS BORN AND RAISED. I LOVED MIAMI FROM THE START. IT'S WHERE MY WIFE AND I RAISED A FAMILY, AND IT'S WHERE WE'VE PLANTED OUR ROOTS

I still believe in the magic of Miami and the solid foundation of a city and a region that has so much to offer to so many. Our growth as a nonprofit healthcare organization is a reflection of the growth of Miami's diverse communities. People come here from both within the United States, as well as from the far reaches of the world. They come here to shop, do business, take advantage of world-class medical facilities, get a first-class education, or to have that once-in-a-lifetime vacation.

Today, Miami is a true international city within a global economy. Our unemployment rate is lower now than both the state and national rates. Our travel industry attracts visitors from other countries who consider America and South Florida a bargain. And our housing market is now more affordable for those want to call this area home. There is always something to do, whether you like the arts, sports, theater, the beach, fishing, golfing, or just enjoying sitting in your backyard, "catching some rays," (a good source of Vitamin D).

Healthcare as an industry continues to provide excellent opportunities for employment, particularly in professions where there is a critical global shortage, such as nursing. Aging baby boomers, as well as retirees who moved here to take advantage of the tropical climate, are increasingly in need of medical care. To meet the rising demand, our philosophy is to "grow our own" staff. This means hiring

BRIAN E. KEELEY,
President & CEO, Baptist Health South Florida

Under Brian Keeley's leadership, Baptist Health South Florida is now the region's largest faith-based not-for-profit healthcare organization. Miami's largest private employer, Baptist Health includes Baptist, Baptist Children's, Doctors, Homestead, Mariners and South Miami Hospitals as well as Baptist Cardiac & Vascular Institute and Baptist Outpatient Services. In addition, work has started on a new West Kendall Baptist Hospital, opening in 2011.

Health Care

BECKMAN COULTER	378
AVMED HEALTH PLANS	380
BAPTIST HEALTH SOUTH FLORIDA	382
UNIVERSITY OF MIAMI HEALTH SYSTEM/LEONARD M. MILLER SCHOOL OF MEDICINE	386
UNIVERSITY OF MIAMI HOSPITAL	388
JACKSON HEALTH SYSTEM	390
LEON MEDICAL CENTERS	391
MIAMI CHILDREN'S HOSPITAL	392
MIAMI JEWISH HOME & HOSPITAL	394
MEDICA HEALTHCARE PLANS	395
SUNRISE COMMUNITY, INC.	396

them when they are young, supporting them through career advancements and changing family needs, and then helping them phase into retirement. At Baptist Health, recruiting the "best and the brightest" is important, but keeping them is even more important.

The magic of Miami helps us by attracting those who thrive on the vitality and the excitement of this grand city that we call home.

BECKMAN COULTER

"There is no satisfactory substitute for excellence."
– Arnold O. Beckman, Ph.D., 1900-2004,
    Founder Beckman Coulter, Inc.

Since its inception in 1935, Beckman Coulter, Inc. has been unwaveringly dedicated to providing high quality, state of the art products for the healthcare and biotechnology industry. The outcome of such dedication speaks for itself: *Beckman Coulter is recognized today as a leading, global manufacturer of biomedical testing instrument systems, tests and supplies designed to simplify and automate laboratory processes.* And by staying true to this business philosophy it fulfills an even greater goal: *improving patient health while reducing healthcare costs.*

Beckman Coulter's diagnostic systems are found in medical facilities and other critical care settings, producing information physicians use to diagnose disease, make treatment decisions and monitor patients. Scientists utilize the company's life science research test instruments to study complex biological problems. Such tools are vital in discovering causes of disease, identifying new therapies and testing new drugs.

Customers include hospitals, physicians' offices, diagnostic reference laboratories, pharmaceutical and biotechnology companies, universities, medical schools and research institutes near and far. The company has more than 200,000 clinical and research instrument systems in operating in laboratories, plus a multitude of long-standing, satisfied clientele. *A major portion of its revenue comes directly from recurring orders for its supplies, test kits and*

service used in laboratory settings.

Beckman Coulter practices its core values of *integrity, leadership and teamwork* to benefit those it serves and employs. It leads the market in its unique ability to collaborate with customers to make their individual processes more efficient and effective. Customers and employees recognize the company's *integrity* and long heritage of quality, superior brand equity and loyal clientele. A highly capable, collaborative workforce of talented people, working as a team consistently delivers innovative technology that impacts healthcare around the globe.

It all dates back to the company's early beginnings, when Arnold O. Beckman, an entrepreneurial college professor in California, started the firm more than 70 years

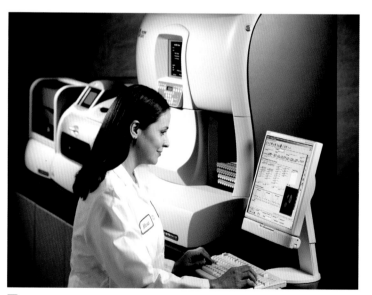

Laboratory technician checks results on a Coulter(R) LH 785 Cellular Analysis system from Beckman Coulter. The system performs CBC (complete blood count) tests -- the most commonly ordered medical diagnostic test.

A typical hospital laboratory processes thousands of patient samples in a day; Beckman Coulter supplies the instruments and tests for nearly 100 percent of routine hospital laboratory testing. Labs rely on the company for tests to help physicians diagnose conditions as diverse as cancer, thyroid disease, reproductive disorders, and cardiovascular disease.

ago. His vision has endured for decades with continuous, steady growth thanks in part to various acquisitions. One of the most significant was acquiring the highly successful Coulter Corporation in 1997, resulting in the name change to Beckman Coulter.

In unison with its core values, Beckman Coulter has built its technological prominence in the marketplace by focusing on systems that simplify and automate laboratory processes. Such traits can vividly be seen, for instance, in its line of cutting-edge hospital laboratory instruments that speed essential information to physicians to help them diagnose and treat patients. It also has made Beckman Coulter a recognized leader in vitro diagnostics systems to hospital laboratories. In fact, *it is the only company that can provide instrumentation to meet up to 75% of any lab's total testing needs and 100% of routine testing requirements.* Life science tools have helped researchers make breakthrough medical science discoveries and expand the boundaries of biological technology.

Of course, early detection is of the utmost importance for many life-threatening diseases. Beckman Coulter places great emphasis on producing tools and tests for diagnosis and disease management. For patients this means being able to receive greater insight than ever before from their physicians regarding their medical conditions-- the kind of information today's patients demand from medical professionals involved in their care.

At Beckman Coulter, the company strives to connect the brightest minds with the best technology to impact the next generation of biomedical testing innovation. Everything stems from the goal to enable new discoveries in biomedical research, drug development and the diagnosis and monitoring of disease. Toward this end, Beckman Coulter seeks motivated and energetic people who want to build their careers in the biotechnology industry.

The company is also synonymous with outstanding community involvement in locations where it has a physical presence. Its exceptional support has earned it a reputation for being a wonderful partner to various charitable causes. In Miami, this has meant strong employee participation in walk-a-thon fundraisers for the South Florida Juvenile Diabetes Association, March of Dimes, American Heart Association and the Cancer Charities Foundation's Breast Cancer Walk among others.

Beckman Coulter: *dedicated to excellence, improving patient health and reducing the cost of care.*

The Beckman Coulter facility in Kendall, Florida, is home to the company's Cellular Analysis Business Center, which contributed a substantial portion to the company's $2.7 billion in revenue in 2007.

AvMed Health Plans

Florida-Based, Florida-Focused

vMed Health Plans was first established in 1969 as Aviation Medicine for the airline industry in Miami. Today, we offer comprehensive health coverage solutions to large and small group employers in most areas of the state and Medicare Advantage to seniors in Miami-Dade and Broward counties.

AvMed serves very loyal members. Many of them have been with us for more than 10 years. Our corporate offices are located in Miami and Gainesville, and we have regional offices in Ft. Lauderdale, Orlando, Tampa and Jacksonville. AvMed is part of SantaFe HealthCare, Inc., a not-for-profit holding company, which also operates the North Florida Retirement Village, Haven Hospice of North Central Florida, Bayview Gardens retirement community in Clearwater and East Ridge Retirement Village in Miami.

Our Mission and Values

AvMed's mission is to improve the health of our members. We provide members with quality, cost-effective plans and highly personalized member services with an emphasis on quality and convenience.

Our vision is to be the health plan of choice. Our corporate culture is defined by compassionate, collaborative and ethical behavior focused on delivering superior member service. As a not-for-profit, we reinvest earnings to continually enhance our services.

Corporate Facts at a Glance

- AvMed has been serving Floridians for more than 35 years.
- AvMed employs more than 750 employees.

- Over 240,000 members around the state count on AvMed for their health coverage.
- The majority of doctors participating with AvMed are board-certified in their specialty.
- The National Committee on Quality Assurance (NCQA), the country's leading healthcare quality evaluator, awarded AvMed an excellent accreditation for both the commercial and Medicare products.
- The Street.com Ratings awarded us an A- (Excellent Financial Strength) for our excellent financial security and our ability to maintain a conservative stance in investment strategies, business operations and underwriting commitments. This rating places us in an elite group of 101 health insurance companies receiving an Excellent rating.
- AvMed also received an AM Best's Rating of B++(Good) for its financial strength, reflecting four years of strong operating performance after restructuring its commercial account business, membership growth and a good capital position. (Category: $100 million to $250 million)

■ AvMed's corporate headquarters are located in Miami with regional offices throughout the state.

Products, Programs & Services

At AvMed, we offer competitively priced health benefit plans for large and small businesses so that our clients and members have more choice and freedom. Whether it's a consumer driven plan with a Health Savings Account, or our Choice plan that's popular with employers because members can access any doctor or hospital in the U.S. without a referral, members can count on quality and superior service.

■ AvMed arranges health fairs and screenings for its employer group accounts.

Personalized, Local Service

AvMed clients receive the benefits of highly personalized and local service, with all the advantages of a nationally competitive health plan.

AvMed staffs a state-of-the-art call center to offer Member Services 24/7, 365 days a year. Registered nurses are available 24/7 through the Nurse On Call program.

The National Research Corporation has ranked AvMed the health plan with the highest customer care in Florida. (Based on 200,000 consumers nationwide across multiple customer care.)

AvMed's local presence ensures a seamless transition for employers—from a quick turnaround on ID cards, to explaining administrative guidelines and the payment process, we bring employer groups online quickly.

AvMed uses "predictive modeling" to identify health patterns in employee groups and forecast potential health-related problems. Once identified, we help members avoid complications and stay healthy and productive. We also make sure employer groups get the benefits and administration support they need.

Focus on Health and Wellness

Empowering members with the resources and tools to improve and maintain personal health is a priority for AvMed. Members receive education and incentives to participate in a wide range of wellness and prevention programs, and complementary and alternative medicine programs. Incentive programs range from reimbursements for Weight Watchers™ to rewards for prenatal and well-child visits. We also provide our members with decision support tools to help them make better health care choices and save money.

For members with chronic conditions, such as asthma, diabetes and heart disease, our team of registered nurses offers individualized attention and educational information to help them manage their health.

Access to Quality Care

We have an expansive network of specialists, flexible authorization polices and plans without referral requirements.

AvMed continually evaluates service and network providers to offer the highest quality health care. We emphasize efficiencies that help control health care costs for members, employers and society at large.

The NCQA named AvMed as a health plan of "Distinction" for its early adoption of new national standards related to care management and health improvement, which was done before it was required of all health plans.

■ AvMed offers a variety of benefit plans that provide easy access to a comprehensive network of doctors.

BAPTIST HEALTH SOUTH FLORIDA

Part of the magic

*M*iami is truly a Magic City. At Baptist Health South Florida, we have known this for years. We know South Florida intimately, and are inextricably linked to it. The flavor of it. The sounds. The sights. The natural beauty and the dazzling architecture. From the warmth of its climate to the warmth of its people, we feel the magic that makes Miami a vibrant, unique place, and are privileged to call South Florida home.

Baptist Health is a faith-based, not-for-profit healthcare organization comprised of Baptist Hospital, Baptist Children's Hospital, South Miami Hospital, Mariners Hospital, Homestead Hospital, Doctors Hospital and an expanding network of Baptist Medical Plazas. We've been caring for our neighbors in the South Florida community for more than half a century.

Our mission extends beyond caring for the sick: We strive to keep people healthy. Through community outreach, prevention and education programs, diagnostic and urgent care services, we are deeply involved in the health of the Greater Miami community.

And that includes less fortunate residents. In 2008, we provided more than $500 million in charity care, community health programs, free screenings and support of many health-related non-profit organizations in our community.

We do more than serve the community. We are the community. Baptist Health employs more than 12,000 people, which makes us the area's largest private employer. We are consistently named to FORTUNE magazine's list of

Baptist Hospital

South Miami Hospital

100 Best Companies to Work For, and are in Working Mother magazine's Hall of Fame as one of the nation's Top 10 companies for working moms.

Quality and Satisfaction

The secret of Baptist Health's success is the same as the secret of Miami's charm: people. Everyone in the Baptist Health family shares a commitment to quality patient care. It's not just a catch-phrase. From top to bottom, across the organization, a culture of excellence through patient safety and satisfaction permeates everything we do.

On average, Baptist Health hospitals score more than twice as high as other hospitals in Miami-Dade and Monroe Counties in numerous quality measures compiled by the U.S. government.

And in 2008, Baptist Health hospitals were rated among the best in patient satisfaction in the nation, ranking above many of the U.S. News & World Report Honor Roll Hospitals. In addition, Baptist Health hospitals were the top five hospitals in Miami-Dade and Monroe Counties, according to the federal government study.

Who we are

Since 1960, Baptist Hospital has been one of South Florida's most respected and preferred medical centers. The campus

Doctors Hospital

Mariners Hospital

houses Baptist Children's Hospital and Baptist Cardiac & Vascular Institute. The Italian Renaissance architecture and lush surroundings create a welcoming atmosphere. Inside, Baptist Hospital offers a full range of medical services and a highly regarded staff. Baptist Hospital was the first in Florida to be named a Magnet Hospital for Nursing Excellence by the American Nursing Credentialing Center.

Baptist Children's Hospital brings together a wide spectrum of health care services for children from birth to age 18. Young patients are treated by a medical staff that includes more than 200 pediatricians and 100-plus pediatric subspecialists in nearly every field. The 24-hour Children's Emergency Center cares for nearly 20,000 patients a year.

Baptist Cardiac & Vascular Institute celebrated its 20th anniversary in 2007. Under the direction of Founder and Medical Director Barry Katzen, M.D., the

Institute's multidisciplinary philosophy — to treat the entire cardiovascular system as a single entity — sets it apart. It is known for pioneering research in less invasive treatments.

South Miami Hospital opened in 1960 as a 100-bed hospital in a small suburban community. As the community grew, so did South Miami Hospital. A beautiful Medical Arts Building was completed in 2005 — phase one of an expansion and renovation project, with expanded emergency and surgical centers still to come. The South Miami Heart Center boasts a new Heart Rhythm Center. South Miami is also a Magnet Hospital for Nursing Excellence.

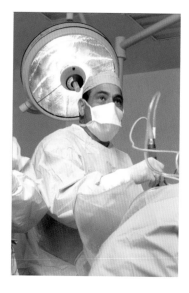

Doctors Hospital has been located in the heart of historic Coral Gables since 1949. The hospital's focus on warm, friendly patient care reflects its integration within this charming community. A nationally recognized Center for Orthopedics and Sports Medicine serves the Florida Marlins, Florida Panthers and the Miami Heat, as well as Florida International University teams. The neuroscience team at Doctors developed the first Gamma Knife program in Florida, and is one of the leading programs in the nation. Gamma Knife is a sophisticated, computer-guided technology that uses laser-thin gamma rays to target tumors.

Homestead Hospital

Baptist Medical Plaza at Tamiami Trail

Homestead is one of the fastest areas of growth in Miami-Dade County. A completely new Homestead Hospital opened in 2007. It's a bright, shining gem in a semi-rural setting, with the latest technology, all private rooms, a 24-hour Emergency Center, Children's Emergency Room and Birthing Suites that welcome more than 1,300 babies a year.

Mariners Hospital has been an integral part of the Upper Keys since 1959. Today, it's a 42-bed community hospital that provides inpatient care, hyperbaric medicine and a 24-hour Emergency Center. The Tassell Medical Arts Building houses the Mariners Wellness Center, outpatient diagnostic services, and physician offices.

West Kendall Baptist Hospital will be located at Kendall Drive and 162 Avenue. Scheduled to open in 2010, the hospital will provide inpatient care for adult medical-surgical patients, outpatient diagnostic services, maternity care and emergency services.

Baptist Outpatient Services

Baptist Health's urgent care centers, located in most of the Baptist Medical Plazas across Miami-Dade County, provide convenient access to patients while helping to reduce overcrowding in hospital emergency rooms. Our outpatient centers provide diagnostic services and are equipped with the latest digital imaging technology.

Baptist Health is proud to be a part of the magic of Miami. Our neighbors know us and rely on us. Our doctors, nurses and staff are dedicated to providing quality, compassionate care. And we look forward to a bright future as a valued member of our South Florida community.

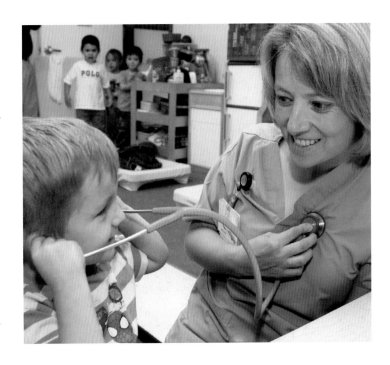

University of Miami Health System/Leonard M. Miller School of Medicine

Entrepreneurial in style and spirit, the University of Miami Health System/Leonard M. Miller School of Medicine has become an international academic medical center known for its excellence in patient care, medical education, scientific research, and community service.

Over the last 56 years, UHealth/Miller has grown so dramatically that it is often easy to overlook the many components that comprise this burgeoning enterprise—one that welcomes more than 400,000 patients and has nearly $200 million in research support annually.

To fulfill its mission and unique position as the only university-based medical center in the region, UHealth/Miller has made significant investments to build a world-class destination for preeminent care. In 2008, the UHealth brand was launched to convey the institution's excellence in lifesaving clinical care powered by the Miller School's groundbreaking research and innovative medical education. Under the UHealth umbrella, patients have access to great physicians who continue to raise the level of medicine in South Florida.

Hospitals, Facilities, and Institutes

UHealth provides care at its flagship University of Miami Hospital as well as at nationally-recognized Sylvester Comprehensive Cancer Center and Bascom Palmer Eye Institute along with our affiliates, Jackson Memorial Hospital, Holtz Children's Hospital, and the Miami VA. UHealth has more than two dozen outpatient facilities in Miami-Dade, Broward, Palm Beach, Collier, and Monroe counties.

Through scientific endeavors at research centers such as the Diabetes Research Institute, the Lois Pope LIFE Institute, the Miami Institute for Human Genomics, the Interdisciplinary Stem Cell Institute, and the Batchelor Children's Institute, treatments and medical breakthroughs are fast-tracked to patients. The bench to bedside cycle is the key distinction of university-based care, and we are fortunate to have this resource in our backyard.

■ Miller School Medical Students

With the ready availability of critical trials, patients have access to the newest and often most revolutionary treatments available.

Community Relations

UHealth/Miller is dedicated to the community. The Miller School adopted Allapattah Middle School and is focused on providing support and information on careers and healthy living for the students and their families. With funding provided by the Dr. John T. Macdonald Foundation, the Miller School of Medicine implemented a comprehensive school-based health program with on-site access to comprehensive health services from elementary through high school.

■ *Clinical Research Building, 2008*

The Miller School of Medicine's volunteer Mitchell Wolfson, Sr. DOCS Program is a student-run, non-profit organization that holds clinics and several annual health fairs in various Florida communities, providing free health care services.

As part of a civic partnership, the University of Miami joined representatives of governmental organizations, educational institutions, and community associations to create the Miami Health Partnership with the goal of rejuvenating the area surrounding the University of Miami and giving it a new identity and a new name, "The Miami Health District." The members of The Miami Health Partnership are committed to making the Miami Health District a more appealing place to live, work, shop, and receive medical care.

Economic Impact

With an annual operating budget of more than $700 million and an endowment of $220 million, UHealth/Miller plays an integral role in the economic health of the South Florida community. Many citizens of Miami-Dade County are employed through the development of new facilities, such as the 188,000 square foot Biomedical Research Building. When finished, the building will significantly increase the Miller School's research space and collaborations will promote increased disease-based research. The building's complementary facility, the 15-story Clinical Research Building, houses more than 900 physicians and scientists along with their teams.

UHealth/Miller in Palm Beach County Area

UHealth/Miller's clinical and educational presence extends far beyond Miami, particularly north in Palm Beach County. The University of Miami Miller School of Medicine at FAU, a four-year medical school program in Boca Raton, expects to enroll 256 medical students on the FAU campus by 2011.

The Miller School at JFK Hospital and the VA has created Palm Beach County's first allopathic (M.D.) residency program. A select group of residents will train in internal medicine at both JFK Medical Center in Atlantis Florida as well as at the West Palm Beach Veterans Affairs Medical Center.

A New Era

A new era was ushered in with a historic $100 million gift from the Leonard M. Miller family, which emboldened the school of medicine to take great strides. Coupled with the visionary, dynamic leadership of a new dean, Pascal J. Goldschmidt, M.D., along with a top tier of preeminent physicians and scientists, UHealth/Miller has capitalized on the possibilities of growth and expansion and is changing the face of medicine in South Florida and beyond. Indeed, we are becoming the destination for the best in leading-edge patient care.

■ *Pascal J. Goldschmidt, M.D., Senior Vice President for Medical Affairs and Dean, Miller School of Medicine, and CEO, the University of Miami Health System — UHealth*

University of Miami Hospital 2008

UNIVERSITY OF MIAMI HOSPITAL

University of Miami Hospital, formerly Cedars Medical Center, is the flagship hospital of the University of Miami Health System.

op physicians from the University of Miami Health System (UHealth), along with some of the very best community doctors, practice at University of Miami Hospital.

As part of UHealth, the region's only university-based health system, patients at University of Miami Hospital benefit from the latest advances in patient care, research, and education developed at the Miller School of Medicine. Another advantage of the UHealth network is that University of Miami Hospital physicians can refer patients to preeminent specialists not only within the hospital, but also at Jackson Memorial Hospital, Holtz Children's Hospital, the Miami Veterans Administration Health Care System, Bascom Palmer Eye Institute, and Sylvester Comprehensive Cancer Center – all significant resources for patients needing immediate specialized attention.

University of Miami Hospital is a fully-accredited 560-bed facility, recognized not only as a health care leader in Miami-Dade County, but throughout our nation. The hospital has earned this distinction by staying steadfastly committed to one important mission: providing the highest standard of university-based medical care.

You don't have to look far to see this pledge being fulfilled. University of Miami Hospital's patient accommodations are all private rooms, the latest technology for diagnosis and treatment is a heavy focus in terms of patient care, and the hospital personnel has earned a reputation for dedication and caring. Its approximate

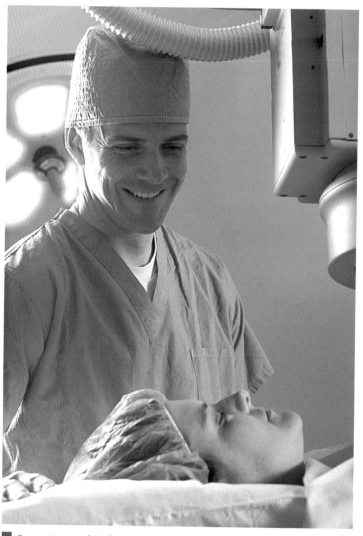

Compassionate and Quality Care

Original Cedars of Lebanon Hospital in 1961

1,600 employees and 900 plus physicians share a strong commitment to delivering a level of excellence in health care services unparalleled in our region.

You also have to admire University of Miami Hospital for its exceptional "customer service." Special patient care conveniences include multi-lingual staffing; specialized services for international patients; physical, occupational, and speech therapists; the very popular "Bingo in bed"; a non-denominational chapel and/or in-room clergy visits; and an on-site outpatient pharmacy.

Equally admirable is its leadership role, beyond the hospital setting, providing extensive community outreach and educational programs designed to help all residents of South Florida enjoy better health.

The University of Miami Hospital also employs outstanding technology. In fact, with the exciting new initiatives and groundbreaking advances in medical care developed at Miller School of Medicine – recognized by *U.S. News & World Report* in 2008 as one of the top medical schools in the nation – the hospital sits at the forefront of medical technology advancement.

Great emphasis is placed on quality assurance. University of Miami Hospital is fully accredited by The Joint Commission on Accreditation of Healthcare. Hence, patients can rest assured that the highest performance standards are being met in all areas of the hospital.

Another top priority is patient safety. Staff members work diligently to provide a safe, secure environment for patients at all times. Moreover, the hospital is constantly implementing new quality-improvement initiatives for the benefit of patients, such as Hand Hygiene, Rapid Response Teams, and Interdisciplinary Team Huddles.

When you consider the prominent status University of Miami Hospital has on a national level, it is truly remarkable how far this hospital has come in the last 45-plus years. The early beginnings of this hospital go back to the 1950s when there was a lack of adequate hospital facilities for patients in the Greater Miami area. This shortage caused local physicians to discuss this problem, with the obvious solution being an organized effort to build a new hospital.

In 1961 the new hospital was complete and was opened as "Cedars of Lebanon." In the decades that followed, the hospital underwent growth and transitions, characterized by new facilities, departments, staff and physicians, ownership and even a name change (twice). However, throughout this journey, one thing has remained constant. The hospital has always strived to meet one most important mission: to provide the best possible medical care available.

This commitment became vividly evident when the University of Miami and its Miller School of Medicine took over ownership of Cedars Medical Center on December 1, 2007, becoming University of Miami Hospital. In doing so, this purchase exemplified a sincere, unwavering dedication to bringing university-based health care to South Floridians and international patients seeking quality health care.

It's no wonder University of Miami Hospital is considered one of the leading hospitals in our nation. For more information, visit www.umiamihospital.com.

Destination Health Care

Jackson Health System's main campus, Jackson Memorial Hospital, is located in downtown Miami.

JACKSON HEALTH SYSTEM

90 Years of Pioneering Medicine

For more than 90 years, Jackson Health System (JHS) has been a cornerstone of the Miami community. Since opening its doors in 1918, Jackson has grown from a small, 13-bed community hospital to an internationally recognized medical system offering services ranging from routine care to rare, life-saving procedures.

Jackson Health System consists of Jackson Memorial Hospital, Jackson North Medical Center, Jackson South Community Hospital, Holtz Children's Hospital, Jackson Rehabilitation Hospital, and Ryder Trauma Center. JHS also has multiple community primary care centers, mental health centers, school-based programs, mobile health care-a-vans and long-term nursing homes. Jackson Memorial Hospital is continually ranked in *U.S. News & World Report* among the "Best Hospitals in America," and its physicians continue to top the "Best Doctors" in America list.

Affiliated with the University of Miami Leonard M. Miller School of Medicine and governed by the Public Health Trust, Jackson is home to numerous nationally acclaimed centers and programs. Jackson Memorial's transplant center is ranked among the 10th busiest in the nation and the only one in Florida to perform every type of solid organ transplant.

Ryder Trauma Center is the only adult and pediatric Level I trauma center in Miami-Dade County and one of the busiest trauma centers in the nation. It is also the only one chosen by the U.S. Army to train their military surgical teams before being deployed to areas of conflict.

Holtz Children's, one of the largest children's hospitals in the Southeast United States and a national leader in pediatric medical specialties, has a 126-bed Newborn Special Care Center that is a regional referral facility. It includes a 66-bed, Level III Neonatal Intensive Care Unit – the largest in Florida – which cares for the tiniest, most complicated newborns with some of the best outcomes in the world.

As Miami-Dade County's only public hospital system, JHS acts as a "safety-net" for the less fortunate in Miami. Every year, JHS spends approximately half a billion dollars to provide care to Miami-Dade residents who cannot afford health services.

Jackson Health System continues to grow and strive for new and better ways to offer innovative, leading-edge care to all residents in Miami-Dade County. For more information, visit www.jhsmiami.org.

The Miami City Hospital, which was later renamed Jackson Memorial Hospital, opened its doors in 1918.

LEON MEDICAL CENTERS

When Benjamín León, Jr. arrived in the U.S. from Cuba as a teenager in 1961, he couldn't have imagined the difference he would make in the lives of other Hispanic immigrants.

In 1964, León's father, Benjamín León, Sr. and his partner Moises Lieber, assembled a group of physicians and other professionals to create Miami's first pre-paid medical center, Clinica Cubana. The clinic served the growing community's healthcare needs and became one of the largest medical service providers in Miami-Dade County.

Six years later, León, Jr. and Sr. founded the Clinica Asociacion Cubana (CAC), which introduced the concept of managed care to Florida. In fact, the Leon family was instrumental in the development of the original Health Management Organization (HMO) and in 1973, CAC was granted the state's first HMO license.

A pioneer in the medical field, León, Jr. dedicated himself to improving the healthcare industry. He participated in government sponsored pilot programs to determine if Medicaid and Medicare could be operated through managed care organizations.

After two decades at the helm of CAC, León, Jr. founded Leon Medical Centers, Inc. (LMC) in 1996. LMC's mission is to improve the quality of life for Medicare recipients and the elderly by offering unparalleled medical care. Focusing on the Hispanic community, LMC remains true to its roots in the community.

LMC was established to bring quality healthcare services to the Medicare population in Miami-Dade County, while maintaining an environment of respect, dignity and compassion for the cultural nuances of the population it serves. The medical centers are located in five facilities in Miami, East Hialeah, Bird Road, West Hialeah and Westchester. Medical services include primary care, specialist care, on-site pharmacy and free delivery of medications, dentistry and ophthalmology. More than 1,000 dedicated healthcare professionals serve more than 26,000 patients.

Under León, Jr.'s leadership, LMC has become a model for successful healthcare institutions both locally and nationally. Moreover, LMC has received national recognition for its philosophy of focusing on the patient's medical needs as well as providing comprehensive individual attention.

In 2005, León, Jr. introduced Leon Medical Centers Health Plans, Inc., an HMO with a Medicare Advantage contract. LMC Health Plans is designed, like LMC itself, to serve the unique healthcare needs of the Hispanic community's Medicare patients.

Over the years, LMC and León, Jr. have redefined the status quo in the healthcare industry by staying true to their original vision of providing superior health care along with respect, dignity, and compassion.

MIAMI CHILDREN'S HOSPITAL

Since 1950, countless children have benefited from the exceptional medical care provided at Miami Children's Hospital.

The only licensed specialty hospital for children in South Florida, Miami Children's 289-bed free-standing facility is widely recognized as one of the nation's top pediatric hospitals. Using the very latest in medical technology and a staff of caregivers whose only focus is serving their young patients, *children confronting complex injuries, illnesses and diseases are having their lives changed for the better thanks to life-saving surgeries, medical research and the development of effective treatment programs.*

With a medical staff of 650-plus physicians and more than 130 pediatric subspecialists and 2,400 employees, Miami Children's carries out its mission literally worldwide serving many thousands of *pediatric patients and their families from throughout Florida and the U.S., as well as the Caribbean, Latin America, Europe and beyond.* This private non-profit facility annually provides millions in uncompensated charitable care. This philanthropic work is supported through the Miami Children's Hospital Foundation, a 501 (c) (3) charitable foundation, which raises funds and awareness to support state-of-the-art care at Miami Children's.

Among the highly acclaimed entities that comprise Miami Children's is the Congenital Heart Institute, which treats some of the most complex cases on the planet, while maintaining one of the best survival rates anywhere in the world. Another

is the Brain Institute. It takes into its care children with brain anomalies, including many who come from afar for treatment of the most challenging conditions.

The hospital's Cancer Center is also a care leader. Accredited by the American College of Surgeons Commission on Cancer, it is the largest provider of pediatric cancer services in the region. Similarly, the Department of Orthopaedic Surgery has earned accolades on a national scale for its innovation and is renowned for its scoliosis surgery program.

Miami Children's Emergency Department is one of the most recognized and best pediatric emergency services in the nation. In 2007, *Child* magazine identified the hospital as having one of the nation's top 10 emergency departments based on patient volume and service excellence. The department is also consistently identified as a regional parent favorite by *South Florida Parenting* magazine.

Another remarkable facility is Miami Children's Research Institute. It is the only entity in Florida dedicated exclusively to pediatric research. Recognized for its innovative, pediatric clinical research, the institute has participated in hundreds of studies of new treatments, interventions and assessment methods.

Training has long been an important part of Miami

Miami Children's Hospital's main campus, located immediately west of Coral Gables in Schenley Park offers treatment for children with complex medical needs.

Children's formula for success, with several generations of pediatricians and pediatric specialists having been trained on campus. *Miami Children's is home to the largest pediatric teaching program in the southeastern U.S., offering training for 69 pediatric residents and 17 subspecialty fellows every year.*

To decompress the hospital's main campus and make services more convenient for families in burgeoning South Florida, Miami Children's is committed to developing and expanding its outpatient service facilities. These include:

- Miami Children's Hospital Dan Marino Center in Weston, which provides comprehensive care for children with neurodevelopmental issues, including rehabilitation, imaging services, neurological services and much more.

- The Miami Children's Hospital South Dade Center in Palmetto Bay, offering urgent care, rehabilitation, imaging services, adolescent medicine and preventive medicine services, as well as an intervention program for children at risk of developmental delays.

- Miami Children's Rehabilitation Services – Miami Lakes, offering comprehensive rehabilitation services, including physical, occupational and speech therapies.

- New outpatient centers in Doral and Kendall, slated to open in 2008, will feature urgent care and rehabilitation and diagnostic services.

Miami Children's excellence is highly acclaimed. It holds the unique distinction of being the only Florida pediatric hospital to be included in *U.S.News & World Report's* 2007 listing of "America's Best Children's Hospitals." It also has earned distinguished recognition for being designated an American Nurses Credentialing Center (ANCC) Magnet facility – the nursing profession's most prestigious institutional honor.

With accolades such as these and given its extraordinary high level of commitment to providing the very best in pediatric medical care, Miami Children's Hospital will continue to be a beacon of hope to families of children with complex medical needs.

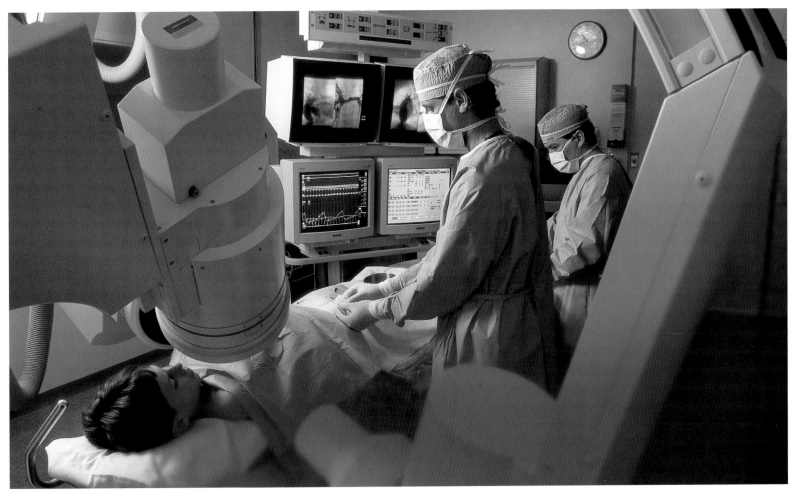

Miami Children's Hospital offers the most current medical interventions.

MIAMI JEWISH HOME & HOSPITAL

The Miami Jewish Home & Hospital at Douglas Gardens is both a serene sanctuary and a vital community trust.

With a main 20-acre tropically landscaped campus in the heart of the city and other sites from Miami Beach to Deerfield Beach, the Home has grown from humble beginnings in 1945 into South Florida's premier healthcare center for seniors, offering a continuum of care unmatched by any other facility.

In addition to providing independent and assisted living, specialized care for ventilator patients, and a outpatient medical clinic, the Miami Jewish Home cares for patients of all ages from around the world in its biofeedback, comprehensive pain and rehabilitation centers.

The Douglas Gardens campus has the largest skilled nursing facility in the state, with 462 inpatient beds and the 32-bed Olson Hospital. The Home is also known for its Alzheimer's programs, which include facilities for inpatient care, day care services, and a memory center for treatment and research.

Another component in the continuum is the wide array of community-based services designed to give people the support needed to maintain their independence and remain in their own homes for as long as possible. These programs include Douglas Gardens Hospice, Douglas Gardens Home Care and New Beginnings, a program providing outpatient

The Douglas Gardens campus is a complete living environment, pleasurable for residents, their visitors, and the community.

geriatric mental health services. The Miami Jewish Home serves more than 5,000 people a year through its extensive community outreach.

Among many firsts, the Miami Jewish Home established the first adult day care center in Miami-Dade County, the first freestanding geriatric mental health center in South Florida at its affiliate on Miami Beach, and Florida's first Program of All-Inclusive Care for the Elderly (PACE), which provides healthcare services to nursing home-eligible elderly living at home. In addition, the Home is the site for Florida's only Teaching Nursing Home program, a statewide educational initiative created by the Florida Legislature in 1999.

In 2006, the Miami Jewish Home opened Douglas Gardens North in Pembroke Pines, which is currently home to a HUD-sponsored apartment building for 100 low-income elderly residents. Additional apartments and healthcare facilities are planned for the 26-acre site. In displaying an extraordinary commitment to the community since its founding, the Miami Jewish Home & Hospital at Douglas Gardens has proven to be a truly outstanding community resource that will continue to serve countless South Floridians for generations to come.

The Sam and Isabel May Visitors Center is Douglas Gardens' "front parlor," a reception area to welcome family and friends.

MEDICA HEALTHCARE PLANS

When he founded Medica Healthcare Plans in 2004, Rafael Perez wanted doctors to be an integral part in the success of the company.

Administration from Nova Southeastern University's Executive MBA Program while continuing to work fulltime. In fact, he wound up in managed care by accident. As a father with young children, he wanted to be home on the weekends. The managed care industry fit his lifestyle. Perez's experience in managed care continued at other health care companies, where he served in multiple positions including Executive Director and Senior Vice President.

Fortified by 16 years of healthcare experience, Perez pursued his dream of starting his own HMO in 2003. His dream was to have his family work with him; his brother and son are by his side in the business, all he needs now is for his daughter to join them.

Medica avoids many of the pitfalls other managed care companies encounter by focusing on the details, superior customer service and employee accessibility to members and providers. The large number of satisfied members is a testament to a flourishing healthcare plan which happens to have a successful business plan.

erez founded Medica with the help of his brother Martin and a group of approximately 30 physicians. Some of the primary care physicians, who are part of the Medica network, are shareholders and have a voice in the company, which distinguishes it from its competitors.

Perez created two HMOs which serve Miami-Dade and Broward counties: Medica Healthcare Plans – a Medicare HMO with over 12,000 Medicare members, and Medica Health Plans of Florida offers commercial and individual group insurance, which was started in 2007 to address the needs of the uninsured population. Medica network of providers include more than 2,300 physicians and specialists, all of whom see patients in their private offices.

Medica's business model of physician-shareholders and superior customer service has proven to be financially successful. Since its inception, annual income has grown from $30 million to over $136 million in only three years. Perez believes healthcare is relationship-based, therefore, physicians and employees play a crucial role in the firm. To better serve the members, employees are empowered to make decisions locally without relying on the typical, medical insurance bureaucracy. High-quality customer service is Medica's hallmark.

Perez, a Cuban immigrant, began his career as a pharmacist after earning a pharmacy degree from the University of Florida. Realizing he wanted to use his degree as a platform to launch a more comprehensive career in the healthcare industry, Perez earned his Masters in Business

Rafael Perez

SUNRISE COMMUNITY, INC.

Prior to 1965, the prevailing philosophy regarding care for people with developmental disabilities was institutionalization managed by state-run organizations.

This approach to care evolved over the next 10 years as health professionals, caregivers, advocates and parents had access to information supporting life-enhancing environments for people with developmental disabilities.

In Florida, the move to deinstitutionalize created opportunities for people with special needs to live in familial surroundings with personalized and compassionate care known as group homes. Though the system was poised for change, the community needed a champion who could be innovative, flexible, and holistic in their understanding of managing quality group homes. Sunrise emerged as a leading organization to assist in this ardent and complex transitioning of Florida's citizens into this new environment.

Today, Sunrise Community is one of the largest not-for-profit organizations in the country dedicated to serving the needs of people with intellectual and physical challenges. Sunrise serves 2,750 people in six states – Florida, Alabama, Connecticut, Maryland, Tennessee, and Virginia with residential and day programs. Approximately 1,000 people live in Sunrise group homes which provide support for community socialization and inclusion, while offering residents an opportunity to live a dignified and fulfilling life.

For the past 43 years, Sunrise has worked diligently in assisting people with developmental disabilities to reach their potential in every aspect of their lives. Under the leadership and strategic vision of the Board of Directors and Les W. Leech, Jr., President and CEO since 1976, Sunrise has established a business model of best practices for other agencies around the nation to emulate.

The Sunrise philosophy and methodology has a proven track record which comes full circle – our primary focus is to fulfill the needs and desires of the people we serve. Perhaps, the pinnacle of the organization's success is the size and scope of Sunrise operations, having risen from serving 50 children to thousands of individuals whose lives have been transformed.

Improving the lives of people with developmental disabilities requires tenacity, passion, and sensitivity – values that are integral to the Sunrise mission. Sunrise Community remains steadfast in its commitment to advocate for the rights of people with developmental disabilities, a worthy challenge indeed.

The campus of the Sunrise Community 120 person facility.

A
PIONEERING
SPIRIT

S A LONG TIME RESIDENT OF MIAMI AND AN ACTIVE BUSINESS LEADER, I HAVE SEEN THE MANY FACETS OF MIAMI AND HOW THE DEVELOPMENT CHANGES HAVE IMPACTED BUSINESSES IN A POSITIVE WAY. MIAMI HAS NOW BECOME THE HEADQUARTERS FOR SCORES OF COMPANIES AND A PLACE WHERE BUSINESSES OF ALL SIZES CAN TAP INTO A DIVERSELY TALENTED AND EXPERIENCED WORKFORCE. IN THE "MAGIC CITY", YOU CAN FIND A WEALTH OF OPPORTUNITY AND THE PERFECT BUSINESS CLIMATE IN WHICH BUSINESS OLD AND NEW CAN THRIVE.

In addition to the many economic and entrepreneurial opportunities, Miami has the unique quality of providing the perfect blend of sophistication and cosmopolitan flair of a large city but still provide the charm of a hometown feel. It provides a quality of life that makes raising a family in Miami the ideal location. Where else can you relax on one of the many sandy beaches, attend a culture event in a state of the art facility, or visit numerous historical and educational attractions and do this all in your own "backyard"? Miami is rich in cultural landscape with businesses and residents alike sharing and working together.

Miami's airports and seaport along with it's expertise in the import and export industry make it the ideal setting for Latin American companies who make their headquarters in Miami. Providing the setting for international companies to be successful has supported our economy and provided numerous opportunities for Miami to remain competitive in the workforce.

GEORGE G. JOSEPH
President & CEO
Dade County Federal Credit Union

George Joseph has over 22 years of experience working with financial institutions, 12 years specifically with credit unions. He is member of the Loan Review Committee for the Development and Loan Administration Division of Miami-Dade County's Finance Department and is a Director of the Florida Credit Union League.

Banking & Finance

DADE COUNTY FEDERAL CREDIT UNION	400
BANK OF AMERICA	402
BAC FLORIDA BANK	403
BANKUNITED	404
NORTHERN TRUST	405
1 FIRSTBANK	406
HELM BANK	408
WACHOVIA	410

Dade County Federal Credit Union has been a pillar in Miami since 1939. And we are proud to be part of a city that has grown through the years and has created an environment that embraces its communities, its diverse population and continues to thrive and flourish.

DADE COUNTY FEDERAL CREDIT UNION

Growing together with Miami since 1939

By most standards, Miami is a young city, and many of its financial institutions share this trait. However, the Dade County Employees Credit Union, as it was originally known, was founded a mere 43 years after the city was incorporated and decades prior to many other local institutions. During the years hence, the credit union has grown alongside the vibrant and diverse area that we call home.

The austere beginnings of Dade County Federal reflect the times when it was founded: Florida was climbing out of the Great Depression and Europe was about to go to war. On April 13, 1939, a group of 10 Dade County employees met, pooled $135 in an old cigar box, and signed a certificate of origination to form a credit union for their fellow employees under the Florida Credit Union League. In just a single year, the original $135 grew to more than $3,000, and county employees were joining in significant numbers to gain financial security and independence.

The credit union, which is owned by its members as a not-for-profit, was operated exclusively by volunteers at its original location at 73 West Flagler Street in the Dade County Courthouse. On January 1, 1950, the Board of Directors created the first paid position when they hired a clerk. Other employees soon followed, enabling the financial institution's total assets to reach $1 million in 1958 with more than 3,200 members and 2,250 borrowers.

The institution continued to add county employees as well as those of other municipalities and, in response to the growth, the home of the credit union changed several times. From its original courthouse location, the credit union moved to the Miami Realtors Building on 7th Street. In 1955, the institution moved to 864 NW 23 Street, where it remained until 1982 when it moved to 3rd Street on South Miami Avenue. Just three years later in 1985, the credit union moved to a central downtown Miami locale at 172 West Flagler, which remains today as the location of the Downtown Branch.

Interior of the Miami Gardens Branch at 20645 NW 2nd Avenue

As the local area's population grew larger and more diverse, the financial institution grew with it to continue meeting the needs of county and municipal employees. It became a federally chartered credit union and changed its name to Dade County Federal Credit Union in 1994, a move that would foreshadow the future of the institution in the years to come.

With more than 34,000 members and $169 million in total assets by the mid-1990s, the time had come for Dade County Federal Credit Union to invest in a facility that would accommodate further growth and expansion. In July of 1995, the credit union celebrated the opening of its new Main Branch and Headquarters at 1500 NW 107 Avenue in Miami-Dade's fast-growing Doral area.

From this location, the credit union and its management have made some of the most significant strides in the history of the financial institution. Additional branches were opened in strategically located corners of the county to better serve the growing membership, and in 2003 the institution converted to a community charter and opened its membership to everyone who lives, works, worships or attends school in Miami-Dade.

Since the change to a community charter, membership in DCFCU has grown from approximately 56,000 to more than 86,000 and the credit union has opened six new branches to reach 11 in 2007. The branch openings included a large branch with additional space for its growing staff and departments in the heart of Kendall in southwest Miami-Dade on Kendall Drive at 109 Avenue. The credit union's plans call for a total of 16 branches by 2010, all of which will be in Miami-Dade County.

DCFCU began to offer commercial accounts and loans for local business owners in 2006. These enterprises are part of the lifeblood of the South Florida economy, and the institution plans to continue working with local businesses to help them grow and reach their fullest potential.

As a non-profit that is owned by the members and operated exclusively for their benefit, the spirit of service to the community has always been strong at DCFCU. The institution is a proud supporter of the Police Officer Assistance Trust, the Police Athletic League, the American Cancer Society, Mothers Against Drunk Driving, the March of Dimes and other worthwhile organizations.

As greater Miami continues to grow, the residents of the area can expect that the credit union will grow along with it. As one of the organization's slogans says: "We have been here all along." The credit union will be an integral part of Miami for many years to come, and the leadership, staff and Board of Directors are committed to continuing to provide its members with the very highest level of financial products and customer service with professionalism and integrity.

The Kendall Branch at 10900 North Kendall Drive

BANK OF AMERICA

Tracing our history in Miami back to 1925, Bank of America and its predecessor banks have a rich legacy of community impact and civic responsibility, having played a key role in making many of the community's most ambitious dreams a reality.

Today, as the leading bank in Miami, Bank of America leverages its extensive resources to deliver world-class financial services and continue to create opportunities that have a positive impact in the community we call home. With over 1400 associates, 65 banking centers and 180 ATMs, we look forward to continued growth as we meet the financial needs of consumers, businesses and the community overall.

Long a supporter of community organizations, Bank of America is a leader at both the local and national level. Bank of America recently restated its national community development goal to lend and invest $1.5 trillion over ten years, with a focus on affordable housing, economic development, and consumer and small business lending. The bank also announced a new ten-year commitment to donate $2 billion to nonprofit organizations engaged in improving the health and vitality of neighborhoods. The bank's approach to community impact utilizes our scale and breadth of resources for the benefit of the communities where we do

business, where we live and work. Simply stated, we understand that our success and that of our communities go hand in hand.

In Miami, our contributions are as diverse as the community, with local giving focused on education, neighborhood revitalization and arts and culture. Bank of America strives to make a difference in Miami through a combination of resources and programs that include community development, grants from the Bank of America Charitable Foundation, sponsorship of community events, volunteer activities led by our associates, and the participation of senior leadership on nonprofit and civic boards. Expanding our reach and impact, the Bank of America Neighborhood Excellence Initiative is an innovative program that allows us to recognize, nurture and reward nonprofit organizations, local heroes and student leaders working to improve Miami.

As we move forward, and Miami becomes the world-class, global metropolis it aspires to be, Bank of America looks forward to continuing to play an integral role in the fulfillment of its destiny.

BAC FLORIDA BANK

Offering financial and banking solutions to individual and corporate clients domiciled in Latin America and South Florida.

s of June 30, 2008, BAC Florida Bank and subsidiaries had just over 5,200 customers, 135 employees, $ 963 million in assets and $ 669 million in deposits. We are part of the Pellas Group and are a member of the BAC Credomatic Network.

Although the majority of our customers live abroad, mainly in Latin America, we also offer products and services to customers based in South Florida. We provide a wide array of banking and financial products and services to a variety of individual, corporate, and institutional customers in the areas of:

- Personal Banking and Wealth Management
- Corporate Banking
- Institutional Banking
- Real Estate Financing

Our wide variety of products and services, together with our 25 years of banking expertise and our membership in the BAC Credomatic Network, allow us to provide banking solutions for customers that are individuals, companies or financial institutions seeking investment, online services, cash management and credit products.

We are a bank with a boutique strategy. Our size allows us to provide a close and customized service, and our business model is based on strong and personal relationships with our customers.

The BAC Credomatic Network has over 260 branches throughout Panama, Costa Rica, Nicaragua, Honduras, El Salvador, Guatemala, Mexico and Florida. Credomatic is the largest issuer and processor of credit card transactions in the Central American region.

The Pellas Group is one of the largest and most diversified business consortiums of Central America. It is present in the financial, agribusiness, energy, manufacturing, real estate, tourism, health, and retail industries in Central America, Panama, Mexico, and the United States.

At BAC Florida Bank we have two subsidiaries that provide investment products and wealth management services:

BAC FLORIDA INVESTMENTS – Registered Broker/Dealer

BAC Florida Investments (BFI) was created in 1986 as a broker/dealer initially serving other member institutions of the BAC Credomatic Network and their clients. Over time, BFI expanded its customer base to include individuals and institutions from Latin America and the United States.

BFI does its securities custody, clearing, and settlement through Pershing LLC., a wholly owned subsidiary of the Bank of New York Mellon. BFI is a member of FINRA (formerly NASD) and is subject to its rules and regulations. BFI is also regulated and supervised by the Securities and Exchange Commission (SEC).

BAC GLOBAL ADVISORS (BGA) – Registered Investment Advisor

BAC Global Advisors (BGA) was created in 2002 to provide fee based investment advisory and portfolio asset allocation services to institutions and high net worth individuals.

BANKUNITED

BankUnited is the largest bank headquartered in Florida, but despite its size, the community bank prides itself on personal service.

Built on the "old fashioned" model of banking by founder Alfred R. Camner, the big bank with the homegrown focus has more than 90 branches throughout Florida, each with their own individual identity. Camner serves as the chairman of the board and chief executive officer of BankUnited Financial Corporation and Ramiro Ortiz is president and chief operating officer.

Headquartered in Coral Gables with a campus of support areas strategically located in Miami Lakes, BankUnited offers the full spectrum of deposit, loans, investments and cash management products for consumers and businesses. The bank also offers online products and a wide array of residential, consumer and commercial loans.

With customer service and community as the cornerstones of the financial institution, BankUnited's branches are immersed in the places in which they serve. Many employees not only work in the neighborhood, but live in the communities, so their customers are also their neighbors and friends. Financial advisers are available in most branches and are dedicated to working one-on-one with customers to meet their particular goals. And unlike "big box" banks, the neighborhood branch reflects the community. Walk into BankUnited in Hialeah, for instance, and help yourself to a Cuban coffee, while watching regulars relax and play a game of Dominos. The Key Biscayne

branch has a lighthouse theme, from artwork to the chocolates customers enjoy each time they visit.

BankUnited's dedication to its customers also means providing the latest technology, including online banking services, remote deposit capture and online bill pay for small business. Commercial and small-business banking has grown in the past five years.

To further solidify its role as a community partner, The University of Miami and BankUnited entered into a multi-year agreement to rename the university's Convocation Center the BankUnited Center. While it does give the bank visibility, the move wasn't approached as a sponsorship deal, rather it was an important way to be part of the community.

The lawyer with a vision, who started the company as a wholesale mortgage operation in 1983, continues to grow a down-to-earth full-service community bank. With more than 1,500 employees based in Florida, BankUnited's biggest investment is in the communities in which it serves. BankUnited – it's a local thing.

■ *Alfred R. Camner, chairman of the board and chief executive officer, and Ramiro Ortiz, president and chief operating officer of BankUnited Financial Corporation.*

■ *The BankUnited Center, a 7,000 seat multipurpose facility located on the University of Miami's Coral Gables campus.*

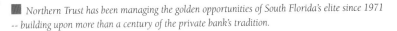

Northern Trust has been managing the golden opportunities of South Florida's elite since 1971 -- building upon more than a century of the private bank's tradition.

NORTHERN TRUST

Northern Trust has been the trusted advisor to families of means since 1889.

trength and stability are hallmarks of Northern Trust, guiding it toward becoming one of the largest managers of personal trust assets in the United States. Founded in Chicago by Byron Laflin Smith, the company has grown to 85 offices in 18 states and 13 international locations. As of mid-2007, Northern Trust Corporation had assets under custody of $4.0 trillion, and $766.5 billion in assets under investment management.

In 1971, Northern Trust entered the Miami market by purchasing Security Trust Company, Florida's largest and oldest pure trust company. Security Trust was founded in 1938 by a prominent Miami family, Lindsey Hopkins and his sister, Sara McKillips. Northern Trust's acquisition of the smaller company was strategic, as more and more of its longtime customers began to retire and buy second homes in South Florida.

Further acquisitions of pure trust companies in Sarasota, Palm Beach, and Naples enabled Northern Trust to grow from $100 million in trust assets in 1971 to $1.1 billion by 1981. In 1984, Northern Trust of Florida was incorporated as the holding company for all its banks in Florida.

The company also began to distinguish itself from the glut of banks in the state by modeling itself after the private banks of Europe. As such it developed a mantra of deep client relationships and an unmatched dedication to quality.

Northern Trust's growth rate has exploded with the local population. In 1992, the company had nine offices, concentrated in a handful of wealth centers. By 2007, there were 25 offices operating on both coasts from Miami to Vero Beach and from Naples to Tampa.

Sheldon T. Anderson, president of Northern Trust for Miami-Dade County, is one of those seemingly rare Miami natives. His community roots and involvement exemplify Northern Trust's reputation as a socially responsible and philanthropic company that actively supports a wide variety of social and cultural causes. These include the Carnival Center for the Performing Arts, the New World Symphony, Miami City Ballet, the United Way, Miami Dade College, and the University of Miami, among many others.

In just 36 years of its 118-year history, Northern Trust has become not only the best private bank around, but an integral part of Miami.

Northern Trust is a premier provider of banking, asset management and asset servicing to affluent families and individuals and leading institutions worldwide.

■ FirstBank is celebrating its 60th anniversary in 2008.

1 FirstBank

Since its founding in Puerto Rico in 1948 under the name First Federal Savings and Loan Association, FirstBank has played a fundamental role in improving the quality of life of citizens in Puerto Rico, the U.S. British Virgin Islands, and in the United States.

ogether we are one" is the motto of FirstBank and by establishing relationships with its customers, FirstBank has helped thousands of people build their dreams.

In 1987, FirstBank became a stockholder-owned savings bank and went public, on the NASDAQ Exchange. In 1993, it was listed on the New York Stock Exchange under the symbol FBP and a year later converted to a commercial bank charter and changed its name to FirstBank Puerto Rico. It reorganized into a holding company under the name First BanCorp in 1998.

In 2002 and after acquiring Chase Manhattan Bank, FirstBank became the largest bank in the Virgin Islands (USVI & BVI), serving St. Thomas, St. Croix, St. John, Tortola and Virgin Gorda, now with 17 branches. In the United States and British Virgin Islands, the corporation operates FirstBank in addition to the subsidiaries First Express, a finance company specializing in the origination of small loans; FirstBank Insurance Agency, V.I.

In March 31, 2005, FirstBank acquired Ponce General Corporation and its subsidiaries FirstBank Florida, a federal savings and loan association, and Ponce Realty Corporation, a company with real-estate holdings. FirstBank also operates a loan agency in Miami, FirstBank Corporate Banking, providing wholesale loans. This office concentrates on Corporate and Commercial lending including Lines of Credit and Commercial Real Estate.

Opened in Coral Gables in 2004, FirstBank Corporate Banking has grown from not only serving the Puerto Rican and Latin American communities, but by also providing loan services to foreign nationals from the United Kingdom, Ukraine, Ireland, Australia, and others seeking to do business in Miami. Entrepreneurs and developers who want to invest in Miami continually choose FirstBank as a partner for their commercial lending needs.

Looking to the future, FirstBank continues to diversify its portfolio of lending. FirstBank Corporate Banking is an integral part of Miami's economic growth, and is actively seeking to provide more loans for commercial properties, warehouses,

■ The Kendall branch of FirstBank Florida.

shopping centers and other income-producing businesses.

As of Dec. 31, 2007, the bank, headquartered in San Juan, Puerto Rico, had total assets of $17.2 billion. It is among the three largest financial holding companies headquartered in Puerto Rico.

James J. Partridge, Senior Vice President of FirstBank Corporate Banking explained that the bank chose Miami as the place to lay its U.S. roots because of the city's vibrancy, and its great economic potential.

FirstBank has evolved with the city as a solid citizen, building and maintaining relationships, and continues to expand its franchise in South Florida. The bank helps members of the local community by sponsoring economic development events, hosts seminars to inform the public about lending products, savings accounts, and personal financial management, and provides technical assistance to community-based organizations. FirstBank's priority is to support the neighborhoods in which it operates. Through employee volunteerism, financial services, and grants, the company's belief is that its support of community organizations improves our quality of life.

Its Community Reinvestment Program is a vital tool which focuses on supporting affordable housing, economic development organizations, health, social services and education. The program focuses on communities where FirstBank maintains a strong presence, and helps to promote self-help and community stabilization, from education and financial literacy, to environment and community revitalization. FirstBank also works with non-profit organizations, associations, and public and private agencies that thrive on improving the lives of low and moderate income individuals.

FirstBank continues to be an integral part of Miami as it builds relationships and grows dreams.

■ *"Together we are one" is the motto of FirstBank.*

HELM BANK

For international customers who wish to do business in the United States, having a strategic financial partner on U.S. soil is of the utmost importance.

That's why Helm Bank has become an integral part of Miami's financial sector, both here and abroad. Its business model is distinctive for a full-service commercial bank as the main focus of Helm Bank is devoted to the financial needs of international customers.

Headquartered in the city known as the Gateway to Latin America, the bank is a financial bridge between Miami and the country of origin of its international customers through the local support and service provided by its foreign representative offices. High net worth professionals and business owners from Latin America come to Miami for business and find themselves in need of credit support for themselves and their businesses. These customers may have an established track record and excellent bank references in their own country, but they need a financial partner in the U.S. That's where Helm comes in with the goal of making its customers feel important not only in their own country, but also in the U.S., plus give them the safety and stability of a U.S. based bank account.

The bank is funded primarily with deposits from international clients with 80 percent of total deposits coming from outside the U.S. The financial institution provides access for customers that need a dollar denominated account with

a bank in the States, however, what sets Helm Bank apart is the access customers have to the bank from their own countries. The bank's important foreign affiliations allow it to serve the financial needs of a select group of international clients. But make no mistake, Helm Bank is 100 percent a U.S. bank. The Federal Deposit Insurance Corporation (FDIC) is the regulatory agency charged with overseeing the bank's operations and insuring its deposits.

For international customers seeking a loan, Helm Bank uses several background reporting agencies. They also obtain an international credit report, which checks and verifies information with foreign embassies. The financial institution

The reception area welcomes customers

also requests the direct assistance of its representative offices or affiliate banks to verify information – to go out and "kick the tires," so to speak. The direct access to a customer's information from his or her own country of origin obtained with the help of foreign representative offices is Helm Bank's main competitive advantage.

Helm Bank began its operations on Dec. 8, 1989, licensed by the state of Florida, as a full service, state chartered commercial bank headquartered in Miami. In 1990, the bank moved its operations from the northwest section of Greater Miami to the financial district of Brickell Avenue. On Jan. 22, 1996 the regulatory banking agency of Colombia, "La Superintendencia Bancaria," authorized the opening of a Helm Bank Representative Office in Colombia. In 1996, a correspondent alliance agreement was signed with Banco de Crédito of Colombia seeking to expand Helm Bank's banking activities in that country. Today, Helm Bank has nine representative offices in four countries with four offices in Colombia, two in Venezuela, two in Ecuador and its most recent addition, a representative office in Mexico.

Competition for large corporate accounts is staggering, but Helm Bank has succeeded by offering personalized service and investing heavily in technology. Its strategy has earned the bank one of the highest ratings from the FDIC and the Florida State Comptroller's office. It also holds a "Four Star" rating from Bauer Financial Reports. Over the last seven years, Helm Bank has continuously placed in the Top Ten list of most profitable banks headquartered in Florida.

While building on its strength as a full-service commercial bank, Helm Bank's future vision is to continue to grow through its foreign representative offices rather than developing a domestic network of brick-and-mortar branches on every corner. Its mission continues to be to attract and provide services to its international customers and to help those customers realize their dreams by providing a sound financial partner in the United States, Latin America and Mexico.

Helm Bank – Su banco personalizado en los Estados Unidos. Your personalized bank in the United States.

■ The lobby at 999 Brickell

WACHOVIA

Aiming to be "the best, most trusted and admired financial services company."

At Wachovia, giving back is a vital component of the culture. They know that they grow stronger, as a corporation and as individuals, when they are fully engaged in serving their communities. In 2007, Wachovia contributed $129 million to charitable organizations through company and foundation giving; completed year of innovative Teachers and Teaching Initiative funding in the amount of $5.2 million, which provides funding to help teachers develop skills that advance student achievement in under-resourced schools; and provided more than $47 billion in community development loans and investments to revitalize neighborhoods. Companywide, Wachovia employees logged more than 703,000 hours of employee volunteer community service.

Wachovia strives to build a strong and vibrant community by providing employee-volunteer programs and financial support for education, the arts and culture, affordable housing, economic development and other community needs. Among the organizations and programs Wachovia has supported in Miami-Dade, include: the United Way, Camillus House, Community Partnership for Homeless, Florida International University, Overtown Youth Center, Teach for America, and Performing Arts Center Foundation of Greater Miami.

Wachovia invites you to stop by any financial center or brokerage office to discover the best service in the financial services industry and how its dedicated employees can help you achieve your financial dreams.

achovia Corporation (NYSE:WB) is one of the nation's largest diversified financial services companies, servicing 15 million customers with a broad range of retail banking and brokerage, asset and wealth management, and corporate and investment banking products and services.

It operates the nation's fourth largest banking company, serving retail and commercial banking customers through 3,400 retail financial centers in 21 states from Connecticut to Florida and west to Texas and California. In addition, the retail brokerage operations under the Wachovia Securities brand name manage more than $1.2 trillion in client assets through 14,600 financial advisors in 3,700 locations nationwide. Wachovia also serves corporate and investment banking clients globally and provides international correspondent banking services and trade finance through more than 40 international offices.

In Miami-Dade County, Wachovia offers customers a network of complete financial services that include nearly 70 financial centers and over 120 ATMs, along with a dedicated workforce of 2,000, who focus on providing the highest level of customer service. In fact, for seven straight years, Wachovia has been ranked No. 1 in customer satisfaction in the retail banking industry, according to the American Customer Satisfaction Index.

Wachovia employees walk to raise funds for healthy babies at the March of Dimes event in Key Biscayne.

ENTREPRENEURIAL SPIRIT

*M*IAMI IS ONE OF THE MOST VIBRANT AND DYNAMIC COMMUNITIES IN THE WORLD TO LIVE, WORK AND PLAY! MIAMI OFFERS YOU A BUSINESS CLIMATE LIKE NO OTHER. I HAVE SEEN MIAMI'S ECONOMY EXPAND AND DIVERSIFY MORE AND MORE OVER THE YEARS. FROM BEING THE BANKING AND FINANCIAL CENTER OF THE AMERICAS, TO BOASTING WORLD-CLASS INTERNATIONAL AIR AND SEA PORTS, EMERGING AS A GLOBAL SCIENCE AND TECHNOLOGY HUB AND HAVING A BUSINESS FRIENDLY GOVERNMENT.

More than 1,200 multinational corporations have chosen Miami as their business center. Companies from around the world are attracted by Miami's infrastructure and location as an international hub, allowing businesses to reach key markets throughout the United States, Latin America, Europe and Asia. Miami's multilingual and multicultural workforce and diversified economy are what drive many enterprises to sunny Miami.

Miami alone represents more than 150 ethnicities and 100 languages. Miami is constantly ranked high in business excellence, and also ranks as a top spot for its beaches, nightlife, shopping, and recreational activities including golf, fishing, tennis, biking, running and shopping.

America Economía magazine ranked Miami as the "#1 Best City to do Business in Latin America;" one of "America's 50 Hottest Cities" for relocation and expansion; and a "Top Ten City of the Future." American Express Travel agents ranked Miami as the #1 U.S. destination for families. Travel channel also voted South Beach as one of the "Top 10 Best Beaches in the World."

Above all, Miami is a state of mind. It is a city that has

SERGIO PINO
President of Century Homebuilders of South Florida.

Century is the largest Hispanic homebuilding company in the country. At the age of 20, he bought Century Plumbing, turning it into the largest Hispanic-owned plumbing company in the nation. As Chairman and President of Century Partners Group, which he founded in 1997, and Vice Chairman of U.S. Century Bank, one of the fastest-growing and best-capitalized community banks in the state of Florida, Pino has also established 13 other companies bearing the Century name.

Building & Development

FORTUNE INTERNATIONAL	414
FLORIDA EAST COAST REALTY	416
CENTURY HOMEBUILDERS OF SOUTH FLORIDA	420
THE GRAHAM COMPANIES	422
THE RELATED GROUP	424
ROK ENTERPRISES, INC.	426
ESSLINGER-WOOTEN-MAXWELL, INC.	428
HILL YORK	430
RILEA GROUP	432
TERRA GROUP	433
R.J. HEISENBOTTLE ARCHITECTS	434
SUPERMIX CONCRETE	436
THE ALLEN MORRIS COMPANY	438

welcomed millions of tourist over the years, as well as
hundreds of thousands of new residents from around the
globe. A city that makes you feel right at home the moment
you feel its warm tropical breeze. It is where I call home.
Home to my friends. Home to my business, and above all,
home to my family. Miami is truly the Magic City!
– Sergio Pino

■ *Jade Residences at Brickell Bay*

FORTUNE INTERNATIONAL

Since its inception in 1983, Fortune International has taken high-end Miami real estate to a level of excellence unsurpassed by any other development company in South Florida.

*B*uilt around sound leadership, a clear corporate vision, talented people and an "anything is possible" attitude, Fortune International's blueprint for success stems from its ability to forge ahead into new frontiers in real estate development – while maintaining its position as a leader in sales and marketing of luxury real estate property.

For example, Miami's impressive skyline wouldn't be what it is today without the magnificent buildings developed by Fortune International. It was the first to pioneer the use of smart home technology, incorporating it into every real estate project it develops. This, along with partnering with some of the most renowned architects in the world for innovative building designs, has produced impressive results like trademark colossal residential structures such as:

• Jade Residences at Brickell Bay: This work of art in luxury condo

living overlooks Biscayne Bay and features 326 deluxe residences. Amenities include touch-screen communication technology for ease and quickness to entertainment, information, business and security. The top of the 48-story structure is configured with a rooftop sky-lounge, media room, library and observation deck, all adding to the building's distinctive nature.

• Jade Beach: This sister property is a 51-story oceanfront tower rising majestically in Sunny Isles Beach. Superbly designed by world-renowned architect Carlos Ott (often commissioned by Fortune International for his extraordinary talents), Jade Beach features a three-story Grand Entrance Lobby with breath-taking direct ocean and pool views. Wireless high-speed Internet access is available throughout the Tower and Resort Deck; security-controlled high-speed elevators open to private foyers in most residences; and a state-of-the-art security surveillance system gives residents uncompromising safety.

■ *Artech, Aventura*

Jade Ocean, Sunny Isles Beach

• Ritz-Carlton Club & Residences, South Beach: Spanning from the Atlantic Ocean to Indian Creek in South Beach, this luxury development represents the perfect combination of The Ritz-Carlton's legendary quality, services and amenities in the midst of South Beach's excitement. Located on Collins Avenue, with elegantly-designed towers, the residential community will include the restoration and incorporation of the historic Seville Beach Hotel – a onetime pleasure haven for the famous Rat Pack, among other celebrities – symbolizing the grandeur of this luxury complex.

South Florida has long been a Mecca for international business and pleasure travel, and with Fortune International's history of focusing on prime waterfront residences, a logical step was to diversify into the hospitality industry. This bold initiative has been yet another successful venture thanks to its strategic alliances. Its affiliation with Ritz-Carlton on the project in South Beach is an excellent case in point. Other hospitality success stories include its involvement with Mandarin Oriental, and Le Meridien Sunny Isles Beach – Fortune International's first condo hotel.

But Fortune International hasn't stopped there. It also has championed the movement in South Florida into office-condominium development. Fortune International's 1200 Brickell in the heart of Miami's Central Business District is a prime example. With beautiful views of Biscayne Bay and the Magic City's growing skyline, this landmark building is a coveted location on South Florida's Brickell Avenue and Coral Way.

At Fortune International, the mission to be the very best in all facets of high-end Miami real estate never ends.

• Jade Ocean: With this neighboring structure, Fortune International is introducing a whole new class of luxury to Sunny Isles Beach. This 50-story tower architectural wonder is another fascinating Ott creation. For residents, Jade Ocean will provide supreme elegance, glamour and technology. There will be a six-story cascading waterfall along the entranceway, leading into an oceanfront drop-off at the main entrance, as well as a unique pool, flowing through the building from ocean to city. Floor-to-ceiling glass walls, a 24-hour business center, state-of-the-art technology and premiere concierge services from Quintessentially are just some of its extraordinary features.

• Artech: One of the latest projects by Fortune International, this Ott-designed, distinctive structure is immaculately detailed, and sits on the waterfront in the midst of the most buzzing area of Aventura. Fashioned in a boomerang shaped design, the 234-residence condominium features curvilinear floorplans offering longer windows that maximize views and take advantage of close to 900 feet of direct waterfront.

Ritz-Carlton Club & Residences, South Beach

One Bayfront Plaza rendering

FLORIDA EAST COAST REALTY

Tibor Hollo is known as the father of modern Miami, the patriarch of downtown development.

His company, Florida East Coast Realty, Inc., [FECR], has been at the forefront of Miami's growth since 1956 by developing more than 60 million square feet of residential and commercial space.

Hungarian-born Hollo, a Holocaust survivor who trained as an architect in France, began his career in New York City in 1948. When he couldn't get a job as an architect, Hollo went to work for a New York contracting firm. The following year he started his own company. He moved the company to Miami seven years later, when it had the distinction of being one of the largest contracting companies in the country.

Miami proved to be Hollo and FECR's "blank canvas". Working to make Hollo's vision of urban living a reality, FECR changed the face of the city with every new building. Forty years later, to Hollo's enormous gratification, that dream of a vibrant live, work and play urban core has been realized.

FECR defined the future of the Brickell Avenue corridor with the construction of Vizcaya Towers, the first urban residential building on Brickell in 1966. Around the same time, the company developed the Civic Center, which at 22 stories was the tallest building in Miami and the first mixed-use high rise in South Florida. Other buildings, including the first high-rise office building on Brickell Avenue, Rivergate Plaza, followed.

But perhaps Hollo and FECR's most innovative accomplishment is the development of the Omni-Venetia area. In the 1960s the area, which now encompasses the Performing

Arts District, was nothing more than a blighted neighborhood north of downtown. Hollo saw great potential there and purchased 58 parcels of land between 1968 and 1971. The Omni, built in 1973, jumpstarted the transformation of the area, which continued with the development of Plaza Venetia and The Grand, the landmark hotel/condominium tower which boasts 15 percent more space than the Empire State Building. The newest, Opera Tower, is 60-story luxury condo with 635 units. FECR is planning to build the Mikado Hotel and Residences on the company's last remaining parcel in Omni-Venetia.

Overall, Hollo has shaped Miami with more than $10 billion worth of high-rise residential and mixed-use buildings. Currently, FECR is developing 2020 Ponce, an upscale Class-A office condominium in Coral Gables. Completed projects include Bay Parc Plaza, the Biscayne Bay Marriott Hotel and Marina, Flamingo Plaza, Vizcaya North, Center House, Sans Souci Manor, Tropicana East and Tropicana West Apartments, and Twin Lakes Racquet Club. Other projects have included 888 Brickell Avenue, two United States Treasury Buildings and the United States Justice Department Building in downtown Miami. One of FECR's latest projects is Casa Majorca, a boutique residential condominium with only 36 exclusive residences located in the heart of Coral Gables.

A major project on the horizon for FECR is One Bayfront Plaza, a redevelopment of one of downtown Miami's most desirable sites at 100 South Biscayne Boulevard. One Bayfront Tower, currently in the design phase, will be a 70-story, 1,049-foot tall building that will become a landmark in the city. The 4.2 million square foot building will encompass 2.2 million square feet of Class-A office space, an 850 room convention hotel with 150,000 square feet of exhibition space, 112,000 square feet of retail, a 2,700 space parking garage and a pedestrian bridge to the Bayfront Park MetroMover station. According to the Miami Downtown Development Authority, One Bayfront Plaza will provide 30% of the city's retail needs. The project should be a catalyst for other investment activity and will certainly attract national and international business.

One Bayfront Plaza will be constructed to LEED's Green standards to obtain the Silver certification. An existing building on the site, which includes the headquarters for FECR, will be demolished to make room for the new project. In addition to becoming Miami's largest and most prestigious office tower, the

■ *One Bayfront Plaza*

WORKING TO MAKE HOLLO'S VISION OF URBAN LIVING

A REALITY, FECR CHANGED THE FACE OF THE CITY WITH EVERY

NEW BUILDING. FORTY YEARS LATER, THAT DREAM OF A VIBRANT

LIVE, WORK AND PLAY URBAN CORE HAS BEEN REALIZED.

From top left: rendering of the Opera Tower, the Eden Roc Hotel, Yacht and Cabana Club (bottom); Colonnade Plaza on Brickell Avenue (middle); President and Chairman of Florida East Coast Realty Tibor Hollo with Jerome and Wayne Hollo (far right). Opposite page: Sea Isle Marina located behind Biscayne Marriott.

building is poised to become the signature building which will define the city for years to come. FECR is now setting its mark on Las Vegas, New York, and St. Petersburg, Florida.

While Hollo's business activities are largely devoted to commercial and residential developments and management, he is an active participant in over 40 civic, fraternal and religious organizations and is a respected member of the community. Hollo is a fierce proponent of giving back to the community which gave so much to him. Today he splits his time between work, charities and civic activities.

It is a natural progression that Hollo's vast contribution to society often leads to accolades and awards. Recently, he was honored by the House of Representatives for his contribution to Miami's growth. At the request of The Honorable Ileana Ros-Lehtinen of Florida, a flag was flown over the United States Capitol in Washington D.C. in Hollo's honor.

In 2006, Catholic Charities Legal Services and the Archdiocese of Miami presented Hollo with the New American Award, which recognizes individual immigrants' contributions to society. Under Hollo's leadership, Florida East Coast Realty was honored by South Florida CEO magazine as Best Condo Developer for 2006. The U.S. Congress recognized and honored him as an Outstanding Floridian in 1981 and again in 2005. Simon Wiesenthal Center honored Hollo and his wife

Sheila in 2005; and he was the first recipient of the prestigious City of Miami Visionary Award in 1990.

Hollo is a member of the Society of Founders of Mount Sinai Hospital and the University of Miami. He has served on Florida's Task Force on Housing and Community Affairs as well the Governors Advisory Council on Factory Built Housing. Hollo is a member of the Downtown Advisory Committee and the Committee on Ecology and Beautification. He served on the Executive Board as Trustee of Barry University as well as on the City of Miami Beach's ad hoc committee for Economics Adjustment Strategy. He is also on the County's Performing Arts Center Strategic Planning Committee and serves on the Board of Directors of the Latin Builders Association.

Despite his many achievements, Hollo believes the greatest one is his family. He and his wife Sheila have lived in the same home for 40 years, where they raised their three children Wayne, Jerome and Arlene. Wayne and Jerome work with their father at FECR. Wayne is involved in the financial side of the company and specializes in acquisitions and capitalization; Jerome is the firm's vice president and general counsel.

The history of Miami has been written by visionaries like Hollo, who had a dream for the city and has seen it come to fruition. Fortunately for the city, Miami's future will be influenced by Hollo's legacy, foresight and imagination.

CENTURY HOMEBUILDERS OF SOUTH FLORIDA

Century Homebuilders of South Florida, developer of Miami-Dade's largest planned community, began because Sergio Pino had a passion for real estate, architecture and investing.

In 1997, the opportunity to combine his passions arose when he bought an existing home development company and remade it to fit his vision for the community. He took the company private in 2001 and by 2002 Century had become the largest home builder in Miami-Dade County.

It is clear this Cuban immigrant's story is rooted in the American Dream. As a 12-year old arriving in a new country, Pino knew his future could be as great as his dreams. By the age of 20 he owned a plumbing supply company, which he transformed into the largest Hispanic plumbing company in Miami. Pino was always interested in real estate and an active investor; at one time he even considered becoming an architect. However, his aspiration to build homes and create communities defined his path in life.

Century Homebuilders approaches home development with the credo that a new home is not only the most important purchase someone will make, but it is where the future lies. Pino realizes a home is where family experiences are shared, memories are made and values are passed along to the next generation. Nothing is as important to Pino as providing homes for families.

To date, Century has built more than 25 distinctive communities throughout Miami-Dade and Broward counties. Its largest development is Century Grand, set on 350 acres in the Doral area of Miami-Dade, which will have 4,200 homes when complete.

Century Grand main entrance

Century Grand is designed to be a complete community consisting of numerous neighborhoods, schools, parks, a town center, houses of worship, retail outlets and offices. The neighborhoods each have unique personalities and include single family, townhomes, condominiums and villas to fit any lifestyle. The small town feeling begins with the unique character of each street. Although there are 72 models to choose from, they will not be repeated next to one another. The appeal of these "old-school" style communities fits with the concept of a small town within a large metropolitan area. Thus, Century Grand will set the standard for the perfect live-work-play lifestyle.

The city of Doral is centrally located in Miami-Dade County, making it the ultimate location for Century Grand with its easy access to highways and the airport. The city has a strong employment base and low taxes, making it ideal for a growing population.

Century Homebuilders has delivered thousands of homes over the years, and takes pride in the high-quality homes offered at reasonable prices. The company listens to the customer and provides a home that meets their needs.

The commitment to creating real communities, improving the quality of life and offering professional excellence contributes to Century's impeccable reputation.

To Pino, "value" means more than just affordability. It includes design, attention to detail, abundant amenities and an enjoyable lifestyle. Pino's enthusiasm and dedication to customer service is a value shared by all in the company. Century strives to give the home buyer a positive experience along with a quality home. Customers get peace of mind knowing the company takes great pride in the quality of the communities and of each individual home.

Making Century the powerhouse in the home development field that it is today, is something Pino credits to hard work, a good management team and a love for the business. He believes there is nothing quite as satisfying as taking an empty piece of dirt and creating a real community for families to live.

Pino's belief that a home provides the foundation for family has influenced everything he has done professionally. It seems a 12-year old immigrant has realized his American dream by making it available to everyone else.

■ *Aerial view of Century Grand*

Executives of The Graham Companies, posing with a cow sculpture that is part of the Town of Miami Lakes Art Around Town program, are (from left) Sandra G. Younts, Chairman of the Board; Carol G. Wyllie, Executive Vice President; Stuart S. Wyllie, President and Chief Executive Officer; Elizabeth G. Martinez, Executive Vice President; and Luis O. Martinez, Senior Executive Vice President.

THE GRAHAM COMPANIES

The patriarch of what would become The Graham Companies, Ernest R. "Cap" Graham, was a young man filled with optimism and a pioneering spirit when he moved to the Miami area from South Dakota in 1921 to manage the Pennsylvania Sugar Company's Florida sugar operations.

In 1931, the company decided to close its South Florida operation after the devastating 1926 hurricane and a couple of others in succeeding years. Graham was given the opportunity to acquire company land for the cost of carrying it, not an easy feat, being in the depths of the Depression. He wound up taking over approximately 5,000 acres in northwestern Dade County.

Graham's story is the quintessential example of taking life's lemons and making "lemonade." It could be said that The Graham Companies, one of Florida's most successful family businesses, is still pouring Cap's "lemonade" today. In addition, the family has left its mark on the state and the nation – Cap's youngest son Bob Graham had a prestigious public service career serving as a Florida legislator and two-term governor, and ultimately a U.S. Senator before his retirement in 2004. Cap's oldest son, Philip Graham, was president of The Washington Post Company for many years; and middle son William A. Graham was instrumental in the creation of Miami Lakes, Florida.

Cap focused his efforts in Miami on farming, ultimately settling on the dairy business, and accumulating land. Years of hard work yielded a successful business that included milking parlors which were operated on Miami Lakes land until 1981. Today the dairy is located further upstate, where 2,000 cows are milked every day.

In the 1950s, construction of the Palmetto Expressway made the land in northwest Dade more accessible and valuable, enticing many farmers to sell. William A. Graham, who was running the company by then, chose to develop the land instead. He went to Europe to study New Towns developed after World War II, and knew he wanted to develop a planned community instead of the usual sprawl of suburban tract homes.

What started in 1962 is what stands today, the hometown of Miami Lakes with its compact town center, winding roads, ample lakes and parks, and an impressive variety of housing options. The residential neighborhoods, hotel and golf course aren't the only areas that were carefully planned to create an idyllic setting. Miami Lakes' two business parks – located on the east and west sides of town – incorporate lush landscaping that helps create a relaxing work environment which has attracted multi-national companies including the Latin American headquarters of American Express, Caterpillar, Schering-Plough, and MACTEC.

Centerpiece of The Graham Companies development of Miami Lakes is its charming Town Center, a pedestrian-friendly area with restaurants, shops, movie theater, hotel, office space and athletic club, apartments and offices.

Aerial view (looking west to east) of the original five square-mile Miami Lakes community developed by The Graham Companies in northwest Miami-Dade County.

The design for the town came from Harvard professor Lester Collins, grandson of Miami Beach pioneer John Collins. The town center is located at the heart of the nautilus-shaped road system which spirals outward to encompass parks, schools, apartments, townhomes, single family homes and shopping centers. The town's numerous lakes are shaped with twists and turns that add an interesting mystique to the landscape.

Today, The Graham Companies is run by the third generation of Grahams. Members of the family in executive roles include Sandra Graham Younts, Carol Graham Wyllie, Stu Wyllie, Beth Graham Martinez and Luis Martinez. Over time, the company evolved from developer to a property management firm encompassing its hospitality, office, industrial, retail and residential properties, and it remains the largest property owner in Miami Lakes. It owns and operates Shula's Hotel and Golf Club, Shula's Athletic Club, 1,500 rental apartments, and more than two million square feet of office, industrial and retail space.

The centerpiece of the town is its charming Town Center, a pedestrian-friendly area with restaurants, shops, movie theater, hotel, spa and athletic club, apartments and offices. The sidewalks are brick-paved and lined with flowers, trees and shrubs, and encourage people to stroll leisurely through the shaded town. Special events, including concerts, classic car shows and holiday festivities, are a regular feature on Main Street.

In 2000, Miami Lakes was incorporated as a municipality with 23,000 residents, and more than 250 businesses which employ approximately 12,000 people. Living in Miami Lakes is tantamount to living in a small town within a large city. The community is family oriented and boasts a plethora of activities including sports, arts and culture along with that intangible, small-town feeling. Miami Lakes, a vibrant 21st century city, offers the perfect live-work-play lifestyle.

For over 80 years, The Graham Companies has been an integral part of Miami. The company has created a lasting legacy in Miami Lakes, as well as a strong family tradition of service to the community. Family members have been active participants with the United Way, Boy Scouts of America, Greater Miami Chamber of Commerce, Greater Miami Visitors and Convention Bureau, the Beacon Council, the Historical Association of South Florida, the Miami Museum of Science and numerous other organizations.

The "lemonade" Cap Graham made when the sugar operation closed down continues to flow and is a sweet reminder of a man of vision, who passed that trait on to his many heirs.

Patriarch of what would become The Graham Companies, Ernest R. "Cap" Graham, established a successful dairy business and accumulated land in the northwest area of Miami-Dade County.

THE RELATED GROUP

The Related Group, which has been instrumental in developing much of Miami's high-rise, sparkling skyline, had much more humble beginnings.

Since 1994, The Related Group has dominated the luxury condominium market in South Florida. The development of Portofino Tower on South Beach was the first of the SoFi (South of Fifth Street) luxury developments and created a hot, new market. Portofino set the standard, which was followed by the Yacht Club at Portofino, Murano at Portofino, Murano Grande, Icon South Beach and Apogee.

Across the bay on Brickell Avenue, Icon Brickell has become a landmark project on ten acres at the mouth of the Miami River. Designed by famed architect Phillipe Starck, the innovative condominium is a multiple award-winner. Related's collaboration with Donald Trump has resulted in the elegant Trump Towers in Sunny Isles Beach and Trump Hollywood in Hollywood Beach.

Company founder Jorge M. Perez began his career creating affordable housing in South Florida neighborhoods such as Little Havana and Homestead. More than a quarter of a century later, The Related Group is one of the nation's premier development firms. Specializing in luxury condominiums, multi-family residences and mixed-use developments, Related is also the largest Hispanic-owned business in the United States.

Perez, Chairman and CEO, had the foresight to pioneer an urban revolution in Florida, the state with more development of urban high-rise luxury condominiums than any other. Since 1979, Related has built and managed more than 70,000 residential units in Florida, reshaped the skyline of downtown Miami and helped redefine South Beach as desirable residential location.

In Miami, The Related Group led the new downtown urbanism movement by developing One Miami on one of the last pieces of waterfront land at the intersection of the Miami River and Biscayne Bay. With that project, a trend was born. A bit further north, Related contributed to the transformation of Sunny Isles Beach from a sleepy sea-side town to the chic metropolis it is today. The skylines of Broward and Palm Beach Counties have also been impacted by the company's developments, adding an excitement and dynamism to the region.

The Related Group's roots may be in South Florida, but the business has expanded to markets including Mexico, Panama, Argentina, Uruguay and the Caribbean. Subsidiary Related International is dedicated to the same high standards of excellence and quality in its projects starting with the new Icon Vallarta in Puerto Vallarta, Mexico.

With a development portfolio valued in excess of $10.7 billion, the firm reported sales of more than $3.2 billion since 2005. Employing more than 500 in South Florida, The Related Group also operates subsidiaries that handle real estate financing, sales and property management.

The company's corporate philosophy is simple; only the best is good enough. From the luxurious finishes in a lavish condominium to the right location for the next mixed-use project, The Related Group is committed to excellence. That commitment includes its people; the team of skilled professionals is among the firm's greatest assets.

Take another look at Miami's modern skyline or those gleaming high-rises on the water. What stands there is Jorge Perez and The Related Group's vision of a vibrant, modern city.

Although The Related Group has reached the pinnacle of success through the luxury market, Perez has not forgotten his roots in the affordable housing market. In fact, the firm has an entire division devoted to that constituency, the Attainable Housing Division. The division focuses on housing for the numerous people working in supportive positions in the thriving South Florida economy. With this division, Perez has brought the company back to where it first began.

The Loft developments in downtown Miami are the embodiment of The Related Group's commitment to the market. The four luxury, high-rise condominiums are located in the heart of Miami's central business district and feature amenities normally not associated with affordable housing. With the advent of the Loft projects, downtown Miami is poised to join the ranks of other major cities in the world where people of all walks of life enjoy the live – work – play dynamic.

In addition to its residential developments, The Related Group is widely regarded as an innovator in the field of mixed-use centers. CityPlace in West Palm Beach has become the model for modern, mixed-use urban centers by converting a deteriorating area into a hub of activity where people can live, work and play. The firm's vision of a vibrant urban lifestyle center – including residences, offices, retail shops, theaters and restaurants – has been realized at CityPlace.

Natan R. Rok

ROK ENTERPRISES, INC.

Rok Enterprises has its finger on the pulse of downtown Miami's retail scene.

tenants often; he was a regular fixture on Flagler Street. In 1986, the company opened Flagler Station a 120,000 square foot retail and office building located in the heart of the city. At around the same time, the company bought a controlling interest in TransAtlantic Bank. Rok, who passed away in 2004, spent most of his time cultivating and expanding the bank's business. His son Sergio, who

The company is so entrenched in the community that its founder Natan Rok was also known as the Mayor of Flagler Street and the street has been designated Natan R. Rok Boulevard in his honor. For more than 40 years, the family-owned real estate management firm has been a catalyst for the growth of businesses in the central business district and plans to continue and increase that role through the 21st century.

An immigrant from Cuba, Rok started his business with a small menswear shop in 1964. Dandy's Men's Wear was so successful, it expanded to six shops. Rok parlayed that success into an impressive amount of real estate holdings, ultimately making Rok Enterprises the largest landlord in downtown Miami. Rok created a unique business model in 1971 when he purchased an old downtown drugstore and converted it into five separate stores. The concept worked, so Rok expanded it to ever larger buildings.

Eventually, Rok had 300 merchants, many of whom were immigrants like him, who were accustomed to doing business on a handshake and personal interaction. It was not uncommon for Rok to visit his

Sergio Rok

Flagler First Condominiums renovated back to its 1926 facade.

Flagler Station.

had been working at Rok Enterprises since 1984 managed the company's real estate portfolio and serves as its president today. Although the bank was sold in 2007, the company continues to do a significant amount of business with TransAtlantic.

The key to the Rok Enterprise's success is the fact they only manage company-owned buildings, most of which are located in Miami-Dade County with a few in Broward and Palm Beach counties. The vast majority of the 26 buildings in their portfolio are commercial and retail properties, with more than 1,5 million square feet of space. Once a building is part of Rok Enterprises, it remains so. In 25 years, only two properties have been sold. The company excels at purchasing, remodeling, leasing and holding its properties and is always looking for the next building to redevelop. One exception is Flagler First Condominiums, a mixed-use condominium project that turned a historic downtown building, First National Bank, into livable space with retail attached.

The vision for Rok Enterprises going forward is in line with that of Miami in general; to become a world-class, livable city with 24/7 services, shops and restaurants for residents and visitors. With the construction of numerous condominiums in the downtown area, the future looks bright. The residential component of Miami is key to every downtown business's success and Rok Enterprises

plans an aggressive campaign to attract national retailers, boutiques and other retail outlets once the condominiums are occupied. The residents will be good for downtown businesses, which will draw more residents.

Sergio, who served on the Downtown Development Authority for 18 years, started working at the company right out of college. His expertise in marketing and business management has helped expand Rok Enterprises. As President of Rok Enterprises, Sergio's vision for the city includes a comprehensive urban retail center. A lot of work has been done, but Rok sees a lot more to do in the next decade. When complete, Miami could rival cities like Chicago, San Francisco and New York. Rok Enterprises's projects are a crucial part of the revitalization of downtown Miami's central business district, which will transform the city into an appealing, sophisticated metropolis.

Rok Enterprises is still a family business with the motto it has always maintained; family first. One of the first things Sergio learned from his father was that true happiness and success isn't found in one's business; it is measured by the love of your family. A few members of the family help operate the business and are an integral part of its success, Robert Moskovitz, Vice president and Bryan Morjain. The next generation is already showing an interest in the business. The integrity upon which Rok Enterprises was built remains the essence of the company business model.

Miami would be a very different city had it not benefited from Natan Rok's vision. His legacy is vast and can be see on the bustling streets and the busy storefronts of downtown Miami every day.

Building with Company's logo.

ESSLINGER-WOOTEN-MAXWELL, INC.

Esslinger-Wooten-Maxwell Realtors (EWM) is a real estate powerhouse in no small part by sticking to the values upon which it was founded in 1964.

Three ladies -- Anna Mae Esslinger, Dodie Wooten and Arline Maxwell – built EWM into a highly respected boutique real estate firm based on a commitment to good old-fashioned personalized customer service.

Recognizing the quality of the firm, a partnership team that included current President Ron Shuffield purchased the company in 1984. Since then, the company has seen its success soar and is now established as one of the largest real estate services firms in America, rising from $50 million in sales in 1984, to average some $2.5 billion today.

Early on, EWM's growth strategy focused heavily on its sales associates. Recognizing the vast diversity of the South Florida market, the company realized the importance of

■ EWM's Weston Town Center office is positioned at 2000 Main Street in the heart of Weston

providing its associates and staff members access to the latest technology, facts and figures, and up-to-the-minute market knowledge. The result: a diverse group of professionals from every corner of the globe. Today, EWM has more than 850 associates and staff members, speaking 13 different languages.

With offices throughout Miami-Dade and Broward counties, EWM actively began merging real estate firms in the early 1990's, and does so to this day, embracing quality brokerages who share common values.

EWM's early view toward the future included offering a vast array of services to its clients. The organization became a veritable one-stop-shop offering residential and commercial real estate services, corporate relocation, and international services.

■ EWM's Coral Gables - South Miami Office is located in our new EWM-owned, state-of-the-art building at 550 South Dixie Highway in Coral Gables

The firm offers mortgage, title closing services, and property insurance through subsidiary companies HomeServices Lending, LLC; EWM Title; and EWM Insurance.

EWM is the exclusive Miami-Dade and Broward Counties affiliate for Christie's Great Estates, the largest network of luxury, independent, real estate firms in the world, and a

◼ Wide expanses of glass invite natural light in and offer panoramic views from EWM's Coral Gables - South Miami Office at 550 South Dixie Highway in Coral Gables

subsidiary of Christie's International PLC, the London-based art auction company founded in 1766. With more than 500 offices and approximately 14,000 real estate agents in 15 countries, the affiliate members of Christie's Great Estates market the finest homes around the globe.

The company became the 'standard' for brokerage firms in the South Florida market, serving generations of customers. "We have individuals and families whose parents and grandparents have purchased from our company," says Shuffield. "When you treat someone honestly and with respect, they not only remember you, but their families do as well. It's an honor and privilege to be thought of that way."

◼ Graceful architecture details add to the visual appeal of EWM's Miami Beach office, located at 419 Arthur Godfrey Road.

As one of the nation's elite brokerages, in 2003 EWM caught the eye of Berkshire Hathaway affiliate, HomeServices of America, the second largest residential brokerage firm in the nation.

Through its affiliation with HomeServices of America, EWM is part of a real estate family of 20,000 sales associates spanning 19 states, with an annual sales volume exceeding $60 billion.

◼ The interior of EWM's Southeast Broward office, located at 4410 Weston Road, reflects the company's appreciation for classic design.

"Becoming a part of HomeServices was a natural transition for us," adds Shuffield. "We share the same values and business philosophies practiced by our sister companies across the US. It is a privilege for us to be a part of an organization that honors the same values upon which EWM was founded in 1964."

It is these qualities that have allowed the company to expand, mature, and find its place as a major attractor for people looking for Miami's promise. EWM has supported some 150 different charitable groups through the work of its large stable of associates and staff members. This creed supports the concept of a quality of life for all.

If the business of EWM is any indication, Miami has a bright future in store.

◼ EWM's Aventura Office is located at 2750 NE 185 Street in Aventura

HILL YORK, THE AIR-CONDITIONING PEOPLE

Making Life More Comfortable for Miami Since 1936

Imagine the luxury hotels of Miami Beach without air conditioning, closed in the summer, and cooled only by fans in the winter months. One South Florida company changed all that.

As Florida's first air-conditioning company, Hill York pursued the challenge of designing and installing air conditioning in more than half of the luxury hotels in Miami Beach just after World War II, making way for more tourism in South Florida with visitors and conventioneers flocking to the area. To this day, the company is credited with making Miami Beach a year-round community.

Hill York didn't start off specializing in air conditioning, however. It was an evolution begun by two hard-working men with a vision, and a business partner they met who shared that vision. In 1936, the two founders, Ren Nitzsche and Everett Carroll were in the equipment business, serving as a distributor for Hill refrigerated cases and York air conditioning. During World War II, the company refurbished and installed used refrigerators, and renamed their company by combining the names of the two companies for which they were distributors.

Ten years after the duo began their business, they met Robert S. Lafferty, Sr., whose vocation was selling oil heaters in New Jersey. Lafferty saw an opportunity in the warm climate of the South to bolster the air-conditioning business of Hill York. He sold the first complete air-conditioning system to The Roney Plaza Hotel on Miami Beach. Other hotels started following suit, and Lafferty soon had nearly every major hotel lined up for air conditioning. Eventually, he became a part owner of the company.

His son, Robert S. Lafferty, Jr., is now chairman of the board of Hill York, while his grandson, Robert W. "Chip" Lafferty, a professional engineer, presides as chief executive officer. The company still maintains a branch in Miami where it got its start, but Fort Lauderdale is now the location of its headquarters. Other branches are located in West Palm Beach, Melbourne and Sarasota. The company has grown to more than 500 employees and is one of the largest HVAC contracting firms in the country. It provides engineering,

Chief Executive Officer Robert W. "Chip" Lafferty and Chairman Robert S. Lafferty

preconstruction, installation, start up, service and maintenance for any size HVAC project. Hill York has built a reputation for providing clients with an immediate response because of its ability to cover many geographical areas.

In addition to being recognized for its superior craftsmanship in the design and installation of state-of-the-art equipment, one of the keys to Hill York's success is its longevity. It was Robert Lafferty, Sr., who sold the Delano Hotel on Miami Beach its first air-conditioning system. When Miami Beach turned into trendy South Beach, it was time for the Delano to reassess every inch of the hotel, including its air conditioning. More than five decades later, Chip Lafferty worked with the Delano for the installation of

■ The chiller plant at the University of Miami's Rosenstiel School of Marine and Atmospheric Science

its new system. It isn't unusual for Hill York, which has been servicing the area for more than half a century, to replace or rebuild a system for the same company multiple times.

In 1983, when The Biltmore Hotel was renovated, it was Hill York that was charged with installing its air-conditioning system. Most recently, a Hill York team completely renovated the entire chiller plant at the University of Miami's Rosenstiel School of Marine and Atmospheric Science on Biscayne Bay. The team removed the school's antiquated, ammonia ice plant, recovering 3,000 pounds of ammonia refrigerant and 6,000 gallons of glycol. They were able to perform this monumental task without affecting the Rosenstiel School's production schedule. The new plant has resulted in an average of 30 percent in energy savings since its installation Jan. 1, 2008.

Since the mid-1990s, Hill York has been part of Nova Southeastern University's design development and construction team. Hill York maintains a full-time construction office and a permanent staff of project managers and technicians on the campus, fulfilling all of NSU's air-conditioning needs.

Always a leader and innovator at the forefront of technology in its industry, Hill York recently initiated a Performance Management Group, cleverly named *hygreen*, which embraces the growing green building philosophy. Hill York is an Energy Star Service and Product Provider, and a high percentage of its tactical leadership team has earned the U.S. Green Business Council's LEED accreditation (Leadership in Energy and Environmental Design). The Performance Management Group includes a focus on building oversight management, which is powered by Utilivisor. This state-of-the-art, real-time, web-based building optimization tool monitors and analyzes the operation and efficiency of HVAC systems and is an invaluable tool to reduce energy usage and maintain LEED-compliant properties.

One could hardly mention Hill York without making special note of its philanthropy. A quick look at its website reveals more than 50 organizations to which it reaches out in community support. With a mission built on faith, family and business, as well as corporate core values that center on communication and accountability, Hill York believes in cultivating lasting relationships with its clients, always keeping its vision in mind: Making Life More Comfortable.

■ Hill York's pledge...Making Life More Comfortable

RILEA GROUP

Miami-Based Rilea Group is a full real estate development company that since 1981 has been developing real estate projects in South Florida.

Standing tall as one of Miami's most recognizable buildings is One Broadway in the heart of Brickell Avenue. The elegant 371 unit, 36 story "City Residences for Rent" represents what Alan Ojeda, president and CEO of the Rilea Group, likes to think of as the true standard of living in a growing urban city.

When Ojeda started the Rilea Group in 1981 after arriving in Miami from Madrid, he saw the potential of the city, he says. Through his development of properties in Miami, he continues to help to define a new skyline and establish an urban-defined community where everything is easily accessible.

One Broadway, completed in 2006, was Phase 1 of a two-tower project from the Rilea Group. Phase 2 includes a 35-story office, 588,000 square foot-tower located at 1450 Brickell Avenue, and like One Broadway also includes ground level retail stores and is the first green Class "A" office building to be pre-certified LEED gold in Miami by the US Green Building Council. Both One Broadway and 1450 Brickell typify Ojeda's vision that buildings should work on all levels, and what he says is "designing for people with real lives and daily needs."

Because of the long-term philosophy of the Rilea Group, a building's design needs to withstand the test of time --

how they will look fifteen or twenty-five years after opening. Another signature of a property developed by the Rilea Group is that the building must work as a pedestrian urban experience relating to people at ground level, not only at five, ten or 20 stories up from the pavement.

For the Rilea Group, developing its sixth high-rise building in Miami is a major milestone, something that reflects a shift in the global perception of the city, with people from not only South America flocking here, but from Europe, too. With the influx comes a city with a more modern and sophisticated crowd, a more urban city with more needs, and a place that thrives with an urban lifestyle.

But Ojeda doesn't cater only to sophisticated urbanites. He treasures the work he does with Carrfour Supportive Housing as a board member, an executive committee member and chairman of construction, an organization that builds homes for homeless. Also his participation in the board and executive committee of the Miami Children's Hospital Foundation is part of his "giving back" to a community that he says accepted and helped him.

Whether on the leading edge of suburban growth or developing multi-use urban centers, the Rilea Group creates buildings that aren't only beautiful, but that leave a legacy.

TERRA GROUP

Miami-based Terra Group is a real estate development firm that focuses on creating environments that enhance people's lives.

ts innovative projects integrating culture, the environment and residential development are the perfect compliment to Miami's burgeoning cultural and urban communities.

Founded in 2002, by father and son team Pedro Martin and David Martin, Terra Group has become a leading force in the South Florida real estate industry. In the past six years, the company has demonstrated a keen eye for bold decisions, investments and the identification of new neighborhoods, paving the way for the transformation of Miami into a world-class cosmopolitan city. The company has also cultivated strategic partnerships with the best architectural firms and designers giving their projects top-notch quality and design.

Terra Group is committed to innovative projects and to the renewal of Miami's downtown, arts and entertainment districts. The company is at the helm of the revitalization currently taking place in the Biscayne Corridor; inspired by their vision of transforming Miami to a world-class cosmopolitan city with its most current projects, Quantum on the Bay and 900 Biscayne Bay.

Taking the lead in the resurgence of Downtown Miami, Terra Group has developed 900 Biscayne Bay, a 1.5 million –square foot tower overlooking Biscayne Boulevard. The development's innovative architecture offers stunning bay and city views. With its superb design and fresh perspective on sophistication, 900 Biscayne Bay offers residents two main pool areas, wet bar, spa lounge, a private theatre room, state of the art gym, and an observation deck offering full bay views and adorned with a grand piano.

Terra Group's Quantum on the Bay is a spectacular mixed-used development located in Miami's dynamic Arts and Entertainment district that offers breathtaking views of Biscayne Bay and downtown Miami. Quantum on the Bay has been drawing accolades for its spectacular amenities and prime location. Just recently the Builders Association of South Florida awarded Quantum on the Bay the prestigious Blue Ribbon Award for Outstanding Overall Project Execution. In addition, the building is located on the revitalized Biscayne Boulevard, placing it in close proximity to many attractive cultural and entertainment options. With amenities that rival even 5-star hotels, residents will enjoy the ultimate in style and comfort.

Terra Group has cultivated a reputation as a trendsetter, creating high-end residential and mixed-use projects notable for their originality. Terra Group's roster of innovative projects also include: Metropolis at Dadeland, the first development to bring high-rise living to downtown Dadeland, Nautica, a chic and luxurious 33-unit building on Miami Beach, and The Reserve, a village in Doral awarded the Platinum winner in 2006 for the best planned community by Florida's Best. Terra Group has achieved insurmountable growth, developing a myriad of communities that aim to enrich the sense of community and create environments that enhance people's lives.

■ *Quantum on the Bay, Downtown Design and Arts District*

R.J. HEISENBOTTLE ARCHITECTS

Everywhere you look in Miami,
R.J. Heisenbottle Architects has
a presence.

The firm is well known in South Florida for having restored some of the area's oldest and most prestigious buildings, including the Gusman Center for the Performing Arts, The Colony Theater, the Freedom Tower and Miami Edison Middle School, but its vast portfolio of projects also includes innovative new structures. The striking Lou Rawls Center for the Performing Arts at Florida Memorial College, Fulford Elementary School and the Beach and Marine Life Safety Facilities at Haulover Beach Park are among the firm's unique contributions to the new face of architecture in Miami.

"We look for great clients and great projects. We look for opportunities for accomplishment," says Richard J. Heisenbottle, FAIA, president of the Coral Gables architecture firm.

The accomplishments are numerous. RJHA has become a sought after firm for many high-profile projects, including the new Kings Point Theatre for the Performing Arts in Tamarac, Fla., and the restored Athens Theatre in Deland, Fla. Not only does RJHA help clients meet the technical challenges of designing performing arts theaters, but it also emphasizes award winning designs that invigorate cultural arts scenes in communities.

The company's architectural solutions are often unique and innovative, yet the end results are timeless, well-crafted buildings with durable materials, sensitive to their context. RJHA's restoration of Miami City Hall (originally

Pan American Airway's first seaplane terminal) and of Miami's National Historic Landmark Freedom Tower brought new life to neglected structures that represent milestones in the city's history.

The Freedom Tower
Photographer: Dan Forer

Miami Edison Middle School
Photographer: Dan Forer

From the architect's first preservation project in the Cast Iron District of New York City in 1972, Heisenbottle's firm has evolved to offer unparalleled expertise in preservation planning, consulting, restoration and adaptive reuse of historic structures. The Master Plan for Vizcaya Museum and Gardens, one of only three National Historic Landmarks in Miami, represents one of the firm's most important preservation

Lou Rawls Center for the Performing Arts
Photographer: Dan Forer

planning accomplishments. RJHA's commitment to Miami's architectural past strengthens ties to the future and pays respect to the city's unique architectural legacy.

The team of professionals at RJHA brings an impressive depth of resources and expertise in a variety of building types and state-of-the art technology. In 1998, R.J.

Heisenbottle Architects was awarded a National Preservation Award by the National Trust for Historic Preservation for the Restoration of Miami Edison Middle School. To date, the firm has received more than fifteen state and local design awards from the American Institute of Architects, and five awards from the Florida Trust for Historic Preservation.

Colony Theatre
Photographer: Raul Pedrosa

Many of its projects have been featured in both local and national publications. Mr. Heisenbottle earned the coveted Silver Medal for Design from the AIA Miami in 2004, and was elevated to AIA Fellow in 2005.

RJHA is currently the architect for the restoration of the 1897 Belleview Biltmore Hotel and Resort in Bellaire, Fla., one of the largest preservation projects in the state of Florida.

Miami City Hall
Photographer: Dan Forer

SUPERMIX CONCRETE
THE ON TIME CONCRETE COMPANY

From its contributions to the city's biggest high-rises and road projects to its residential jobs, Supermix has played a large part in helping to build Miami.

The On Time Concrete Company® has developed a reputation for the use of innovative techniques, outstanding service and attention to detail. And it has done so with a focus on traditional values and doing business the old-fashioned way without sacrificing quality.

In 1976, the Dias family began work in Brazil and in 1989 expanded to the United States, opening Supermix Concrete in Miami. Supermix has steadily grown and now serves Southeast and Southwest Florida, including the counties of Miami-Dade, Broward and South Palm Beach.

According to Bernardo Dias, executive vice president of Supermix, quality, safety, honesty and dignity are attributes that are not negotiable in his business. Furthermore, not a penny is spared in guaranteeing the quality of Supermix. Add to that the company's mission that includes keeping customers and employees at the center of its daily operations, and it's no wonder that Supermix has earned a reputation of creating an exceptional atmosphere in which to work and do business while delivering a superior product.

The company's reputation is a point of pride for Dias, whose father started the family's operations in the United States after buying an already existing company. When the family purchased the business, they operated only two plants with some 20 trucks in South Florida. Supermix was the first independent concrete supplier to use air conditioning in its mixer cabs and operated trucks with automatic transmissions.

Today, the business has seven locations, 10 concrete batch plants and 135 trucks serving commercial, single-family residential and high-rise customers in the Southeast and Southwest Florida markets. The family also continues to own and operate more than 90 plants and 700 trucks in South America. Its continued growth makes Supermix poised to gain the competitive edge in a global marketplace.

Supermix not only delivers quality service, but it brings together the best equipment, technology and innovative

State Road 836 Toll.

Brickell Courts, Carbonell and Asia Condominiums on Brickell Key.

techniques. In 2007, the company expanded its product line by opening its Superblock™ state-of-the-art block plant in Medley, Fla., with a manufacturing facility that is one of the most highly advanced in the country. As an independent company, Supermix has the ability to use local materials thus contributing to the economy of Miami-Dade County. In the production of its own concrete and masonry block, the company is committed to the highest environmental standards and maintains awareness of its social responsibility.

Under the leadership of Pepe Canco Sr., president and CEO since 1989, the company has been engaged in projects ranging from 5,000 to 80,000 cubic yards of concrete. Supermix has supplied some of Miami's highest profile projects including Murano at Portofino, Icon and Apogee Condominiums on South Beach, Carbonell and Asia Condominiums on Brickell Key, the 50 Biscayne Plaza, the Icon Brickell in downtown, the Ritz Carlton hotels in both Key Biscayne and Coconut Grove, and city projects including Concourse D Extension at Miami Airport and the State Road 836 Toll Plaza reconstruction. And while Supermix is available to supply customers with large-scale demands, it doesn't take its smaller customers for granted, always at the ready to accommodate any job big or small.

An active involvement in helping to build Miami doesn't only include its products, but in community service, too. Supermix sponsors various local and civic associations such as La Liga Contra El Cancer (League Against Cancer), Habitat for Humanity, MADD, PBA, Boys and Girls Clubs, The Alzheimer's Foundation and The Estela Project, to name a few. The company maintains memberships in the Latin Builders Association, Builders Association of South Florida, Associated Builders & Contractors, Inc., Construction Association of South Florida, the National Ready Mixed Concrete Association, and The Florida Concrete and Products Association, and has been the recipient of numerous awards for service, quality of product and responsible environmental practices.

What makes this independent concrete supplier the customer's choice is not only its outstanding product and state-of-the art equipment, but also the ability to guarantee and deliver its product to the job-site in a timely, efficient manner. It's a foundation that was built by families devoted to quality and service, and a mission that continues into the 21st century.

Supermix has supplied some of Miami's highest profile projects.

THE ALLEN MORRIS COMPANY

In 1947, Miami was an undeveloped city with nothing but promise for the future.

Ever the optimist, L. Allen Morris made the move from Atlanta to Miami to work for the Keyes Company. About a decade later, Morris became a real estate developer himself and in 1958 he founded what has proven to be one of Miami's powerhouse real estate firms, The Allen Morris Company, (AMCo).

Located in a small office in downtown Miami, Morris helped create the city that exists today. His influence can be seen from Key Biscayne to Kendall to Brickell Avenue. L. Allen Morris's legacy extends to Coral Gables, where his son W. Allen Morris built the landmark Alhambra Towers.

Since its inception, AMCo has become one of the largest diversified real estate firms in the Southeast with a specialty in commercial and industrial property sales; office, industrial and retail, leasing, development and property management; as well as marketing and consulting. Over the years, the company has developed more than 78 office and industrial buildings for businesses and major corporations throughout Florida and Georgia.

The firm has prospered due to its philosophy of serving clients with integrity, responsiveness, professional expertise and market information. AMCo's remarkable success is due to a conservative development philosophy in which the firm builds projects only in carefully selected market areas.

In 1980, the baton of leadership was passed from L. Allen Morris to his son, W. Allen Morris, who assumed the position of president and chief executive officer and has led the company to the heights it occupies today.

A privately held company, AMCo has been recognized for its excellence and won nine (9) awards including the Builders Association of South Florida (BASF) "Builders Best Overall Product Commercial Office" Platinum award, and the National Association of Industrial and Office Properties (NAIOP) "Project of the Year" for Alhambra Towers.

Alhambra Towers has become AMCo's signature project and it's most ambitious to date. The architecture for the award-winning, 16-story, 174,000 square-foot office building encompasses both Spanish and Italian design features, including a 12-foot tall working weathervane, an exact replica of the original Giraldillo(Lady of Faith) found atop the Giralda Tower of the Cathedral in Seville, Spain.

Looking to the future, AMCo plans to develop Ponce de Leon Towers, a 16-story, 215,000 square-foot world class office building in Coral Gables, which will be the first office building in Coral Gables built to LEED certification from the U.S. Green Building Council. The project is expected to be completed in 2010.

Ponce de Leon Towers.

A
METROPOLITAN
CITY

*T*HE **GREATER MIAMI** AREA IS AN EXCITING PLACE TO LIVE FOR A VARIETY OF REASONS — THE DIVERSITY OF CULTURE, A FABULOUS CLIMATE, AND SUPERB RECREATIONAL ACTIVITIES. AND ALL THIS COMBINED WITH A LANDSCAPE OF TROPICAL GREEN, AND GLISTENING WATERS NESTLED INTO WARM SANDY BEACHES. WHAT A BEAUTIFUL PICTURE! ADD TO THIS THE NECESSARY PIECES OF A THRIVING ECONOMY — A BUSTLING FINANCIAL SECTOR, A MAJOR PORT, AND THE COMMUNITY'S ROLE AS THE BRIDGE BETWEEN THE AMERICAS..

Physical beauty and proud institutions are one thing. But it is people who make up the greatness of a community, and from my perspective, Miami is rich with outstanding community and business leaders, who have been instrumental in the growth of our area of more than 2.5 million people. Along with my family and friends, both personal and professional, we have watched greater Miami explode with industry and tourism over the past few decades. With that growth comes responsibility. In that regard, many neglected neighborhoods are experiencing a renaissance through the addition of affordable housing, infrastructure, and recreational venues like parks, performing arts centers, and now, the culmination of a new major league baseball stadium.

Big business is important, but the hidden strength of Greater Miami is the small and medium size businesses that complement the large, domestic and multinational companies. Our CPA firm has witnessed extraordinary growth. In fact, many area CPA and law firms started with only a few partners, and like us, have grown over the years into national practices with some boasting hundreds of partners and associates. We owe this growth to the climate that the Miami community has fostered to motivate business and cultivate jobs.

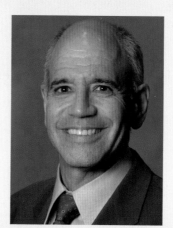

MONTE KANE
Founder and managing director of Kane & Company, PA, CPAs.

Under Mr. Kane's leadership, the firm has a proud history of cutting edge services to its domestic and international clients including assurance, advisory, tax and technology services. The firm believes in giving back to the Greater Miami community and is active in civic and charitable activities.

Professional Services

SHOOK, HARDY & BACON, L.L.P.	442
MORRISON, BROWN, ARGIZ & FARRA, LLP	446
GOLDSTEIN SCHECTER KOCH	448
THE FERRARO LAW FIRM	449
MORGAN, LEWIS & BOCKIUS LLP	450
ZUMPANO, PATRICIOS, & WINKER, P.A.	451
KANE & COMPANY, P.A.	452
FUERST, HUMPHREY, ITTLEMAN	454
HALL, LAMB AND HALL, P.A.	456
VICTORIA & ASSOCIATES CAREER SERVICES	458
BUSINESS CENTERS INTERNATIONAL	459
ASSOCIATED PHOTO & IMAGING	460
McKINLEY FINANCIAL SERVICES	462
HARVEY BILT PHOTOGRAPHY	463

Like so many others, I came here as a toddler. I've been witness to a half century of growth, watching my small town grow into one of the outstanding commercial markets in America, and all the while, never losing its unique charm and extraordinary quality of life.

SHOOK, HARDY & BACON L.L.P.

SHB has achieved favorable results for national and international clients under the most contentious circumstances both inside and outside the courtroom.

ttorneys from the firm's Miami office have built successful practices in a variety of specialties for a wide spectrum of clients, while at the same time evincing a deep commitment to the Miami community on a number of levels.

Legal Services

SHB's Miami office was created in June 1988 as a result of a merger with Anderson, Moss, Sherouse & Petros, P.A., a long-time Miami trial boutique. A second merger in 2000 with Coll, Davidson, Smith & Barkett, another well-known Miami trial firm, established SHB-Miami as one of the premier litigation and trial firms in Florida. Since that time, the office has specialized in, among other areas, commercial, business, products liability, environmental, toxic tort, employment, and trade secret litigation; all forms of class action litigation; complex litigation; and arbitration of commercial, construction and other types of disputes.

For a number of *Fortune* 100 and local companies, SHB's Miami office has "go to" lawyers who have directed, managed and, when necessary, tried many high-profile cases, including numerous class actions. SHB-Miami's extensive trial and litigation experience truly sets it apart, as its attorneys have

collectively tried or won judgments before trial in hundreds of cases in federal (Southern, Middle and Northern District, and outside of Florida) or Florida court (from Monroe County in the south to Duval county in the north).

■ *Front Row (L to R): Dick Smith/Partner, Lea Souza Rasile/ Managing Partner, Luis Perez/ Partner. Back Row (L to R) Paul Reid/ Partner, Tom Sherouse/Partner, Sergio Pagliery/Partner*

Back Row: Ed Moss/Partner, John Barkett/Partner. Front Row: Eileen Moss/Partner, Lea Souza Rasile/Managing Partner

SHB-Miami is equipped to handle matters of any size and to devote the appropriate level of resources to service its clients' needs. Coordination of work with the firm's Tampa office also gives SHB the geographic flexibility to address a client's

litigation needs in Florida in a cost-effective manner.

In recognition of the knowledge, judgment, strategic thinking, and dispute avoidance and dispute resolution capabilities of its lawyers, SHB-Miami has enjoyed numerous "Super Lawyers," "Best Lawyers," "Top Lawyers," "Legal Elite," "Up-and-Comers," and *The National Law Journal's* "Top Defense Verdict" honorees within its ranks.

So far in 2008, *The American Lawyer* named SHB the Litigation Department of the Year in the Product Liability category and the firm was named Global Product Liability Firm of the Year for the fourth consecutive year by *Who's Who Legal*. In 2007, SHB was recognized by the *National Law Journal* on its "Defense Hot List" for the second consecutive year, and the firm was listed in Chambers USA as one of just seven elite "Band One" firms for national product liability defense.

Community and Civic Leadership

Shook, Hardy & Bacon's Miami office is just as proud of it pro bono work and commitment to community service. In 2007, one partner served his third term as president of the board of directors for Legal Services of Greater Miami, Inc., the largest provider of free legal services for the poor in Miami-Dade

Former Managing Partner Kenneth Reilly (left) is joined by Alicia Menendez/Of Counsel, Tara Elfering/Associate, Stacey Koch/Of Counsel, Dan Gardner/Associate, Victoria Kush/Associate, Jared Sherr/Associate, Marc Levinson/Of Counsel

Back Row: Geri Howell/Associate, Heather Cohen Szkaradek/Associate, Tara Elfering/Associate, Jennifer McLoone/Associate, Lea Souza Rasile/Managing Partner.
Front Row: Hildy Sastre/Partner, Eileen Moss/Partner, Lisa Leontiev/Associate

and Monroe Counties. Firm attorneys have been honored for their pro bono efforts by Lawyers for Children America, Florida Immigrant Advocacy Center, and the Dade County Bar Association's Put Something Back Pro Bono program.

SHB-Miami has also adopted the JESCA Head Start Center in Overtown and has filled the center's library, the children's Halloween bags and holiday stockings, and supplied the center with a new refrigerator, laptop computer, printer, and enough construction paper and poster board to keep the center's three- to five-year-olds busy for months. Supporting the center is

Back Row (L to R): Adam Klarfeld/Associate, Salo Kozolchyk/Associate, Geri Howell/Associate, Dan Rogers/Associate, Jennifer McLoone/Associate, Tara Elfering/Associate, Heather Cohen Szkaradek/Associate, Stephen Darmody/Partner, Todd Wallen/Partner, Rafael Cruz-Alvarez/Partner, Mihai Vrasmasu/Associate. Front Row (L to R): Darrell Payne/Partner, Eileen Moss/Partner, Lea Souza Rasile/Managing Partner, John Barkett/Partner, Ed Moss/Partner, Hildy Sastre/Partner

Stephen Darmody/Partner, John Barkett/Partner, Camila Tobon/Associate

SHB-Miami was the 2004 law firm recipient of the prestigious "Angels of Justice Award," presented by the Florida Immigrant Advocacy Center to recognize SHB-Miami for its pro bono work on behalf of unaccompanied minors going through the immigration system, work that continues to involve numerous SHB-Miami lawyers. Also, as part of the *South Florida Business Journal's* first annual "Diversity Works!" awards, SHB was honored as a 2004 finalist for the Best Corporate Diversity Award, recognizing a track record of successful diversity-based programs designed to cultivate cultural change, increase diversity in management, and build relationships with minority suppliers.

The Future

As the firm's vision statement states, "Shook, Hardy & Bacon is committed to being the best in the world at providing creative and practical solutions at unsurpassed value." The firm's Miami attorneys have played an integral role in making this vision a reality and looks forward to continuing their partnership with the city of Miami for years to come.

an on-going effort for the Miami office. The firm is also a proud supporter of the Kristi House, a home for sexually abused children; the Miami Science Museum; and the Muscular Dystrophy Association, where one Miami partner broke the MDA's record for "bail" by raising over $9,000 to get out of "jail" as part of an annual fundraiser.

Commitment to Diversity

Shook, Hardy & Bacon recently received the inaugural Living the Values Award, presented by The Coca-Cola Company to its outside counsel that best shares the Company's diversity values. SHB-Miami also is a proud sponsor of the ABA's Judicial Intern Opportunity Program, which places minority law students in summer clerkships with state and federal judges. This program has been recognized by the bar as one of the most effective tools to increase minority representation in these prestigious positions.

Salo Kozolchyk/Associate, Victoria Kush/Associate, James Feeney/Associate, Stacey Koch/Of Counsel

Tony Argiz, Managing Partner, in front of MBAF's Miami office located at 1001 Brickell Bay Drive.

MORRISON, BROWN, ARGIZ & FARRA, LLP

Sharing the Vision™ of successful Miami entrepreneurs has led MBAF to its current position as accountant and advisor of choice to the business community.

trusted accountant and advisor for many of the successful entrepreneurs who have built Miami into a center for international business, Morrison, Brown, Argiz & Farra (MBAF) is the largest certified public accounting firm based in Florida and ranked 43rd in the nation.

With a broad portfolio of management and consulting services, MBAF offers a single source for many of the business solutions that clients need to succeed in today's competitive landscape. For high net worth individuals and families, private wealth services help to preserve and maintain financial prosperity for generations to come.

MBAF's story reflects Miami's transformation and growth over four decades. Founded in 1969 through the merger of *Zaiac and Morrison* with *Caplan, Brown and Brown*, Albert Morrison, Sanford Caplan, Bert Brown and Alvin Brown formed Caplan, Morrison, Brown with a staff of 10. Within four years the firm had grown to almost 15 employees and

moved to South Miami to focus on general accounting, tax consulting and auditing services. For nearly two decades, MBAF continued to grow while establishing an impeccable reputation in the South Florida business community. In 1990, with 40 employees, the firm began to formalize specialty practice groups, in order to better meet client needs and optimize the knowledge base.

In 1997, Antonio (Tony) Argiz became managing partner, signaling a phase of double-digit growth for the firm. That decade saw then Morrison, Brown, Argiz & Co. expand operations outside Florida through the opening of an office in Colorado and relocation of the firm's burgeoning headquarters to its current location. With the new century came increased expansion north into Broward and Palm Beach counties as well as into the Orlando area and most recently further north into Maryland. Greater focus was placed on serving the tax and accounting needs of business clients and high net worth individuals. In 2001, Miguel G. Farra joined the firm to lead the tax and accounting practice, becoming a name partner in 2003 as the firm became Morrison, Brown, Argiz & Farra, LLP. Throughout its history, MBAF has continued to reflect the multi-lingual and multi-ethnic diversity of Miami.

Today, MBAF provides accounting-based professional services in auditing, tax, litigation support, and business and computer technology to successful entrepreneurs and business owners, wealthy individuals, and public and private companies throughout Florida as well as in 29 states and 30 nations.

Vertical Markets

Headquartered in Miami's financial and legal center, the firm's CPAs and consultants serve clients in both the corporate and non-profit sectors. The firm pioneered a

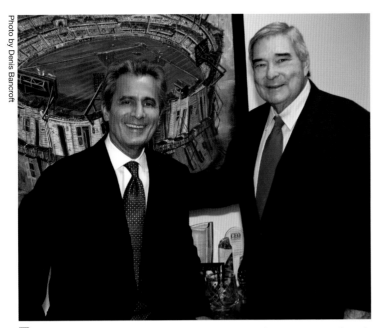

Photo by Denis Bancroft

■ *Tony Argiz and Al Morrison, one of the founding partners of Morrison, Brown, Argiz & Farra, LLP.*

vertical market approach in accounting services and now holds a leadership position across a range of industries, serving automotive dealerships, health care providers, cruise lines, hotels and restaurants, domestic, commercial and international financial institutions, sports athletes and entertainment personalities, high net worth individuals, and real estate and construction companies.

Litigation Support

The firm provides complex business litigation support and business valuation services to leading legal firms and has special capabilities in forensic accounting, family law, anti-money laundering, computer modeling and business disputes. For the last four years since its inception of its rankings, *South Florida Legal Guide* has independently recognized the top litigation support team at MBAF in its annual survey.

Computer Technology

MBAF is unique among accounting firms in having developed a highly successful computer and information services division, *Solutions@MBAF LLC*, which provides the largest South Florida-based team for Microsoft Dynamics Great Plains, and has been honored as a technology pacesetter by *Accounting Today*. *Solutions@MBAF LLC* also developed nationally-recognized *PaperSave®*, a document imaging and storage solution, which in less than three years has been sold in over 46 states to not-for-profits and successful businesses.

Hallmark Service

MBAF is recognized in Florida and nationally for its hallmark hands-on leadership and the quality service of its partners, consultants and staff. The firm serves its clients from convenient offices in Miami, Fort Lauderdale, Boca Raton, Orlando, Boulder (Colorado), and, through cyberspace technologies, from Kansas, South Carolina, Maryland and India.

Each year since 1998, *Inside Public Accounting* has honored MBAF as one of the country's 25 "**Best of the Best**" accounting firms, including one year as honorable mention. MBAF was selected as **2007 Business of the Year** by the *South Florida Business Journal* and was recognized by the Greater Miami Chamber of Commerce with its **2008 Good to Great Award**. These accolades reflect upon the strength of the firm, its people. A much-sought after employer, MBAF is known for its progressive employee policies, its family orientation and its flex time, flex locations and benefits.

The firm slogan *Sharing the Vision™* guides MBAF partners and staff within the firm, with clients and with the community. MBAF extends its focus on people even further through extensive charitable involvement with over 100 charitable and civic organizations. In addition, Tony Argiz chairs the United Way of Miami-Dade County and is vice-chair of the Orange Bowl Committee, Chair of the Board of Trustees, Carrollton School of the Sacred Heart, and past Chair of the Archbishop's Charity and Development Drive.

MBAF looks forward to its ongoing role as the accountant and advisor of choice to the successful entrepreneurs and other business leaders who will write the next chapters in Miami's story as the Magic City.

Photo by Bob Soto

■ *Miguel G. Farra, CPA, JD, Partner, Tony Argiz, Managing Partner and Stuart Rosenberg, CPA/ABV, Partner.*

GOLDSTEIN SCHECHTER KOCH

For 60 years, Goldstein Schechter Koch has been South Florida's most trusted certified public accounting firm. Yet despite the company's long history, it maintains a modern view to consistently meet the needs of its clients.

hile proud of its traditions, the company's current practice is anything but traditional, even though it still provides all that you would expect from an experienced accounting firm. Coral Gables and Hollywood-based GSK provides assurance and attest services, internal audit and operational analysis, tax compliance, planning and research, business valuations, consulting and management advisory services, litigation support, Sarbanes-Oxley compliance and consultation, estate planning and wealth preservation, and inbound foreign tax assistance.

The GSK team draws on its experience to provide services often not found at other CPA firms. One of the most unique services offered by GSK is its Outsourced CFO Services, which helps businesses and not-for-profit organizations restructure their accounting practices, create new procedures and internal controls and implement those mechanisms to help run operations more efficiently. GSK also developed its Financial Concierge service which assists an executive in time management by taking over daily tasks of bookkeeping, bill payment, tracking and organizing personal finances.

Through its affiliate, KR Financial Services, Inc., GSK is able to provide the highest quality investment advisory services. Using strategic asset allocation techniques, it guides clients through the maze of investment opportunities to maximize returns at the least possible risk.

In addition to building relationships, GSK also has a commitment to Miami's financial well-being. Therefore, GSK works with many non-profit clients within the community. Howard Lucas, CEO of the firm, says working with non-profit organizations is a "win-win" because it is a way to give back to the community that has been so much a part of GSK for so many years.

The company views itself as trusted confidants proactively leading clients to achieve their business, personal and financial goals. It also invests in the latest technology to efficiently

serve its clients, while still helping to balance convenience of information with the highest standards of security.

GSK also makes its employees a priority with the belief that a good working environment is essential to a successful business. In 2008, GSK won the prestigious award through The South Florida Business Journal as one of the Best Places to Work.

Goldstein Schechter Koch's mission is to surpass expectations and to offer leading edge financial advisory and planning skills to a broad range of clients.

THE FERRARO LAW FIRM

Since 1985 the trial attorneys at The Ferraro Law Firm have vigorously and successfully fought for the rights of those seriously injured by the wrongful acts of others.

To date, the firm has represented more than 20,000 asbestos claimants, with judgments and settlements totally more than $1 billion in compensation for injured clients. The result of the firm's multi-million dollar verdicts has earned The Ferraro Law Firm a national reputation for being among the best at handling asbestos, malignant mesothelioma and environmental toxic tort lawsuits.

The driving force behind this renowned, Miami-based firm's success since day one has been Founding Partner James L. Ferraro. His actions speak louder than words. In 1995, he received what was at the time the largest compensatory award in Florida history for a mesothelioma case. In 1997, he had the highest jury verdict ever in our nation for a non-malignant asbestos case. In 2002, the firm successfully persuaded the Delaware Supreme Court to weaken a law that protected large corporations from being sued more than two years after their products caused injuries to consumers. In 2004, the firm won the first-ever asbestos case against Union Carbide for its raw asbestos; and in 2008, received the largest compensatory jury verdict in Florida history for a mesothelioma case against Honeywell ($24.17 million).

Most remarkable, in 1997 Mr. Ferraro was a national finalist for "Trial Lawyer of the Year" for successfully trying the first case ever against a chemical company for causing a birth defect. In *Castillo vs. DuPont*, he proved that a pregnant woman's exposure to DuPont's fungicide, Benlate, caused her son to be born without eyes. The trial was covered on Court TV and received worldwide attention. The case involved 63 depositions in 4 different countries with 13 expert witnesses testifying from geneticists to neurotoxicologists.

Beyond the prestige Mr. Ferraro and The Ferraro Law Firm have earned in the legal profession, he is recognized as an outstanding community partner and leader. Mr. Ferraro is a Trustee of the William J. Clinton Presidential Foundation. He serves on boards of key nonprofits in the Miami area and has contributed millions of dollars to various charities in South Florida including: Make-A-Wish Foundation, the Miami Project To Cure Paralysis, Jackson Memorial Hospital and the Children's Home Society, among others.

James Ferraro and The Ferraro Law Firm: *far more than just another attorney or law firm in the legal industry.*

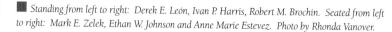

Standing from left to right: Derek E. León, Ivan P. Harris, Robert M. Brochin. Seated from left to right: Mark E. Zelek, Ethan W. Johnson and Anne Marie Estevez. Photo by Rhonda Vanover.

MORGAN, LEWIS & BOCKIUS LLP

Client-Focused Culture and Global Legal Talent Propel Award-Winning Law Firm

In 2007, as Morgan, Lewis & Bockius LLP celebrated its 30th anniversary in Miami, the firm also celebrated the longest, most distinguished track record of any national law firm in the city. Founded in 1873 in Philadelphia to represent corporate clients, and today one of the largest U.S. law firms, Morgan Lewis recognized Miami as a gateway for global business in 1977 and opened a local office.

Key to the longevity and success of the Miami office has been its vision of deliberate, strategic growth. As Morgan Lewis vaulted to 22 offices with 1,400 attorneys worldwide, it built its 30-attorney Miami presence incrementally in the same practice areas in which it was prominent nationally. Seamless teamwork among the firm's offices gives its Miami lawyers a decisive edge.

Partners in Morgan Lewis's complex commercial litigation, securities, and labor and employment practices excel in summarily defeating civil class and collective actions brought against Fortune 500 companies, saving clients the cost and strain of high-profile litigation. Office partners also handle high-powered transactions in real estate law and advise top investment management clients.

One of Morgan Lewis's greatest distinctions is the global firepower its attorneys can tap as members of *The American Lawyer* magazine's 2006-2008 "Labor & Employment Litigation Department of the Year." Both the firm's national and

Miami-based labor and employment practices routinely receive top-tier rankings from *Chambers*.

The Miami office also serves as the firm's portal to Latin America, counseling U.S. companies on diverse Latin American labor laws. Similarly, Miami attorneys helped organize, and still support, the South Florida Group of Regional Counsel, a professional association for in-house counsel to multinationals with regional headquarters in Miami. And, a Morgan Lewis attorney spearheaded a joint venture between the American Arbitration Association and the Inter-American Bar Association to make Miami a headquarters for international commercial arbitration.

Morgan Lewis also supports and reflects the vibrant diversity of Miami. Firm partners have mentored female and minority attorneys to federal court clerkships, and a Morgan Lewis alumna is Miami's first female African American District Court of Appeals judge. Other Morgan Lewis Miami attorneys and alumni have distinguished themselves in public service as former Chairman of the National Labor Relations Board, Florida Inspector General, Deputy General Counsel to the Governor, and Speaker of the Florida House of Representatives.

Also key to Morgan Lewis's continuing success in Miami is its commitment to civic leadership and community service. In 2007, a Miami Morgan Lewis partner helped found LegalLine of Miami-Dade, the region's only free legal help-line. Miami attorneys mentor inner city elementary students and have served on the boards of the Greater Miami Chamber of Commerce, Greater Miami Society for Human Resource Management, The Education Fund, Hands on Miami, and have won the Put Something Back Pro Bono Service Award of the Dade County Bar Association.

ZUMPANO PATRICIOS & WINKER, P.A.

Zumpano Patricios & Winker, P.A. is a hometown firm with a global perspective.

Like Miami, ZP&W is dynamic, multi-lingual and multi-cultural. Founded by Joseph Zumpano, Leon Patricios and David Winker, the law firm has expanded to 50 attorneys with locations in eleven foreign countries, including Freeport and Nassau, The Bahamas; Sao Paulo, Brazil; Santiago, Chile; San Jose and Quepos, Costa Rica; Santiago, Dominican Republic; Bremen and Frankfurt, Germany; Milan and Pesaro, Italy; Mexico City, Mexico; Panama City, Panama; Madrid, Spain and Buenos Aires, Argentina.

ZP&W has attracted top talent both in the U.S. and abroad, under a theory which numerous publications have dubbed "New Globalism." New Globalism is based on the theory that a business enterprise looking to participate in the international market can redefine its target market as the stream of commerce between nations. This business model seeks to prevent the conflict and inefficiency caused when law firms seek to remove market share from other law firms in foreign markets. New Globalism is implemented via foreign satellite offices operating through ZP&W Attorney Coordinators located inside prominent foreign law firms. ZP&W and the foreign law firms regularly co-counsel matters to provide added efficiency and value through the integrated participation of both law firms.

ZP&W is focused on the delivery of high impact legal services and has been involved in numerous significant cases.

In 2004, ZP&W attorneys Joseph Zumpano and Leon Patricios obtained an $86.5 million judgment against Fidel Castro, Raul Castro, the Army of Cuba, and the Republic of Cuba. ZP&W represented Janet Weininger, the daughter of CIA Pilot Pete Ray, who was shot down over Cuba during the Bay of Pigs Invasion and was later ordered executed by Fidel Castro. Joseph Zumpano assembled and led the legal team that in 2006 collected more than $23.7 million on the judgment.

ZP&W is proud of its South Florida heritage and its members are grateful for the myriad opportunities for business and recreation in Miami. The firm's attorneys are down-to-earth and passionate about Miami and its prominent role in international commerce. True to the entrepreneurial spirit of its founders, ZP&W has from its beginning used profits from the firm to invest in waterfront property that attorneys and staff members of the firm are encouraged to use. The members of ZP&W practice law together, enjoy South Florida together, and live life to its fullest.

CIA Pilot Pete Ray was shot down over Cuba during the Bay of Pigs Invasion and was later ordered executed by Fidel Castro.

KANE & COMPANY, P.A.

From his Brickell Avenue office, Monte Kane has watched Miami literally grow right outside his window.

The accounting firm he founded in 1990, Kane & Company, P.A., has also grown, from one of Miami's premier regional accounting and consulting firms to a sizeable company with offices in Boca Raton, Orlando, and Las Vegas.

Kane, who began his career in 1972 with an international CPA firm, founded accounting firm Kane & Company, P.A., on the principles of personalized service and connection. The company was originally called Monte Kane & Associates. It merged with another company for five years before evolving into its current incarnation in 2003.

One thing that has never changed is helping clients achieve their life goals. The key is to both listen to what the clients are saying, and to push them, delicately, toward the cutting edge of their profession.

Kane & Company has become well known for their expertise in a wide diversity of areas, including health care, entertainment, hospitality, real estate and condominiums, legal and other service professionals, as well as litigation support and forensic accounting services. The firm also provides full audit and tax services in addition to financial planning and trust and estate services. Kane & Company is a member of AGN International, a prestigious worldwide association of separate and independent accounting and consulting firms throughout the world.

Kane's model for success has been to focus his energies on attracting top quality accountants who share his service-oriented philosophy. To that end, Kane spent years refining the art of keeping his staff happy. He offers excellent benefits, a supportive work environment, and lots of extras, such as gym memberships, PDAs, and a high degree of autonomy.

That personal touch translates directly into CPAs who make clients their first priority. Each client, no matter how large or small, is treated as if they are the only client the firm has. The feel of being coddled by a boutique firm is aided by Kane's enthusiastic embrace of the latest technology, aimed at creating a nearly paperless work flow and highly responsive client handling.

That sensibility made a natural leap in 2007, when Kane & Company launched Kane Technology Advisors, LLC, to offer clients a suite of information technology services, such as a support call center, site relocation, and network implementation.

Kane & Company has been widely recognized in its field. The firm was named among the South Florida Business Journal's largest Accounting Firms in 2004. Kane himself was also listed as a 2004 Heavy Hitter in Finance and one of 2004's Excellence in Accounting Honorees. In 2006, the publication honored Kane again by naming him a Key Partner, an award reserved for South Florida's leading legal and accounting professionals.

■ *Monte Kane, Kane & Company, P.A., Managing Director*

Besides his duties as managing director of Kane & Company, Monte Kane has been active both in his

■ *Firm Directors: Monte Kane, Jeffrey L. Ducker, Laurie Baad, Carl Gadinsky, Candido Fernandez*

profession and in the community. He has served on the Board of Governors of the Florida Institute of CPAs and is past president of its Dade County Chapter. Kane co-authored the American Institute of Certified Public Accountants (AICPA) influential Accounting and Audit Guide for Common Interest Realty Associations.

Kane serves on the elder care committee and condominium section committee of the Florida Institute of CPAs and is Vice President and Trustee of the FICPA Educational Foundation. He also frequently lectures about continuing education for CPAs in the areas of accounting, taxation, and consulting services.

Kane's schedule of community work is just as daunting.

He also encourages every member of his staff to be involved in the community. Kane has donated time and money to a number of non-profit organizations and has served on the Board of Directors of several. He is one of the founders and currently co-chairs the Florida Institute of CPAs 1040K Run and Fitness Walk, which awarded more than 40 scholarships and thousands of dollars in the last 15 years. He is a past treasurer of the South Florida Multiple Sclerosis Society. In 2005, he was appointed to the Board of Directors of Biscayne Bank.

Kane & Company's founder is not complacent with these successes, however. Kane is constantly working on his vision for the accounting firm of the future. No doubt whatever that future holds, the company will keep pace with Miami's growth.

FUERST, HUMPHREY, ITTLEMAN

Fuerst Humphrey Ittleman is a Miami-based law firm that has quickly become an international success story by providing specialized legal services to businesses near and far.

These services have grown to be in high demand as a result of what has been occurring historically for decades in South Florida: a transformation of the greater Miami area into a Mecca for worldwide trade and commerce.

Founded by Attorneys Mitchell S. Fuerst, Christine Humphrey and Andrew S. Ittleman, the firm takes pride in serving a growing portfolio of international clients: companies and business individuals in need of legal counsel related to U.S. trade policies in the global marketplace. This thriving practice's success stems not only from clients' appreciation of the firm's outstanding international legal expertise, but also for the way FHI conducts business. It's a philosophy built on teamwork and always an unwavering commitment to excellence, efficiency and effectiveness.

In implementing this formula, FHI has discovered a unique ability to nurture responsive and proactive relationships with its clientele. The result has been long-

■ *FHI's Founders: Attorneys Mitchell S. Fuerst, left, Christine Humphrey and Andrew S. Ittleman*

lasting relationships with those it has served; along with building a distinguished client portfolio featuring some of the most "international elite" companies in the business world.

What further enhances these relationships and the firm's track record for success is instituting a team approach to doing business. Everyone in the company is considered an integral part of the business including the support staff that help to make it possible for FHI to maintain its high standards of excellence.

■ Under the leadership of Mitchell S. Fuerst, Esq., Managing Partner, FHI is building its business through teamwork and an unwavering commitment to excellence, efficiency and effectiveness.

And FHI hasn't stopped there. The team concept is also utilized in the practice by having attorneys pool their know-how and experience together with that of the client. FHI has found with everyone working in unison, problem-solving strategies develop, producing an optimal resolution. A further benefit: it saves time and money.

A Distinct Presence In The Global Legal Marketplace

Fuerst Humphrey Ittleman intentionally limits its international practice to certain specialty areas of the law. In doing so, the firm is able to deliver the highest level of professional service in these areas, further enhancing its presence in the global marketplace. The main areas of FHI's specialized practice are: Tax Planning and Litigation; Food, Drug and Cosmetic Law Compliance; Complex Litigation; Customs, Import and Trade Law; Anti-Money Laundering; and White Collar Defense.

- Tax Planning & Tax Litigation work is headed up by Mitchell S. Fuerst, Esq. and covers all aspects of taxation

issues, especially proactive business planning, where tax implications are paramount.

- Food, Drug & Cosmetic Law under the supervision of Christine M. Humphrey, Esq., focuses on personalized, one-on-one relationships with each corporate client; creative and pro-active problem-solving with every client; and the best possible assistance and follow-up in implementing solutions.

- Complex Litigation is commonplace in international commerce and requires experience and skill particularly when laws and forums of several countries must be considered and weighed. FHI has proven to excel in meeting such challenges in and out of the courtroom in reaching satisfactory resolution.

- Customs, Import & Trade Law are extremely important in the global marketplace. Having legal counsel in negotiating with U.S. Customs, Border Patrol and Immigration and Custom Enforcement Services is imperative. FHI attorneys have demonstrated time and again they know how to grasp not only the complexities of commercialized globalization, but understand the multi-faceted impact of trade regulation.

- Anti-Money Laundering legislation passed by the U.S. government since September 11, 2001 and the Bank Secrecy Act (AML-BSA) have become a major focus of both U.S. and foreign bank regulators and financial leaders alike. Under the leadership of Andrew S. Ittleman, Esq., a certified Anti-Money Laundering specialist, FHI has developed a strong presence in providing legal counsel to businesses working to meet compliance by U.S. regulatory agencies.

- White Collar Defense, also headed up by Andrew S. Ittleman, Esq., FHI is earning a reputation for providing excellent legal counsel for those involved in complex Civic and White Collar Litigation.

As Fuerst Humphrey Ittleman continues to span the globe providing its unique brand of legal services, there will obviously be change. But present and future clients can be rest assured, the firm's formula for doing business will remain unchanged. It will always be about providing counsel with a strong focus on teamwork and an unwavering commitment to excellence, efficiency and effectiveness…wherever its clientele are in the world.

HALL LAMB AND HALL, P.A.

Miami attorney Andrew C. Hall formed Hall, Lamb and Hall, P.A. in 1975, shortly after defending John D. Ehrlichman, President Richard Nixon's former senior advisor for domestic affairs, in the Watergate trials.

Since then, Hall has earned a reputation for success representing several high-profile individuals, organizations and corporations nationally and in South Florida. On several occasions, his work has sparked changes to the law, earning him the nickname "David," to the government's "Goliath."

Hall got a taste of what it's like to stand up to government at the age of 24. He represented his brother, Allan Hall, in a case that went to the Florida Supreme Court. There, he successfully argued that real estate agents had a constitutional right to keep their state-issued licenses, regardless of the state in which they lived. That success protected brokers when they moved and Hall's reputation as a champion for civil rights began to take shape.

Hall's next case that changed the law was in 1972. Hall successfully represented landlords in their efforts to prevent rent control for apartments in Miami Beach, arguing that such a policy conflicted with state law. In 1979, he represented homeowners residing on Miami Beach's prestigious Hibiscus, Star, and Palm islands in their winning quest to thwart the development of a Coney Island-type of amusement park on nearby Watson Island.

Throughout the 1980s, Hall handled a variety of matters, ranging from the defense of former Ambassador Marvin L. Warner in various cases as a result of the failure of Ohio's state-insured savings and loan industry, to the representation of the Miami-based Burger King Corporation in litigation against franchisees.

The final decade of the twentieth century saw Hall embark on a new venture: representing American victims of terrorism in their lawsuits against sovereign nations that sponsor terrorist activities. In 1992, he took on the case of a former American soldier who was kidnapped and tortured by Iraqi soldiers seeking nuclear codes. In response to these atrocities, Hall brought a lawsuit against Iraq. The case was dismissed in the U.S. federal court, which claimed Iraq was protected by sovereign immunity. But Hall – never one to back down – persevered and the law was changed. Eleven years later, after going toe-to-toe with the judicial system, the White House and the U.S. State Department, Hall won the case and the soldier received full compensation.

The Iraq case led to the passage of laws that enabled victims of terrorism to recover damages from a foreign sovereign state that sponsors terrorism.

■ Formed by Andrew Hall in 1975, Miami, Florida-based Hall, Lamb and Hall, P.A. handles matters involving complex corporate and business litigation, including securities, intellectual property, employment, real estate, professional malpractice cases and family law cases.

Under that law, Hall sued and recovered money for victims of terrorism against Libya and Iraq. In 2002 Hall lobbied Congress for a new change in the law that further insured that judgments were paid. In 2007, Hall successfully represented the families of U.S. sailors who died in the USS Cole terrorist attack and recovered a multi-million dollar award from the government of Sudan for its sponsorship of Al Qaeda.

In 2008, Hall successfully represented the Coral Gables-based Dr. John T. Macdonald Foundation in a multi-million dollar trust dispute against Baptist Health South Florida. This year, Hall also won a million dollar case against Fisher Island, widely recognized as the wealthiest community in America, on behalf of a resident of the private community. Hall also successfully resolved a twelve year court fight for a doctor who had been blacklisted from employment by the cruise industry because the doctor refused to falsify medical records. Finally, in 2008, Mr. Hall negotiated a million-dollar wrongful death settlement on behalf of a woman who died

as a result of the refusal of a Miami-area retirement home to provide medical care.

It goes without saying that Andrew Hall has left an imprint on South Florida.

Much of this success derives from the unmatched perseverance he has demonstrated throughout his career. This determination may be a product of his upbringing. Born in Warsaw, Poland in 1944 while his Jewish parents hid from the Nazi occupiers, Hall has always sought opportunities to stand up to oppression and abuse of power. It's a guiding principle that he still carries with him today, more than 60 years later.

When Hall's father relocated his family to Miami Beach in 1952, the city was "a sleepy little southern town," as Hall describes it. Today, South Florida is a thriving metropolis. Throughout this period of unprecedented growth, Andrew Hall's commitment to fighting for justice on behalf of his neighbors has remained an invaluable constant.

VICTORIA & ASSOCIATES CAREER SERVICES

Victoria E. Villalba considers herself one of the blessed ones; she has a real passion for her work, which has made her business a success.

When she founded Victoria & Associates Career Services in 1992, Villalba was a former temporary worker who saw an opportunity in the cruise line industry and never looked back.

A Miami native, Villalba went to work for Eastern Airlines after graduating college. The airline went out of business shortly thereafter, so Villalba went to work for a staffing company. It was there she learned to love the industry she would call her own.

Victoria & Associates got its start as an on-site vendor handling Royal Caribbean Cruise Line's temporary staffing needs. From her desk at RCCL, Villalba was able to grow her business to the point of expansion. She opened a second office in the Doral area and another in Broward.

Since that humble start, Victoria & Associates has diversified and maintains clients in a variety of industries including insurance, cruise lines, mortgage companies, financial institutions, accounting firms and health care. Numerous Fortune 500 companies use the services of Victoria & Associates because of the care given to matching the right person for each job. The company specializes in direct hire, temp to hire and temporary placement at all levels, from the mailroom to the board room. Victoria & Associates prides itself on the depth of its workforce and contract employees and places hundreds of people in jobs every week. The dedication of the Victoria & Associates team is paramount to the success of the organization itself.

Villalba's success may be attributed in part to the support of her family, her exemplary work ethic, but credit must also be given to her commitment to the community. In addition to her membership in a multitude of South Florida business and service organizations, Villalba sits on the board of directors of Baptist Hospital, Coral Gables Chamber of Commerce and His House Children's Home. She is the recipient of many awards and accolades, including the Greater Miami Chamber of Commerce "Minority Business of the Year Award", "America's Promise for Youth Good Hands Award" presented by Colin Powell, "Inc. 5,000" list of top businesses in the country and the FIU Commonwealth Institute's "Top 50 Women-Led Businesses in Florida", to name a few.

Passionate about recruiting, Villalba plans to expand Victoria & Associates and open offices around the state and perhaps franchises. After placing tens of thousands of workers in South Florida alone, the future looks bright for all the others who will benefit from the work of this home-grown staffing company.

BCI's Ponce de Leon office is strategically located in the heart of the Coral Gables business district.

BUSINESS CENTERS INTERNATIONAL

Business Centers International is Miami's premier workspace solution. The company is the brainchild of CEO Carolina Rendeiro, who started the business in Houston in 1986, and moved it to Miami in 2001

Rendeiro, with 30 years experience running business centers, has taken an innovative approach to providing a well-equipped executive business environment tailored to meet the needs of local, national, and international businesses.

Furnished offices are provided, complete with staff who can speak English, Spanish, and Portuguese, integrated voice IP, video conferencing, conference rooms, and other customizable services. BCI has 122 office spaces in two locations, on Brickell Avenue and in Coral Gables.

The offices at BCI are not only full-service; they are much more chic than the typical office. For instance, the Coral Gables office also functions as an art gallery, displaying the work of artist Carlos Navarro in the hallways, as well as small paintings and drawings from University of Miami art students. Everything is for sale, so the collection is always fresh.

BCI doesn't advertise or market in the traditional sense. Instead, Rendeiro lets her community involvement speak for itself. Rendeiro is the incoming chairwoman of the Coral Gables Chamber of Commerce, treasurer of the Historical Museum of South Florida, a trustee member of both the Greater Miami Chamber of Commerce and the Beacon Council, board member of the Rhythm Foundation, and second vice president of the Miami Council for International Visitors, among many other affiliations.

Many companies in transition – from start-ups to those that are downsizing -- find BCI's virtual office plan the perfect fit for their needs. In addition, many international companies require Miami offices to effectively interface between the United States or Europe, and Latin America. A majority of BCI's clients fall into this category, including divisions of Adobe, Time Warner, Microsoft, and BBC Worldwide. Still other companies use BCI as an emergency management backup during hurricanes.

Business Centers International also partners with centers in other countries for the convenience of clients. Rendeiro also plans to expand BCI directly into Costa Rica in the near future. Rendeiro has embraced the truly international nature of Miami's business climate, which she describes as "working global on a local level."

Business Centers International founder and CEO is Carolina Rendeiro.

BCI's Brickell office is located in the Espirito Santo Plaza, downtown Miami's premier 35-story office tower, condominium and luxury hotel. Its ultra-modern and imposing design has already made it a well-known Miami landmark.

ASSOCIATED PHOTO & IMAGING

Associated Photo & Imaging President Larry Apple is a storyteller by nature, something of a family trait.

That's a good quality to have in the "a picture is worth a thousand words" business. In its 60-year history, the company has told the story of Miami through countless photographs, and in the process transformed itself from a small family photography shop to Miami's premier commercial imaging company. Associated Photo & Imaging was founded by Arthur "Art" Apple in 1946. The senior Apple had served as a member of a photo reconnaissance team for the Army during World War II. President Franklin Roosevelt's son Elliott was the head of Apple's platoon and later hired him to be the photographer at his wedding.

When Apple got back from the war, he founded Associated Photo & Imaging, and became a commercial photographer specializing in South Florida hotels. As a result, Apple captured the '50s and '60s boom, during

■ *Donna Karan New York, DKNY Red Delicious*
San Juan, Puerto Rico

which many South Florida landmarks were built, including the Imperial Hotel, the Fontainebleau Hotel and Joe's Stone Crabs. Joe's still has some of Apple's photos on display today. Art also did product photography for well-known legacy companies in Miami including Burdines (now Macy's) and the original Burger King restaurant.

Larry Apple remembers the family restaurant from which Burger King originated. It was called McLamore's and was located on Brickell Avenue. When James McLamore and his partner David Edgerton opened the first fast-food burger joints in Miami in the 1950s, they hired Associated Photo & Imaging to do the food photography. "My Dad took pictures of the original Whopper," Apple recalls.

Apple has a hundred similar stories about Miami's imaging history, and the part that Associated Photo & Imaging has played. Tragically, a massive hurricane in the 1960s destroyed most of the film negatives from Associated Photo's extensive work in the previous two decades. But out of this loss, positive changes emerged as the business began to take a new direction toward becoming a commercial

■ *Davidoff, Cool Water Deep*
New York City

photo printer rather than a photo shop.

During the 70s, photographic technological advances produced innovations such as roller transport processing. Apple bought one of the first processors. In the early 80s, Larry Apple, who had spent 13 years in the book publishing industry, rising to become Editor-in-Chief of one of New York's premier publishing companies, returned to Miami to take over the company from his father.

Larry Apple brought with him the famous New York urban work ethic and the goal of molding Associated Photo & Imaging into a company that could compete with the best New York firms. His arrival came just as Miami was steadily becoming more cosmopolitan, and attracting international advertising agencies.

Apple's emphasis on teamwork, professionalism, and quality earned the company loyal clients such as Chanel, Celebrity Cruises, the Florida Marlins, Macy's/Federated, Norwegian Cruise Lines, Proctor & Gamble, Miami Dolphins, The Related Group, Fortune Realty, Miami Children's Museum, Royal Caribbean Cruise Lines, Miami International Airport, Bijoux Terner, and Givenchy.

Another hallmark of Associated Photo & Imaging is its

dedication to investing in the latest technology to produce the highest quality results. The company evolved from solely commercial photography to digital imaging and visual merchandising including high-end, large-format reproductions and museum quality imaging.

The digital revolution in photo imaging came in the early '90s, forcing rapid changes into the industry and requiring a large investment from Associated Photo & Imaging. Those changes have continued to accelerate. In 2006, the company purchased a state-of-the-art digital Durst Rho 205 Large-Format Flatbed UV inkjet printer and is positioned for further innovations and services.

Another challenge is managing the company's success. After 60 years in the same downtown location by the Miami River, Apple had the nice problem of having to find a larger space for his burgeoning business.

Meanwhile, the Apple family, which has been in Miami since the 1930s, continues to be an active part of the community. Larry Apple is on the Community Advisory Board for Miami's Design and Architecture Senior High School (DASH), the Board of Directors for the Association of Imaging Executives (AIE), and was a founding Board Member for the Miami International Book Fair.

"We're part of Miami's history and we're proud of that," says Apple. "We love the idea that we'll continue to be a part of Miami's growing imaging future."

McKinley Financial Services

For Jim McKinley, the skills used to grow a successful business were the same tools he used from his first career as a championship college and professional football coach.

tilizing a mix of teamwork, a philosophy that incorporated staying ahead of the game, and taking on the toughest of opponents helped propel McKinley Financial Services from a one-man company to one of the largest minority-owned insurance agencies in the United States.

Headquartered in Fort Lauderdale and incorporated in 1987, McKinley Financial Services provides insurance to companies and public institutions as well as individuals. With access to more than 100 different insurance carriers, the insurance broker has the ability to provide a variety of products including life and health insurance, pension plans, group benefits, commercial property and casualty, sports activities and events coverage, athletic coverage, student accident and sickness policies, and is also proud of its large charitable gifts program.

McKinley's response and dedication has earned the respect and trust of some of the most recognizable government entities in South Florida. The diverse customer base includes Broward County Government, Broward County School Board, Broward Sheriff's Office, the North and South Broward hospital districts, the state of Florida, the Tri-County Community Rail Authority, and the South Florida Super Bowl Host Committee, to name a few.

Jim McKinley never expected to have a second career running a company that now serves more than 400,000 individuals, with a dedicated team of more than 50 agents, brokers and customer-service personnel. Originally from

Kalamazoo, Mich., McKinley retired to South Florida after 22 years in the world of college and professional sports. His idea was to sell insurance to supplement his retirement. But with McKinley's winning attitude and perseverance, the company took off and continues to grow. Recently, the company began to expand its reach from the Southeast to include servicing Fortune 500 companies throughout the United States.

But McKinley's allegiance remains in South Florida, and to a community that helped him build a successful company beyond his dreams. McKinley Financial Foundation helps to build Broward County's future with its scholar athlete award, a four-day Big 8 basketball tournament for young athletes, and an annual scholarship awarded to a student who shows an interest in a career in public administration.

From serving a variety of clients to community involvement, it's all part of the McKinley mission of "service is our specialty," ready to serve anytime, anywhere and any place.

McKinley Financial Services, based in Fort Lauderdale, is one of the largest minority-owned insurance agencies in the United States.

HARVEY BILT PHOTOGRAPHY

Since 1983, Harvey Bilt Photography has more or less been Miami's unofficial photographer.

Ensconced in his offices at the Intercontinental Hotel in downtown Miami, Bilt has been there, camera poised, to capture some of the city's most memorable moments.

Nearly every notable who has ever set foot in Miami has been photographed by Harvey Bilt. The Queen of England, the Pope, several presidents of the United States, and various heads of state from around the world have been captured in his lens.

But Bilt's bread and butter is corporate photography. He shoots conventions, workshops, summits, and cruises. Widely known for his attention to detail and extreme efficiency, Bilt also specializes in making retail products stand out in photographs used for marketing and advertising. Whether the product is a watch, a clothing line, or just about anything that can be sold, Bilt has a knack for making it look good on paper. The key is anticipating a client's needs and planning far in advance so the process appears effortless.

Bilt, originally from New York, came to Miami after spending 12 years running a photography business in Freeport, Bahamas. When he first arrived in Miami, he worked out of the Four Ambassadors in downtown Miami, before making a permanent move to the iconic Intercontinental Hotel, scene of such international events as the Free Trade Area of the Americas conference in 2003.

Bilt's clients have included Pan American World Airways, the legendary airline once based out of today's Miami City Hall in Coconut Grove. He also spent seven years shooting theater productions for the Coconut Grove Playhouse.

Bilt's success can be traced to his work ethic and his policy of returning his fee if any customer is unhappy with his work. So far, he hasn't had any takers. And that's all part of the plan.

Vicki L. Smith-Bilt, Business Director, Greenberg Traurig

Randy G. DeFrehn, Executive Director-NCCMP

A GREAT PLACE TO LIVE AND WORK

EW WHO SPEND EVEN ONE NIGHT IN MIAMI CAN DENY THERE'S SOMETHING SPECIAL HERE. MAYBE IT'S IN THE WARM TRADE WINDS, OR THE AROMAS OF FLAVORFUL CUISINES, OR THE FAINT NOTES OF A MELODY THAT EMERGE AND RECEDE. ELUSIVE THOUGH THAT SOMETHING MAY BE, PEOPLE THE WORLD OVER APPEAR TO HAVE FOUND ITS ALLURE IRRESISTIBLE AND NOW CALL OUR CITY HOME.

Or maybe their decision has less to do with intangibles than with a very real sense of the opportunities that beacon. For decades, people of diverse backgrounds have chosen Miami as their adopted home in increasing numbers; the tenacity and creativity with which they have rebuilt their lives lend a rare dynamism and entrepreneurial mindset to our workforce. It is our distinctive position as the Western Hemisphere's gateway between North and South which has created this hothouse atmosphere, nourishing an economy and culture whose reach is felt globally.

Companies wishing to expand into Latin America base themselves in Miami not only for proximity, but to take advantage of this unique business environment as well as a cultural vibrancy and vacation-worthy climate. Meanwhile, their counterparts from Latin America do likewise to house North American operations. Together, these businesses provide the motivation and sustenance fueling the growth of enterprises which facilitate trade, legal and financial transactions, real estate development, education and countless services. They have flourished despite strong international competition and grow agile by tapping into the strong work ethic of their associates, whose warmth and creativity underscores their willingness to try new approaches and meet new challenges.

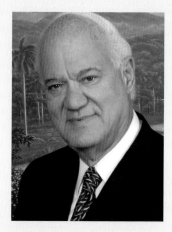

GEORGE FELDENKREIS
Chairman and CEO
Perry Ellis International

Himself a beneficiary of Miami's fertile business atmosphere, George Feldenkreis arrived here in 1961 after fleeing Fidel Castro's Cuba with only $700 in his pocket. His subsequent creation of Perry Ellis International, a leading fashion company with over 30 influential brands distributed throughout more than 50 countries, is a true American success story.

Marketplace

RYDER SYSTEM, INC.   466

BACARDI   470

BADIA SPICES   472

DEL MONTE FRESH PRODUCE NORTH AMERICA   474

ROWLAND COFFEE ROASTERS   476

MERCEDES-BENZ OF CORAL GABLES   478
MERCEDES-BENZ OF CUTLER BAY

BRICKELL MOTORS   480

FAIRCHILD TROPICAL BOTANIC GARDENS   484

FLAGER DOG TRACK   485

MIAMI CHILDREN'S MUSEUM   486

OLYMPIA THEATER AT GUSMAN CENTER   487

MIAMI SCIENCE MUSEUM   488

PERRY ELLIS INTERNATIONAL   490

RCI GROUP   492

THE OCEANAIRE SEAFOOD ROOM   494

NEWS CAFÉ   496

MIAMI RIVER INN   498

WOMETCO ENTERPRISES   499

THE RUSTY PELICAN   500

To set foot in Miami is to bridge multiple divides:
North and South, domestic and international, heritage
and invention. Far greater than the sum of its parts, the
city's inimitable character is born from a vital fusion of
perspectives and interests, giving rise to a worldwide
reputation which tantalizes with promises of prosperity,
excitement and homecoming.

RYDER SYSTEM, INC.

Whether a product travels by plane, ship or train, it eventually ends up being loaded onto a truck for delivery to its final destination. Jim Ryder knew that, but he had a bigger vision of a company that would integrate all forms of transportation.

Today, Ryder's vision of transportation and supply chain management solutions is an integral behind-the-scenes element of everyday life, helping many of the most significant brands in every industry. More than half of Ryder's business is in its Fleet Management Solutions area, providing trucks, tractor-trailers and other vehicles typically painted with the colors and brands of thousands of commercial customers in the United States, Canada, and the United Kingdom. Another segment of the company's business is Dedicated Contract Carriage, which provides transport equipment and drivers who wear the customers' uniforms and are dedicated to a specific Ryder customer. The Supply Chain Solutions segment provides logistical engineering, management, hands-on operational support and innovative technologies to orchestrate the efficient movement of materials, components and finished goods from parts suppliers, to manufacturing plants, to warehouses, and finally to end users.

A painting that hangs in Ryder's headquarters, commissioned by founder Jim Ryder more than a half century ago, shows how he envisioned a system that would integrate all forms of transportation to efficiently serve the needs of business. It depicts the "Ryder System" – an interrelated system of trucks, ships, trains, planes and warehouses, supported by innovative technology meeting the demands of business. The vision wasn't far off; his futuristic concept is now an essential element of the global sourcing and production of goods.

While Jim Ryder dreamed big, he started small. He began his business during the midst of the Great Depression. Just 19 years old, he quit his job as a 25-cent-an-hour laborer hoping

Jim Ryder is shown wearing two watches, a way to remind customers of his commitment to on-time deliveries.

to earn an extra 10 cents an hour by hauling concrete blocks to construction sites in Miami Beach. In 1933, he bought a used 1931 Ford Model A truck for $35. He figured that if he stacked the blocks a certain way, he could deliver more blocks than others performing the same service. By employing a high-school classmate to share the driving duties, he was able to keep the truck running 22 hours a day hauling the blocks.

A photo of Jim Ryder taken in those early days shows the hard-working entrepreneur wearing two watches, one on each arm. A conversation starter, it was a way to remind customers of his commitment to on-time deliveries.

In 1934, Ryder bought his second truck, a new Ford V-8, doubling the size of his fleet. Within four years, he secured a five-year lease deal with a Miami beverage distributor of

Champagne Velvet Beer, increasing the fleet to 20 trucks. By the following year, the fleet would rise to more than 50. During World War II, the company's services proved to be significant to the growing needs of a nation at war. Local military bases expanded and an Air Corps Training Command was established in Miami Beach. Ryder trucks were used by the U.S. Government to transport supplies for more than 500,000 soldiers through the end of the war. Of course, the fleet grew again, making it necessary for Ryder Truck to open its first outsourced warehouse. Throughout the 1940s, revenue rose from under $100,000 to more than $1 million.

▪ *During World War II, Ryder trucks were used by the United States government to transport supplies to more than 500,000 soldiers stationed in South Florida.*

In 1945, Ryder landed its longest-standing customer and moved into a segment of its business that would solidify the future of the company and propel it to leadership status in the transportation field. Ryder provided a dedicated fleet and drivers for daily distribution of *The Miami Herald*. The two companies continue to work together today.

One of the most defining eras for Ryder came soon after when, in the 1950s, the company made history after it loaded trailers of cargo onto railroad flatcars for the first "piggyback" operation in the southeastern United States. By doing this, Ryder created one of the first transportation logistics solutions. In 1955, the company was incorporated as Ryder System, Inc. and issued 160,000 shares of common stock over-the-counter at $10 per share.

The firsts at Ryder continued at a rapid pace. In 1960, Ryder began to establish its brand at the national level when it began trading on the New York Stock Exchange. In 1968, it introduced itself to the consumer market with its familiar yellow "One-Way" truck rental business to target self-move

customers. In 1969, Beverly Nannenga became Ryder's first female driver. In 1971, the company expanded its truck leasing and rental offering to the United Kingdom.

For 45 years, Jim Ryder guided his company, never forgetting the humble beginnings that drove him to be a life-long champion of the front-line employees who served the customers. Through more than seven decades of progress in an ever-changing and volatile business world, Ryder has been led by only four chief executives.

In 1975, Leslie O. Barnes, a former Allegheny Airlines executive, became chairman and chief executive officer, standardizing corporate practices and ensuring that Ryder was on a solid financial footing during a critical point in the company's history. In 1983, M. Anthony Burns took over, pioneering the company's entry into the field of logistics and supply chain management among other important milestones. During Burns' tenure, Ryder launched its Latin American operations in Mexico, Argentina, and Brazil. The company also sold its familiar yellow "One-Way" consumer rental business and rebranded its fleet with a new logo and colors to focus on its commercial customers. Currently, Greg Swienton is chairman and chief executive officer, having joined Ryder in 1999 and later taken the reins as chief executive officer in 2000 and chairman in 2002. Today, companies around the globe look to Ryder for innovative ways to gain a competitive edge through increased productivity. It has become a trusted partner to more than 15,000 customers in North America, Latin America, Asia, and Europe with more than

▪ *In 1960, Jim Ryder (left) is shown at the New York Stock Exchange when Ryder System, Inc., begins trading on the exchange.*

Ryder has more than 28,000 employees around the globe.

28,000 employees and a fleet of 165,000 trucks. Jim Ryder's pioneering spirit has created a $6.6 billion business.

It's a new era for Ryder, as the company moves forward in the 21st century. Continuing on the visionary path begun in the 1930s, it is setting the standard for tomorrow's best practices not only in transportation, but in operational efficiency, safety performance, and environmental responsibility. Many current initiatives involve the use of new technology to make Ryder's fleet more effective, cost-efficient, safer, and more environmentally friendly.

With Ryder Fleet Care technology, a web-based program that provides Ryder customers with instant access to information on the performance of their fleets through the Internet, transportation managers can analyze trends and recognize opportunities for increased efficiencies. Ryder Fleet Care displays a variety of performance metrics such as vehicle maintenance schedules, service calls, rental activity, and fuel purchases, while allowing for the customer to customize and sort reports in unique ways to analyze information by location or vehicle.

In 1996, the company changed its familiar yellow "One-Way" logo and rebranded its fleet with a new logo and colors to focus on commercial customers.

Another innovation is RydeSmart, which uses a Global Positioning System linked with computers and wireless communications to monitor a truck's whereabouts and vital statistics. RydeSmart provides business managers with real-time information to track the vehicle's location, driver performance, and odometer readings. Fuel consumption, idle time, speed and other statistics are also recorded to monitor driver performance, which also improves safety and lowers operating costs.

Due to the nature of its business, Ryder's environmental program is deeply integrated into its operations and the services it offers to customers. It is an environmental leader in everything from preventive fleet maintenance, waste reduction and storage tank management, extensive facility audits, and

RydeSmart provides real-time information to track a vehicle's location, driver performance, system diagnostics and odometer readings.

overall environmental performance throughout a customer's entire supply chain. Ryder is also in the forefront of delivering reduced carbon emissions through its partnership with the Environmental Protection Agency's SmartWay program and with its new equipment line, RydeGreen.

But the corporation's commitment to safety and fuel conservation began long before the concepts became buzzwords. For more than a decade, Ryder has been dedicated to pro-active waste management practices with on-site and off-site recycle and reuse technologies. Furthermore, the company is closely monitoring emerging issues and opportunities related to the environment and has partnered with the EPA to promote energy efficiency and reduce greenhouse gas emissions.

Safety for its employees and all those who share the roadways is also a top priority at Ryder. In 2002, Ryder became the first transportation company to receive the National Safety Council's highest honor, the Green Cross for Safety medal. Since 1995, the company has reduced its employee injury rate by nearly 50 percent by maintaining best practices, and devising new and innovative technologies that improve safety.

While Ryder is dedicated to its customers and employees around the world, it is committed to the local community. Now a recognized global leader in transportation and

Today, Ryder has become a trusted partner to more than 15,000 customers in North America, Latin America, Asia and Europe, with a fleet of 165,000 trucks.

Ryder's Transportation Management Center manages customer freight shipments through a web-enabled network of more than 1,500 transporters of air, ground, rail and ocean cargo.

logistics, the company has made a conscious choice to keep its operations based in South Florida. Its leaders believe that the Miami area is especially compatible to a global business because of its diverse population and close proximity to airports and ports. Ryder's original headquarters was located in downtown Miami and later moved to Coconut Grove in the 1960s. In 1973, the company moved to larger facilities in Miami's Doral area. In 2005, it moved to its current, more modern and efficient Global Headquarters in northwestern Miami-Dade County.

With its roots in Miami, Ryder contributes in many ways to the citizens of South Florida. The Ryder Charitable Foundation, founded 1984, donates funds to the United Way and other causes in communities in which Ryder operates. The Ryder Trauma Center at Jackson Memorial Hospital in Miami is South Florida's only Level I trauma center and bears the Ryder name. And the Ryder Center for Supply Chain Management at Florida International University is an emerging voice that is advancing the discussion of important industrial issues such as green supply chains.

From its employees, to its customers, and the community, Ryder is a company that takes pride in its past while looking ahead to its future. *Delivering On Promises. Then. Now. On The Road Ahead.*

Ryder's Global Headquarters in Miami.

BACARDI

The story of Bacardi echoes the American dream, but with a Cuban twist.

by opening a bottling company in New York City in 1915.

Bacardi incorporated in 1919 as an LLC. Founders were Emilio Bacardí, president; Facundo Bacardí, 1st vice president; Enrique Schueg, 2nd vice president. Prohibition in the U.S., which made the consumption of alcohol illegal, went into effect eight months later. With an inventory of 60,000 cases and a law prohibiting its consumption, Schueg issued "wet stock" to shareholders. One case of Bacardi equaled one share of stock. After the disbursement of the cases, the New York bottling plant was dismantled.

American tourists discovered Cuba as a destination, where they could imbibe legally. Tourism and Bacardi prospered and the Company expanded to a larger distillery. The opening of the new facility on February 4, 1922, the Company's 50th anniversary, was cause for celebration. In fact, that celebration of the Bacardi legacy is still commemorated annually by family members and employees around the globe.

Family patriarch, and Facundo's son, Emilio was long considered Santiago de Cuba's favorite son. Over the course of his life, he established hospitals and schools, financed municipal projects including a museum and numerous parks, and enhanced the beauty of the city with monuments

xiled from Cuba, the Bacardí family had moved their assets off shore. In Miami, they embraced their new home, met with great success in business and gave back to the community in which they prospered. That rich tradition of business and philanthropy is the true essence of Bacardi.

But the Company itself had humble beginnings. Bacardi was founded in Santiago de Cuba in 1812 by Spanish immigrant Facundo Bacardí Massó, whose initial vision for the Company was as a wine merchant and importer. During the early years, the Company was in and out of a state of bankruptcy more than once. Sacrifices were made to save the Company time and again.

The story of the infamous BACARDI logo is as colorful as the tropical environment from which it emerged. In Cuban lore, the fruit bat symbolizes good health, fortune and family unity. When the first distillery was acquired in 1862, fruit bats were frequently found hanging from the rafters. Apparently, they enjoyed the fermenting molasses. The Bat was adopted as the Company logo and has proven to be the most successful Trademark in the spirits industry.

The iconic Mojito was created in 1862, the Daiquirí was created in 1898, followed by the Cuba Libre in 1900. The three cocktails were used as a marketing tool and Bacardi finally saw a profit. The family expanded the Company to Barcelona, Spain in 1910, making Bacardi Cuba's first multinational corporation. The Company followed that success

and sculptures. When he died a few months after the expansion in 1922, all shops and businesses closed and the entire city went into mourning. The esteemed family tradition of philanthropy began in Santiago and continues to this day.

Another tradition, embracing architectural landmarks, opened in 1930 with the construction of the

Enrique Schueg

Edificio Bacardi de la Habana, an Art Deco masterpiece in the Cuban capitol city. The building's mezzanine bar became a favorite of celebrities and tourists alike, who flocked to the venue to sip BACARDI drinks such as the Mojito, Daiquirí, Cuba Libre, and BACARDI Cocktail.

With the end of prohibition in 1933, Bacardi established a New York office in the Chrysler Building, another Art Deco jewel. A distillery in Puerto Rico opened in 1936. Two years later, the Company's New York office moved into another iconic building, the Empire State Building. The famed Bacardi mural, by Cuban artist Antonio Gattorno, a long-time friend of Ernest Hemmingway, was painted on-site. Entitled "Waiting For Coffee", the colorful mural depicts Cuban country life – sugar cane fields, a sugar mill, a train to bring the molasses to the distillery and guajiros [country people].

Antonio Gattorno mural titled "Waiting for Coffee"

In New York, the Company fought in court to protect its proprietary name. A restaurant owner was selling a drink called the BACARDI Cocktail, which contained no BACARDI. A year of litigation resulted in the court ruling in the Company's favor, which validated the importance of the BACARDI rum in a BACARDI Cocktail.

Prior to Castro seizing power in Cuba, Company president Pepín Bosch transferred all Bacardi assets, ownership and proprietary formulas and distribution rights out of Cuba. By the time Castro gained full control in 1959, Bacardi was protected but the Company's Cuban possessions were not. Since the unique yeast strain which had been developed by Facundo Bacardí in 1862 had already been safeguarded off shore, the rest was destroyed to prevent the Cuban government from appropriating it. The formula was safe.

The Company moved its U.S. headquarters to Miami in 1965. The headquarters on Biscayne Boulevard, designed by Cuban architect Estéban Gutierrez, quickly became a landmark in the city. The huge, exterior blue and white tile murals add to the building's iconic stature. Bacardi found the formula for success in Miami and sales tripled.

Bacardi U.S.A., Inc. corporate headquarters in Miami, Florida

Financial success led to generous philanthropic activities throughout Miami and beyond. More than $1 million was dedicated by Amalia Bacardí to the University of Miami for the Amalia Bacardí / Emilio Bacardí Chair and the Bacardí Family Foundation / Casa Bacardi. The Bacardi Heritage Foundation created the Bacardi Museum on the ground floor of the Miami headquarters. In the 1990s, the Company funded a program to teach English to 12,000 Cuban migrants, who were housed at the U.S. Naval Base in Guantanamo Bay, Cuba at the time.

Bacardi has been a family business for eight generations and is comprised of 500 family members in countries around the world. It is a global company run by a global family of employees. With the Company as the family touchstone, the Bacardi legacy will endure for generations to come.

Site of the first Bacardi distillery in Santiago de Cuba, circa 1940s

BADIA SPICES

Drive down the end of the street to the Badia Spices factory and you'll be in olfactory heaven. The smell of pepper, paprika, garlic, curry powder and cinnamon drifts through the air.

The complex, at 92,000-square-feet, includes corporate offices and a warehouse where pallets are stacked with items such as teas and seasonings that are labeled to be shipped throughout the United States, Central America and the Caribbean. Meanwhile, in another part of building, large mixers are creating the sumptuous spices, and in another area, bottles, bags, boxes, and cans are being filled to be distributed both domestically and internationally.

More than 350 products are produced, packed and shipped from the West Miami-Dade facility. Today, there are 10,000 points of sale in the United States, international markets in three continents, international distribution, and a dynamic, high-tech production line. All of this combines to position Badia as a global leader in the manufacturing and distributing of spices and other cooking products.

Joseph "Pepe" Badia heads the company, which was founded 40 years ago by his father, Jose, who supplied Miami's Hispanic grocers with basic spices and a secret family blend. The company's Mojo and Complete Seasoning blends continue to be the top sellers today.

In the early 1960s, Spanish-born Jose Badia ran a hardware store in Cuba. But in 1966 with difficulties facing the island, he left for Puerto Rico. It was there where he entered the world of spices, helping a company that sold spices to small grocery stores. Badia pondered an expansion of the

Puerto Rican venture to Miami because of the large Hispanic population there. He made his dream a reality when he moved to Miami in 1967, and began selling his own blend in small plastic bags with labels handwritten in Spanish. He found a friend in Sedano's supermarket, the Hispanic grocer, who began carrying Badia's spices. In a tiny space in Miami, Jose, his wife, Azucena, and their son, Joseph "Pepe," would hand

■ More than 350 products are produced, packed and shipped from the West Miami-Dade facility, which also houses the corporate offices.

pack spices in the evening and wake at dawn to distribute the orders to more than 30 small stores across Miami Beach.

It was Pepe who continued to expand the scope of Badia Spices, eventually distributing to 60 to 70 bodegas in Miami Beach. Varadero Supermarkets started selling Badia Spices in 1979. Winn Dixie began displaying the products in some of its stores in 1985. But it was interest from Publix supermarkets in 1989 that was the turning point for Badia Spices. The initial trial began in 100 stores; now a full 520 Publix supermarkets stock Badia products.

■ *Badia Spices uses dynamic and high-tech production equipment to maintain and keep its items fresh.*

As its sales continued to grow, so did its offerings, and demand. New items were introduced including olive oils and canned foods, such as hearts of palm and malanga, to usher in the year 2000. The following year, the company launched subcategories of its traditional favorites, including new gourmet mixes. Marinades and hot sauces, extracts, and some organic products, are now all part of the lineup. Products are packaged in everything from economy sized gallons to pails and pints, and zip locked in cellophane. Badia also supplies to large warehouse retail chains including Costco and Sam's Club, Wal-Mart and Albertsons, and companies that service the food industry. While its main strongholds in the United States are in Florida and New York, regional distributors continue to keep store shelves stocked and help make Badia a formidable competitor in mid Atlantic states, and also southern states including Texas, Tennessee, South Carolina, and Georgia. The product is also starting to be distributed throughout California.

While Badia is a growing presence around the globe, it remains loyal to Miami as the place that gave Jose Badia his start. The company uses many local firms in its business, including a Miami-based plastic container manufacturer, and a North Miami firm to create its package design and store display materials.

Badia is also environmentally conscious and is working toward converting its fleet of energy efficient distribution trucks to hybrid trucks. Already on the drawing board is a plan to have Badia's factory receiving 20 percent of its power from solar and wind. Badia is working with Florida International University to formulate the plan for the company.

While active in many community endeavors, Pepe Badia is most proud of the Badia/Publix Culinary School he established at Here's Help, a Miami-Dade County substance abuse treatment provider and facility, that features an occupational training program for its youngsters. The program is run by John "Footy" Kross, a legendary South Florida radio personality. The cooking training program, utilizing the Badia/Publix Culinary School, is one of the most successful programs at Here's Help. Pepe Badia is also a member of Florida International University's Torch Society. Badia Spices created an endowment that will provide scholarships to ten students per year indefinitely.

From Jose Badia's small kitchen to a multi-million dollar company, Badia Spices, the Soul of Cooking, stays true to its mission: to have the strongest ethnic line in the marketplace with the most competitive prices, and products that not only please consumers, but add spice to their lives.

■ *Badia products are created in Miami, then shipped from the warehouse to stores and distributors in the United States, Central America and the Caribbean.*

DEL MONTE FRESH PRODUCE NORTH AMERICA

With its familiar red label recognized around the world, Fresh Del Monte Produce Inc. isn't just a company recognized in the United States, but a way of life for consumers.

The company prides itself on its dedication to delivering products that are essential for healthy and wholesome living. The Del Monte® brand has been a symbol of quality since the now famous shield appeared in 1909. First established as California Packing Corporation (CalPak), the company processed a wide range of canned fruit and vegetables. Its early ads assured customers that it wasn't just a label, but a guarantee. Fresh Del Monte Produce markets its products worldwide under the Del Monte brand, a symbol of product quality, freshness and reliability since 1892. Furthermore, it is recognized as one of the world's leading producers, marketers and distributors of fresh fruit and fresh-cut fruit and vegetables.

Since 1996, the Del Monte team has been lead by Mr. Mohammad Abu-Ghazaleh, chairman and chief executive officer, and Mr. Hani El-Naffy, president and chief operating officer. Following the acquisition of the company, Fresh Del Monte Produce Inc. went public on NYSE trading as FDP; the company's melon program was expanded, and new global distribution centers were added in key markets. Abu-Ghazaleh and El-Naffy are dedicated to the growth of the company and in ensuring that Fresh Del Monte continues to be a significant player in the produce industry. One of the achievements the company is most proud of is the introduction of the first new pineapple variety in more than 15 years and

a current market leader, the Del Monte Gold® Extra Sweet Pineapple. The pineapple is twice as sweet and contains four times the Vitamin C of traditional varieties. The Del Monte Gold® Extra Sweet Pineapple grows to a uniform size and ripens evenly, allowing Del Monte to keep the guarantee promise to its customers. In 2004, the company acquired Del Monte Foods Europe establishing a significant new growth platform as a leading producer and distributor of prepared food in Europe, Africa and the Middle East.

At the core of its mission, the company delivers products that make an impact daily in consumer's lives, but there is also an importance placed on improving the quality of life for its employees and citizens. At sourcing and production locations where many residents are economically challenged, an emphasis is placed on social and support programs. In Africa, educational programs focus on AIDs prevention and

■ *Mohammad Abu-Ghazaleh, chairman and chief executive officer, and Hani El-Naffy, president and chief operating officer, Del Monte Fresh Produce North America.*

training. At the Costa Rica facility, recreation, education and medical programs play an integral role in the lives of workers. Every region where the company has a presence, programs are provided that address the particular challenges in that community, according to Dionysios Christou, vice president/marketing of Del Monte Fresh Produce North America.

Contributing locally to the betterment of the community is also important to the company's leaders. In South Florida, Del Monte Fresh Produce North America joins forces with non-profit organizations that provide food for individuals and families in need, including participation with hunger-relief organization Second Harvest.

As one of the cornerstones of the Miami business community, Del Monte Fresh Produce's operations have been a formidable presence in South Florida. From its shiny North America regional offices on Sevilla Avenue, its Coral Gables base positions the company to be at the epicenter of a diverse landscape. South Florida is the perfect home for Del Monte Fresh Produce North America due to its proximity to Central and Latin America and the Miami International Airport which provides access to global markets. The company has become a supplier that grows, packs, processes and distributes fresh and fresh-cut produce throughout the United States and Canada.

Fully embracing its past, the company also focuses on its future. Keeping on par with technology is a priority in order to provide consumers with fresh fruits all year 'round, no matter their location, while maintaining the integrity of the natural product. Innovations in refrigeration and transportation offers consumers a wider range of products delivered to them rather than the limitations of seasonal products. According to Christou, fresh-cut technology allows Del Monte to package and transport produce to the consumer in a fresh state. And delivering the product so that it is cosmetically appealing is of utmost importance, too.

With the trend continuing to healthier snacking on the go, Del Monte Fresh Produce North America is poised to keep pace with ever-changing consumer needs. New packaging of healthy fruit and vegetable mixes for on-the-go eating are constantly being developed by teams at Del Monte.

Steeped in legacy, Del Monte Fresh Produce North America continues to inspire and encourage consumers to lead a healthy lifestyle. As it has done for more than 100 years, the brand will continue to maintain its relationship and stay relevant to consumers. Future generations will grow to depend on Del Monte Fresh Produce North America and its healthy freshness guarantee for decades to come.

The Del Monte® brand has been a symbol of quality since the now famous shield appeared in 1909.

ROWLAND COFFEE ROASTERS

Rowland Coffee Roasters is an all-American company with strong Cuban roots.

The company started with one brand of coffee, Pilon, in Cuba in the 1860s by the Souto family. By the time Jose Angel "Pepe" Souto brought his family to Miami in 1960, the brand was by far the most popular in Cuba and commanded 85% of the market.

Miami, however, was a very different story. Pepe, always an industrious business man, found a company to roast the same blend of beans the way as it was done in Cuba. Once he was satisfied with the product, he proceeded to sell Pilon from his car, door to door. The company grew with the Cuban exile community in Miami; most were familiar with Pilon and embraced it in their new hometown. By 1967, Souto purchased the roasting plant and renamed the company.

From that humble start, Rowland Coffee Roasters flourished. Pepe's three sons, Jose Enrique, Jose Alberto and Angel L. Souto, were brought into the business as soon as they could drive. With their newly minted drivers' licenses, the sons each received a Volkswagen Beetle with which they made coffee deliveries. The sons all went on to college and to careers with top American companies; Jose Enrique was a buyer for Jordan Marsh department stores, Jose Alberto was a sales executive with Pillsbury, and Angel worked at Campbell's.

Pepe never insisted his sons join the family business, but made it clear if they ever wanted to, Rowland would be there for them. By 1975, all three sons had joined

their father in the company, which at the time had only a five-percent market share in Miami. It was the perfect opportunity to grow the business, which they did with gusto. The largest competitor was Bustelo, which had 75% of the market. Hard work and perseverance led to Rowland's success, but two other factors contributed as well.

In the late 1970s, Brazil endured a freeze, which decimated the coffee crop. Fortunately, since Rowland's

Rowland Coffee Roasters brands

■ *Café Bustelo in the Hotel Gansevoort South in Miami Beach*

Paramount to Rowland's success is the high quality of the coffee itself. The company purchases beans from around the world, including Central and South America, Vietnam and Africa. Coffee needs plenty of shade, the cool climate of a high elevation and fertile soil to thrive. The best beans, which are harvested by hand, command a hefty price and coffee made from the finest beans is coveted by coffee connoisseurs.

The key to making the highest quality coffee depends on the right blend of beans, the perfect geography to grow the beans, and the proper treatment of them. When all the right components are in place, the outcome is a sublime cup of coffee. Rowland, a $100 million company, succeeds in making sure their coffee is the finest available.

The Souto family's passion for great coffee has been passed on to yet another generation. Seven of the brothers' children are involved in the company today. The cousins have introduced a new concept, Bustelo Café, a place where people enjoy coffee and modernized Cuban-style snacks and pastries.

Family patriarch Pepe Souto, who lived to age 91, enjoyed his years in business and loved that his sons chose to join him at Rowland. He was a lucky man who left a lasting legacy and lived to see his children and grandchildren embrace his passion in the city he loved.

sales were increasing, Pepe had purchased a massive amount of coffee before the freeze. That stockpile allowed the company to compete and grow.

The 1980 Mariel boatlift, in which thousands of Cubans landed on Miami's shores, was another landmark period for Rowland. After nationalizing Pilon in 1960, the Cuban government continued to produce the brand until the 1980s. Subsequently, the Mariel refugees became instant customers of the familiar coffee when they arrived in Miami.

Indeed, the 1980s were key growth years for the company, which began the first Office Coffee Service (OCS) featuring espresso machines. Today OCS boasts 3,000 customers, mostly small businesses. At that time, Rowland also opened an office in New York to service the large Cuban community in the Northeast.

In 2000, Rowland purchased New York-based Bustelo, their most formidable competitor, and other Latin-style coffee brands including Medaglia D'Oro, Estrella, Caffee Signore, Ideal, Moke d'Oro, El Pico and Oquendo. The family moved production of all the brands to Miami in order to maintain quality control.

■ *Joey Souto, Joseph Souto, Jose E. Souto, Jose A. Souto, Angel Souto, Angel R. Souto, Nicolas Souto. Not pictured, but also part of the operations, are John Paul Souto, Jolie Souto Duenas, Ana Souto Vila.*

Bill Ussery Motors in 1954.

MERCEDES-BENZ OF CORAL GABLES MERCEDES-BENZ OF CUTLER BAY

In South Florida, Mercedes-Benz automobiles offer the perfect marriage of craftsmanship, technology, comfort, safety and luxury.

And for more than 50 years, family-owned Bill Ussery Motors, parent company of Mercedes-Benz of Coral Gables and Mercedes-Benz of Cutler Bay, has delivered the ideal combination of exceptional Mercedes-Benz sales and service.

"Since the time my grandfather established the company more than five decades ago, our customer philosophy has never changed," says Robert "Bob" Brockway, chairman and CEO of the South Florida dealership. "We follow the golden rule: treat people fairly and honestly in the same way you would want to be treated, and you will have a customer for life."

The company's tradition of service dates back to 1953, when founder Bill Ussery, opened the dealership, initially selling used cars and Studebakers. A few years later, Ussery took a chance, added the Mercedes-Benz line, and never looked back. In fact, Bill Ussery Motors is one of the oldest Mercedes-Benz dealerships in the U.S.

In the 1960s and '70s, Mercedes-Benz sales continued to rise, fueled by innovative technology and an unswerving reputation for quality. In fact, the vehicle's icon – a three-pointed star – became a brand that portrays luxury, reliability and craftsmanship. Then in 1974 Ussery sold the dealership to his son-in-law John Brockway Sr. and his daughter, Patricia – the second generation of family owners. "My father walked from bank to bank in Coral Gables, finally securing a loan for $100,000 to maintain the business," recalls Brockway.

Brockway Sr. focused on the hiring of talented people, such as general manager Bill Newcomb who ran the dealership from 1973 to 1995. In 1992, the Gables dealership moved across the street to a more spacious and attractive facility that remains its location today.

Bob Brockway joined the family business in 1986 as vice president and operations manager, and was named president in 1996, taking over active operations after Newcomb retired. In 2001, Greg Barnes became general manager, and the dealership continued to grow its client base and enhance its services. For instance, Bill Ussery Motors recently introduced its OnSite Mobile Service, offering its Miami-Dade customers the ability to have their car serviced at their home or office.

In 2006, Bob Brockway and wife Paula purchased the dealership from the family outright and Bob assumed the role of Chairman and CEO.

Today, Bill Ussery Motors consistently ranks as the top volume Mercedes-Benz dealer in the Southeastern U.S. and has been recognized every year since 2000 with the "Best of the Best Award" from Mercedes-Benz USA for outstanding performance and an exceptional customer experience.

Bill Ussery Motors dealership has graced Coral Gables for more than 50 years.

A major supporter of South Florida's civic, charitable and educational institutions, Bill Ussery Motors contributes to more than 30 non-profit organizations each year. The Brockways provide significant financial support and volunteer their time to help worthy organizations like the American Red Cross, American Cancer Society, CHARLEE Homes for Children, Community Partnership for Homeless and Miami Science Museum.

On the business side, Bill Ussery Motors recently took a major step forward with the opening of a second dealership, Mercedes-Benz of Cutler Bay, under the leadership of general manager Pete Blackwell. It's a convenient new location for Mercedes-Benz owners from Pinecrest to Homestead and the Florida Keys.

"Our state-of-the-art second facility is a showpiece for southern Miami-Dade County and the Mercedes-Benz brand," says Brockway. "We are fast becoming an integral part of the southern Miami-Dade community and are excited to be part of the phenomenal growth that is taking place in the area."

Brockway attributes the continued growth and success of Bill Ussery Motors to the personal relationships forged with its loyal customers, as well as a workplace where employees are treated like family. In fact, top salesman Robert Corso, who has been with the company for more than 30 years, was a member of Bob and Paula's wedding party.

Looking to the future, Brockway says his son Cole and daughter Madelaine have expressed an interest in running the dealership when they grow up, and there's also toddler Edith to consider. So, it seems likely that a fourth-generation may continue the family's service-oriented business tradition.

As Brockway says, "All of us at Bill Ussery Motors recognize that our valued clients are responsible for our five decades of success. Our dealership's skilled and professional 'family' will continue to provide them with the highest possible level of customer service."

■ *"The Brockway family, clockwise from top: Cole, Bob, Edith, Paula and Madelaine."*

■ *The latest edition to the Bill Ussery Motors family is the new dealership in Cutler Bay, as seen in this artist's rendering.*

■ Mario Murgado, President & CEO

BRICKELL MOTORS

Formerly known as Packard Pontiac, then Brickell Automotive in the 1980s, Mario Murgado purchased the dealership in 2003 and changed the name to Brickell Motors. Under Murgado's leadership, Miami's oldest Pontiac dealership was rejuvenated and reinvented. Today, the Brickell Motors' name has become synonymous with quality, reliability and dependability for every new or certified vehicle it sells.

Since the 1980s the name Brickell Motors has become as commonplace to the people of Miami as Biscayne Bay, Little Havana or Lincoln Road Mall when thinking about their City of Magic. But this renowned auto retailer in South Florida hasn't always had the best image. For a time the company went through a period when service was far from excellent, quality was questionable and ever-declining sales was leading to its demise. However, that has all changed in the past several years. Today, it has a reputation any auto dealership would love to have. The Brickell Motors' name has become synonymous *with quality, reliability and dependability for every new or certified vehicle it sells.*

The result of earning this distinction has been unprecedented sales. In addition, this multi-faceted firm comprised of Honda, Pontiac, GMC and Buick dealerships, is now considered one of the top retail car companies in the entire Miami area. In fact, Brickell Motors is ranked as the number one Pontiac dealership in South Florida and has won the distinguished GM Mark of Excellence Award five years in a row.

"It is often said that any organization will ultimately be reflected by the character of its leadership. In your case, Mario, there is no doubt that this is true with Brickell Motors. And it is this level of character that gives me the confidence as a client to keep coming back, knowing that I will always enjoy a quality buying experience." – Nic Bustle, Sun Trust Bank.

Many reasons can be cited for Brickell Motors' transformation. But it is vividly clear one person, in particular, has been the main component in steering this company out of a dead end into an auto retail industry leader in greater Miami.

That person is Mario Murgado, president and chief executive officer of Brickell Motors, who purchased the struggling company in 2001. From day one, Murgado knew with his driven leadership style, extensive sales management experience, first-hand knowledge of the auto industry, bi-lingual communication abilities and a proven record of cultivating diverse team leadership achievements, he could turn Brickell Motors around. And with the help of his partners and lifetime friends, Alex Andreus and Rick Barraza, who have

■ Outside the Honda showroom

■ Inside the Honda showroom

a shared passion for cars and the automobile industry, he did just that. Together they achieved this by instituting a number of business-savvy measures into the work place to promote higher standards using a three-prong approach that included:

(1) Establishing a steadfast commitment to quality, reliability and dependability, with the intent of making these traits how every customer from now on would remember Brickell Motors. Furthermore, as noted in Brickell Motors' mission statement to its clientele, it is the company's goal "to make buying a vehicle and serving your vehicle a pleasant experience in a relaxed and professional atmosphere. We want to answer all your questions knowledgeably and always treat you with courtesy and respect."

Then Murgado went a step further with letting customers know that Brickell Motors is not merely dedicated to providing great service on a one-time basis, but is committed to "you and your family for generations to come. We want to earn your business by providing outstanding value, excellent service and reliability."

(2) Instituting a set of moral values to ensure the highest ethical standards are practiced in the workplace. As stated to customers, "We're dedicated to serving you with honesty, integrity and professionalism. We respect

you and your time. You honor us with your business and we express our appreciation with courteous and attentive personnel, who are knowledgeable, accessible and devoted to serving all your automotive needs."

(3) Creating a vision for the company in serving customers that goes beyond the present stating, "We're here to serve you not only today, but well into the future. Our goal is to establish a lifetime relationship with our customers by offering our unparalleled Brickell service."

Toward this end, Murgado, along with Andreus and Barraza gave Brickell Motors a new look, bringing the dealership into the 21st Century with state of the art equipment and an ambiance that entices people into the dealership's lobby. This includes a "full service" food and beverage counter with attractive seating for a more comfortable place to wait while your vehicle is being serviced. To come will be a parking garage for further customer convenience and a covered walkway between buildings in the complex and a hi-tech, energy efficient air conditioning system.

These capital improvements will be the latest in Brickell Motors' long-term commitment to staying in the heart of historic Little Havana, through physical plant enhancement, employment of residents and patronization of neighboring businesses by its employees.

■ Mario Murgardo and his partners: Alex Andreus, Rick Barraza.

Honda showroom

"I have purchased three cars from Brickell Motors and each time the experience was great. It is not just the buying experience, but how the dealership takes care of you once you need service or any other help. I have sent many friends and relatives to Mario and everyone has thanked me for the referral and today they are all customers of Brickell Motors. You couldn't ask for a better dealer." – Mark Levin, Coral Springs

The results of Mario Murgado's efforts clearly indicates when it comes to discovering the formula for auto retail success, he has surely found it. When Murgado purchased Brickell Motors, he could count his entire workforce on less than one hand. Today, he oversees more than 100 well-qualified sales, customer service and administrative personnel. It's no wonder he has earned a position as a true business leader in South Florida. And rightly so.

Through energy, hard work and perseverance the partners transformed a tired, rundown store, turning it into one of Miami's premiere auto dealerships, which exemplifies leadership and commitment to the community.

"Brickell Motors and its CEO Mario Murgado are great examples of thriving entrepreneurship and a commitment to bettering our community. As a company, they go beyond a great product, people and service. Their investment in Miami and revitalizing a core property has been an outstanding example of urban redevelopment. As a business leader, Mario's personal commitment to Miami-Dade County is an example we all can follow." – Tom Cornish, Coral Gables

G.M. showroom

Certainly, Murgado's auto industry experience played a big role in the metamorphosis of Brickell Motors. After earning a bachelor's degree in business administration at Louisiana's La Salle University, Murgado, who has always had a fascination for cars, decided to pursue a career in retail auto sales and went to work for Braman Imports, one of South Florida's largest dealerships. In the years to follow, he steadily moved up the ranks, until he reached the top as managing partner, president and CEO. Like every job he previously held with the company, as head of Braman Imports he continued to excel: sales figures rose dramatically as did profits. Producing such exceptional results Murgado truly was ready for the challenge as owner of the "tarnished, dilapidated and poor" Brickell Motors, as he remembers it, when he purchased the company in 2001.

Café open daily for our customer's convenience.

Along with bringing higher ethical standards to Brickell Motors, Murgado also brought a new kind of business philosophy that he regards as "the backbone of any organization." This was a direct focus on "attitude and teamwork to function in an efficient and competent manner to maximize synergy and profits."

But he didn't stop there. Murgado is all about personal community service – a mindset he has established by example. Murgado serves on the board of trustees of St. Thomas University and Miami Children's Hospital Foundation. He is also a member of the Orange Bowl Committee, an ambassador for the South Florida Golf Foundation and the statewide chairman for Mothers Against Drunk Driving (MADD).

One of Brickell Motors' most impressive charitable efforts under his leadership was a huge telethon at the dealership for Camillus House, the area's preeminent institution for assisting the homeless. The event raised more than $600,000 for this very needy cause.

Such impressive benevolent work for Murgado has earned him distinguished recognition. In 2007, Murgado was the proud Florida recipient of the *Time Magazine Quality Dealer Award* for outstanding community service.

The Brickell Motors Café.

When you consider what a wonderful business and community asset Brickell Motors has become in just a matter of years under the ownership/leadership of Mario Murgado, it comes as no surprise why the company is winning accolades for its work and customers like Ellen Kushner say, "Brickell Motors is superb and can't be beat! It is truly a carefree experience and a pleasure to do business with. Service of this caliber is a rarity these days. I would recommend them to anyone!"

Brickell Motors: *a name synonymous with quality, reliability and dependability for every new or certified vehicle it sells.*

FAIRCHILD TROPICAL BOTANIC GARDENS

Fairchild Tropical Botanic Garden has been Miami's "Secret Garden." Fortunately, for residents and visitors, it no longer bears that designation, since hundreds of thousands of people visit it each and every year.

A tropical paradise set within suburban Miami, the garden is vibrant with rare species, flowering plants, palms and cycads and fine art displayed in a natural environment. South Florida's weather is perfect for palms and cycads, and the garden has the largest collection of them in the nation. The garden also boasts the only natural rainforest on the U.S. mainland.

The 83-acre garden is the oldest institution in South Florida. Founded by several people in 1938 including Dr. David Fairchild, one of the greatest plant explorers of his time, the garden was designed by renowned landscape architect William Lyman Phillips, a member of Frederik Law Olmsted partnership. Many of the original specimens planted by Dr. Fairchild, including a magnificent giant African Baobab tree, still grace the grounds.

With a mission to save tropical plant diversity, Fairchild Tropical Botanic Garden is committed to the conservation of endangered species from around the world. The Center for Tropical Plant Conservation focuses its efforts on species from specific regions, including Madagascar, tropical Africa, South Florida and the Caribbean. Conservation efforts extend to specific plant groups including cycads, palms, tropical fruit and tropical trees.

The garden, accredited by the American Association of Museums, provides educational programs for thousands of school children annually, daily tours and special events.

In 2002, the garden began an artists' series, which showcases the sculptures of major international artists. The works of Dale Chihuly, Fernando Botero and Roy Lichtenstein have been on display in the garden and conservatory. The juxtaposition of man-made art and natural beauty is breathtaking.

Festivals and events occur in the garden throughout the year. Some highlights include the Mango Festival in July, the Orchid Show in March and the Chocolate Festival in January which coincides with the harvest of the cocoa plant. In addition, concerts are held regularly in the small amphitheater and the Garden House lawn. An abundance of wildlife, including wading birds, turtles, alligators, osprey and macaws, call Fairchild home.

Open every day of the year except December 25, Fairchild Tropical Botanic Garden is dedicated to ensuring that the beauty of our natural world live on.

■ *Glade Lake vista*

FLAGLER DOG TRACK

Steeped in history, Flagler Dog Track is a Miami entertainment destination that has been evolving for over 50 years. And the excitement is growing.

nchored by its mainstay -- greyhound racing, the venue continues to add attractions to keep regular customers and its many visitors from around the world coming back for more. One of the newest and successful additions has been the Flagler Magic City Poker Room. With 18 tables, plasma televisions, and a full service kitchen and bar, it's filled to capacity, especially on weekends. Card players can find whatever suits their fancy from No Limit Hold-'Em Cash Games to Multi-Table Tournaments.

Despite being one of the oldest businesses in Miami, the enterprise pays close attention to advances in technology, primarily when it comes to video and audio, an important component in the racing business. Races are broadcast live on the Flagler Dog Track website at www.flaglerdogs.com. The poker room televises the track at Flagler, so card players don't miss a race, and there are also simulcasts from other dog and horse tracks around the country. On Saturdays and Sundays, it features the longest-operating and largest flea market in South Florida, attracting more than 500,000 visitors each year.

While its many attractions sets Flagler Dog Track apart from other entertainment destinations, its long-term commitment to Miami is what truly stands out. Flagler Dog Track has been a family-owned operation

Casino gambling will join dog racing when Flagler Dog Track opens The Magic City Casino in November of 2009.

Isadore Hecht, shown with his wife, renowned South Florida philanthropist Florence Hecht, bought Flagler Dog Track in 1952. It has been a family-owned operation ever since.

for more than half a century. The president of the company is Barbara Hecht Havenick, whose father, Isadore Hecht, bought the track in 1952. Fred Havenick, who ran the track until he passed away suddenly last year, was a true visionary and was instrumental in the push to bring slot machines to the racetrack and to Miami-Dade County. Their two sons, Izzy and Alex, run the day-to-day operations and will soon be joined by brother Michael, and are the third generation to preside over the business.

Because of its staying power, Flagler Dog Track is globally renowned. *Time* magazine trumpeted the track as the "White House of the national dog racing scene" in a 1974 article. In the 1980s, Flagler was known internationally as the marquee dog track in the United States. Flagler is now in the midst of a major construction project and will open its newest addition, The Magic City Casino, in November of 2009. A new Miami landmark is on the horizon.

MIAMI CHILDREN'S MUSEUM

Conceived from the idea that playing is learning, the Miami Children's Museum is a wonderland of imagination, creativity and education.

iami Children's Museum's slogan defines their fundamental purpose; play, learn, imagine, create. Their mission, to enrich the lives of children by fostering a love of learning and enabling children to realize their highest potential, is fulfilled with every smiling face and gleeful giggle.

As children walk through the doors of the museum, they are immediately drawn in to a world of make-believe filled with stimulating exhibits to explore. When they leave, the children have gained a feeling of accomplishment along with their day of fun.

The first exhibit to greet the children is the Castle of Dreams, a dazzling, two-story sand castle containing sand from beaches around the world. At the Kidscape Village, children can play-act at a grocery store, bank, health and wellness center, veterinarian office and a television studio. Or they can pretend to be a firefighter or police officer in the Safety Zone. All the while, children are learning about food and where it comes from, how to use and save money, proper nutrition and exercise and how a TV newsroom operates. Is this fun or education?

It turns out, it's both. Today MCM is one of the ten largest children's museums in the country. The museum has seamlessly merged entertainment with education, to the delight of children, their parents and educators. The museum was founded in 1983 by two educators, Barbara Goldman and Denise Glasser, who realized most major cities had children's museums, and Miami needed one as well. They did research on the value of early childhood education and created the perfect place for young children to learn through play.

The real value in a children's museum is how well the children are engaged. The museum has 14 galleries, one of which is reserved for traveling exhibits. Every exhibit is interactive and bilingual. MCM, a favorite stop for elementary school field trips, hosts after school and camp programs throughout the year.

As children leave the museum, their reaction is always the same; they want to know when they can come back. There is no stronger vote of confidence for this important Miami institution than the one given by the children who love it.

■ The Castle of Dreams is covered in a mosiac created by local Miami artist, Carlos Alves

PHOTOS: DAN FORER

The theater's intricately detailed turrets and balconies suggest a peaceful Mediterranean courtyard.

OLYMPIA THEATER AT GUSMAN CENTER

Downtown Miami has been a magnet for the performing arts since 1926, thanks to the Olympia Theater at the Gusman Center for the Performing Arts.

Silent movies, Vaudeville shows, operatic arias, pop stars and rock and roll concerts have all had their moment in the spotlight on the Gusman's venerable stage. Today, the theater welcomes a wide variety of popular performers and is home to the Miami International Film Festival and Ballet Gamonet.

The historic theater in the heart of downtown Miami features superb acoustics, dramatic Moorish-style architecture, and a simulated night sky complete with wafting clouds and twinkling stars. Along with its architectural magnificence, the theater boasts an intimate ambiance in its 1,567 seats. Today, the theater is a beacon of the South Florida arts community and an important component of Miami's cultural scene. Its online event calendar, at www.gusmancenter.org, demonstrates the breadth of its programs.

For more than 40 years, the Olympia Theater was the top entertainment center in Miami and was one of the last in the nation to showcase Vaudeville acts. It also has the distinction of being the first air-conditioned building in Miami. In the early 1970s the aging theater was earmarked for demolition. Fortunately, South Florida business tycoon and philanthropist Maurice Gusman ensured its survival by donating it to the City of Miami. After extensive renovations overseen by famed architect Morris Lapidus, the renamed Gusman Center for the Performing Arts was named to the National Register of Historic Places in 1984. Friends of Gusman, the theater's fundraising arm, supports continuing improvements.

After decades of hosting crowds at its cultural events, the Gusman Theater was in need of another massive renovation. This time, the process included structural, systemic and aesthetic restorations. When the project was completed, the majesty of the theater was restored to its 1926 grandeur.

Entering the Gusman is like stepping into a time machine for the arts. The theater's unique character was devised by architect John Eberson, internationally known as the master of "atmospheric" theater design. The Gusman is one of the few Eberson-designed theaters still in use. The design scheme has been restored to its original condition and the new carpeting was custom-loomed to match the original. Historically appropriate details, including wood-and-brass seats, elegant appointments, classical statuary and ornate ironwork, add to the refined ambiance of the theater.

Outside, the hustle and bustle of a vibrant downtown is a stark contrast to the graceful and serene ambiance inside. Thanks to the Olympia Theater at Gusman Center, people in this thriving urban center can always take refuge in the arts while enjoying the atmosphere of one of the world's most distinctive classic theaters.

PHOTOS: DAN FORER

MIAMI SCIENCE MUSEUM

"We inspire people of all ages and cultures to enjoy science and technology, in order to better understand ourselves and our world."
– Miami Science Museum's mission statement

For more than 60 years, the Miami Science Museum has worked to fulfill its mission through innovative exhibits, collections and activities that are entertaining yet education-focused. The results of the Museum's efforts have been impressive. During the last decade alone, the Museum has grown tremendously: *today it has more than 4,000 member families and accommodates close to 300,000 visitors every year on and off site, making it the largest educational facility in South Florida.*

Furthermore, it annually hosts *one of the biggest summer science camps in the nation for children 3 to 14 years of age.* More than 250 classes are offered that explore the sciences, environment, rocketry, photography, digital video, computers, sailing, snorkeling, magic and engineering, among others. In addition, birthday parties have become popular and unforgettable with hands-on exhibits, real live animals and planetarium shows for all to enjoy.

But the Museum is a special venue, people of all ages appreciate, as evident by its Website traffic: *the site gets more than 4 million hits every month.*

Equally striking is what the Museum has planned for the future. A new Miami Science Museum is in the works to be located in downtown Miami's Bicentennial Park (also known as Museum Park). Museum officials say the new facility without question will enhance tourism, while becoming an important education destination for locals and tourists alike. The magnificent new building will feature more than 200,000 sq. ft. of exhibits, galleries, laboratories, presentation and public use spaces.

The Learning Center provides a wide range of hands-on science learning opportunities for students, parents, teachers and the learning professionals.

From Humble Beginnings
To Award-Winning Stature

In 1949, the Junior League of Miami determined that Miami-Dade County's children needed a science museum. The Junior Museum of Miami, a private non-profit organization, was established in 1950 in a house on the corner of Biscayne Boulevard and 26th Street. The Junior Museum expanded so quickly that in 1952 it moved to the Miami Women's Club building on Bayshore Drive, christened as the Museum of Science and Natural History.

■ The Museum's Wildlife Center offers a hands-on introduction to living creatures in South Florida.

In 1953, the Guild of the Museum of Science was formed, providing volunteer assistance to staff, the operation of the Museum Store, and doing tours and outreach programs. Soon after the Museum was already out of space, leading the Dade County Commission to establish a major independent science museum to service citizens of all ages. Hence, in 1960, the first building of the community's new science museum was opened on three acres of the historic Vizcaya complex. It quickly gained national recognition for innovative programs spanning from astronomy to zoology.

With the construction of the Planetarium in late 1966, the renamed Miami Museum of Science and Planetarium grew into a landmark institution for learning science and technology in fun, creative ways. Since then the Museum has continued to earn acclaim for its training of educators, exemplary youth programs and highly visited Website, along with growth through its Planetarium programming and Wildlife Center operations.

Such achievements deserve recognition, and the Miami Science Museum has seen its share. In 2004, for example, the Museum beat out more than 3,000 entries from around the world to win a bronze award for its redesigned "MiamiSci" newsletter at the Summit Creative Awards. That same year, it was voted the "Best Children's Museum" in Miami-Dade County, earning a Silver Award from *South Florida Parenting Magazine* and the "Greatest Museum" by the *Coral Gables Gazette*.

It also received a grant from the National Institutes of Health for the national dissemination and replication of the Museum's Bio Trac educational program to be used as a prototype in museums across the country. Other special recognition has included a 2005 Eleanor Roosevelt Fund Award presented to Dr. Judy Brown for her success in encouraging young girls to explore careers in math and science; and to the Museum a 2005 Presidential Award for Excellence in Science, Mathematics and Engineering Mentoring. More recently, the Miami Science Museum was named to the *South Florida Parenting Hall of Fame* in 2008. It was also named best museum by both *New Times* and *Sunpost Magazine* in the summer of 2008.

The Miami Science Museum: *since 1949 inspiring people of all ages and cultures to enjoy science and technology, in order to better understand ourselves and our world.*

■ The Miami Science Museum focus has always been about education of our world and beyond. That will be reflected more than ever with the opening of the new museum that has been labeled to be "a living laboratory of learning."

PERRY ELLIS INTERNATIONAL

A global giant in the apparel industry, Perry Ellis International (NASDAQ: PERY) makes its home in Miami, but globalist reach is felt throughout the world.

hief Executive Officer George Feldenkreis is the epitome of the American dream. With little money in his pocket when he first came to Florida as a Cuban immigrant, Feldenkreis recently celebrated his company's 40th year of vision and success.

This leading apparel conglomerate boasts nearly $900 million in sales and an average growth of 20% in revenues and profits over the last six years. PEI has 34 worldwide offices, which employ over 2,000 associates. Its portfolio of 29 national and international brands is available in over 15,000 doors in the U.S. Of these, the Perry Ellis brand alone sells over $1.5 billion at retail worldwide.

In the late 1960s, George and his brother, Isaac, started Supreme International, importing guayabera shirts — the pleated, four-pocket shirts traditional to Latin America — which earned him the nickname, "Guayabera King." In 1980 his son, Oscar, joined Supreme International and they began an aggressive brand acquisition strategy which included names such as Munsingwear, the 110-year old menswear company, Jantzen, the world's first swimsuit label, and the company's current namesake, Perry Ellis.

With so many recognizable brands positioned in diverse channels, it is no surprise that PEI is one of the most sought after apparel manufacturers by leading retailers. Retail experts commend the clothier not only for covering all channels of distribution from Wal-Mart to Neiman Marcus, but for an almost uncanny ability to spot niche market opportunities and revitalize dying brands.

Although renowned for its keen understanding of menswear categories, the company has been strengthening its position in markets for swimwear, outerwear, and sportswear for women, juniors and boys. It has recently

Perry Ellis International Corporate offices, Doral, FL.

entered the women's contemporary category, with luxury department store specialty labels Laundry By Shelli Segal® and C&C California®. The company consistently seeks new niche businesses to expand its customer base. Its Hispanic-inspired brands, Cubavera®, available in major department stores, the Havanera Company® in J.C. Penney and Centro™ at Kohl's, attract both the Hispanic customer and the fashion consumer who is responding to the relaxed lifestyle and cultural influences of Latinos on today's pop culture. In the global marketplace, the company's Original Penguin brand is embraced by consumers in the U.K, Italy, Spain and 13 other countries across Europe. Meanwhile, Farah remains the most popular trouser for men in the United Kingdom.

PEI is also a champion in the sports world. A licensing agreement with Nike creates swimwear for men, women, juniors, boys, and girls. Its golf lifestyle apparel includes names such as PING, PGA Tour, Champions Tour and Grand Slam, while action sports brands include Gotcha, Redsand and MCD.

Embroidered products, used as commercial attire for corporate businesses, provide further revenue opportunity. Major corporations like to have their brands associated with the recognized quality of Cubavera, Tricots St. Raphael and PING. In fact, each year chefs and other uniformed personnel wear designs from PEI during the South Beach Wine and Food Festival.

While lauded as a major contributor to South Florida's economy, the members of the Feldenkreis family are also recognized for their contributions to civic enrichment. The Miami-Dade community has so benefitted from George Feldenkreis' generous support of local charities, universities, hospitals and Jewish philanthropies that in April 2007 Miami-Dade County Commissioners designated a street in the city of Doral as "George Feldenkreis Way."

As a company constantly on the move with new product lines and an ever expanding roster of licensing agreements, Perry Ellis International is poised to continue its growth while remaining true to its core values of quality, innovation and evolution.

PERRY ELLIS INTERNATIONAL
MIAMI CORPORATE OFFICE

RCI GROUP

RCI Group is more than a developer of marinas; the company creates waterfront destinations for boaters and land lovers alike by combining premier boating services with popular restaurants and retail shops.

ounded by Robert Christoph in the early 1980s, RCI has developed waterfront properties from the Long Island Sound in Connecticut to Key West.

RCI's philosophy is that a marina is more than a parking lot for boats; it is a complete lifestyle for boaters. Facilities for entertainment, dining, shopping and leisure activities exist in conjunction with a full menu of boating support facilities. The goal is to deliver the ultimate lifestyle for boaters and introduce non-boaters to a rich and entertaining environment.

In Miami, the company owns and operates the Miami Beach Marina in South Beach, and Bayshore Landing in Coconut Grove. Each location has its own personality and offers a range of services.

Miami Beach Marina is often used as a gateway to the Caribbean by boaters from around the world. Its 400 slips can accommodate boats up to 250 feet in length and has a deep water entrance at the mouth of Government Cut, which leads from the ocean to the Port of Miami. Lift slips, floating docks and wet slips are available as well as a fuel dock. Amenities include a control tower with state-of-the-art weather service, 24-hour dock attendants and security, a heated swimming pool, laundry facilities, U.S. Customs clearing and wireless internet service. The ambiance is a tropical oasis, overlooking the gleaming high-rises of Miami and Miami Beach.

Bayshore Landing, in the heart of Coconut Grove, is home to many local boaters. The marina has 150 slips and offers easy access to the Intracoastal Waterway, Biscayne Bay and the Atlantic Ocean. Located within walking distance are the numerous restaurants, shops and art galleries of Coconut Grove. Amenities at the secured facility include overnight security, electricity and water, as well as laundry facilities.

Both marinas host special events throughout the year including sailing regattas, fishing tournaments and motorboat races. Bayshore Landing is home to three annual fishing tournaments; the Sailfish Kickoff in December, the Mayor's Cup for Sailfish in January and the Grove Slam in May, a dolphin tournament.

Miami Beach Marina hosts between eight and ten fishing tournaments annually including the Bob Lewis Fishing tournament in March, the Miami Billfish tournament in April, the Miami Dolphins Charity tournament in June. Smaller tournaments are also held including ones sponsored by the Miami Beach Police and Fire Departments and the Miami-Dade Transit Authority. Sailing regattas headquartered at the Marina include the Acura Southern Ocean Racing Regatta, featuring 100 boats in five classes over ten days. The Farr 40 Regatta World Championship includes 40 boats from 19 countries.

Originally from the Midwest, Christoph grew up boating on the Great Lakes. Prior to starting RCI, he spent about 15

■ *Public Promenade*

Fuel Dock and Dock Masters Tower

years as a developer of multifamily residences and marinas on lakes and reservoirs in the Midwest and Southeast. His experience with waterfront development led Christoph to consider multifamily communities with both upland and waterside features, creating the optimum waterfront lifestyle.

His attraction to the Art Deco district brought him to Miami Beach, where he bought and renovated numerous historic buildings. In the early 1980s, the site of the Miami Beach Marina was nothing more than a refuse transfer point and was filled with tanks. Christoph realized the area could be a catalyst for development and become a destination

instead of an industrial site. Christoph's life-long love of boating and knowledge of what boaters want and need led him to concentrate his efforts on marinas.

Building upon the success with multifamily communities and extensive knowledge of the waterfront, RCI developments include the best of water and land-based destinations. Today, RCI encompasses all aspects of each marina, from design, construction, leasing, management and support. The company is responsible for everything from blueprints to bricks to management of the marine and upland, or land-based, components. RCI is also a family business. Christoph serves as president and his sons Robert Jr. and Hunter are both vice presidents. Together, this boating family brings the lifestyle to all who desire it.

Christoph believes the future of boating may include a shift from powerboats to sailboats because of fuel prices. Regardless of the size or type of boat a boater uses, the boating community is well known for their camaraderie. RCI's marinas offer boaters a place to keep their boats, share their experiences and enjoy the company of other like-minded boating enthusiasts.

Newly Renovated Facilities

■ Outside of The Oceanaire Seafood Room at 900 South Miami Avenue.

THE OCEANAIRE SEAFOOD ROOM

Walking into the cool of The Oceanaire Seafood Room on a hot Miami day is like jumping into the sea and descending into a different time and place.

That's by design, as in a 1930s-era luxury ocean liner. Beautiful dark cherry woods complement the gracious curves of the dining room, the Art Deco lighting fixtures, and the damp luster of the shellfish bar.

There is a sensation of having ducked under the velvet ropes at the museum, and entered a time warp, where, strangely, the staff seems to have been waiting for you. The air is fragrant with a salty tinge of ultra-fresh seafood. The glasses and silverware are polished by hand before each shift. Big band and swing music issues gently from the ceiling.

The 280-seat restaurant offers a curiously comfortable blend of top-notch seafood and service in a beautiful setting that welcomes diners in jeans and tropical shirts just as warmly as those in formal evening wear.

Every day a new menu is printed according to what has been caught locally that day, or specially flown in. The rest of the menu's vagaries are due to the mood of executive chef and operating partner Sean Bernal. He's a hands-on chef, and likes to keep things interesting. The restaurant will even print custom menus with personal messages for private parties.

Bernal is a veteran Miami chef, having served at restaurants including The Bistro and Pescado in Coral Gables, the Omni Colonnade and J.W. Marriott in downtown Miami, and on South Beach at Baleen and Tambo. Bernal's helming of the kitchen at Pescado brought him into partnership with that restaurant's general manager, Kevin Amiott. Amiott is now general manager and operating partner at The Oceanaire Seafood Room.

The Oceanaire Seafood Room is a national success story. The flagship opened in 1996, in Minneapolis. As of 2007, there are 14 restaurants in cities including Dallas, Houston, Baltimore, Atlanta, Philadelphia, San Diego, Seattle, Charlotte, Washington, D.C., and Miami. More are planned for Boston, Phoenix, and Cincinnati.

The Miami restaurant is unique, however, in that Bernal and Amiott were the first operating partners to be hired from outside the close-knit company. One reason is that Miami is an American city like no other; to serve it right, you have to know it well.

Roughly half the menu offers popular standards (such as the to-die-for crab cakes) common to all of The Oceanaire's restaurants, with the other half dictated by Bernal. Bernal's

■ The Oceanaire is available for large dinner parties or small groups celebrating a special occasion.

extensive and varied background in the Miami restaurant world is reflected in the fusion of classic dishes with Caribbean, Latin, South American and Asian cuisine.

"I like to tell people we're at the mercy of the ocean," says Bernal. "You could come here five nights a week and see something different every time. It keeps it exciting."

The ever-changing menu requires Bernal to instruct the black-and-white clad wait staff daily on the flavor and texture of a large list of oysters and fish species, which can include several varieties of tuna, grouper, salmon, snapper, trout, and shark, among other possibilities. Oysters are decanted from their half-shells with the same level of attention to their provenance as is normally reserved for vintage wine. Bernal explains that, like wine, where an oyster grows has much to do with the subtle flavors of the finished product. On any given day, a connoisseur can choose among a half-dozen to a dozen varieties of oyster.

Although The Oceanaire Seafood Room is relatively new to Miami, its ambiance and attention to detail have garnered it a loyal following of regulars from Key Biscayne and Fisher Island to Coral Gables. Lunch is convenient for the downtown business crowd, while dinner is perfect for the patrons of the Carnival Performing Arts Center, but a drink at the bar entices the Miami Heat Basketball fans. There is something for everyone here.

It's clear that the restaurant's ambition is, as Bernal puts it, to become to South Florida seafood what the legendary Joe's Stone Crab is to stone crabs.

By the look (and taste) of it, that's a dream that will come true.

On any given day, a connoisseur can choose among a half-dozen varieties of oyster.

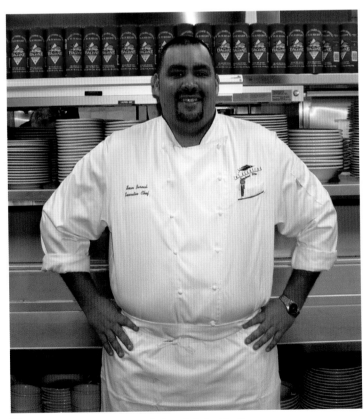

Sean Bernal's cooking blends perfectly with the hot Florida sun.

Sip a Sidecar in the lounge, sidle up to the oyster bar, or kick back in a horseshoe booth before diving into a Sea of Ultra-Fresh fish.

NEWS CAFE

There was a time in Miami Beach history when the prospect of a thriving restaurant culture in the post-Scarface era seemed to have about as much chance as a snowball in, well, South Beach.

Then restaurateur Mark Soyka and then partner Jeffrey Davis opened an ice cream parlor, on Ocean Drive, in 1987. Turns out, Soyka was on to something. Soon they realized that what South Beach really needed was a cool European café, a place where beach dwellers could stroll in from the melting sun, order a coffee, a newspaper, and something to nibble on. So the Sundae crowd turned into the Sunday afternoon crowd as in 1988, a new business was born.

Twenty years later, the News Café is always bustling with life, a fixture on Ocean Drive for thousands of tourists who patronize it each time they come to town. Miami residents, once the main clientele when News Café was a tiny place and South Beach just beginning its transformation into the American Riviera, come back for the nostalgia – and the Eggs (News Cafe).

This is the genius of the News Café – reasonably-priced comfort food with a twist on its enormous menu. Breakfast, lunch, and dinner are available 24 hours a day. It becomes for all a home away from home. Red vinyl booths and café-style chairs compliment the European café on the beach feel of the place. Fans stir the humid air above the outdoor tables as cigar girls hawk their products on the sidewalk and customers gawk at the unique species of Ocean Drive walkers, occasionally spotting a famous face.

General Manager Anthony Magaldi, has worked at the News, as people fondly call it, for 17 years, working his way up from waiting tables (he's been GM now for 11 years). "It's my baby," he explains. "It was the right place and the right time. Soyka was not afraid to take chances when this was a ghost town."

Back then the café wasn't much more than a handful of tables, a tiny staff, and a kitchen capable of producing only basics that could be cooked on a couple of burners. Perhaps 50 people could be served at a time. Now more than 350 people can, and frequently are, served at the same time, in the expanded indoor and outdoor complex, complete with a bar and a store. The News Café employs more than 220 people.

Incredibly, there are probably even more items on the menu than people who work there. This is the ideal place to take a large group of visitors who can never agree on what to eat. The aforementioned Eggs (News Cafe) are quite popular and come with salmon, or spinach, or ham and tomato. But if your mother wants a Greek salad, your father wants a steak churrasco, the children want pasta, and crazy cousin Eddie can't live without a turkey panini, the News Café has got it covered. The dessert and coffee menus are similarly accommodating.

In the mid-Nineties, Italian designer Gianni Versace moved to the Casa Casuarina mansion down the street and became a regular. Every day, Magaldi says, the stylish gent would saunter in for his daily espresso and an Italian newspaper. He even appeared there the day of his untimely death and the international media circus that descended afterward made the News Café a landmark for the curious.

"Twenty years here is some kind of landmark," says Magaldi, wearing one of his ubiquitous Tommy Bahama shirts that became so popular with customers the News store started selling them. "It's an accomplishment."

Soyka went on to make his mark throughout Miami, opening the Van Dyke Café & Upstairs at the Van Dyke on Miami Beach's famous Lincoln Road and partnering with others to open upscale European café Segafredo Zanetti. Two other local favorites are Soyka Restaurant and Andiamo Pizza, both located in Miami's rapidly developing midtown corridor and frequented by many business and political movers and shakers.

MIAMI RIVER INN

Miami's image certainly consists of beautiful beaches, sleek new high-rises and a sophisticated night-life.

But there is also a historic side to the Magic City, one that isn't always found by typical tourists. Hidden like a gem amidst a lush, tropical landscape sits the Miami River Inn, downtown Miami's only historic bed and breakfast.

Listed on the National Register of Historic Places, the Miami River Inn is an assemblage of buildings built between 1906 and 1910 and features 38 antique-filled guest rooms, swimming pool and hot tub, beautiful gardens and a conference center. The enclave is located across the street from the Miami River and encompasses a half of a city block. Entering the gated property is like stepping back in time. A peaceful atmosphere surrounds the wood-frame, two and three-story buildings, which boast wide porches and hardwood floors. However, the niceties of modern life haven't been overlooked; every room has central air conditioning, cable television, wireless internet access and a private bathroom.

The Miami River Inn was lovingly restored to its original splendor. Some of the distinctive features of the buildings remain as they were a century ago and include built-in bookcases, sideboards and wainscoting. The five-year restoration was completed in 1990, when the Inn opened for business. Each room's décor is unique, adding interest to this country-style hideaway. The buildings are named for Miami's founders; Henry Flagler, William Brickell, Julia Tuttle and Carl Fisher. The conference center is named for Marjorie Stoneman Douglas, who celebrated her 101st birthday there.

Guests enjoy the serenity of the property as well as a daily breakfast of homemade breads and jams, fresh squeezed orange juice, cereals and fruit. Additional services include a focus on individual attention, recommendations on sightseeing trips and restaurants. The Inn has hosted numerous weddings, with entire wedding parties filling the rooms. Travelers from all corners of the globe have appreciated the country atmosphere of the Inn, while being a stone's throw from one of the most vibrant and stylish cities in the world.

The eclectic and historic Miami River Inn, an oasis within the city, provides a glimpse into Miami's past while remaining a welcome respite from the hustle and bustle of the 21st century.

WOMETCO ENTERPRISES

Founded in 1925 by Mitchell Wolfson and Sidney Meyer, Wometco Enterprises, Inc., has enjoyed a long life kept vital by its ability to change with the times.

ometco's first venture was the grand Capitol Theater, which opened in 1926 on North Miami Avenue in the heart of downtown. Patterned after the great New York theaters, the Capitol featured an enormous Wurlitzer organ, first-run films, and live stage shows. From one theater, Wometco grew into an entertainment dynasty.

After two decades of successfully running a chain of theaters throughout South Florida and the Caribbean, Wometco leapt into the television industry in 1949. Wolfson built Florida's first TV station – WTVJ/Channel 4/Miami – in a back room of the Capitol Theater. At the time, few South Floridians owned televisions. But Wometco's pioneering decision would prove prescient. The company went public in 1959.

By the 1980s, the company owned several TV stations and fourteen cable systems. Wometco also expanded into vending machines and bottling Coca-Cola products. The best known legacy of Wometco, however, is the Miami Seaquarium, which opened in 1955 and became famous as the site of filming for the 1960's TV series "Flipper."

After the death of Mitchell Wolfson in 1983, a major leveraged buyout firm, Kolberg, Kravis and Roberts, bought Wometco for $1 billion. During the sale of assets that followed, longtime company executives Arthur Hertz and Michael Brown led a group of investors to buy the theaters, the Seaquarium, and the food service operations.

Hertz, the company's chairman and CEO, joined Wometco as an accountant right out of his graduating class at the University of Miami, in 1956. In the post-buyout years, Hertz and Brown refocused the company, eventually selling off the theaters and the vending operation, while keeping a hand in food with the ownership of some 50 Baskin-Robbins/Dunkin' Donuts franchises in Puerto Rico.

The company's most recent focus is on renovating and expanding the Seaquarium. The tourist attraction is building a larger facility on its Virginia Key site to expand a popular swim with the dolphins program. Plans are also in the works to renovate the shark facility.

The family tradition of Wometco continues, with Hertz's son Andrew serving as general manager of the Miami Seaquarium. After more than 80 years of entertaining Miami, Wometco has grown up with the city without growing old.

Miami Seaquarium was built in 1955 and became world famous in the 1960s, when the popular children's television show "Flipper" was filmed there.

THE RUSTY PELICAN

Even in a city built on hyperbole, it can honestly be said that the Rusty Pelican has the best view of any waterfront restaurant in Miami.

From its location on a finger of Virginia Key, the Rusty Pelican's large windows face across Biscayne Bay toward the glass and steel core of downtown Miami.

Virginia Key is a special place, the last bit of big green the City of Miami has yet to harness. Since 1970, the city has leased a portion of the key to the Rusty Pelican. Owner and former military pilot David Tallichet also operates two dozen restaurants across the country, including the 94th Aero Squadron restaurant on the southern border of Miami International Airport. For Tallichet, the view is everything, and that principle has become a hallmark of the locations he opens. That, and fresh seafood.

The Rusty Pelican opened in 1972. In 1985, a fire largely destroyed the restaurant, but it was rebuilt (adding a second story and banquet facilities) two years later. The Rusty Pelican has served as the backdrop for numerous television and movie shoots, including a scene in Caddyshack, and regular appearances on ESPN and the Weather Channel. Numerous stars have also dined here.

The décor, all wood paneling and nautical-themed aesthetics, creates an impression of being submerged in a time capsule of Miami's history. The entrance is a covered walkway with koi ponds on each side. Inside, the chateau-like lobby frames the sunlit dining room.

The staff, led by general manager Peter Knezevic, is uniformly charming. Knezevic, a native of Yugoslavia, has managed the Rusty Pelican since 1990. He has presided over countless weddings, romantic dinners, and business luncheons.

One of the best times to experience the Rusty Pelican is during the legendary champagne brunches on Sundays. A wide assortment of Miamians assembles to gorge on the most opulent buffet in town. Just outside the window, dolphins play among a riot of watercraft, and even the occasional seaplane. Massive cruise ships docked at the Port of Miami are also visible at the horizon.

These are the reasons the Rusty Pelican has been a Miami success story for more than 30 years.

The romantic views of the water and downtown Miami attract many wedding parties to the Rusty Pelican.

1 FIRSTBANK

701 Waterford Way, Suite 810
Miami, FL 33126
Tel: (305) 443-4884
Fax: (305) 443-4833
www.firstbankpr.com......................406

ASSOCIATED PHOTO & IMAGING

19 S.W. 6 Street
Miami, FL 33130
Tel: (305) 373-4774
Fax: (305) 373-7446
www.apimaging.com 460

AV MED HEALTH PLANS

9400 S. Dadeland Blvd.., Suite 409
Miami, FL 33156
Tel: (800) 432-6676
Tel: (305) 671-5437
Fax: (305) 671-6103
www.avmed.org 380

BAC FLORIDA BANK

169 Miracle Mile
Coral Gables, FL 33134
Tel: (305) 789-7000
Fax: (305) 374-1402
www.bacflorida.com 403

BACARDI

2100 Biscayne Boulevard
Miami, FL 33137
Tel: (305) 573-8600
Fax: (305) 576-0374
www.bacardi.com 470

BADIA SPICES

1400 Northwest 93rd Avenue
Miami, FL 33172
Tel: (305) 629-8000
Fax: (305) 629-8100
www.badiaspices.com 472

BANK OF AMERICA

100 SE 2nd Street, 15th Floor
Miami, FL 33131
Tel: (305) 523-4726
Fax: (305) 523-4724
www.bankofamerica.com...............402

BANKUNITED

7815 N.W. 148th Street
Miami, FL 33014
Tel: (305) 231-6400
www.bankunited.com.....................404

BAPTIST HEALTH SOUTH FLOIDA

6855 Red Road, Suite 600
Coral Gables, FL 33143
Tel: (786) 596-6534
Fax: (786) 662-7176
www.baptisthealth.net 382

BARRY UNIVERSITY

11300 North East Second Avenue
Miami Shores, FL 33161
Tel: (305) 899-3100
www.admissions@mail.barry.edu....352

BECKMAN COULTER

11800 S.W. 147 Avenue, M/S 32 CO5
Maimi, FL 33196
Tel: (305) 380-3800
Fax: (305) 380-8312
www.beckmancoulter.com..............378

BELEN JESUIT PREPARATORY SCHOOL

500 S.W. 127th Ave.
Miami, FL 33184
Tel: (305) 223-8600
Fax: (786) 621-4044
www.belenjesuit.org........................354

BRICKELL MOTORS

665 S.W. 8th Street
Miami, FL 33130
Tel: (305) 777-2993
Fax: (305) 250-4176
www.brickellmotors.com 480

BUSINESS CENTERS INTERNATIONAL

2000 Ponce de Leon Blvd., Suite 600
Coral Gables, FL 33134
Tel: (305) 443-1414
Fax: (305) 443-1603
www.bci-coralgables.com................459

CARLOS ALBIZU UNIVERSITY

2173 N.W. 99th Avenue
Miami, FL 33172
Tel: (305) 593-1223
Fax: (305) 592-7930
www.albizu.edu 356

CARROLLTON SCHOOL OF THE SACRED HEART

3747 Main Highway
Miami, FL 33133
Tel: (305) 446-5673
Fax: (305) 529-6528
www.carrollton.org 358

CENTURY HOMEBUILDERS OF SOUTH FLORIDA

2301 NW 87th Ave., 6th Floor
Doral, FL 33172
Tel: (305) 599-8100
Fax: (305) 470-1900
www.centuryhomebuilders.com 420

CHRISTOPHER COLUMBUS HIGH SCHOOL

3000 S.W. 87th Avenue
Miami, FL 33165
Tel: (305) 223-5650
Fax: (305) 559-4306
www.columbushs.com...................353

DADE COMMUNITY FOUNDATION

200 S. Biscayne Blvd., Suite 505
Miami, FL 33131
Tel: (305) 371-2711
Fax: (305) 371-5342
www.dadecommunityfoundation.org . 324

**DADE COUNTY FEDERAL
CREDIT UNION**

1500 N.W. 107 Avenue
Miami, FL 33172
Tel: (786) 845-3105
Fax: (305) 392-2597
www.dcfcu.org 400

**DEL MONTE FRESH PRODUCE
NORTH AMERICA**

241 Sevilla Ave.
Coral Gables, FL 33134
Tel: (305) 520-8400
Fax: (305) 520-8077
www.freshdelmonte.com 474

**ESSLINGER – WOOTEN –
MAXWELL, INC.**

355 Alhambra Circle, Suite 950
Coral Gables, FL 33134
Tel: (305) 960-2500
Fax: (305) 444-0185
www.ewm.com 428

**FAIRCHILD TROPICAL BOTANIC
GARDENS**

10901 Old Culter Road
Coral Gables, FL 33156-4296
Tel: (305) 667-1651
Fax: (305) 661-8955
www.fairchildgarden.org 484

FLAGLER DOG TRACK

401 N.W. 38th Court
Miami, FL 33126
Tel: (305) 649-3000
Fax: (305) 631-4525
www.flaglerdogs.com 485

FLORIDA EAST COAST REALTY

100 South Biscayne Blvd.
Miami, FL 33131
Tel: (305) 358-7710
Fax: (305) 358-1619
www.fecr.com 416

FORTUNE INTERNATIONAL

1300 Brickell Ave.
Miami, FL 33131
Tel: (305) 351-1000
Fax: (305) 351-0989
www.fortune-network.com 414

FUERST, HUMPHREY, ITTLEMAN

1001 Brickell Bay Drive, Suite 2002
Miami, FL 33131
Tel: (305) 350-5690
Fax: (305) 371-8989
www.fuerstlaw.com 454

GOLDSTEIN SCHECHTER KOCH

2121 Ponce de Leon Blvd., 11th Floor
Coral Gables, FL 33134
Tel: (305) 442-2200
Fax: (305) 444-0880
www.gsplh.com 448

**GOODWILL INDUSTRIES OF SOUTH
FLORIDA, INC.**

2121 N.W. 21st Street
Miami, FL 33142
Tel: (305) 325-9114
Fax: (305) 324-7319
www.goodwillmiami.org 336

**GREATER MIAMI CHAMBER
OF COMMERCE**

1601 Biscayne Blvd.
Miami, FL 33132
Tel: (305) 350-7700
Fax: (305) 374-6902
www.miamichamber.com 326

GULLIVER SCHOOLS

6575 North Kendall Drive
Pinecrest, FL 33156
Tel: (305) 666-7937
Fax: (305) 665-3791
www.gulliverschools.org 360

HALL, LAMB AND HALL, P.A.

2665 South Bayshore Drive –
Penthouse One
Miami, FL 33133
Tel: (305) 374-5030
Fax: (305) 374-5033
www.hlhlawfirm.com 456

HARVEY BILT PHOTOGRAPHY

100 Chopin Plaza
P.O. Box 451000
Miami, FL 33245
Tel: (305) 371-5337
Fax: (305) 371-2325
www.biltphoto.com 463

HELM BANK

999 Brickell Avenue
Miami, FL 33131
Tel: (305) 379-4356
Fax: (305) 373-8351
www.helmbank.com 408

HILL YORK

2125 S. Andrews Avenue
Fort Lauderdale, FL 33316
Tel: (954) 525-4200
Fax: (954) 763-7548
www.hillyork.com 430

JACKSON HEALTH SYSTEM

1611 N.W. 12th Avenue
Miami, FL 33136
Tel: (305) 585-7213
Fax: (305) 326-8630
www.jhsmiami.org 390

INDEX

JOHNSON & WALES UNIVERSITY

1701 N.E. 127th Street

Miami, FL 33181

Tel: (305) 892-7000

Fax: (305) 892-7030

www.jwu.edu 364

KANE & COMPANY, P.A.

1101 Brickell Avenue, Suite M-101

Miami, FL 33131

Tel: (305) 789-7900

Fax: (305) 789-7901

www.kanecpas.com 452

LEON MEDICAL CENTERS

11501 S.W. 40th Street

Miami, FL 33165

Tel: (305) 559-5366

Fax: (305) 631-5939

www.leonmedicalcenters.com 391

MCKINLEY FINANCIAL SERVICES

545 N. Andrews Ave.

Fort Lauderdale, FL 33301

Tel: (954) 938-2685

Fax: (954) 938-2695

www.mckinkeyinsurance.com 462

MEDICA HEALTHCARE PLANS

4000 Ponce de Leon, Suite 650

Coral Gables, FL 33146

Tel: (305) 460-0600

Fax: (305) 460-0613

www.medicaplans.com 395

MERCEDES-BENZ OF CORAL GABLES
MERCEDES-BENZ OF CUTLER BAY

300 Almeria Ave.

Coral Gables, FL 33134

Tel: (305) 445-8593

Fax: (305) 447-3766

www.mbcoralgables.com

www.mbcutlerbay.com 478

MIAMI CHILDREN'S HOSPITAL

3100 S.W. 62nd Avenue

Miami, FL 33155

Tel: (305) 666-6511

Fax: (305) 665-8520

www.mch.com 392

MIAMI CHILDREN'S MUSEUM

980 MacArthur Causeway

Miami, FL 33132

Tel: (305) 373-5437

Fax: (305) 373-5431

www.miamichildrensmuseum.org .. 486

MIAMI COUNTRY DAY SCHOOL

601 N.E. 107th Street

Miami, FL 33161

Tel: (305) 759-2843

Fax: (305) 759-4871

www.miamicountryday.org 366

MIAMI DADE CHAMBER OF COMMERCE

11380 N.W. 27th Avenue

Miami, FL 33167

Tel: (305) 751-8648

www.m-dcc.org 329

MIAMI DADE COLLEGE

300 N.E. Second Ave.

Miami, FL 33132

Tel: (305) 237-8888

Fax: (305) 237-3109

www.mdc.edu 342

MIAMI DOWNTOWN DEVELOPMENT AUTHORITY

200 S. Biscayne Blvd.

Suite 2929

Miami, FL 33131

Tel: (305) 579-6675

Fax: (305) 371-2423

www.miamidda.com 332

MIAMI INTERNATIONAL AIRPORT

3600 NW 42nd Avenue

Miami, FL 33122

Tel: (305) 876-7000

Fax: (305) 869-1270

www.miami-airport.com 330

MIAMI INTERNATIONAL UNIVERSITY OF ART & DESIGN

1501 Biscayne Blvd.

Miami, FL 33132

Tel: (305) 428-5700

Fax: (305) 374-7946

www.aimiu.aii.edu 368

MIAMI JEWISH HOME & HOSPITAL

5200 NE 2nd Avenue

Miami, FL 33137

Tel: (305) 751-8626

Fax: (305) 762-1516

www.mjhha.org 394

MIAMI PARKING AUTHORITY

190 N.E. 3rd Street

Miami, FL 33132

Tel: (305) 373-6789

Fax: (305) 371-9451

www.miamiparking.com 335

MIAMI RIVER INN

118 S.W. South River Drive

Miami, FL 33130

Tel: (305) 325-0045

Fax: (305) 325-9227

www.miamiriverinn.com 498

MIAMI SCIENCE MUSEUM

3280 South Miami Ave.

Miami, FL 33129

Tel: (305) 646-4200

Fax: (305) 646-4300

www.miamisci.org 488

INDEX

**MONSIGNOR EDWARD PACE
HIGH SCHOOL**

15600 NW 32nd Avenue
Miami, FL 33054
Tel: (305) 623-7223
www.msgr-pace.com........................348

MORGAN, LEWIS & BOCKIUS LLP

5300 Wachovia Financial Center
200 South Biscayne Boulevard
Miami, FL 33131
Tel: (305) 415-3000
Fax: (305) 415-3001
www.morganlewis.com....................450

**MORRISON, BROWN, ARGIZ
& FARRA, LLP**

1001 Brickell Bay Drive (9th Floor)
Miami, FL 33131
Tel: (305) 373-5500
Fax: (305) 373-0056
www.mbafcpa.com..........................446

NEWS CAFÉ

800 Ocean Drive
Miami Beach, FL 33139
Tel: (305) 538-6397
Fax: (305) 538-7817
www.newscafe.com..........................496

NORTHERN TRUST

700 Brickell Avenue
Miami, FL 33131
Tel: (305) 372-1000
Fax: (305) 789-6253
www.ntrs.com.................................405

**OLYMPIA THEATER AT
GUSMAN CENTER**

174 East Flagler Street
Miami, FL 33131
Tel: (305) 373-6789
Fax: (305) 371-9451
www.gusmancenter.org...................487

ORANGE BOWL COMMITTEE

703 Waterford Way #590
Miami, FL 33125
Tel: (305) 341-4700
Fax: (305) 341-4750
www.orangebowl.org.....................333

PALMER TRINITY SCHOOL

7900 Southwest 176th Street
Palmetto Bay, FL 33157
Tel: (305) 251-2230
Fax: (305) 251-2917
www.palmertrinity.org....................370

PERRY ELLIS INTERNATIONAL

3000 N.W. 107 Avenue
Miami, FL 33172
Tel: (305) 873-1111
Fax: (786) 221-8388
www.perry.com...............................490

PORT OF MIAMI

1015 American Way 2nd Floor
Miami, FL 33132
Tel: (305) 371-7678
Fax: (305) 347-4820
www.miamidade.gov.......................331

R.J. HEISENBOTTLE ARCHITECTS

2199 Ponce de Leon Boulevard, Suite 400
Coral Gables, FL 33134
Tel: (305) 446-7799
Fax: (305) 446-9275
www.rjha.net...................................434

RANSOM EVERGLADES SCHOOL

3575 Main Highway
Coconut Grove, FL 33033
Tel: (305) 460-8847
Fax: (305) 460-7603
www.ransomeverglades.org.............340

RCI GROUP

300 Alton Road, Suite 303
Miami Beach, FL 33139
Tel: (305) 672-5588
Fax: (305) 673-5995.......................492

RILEA GROUP

1000 Brickell Avenue
Suite 1015
Miami, FL 33131
Tel: (305) 371-5254
Fax: (305) 371-4642
www.rileagroup.com.......................432

ROK ENTERPRISES, INC.

48 E. Flagler Street – PH #105
Miami, FL 33131
Tel: (305) 377-4921
Fax: (305) 358-7429
www.rokenterprisesinc.com.............426

ROWLAND COFFEE ROASTERS

5605 N.W. 82nd Ave.
Doral, FL 33166
Tel: (786) 336-5020
Fax: (305) 594-7603
www.javacabana.com.......................476

RYDER SYSTEM, INC.

11690 N.W. 105th Street
Miami, FL 33178
Tel: (305) 500-3726
www.ryder.com...............................466

SHOOK, HARDY AND BACON, L.L.P.

201 South Biscayne Blvd.
Suite2400
Miami, FL 33131
Tel: (305) 358-5171
Fax: (305) 358-7470
www.shb.com..................................442

INDEX

SOUTH FLORIDA HISPANIC CHAMBER OF COMMERCE

30l Arthur Godfrey Road
Suite 500
Miami Beach, FL 33140
Tel: (305) 534-1903
Fax: (305) 534-8365
www.sflhcc.com..............................328

ST. STEPHEN'S EPISCOPAL DAY SHCOOL

3439 Main Highway
Coconut Grove, FL 33133
Tel: (305) 445-2606
Fax: (305) 445-7320
www.sseds.org 363

ST. THOMAS UNIVERSITY

16401 N.W. 37th Avenue
Miami Gardens, FL 33054
Tel: (305) 474-6880
Fax: (305) 620-8298
www.stu.edu 372

SUNRISE COMMUNITY, INC.

9040 Sunset Dr.
Miami, FL 33173
Tel: (305) 596-9040
Fax: (305) 273-3071
www.sunrisegroup.org....................396

SUPERMIX CONCRETE

4300 S.W. 74th Ave.
Miami, FL 33155
Tel: (305) 262-3250
Fax: (305) 267-0698
www.supermix.com.........................436

TERRA GROUP

1200 Brickell Ave.
Miami, FL 33131
Tel: (305) 416-4556
www.terragroup.com 433

THE ALLEN MORRIS COMPANY

121 Alhambra Plaza
Suite 1600
Coral Gables, FL 33134
Tel: (305) 443-1000
Fax: (305) 443-1462
www.allenmorris.com 438

THE CUSHMAN SCHOOL

592 North East 60th Street
Miami, FL 33137
Tel: (305) 757-1966
Fax: (305) 757-1632
www.cushmanschool.org 374

THE FERRARO LAW FIRM

4000 Ponce de Leon Boulevard
Suite 700
Miami, FL 33146
Tel: (305) 375-0111
Fax: (305) 379-6222
www.ferrarolaw.com 449

THE GRAHAM COMPANIES

6843 Main Street
Miami Lakes, FL 33014
Tel: (305) 821-1130
Fax: (305) 557-0313
www.miamilakes.com 422

THE OCEANAIRE SEAFOOD ROOM

900 South Miami Ave.
Miami, FL 33130
Tel: (305) 372-8862
Fax: (305) 372-8170
www.miami.theoceanaire.com 494

THE RELATED GROUP

315 S. Biscayne Blvd.
Miami, FL 33131
Tel: (305) 460-9900
Fax: (305) 460-9911
www.relatedgroup.com...................424

THE RUSTY PELICAN

3201 Rickenbacker Causeway
Key Biscayne, FL 33149
Tel: (305) 361-3818
Fax: (305) 361-5931
www.therustypelican.com...............500

THE SAMUEL SCHECK HILLEL COMMUNITY DAY SCHOOL

19000 N.E. 25th Ave.
North Miami Beach, FL 33180
Tel: (305) 931-2831
Fax: (305) 932-7463
www.hillel-nmb.org 362

UNITED WAY OF MIAMI-DADE

3250 SW 3rd Avenue
Miami, FL 33129
Tel: (305) 860-3000
Fax: (305) 646-7127
www.unitedwaymiami.org 334

UNIVERSITY OF MIAMI

1320 South Dixie Highway #950
Coral Gables, FL 33146
Tel: (305) 284-6047
Fax: (305) 284-2532
www.miami.edu..............................350

UNIVERSITY OF MIAMI HOSPITAL

1400 N.W. 12th Avenue
Miami, FL 33136
Tel: (305) 325-5511
Fax: (305) 325-4673
www.umiamihospital.com 388

UNIVERSITY OF MIAMI HEALTH SYSTEM/LEONARD M. MILLER SCHOOL OF MEDICINE

1600 N.W. 16th Avenue
Suite 1125
Miami, FL 33136
Tel: (305) 243-3453
Fax: (305) 243-8203
www.med.miami.edu......................386

VICTORIA & ASSOCIATES CAREER SERVICES

8181 N.W. 36th Street
Suite 22
Miami, FL 33166
Tel: (305) 477-2233
Fax: (305) 477-2149
www.victoriaassociates.com 458

WACHOVIA

200 South Biscayne Boulevard
15th Floor
Miami, FL 33131
Tel: (305) 789-4823
Fax: (305) 789-4904
www.wachovia.com 410

WOMETCO ENTERPRISES

3195 Ponce de Leon Blvd.
Coral Gables, FL 33134
Tel: (305) 529-1400
Fax: (305) 529-1485
www.wometcoenterprises.com 499

ZUMPANO, PATRICIOS & WINKER, P.A.

312 Minorca Avenue
Coral Gables, FL 33134
Tel: (305) 444-5565
Fax: (305) 444-8588
www.zpwlaw.com 451

ACKNOWLEDGEMENTS

So many people have helped me bring this new edition to life that I almost need another book to thank them all.

First comes Ray Spagnuolo of Community Media and the corporate sponsors who made this larger, four-color book possible. I am grateful for their faith in me and in the project.

Sadly, several of my mentors and closest friends have died since the last edition. Dr. Charlton W. Tebeau gave me years of guidance and inspiration and Dr. Thelma P. Peters constantly encouraged my growth as an historian and a woman. Mary Munroe and Patty Catlow, who helped launch my career, are sorely missed.

Others deserve special mention. My friend, historian and editor Howard Kleinberg continues to provide good humor and share his expertise. Historian Dorothy Jenkins Fields adds her essential perspective. Joe Knetsch, another outstanding historian, is always ready to answer questions and send new information my way. Archaeologist Bob Carr teaches me new secrets about Miami's distant past. William Straight, M.D., who started out as a medical doctor and became an historian, is a valued contributor. Don Gaby and Jim Broton are always eager to share their excellent Miami River research and writing. Carolyn Klepser always provides superior research and counsel.

We are fortunate that another generation of historians is ready to pick up the torch and continue to explore Miami's past. Two of the best are Laura Pincus and Larry Wiggins, both of whom helped me write this book. Another, Judge Scott Silverman, is doing superior research and writing about Miami-Dade County's legal and judicial history while preserving it.

Many others have contributed to this effort. Childhood friend Joe Fitzgerald, M.D., shares his rare South Florida maps and his prodigious knowledge. Alberto Ibargüen, Dave Lawrence Jr., Laura Pincus, Merrett Stierheim and Hugh MacRae II took the time to write for the book.

My dear friend Mildred Merrick has shared her time and expertise and has trusted me with material from the Merrick Collection. Estelle Overstreet, who has celebrated her 101st birthday, is an absolute font of information.

Photographs tell their own stories and this book is enriched with images that speak volumes. For that, I am indebted to many people and organizations.

Since the day I first laid my eyes on Ralph Munroe's photographs, I have appreciated Miami's unique photographic history. This new edition is loaded with both old and new images. Once again the Historical Museum of Southern Florida has allowed me the use of their incomparable collection and Dawn Hugh has, as usual, been invaluable. Jorge Zamanillo and Christina Blanco also provided assistance.

When it comes to new images, several friends stand out. Harry Emilio Gottlieb took hundreds of photographs from early morning to late at night. Although not a professional photographer, he performed like one as his work attests. Randy Groh did as well. Their evocative images are on the cover, end sheets and are sprinkled throughout the book. Frank and Fran Rollason made a special effort to capture the MiMo/BiBo district. Mary Carolyn Smith Pohl, Fred Kirtland and Charlotte Wise Powers shared vintage photographs of their pioneer families, and dear friend Jean Batten of her late husband. Jim Reeder and Jerry Wilkerson also added valuable images.

Nationally known photographer Steven Brooke, who took many of the photographs in the earlier book, allowed me to use his photos again. Michael Carlebach, Ray Fisher, Michael Stephen McFarland and Bobi Dimond also shared their work. Some of Miami's best architectural photographers are listed under their images provided by architectural and realty firms and museums.

The Miami Herald generously allowed me the use of their photographs critical to illustrating Miami's recent past. Megan Waters, Fernanda Roca and Elissa Vanaver were particularly helpful. Others deserve special mention for taking time to provide information, to locate and send photographs or facilitate their acquisition. They include Kendrick Meek, Don Worth, Les Martines, Rosario Kennedy, Madeleine Parades, Les Pantin, Patricia Rhode, Randall Robinson, Ralph Sanchez and Don Boyd. Institutional help came from Donna Shalala, Janet Gavarret, Christine Casas, Liz Plater-Zyberk and Maria Estorino at the University of Miami; Carol Damien, Hope Herman and Judith Dabdoub at Florida International University; Juan Mendieta and Irene Muñoz at Miami Dade College; Paula Musto at Miami-Dade County; Mayor Manny Diaz, Isabel de Armas and Jorge R. Perez at the City of Miami; Gene Tinnie, Virginia Key Park Trust; Alyce Robertson and Yami Roa, Downtown Development Authority; Luis Wong, City of Miami Beach; Madeleine Parades, Greater Miami Visitors and Convention Bureau; and Iris Romero, Sunny Isles Beach Association. Cultural institutions also added their perspective and images. They include: Sherwood "Woody" Weiser and Suzette Espinosa, Adrienne Arsht Performing Arts Center; Rose Ellen Greene and Mitchell Snow at MAM; Chi Lam, Rubell Family Collection; Tessa Blumenberg, Margulies Collection; Gillian Thomas, Adriana Villar and Jose Lima at the Miami Museum of Science; Mireille Chancy-Gonzalez at the Haitian Cultural Alliance; and Gepsie Metellus at Sant La Haitian Neighborhood Center.

Eric Pons and Larry Wahl of the Orange Bowl Committee, Kristen Hingston of the Miami Dolphins, Andrew Hertz at the Miami Seaquarium, Robert Vignon of the Florida Marlins and Nick Maiorana of the Miami Heat helped with the sports scene.

Architects Jose Gelabert-Navia, Thorn Grafton, John Fullerton, Richard Heisenbottle, John Nichols and Luis Revuelta shared images of their work. Dennis Wilhelm of Arquitectonica, Cheryl Jacobs of Zyscovich Architects and Daisy Fernandez of Fullerton Diaz were particularly helpful.

Business organizations also provided photographs, including Megan Kelly, Swire Properties; Tony Goldman, Goldman Properties; Alex Rico, Related Cervera Realty Services; Anuca Valverde, Cervera Realty; and Jennifer Toledo, Dacra Development.

Eleanore Keim and Cecy Williams added their artistic touch by hand-coloring vintage photographs. Those who were helpful in the earlier editions are acknowledged in the photo credits.

This book would not have happened without the support of my husband, Bob McCabe, the talents of designer Rhondda Edmiston and editor Patty Shillington, and the assistance of Nuria Santizo. The keen eye and professionalism of Eladio Robertson, who oversees the printing, makes us all look good.

Before I end, I need to thank ever-changing Miami, the place of my birth, for giving me so much to write about. My late parents Jack and Anne Parker Moore, who, like so many others, moved to Miami from someplace else, gave me my sense of history and taught me to appreciate Miami and its diverse people.

Arva Moore Parks
September 2008

SELECTED BIBLIOGRAPHY

The following bibliography is limited to books that are available in South Florida libraries. Most of the research material for *The New Miami: The Magic City* came from primary sources—manuscript collections, diaries, government documents and reports found in the following research libraries.

Black Archives History and Research Foundation, Inc., Joseph Caleb Center, Miami, Florida

Charlton W. Tebeau Library of Florida History, Historical Museum of Southern Florida, Miami, Florida

Florida Collection, Miami-Dade Public Library, Miami, Florida

Florida Collection, Monroe County Library, Key West, Florida

Cuban Collection and Special Collections, Richter Library, University of Miami, Coral Gables, Florida

Florida Collection, Strozier Libraries, Florida State University, Tallahassee, Florida

Louis Wolfson II Media History Center, Miami-Dade Public Library, Miami, Florida

P.K. Yonge Library of Florida History, University of Florida, Gainesville, Florida

The most valuable printed sources on the history of Miami are *Tequesta* and *South Florida History* magazine, publications of the Historical Association of Southern Florida. Other valuable articles are found in the *Florida Historical Quarterly*, the *Florida Anthropologist* and *Broward Legacy*. Newspaper sources include *The Miami News*, formerly *The Miami Metropolis* (1896-1988), *The Miami Herald*, *The Miami Times*, *The Tropical Sun* and *Miami Today*.

BOOKS

Akin, Edward. *Flagler: Rockefeller Partner and Florida Baron*. Kent, Ohio: Kent State University Press, 1988.

Allman, T.D. *Miami: City of the Future*. New York: Atlantic Monthly Press, 1987.

Ammidown, Margot and Ivan Rodriguez. *Wilderness to Metropolis*. Miami, Florida: Metropolitan Dade County, 1982.

Anderson, Edward C. *Florida Territory in 1844*. Edited by W. Stanley Hoole. Alabama: University of Alabama Press, 1977.

Anderson, Marie. *Julia's Daughter: Women in Dade History*. Miami, Florida: Herstory of Florida, Inc., 1980.

Ardalan, Christine. *Warm Hearts and Caring Hands*. Miami, Florida: Centennial Press, 2005.

Arend, Geoffrey. *Great Airports: Miami*. New York: Air Cargo News, Inc., 1986.

Armbrister, Ann. *The Life and Times of Miami Beach*. New York: Alfred A. Knopf, 1995.

Ballinger, Kenneth. *Miami Millions*. Miami, Florida: Franklin Press, 1936.

Barrientos, Bartolome. *Pedro Menendez de Aviles*. (1567). Trans. by Anthony Kerrigan. Gainesville, Florida: University of Florida Press, 1956.

Biondi, Joann. *Miami Beach Memories: A Nostalgic Chronicle of Days Gone By*. Guilford, Connecticut: Globe Pequot Press, 2007.

Blackman, E.V. *Miami and Dade Country, Florida*. Miami, Florida: Victor Rainbolt, 1921.

Blake, Nelson M. *Land into Water-Water into Land*. Gainesville, Florida: University Presses of Florida, 1980.

Blank, Joan Gill. *Key Biscayne*. Sarasota, Florida: The Pineapple Press, 1996.

Blight, James G, et al. *Cuba on the Brink: Castro, The Missile Crisis, and the Soviet Collapse*. New York: Pantheon, 1993.

Born, Donna. *The Road to Somewhere*. Miami, Florida: Arva Parks & Co., 1990.

Boswell, Thomas D. ed. *South Florida: The Winds of Change*. Miami, Florida, Annual Conference of the Association of American Geographers, April 1991.

Branson, Seth H. *Speedway to Sunshine*. Erin, Ontario: The Boston Mills Press, 1984.

Brookfield, Charles M. and Oliver Griswold. *They All Called it Tropical*. Miami, Florida: Banyan Books, 1977.

Broton, Jim. *Home on the River*. Miami, Florida: The Broton Group, 2007.

Buker, George E. *Swamp Sailors*. Gainesville, Florida: University Presses of Florida, 1975.

Capitman, Barbara. *Deco Delights*. New York: E.P. Dutton, 1988.

Ceo, Rocco J. and Margot Ammidown. *Redland*. Miami, Florida: Metropolitan Dade County, 1993.

Cerwinske, Laura. *Miami, Hot and Cool*. New York: Clarkson N. Potter, Inc., 1990.

_____. *Tropical Deco*. New York: Rizzoli, 1981.

Chesney, Ann Spatch, et. al. *Miami Diary 1896*. Miami, Florida: privately printed, 1996.

Clemence, Paul and Julie Davidow. *Miami Contemporary Artists*. Atglen: Schiffer Publishing, 2007.

Cohen, Isidor. *Historical Sketches and Sidelight of Miami, Florida*. Miami, Florida: privately printed, 1925.

Confronting Racial Isolation in Miami. Washington, D.C.: U.S. Commission on Civil Rights, 1982.

Croucher, Sheila. *Imaging Miami: Ethnic Politics in a Post Modern World*. Charlottesville, Virginia: University of Virginia Press, 1997.

Culot, Maurice and Jean-Francois LeJeune. *Miami: Architecture of the Tropics*. New York: Princeton Architectural Press, 1993.

Deadlock: The Inside Story of America's Closest Election. New York: Public Affairs, 2001.

DeCroix, F. W. *Miami and Ft. Lauderdale*. St. Augustine, Florida: Record Co., c1911.

Deer, Mark. *Some Kind of Paradise*. New York: William Morrow and Company, Inc., 1989.

Didion, Joan. *Miami*. New York: Simon and Schuster, 1987.

Doner, Michele Oka and Mitchell Wolfson, Jr. *Miami Beach: Blueprint of an Eden*. Cologne: Feierabend Unique Books, 2005.

Douglas, Marjory Stoneman. *The Everglades: River of Grass*. Miami, Florida: Banyan Books, 1978.

_____. *Voice of the River*. Englewood, Florida: Pineapple Press, Inc., 1987.

Downs, Dorothy. *Art of the Florida Seminole and Miccosukee Indians*. Gainesville, Florida: University Presses of Florida, 1995.

Dunlop, Beth. *Aqua: Miami Modern by the Sea*. New York: Rizzoli, 2007.

_____. *Miami: Mediterranean Splendor and Deco Dreams*. New York: Rizzoli, 2007.

_____. *Arquitectonica*. New York: Rizzoli, 2004.

Dunn, Marvin. *Black Miami in the Twentieth Century*. Gainesville, Florida: University Press of Florida, 1997.

DuPuis, John G. *History of Early Medicine in Dade County*. Miami, Florida: privately printed, 1954.

Erdman, Barbara Putman, editor. *Beyond Julia's Daughters*. Coconut Grove: Herstory Committee of the Women's History Coalition, 2006.

Escalante Fontaneda, Hernando D'. *Memoir*. (c.1575). Trans. by Buckingham Smith. Edited by Buckingham Smith. Edited by David O. True. Coral Gables, Florida: University of Miami Press, 1947.

Fairchild, David. *The World Grows Round My Door*. New York: Charles Scribner's Sons, 1947.

Firmat, Gustavo Perez. *Life on the Hyphen: The Cuban-American Way*. Austin, Texas: University of Texas Press, 1994.

_____. *Next Year in Cuba: A Cubano's Coming-of-Age in America*. New York: Anchor Books, 1995.

Fisher, Jane. *Fabulous Hoosier*. Chicago: Harry Coleman and Co., 1953.

Fitzgerald Bush, Frank S. *A Dream of Araby*. Opa-locka, Florida: South Florida Archaeological Museum, 1976.

Foster, Mark S. *Castles in the Sand*. Gainesville: University Presses of Florida, 2000.

Frazure, Hoyt. *Memories of Old Miami*. Miami, Florida: *The Miami Herald*, 1969.

Gaby, Donald. *The Miami River and Its Tributaries*. Miami, Florida: Historical Association of Southern Florida, 1993.

Garcia, Maria Christina. *Havana U.S.A.: Cuban Americans in South Florida 1959-1994*. Berkeley, California: University of California Press, 1996.

George, Paul. *A Journey Through Time: A Pictorial History of South Dade*. Virginia Beach, Virginia: The Donning Company, 1995.

_____. *Little Havana*. Charleston, South Carolina: Arcadia Publishing, 2006.

Gibson, Thelma Vernell Anderson. *Forbearance*. Homestead, Florida: Helena Enterprises, Inc. 2000.

Gifford, John C. *The Everglades and Other Essays Relating to South Florida*. Miami, Florida: Everglades Land Sales, 1911.

Giller, Norman and Sarah Giller Nelson. *Designing the Good Life: Norman M. Giller and the Development of Miami Modernism*. Gainesville, Florida: University Press of Florida, 2007.

Gonzalez-Pando, Miguel. *Greater Miami: Spirit of Cuban Enterprise*. Fort Lauderdale, Florida: Copperfield Publications, Inc., 1996.

SELECTED BIBLIOGRAPHY

Grenier, Guillermo and Alex Steppick, eds. *Miami Now! Immigration, Ethnicity, and Social Change*. Gainesville, Florida: University Press of Florida, 1992.

Grunwald, Michael. *The Swamp*. New York: Simon & Schuster, 2006.

Guide to Miami and Environs. Work Progress Administration. Northport, New York: Bacon Percy and Daggett, 1941.

Hann, John H. *Missions to the Calusa*. Gainesville, Florida: University Presses of Florida, 1991.

Harwood, Kathryn Chapman. *The Lives of Vizcaya*. Miami, Florida: Banyan Books, Inc., 1985.

Hatton, Hap. *Tropical Splendor*. New York: Alfred A. Knopf, 1987.

Hoffmeister, John Edward. *Land from the Sea*. Coral Gables, Florida: University of Miami Press, 1974.

Hollingsworth, Tracy. *History of Dade County Florida*. Coral Gables, Florida: Parker Art Printing, 1949.

Hourihan, J.B. *My Daddy Made the Sidewalks*. Miami, Florida: Centennial Press, 2005.

Kanter, Rosabeth Moss. *World Class: Thriving Locally in the Global Economy*. New York: Simon & Schuster, 1995.

Kearney, Bob, ed. *Mostly Sunny Days*. Miami, Florida: *The Miami Herald*, 1986.

Kent, Gertrude M. *The Coconut Grove School*. Coral Gables, Florida: Parker Printing, 1972.

Kersey, Harry A., Jr. *Pelts, Plumes and Hides*. Gainesville, Florida: University Presses of Florida, 1975.

Kinerk, Michael, Dennis W. Wilhelm and Barbara Capitman. *Rediscovering Art Deco U.S.A.* New York: Penguin Books, 1994.

Kleinberg, Howard. *Florida Hurricane and Disaster*. Miami, Florida: Centennial Press, 1992.

_____. The Florida Hurricane and Disaster, 1992. Miami, Florida: Centennial Press, 1992.

_____. *Miami: The Way We Were*. Tampa, Florida: Surfside Publishing, 1989.

_____. *Miami Beach: A History*. Miami, Florida: Centennial Press, 1994.

_____. *The Stingaree Century*. Miami, Florida: Centennial Press, 2003.

_____. *Woggles and Cheese Holes: The History of Miami Beach Hotels*. Miami Beach, Florida: Greater Miami and Beaches Hotel Association, 2005.

Lapidus, Morris. *Too Much is Never Enough: The Autobiography of Morris Lapidus*. New York: Rizzoli, 1996.

LaRoue, Samuel and Ellen Uguccioni. *The Biltmore Hotel: An Enduring Legacy*. Miami, Florida: Centennial Press, 2002.

Lejeune, Jean Francois and Allan Shulman. *The Making of Miami Beach 1933-1942: The Architecture of L. Murray Dixon*. New York: Rizzoli, 2001.

Levine, Robert and Moises Asis. *Cuban Miami*. New Brunswick: Rutgers University Press, 2000.

Liebman, Malvina W. and Seymour B. Liebman. *Jewish Frontiersmen*. Miami Beach, Florida: Jewish Historical Society of South Florida, Inc., 1980.

Llanes, Jose. *Cuban Americans: Masters of Survival*. Cambridge, Massachusetts: Abt Books, 1982.

Lummus, J.N. *The Miracle of Miami Beach*. Miami, Florida: Miami Post Publishing Co., 1940.

Lyon, Eugene. *The Enterprise of Florida*. Gainesville, Florida: University Presses of Florida, 1965.

_____. *The Search for the Atocha*. New York: Harper and Row, 1979.

Mahon, John D. *History of the Second Seminole War*. Gainesville, Florida: University of Florida Press, 1967.

Mahoney, Lawrence. *The Early Birds*. Miami, Florida: Pickering Press, 1987.

Martin, Sidney Walter. *Florida's Flagler*. Athens, Georgia: University of Georgia Press, 1949.

McIver, Stuart. *The Greatest Sale on Earth*. Miami, Florida: E.A. Seeman Publishing, Inc., 1980.

Merzer, Martin and Staff. *The Miami Herald Report: Democracy Held Hostage*. New York: St. Martin's Press, 2001.

Miami Herald Staff. *Miami: In Our Own Words*. Kansas City, Kansas: Andrews and McMeel, 1995.

Milanich, Jerald T. and Charles H. Fairbanks. *Florida Archaeology*. New York: Academic Press, 1980.

Milanich, Jerald T. and Samuel Proctor, eds. *Tacahale*. Gainesville, Florida: University Presses of Florida, 1976.

Miller, Randall M. and George E. Pozzetta, eds. *Shades of the Sunbelt: Essays on Ethnicity, Race and the Urban South*. Boca Raton, Florida: Florida Atlantic University Press, 1989.

Mohl, Raymond. *South of the South: Jewish Activists and the Civil Rights Movement in Miami 1945-1960*. Gainesville, Florida: University of Florida Press, 2004.

Moore, Deborah Dash. *To the Golden Cities: Pursuing the American Jewish Dream in Miami and L.A.* New York: The Free Press, 1994.

Morrisey, Pat. *Miami's Neighborhoods*. Miami, Florida: The Miami News, 1982.

Motte, Jacob Rhett. *Journey into Widerness*. Edited by James F. Sunderman. Gainesville, Florida: University of Florida Press, 1963.

Muir, Helen. *Baby Grace Sees the Cow*. Miami, Florida: The Prologue Society, 2004.

_____. *Miami U.S.A.* New York: Henry Holt, 1953, 2nd Edition, 1990.

_____. *The Biltmore: Beacon for Miami*. Miami, Florida: Pickering Press, 1993.

Munroe, Ralph Middletown and Vincent Gilpin. *The Commodore's Story*. Reprinted from 1930 edition by the Historical Association of Southern Florida. Norberth, Pennsylvania: Livingston Co., 1966.

Murrell, Muriel V. *Miami: A Backward Glance*. Sarasota, Florida: Pineapple Press, 2003.

Nash, Charles Edgar. *The Magic of Miami Beach*. Philadelphia: David McKay, 1938.

Nash, Eric and Randall Robinson. *MiMo: Miami Modern Revealed*. San Francisco: Chronicle Books. 2004.

Marina, William and Charlton Tebeau. *Rendezvous with Greatness*. Coral Gables, Florida: University of Miami Press, 2001.

Morrissey, Pat, ed. *Miami's Neighborhoods*. Miami, Florida: The Miami News, 1982.

Olson, James F. and Judith E. Olson. *The Cuban American: From Trauma to Triumph*. New York: Twayne Publishers, 1995.

Parks, Arva Moore. *George Merrick's Coral Gables: Where Your Castles in Spain are Made Real*. Miami, Florida: Centennial Press, 2006.

_____. *Miami Memoirs, A New Pictorial Edition of John Sewell's Own Story (1931)*. Miami, Florida: Arva Parks & Company, 1987.

_____. and Greg Bush with Laura Pincus. *Miami: The American Crossroad*. Needham, Massachusetts: Simon & Shcuster, 1976.

_____. *The Forgotten Frontier*. Miami, Florida Banyan Books, Inc. 1978, revised edition Miami, Centennial Press, 2004.

_____. *Miami: The Magic City*. First edition, Continental Heritage Press, Tulsa, Oklahoma, 1980; Second edition, Miami, Florida: Centennial Press. 1990.

_____. ed. *Miami Sense of Place*. Miami, Florida: Greater Miami Visitors and Convention Bureau, 2004.

_____. *Miami Then and Now*. Miami, Florida: Centennial Press, 1992.

_____ and Carolyn Klepsler. *Miami Then and Now*. San Diego, California: Thunder Bay Press, 2002.

_____. *Pathway to Greatness: Building the University of Miami: 1926-2001*. Miami, Florida: Centennial Press, 2001.

Patricios, Nicholas M. *Building Marvelous Miami*. Gainesville, Florida: University of Florida Press, 1994.

Perrine, Henry E. *The True Story of Some Eventful Year in Grandpa's Life*. Buffalo, New York: E. H. Hutchinson, 1885.

Peters, Thelma. *Biscayne County*. Miami, Florida: Banyan Books, 1976.

_____. *Lemon City*. Miami, Florida: Banyan Books, 1976.

_____. *Miami 1909*. Miami, Florida: Banyan Books, 1984.

Picchi, Blaise. *The Five Weeks of Giuseppe Zangara*. Chicago: Academy Chicago Publishers, 1998.

Pierce, Charles W. *Pioneer Life in Southeast Florida*. Edited by Donald Walter Curl. Coral Gables, Florida: University of Miami Press, 1970.

Places in Time. Miami, Florida: Florida International University, 1994.

Porter, Bruce and Marvin Dunn. *The Miami Riot of 1980*. Lexington, Massachusetts: Lexington Books, 1984.

Portes, Alejandro and Alex Stepick. *City on the Edge: The Transformation of Miami*. Berkeley, California: University of California Press, 1993.

Redford, Polly. *Billion-Dollar Sandbar*. New York: E.P. Dutton and Co., 1970.

Reiff, David. *The Exile: Cuba in the Heart of Miami*. New York: Simon and Schuster, 1991.

_____. *Going to Miami*. Boston, Massachusetts: Little Brown and Co., 1987.

Robinson, Tim. *A Tropical Frontier*. Port Salerno, Florida: Port Sun Publishing, 2005.

Rybczynski, Witold and Laurie Olin. *Vizcaya*. Philadelphia, Pennsylvania: University of Pennsylvania Press, 2007.

Sandiford, Les. *Last Train to Paradise*. New York: Crown Publishers, 2002.

SELECTED BIBLIOGRAPHY

Sandoval, Mercedes Cros. *Mariel and Cuban National Identity*. Miami: Editorial SIBI, 1985.

Smiley, Nixon. *Knights of the Fourth Estate*. Miami, Florida: E.A. Seemann, 1974.

Solis, de Meras, Gonzalo. *Pedro Menendez de Aviles*. A facsimile reproduction of 1567 manuscript. Translated by Jeannette Thurber Connor. Gainesville, Florida: University of Florida Press, 1964.

Stearns, Frank F. *Along Greater Miami's Sun-Sea-Ara*. Miami, Florida: Privately printed, 1932.

Stepick, Alex, Gullermo Grenier, Max Castro and Marvin Dunn. *This Land is Our Land: Immigrants and Power in Miami*. Berkeley: University of California Press, 2003.

Stofik, Mary Barron. *Saving South Beach*. Gainesville: University Press of Florida, 2005.

Stuart, John. and John Stack. *The New Deal in South Florida: Design, Policy and Community Building, 1933-1940*. Gainesville: University Press of Florida, 2008.

Taylor, Jean. *The Villages of South Dade*. St. Petersburg, Florida: Byron Kennedy and Company, 1987.

Tebeau, Charlton W. A. *History of Florida*. Coral Gables, Florida: University of Miami Press, 1971.

_____. *Florida's Last Frontier*. Coral Gables, Florida: University of Miami Press, 1956.

_____. *Man in the Everglades: 2,000 Years of Human History in the Everglades National Park*. Coral Gables, Florida: University of Miami Press, 1968.

_____. *Temple Israel of Greater Miami*. Coral Gables, Florida: University of Miami Press, 1972.

_____. *The University of Miami: A Golden Anniversary History*. Coral Gables, Florida: University of Miami Press, 1976.

Vickers, Raymond B. *Panic in Paradise*. Tuscaloosa, Alabama: The University of Alabama Press, 1994.

Weigall, T.H. *Boom in Paradise*. New York: Alfred H. King, 1932.

West, Patsy. *The Enduring Seminoles*. Gainesville, Florida: University Press of Florida, 1998.

Willbanks, William. *Forgotten Heroes*. Paducah, Kentucky: Turner Publishing Company, 1996.

Wyden, Peter. *Bay of Pigs: The Untold Story*. New York: Simon and Schuster, 1979.

Zuckerman, Bertram. *The Dream Lives On: A History of Fairchild Tropical Garden, 1938-1966*. Miami, Florida: Fairchild Tropical Garden, 1988.

_____. *The Kampong: The Fairchild's Tropical Paradise*. Miami, Florida: Fairchild Tropical Garden, 1993.

(TP)

PHOTO CREDITS

A	Arquitectonica
AC	Alvah Chapman
AHC	Archaeological and Historical Conservancy
APC	Arva Parks & Company
AW	Alice Wood
BA	Black Archives History and Research Foundation
BC	Bob Carr
BD	Bobi Dimond
BG	Bob Graham
BL	Bob Lamme
BS	Beber Silverstein Group
CG	City of Coral Gables
CH	Chris Hansen
CM	City of Miami
CMC	Claude Matlock Collection Historical Museum of Southern Florida
CSP	Connie Seybold Prunty
CT	Children's Trust
CWP	Charlotte Wise Powers
DB	Don Boyd
DDA	Downtown Development Authority
DDD	Dorothy Dean Davidson
DPZ	Duany-Plater-Zyberk
DES	Donna E. Shalala
DS	Don Shula
DAW	David A. Wilson
DW	Don Worth
EF	Enterprise Florida
EPM	Eunice Peacock Merrick Collection
EV	Elizabeth Virrick
FC	Fisbaugh Collection, State of Florida Photographic Archives
FIU	Florida International University
FK	Fred Kirtland
FM	Florida Marlins
FR	Frank Rollason
GA	Grimshaw Architects
GP	Goldman Properties
HFM	Flagler Museum
HG	Harry Emilio Gottlieb
HMSF	Historical Museum of Southern Florida
HSPBC	Historical Society of Palm Beach County
IP	Isabelle Peacock
JB	Jo Ann Bass
JF	Joseph Fitzgerald, M.D.
JGB	Joan Gill Blank
JGN	Jose Gelabert-Navia
JK	Jim Kitchens
JP	Joe Pero
JS	Jeannette Slesnick
KM	Kendrick Meek
KSD	Kate Stirrup Dean
KT	Ken Treister
LC	Library of Congress
LL	Lynn Lummus
LM	Lee Martines
LW	Larry Wiggins
MAM	Miami Art Museum
MB	City of Miami Beach
MC	Munroe Collection, Historical Museum of Southern Florida
MCSP	Mary Carolyn Smith Pohl

MCW	Margulies Collection at the Warehouse
MD	Miami Dolphins
MDC	Miami Dade College
M-DC	Miami-Dade County
MDPL	Miami Design Preservation League
MH	*Miami Herald*
MM	Mildred Merrick
MN	*Miami News* Collection, Historical Museum of Southern Florida
MSV	Village of Miami Shores
MSMc	Michael Stephen McFarlane
MT	Museum Towers
NA	National Archives
NBA	NBA Photos
NOAA	National Oceanic and Atmospheric Administration
NBWWA	Nichols Brosch Wurst Wolfe & Associates
PAC	Performing Arts Center
PR	Patricia Rhode
RC	Romer Collection, Miami Dade Public Library
RCRS	Related Cervera Realty Services
RFC	Rubell Family Collection
RG	K. Randall Groh, D.D.S.
RK	Rosario Kennedy
RL	Revuelta Vega Leon
RLG	Related Group
RM	Richard Maxwell
RR	Randall Robinson
RSAN	Ralph Sanchez
RS	Ruth Shack
RTG	Russell Thorn Granfton
MS	Miami Seaquarium
SDL	Sam D. LaRoue
SL	Sant La
SP	Swire Properties
SIB	City of Sunny Isles Beach
SPA	State of Florida Photographic Archives
SPSC	St. Patrick's School Collection
SS	Scott Silverman
RK	Rok Enterprises
TA	Thomas Abraham
TC	Trinity Cathedral
TG	Tucker Gibbs
TP	Thelma Peters
UF	University of Florida Archivo General de Indians, Stetson Collection
UM	University of Miami
USN	U.S. Navy
USNAM	U.S. Naval Academy Museum
USS	U.S. Senate
V	Vizcaya Museum & Gardens
VW	Verne Williams
W-FIU	Wolfsonian-Florida International University
WH	White House
WS	William Straight, M.D.
ZA	Zyscovich Architects

INDEX

A

Abraham, Thomas G. 284
Actor's Playhouse 311
Adams, John 47
Addison, John 53, 58, 59
Adrienne Arsht Center 317
Agam, Yaacov 254
Albaisa, Adolfo, 243
Allman, T.D. 245, 260
Alvarez, Carlos (Mayor) 306
Americana Hotel, 213, 214, 215
Anderson, Edward 34
Anderson, Perry 264
Andrews, Samuel 86
Anderson, Marian 208
Ansin, Toby 267
Anti-Saloon League 111
Arison, Ted and Lynn 265
Armstrong, Neil 230
Arquitectonica International 254, 255, 298, 312, 315
Arriola, Ricky 317
Arsht, Adrienne 317
Art Basel Miami Beach 398, 300, 301, 302, 305
Art Deco 240, 241, 256, 258, 259, 272, 294, 302
Art in Public Places 265, 284, 305
Astor, Vincent 180
Atkins, C. Clyde 234
Atlantis 254
Audubon, John James 25
Auer, Joe 231
Austin, Silas 86

B

Babcock, Charles 251
Babylon 255
Baggs, Bill 230
Bahamas 15, 17, 18, 47, 73, 262, 264,
Bahamas Royal Gazette 18
Bahn, Nancy 284
Bakehouse Art Complex 300
Ball Building (Miami Center) 255
Ballinger, Kenneth 166
Bank of Bay Biscayne 90, 91, 92, 99, 117, 129
Bank of Fort Dallas 117
Barefoot Mailman 47
Barnacle 70
Barnes, A.D. 182, 183
Barrios, Jarrett 293
Barry University 267, 308
Barry, Dave 272
Bass Museum 235, 398
Batista, Fulgencio 220
Batten, Jim 283, 311
Bay of Pigs, the 224, 225
Bayfront Park 145, 233, 256, 282, 284
Bayside 256, 258, 272
Bayview House 58, 59, 69
Beasley, Anna 49 63
Beasley, Edmund 37, 47, 49, 63, 139
Beatles, the 229
Bellusschi, Pietro 255
Bethel A.M.E. Church 135
Bicentennial Park 236, 237, 296
Bills, Jeanne Bellamy 243
Biltmore Hotel 156, 160, 161, 164, 258

Biscayne Bay 4, 6, 15, 34, 57, 68, 78, 104, 119, 134, 152, 164, 165, 238, 252
Biscayne Bay Company 52, 53, 57, 74, 78, 81
Biscayne Bay Yacht Club 68, 112, 273
Biscayne Boulevard 170, 172, 180, 191, 217, 238, 239,258, 266, 285, 298,
Biscayne Hotel 109
Biscayne House of Refuge 54, 55
Biscayne National Monument (Park) 230
Biscayne View Apartments 54, 112
Black Archives History and Research Foundation 261
Blackman, E.V. 94, 100
Blanchard, Allan
Bolton, Roxcy 235
Booker T. Washington Middle School 271
Bower, Matti Herrera (Mayor) 259, 317
Bowlegs, Billy 39
Bowles, William Augustus 17, 18
Boyd, Joe 234
Brady, E.L. 84, 110
Brady's Grocery Store 93, 109
Braman, Norman 315
Breckenridge, John C. 41
Brickell Avenue 65, 102, 108, 112, 123, 133, 134, 228, 254, 255, 257, 286, 287, 295, 296, 309
Brickell, Edith 140
Brickell Hammock 65
Brickell, Mary 42, 50, 65, 82, 140
Brickell Trading Post 50, 51
Brickell, William B. 50, 83, 87, 101
Bright, James 149, 158
Britto, Romero 284, 285
Brodie, M.J. 264
Broward, Napoleon Bonaparte (Governor) 119
Brown, A.W. 76, 83
Brown, John 56
Brown, John O., M.D. 206
Brown, Mariah 61, 63
Browner, Carol 283
Bryan, William Jennings 114, 115, 127, 133, 155, 157
Bryan, Mary Baird 127
Budge's Hardware Store 105, 109
Buena Vista East 260
Burdine, Bess (Mrs. Albert Cushing Reed) 110, 139
Burdine, W.M. 110, 139
Burdines Department Store 110, 118
Burgee, John 255
Burlingame, Margaret 136
Burrows, Alice 67
Bush, George H. (President) 280, 293, 308, 309
Bush, Gregory 313
Bush, John Ellis (Governor) 287
Button, Frank 147, 154
Byoir, Carl 177

C

Caldwell, Millard (Governor) 202, 239

Caldwell, Russell 180, 181
Call, Richard Keith (Governor) 28
Calle Ocho 240, 263, 271
Canseco, Jose 272
Cape Canaveral 190, 230
Cape Florida Lighthouse 36, 40, 54, 71, 98, 112,139, 230
Cape Florida Settlement 18, 22, 24, 25, 26, 28
Capitman, Barbara 256, 259, 272, 298
Capone, Al "Scarface" 175, 204
Carbonell, Manuel 8, 286
Caribbean Marketplace 263
Carlos, Chief 6, 9
Carlton, Doyle (Governor) 175, 176
Carney, Dick 64
Carnival Center for the Performing Arts 296, 304, 305, 306 (See also Adrienne Arsht Center)
Carr, Robert (Bob) 261, 286
Carrollo, Joe (Mayor) 301
Carter, Aaron 20, 29
Carter, Jimmy (President) 246
Carver Village 207
Casas, Roberto 262
Castro, Fidel 220, 224, 246, 271, 300, 301
Cejas, Paul 262
Center for the Fine Arts 240, 243
CenTrust 272, 276, 285
Cermak, Anton 180, 181
Chaille Block 260
Chaille, Josiah 144
Chaille's Racket Store 110
Challenger Seven Memorial 257
Chamber of Commerce 144, 145, 173, 236, 243, 251, 262
Chamberlain, J.N. 83, 85, 104
Chapman, Alvah 237, 280, 315
Chapman, Bill 258
Chappell, Dan 176
Chase, C.W. "Pete" 149
Chekaika, Indian Leader 30, 32, 33
Christo (Javacheff) 252
City of Miami Commission 281, 313
Civic Theatre 175, 178
Clark, Dan 47
Clark, John 205
Clark, Steve (Mayor) 236, 266, 271, 282, 283, 310
Claughton, Edward 136
Clinton, William J. (President) 283, 301, 308
Coconut (Cocoanut) Grove 27, 37, 39, 47, 48, 49, 53, 57, 61, 63, 171, 174, 200, 201, 226, 235, 259
Coconut Grove Art Festival 235
Coconut Grove Playhouse 311
Codina, Armando 262
Coe, Ernest 202
Coffey, Kendall 293
Cohen, Isidor 83, 88. 92, 110, 318
Cohen, Samuel P. 204
Collins, John 123, 124, 125, 126, 128, 129, 188
Collins, Leroy 207, 272
Colonnade Building
Colored Town 134, 135,137, 140
Columbus Hotel 217

Congregational Church 91
Cooley, Brad 16
Cooley, Brad Jr. 16
Cooley, William 28
Cooper, Frank 265
Cooper, Myers Y. 165
Coral Gables, City of 53, 146, 147, 148, 149, 152, 153, 154, 155, 156, 157, 160, 162, 163, 164, 165
Coral Gables Country Club 155
Costa Indians 12
Cox, James M. 161
Crandon, Charles 182, 204
Creek Indians 10, 11, 14, 15
Crime Commission of Greater Miami 204, 205
Cruz, Celia 280
Cuban Missile Crisis 225
Cuban refugees 220, 221, 222, 224, 226, 231, 236, 240, 243, 246,
Cullom, Bill 251
Culmer, Father John 184
Curtiss' Flying School 137
Curtiss, Glenn 130, 137, 139, 149, 158, 165, 166

D

D'Amico, Teri 298
Dade County 28, 34, 46, 47, 53, 56, 68, 71, 74, 94, 100, 104, 174, 176, 179, 180, 182, 187, 189, 198, 200, 204, 205, 207, 208, 211, 214, 226, 228, 234, 235, 239, 240, 243, 246, 256, 257, 259, 260, 261, 262, 264, 267, 271, 278, 265, 280, 282, 283, 286, 299, 306,
Dade County Administration 265, 293
Dade County Courthouse 108
Dade County Cultural Center 235, 240, 243, 266,
Dade County Public Schools 267, 306
Dade Heritage Trust 286, 309, 313
Dade Massacre 28
Dade, Francis Langhorn 28
Dallas, Alexander 29
Dammers, Edward E. "Doc"" (Mayor) 126, 148, 149
Davidson, Dorothy Dean 115
Davis, Mary Ann 24
De Bovenkamp, Hans Van 302
De Brahm, William Gerard 14, 15, 17
De Grandy, Miguel A. 293
Dean, S. Bobo 115
Deering, Charles 260
Deering Estate 53, 165, 260, 273
Deering, James 132, 133, 134
Depression, the 176, 177, 178, 182, 185, 186, 187, 188, 189, 195, 199, 202, 241, 250, 264, 311
Design Preservation League 241
Diaz, Manuel A. "Manny" (Mayor) 296, 306, 309, 315
Didion, Joan 260
Dinner Key Naval Air Station 138, 139

INDEX

Doherty, Henry L. 177, 187
Dolphin Stadium 311
Doral Open Golf Tournament 270
Dorschner, John 283
Dorsey, D. A. 135
Doubleday, Abner 39, 40
Douglas, E.B. 110
Douglas, Marjory Stoneman 96, 100, 111, 136, 310
Downtown Development Authority 237, 256
DPZ (Duany Plater-Zyberk) 255, 309
Drucker, Judy 305
Du Puis, John G., M.D. 74
Duany, Andres 254, 255
Dubose, John 26, 29
Dunlop, Beth 253
DuPont Building, the Alfred 190, 191, 312

E

Earhart, Amelia 179
Eastern Airlines 187, 272
Ebenezer M.E. Church 135
Eden Roc Hotel 212, 213
Egan, James 22, 24, 25, 26, 27
Egan, John 17, 18, 22, 24
Egan, Rebecca 24
Elizabeth II (Queen) 271
Elser's Pier 134, 256, 258
Embry-Riddle Aviation School 189
English, Earl 41
English, William H. 34, 35, 36, 38, 46, 49, 53, 81, 94
Enola Gay, the 195
Epic Residences 312
Ernst, John Augustus 15, 17
Esquiroz, Margarita 262
Estefan, Emilio 271, 280, 291
Estefan, Gloria 271, 272, 280, 291
Everglades National Park 171, 174, 178, 201, 202, 203, 224, 230, 239, 294, 310
Ewan, J.W 52, 53, 78, 81

F

Fascell, Dante (Conrgessman) 230
Ferguson, George W. 36, 37, 38
Ferre, Maurice (Mayor) 260
Fisher, Carl Graham 120, 123, 126, 127, 128, 129, 135, 149, 150, 151, 152, 155, 163, 165, 174, 188
Fitzpatrick, Richard 24, 26, 27, 28, 29, 34
Flagler, Henry M. 76, 79, 80, 81, 82, 83, 85, 86, 87, 88, 90, 91, 92, 94, 98, 99, 100, 101, 102, 104, 105, 112, 118, 122, 123, 126, 127, 134, 135, 137, 149, 228, 266, 284, 313
Flagler, Mary
Fletcher, Robert R. 35
Florida Adirondack School, 61
Florida Airways Corporation 178
Florida Center for the Literary Arts 306
Florida East Coast Railroad 100, 122, 162, 163, 303
Florida Federation of Womens' Clubs 121, 202
Florida Grand Opera 305
Florida International University

234, 238, 267, 298, 299, 307
Florida Marlins 268, 270, 288
Florida Memorial College 267, 308
Florida State University 246,
Fontainebleau Hotel 212, 213, 214, 265, 310,
Fontaneda, Escalante 6, 9
Foote, Edward T. 308, 315
Fornells, Pedro 17, 24
Fort Dallas 29, 30, 33, 35, 36, 38, 39, 40, 41, 45, 46, 47, 52, 74, 85, 94, 108, 109, 111
Fort Dallas National Bank 109
Fort Dallas Park 108
Fort Lauderdale 18, 24, 26, 39, 40, 47, 82, 119, 288, 300
Fort Taylor 40, 41
Fort-Brescia, Bernardo 254, 255
Four Seasons Hotel and Residences 295
Fraser, Ron 268
Frazier, Hoyt 120
Freedman's Bureau 44, 45
Freedom Tower 222, 223, 226, 306, 316
Freeman, William 74
Friedman, Charles 204
Friedman's Bakery 258
Fritz Hotel 160
Fritz, Joachim 149, 160
Frost, Patricia, Ph.D. 298
Frost, Phillip, M.D. 298
Frow, Joseph 63
Fuentes, Alex 311

G

Gable, Clark 190, 191
Gadsden, James 22
Garcia, Andy 272, 291. 301
Garcia-Pedrosa, Jose 262
Gardner, John W 272.
Gautier, Petsy 199
Gautier, R.B. (Mayor) 180
Gelabert-Navia, Jose 298
Gibson, Father Theodore 200, 201, 207, 272
Gill, Howard 130
Gill, Mabel 180
Giller, Norman 298
Gilman, James H. 145, 171, 172
Girtman Grocery 110
Gleason, Jackie 198, 229, 272
Gleason, William H. 44, 45, 46,47, 49, 52, 53, 56, 57, 71, 83
Godfrey, Arthur 206, 253
Goldman, Joey 302
Goldman, Tony 302, 303
Gonzalez, Angel 281
Gonzalez, Elián 290, 291, 292, 293
Gonzalez, Juan Miguel 290
Gonzalez, Lazaro 290, 291, 292
Goombay Festival 262, 263
Gordon, R.W. 135
Gorman, Maggie 208
Government Cut 162
Graham, Bob (Governor; Senator) 239, 253, 266, 273, 287
Graham, Donald L. (Judge) 280
Graham, Ernest R. "Cap" (Senator) 239
Graham, Reverend Edward T. 208
Grand Bay Hotel 259

Grant, James (Governor) 14
Grant, James 137
Graves, G.E. 200, 208
Greater Miami Air Association 178
Greater Miami Chamber of Commerce 236, 243, 251, 262
Greater Miami Citizens Against Crime 251
Greater Miami Opera Association 265, 267,
Green Tree Inn 110
Greene, Rose Ellen Meyerhoff 296
Greynolds Park 182, 183
Grimm, Fred 290, 291
Gusman Theatre of the Performing Arts 117, 287, 306, 309
Gwathmey, Charles 298

H

Haas, Richard 265, 266
Hagan, James Fletcher 22, 47
Haitians 250, 262, 263, 264, 281, 289, 290, 312, 317
Halcyon Hall 110, 136, 137
Hammon, Briton 12
Hardie, Dan 112, 128, 129
Hardie's Casino 128, 129
Harlem Square Club 200
Harney, William S. 30, 32, 33, 54
Harrington, Eugene C. 71
Harris, Jeptha V., M.D. 46, 47, 49, 52
Harrison Construction Company 165
Hayes, Rutherford B. (President) 45, 56
Henry, John 288
Hernandez, Pete 313
Herzog & de Meuron 296
Hewitt, Amelia 57
Hialeah 120, 148, 149, 158, 162, 163, 171, 175, 176, 205, 239, 262, 311
Hialeah Park 311
Hicks, Reverend W.W. 47
Highleyman, Locke 123
Hispanic Heritage Celebration 263
Historical Museum of Southern Florida 235, 240, 243, 266, 296,
Hoffman, Burrall 132
Holland, Spessard (Governor; Senator) 202
Holly, Alonzo P. 264
Holocaust Memorial 263, 266
Homestead Act, 1862 94
Homestead Speedway 288, 289
Horowitz, Leonard 258
Hotel Miami 83
Housekeepers Club, the 64, 68
House of Refuge 53
Housman, Jacob 26, 30
Huizenga, Wayne 270, 288
Hunt, William H. 44, 45, 46, 47, 49
Hurricane Andrew 276, 277, 278, 279, 280, 288
Hurricane Wilma 309
Hurricane, 1926 166, 167, 170, 171, 172, 173
Hurricane, 1945, 201
Hurricane, 1947, 202
Hutson, Thomas W,. M.D. 139

I

Ibargüen, Alberto 275
Icon on Brickell 312
Ideal Saloon, the 111
Iglesias, Julio 270, 272
Imperial 254
Indian Key 24, 32, 33
Ingraham, James E. 80, 81, 82
Interama 238
Intercontinental 255
International Tobacco Growers 100
Interterra Building 255
Ishida, Kentaro 296
Isosaki, Arata 298

J

Jackson Memorial Hospital 126, 130, 140, 181, 182, 204, 229, 235,
Jackson, Ethel 139
Jackson, James M., M.D. 139
James, Levi 18
Jason, Jean Yves 281
Jaudon, James F. 109, 128
Jewish Museum 299
John Paul II, 270
Johnson, Carrie 72
Johnson, Don 253, 271
Johnson, Nevil Jr.
Johnson, Peter 39
Johnson, Philip 240, 243, 255, 257
Johnson, S.H., M.D. 200
Johnston, George
Jones, Johnny 243, 246, 249
Jones, Michelle Spence (Commissioner) 281
Jude, Sallye 260
Jungle Island 298, 299
Junior League of Miami 235,
Junior Museum, the 235

K

Katzentine, Frank 205
Kebo 63, 66, 67
Kefauver, Estes (Senator) 204, 205
Kelly, Alonzo "Pop" 184
Kelly's Theater 112
Kendall 17, 279, 309
Kennedy, John F. (President) 225, 233
Kennedy, Rosario 262, 287
Kershaw, Joe Lang 227
Key Biscayne 18, 24, 27, 29, 33, 34, 41, 54, 154, 228, 231, 236, 259
Khoury, Adele (Graham) 239
King Mango Strut 272
King, Lawrence D. (Judge) 293
Kleinberg, Eliot 279
Kleinberg, Howard 111, 273, 279
Knight, James L. 205, 243
Knight, John S. and James L. Foundation 275, 310, 311
Knight Ridder 280, 282, 310, 311
Knox, George 264, 270
Kosar, Bernie 268
Krebs, Rockne 244, 265
Krome, William J. 123

L

Lanier, Sidney 47
Lapidus, Moris 213

INDEX

Lee, Fitzhugh 181
Lehman, William (Congressman) 310
Leigh, Douglas 256
Lemon City 71, 72, 73, 74, 119, 134
Levitt, Jules 204
Lewis, Charles 18
Lewis, Frankee 26
Lewis, George 40, 41
Lewis, Jonathan 24, 40
Lewis, Mary "Polly" 24, 49
Lewis, William 18
Lewis, Winslow 29
Liberty City 184, 226, 228, 249, 251
Lincoln, Samuel 26
Lindbergh, Charles 179
Lipton Tennis Tournament 268
Little Haiti 281, 312
Little Havana 231, 260, 270, 290, 291, 292,
Loews Hotels 294
Lowe Art Museum 298
Lummus, Helen 125
Lummus, J.E. 76, 109, 110
Lummus, J.N. (Mayor) 85, 86
Lummus, Lula 85
Lyric Theater 134, 260, 261, 310

M

Miami Vice 253, 254, 256, 271
"Miami's For Me" 251
M & M cafeterias 198
MacRae, Hugh II 194
Magic City Coronet Band 137, 140
Magic City Printery 264
Magic Knights of Dade 163, 187
Mahoney, Dan 205
Maidique, Modesto "Mitch" 262, 307
Majestic Saloon 111
Mallory, Stephen 26, 29, 40
Mandela, Nelson 271
Mann, Michael 253, 256, 258
Margulies, Martin 303
Mariel boatlift 246, 247, 249, 250, 251, 260, 265
Marielitos 246
Marino, Dan 268, 269
Marques, Pedro Menéndez 6, 9
Marshall, Thurgood (Justice) 200
Martinez, Dennis 272
Martinez, Raul (Mayor) 262
Marx, Roberto Burle 266
Mas Canosa, Jorge 310
Matheson, William 40, 52, 133, 182, 183,
Maxwell, Cora 162
Mayfair 259
McAllister Hotel 134, 144, 170
McAllister, E.C. (Mrs.) 134
McCabe, Robert H., Ph.D. 267, 306, 315
McCarthy, Joseph 206
McClatchy Company 310
McDuffie, Arthur 249
McFarlane, Flora 68, 79
McGregor, Smith 205
Meek, Carrie (Congresswoman) 317
Meek, Kendrick (Congressman) 317
Menéndez de Avilés, Pedro 4, 6, 7, 9
Menéndez, Antonia 6
Meredith, J.C. 123
Merrick, George Edgar 146, 147,

148, 154, 155, 156, 157, 160, 161, 162, 163, 164, 165
Merrick, Solomon G. 146
Merritt, Ada 74
Metellus, Gepsie, 281
Met Miami 312
Metropolitan Charter Board 211
Metrozoo 190, 191, 289
Metro-Dade Administration 255
Metromover 254, 256, 289
Metrorail 244, 256, 265, 289
Mettair's Bight, Billy 63, 71
Meyer, Hank 206, 229, 237, 239
Meyer, Sylvan 243
Miami 21, 309
Miami Arena 270
Miami Art Museum (MAM) 243, 296, 297
Miami Beach 54, 55, 85, 112, 118, 119, 123, 124, 125, 126, 127, 128, 129, 130, 131, 134, 149, 150, 151, 152, 154, 161, 163, 167, 256, 258, 263, 265, 266, 267, 272, 276, 282, 283, 294, 296, 298, 299, 300, 301, 303, 305, 310, 317
Miami Book Fair International 306
Miami Canal 120, 121, 149, 158
Miami Centennial 284, 285
Miami Children's Museum 298, 299
Miami Circle 3, 8, 286, 287
Miami Citizens for a Drug Free Community 315
Miami City Ballet 266, 267, 305
Miami City Commission 109, 145
Miami Conservatory of Music 145
Miami-Dade Community College 240, 263, 267, 306, 313, 315
Miami Dade County 181, 243, 283, 286, 289, 291, 293, 305, 306, 313, 315
Miami Design District 302, 303
Miami Design Preservation League 241
Miami Dolphins 229, 231, 268, 288
Miami Edison 216
Miami Evening Record, the 111
Miami Grand Prix 268
Miami Heat 268, 270, 288, 289
Miami Herald, The 121, 136, 176, 178, 182, 184, 189, 197, 198, 202, 205, 206, 207, 211, 231, 236, 237, 243, 250, 253, 270, 272, 276, 280, 283, 286, 289, 291, 292, 293, 294, 301, 302, 310, 315
Miami High 216
Miami International Airport 204, 229
Miami Lakes 239, 289
Miami Line 244, 265
Miami Marine Stadium 226, 311
Miami Metropolis, The 88, 89
Miami Modern 295, 298
Miami News 171, 205, 222, 226, 243, 250, 260, 272, 273,
Miami River Inn 260
Miami Science Museum 296
Miami Senior High School 239
Miami Shores 46, 78, 81, 152, 153, 154, 171, 182, 183, 207,
Miami Stadium 311
Miami Times, the 264

Miami Vice 253
Miccosukee Indians 228, 233
Midtown Miami 303, 304
Milledge, John 200
Miller School of Medicine 308
Miller, Leonard 308
Mizner, Addison 154
Monaco, Father Josepha Maria
Montes, Marta 262
Montgomery, Nell Foster
Montgomery, Robert M.
Moore, T.V. 149
Morin, Jim 283
Morley, Nicholas 254
Morningside 260
Mount Zion Church 135
Muhammad, Ali (Cassius Clay) 234
Muir, William 175
Mumford, Bobbi 284
Mumford, Bobby 284
Munroe, Charlie 273
Munroe, Edith 63
Munroe, Eva 57, 62
Munroe, Kirk 64, 68. 69, 82
Munroe, Mary Barr, 68, 69, 121
Munroe, Ralph 43, 49, 55, 57, 62, 63, 68, 70, 82, 166, 226, 273
Murano Grande 315
Musa Isle 112, 198
Museum of Contemporary Art (MOCA) 298, 299
Museum Towers 265, 266
Muxo, Alex 262

N

National Foundation for the Arts 265
Negro Civic League 184
Negro Merchants Association 135
Neighborhoods United 309
New World Center 219, 237, 239, 240
New World Festival of the Arts 265
New World School of the Arts 267, 306
New World Symphony 304, 305
Nichols Brosch Wurst Wolfe & Associates 310, 312, 315
Nixon, Richard 228, 231, 236
Noguchi, Isamu 256, 257,
Norcross, Bryan 278, 279
Nuta, Louis 174

O

O'Neal, Shaquille 289, 312
Obata + Kassabaum 298
Ocean Beach 112, 118, 123, 125, 126, 128,
Ocean Beach Real Estate 125
Odd Fellows Hall 134
Odio, Cesar 248
Ogden, William 111
Oldenberg, Claes 265
Oliveros, Gilda 262
Olmstead, James 100
Olympia Theater 115, 117, 287, 309
Omni 178, 239, 254, 266
One Biscayne Tower 236, 243
One Miami 312
Opa-locka 120, 165, 166, 179, 201, 224, 251
Operation "Greenpalm" 283
Orange Blossom Classic 200

Orange Bowl Festival 187, 189
Orange Bowl Stadium 200, 201, 288, 311
Osborn, Ezra 54, 123
Overtown 134, 135, 184, 194, 200, 227, 241, 256, 260, 261, 270, 271, 310
Overtown Folklife Village 261
Overtown/Park West 256, 270

P

Padron, Eduardo J., Ph.D. 262, 266, 306
Paine, James 40
Paist, Phineas 154
Palace 254
Pan American Airways 178, 179, 187, 189, 273
Pan American Field 178, 204
Pancoast, Lester 243
Pancoast, Thomas J. 123, 125, 128, 129, 226
Parks, Arva Moore 284
Parrot Jungle, the 298, , 315
Parson, George 50, 78
Patten, Arthur H. Jr. 234
Paul, Dan 211
Paul, David 256
Pawley, Charles 263, 281
Peacock, Alfred 63
Peacock Inn 58, 59, 60, 61, 68, 82
Peacock, Charles 37, 63, 68, 83
Peacock, Charles John 63
Peacock, Harry 63
Peacock, Isabella 57, 61, 63, 68
Peacock, Jack 49, 63
Peebles, Donald 294
Pei, I.M. 255, 257, 314
Pelli, Cesar 296, 304, 305
Penelas, Alex (Mayor) 280, 286, 291
Pennekamp State Park, John 230
Pennekamp, John 189, 202, 211
Pent, Edward "Ned" 71
Pent, John 71
Pent, Temple 24, 71
Pent, William 71
Pepper, Claude (Senator) 206, 207, 272
Pereira, Sergio 262
Perez, Jorge 312
Perrine 53, 100
Perrine, Henry Jr. 29, 30, 53
Perrine, Henry E. (son of Henry) 31, 53
Peters, Solomon J. 72
Peters, Thomas J. 122
Phillips, Roy 264
Phipps family 173, 178, 239
Pier 5, 198
Pinckney, Enid 313
Pine Needles Club 68
Pitcairn, Harold 178
Plant, Henry B. 81, 82, 100
Plater-Zyberk, Elizabeth 254, 255, 309
Plummer, J.L. (Commissioner) 266, 284
Ponce de León, Juan 3, 4, 6, 147, 154, 162
Pope, Edwin 288
Port of Miami 94, 120, 191, 192, 234, 237

INDEX

Porter, David 22, 23
Porter, Horace P. 63
Potter, George 49
Potter, Richard B., M.D. 49
Powell, L.M. 29
Presley, Elvis 212
Preston, Robert 190
Price, Andrew 46, 47
Price, W.T. 138
Prio, Carlos 320

Q

R

Ramblas Service Station 248
Range, Athalie 227, 310, 313
Read, Albert Cushing 139
Reagan, Ronald (President) 270
Red Cross Pharmacy 110
Reeves, Garth C. 200, 264
Reeves, Henry Ethlebert 264
Reeves, Rachel 264
Regalado, Tomas (Commissioner) 281
Reid, John C. 56
Reiff, David 260
Reilly, John B. (Mayor) 86, 109, 138, 139
Renick, Ralph 205, 220, 272
Reno, Janet (Attorney General) 283, 291, 292
Revuelta, Leon Vega 312, 315
Ricardo, Jennifer 268
Rickenbacker, Eddie 24, 178,
Riddle, Paul 189
Riley, James Whitcomb 133
Robbie Stadium, Joe 268, 270
Robbie, Joe 268, 288
Robins, Craig 302, 303
Robinson, Randall 298
Rockefeller, John D. 80, 81, 133
Rockledge, The 83
Roedel, Kitty 256
Rodriguez, Jose Luis 272
Rogers, Will 152
Rogers, Woodes (Governor) 15
Roland, Gilbert 190
Romans, Bernard 15, 17
Romfh, Ed (Mayor) 145
Romney, Hervin 254
Roosevelt Hotel 160
Roosevelt, Eleanor 194
Roosevelt, Franklin Delano (President) 180, 181, 183
Rosenbaum, Eddie 204
Rosenquist, James
Ros-Lehtinen, Ileana (Congresswoman), 261, 262
Ross, Calvin 264
Rourke, Mickey 272
Rouse Company, The 256, 258
Royal Palm Lodge 121
Royal Palm Crown Resort 294
Royal Palm Hotel 86, 90, 92, 96, 97, 98, 99, 106, 107, 114, 133, 145, 146
Royal Palm Park 114, 115, 116, 117, 121, 140
Rubell Family Collection 300, 302
Rubell, Don 300, 302
Rubell, Mera 300, 302
Rubin, Robert 283

Russell, Fort 30
Russell, S.L. 30

S

S&G Syndicate 204
Sabatini, Gabriela 268
Sampson, Nat 67
Sampson, Reverend Samuel A. 264
San Carlos Hotel 110
Sanchez, Joe (Comissioner) 313
Sanchez, Ralph 268, 288, 289
Santa Maria de Loreto, Pueblo de 12, 13
Santiago, Sandra 271
Saunders, John 71
Scott, James E. 184
Scruggs, Frank 264
Seaboard Airline Railway 174
Seaquarium 210
Second Seminole War 20, 21, 28, 54
Seiler, Ernie 311
Seminole Indians 14, 16, 28, 30, 37, 39, 51, 59, 62, 93, 149
Seminole Wars 20, 21, 27, 28, 39, 40, 53, 94
Senator Hotel 259
Serpentarium 210
Sewell, E.G. "Ev" 76, 130, 131, 133, 137, 140
Sewell, John 76, 83, 85, 86, 87, 88, 109, 110, 117, 119
Seybold, John 110, 136, 137
Seybold's Ice Cream Parlor 110
Shack, Ruth 256, 261
Shalala, Donna, Ph.D. 283, 308, 309
Shannon, Duncan W. "Red" 174
Shula, Don 231, 268, 288
Sierra, Gregory 253
Silverman, Scott (Judge) 181
Simonton, John 24
Simpson, George 208
Simpson Park 65
Sinnott, Bill 180
Skidmore Owings Merrill 255, 257
Smathers, George (Senator) 206, 207, 310
Smiley, Nixon 211
Smith, Avery 118
Smith, H.T. 271, 283, 294
Smith's Casino 112, 119, 128, 129
Sorenson, Katy (Commissioner) 284
Southeast Financial Center 255, 257
Spanish-Cuban-American War 61, 101, 102, 103, 104, 137
Spear, Laurinda 254, 255
Spence-Jones, Michelle (Commissioner) 281
Sports and Exhibition Authority 271
St. Agnes Baptist Church 68
St. Agnes Episcopal Church 135
St. Augustine, Florida 4, 7, 10, 17, 22, 34, 80, 81
St. John's Baptist Church 135
St. Moritz Hotel 294
St. Thomas University 267
Stallone, Sylvester 287
Steinback, Robert 292
Stewart, Israel 56
Stierheim, Merrett 283, 289
Stirrup, E.W. F. 135
Stoneman, Frank 111, 184

Stowe, Harriet Beecher 68
Strobel, Benjamin 25, 34
Stubbins, Hugh 255
Sturgiss Boarding House 90
Sturtevant, Ephraim T. 48, 49, 56, 74, 78, 81
Suarez, Diego 133
Suarez, Xavier (Mayor) 262, 265, 283
Sub-Chaser School, U.S. Navy 191
Sullivan, "Smiling Jimmy" 205
Sullivan, Daniel P. 204, 205
Summit of the Americas 282. 283
Sunny Isles Beach 295
"Surrounded Islands" 252

T

Tamiami Trail 128
Tatum Brothers, the 109, 118, 120, 149, 158
Tebbets, Merle 165
Teele, Arthur (Commissioner) 280, 282, 310
Tequesta, Chief 6, 9, 10
Tequesta Indians 4, 6, 7, 8, 9, 10, 11, 12, 30, 76, 286
Testaverde, Vinny 268
The Espirito Santo Plaza 295
Third Seminole War 39, 40
Thomas, L.E. (Judge) 200
Thomas, Michael Tilson 266, 304
Thomas, Philip Michael 253, 271
Thompson, Charlie 118
Thompson, George F. 45
Thompson, John 20, 29
Thomson, Parker 305
Thompson, Uly 0. 181
Thomson, Leonard K. (Mayor) 204
Three Kings Parade 290
Tibbits, Paul 195
Tilden, Samuel 56
Tinnie, Gene 313
Toomey, R.E.S. 137
Torch of Friendship 232, 233
Touchett, Samuel 15, 17
Tower Theater 240
Townsend, F. Trench 54
Treister, Ken 263
Trippe, Juan Terry 178
Truman, Harry (President) 203
Turner, William 264
Tuttle, Fannie 75
Tuttle, Frederick 81
Tuttle, Harry 81
Tuttle, Julia 48, 49, 74, 75, 78, 79, 80, 81, 82, 83, 84, 85, 87, 90, 91, 92, 93, 94, 95, 104, 108, 111, 117, 134, 219, 237, 266, 284

U

Ullendorf, Phillip 110
Union Chapel (Plymouth Congregational Church) 68
U.S. Southern Command 282
University of Miami 165, 172, 187, 189, 199, 211, 229, 235, 240, 243, 254, 256, 266, 267, 269, 271, 283, 288, 298, 308, 309, 315
University of Miami Ring Theater 235
University of Miami Symphony 235
Urban Environmental League 309

V

Vail's Floating Hotel 83, 84
Valdez, Jorge 262
Van Bruggen, Coosie 265
Venetian Pool 154, 155, 157, 258
Villa Regina 254, 255
Villa Vizcaya 18, 127, 132, 133, 134, 235, 270, 271, 283
Villareal, Brother Francisco 7, 9, 10, 11
Villela, Edward 267
Vinton, J.R. 27, 30
Virginia Key Beach Park 194, 200, 311, 312, 313
Virrick, Elizabeth 200

W

Wall Street 240, 254
Walker, Hester Perrine (sister of Henry) 52
Ward, Elmer 200
Warren, Fuller (Governor) 205
Washington Graded and High School 135
Washington High School, Booker T. 241, 271
Webster, L.B. 29
Weiser, Sherwood "Woody" 305, 317
Weiss, Jennie 128, 129
Weiss, Joe 128, 129
Wertheim Performing Arts Center 307
Weymouth, Yann 298
WGBS radio 205
Wharton, Frank H. 162
Whited, Charles 272
Whitten, George 205
Whitworth, Lew 234
Widener, Joseph 176
Williams, John 271
Winfield, T.A. 149
Winton, Johnny (Commissioner) 298
WIOD radio 205
Wister, Owen 64
WKAT radio 205
Wolfson, Louis Media History Center 266
Wolfson, Mitchell Jr. 267, 298
Wolfsonian-FIU Museum of Decorative and Propaganda Arts 267, 298, 299
Women's Christian Temperance 111
Woods, Alice 127
World War I 137, 138, 140
World War II 189, 190, 192, 193, 194, 195
Worth, Don 298
WQAM radio 205
Wright, James 26, 29
Wynwood 302, 303

Y

Yerkovich, Peter 253

Z

Zaminco International 260
Zangara, Guiseppe 180, 181
Zyscovich, Bernard 280, 281, 303, 304, 315

The past views the future at the Barnacle.